Fod
Aff
France

Portions of this book appear in
Fodor's France '93 and *Fodor's Paris '93*

Fodor's Travel Publications, Inc.
New York • Toronto • London • Sydney • Auckland

ISBN 0–679–02253–8

Fodor's Affordable France

Editor: Jillian L. Magalaner
Editorial Contributors: Judy Allen, Stephanie Curtis, Donna Dailey, James Etheridge, John P. Harris, Andrew Heritage, Simon Hewitt, Holly Hughes, Amanda Jacobs, Philip Joseph, Caroline Liou, Alexander Lobrano, Ann O'Connor, Gillian O'Meara, Conrad Little Paulus, Carla Power, Marcy Pritchard, Linda K. Schmidt, Richard Smart, Caroline B.D. Smith, Anne Willan, Claire Wilson
Creative Director: Fabrizio La Rocca
Cartographers: David Lindroth, Maryland Cartographics
Illustrator: Karl Tanner
Cover design: Tigist Getachew
Cover Photograph: Peter Scholey/TSW

Design: Vignelli Associates

Special Sales

Fodor's Travel Publications are available at special discounts for bulk purchases (100 copies or more) for sales promotions or premiums. Special editions, including personalized covers, excerpts of existing guides, and corporate imprints, can be created in large quantities for special needs. For more information, write to: Special Marketing, Fodor's Travel Publications, 201 East 50th Street, New York, NY 10022. Inquiries from Canada should be sent to Random House of Canada, Ltd., Marketing Dept., 1265 Aerowood Dr., Mississauga, Ontario L4W 1B9. Inquiries from the United Kingdom should be sent to: Fodor's Travel Publications, 20 Vauxhall Bridge Rd., London, England SW1V 2SA.

MANUFACTURED IN THE UNITED STATES OF AMERICA
10 9 8 7 6 5 4 3 2 1

Contents

Maps

Foreword

We'd like to express our gratitude to Simon Hewitt for his help in preparing this edition.

Special thanks also to Marion Fourestier of the French Tourist Office in New York; Colette Martin of Paris's Tourist Board; Alexandre Lévy of the Toulouse-Midi-Pyrénées regional tourist board; and also to Brigitte Doignon and Florence Danjean.

While every care has been taken to ensure the accuracy of the information in this guide, the passage of time will always bring change and, consequently, the publisher cannot accept responsibility for errors that may occur.

All prices and opening times quoted here are based on information supplied to us at press time. Hours and admission fees may change, however, and the prudent traveler will avoid inconvenience by calling ahead.

Fodor's wants to hear about your travel experiences, both pleasant and unpleasant. When a hotel or restaurant fails to live up to its billing, let us know and we will investigate the complaint and revise our entries where the facts warrant it.

Send your letters to the editors of Fodor's Travel Publications, 201 East 50th Street, New York, NY 10022.

Fodor's Choice

No two people will agree on what makes a perfect vacation, but it's fun—and can be helpful—to know what others think. We hope you'll have a chance to experience some of Fodor's Choices yourself while you're visiting France. For detailed information about each entry, refer to the appropriate chapters within this guidebook.

Best Budget Hotels

Auberge de la Commanderie, St-Emilion

Bannière de France, Laon

Central, Beaune

Dormy House, Etretat

Esméralda, Paris

Gutenburg, Strasbourg

Image Sainte-Anne, Vannes

Little Palace, Nice

Louvre, Nîmes

St-Michel, Chambord

Best Value Restaurants

Au Plasir Gourmand, Chinon

Bistrot d'André, Paris

Brasserie Georges, Lyon

Le Buisson Ardent, Chartres

Café de la Bourse, St-Malo

Dar Djerba, Marseille

Les Gourmandins, Senlis

Hiély-Lucullus, Avignon

Historic Towns and Villages

Les Baux-de-Provence

Beaune

Cluny

La Rochelle

Laon

Rocamadour

St-Jean de Luz

St-Emilion

Troyes

Vendôme

Most Scenic Rail Routes

Aix-les-Bains–Chamonix

Bayonne–St-Jean Pied de Port

Dieppe–Rouen

Lisieux–Caen–Pontorson

Strasbourg–Mulhouse

Museums

Musée des Beaux-Arts, Dijon

Condé Collection, Chantilly

Musée Ingres, Montauban

Musée Matisse, Le Cateau-Cambrésis

Musée National de l'Automobile and Musée Français du Chemin de Fer (National Car and Train Museums), Mulhouse

Musée de l'Oeuvre Notre-Dame, Strasbourg

Musée d'Orsay, Paris

Musée Unterlinden, Colmar

Works of Art

Bayeux Tapestry, Bayeux (Musée de la Tapisserie)

Géricault's *Raft of the Medusa*, Paris (Louvre)

Grünewald's *Issenheim Altarpiece*, Colmar (Musée Unterlinden)

Janmot's *Poem of the Soul* painting cycle, Lyon (Musée des Beaux-Arts)

Rodin's sculpture *The Burghers of Calais*, Calais

Stained glass, Chartres (cathedral)

Churches and Abbeys

Basilica of Ste-Madeleine, Vézelay

Cathedral, Amiens

Cathedral, Bayeux

Cathedral, Bourges

Cathedral, Strasbourg

Mont-St-Michel

Notre-Dame-la-Grande, Poitiers

St-Sernin, Toulouse

St-Urbain, Troyes

Gardens

Château of Vaux-le-Vicomte

Château of Versailles

Château of Villandry

Jardin du Thabor, Rennes

Jardin Exotique, Monaco

Musée Rodin, Paris

Orangerie, Strasbourg

Claude Monet's Garden, Giverny

Streets and Squares

Cours Mirabeau, Aix-en-Provence

La Croisette, Cannes

Place des Héros, Arras

Place de la Bourse, Bordeaux

Place du Capitole, Toulouse

Place Stanislas, Nancy

Place des Vosges, Paris

Rue de la Citadelle, St-Jean Pied de Port

Châteaus and Castles

Angers, Loire Valley

Chambord, Loire Valley

Chenonceau, Loire Valley

Fontainebleau, Ile de France

Haut-Koenigsbourg, Alsace

Palais des Papes, Avignon

Pierrefonds, Oise

Versailles, Ile-de-France

Vitré, Brittany

France by Rail

BELGIUM
Lille
Arras
Cambrai
St-Quentin
Beauvais
LUXEMBOURG
Reims
Metz
Paris
Châlons-sur-Marne
Nancy
Rhine
Strasbourg
GERMANY
Troyes
Auxerre
Mulhouse
Belfort
Clamecy
Dijon
Bourges
Beaune
Besançon
Nevers
SWITZERLAND
Montluçon
Saône
Mâcon
Bourg-en-Bresse
Clermont-Ferrand
Lyon
Rhône
Chambéry
ITALY
Aurillac
Le Puy
Grenoble
Rhône
Rodez
Montélimar
Millau
Avignon
Nîmes
Nice
MONACO
Monte Carlo
Aix-en-Provence
Montpellier
Cannes
Marseille
Narbonne
Toulon
Perpignan
Mediterranean Sea
Corsica

France by Road
ENGLAND
Boulogne
La Manche
(English Channel)
Cherbourg
Dieppe
Le Havre
N28
N13
A15
Rouen
Caen
A13
Seine
Roscoff
N175
Brest
N12
St-Malo
NORMANDY
Morlaix
St-Brieuc
Chartres
BRITTANY
A11
Quimper
N165
Rennes
N24
A10
A81
Lorient
Vannes
Le Mans
Angers
Blois
A11
Nantes
PAYS-DE-LOIRE
Tours
Loire
A10
ATLANTIC
OCEAN
N137
Les Sables d'Olonne
Poitiers
Niort
La Rochelle
POITOU CHARENTES
N20
Limoges
Saintes
Royan
Angoulême
Bay of Biscay
A10
Périgueux
Bordeaux
Brive-la-Gaillarde
Arcachon
Garonne
Dordogne
Langon
Cahors
N10
AQUITAINE
A62
Montauban
Bayonne
MIDI-PYRÉNÉES
Albi
N117
Biarritz
Toulouse
Pau
Tarbes
N113
Carcassonne
N
0
50 mi
0
75 km
SPAIN
ANDORRA

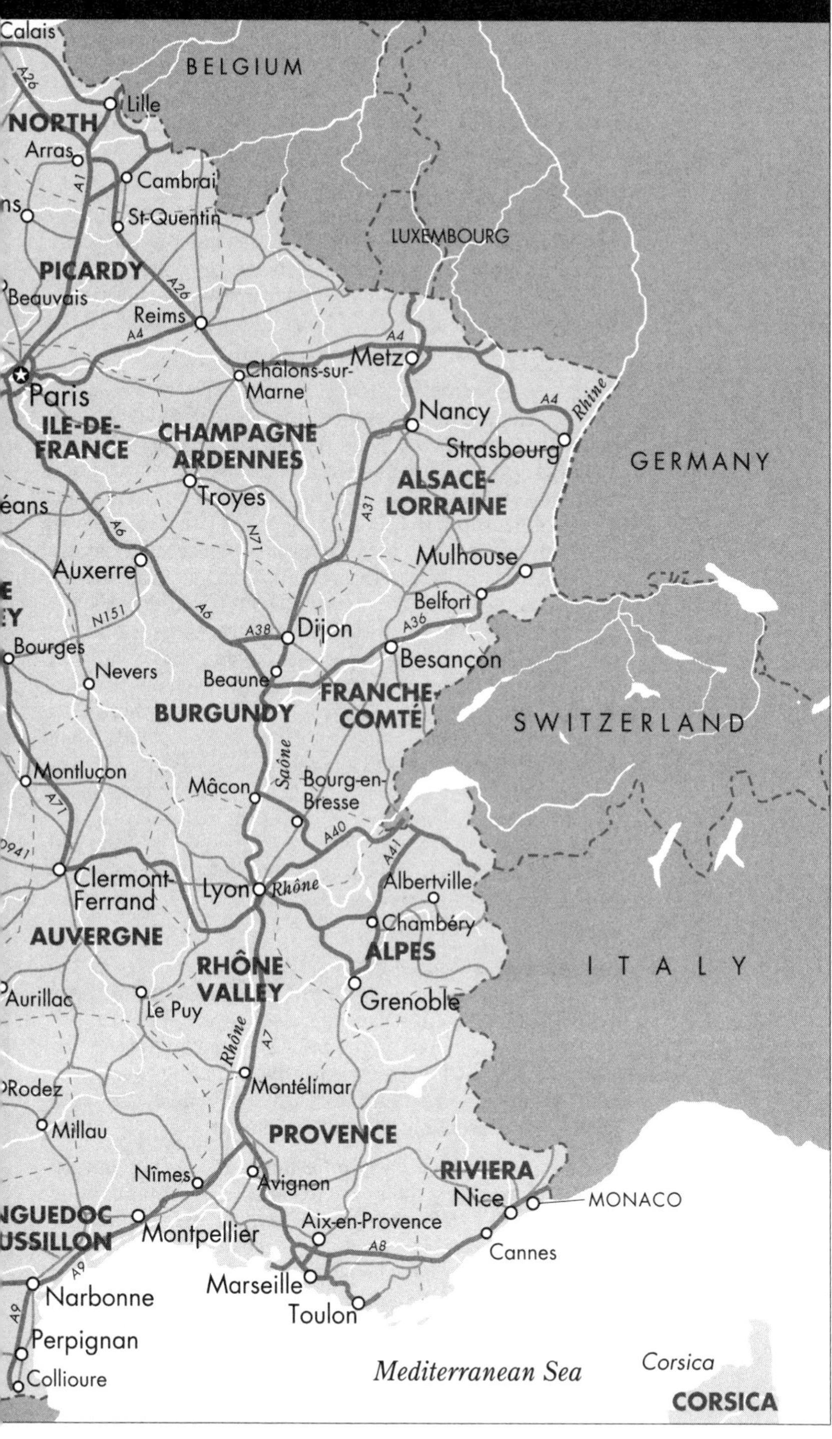
Calais
BELGIUM
Lille
NORTH
Arras
Cambrai
St-Quentin
LUXEMBOURG
PICARDY
Beauvais
Reims
Metz
Châlons-sur-Marne
Paris
Nancy
ILE-DE-FRANCE
CHAMPAGNE ARDENNES
Strasbourg
GERMANY
Rhine
Troyes
ALSACE-LORRAINE
Mulhouse
Auxerre
Belfort
Dijon
Bourges
Nevers
Besançon
Beaune
FRANCHE-COMTÉ
BURGUNDY
SWITZERLAND
Saône
Montluçon
Mâcon
Bourg-en-Bresse
Clermont-Ferrand
Lyon
Rhône
Albertville
Chambéry
AUVERGNE
ALPES
RHÔNE VALLEY
ITALY
Aurillac
Le Puy
Grenoble
Rhône
Rodez
Montélimar
Millau
PROVENCE
RIVIERA
Nîmes
Avignon
Nice
MONACO
Montpellier
Aix-en-Provence
Cannes
Narbonne
Marseille
Toulon
Perpignan
Collioure
Mediterranean Sea
Corsica
CORSICA

Introduction

Spring 1992, when a dollar bought 5.50 French francs, was a far cry from the heady mid-1980s, when it bought more than 10.

Yet it would be a mistake to conclude that France has become expensive to visit. French inflation has stayed steady at only about 3% a year, and hotels, restaurants, and rail travel here are some of the best values in Western Europe. In fact, a budget traveler in France can share almost all the experiences of one who goes first class.

Though world-class hotels are as expensive in France as anywhere else, the high number and low price of establishments that are merely good make traveling on a budget fairly easy, even though bed-and-breakfasts are scarce and youth hostels tend to be of poorer quality than throughout the rest of Europe. Hotels offering good value abound even in the smallest country towns, and only Monaco and Cannes are exclusively haunts of the rich. You can spend as little as $15 for double rooms with shower (though that doesn't buy much in the way of comfort or neighborhood charm in cities). No matter where you go, you should be able to find a double room with bath for under $50; and even in the heart of Paris, where lodging and meals cost about 20% more than elsewhere, it is more than possible to locate a double room with shower for under $35 a night. In most areas, $70 will enable you to live in some style. Even popular holiday destinations such as Normandy and the Loire Valley have something to offer the budget traveler, though in July and August you may have to look hard and book ahead. (Just remember that closing times in such areas are erratic out of season.)

France hasn't sprouted fast-food outlets as quickly as the rest of Europe for the simple reason that restaurants here serve fine three-course meals for as little as $8 to $10. For $20, you can often have a virtual feast—usually with wine and as much bread as you wish thrown in at no extra cost. Many fashionable restaurants with astronomic à la carte prices offer reasonably priced fixed menus.

Getting around is similarly affordable. It needn't concern you that domestic airfares are expensive, and that driving means highway tolls, high gas prices, and even higher car rental rates. Travel in France is geared to train lovers. The rail network is comprehensive, and almost every town boasts a train station with a down-to-earth, inexpensive Hôtel de la Gare nearby. Moreover, trains run on time and are comfortable, fast—and relatively cheap. (A 484-kilometer [300-mile] train trip costs about $50.) Even the TGV bullet trains do not require you to pay a hefty supplement except at peak times—the only extra cost is $3 for the obligatory seat reservation.

Money-saving Tips

Being aware of a few money-saving tips can make the cost of your vacation in France even less expensive.

- **Choose when to travel.** European tourism peaks over the summer, and prices are accordingly high. If you're at all flexible, plan to travel during the low season, between November and March, or else the shoulder season—April, May, and mid-September through October. Since many people begin their vacations on Friday or Saturday, airfares are usually more expensive on weekends, so try to travel midweek. Also, since city hotels are often filled with business travelers during the week, you may save money by arranging to stop in big cities over the weekend when the rates may be less expensive. (*See* When to Go *in* Essential Information, *below*.)

- **Consult discount travel clubs and agencies.** Before going away, you may want to look into organizations that specialize in discounted hotel and airfares. Some travel clubs are especially good at arranging cut-rate deals with suppliers. Other clubs and agencies offer smaller discounts through partial rebates of commissions. Several such organizations are **Discount Travel International** (114 Forrest Ave., Narberth, PA 19072, tel. 215/668–7184); **Moment's Notice** (425 Madison Ave., New York, NY 10017, tel. 212/486–0503); **Travelers Advantage** (CUC Travel Service, 49 Music Square W, Nashville, TN 37203, tel. 800/548–1116); and **Worldwide Discount Travel Club** (1674 Meridian Ave., Miami Beach, FL 33139, tel. 305/534–2082).

- **Stay in cheaper regions.** You can save money by spending more time off the beaten track, in regions that tend to accommodate fewer tourists. This means less time in Paris, and at popular seaside summer resorts. But vacations in the countryside may prove to be even more rewarding.

- **Avoid the single supplement fee.** Solo travelers looking to reduce their expenses can contact one of several organizations that help to match up travel companions. All of these groups charge a fee—usually between $20 and $40. Some publish a newsletter and let readers get in touch with one another, others match companions according to their interests. Organizations include **Odyssey Network** (118 Cedar St., Wellesley, MA 02181, tel. 617/237–2400) and **Partners in Travel** (Box 491145, Los Angeles, CA 90049).

- **Think about buying the *Half-Price Europe Book*.** This book includes discount coupons for hotels, restaurants, rental cars, shops, tours, and special events. However, it's fairly expensive—$65 at the time of writing, plus postage and handling. Some travel experts suggest you buy it *only* for the hotel discounts. And if you're intent on a specific hotel at a particular time, you may be disappointed; many hotels offer a limited number of rooms at discount prices. Send $65 to **Entertainment Publications** (2125 Butterfield Rd., Troy, MI 48084, tel. 800/477–3234), or order by phone with a credit card.

- **Make a budget.** Allow yourself a certain amount of spending money each day and try not to exceed that limit. There's no reason to set the same limit every day; you may want to live the Spartan life for a while, then indulge yourself later. But make a habit of adhering to your daily allowances, so the cost of your trip can be kept below a predetermined sum.

- **Categorize expenses.** Travel expenses generally fall into these categories: accommodation, food, transportation, and cultural or recreational activities. Use these headings as guidelines for setting your priorities when you're deciding where you want to cut back. Eating sandwiches and staying at a youth hostel, for example, may save enough for a concert or a night at the theater.

- **Ask about discounts.** Not all discounts are advertised, so make it a rule of thumb to ask about discounts before paying. Watch for weekend rates, student and age-related reductions, and promotional deals. Movies in Paris are cut-rate for Monday shows. Half-price theater tickets for same-day performances can be bought at the booth near Madeleine Church. Note that museum admission fees are often reduced on Sunday and occasionally Wednesday.

- **Be creative about accommodations.** Though France offers an abundance of inexpensive hotels, they are *not* your only budget-wise option. Other possibilities include hostels, university rooms, Chambres d'Hôte (bed-and-breakfasts), and Gîtes Ruraux (cottages or apartments that can be rented by the week or month).

  Hotel rooms with shower or bath cost at least $6 more than rooms with neither. (But opting to go without facilities in your room isn't always the least expensive way to go: It may cost you $3–$6 to bathe or shower down the hall—so inquire about charges in advance.)

- **Go camping.** If you enjoy the outdoors, try spending some, or all, of your nights at the very affordable campsites located throughout France. Equipment is likely to be less expensive at home, so buy what you need before you go.

- **Save money on food.** Bistros and brasseries are often reasonably priced, and foreign restaurants can be bargains as well. You're likely to find less expensive restaurants in the countryside, or on the outskirts of town, away from the heavily populated areas. You can also buy your food at a store, find an attractive park—or a spot by the road—and have a picnic lunch or an early dinner. In big cities especially, this is the best way to lower dining expenses without resorting to fast food.

Be aware that French hotel breakfasts are pretty skimpy. Unless it is obligatory to eat where you've lodged, start the day with a *baguette*, a long, skinny loaf of bread you can buy at the local *boulangerie* (bakery); then order your café at the counter of the nearest bar.

Also remember that in France, as in many other countries, it's cheaper to plan your main meal for lunchtime, when $10 will buy a three- or even four-course feast. In the evening, $6 a head will cover a meal based on bread, cheese, ham, fruit, and wine.

Finally, note that cafés, though great for watching the world go past, are expensive for most drinks. Unless you choose beer, pastis, or a small espresso, expect to pay at least $2.50 for whatever you order, even fruit juice or mineral water. Drink prices in cafés and bars go up in the evening—and a couple of large beers may set you back as much as a restaurant meal. (*See also* Dining and Lodging, *below.*)

- **Save on money exchange.** Inquire with someone at your hotel, or at a tourist bureau, about banks that specialize in changing money. Whatever you do, don't cash your traveler's checks at shops, hotels, or tourist attractions. (*See* Changing Money *in* Essential Information, *below.*)

- **Don't make phone calls from your hotel.** If you make a call from your hotel room, you'll have to pay a surcharge. When calling home, prepare yourself with lots of change or a phonecard, then find a pay phone and dial your call directly. This may be an inconvenience, but it's cheaper than an operator-assisted call.

- **Shop wisely.** Some of the best bargains can be found at small crafts and antiques shops, where owners may be amenable to lowering their prices. Paris, with its high prices and attractive items, is often frustrating, but ask at your hotel, or at the tourist bureau, about flea markets around town. (*See* Shopping, *below.*)

- **Use the V.A.T. refund.** At many stores, you can claim a refund on France's Value Added Tax if you spend more than 1,200 francs on a given purchase. Remember to ask for the refund, as some stores—especially larger ones—offer the service only upon request.

- **Consider your rail travel needs.** Individual tickets aren't always more expensive than the pass you may be considering (EurailPass, Eurail Flexipass, or French Flexipass, formerly the France-Vacances Rail Pass). If you don't plan to cover a lot of ground, it can be cheaper to pay for your trips individually. (*See* Rail Passes *in* Essential Information, *below.*)

- **Travel at night.** Keep in mind that overnight rail travel saves money on accommodations. But take the necessary precautions against thieves, such as sleeping on top of your wallet or valuables or taking shifts with your companion, if you decide to spend the night on a train.

- **Consider a public transportation pass.** In Paris and other cities, you can buy passes for unlimited travel, good for a certain number of days on city buses and trains. There may also be discounts on tickets purchased in quantity; in Paris, a *carnet* (10 métro tickets) is an excellent value. If you plan to rely at all on public transportation inside a city, passes will save you money.

- **Compare car rental companies.** The multinational American companies don't always offer the best deals. You may do better with North American tour operators that arrange for cars from European rental companies. These tour operators include Auto Europe, Connex, Europe by Car, Foremost Euro-Car, and Kemwell. (*See* Car Rentals *in* Essential Information, *below*.)

  Weekly touring packages offer unlimited mileage and a much better rate than the day-to-day deals. To qualify for most of these touring rates, you need to keep the car for at least five days, so plan your itinerary accordingly.

- **Choose inexpensive activities.** A day spent hiking along footpaths or riding through backroads on a bicycle is often more rewarding than a typical day of sightseeing. It's also less expensive. Try to plan some of your days around this kind of recreation.

  Also remember that while admission to castles, châteaus, and monuments averages $4–$6, you can visit churches, cathedrals, and the formal gardens you will find in most towns and cities at no charge. Museums may cost $1–$6 to enter, unless you go on discount days—but visiting art galleries is free.

  Avoid cabarets, nightclubs, and even relatively modest discos, which tend to be pretty expensive.

- **Find out about the arts for free.** Before spending your money on high-priced culture and entertainment, find out what's being offered for free. Local newspapers and magazines are good sources. While theater and concert tickets are expensive, performances in churches are often free—as are some of the *son-et-lumière* performances, sound-and-light extravaganzas staged outdoors at tourist venues in summer.

1 Essential Information

Before You Go

Government Tourist Offices

Contact the French Government Tourist Offices for information on all aspects of travel to and in France.

In the U.S. 610 5th Ave., New York, NY 10020 (tel. 212/315–0888); 645 N. Michigan Ave., Chicago, IL 60611 (tel. 312/337–6301); 2305 Cedar Springs Rd., Dallas, TX 75201 (tel. 214/720–4010); 9401 Wilshire Blvd., Beverly Hills, CA 90212 (tel. 213/271–6665); 1 Hallidie Plaza, Suite 250, San Francisco, CA 94102 (tel. 415/986–4174).

In Canada 1981 McGill College, Suite 490, Montréal, Québec H3A 2W9 (tel. 514/288–4264); 1 Dundas St. W, Suite 2405, Box 8, Toronto, Ontario M5G 1Z3 (tel. 416/593–4723).

In the U.K. 178 Piccadilly, London W1V OAL, England (tel. 071/491–7622).

Tour Groups

Care to balloon over the Loire Valley, sip wine with a countess in Burgundy, or just hop aboard a whistle-stop tour of the country's most famous highlights? Then you may want to consider a package tour. Creative itineraries abound, offering access to places you may not be able to get to on your own as well as the more traditional spots. They also tend to save you money on airfare and hotels. If group outings are not your style, check into independent packages; somewhat more expensive than package tours, they are also more flexible.

When considering a tour, be sure to find out exactly what expenses are included (particularly tips, taxes, side trips, additional meals, and entertainment); governmental ratings of all hotels on the itinerary and the facilities they offer; cancellation policies for both you and the tour operator; and, if you are traveling alone, the price of the single supplement. Most tour operators request that bookings be made through a travel agent (there is no additional charge for doing so). Below is a sampling of the many tour options available. Contact your travel agent or the French Government Tourist Office for additional resources.

General-Interest Tours **American Express Vacations** (300 Pinnacle Way, Norcross, GA 30093, tel. 800/241–1700 or, in GA, tel. 800/421–5785) is a veritable supermarket of tours; you name it—they've either got it packaged or will customize a package for you. **Globus-Gateway** (95–25 Queens Blvd., Rego Park, NY 11374, tel. 718/268–7000 or 800/221–0090) offers the hectic but comprehensive 15-day "La France." **Jet Vacations** (1775 Broadway, Suite 2405, New York, NY 10019, tel. 212/247–0999 or 800/JET–0999) features "Paris & Châteaux Country" and "Paris, Burgundy, Provence & the Riviera." **Trafalgar Tours** (21 E. 26th St., New York, NY 10010, tel. 212/689–8977 or 800/854–0103) offers a moderately priced, two-week "Best of France" program. **Olson-Travelworld** (Box 10066, Manhattan Beach, CA 90226, tel. 800/421–2255, 800/421–5785 in CA, or 310/546–8400) takes you off the beaten path in its 16-day "French Masterpieces" tour.

Maupintour (Box 807, Lawrence, KA 66044, tel. 800/255–4266 or 913/843–1211) hits the highlights of France within 12 days.

Special-Interest Tours

Wine/Cuisine **Travel Concepts** (373 Commonwealth Ave., Suite 601, Boston, MA 02115–1815, tel. 617/266–8450) serves up such specialties as "Champagne and Cuisine with Mrs. Charles Heidsieck" (of Heidsieck Champagne fame), "Burgundy: History, Wine & Cuisine with Countess De Loisy," and, for the serious wine-lover, a week-long seminar at the University of Wine in the Rhône Valley.

Art/Architecture **Past Times Arts and Archaeological Tours** (800 Larch La., Sacramento, CA 95864–5042, tel. 916/485–8140) escorts the curious through the strange world of prehistoric cave art in southern France. Its "Paris Art Museums and Historic Neighborhoods" is a tour that tells as well as shows.

Cycling **Sobek Expeditions** (Box 1089, Angels Camp, CA 95222, tel. 209/736–4524) gets the blood flowing with its "Tour de France" ride through the French countryside from Burgundy to the Bay of Biscay.

Ballooning **Buddy Bombard Balloon Adventures** (6727 Curran St., McLean, VA 22101–3804, tel. 703/448–9407 or 800/862–8537) takes groups of a dozen or fewer into the gentle breezes above Burgundy and the Loire Valley during its three- to six-night tours. Fine dining back on the ground is an added touch.

Singles and Young Couples **Trafalgar Tours** (*see* General-Interest Tours, *above*) offers "Club 21–35," faster-pace tours for travelers who are not afraid of a little physical activity—whether it's bike riding or discoing the night away.

Music **Dailey-Thorp Travel** (315 W. 57th St., New York, NY 10019, tel. 212/307–1555) offers deluxe opera and music tours, including "French Festivals." Itineraries vary according to available performances.

Package Deals for Independent Travelers

Self-drive tours are popular in France, and **The French Experience** (370 Lexington Ave., Suite 812, New York, NY 10017, tel. 212/986–1115 or 800/22–FRANCE) has put together eight different routes, including "The Châteaux Experience," with stays at private châteaux and manor houses. Accommodations at country cottages and Paris apartments can also be arranged. **Abercrombie & Kent International** (1420 Kensington Rd., Oak Brook, IL 60521, tel. 708/954–2944 or 800/323–7308) adds the option of a chauffeur to its somewhat pricier deluxe driving tours. **Air France** (120 W. 56th St., New York, NY 10017, tel. 212/247–0100) offers week-long air/hotel packages to Paris and the Riviera. **TWA Vacations** (800/GETAWAY) has similar flexible packages. "France à la Carte" is a menu of hotel packages available in Paris and Nice from **The French Experience** (*see above*). **Globus-Gateway** (*see* General-Interest Tours, *above*) gives you a week in Paris, including airport transfers, local host service, half-day sightseeing, and shopping discounts.

When to Go

On the whole, June and September are the best months to be in France, since both are free of the mid-summer crowds. June offers the advantage of long daylight hours, while slightly lower prices and frequent Indian summers (often lasting well into October) make September an attractive proposition.

Try to avoid the second half of July and all of August, or be prepared for inflated prices and huge crowds on the roads and beaches. Don't travel on or around July 14 and August 1, 15, and 31. July and August in southern France can be stifling. Paris can be stuffy in August, too, but it is pleasantly deserted (although many restaurants, theaters, and small shops are closed).

The skiing season in the Alps and Pyrénées lasts from Christmas to Easter; do not go in February if you can avoid it (vacation time for schoolchildren). Anytime between March and November will offer you a good chance to soak up the sun on the Riviera, though, of course, you'll tan quicker between June and September. If Paris and the Loire are among your priorities, remember that the weather is unappealing before Easter. If you're dreaming of Paris in the springtime, May (not April) is your best bet.

Climate The following are average daily maximum and minimum temperatures for Paris and Nice.

Paris

Jan.	43F	6C	**May**	68F	20C	**Sept.**	70F	21C
	34	1		49	10		53	12
Feb.	45F	7C	**June**	73F	23C	**Oct.**	60F	16C
	34	1		55	13		46	8
Mar.	54F	12C	**July**	76F	25C	**Nov.**	50F	10C
	39	4		58	15		40	5
Apr.	60F	16C	**Aug.**	75F	24C	**Dec.**	44F	7C
	43	6		58	15		36	2

Nice

Jan.	55F	13C	**May**	68F	20C	**Sept.**	77F	25C
	39	4		55	13		61	16
Feb.	55F	13C	**June**	75F	24C	**Oct.**	70F	21C
	41	5		61	16		54	12
Mar.	59F	15C	**July**	81F	27C	**Nov.**	63F	17C
	45	7		64	18		46	8
Apr.	64F	18C	**Aug.**	81F	27C	**Dec.**	55F	13C
	46	8		64	18		41	5

Current weather information for more than 750 cities around the world may be obtained by calling **WeatherTrak** information service at 900/370–8728 (cost: 95¢ per minute). A taped message will tell you to dial the three-digit access code for the destination in which you're interested. The code is either the area code (in the United States) or the first three letters of the foreign city. For a list of all access codes, send a stamped, self-addressed envelope to Cities, 9B Terrace Way, Greensboro, NC 27403. For further information, phone 800/247–3282.

Public Holidays January 1, Easter Monday, May 1 (Labor Day), May 8 (VE Day), Ascension Day (five weeks after Easter), the Monday after Pentecost, July 14 (Bastille Day), August 15 (Assumption), November 1 (All Saints), November 11 (Armistice), and Christmas Day. If a public holiday falls on a Tuesday or a Thursday, many businesses and shops and some restaurants close on the Monday or Friday, too.

Festivals and Seasonal Events

Contact the French Government Tourist Office for exact dates and further information on the following events.

Mid- to late Feb. Carnival of Nice provides an exotic blend of parades and revelry during the weeks leading up to Lent.

Apr. to Sept. Sound-and-Light Shows (*son-et-lumière*), historical pageants featuring special lighting effects, are held at many châteaus in the Loire Valley.

Mid- to late May. Cannes Film Festival sees two weeks of star-studded events.

Late May to mid-June. Lyon International Festival spells three weeks of artistic celebrations, held at various locations in Lyon.

Late May to early June. French Open Tennis Championships get under way at Roland Garros Stadium in Paris.

Mid-June to mid-July. Festival du Marais, including everything from music to dance to theater, is held in Paris. (Tickets: 44 rue François-Miron, 75004 Paris, tel. 48–87–60–08.)

Early July to early Aug. Festival of Avignon affords almost an entire month of top-notch theater throughout Avignon. (Tickets: Bureau de Festival, 8-bis rue de Mons, 84000 Avignon, tel. 90–82–67–08.)

July 14. Bastille Day, a national holiday commemorated throughout the country, celebrates the Storming of the Bastille in 1789—the start of the French Revolution.

Mid- to late July. Festival of Lyric Art and Music brings nearly three weeks of musical entertainment to Aix-en-Provence. (Tickets: 32 pl. des Martyrs, 13100 Aix-en-Provence, tel. 42–21–14–40.)

Mid-July to late Sept. Festival Estival of Paris hosts classical concerts in churches, museums, and concert halls throughout the city. (Tickets: 20 rue Geoffroy-l'Asnier, 75004 Paris, tel. 48–04–98–01.)

Early Oct. Prix de l'Arc de Triomphe, a venerable annual horse race, is held at Longchamp Racecourse in Paris.

Oct. *Vendanges* (grape harvest) **festivals** are held in the country's wine regions.

Late Nov. Les Trois Glorieuses is Burgundy's biggest wine festival, featuring the year's most important wine auction and related merriment in several Burgundy locations.

What to Pack

Pack light: Baggage carts are scarce in airports and railroad stations, and luggage restrictions on international flights are tight. (*See* Carry-on Luggage *and* Checked Luggage, *below, for exact specifications.*)

Clothing What you pack depends more on the time of year than on any particular dress code. Eastern France is hot in the summer and cold in the winter. You'll need a raincoat or an umbrella for Paris any time of the year and a sweater or warm jacket for the Mediterranean areas during the winter.

For the cities, pack as you would for an American city: cocktail outfits for formal restaurants and nightclubs, casual clothes for sightseeing. Jeans, as popular in France as anywhere else, are acceptable for sightseeing and informal dining. However, a jeans-and-sneakers outfit will cause raised eyebrows at theaters or expensive restaurants or when visiting French families. The rule here is to dress up rather than down. The exception is in young or bohemian circles, where casual dress is always acceptable.

Men and women who wear shorts will probably be denied admission to churches and cathedrals, although there is no longer any need for women to cover their heads and arms. For the beach resorts, pack something to wear over your bathing suit when you leave the beach (wearing bathing suits on the street is frowned upon).

Most casinos and nightclubs along the Riviera require jackets and ties. They are the place for chic cocktail dresses and tuxedos, if you like to dress formally. Casual dresses and slacks outfits are also appropriate.

Miscellaneous You'll need an adapter for hair dryers and other small appliances. The electrical current in France is 220 volts and 50 cycles. When you are staying in budget hotels, take along small bars of soap; many do not provide soap or limit guests to one tiny bar per room.

Carry-on Luggage Airlines generally allow each passenger one piece of carry-on luggage on international flights from the United States. The bag cannot exceed 45 inches—length + width + height—and must fit under the seat or in the overhead luggage compartment.

Checked Luggage Passengers are generally allowed to check two pieces of luggage, neither of which can exceed 62 inches—length + width + height—or weigh more than 70 pounds. Baggage allowances vary slightly among airlines, so be sure to check with the carrier or your travel agent before departure.

Taking Money Abroad

Before going, you may want to chart the U.S. dollar for a couple of weeks against the currency of the country you're visiting. This can be risky, but the savings may warrant the trouble. If the dollar is weakening, consider buying traveler's checks in foreign currency and paying in advance for such costly items as hotel rooms and train or plane tickets. If the dollar is improving, buy traveler's checks in U.S. currency, and use a credit card to pay for costly items after you've arrived at your destination. (Overseas credit charges often don't appear on your bill for two or three months, and you pay the exchange rate of the day the vendor posted the charge.) Always carry some cash with you however, especially in smaller cities and rural areas where credit cards and traveler's checks are not widely accepted. Regardless of how the dollar is faring abroad, it's wise to change a small amount of money into French francs before you go to avoid long lines at airport currency-exchange booths. Most U.S. banks will change your money into francs. If your local bank can't provide this service, you can exchange money through **Thomas Cook.** To find the office nearest you, contact the headquarters (630 Fifth Ave., New York, NY 10111, tel. 212/757–6915).

The most widely recognized traveler's checks are **American Express, Barclay's, Thomas Cook,** and those issued through major commercial banks such as **Citibank** and **Bank of America.** Some banks will issue the checks free to established customers, but most charge a 1% commission fee. Buy part of the traveler's checks in small denominations to cash toward the end of your trip. It will save you from having to cash a large check and ending up with more francs than you need. American Express now issues **Travelers Cheques for Two**—a system that allows both you and your traveling companion to sign and use the same checks. Don't forget to take the addresses of offices where you can obtain refunds for lost or stolen traveler's checks.

Changing Money

To make the most of your travel money, it's important to plan ahead. Purchase at least some traveler's checks in smaller denominations, to cash either at the end of your trip when you don't want to be stuck with too much foreign currency, or when you're forced to change money at an unfavorable rate. If you think the dollar may drop in value while you're away, buy some traveler's checks in French francs. Also, change about $50 before leaving, so you won't have to deal with long lines and poor rates immediately upon arrival at a foreign airport.

Many shops and most hotels will cash your traveler's checks, but rates are usually unfavorable. Some foreign exchange offices offer reasonable rates, but as a rule, banks save you the most money. Keep in mind that major French banks (such as Crédit Agricole, BNP, Crédit Lyonnais, and Société Générale) charge a set commission of around $5 for changing foreign currency (including traveler's checks) into French francs; however, rates vary from one to another and the fee is often waived if the traveler's checks are denominated in French francs. So ask someone at the tourist bureau, or your hotel, to recommend one that specializes in foreign exchange. If you plan to be out of the vicinity of any such specialty bank, consult a newspaper daily to learn the current exchange rates, then compare rates posted at various banks. Most French banks are open weekdays 9:30–4:30.

An attractive rate may tempt you to change loads of money at once. Carrying excessive amounts of cash, however, is risky. If lost or stolen, traveler's checks can be replaced, provided you've kept the receipts in a separate location; but missing cash is gone forever. (As an added precaution, write down the check numbers as you cash them. If they disappear, you'll know which ones are missing.) You should change more money before weekends and holidays, and when you plan to be outside a city or town for any extended period.

Getting Money from Home

Cash Machines
Withdrawals

It's easy to use automated-teller machines (ATMs) to withdraw money from your checking account with a bank card. Just get the names of affiliated cash-machine networks before your departure. (For locations for two of the larger networks, **Cirrus** and **Plus,** call 800/4–CIRRUS or 800/THE–PLUS.) Note that you may be charged a fee for withdrawals away from your home turf. Of course, you need to get a personal identification number (PIN) if you don't have one already.

Cash Advances You can also use ATMs to get cash advances on your credit card, providing you have a PIN number for your card. As with cash advances from tellers, you pay interest from the day of posting, and some banks tack on an additional service charge.

For both withdrawals and cash advances, there are usually limits on the amount you can access within given time periods. Know before you go.

Bank Transfers Just have your bank send money to another bank overseas. It's easiest to transfer money between like branches; otherwise, the process takes a couple days longer and costs more.

American Express Cardholder Services The company's **Express Cash** system links your U.S. checking account to your Amex card. Overseas you can withdraw up to $1,000 in a 21-day period (more if you card is Gold or Platinum). For each transaction there's a 2% fee (minimum $2, maximum $6). Call 800/227–4669 for information.

Cardholders can also cash personal or counter checks at any American Express office for up to $1,000, of which $500 may be claimed in cash and the balance in traveler's checks carrying a 1% commission.

Wiring Money To send or receive up to $10,000, you can use an **American Express MoneyGram,** and you don't have to have an American Express card. The sender goes to an American Express MoneyGram agent, specifies an amount, pays up to $1,000 with a credit card (anything over that in cash), and telephones the receiver with the reference number he is given. The receiver goes to the nearest MoneyGram agent, presents identification and the reference number, and picks up cash. Fees are 5% to 10%, depending on the amount and method of payment (AE, D, MC, V are accepted). For agent locations, call 800/543–4080.

If there are no American Express offices nearby, you can use **Western Union** (tel. 800/325–6000). A friend at home can bring cash or a check to the nearest Western Union office or pay over the phone with a credit card. Delivery usually takes two business days, and fees are roughly 5% to 10%.

French Currency

The units of currency in France are the franc (fr.) and the centime. Bills are in denominations of 500, 200, 100, 50, and 20 francs. Coins are 10, 5, 2, and 1 francs, and 50, 20, 10, and 5 centimes. At press time (spring '92), the exchange rate was about 5.50 francs to the U.S. dollar, 4.70 to the Canadian dollar, and 9.80 to the pound sterling.

What It Will Cost

Good values for hotels, restaurants, and rail travel are abundant in France (*see* Introduction).

Sample Prices The following are meant only as a general guide, and may change substantially as exchange rates fluctuate.

Admission to Louvre: $6
Budget Paris hotel (Dhély's): $40 for two

Budget Paris dinner, including wine and coffee (Chartier): $20
Paris taxi (1-mile ride plus tip): $4
Métro ticket: $1
Book of 10 métro tickets: $6.25
Movie ticket: $8
Daily newspaper: $1 French, $2 foreign
Baguette: 65¢
Cup of espresso in café: $1.20
Cup of coffee with milk: $2
½-liter carafe of table wine in budget restaurant: $5
Glass of beer in café: $1.80
Can of Coca Cola: in store, $1.20; in bar or restaurant, $3
Big Mac at McDonald's in Paris: $3.50
Round-trip by train from Paris to Versailles: $5
One-way Paris–Bordeaux rail ticket: $50

Taxes

V.A.T (known as T.V.A.) runs at 18.6% on most goods in France, although a 33% luxury rate applies to watches, cameras, jewelry, and videocassettes. All hotel and restaurant prices must, by law, include taxes (and services). A local *taxe de séjour*, usually from 2 to 5 francs per person per day, is collected by hotels in many towns.

Passports and Visas

Americans All U.S. citizens are required to have a valid passport for entry into France. To obtain a new passport, apply in person; renewals can be obtained in person or by mail. First-time applicants should apply to one of the 13 U.S. Passport Agency offices at least five weeks in advance of their departure date. In addition, local county courthouses, many state and probate courts, and some post offices accept passport applications. Necessary documents include: (1) a completed passport application (Form DSP-11); (2) proof of citizenship (certified birth certificate issued by the Hall of Records of your state of birth, or naturalization papers); (3) proof of identity (valid driver's license or state, military, or student ID card with your photograph and signature); (4) two recent, identical, two-inch-square photographs (black-and-white or color head shot with white or off-white background); and (5) a $65 application fee for a 10-year passport (those under 18 pay $40 for a five-year passport). You may pay with a check, money order, or exact cash amount; no change is given. Passports are mailed to you in about 10–15 working days. To renew your passport by mail, you'll need to send a completed Form DSP-82, two recent, identical passport photographs, your current passport (if less than 12 years old and issued after your 16th birthday), and a check or money order for $55.

U.S. citizens do not need a visa to enter France for a period of 90 days. For further information, contact the Embassy of France, 4101 Reservoir Rd. NW, Washington, DC 20007, tel. 202/944–6000.

Canadians All Canadians are required to have a passport for entry into France. Bring a completed application (available at any post office or passport office) to the Bureau of Passports (Suite 215, West Tower, Guy Favreau Complex, 200 René Lévesque Blvd. W, Montréal, Québec H2Z 1X4). Include $35, two 2 × 2¾–inch black-and-white or color photographs (with white or off-white background), a guarantor, and proof of Canadian citizenship. Applications must be made in person at the regional passport offices in Edmonton, Halifax, Montréal, Toronto, Vancouver, or Winnipeg. Passports are valid for five years and are nonrenewable.

Visas are not required of Canadian citizens to enter France. Obtain details regarding length of stay from the French Consulate or the French National Tourist Office.

Britons All British citizens need passports, for which applications are available from travel agencies or a main post office. Send the completed form to a regional Passport Office or apply in person at a main post office. You'll need two photographs and will be charged a £15 fee. The occasional tourist might opt for a British Visitors Passport. It is valid for one year, costs £7.50, and is nonrenewable. You'll need two passport photographs and identification. Apply at your local post office.

Visas are not required for British citizens entering France.

Customs and Duties

On Arrival There are two levels of duty-free allowance for travelers entering France: one for those coming from an EC country and the other for those coming from anywhere else or for goods purchased in a duty-free shop.

In the first category, you may import duty-free: 300 cigarettes or 150 cigarillos or 75 cigars or 400 grams of tobacco; five liters of table wine and (1) 1½ liters of alcohol over 22% volume (most spirits), (2) two liters of alcohol under 22% by volume (fortified or sparkling wine), or (3) three more liters of table wine; 90 milliliters of perfume; 375 milliliters of toilet water; and other goods to the value of 2,400 francs (620 francs for those under 15).

In the second category, you may import duty-free: 200 cigarettes or 100 cigarillos or 50 cigars or 250 grams of tobacco (these allowances are doubled if you live outside Europe); two liters of wine and (1) one liter of alcohol over 22% volume (most spirits), (2) two liters of alcohol under 22% volume (fortified or sparkling wine), or (3) two more liters of table wine; 60 milliliters of perfume; 250 milliliters of toilet water; and other goods to the value of 300 francs (150 francs for those under 15).

Any amount of French or foreign currency may be brought into France, but foreign currencies converted into francs may be reconverted into a foreign currency only up to the equivalent of 5,000 francs. Similarly, no more than 5,000 francs may be exported and no more than the equivalent of 2,000 francs in foreign currency may be exported.

On Departure
U.S. Customs U.S. residents who are bringing any foreign-made equipment from home, such as cameras, would be wise to carry the original receipt with them or register it with U.S. Customs before leaving home (Form 4457). Otherwise you may end up paying duty on your return. You may bring home duty-free up to $400 worth of foreign goods, as long as you have been out of the country for at least 48 hours and you haven't made an international trip in 30 days. Each member of the family is entitled to the same exemption, regardless of age, and exemptions may be

pooled. For the next $1,000 worth of goods, a flat 10% rate is assessed; above $1,400, duties vary with the merchandise. Included for travelers 21 or older are one liter of alcohol, 100 cigars (non-Cuban), and 200 cigarettes. Only one bottle of perfume trademarked in the United States may be brought in. However, there is no duty on antiques or art over 100 years old.

Anything exceeding these limits will be taxed at the port of entry and may be taxed again in the traveler's home state. Gifts valued at under $50 may be mailed to friends or relatives at home duty-free, but no more than one package per day may be sent to any one addressee and no perfumes costing more than $5, tobacco, or liquor may be mailed. For more information, request *Know Before You Go*, a free customs brochure available from U.S. Customs Service, 1301 Constitution Ave., Washington, DC 20229.

Canadian Customs Exemptions for returning Canadians range from $20 to $300, depending on length of stay out of the country. For the $300 exemption, you must have been out of the country for one week. For any given year, you are allowed one $300 exemption. You may bring in duty-free up to 50 cigars, 200 cigarettes, 2.2 pounds of tobacco, and 40 ounces of liquor, provided these are declared in writing to customs on arrival and accompany the traveler in hand or in checked-through baggage. Personal gifts should be mailed as "Unsolicited Gift—Value under $40." Request the Canadian Customs brochure *I Declare* for further details.

U.K. Customs British residents have two different allowances: one for goods bought in a duty-free shop in France and the other for goods bought anywhere else in France.

In the first category, you may import duty-free: 200 cigarettes or 100 cigarillos or 50 cigars or 250 grams of tobacco (these allowances are doubled if you live outside Europe); two liters of table wine and (1) one liter of alcohol over 22% by volume (most spirits) or (2) two liters of alcohol under 22% by volume (fortified or sparkling wine) or (3) two more liters of table wine; 60 milliliters of perfume; 250 milliliters of toilet water; and other goods up to a value of £32, but no more than 50 liters of beer or 25 lighters.

In the second category, you may import duty-free: 300 cigarettes or 150 cigarillos or 75 cigars or 400 grams of tobacco; five liters of table wine and (1) 1½ liters of alcohol over 22% volume (most spirits) or (2) three liters of alcohol under 22% by volume (fortified or sparkling wine) or (3) three more liters of table wine; 90 milliliters of perfume; 375 milliliters of toilet water; and other goods to a value of £420, but no more than 50 liters of beer or 25 lighters.

No animals or pets of any kind may be brought into the United Kingdom without a lengthy quarantine. *The penalties are severe and strictly enforced.*

Language

The French study English for a minimum of four years at school (often longer) but to little general effect. English is widely understood in major tourist areas and at pricier hotels and restaurants throughout the country. However, no matter where you are, you should be able to find at least one person who can explain things to you if necessary. Be courteous and patient and speak slowly: The French, after all, have plenty of other tourists and are not massively dependent for income on English-speaking visitors. And while it may sound cynical, remember that the French respond more quickly to charm than to anything else.

Even if your own French is terrible, try to master a few words: The French are more cooperative when they think you're making at least an effort to speak their language. Basic vocabulary: *s'il vous plaît* (please), *merci* (thanks), *bonjour* (hello—until 6 PM), *bonsoir* (good evening), *au revoir* (goodbye), *comment ça va* (how do you do), *oui* (yes), *non* (no), *peut-être* (maybe), *les toilettes* (toilets), *l'addition* (bill/check), *où* (where), *anglais* (English), *je ne comprends pas* (I don't understand).

Refer to the Traveler's Vocabulary and Menu at the back of the book for other useful words and phrases.

Staying Healthy

There are no serious health risks associated with travel in France. However, the Centers for Disease Control (CDC) in Atlanta cautions that most of southern Europe is in the "intermediate" range for risk of contracting traveler's diarrhea. Part of this risk may be attributed to an increased consumption of olive oil and wine, which can have a laxative effect on stomachs used to a different diet. The CDC also advises all international travelers to swim only in chlorinated swimming pools, unless they are certain the local beaches and freshwater lakes are not contaminated.

In Washington, the Department of State **Citizens Emergency Center** (tel. 202/647–5225) provides information about health conditions in other nations; what U.S. citizens can do in the event of an emergency overseas; whether any notices, cautions, or warnings exist in the area to which you're traveling; and how to obtain passports and visas.

If you have a health problem that might require purchasing prescription drugs while in France, have your doctor write a prescription using the drug's generic name. Brand names vary widely from country to country.

The **International Association for Medical Assistance to Travelers (IAMAT)** is a worldwide association that publishes a list of approved English-speaking doctors whose training meets British and American standards. For a list of French physicians and clinics that are part of this network, contact IAMAT (417 Center St., Lewiston, NY 14092, tel. 716/754–4883. **In Canada:** 40 Regal Rd., Guelph, Ontario N1K 1B5. **In Europe:** 57 Voirets, 1212 Grand-Lancy, Geneva, Switzerland). Membership is free.

Shots and Medications Inoculations are not needed to enter France. The American Medical Association recommends Pepto Bismol for minor cases of traveler's diarrhea.

Insurance

Travelers may seek insurance coverage in four areas: health and accident, loss of luggage, flight, and trip cancellation. Your first step is to review your existing health and home-owner policies: Some health insurance plans cover health expenses incurred while traveling, some major medical plans cover emergency transportation, and some home-owner policies cover the theft of luggage.

Health and Accident Several companies offer coverage designed to supplement existing health insurance for travelers:

Carefree Travel Insurance (Box 310, 120 Mineola Blvd., Mineola, NY 11501, tel. 516/294–0220 or 800/323–3149) provides coverage for emergency medical evacuation and accidental death and dismemberment. It also offers 24-hour medical phone advice.

International SOS Assistance (Box 11568, Philadelphia, PA 19116, tel. 215/244–1500 or 800/523–8930), a medical assistance company, provides emergency evacuation services, worldwide medical referrals, and optional medical insurance.

Travel Guard International, underwritten by Transamerica Occidental Life Companies (1145 Clark St., Stevens Point, WI 54481, tel. 715/345–0505 or 800/782–5151), offers reimbursement for medical expenses with no deductibles or daily limits, as well as emergency evacuation services.

Wallach and Co., Inc. (Box 480, Middleburg, VA 22117–0480, tel. 703/687–3166 or 800/237–6615) offers comprehensive medical coverage, including emergency evacuation services worldwide.

Trip-cancellation and Flight Consider purchasing trip-cancellation insurance if you are traveling on a promotional or discounted ticket that does not allow changes or cancellations. You are then covered if an emergency causes you to cancel or postpone your trip. Trip-cancellation insurance is usually included in combination travel insurance packages available from most tour operators, travel agents, and insurance agents. Flight insurance, which covers passengers in the case of death or dismemberment, is often included in the price of a ticket when paid for with American Express, MasterCard, or other major credit cards.

Lost Luggage The loss of luggage is usually covered as part of a comprehensive travel insurance package that includes personal accident, trip cancellation, and sometimes default and bankruptcy insurance. Several companies offer comprehensive policies, including **Access America, Inc.,** a subsidiary of Blue Cross–Blue Shield (P.O. Box 11188, Richmond, VA 23230, tel. 800/284–8300 or 800/334–7525); **Near Services** (450 Prairie Ave., Suite 101, Calumet City, IL 60409, tel. 708/868–6700 or 800/654–6700); **Travel Guard International** (*see* Health and Accident Insurance, *above*).

Rail Passes

The **French Flexipass** (formerly the **France-Vacances Rail Pass**) is a good value for those who plan to do a lot of their traveling by train. The Flexipass allows you to stagger your train travel time instead of having to use it all at once. For example, the four-day pass ($175 in first class, $125 in second) may be used on any four days within a one-month period. You must buy the French Flexipass before you leave for France. It is obtainable through travel agents or through **Rail Europe** (226–230 Westchester Ave., White Plains, NY 10604, tel. 914/682–5172 or 800/345–1990).

The **BritFrance Rail Pass** allows you to travel for any five out of 15 days in France and Britain (including Channel crossing by Hovercraft) for $249 (in second class) or $335 (in first class), or for any 10 days in a 30-day period ($385 in second class/$505 in first). You can obtain the pass from travel agencies or through Rail Europe.

The **EurailPass,** valid for unlimited first-class train travel through 17 countries, including France, is an excellent value if you plan to travel around the Continent. The ticket is available for periods of 15 days ($430), 21 days ($550), one month ($680), two months ($920), and three months ($1,150). For two or more people traveling together, a 15-day rail pass costs $340. Between April 1 and September 30, you need a minimum of three in your group to get this discount. For those younger than 26 years old (on the first day of travel), there is the **Eurail Youthpass,** for one or two months of unlimited second-class train travel at $470 and $640.

For travelers who like to spread out their train journeys, there is the **Eurail Flexipass.** With the 15-day Flexipass ($280), travelers get five days of unlimited first-class train travel but can spread that travel out over 15 days; a 21-day pass gives you nine days of travel ($450), and a one-month pass gives you 14 days ($610). The new **Eurail Drive Pass** entitles you to 4 days of train travel and three Hertz rental car days within a 21-day period; the pass costs $269 per person (for two people traveling together). Other rail-and-drive and fly-rail-and-drive programs are available.

The EurailPass is available only if you live outside Europe or North Africa. The pass must be bought from an authorized agent before you leave for Europe. Apply through your travel agent or through **Rail Europe** (*see above*).

Student and Youth Travel

The **International Student Identity Card (ISIC)** entitles students to youth rail passes, special fares on local transportation, Intra-European Student Charter flights, and discounts at museums, theaters, sports events, and many other attractions. If the ISIC is purchased **in the United States,** its $14 cost also includes $3,000 in emergency medical insurance, plus $100 a day for up to 60 days of hospital coverage. Apply to the **Council on International Educational Exchange** (CIEE, 205 E. 42nd St., 16th floor, New York, NY 10017, tel. 212/661–1414). **In Canada,** the ISIC is available for CN $13 from **Travel Cuts** (187 College St., Toronto, Ont. M5T 1P7, tel. 416/979–2406).

The **Youth International Educational Exchange Card** (YIEE), issued by the Federation of International Youth Travel Organizations (FIYTO, 81 Islands Brugge, DK-2300 Copenhagen S, Denmark), provides similar services to nonstudents under age 26. **In the United States,** the card is available from CIEE (address above) or from ISE (Europa House, 802 W. Oregon St., Urbana, IL 61801, tel. 217/344–5863). **In Canada,** the YIEE is available from the Canadian Hostelling Association (CHA; 1600 James Naismith Dr., Suite 608, Gloucester, Ont. K1B 5N4, tel. 613/748–5638).

An **International Youth Hostel Federation** (IYHF) membership card is the key to inexpensive dormitory-style accommodations at thousands of youth hostels around the world. Hostels provide separate sleeping quarters for men and women at rates ranging from $7 to $20 a night per person and are situated in a variety of facilities, including converted farmhouses, villas, and restored castles, as well as specially constructed modern buildings. There are more than 5,000 hostel locations in 70 countries around the world. IYHF memberships, which are valid for 12 months from the time of purchase, are available in the United States through **American Youth Hostels** (AYH, Box 37613, Washington, DC 20013, tel. 202/783–6161). The cost for a first-year membership is $25 for adults ages 18 to 54. Renewal thereafter is $20. For youths (under 18) and senior citizens (55 and older), the rate is $15. Family membership is available for $35. Every national hostel association arranges special reductions for members visiting its country, such as discounted rail fare or free bus travel, so be sure to ask for an international discounts list when you buy your membership.

Economical **bicycle tours** for small groups of adventurous, energetic students are another popular AYH student travel service. For information on these and other AYH services and publications, contact AYH at the address listed above.

Council Travel, a CIEE subsidiary, is the foremost U.S. student travel agency, specializing in low-cost charters and serving as the exclusive U.S. agent for many student airfare bargains and student tours. CIEE's 72-page *Student Travel Catalog* and *Council Charter* brochure are available free from any Council Travel office in the United States (enclose $1 for postage if ordering by mail). In addition to CIEE headquarters in midtown Manhattan (*see address, above*) and a branch office (35 W. 8th St., New York, NY 10009), there are Council Travel offices in Berkeley, La Jolla, Long Beach, Los Angeles, San Diego, and San Francisco, CA; Chicago, IL; Amherst, Boston, and Cambridge, MA; Portland, OR; Providence, RI; Austin and Dallas, TX; and Seattle, WA, among other cities.

Students who would like to work abroad should contact **CIEE's Work Abroad Department** (205 E. 42nd St., New York, NY 10017, tel. 212/661–1414, ext. 1130). The council arranges various types of paid and voluntary work experiences overseas for up to six months. CIEE also sponsors study programs in Europe and publishes many books of interest to the student traveler. These books include *Work, Study, Travel Abroad: The Whole World Handbook* ($12.95 plus $1.50 book-rate postage or $3 first-class postage); or *Volunteer! The Comprehensive Guide to Voluntary Service in the U.S. and Abroad* ($8.95 plus $1.50 book-rate postage or $3 first-class postage).

The Information Center at the **Institute of International Education** (IIE) has reference books, foreign university catalogues, study-abroad brochures, and other materials that may be consulted by students and nonstudents alike free of charge. The Information Center (809 UN Plaza, New York, NY 10017, tel. 212/883–8200) is open from 10 AM to 4 PM weekdays and until 7 PM Wednesday evenings. It is not open on weekends or holidays.

IIE administers a variety of grant and study programs offered by U.S. and foreign organizations, and publishes a well-known annual series of study-abroad guides, including *Academic Year Abroad*, *Vacation Study Abroad*, and *Study in the United*

Kingdom and Ireland. The institute also publishes *Teaching Abroad*, a book of employment and study opportunities overseas for U.S. teachers. For a current list of IIE publications with prices and ordering information, write to Publications Service, Institute of International Education (809 UN Plaza, New York, NY 10017). Books must be purchased by mail or in person; telephone orders are not accepted.

General information on IIE's programs and services is available from its regional offices in Atlanta, Chicago, Denver, Houston, San Francisco, and Washington, DC.

For information on the **Eurail Youthpass,** *see* Rail Passes, *above.* For information on rail passes for those under 26, *see* Getting Around France, *below.*

Traveling with Children

Publications *Family Travel Times* is an 8- to 12-page newsletter published 10 times a year by **TWYCH** (Travel with Your Children, 45 W. 18th St., 7th-floor Tower, New York, NY 10011, tel. 212/206–0688). Subscription includes access to back issues and twice-weekly opportunities to call in for specific advice.

Traveling with Children—And Enjoying it (The Globe Pequot Press, Box Q, Chester, CT 06412; $11.95) offers tips on how to keep kids busy, cut costs, reduce jet lag, and pack properly.

Family Travel Organizations **American Institute for Foreign Study** (AIFS, 102 Greenwich Ave., Greenwich, CT 06830, tel. 203/869–9090) offers family vacation programs in France for high school- and college-age students as well as interested adults. Programs for high school students are handled by **Educational Travel Division, American Council for International Studies** (19 Bay State Rd., Boston, MA 02215, tel. 617/236–2015 or 800/825–AIFS). For information on programs for college students, contact AIFS (102 Greenwich Ave., Greenwich, CT 06830, tel. 203/869–9090).

Families Welcome! (Box 16398, Chapel Hill, NC 27516, tel. 800/326–0724) is a travel agency that arranges French tours brimming with family-sensitive choices and activities. Another travel arranger that understands families' needs (and can even set up short-term rentals) is **The French Experience** (370 Lexington Ave., New York, NY 10017, tel. 212/986–3800).

Hotels The **Novotel** hotel chain allows up to two children under 15 to stay free in their parents' room. Many Novotel properties have playgrounds. (For international reservations call 800/221–4542). **Sofitel** hotels offer a free second room for children during July and August, and over the Christmas holidays. (For international reservations call 800/221–4542.) **Club Med** (40 W. 57th St., New York, NY 10019, tel. 800/CLUB–MED) has a "Baby Club" (from age four months) at its resort in Chamonix; "Mini Clubs" (for ages four to six or eight, depending on the resort), and "Kids Clubs" (for ages eight and up during school holidays) at all its resort villages in France except Val d'Isere. In general, supervised activities are scheduled all day long. Some clubs are only French-speaking, so check first.

Villa Rentals **At Home Abroad, Inc.,** 405 E. 56th St., Suite 6H, New York, NY 10022, tel. 212/421–9165. **Villas International,** 605 Market St., Suite 510, San Francisco, CA 94105, tel. 415/281–0910 or 800/221–2260. **Hideaways, Int'l.,** Box 1270, Littleton, MA 01460, tel. 508/486–8955. **B. & D. de Vogue,** 1830 S. Mooney Blvd. 113, Visalia, CA 93277, tel. 209/733–7119 or 800/727–4748. **Vacances en Campagne,** Box 297, Falls Village, CT 06031, tel. 203/824-5155 or 800/553–5405.

Home Exchange Exchanging homes is a surprisingly low-cost way to enjoy a vacation abroad, especially a long one. The largest home-exchange service, **Intervac U.S./International Home Exchange Service** (Box 590504, San Francisco, CA 94159, tel. 415/435-3497 or 800/756–4663) publishes three directories a year. Membership costs $45 and entitles you to one listing and all three directories. **Loan-a-Home** (2 Park La., Apt. 6E, Mount Vernon, NY 10552, tel. 914/664–7640) is popular with the academic community on sabbatical and with businesspeople on temporary assignments. Although there's no annual membership fee or charge for listing your home, one directory and a supplement cost $35.

Getting There On international flights, children under two not occupying a seat pay 10% of the adult fare. Various discounts apply to children 2 to 12 years of age. Regulations about infant travel on airplanes are in the process of changing. Until they do, however, if you want to be sure your infant is secure and traveling in his or her own safety seat, you must buy a separate ticket and bring your own infant car seat. (Check with the airline in advance; certain seats aren't allowed.) Some airlines allow babies to travel in their own car seats at no charge if there's a spare seat available, otherwise safety seats are stored and the child has to be held by a parent. (For the booklet *Child/Infant Safety Seats Acceptable for Use in Aircraft,* write to the Federal Aviation Administration, APA-200, 800 Independence Ave. SW, Washington, DC 20591, tel. 202/267–3479.) If you opt to hold your baby on your lap, do so with the infant outside the seat belt so he or she doesn't get crushed in case of a sudden stop.

Also inquire about special children's meals or snacks. The February 1990 and 1992 issues of *Family Travel Times* include *TWYCH's Airline Guide,* which contains a rundown of the children's services offered by 46 airlines.

Getting Around The **French National Railways** (SNCF) accommodates family travel by allowing children under four to travel free (provided they don't occupy a seat) and by allowing children four to 11 to travel at half fare. There is also the *Carte Kiwi,* costing 395 francs, which allows children under 16 and up to four accompanying adults to travel at half fare.

Baby-sitting Services First check with the hotel concierge for recommended child-care arrangements. Paris agencies: **American University of Paris** (31 av. Bosquet, 75007 Paris, tel. 45–55–91–73); **Baby Sitting Express** (22 rue de Picardie, 75003 Paris, tel. 42–77–45–44); **Allo Service Maman** (21 rue de Brey, 75017 Paris, tel. 42–67–99–37); **Home Service** (5 rue Yvon-Villarceau, 75116 Paris, tel. 45–00–82–51); **Institut Catholique** (21 rue d'Assas, 75006 Paris, tel. 45–48–31–70).

French baby-sitters charge an average of 25–30 francs per hour.

Miscellaneous Contact the **CIDJ** (Centre d'Information et de Documentation pour la Jeunesse, 101 quai Branly, 75015 Paris, tel. 45–67–35–85) for information about activities and events for youngsters in France.

Hints for Disabled Travelers

In France The situation in France is better than average. The French government is doing much to ensure that public facilities provide for disabled visitors, and it has produced an excellent booklet—*Touristes Quand Même*—with an English glossary and easily understood symbols detailing, region by region, facilities available to the disabled in transportation systems and museums and monuments. The booklet is available from French national tourist offices and from the main Paris Tourist Office, or from the **Comité National Français de Liaison pour la Réadaptation des Handicapés** (38 blvd. Raspail, 75007 Paris, tel. 45–44–33–23).

A number of monuments, hotels, and museums—especially those constructed within the past decade—are equipped with ramps, elevators, or special toilet facilities. Lists of regional hotels include a symbol to indicate which hotels have rooms that are accessible to the disabled. Similarly, the SNCF has special cars on some trains that have been reserved exclusively for the disabled and can arrange for wheelchair-bound passengers to be escorted on and off trains and assisted in catching connecting trains (the latter service must be requested in advance).

A helpful organization in Paris is the **Association des Paralysés de France** (17 blvd. Auguste-Blanqui, 75013 Paris, tel. 40–78–69–00), which publishes a useful hotel list.

Free baby-sitting for physically and mentally disabled children is provided by the **Fondation Claude Pompidou** (42 rue du Louvre, 75001 Paris, tel. 45–08–45–15; phone between 2 and 6). Services are available at all times.

In the U.S. Tours that are especially designed for disabled travelers generally parallel those for nondisabled travelers, albeit at a more leisurely pace. For a complete list of tour operators who arrange such travel, write to the **Society for the Advancement of Travel for the Handicapped** (347 5th Ave., Suite 610, New York, NY 10016, tel. 212/447–7288, fax 212/725–8253). Annual membership costs $45, or $25 for senior citizens and students. Send a stamped, self-addressed envelope.

Moss Rehabilitation Hospital (1200 W. Tabor Rd., Philadelphia, PA 19141–3099, tel. 215/456–9603) answers inquiries regarding specific cities and countries and provides toll-free telephone numbers for airlines with special lines for the hard of hearing and, again, listings of selected tour operators.

The **Information Center for Individuals with Disabilities** (Fort Point Pl., 1st floor, 27–43 Wormwood St., Boston, MA 02210, tel. 617/727–5540) offers useful problem-solving assistance, including lists of travel agents that specialize in tours for the disabled.

Mobility International USA (Box 3551, Eugene, OR 97403, tel. 503/343–1284) has information on accommodations, organized study, and so forth around the world.

The Itinerary (Box 2012, Bayonne, NJ 07002, tel. 201/858–3400) is a bimonthly travel magazine for the disabled.

Hints for Older Travelers

The **American Association of Retired Persons** (601 E St. NW, Washington, DC 20049, tel. 202/434–2277) has two programs for independent travelers: (1) *The Purchase Privilege Program,* which offers discounts on hotels, airfare, car rentals, and sightseeing, and (2) the *AARP Motoring Plan,* provided by Amoco, which offers emergency aid and trip-routing information for an annual fee of $39.95 per couple. The AARP can also arrange group tours, some including apartment living in Europe. AARP members must be 50 or older. Annual dues are $8 per person or per couple.

When using an AARP or other identification card, ask for a reduced hotel rate at the time you make your reservation, not when you check out. At participating restaurants, show your card to the maître d' before you're seated, since discounts may be limited to certain set menus, days, or hours. When renting a car, be sure to ask about special promotional rates that might offer greater savings than the available discount.

Elderhostel (75 Federal St., 3rd floor, Boston, MA 02210, tel. 617/426–7788) is an innovative educational program for people 60 and older. Participants live in dorms on some 1,600 campuses around the world. Mornings are devoted to lectures and seminars; afternoons to sightseeing and field trips. All-inclusive fees for two- to three-week international trips, including room, board, tuition, and round-trip transportation, range from $1,800 to $4,500.

Travel Industry and Disabled Exchange (TIDE, 5435 Donna Ave., Tarzana, CA 91356, tel. 818/368–5648) is an industry-based organization with a $15 per person annual membership fee. Members receive a quarterly newsletter and information on travel agencies and tours.

National Council of Senior Citizens (1331 F St. NW, Washington, DC 20004, tel. 202/347–8800) is a nonprofit advocacy group with some 5,000 local clubs across the country. Annual membership is $12 per person or per couple. Members receive a monthly newspaper with travel information and an identification card for reduced-rate hotels and car rentals.

Mature Outlook (6001 N. Clark St., Chicago, IL 60660, tel. 800/336–6330), a subsidiary of Sears Roebuck & Co., is a travel club for people over 50, offering hotel and motel discounts and a bimonthly newsletter. Annual membership is $9.95 per couple. Instant membership is available at participating Holiday Inns.

In France

Senior citizens (men over 62 and women over 60) enjoy reduced museum admission (usually 50%) and cheap train tickets (the **Carte Vermeil,** available at stations throughout France; the Carte Vermeil costs 165 francs a year and entitles the holder to discounts of up to 50%, depending on when you travel). Senior citizens should keep their passport or an identification card with them at all times.

Arriving and Departing

As the air routes between North America and France are among the world's most heavily traveled, passengers have many airlines and fares to choose from. But fares change with stunning rapidity, so consult your travel agent on which bargains are currently available.

From the U.S. by Plane

Be certain to distinguish among (1) nonstop flights—no changes, no stops; (2) direct flights—no changes but one or more stops; and (3) connecting flights—two or more planes, one or more stops.

Discount Flights The best advice is to begin looking for a suitable offer well before the planned departure date. With a little bit of patience, you should be able to find a ticket that's both dependable and affordable.

The major airlines offer a range of tickets that can increase the price of any given seat by more than 300%, depending on the day of purchase. As a rule, the further in advance you buy the ticket, the less expensive it is and the greater the penalty (up to 100%) for canceling. Check with the airlines for details.

APEX fares The best buy is not necessarily an APEX (advance-purchase) ticket on one of the major airlines. APEX tickets carry certain restrictions: They must be bought in advance (usually 21 days); they restrict your travel, usually with a minimum stay of seven days and a maximum of 90; and they penalize you for changes—voluntary or not—in your travel plans. But if you can work around these drawbacks (and most travelers can), they are among the best-value fares available, especially if you plan to travel during the low season: November through March. The shoulder season—April, May, and mid-September through October—has the next best rates.

If a reservationist tells you that the least expensive seats are no longer available on a certain flight, ask to be put on a waiting list. Some airlines don't offer waiting lists for the lowest fares, in which case you can call on subsequent mornings to see about openings. Cancellations and last-minute adjustments by airlines trying to fill all their seats often result in additional cut-rate tickets.

If you end up paying more than you wish for a ticket, keep your eye on advertisements in the travel sections of newspapers. An airline that anticipates empty seats on a flight may increase the number of tickets at the lowest price, or even introduce a lower fare. Some airlines will then refund the difference in cost to you, provided that you approach them. But don't expect them to contact you. Travel agents can help you with these fluctuations in cost. They have access to computer networks that show the lowest fares before they're advertised; and airlines will be more likely to bend when dealing with productive agents. You can also call the airlines and ask about late-saver fares, which usually must be purchased between one and three days before the flight. These tickets give maximum savings, but it's difficult to predict when, and if, they'll be available.

Consolidators Buying directly from the major airlines is by no means your only choice. Some of the most attractive fares are offered by consolidator companies, which buy blocks of tickets at cut-rate prices from airlines trying to fill up their planes. There are, however, a few drawbacks: Consolidator tickets are often nonrefundable, and ensuing flights may present inconveniences, such as indirect routes, long layovers in connecting cities, and unfavorable seating assignments. You probably won't be accepted on another airline if your flight is delayed, and you may be disqualified for frequent-flier-mileage credit. Also, before buying your ticket, you may want to check the consolidator's reputation with the Better Business Bureau. Most consolidators are perfectly reliable, but it's always best to play it safe.

If you can accept these restrictions and minor risks, a ticket purchased through a consolidator is, more often than not, the most economical option. During the low season in early 1992, round-trip tickets between New York and Paris were as low as $390. Well-known consolidators include **Access International** (701 W. 31st St., Suite 1104, New York, NY 10001, tel. 800/825–3633 or 212/465–0707), **Sunline Express** (607 Market St., San Francisco, CA 94105, tel. 415/541–7800 or 800/786–5463), **UniTravel** (Box 12485, St. Louis, MO 63132, tel. 800/325–2222 or 314/569–2501), and **Up & Away Travel** (141 E. 44th St., Suite 403, New York, NY 10017, tel. 212/972–2345 or 800/275–8001).

Charters Since the deregulation of the airline industry, charter flights have fallen out of favor among budget travelers, especially on trips to Europe. Consolidators and major airlines have lowered many of their fares, allowing travelers to bypass the various risks and inconveniences of charter flights—bankruptcy of the operator, long delays, long lines at check-in, and infrequent flight scheduling. In spite of this, you may find that a charter company is offering the least expensive ticket at the time you wish to travel. If you're set on a charter fare, check the reputation of the company with the Better Business Bureau, and take out trip cancellation insurance, making sure it covers the potential failure of the operator: Some companies have gone bankrupt in the past, leaving travelers stranded in Europe, or without the future trip they had paid for.

Charter flights to Europe are offered by **Council Charter** (205 E. 42nd St., New York, NY 10017, tel. 800/800–8222 or 212/661–0311), a division of CIEE (Council on International Educational Exchange); **DER Tours** (Box 1606, Des Plaines, IL 60017, tel. 800/782–2424); and **Travel Charter** (1120 E. Long Lake Rd., Troy, MI 48098, tel. 800/521–5267 or 313/528–3570).

Courier Travel If you're willing to put up with a few severe restrictions in exchange for a substantially reduced airfare, you may be interested in flying as an air courier—a traveler who accompanies shipments between designated points, on both outbound and inbound flights. Restrictions vary: Many services limit you to one carry-on bag (no check-ins) and cash payment; and they often permit only one courier to a given flight. However, savings can be considerable. Two agents that handle courier travel are **Now Voyager** (74 Varick St., Suite 307, New York, NY 10013, tel. 212/431–1616), which charges a $50 one-year registration fee, and **Courier Travel Service** (tel. 212/836–1989 or 800/922–2359), which has no fee. For "A Simple Guide to Courier Travel," send $15.95 (includes postage and handling) to the **Carriage Group** (Box 2394, Lake Oswego, OR 97035, tel. 800/344–9375).

Travel Clubs Still another option is to join a travel club that arranges discounts for its members. Some clubs specialize in getting substantial reductions from suppliers, others provide smaller discounts by rebating part of their commission. Among the best-known travel clubs are **Discount Travel International** (114 Forrest Ave., Suite 203, Narberth, PA 19072, tel. 215/668–7184 or 800/334–9294; membership $45), **Moment's Notice** (425 Madison Ave., New York, NY 10017, tel. 212/486–0500; membership $19.92), and **Worldwide Discount Travel Club** (1674

Meridian Ave., Suite 300, Miami Beach, FL 33139, tel. 305/534–2082; membership $50).

Commission Rebates Some travel agencies offer rebates on commissions, usually in exchange for a small fee. These include **Smart Traveller** (Box 330106, Miami, FL 33133, tel. 800/226–3338 or 305/448–3338) and **Travel Avenue** (641 West Lake St., Suite 2001, Chicago, IL 60606, tel. 800/333–3335).

Airports and Airlines The U.S. airlines that serve France are **TWA** (tel. 800/892–4141), **American Airlines** (tel. 800/433–7300), and **Delta** (tel. 800/241–4141). All fly to Paris's Charles de Gaulle (Roissy) Airport (tel. 48–62–22–80) and Orly (tel. 49–75–15–15). Delta also flies to Nice.

Flying Time to Paris From New York: 7½ hours. From Chicago: nine hours. From Los Angeles: 11 hours.

Enjoying the Flight Since the air on a plane is dry, it helps, while flying, to drink a lot of nonalcoholic liquids; drinking alcohol contributes to jet lag, as does eating heavy meals on board. Feet swell at high altitudes, so it's a good idea to remove your shoes while in flight. Sleepers usually prefer window seats to curl up against; those who like to move about the cabin should ask for aisle seats. Bulkhead seats (located in the front row of each cabin) have more leg room, but seat trays are attached to the arms of your seat rather than to the back of the seat in front. Bulkhead seats are generally reserved for the elderly, the disabled, and those traveling with babies.

Smoking On international flights, where smoking is permitted, you may request a nonsmoking seat during check-in or when you book your ticket. If the airline tells you there are no seats available in the nonsmoking section on the day of the flight, insist on one: Department of Transportation regulations require that U.S. carriers find seats for all nonsmokers, provided they meet check-in time restrictions. Avoiding smoke can be a serious problem on non-U.S. carriers.

From the U.K. by Plane, Car, Train, and Bus

By Plane The best values are charter flights, including service between Gatwick and Beauvais (north of Paris) provided by Caledonian Airways, the charter division of British Airways (tel. 0293/36321). Contact **Nouvelles Frontières** (1–2 Hanover St., London W1R 9WB, tel. 071/629–7772).

Scheduled service between the United Kingdom and France is provided by **Air France** (tel. 081/759–2311) and **British Airways** (tel. 081/897–4000).

The route from London to Paris (journey time: one hour) is the busiest in Europe, with up to 17 flights daily from Heathrow (Air France/British Airways) and four or five from Gatwick (Air France), all to Charles de Gaulle (also known as Roissy). There are also regular flights—geared mainly to businesspeople—from the new London City Airport in the Docklands; direct flights to Paris from several regional U.K. airports, including Manchester, Birmingham, Glasgow, Edinburgh, and Southampton; and flights from London to Nice, Lyon, Bordeaux, Marseille, Clermont-Ferrand, Caen, Quimper, Nantes, Montpellier, and Toulouse, as well as from Manchester to Nice.

By Car Beginning in late 1993, cars will be able to reach France through the Channel Tunnel aboard special double-decker trains that will shuttle between Folkestone and Sangatte (near Calais) every 15 minutes.

In the meantime, there is no shortage of ferry crossings from England to France; all boats (and Hovercraft) welcome motor vehicles. The quickest and most frequent service, with the lowest overall fares, is between Dover and Calais: Sealink and P & O run about 16 daily departures in summer and at least 10 in winter. The journey time is 75 minutes.

Each of the other routes has geographic advantages to offset its comparative slowness. Ramsgate–Dunkirk (Sally Line, 2½ hours) offers excellent restaurant and duty-free facilities, plus minimum fuss at port terminals; Newhaven–Dieppe (Sealink, 4½ hours) lands you in pretty Normandy; Portsmouth–Caen/St-Malo (Brittany Ferries, six hours) can take you either to Brittany (St-Malo) or within striking distance of Paris (Caen); Portsmouth–Le Havre/Cherbourg (P & O, six hours), Plymouth–Roscoff (Brittany Ferries, eight hours), and Poole/Weymouth–Cherbourg (Brittany Ferries, eight hours) all cater to drivers from Wales and southwestern England.

The Ramsgate–Dunkirk service operates several times daily, the rest at least once a day (Weymouth–Cherbourg summer only). The Hoverspeed crossings between Dover and Boulogne/Calais take just over half an hour but are suspended during heavy winds and, therefore, unreliable in winter.

Fares vary with the season and time of crossing. Winter is cheapest, summer most expensive; it costs less to cross at night than during the day. Contact the relevant ferry operator for details: **Sealink** (tel. 0233/647047), **Sally Line** (tel. 0843/595566), **Brittany Ferries** (tel. 0705/827701), **P & O** (tel. 0171/734–4431), and **Hoverspeed** (tel. 0304/240241).

Whichever route you choose, it is advisable to book ahead.

By Train If your budget is tight, traveling by train may be your best bet, since all London–Paris train prices include the cost of the Channel crossing. Expect hassles, though: purposeless waiting, lengthy lines, and a pervading air of either dilapidation (British Rail) or indifference (French officialdom). In addition, the trip is time-consuming—until the Channel Tunnel opens in late 1993 (slashing journey time to 3½ hours), the journeys from London to Paris via Dover take around seven hours, and the trip via Newhaven–Dieppe—offering the cheapest prices to those aged under 26—takes nine hours—and that's if there are no unforeseen delays.

Check train/ferry prices with Sealink/British Rail, as there are numerous variations, depending on the time, season, crossing, and length of travel. The faster and more convenient Hovercraft service via Dover–Boulogne takes under six hours, but remember that Hovercraft are more affected by high winds and are relatively expensive (around £46 each way, although five-day minivacations are a good value at just around £60). There are also budget-wise five-day trips to such destinations as Lyon, Avignon, and Cannes. For more information contact Sealink or British Rail.

Paris is the hub of the French train system, and a change, both of train and station, is often necessary if your destination lies farther afield. There are, however, direct trains from London to Strasbourg, Lyon, the Alps, the Riviera, and the Pyrénées.

By Bus Unless you're eligible for travel with a Carte Vermeil or Carte Jeune (*see* By Train, *below*), buses offer you the lowest fares of all. The London–Paris bus journey costs only a little over £50 round-trip.

Eurolines (tel. 071/730–0202), the international affiliate of **National Express,** runs four daily *Citysprint* buses in summer from Victoria Coach Station to the rue Lafayette in Paris near the Gare du Nord; these buses use the Hovercraft crossing, and the journey time is around 7½ hours. Three daily buses from Victoria to the Porte de la Villette on the outskirts of Paris use traditional ferries for the Channel crossing and take a bit longer (nine to 10 hours).

Eurolines has buses to the Riviera, leaving Victoria three times a week for such resorts as Nice and Cannes. The round-trip fare to Cannes is £99. The Atlantic coast is also served by Eurolines, with two buses a week to Bordeaux and Biarritz in mid-summer (journey time 24 hours; price approximately £92 round-trip); the Bordeaux service can be extended to Lourdes via Tarbes. There is also regular service from London to Chamonix and the Alps (22½ hours; around £85 round-trip).

In addition, Eurolines (tel. 071/730–0202) operates an express service that runs overnight to Grenoble, where there are connecting services to Nice and Marseille (return trip to Nice costs around £99), as well as a fast bus service to Lyon six days a week in summer, leaving London mid-evening and reaching Lyon the following afternoon (around £75 round-trip).

Staying in France

Getting Around France

By far the best option for budget travel in France is by train. Long-distance bus travel is virtually nonexistent while air travel and car rental can be quite expensive. The price of a second-class Paris–Lyon train ticket is $48; by air, the fare is $142. Paris–Nice costs $84 by train compared with $176 by plane. And the cost of travel from the airport to downtown still has to be added on! Travelers under 26 or over 60 can enjoy discount fares at off-peak times, reducing the price of a Paris–Nice ticket to $42 (rail) or $103 (plane).

By Train The **SNCF** is generally recognized as Europe's best national train service: It's fast, punctual, comfortable, and comprehensive. The high-speed TGVs, or *Trains à Grande Vitesse,* the best domestic trains, average 255 kph (160 mph) on the Lyon/southeast line, 300 kph (190 mph) on the Bordeaux/southwest line between Paris and Lyon/Switzerland/the Riviera, and between Angers/Nantes and Tours/Poitiers/Bordeaux. As with other mainline trains, you may need to pay a small supplement when taking a TGV at peak hours. Unlike other trains, the TGV *always* requires a seat reservation—easily obtained at the ticket window or from an automatic machine (cost: about $3). Seat reservations are reassuring but seldom necessary on other mainline French trains, except at certain busy holiday times.

If you are traveling from Paris (or any other station terminus), get to the station half an hour before departure to ensure yourself a good seat. The majority of intercity trains in France consist of open-plan cars and are known as *Corail* trains. They are clean and extremely comfortable, even in second class (which costs 50% less than first class). Trains on regional branch lines are currently being spruced up but lag behind in style and quality. Note that food on French trains, though usually good, is not worth the money.

Long journeys can often be made without overnight travel. If yours can't, your least expensive option is a *couchette* (a bunk provided with sheet and pillow), six to a compartment. *Voitures-lits* (sleeping cars) offer more privacy at higher cost (370 francs in a compartment for two, 247 francs in a compartment for three). Special summer night trains from Paris to Spain and the Riviera, geared to younger people, are equipped with disco and bar to enable you to dance and talk the night away.

Fares Various reduced fares are available. Senior citizens (over 60) and young people (under 26) are eligible for the **Carte Vermeil** (165 francs) and **Carrissimo** card respectively, with proof of identity and two passport photos. The Carrissimo card costs 190 francs (four trips) or 350 francs (eight trips) and can be used by up to four young people traveling together. The SNCF offers 50% reductions during "blue" periods (most of the time) and 20% the rest of the time ("white" periods: noon Friday through noon Saturday; 3 PM Sunday through noon Monday). On major holidays ("red" periods), there are no reductions. A calendar of red/white/blue periods is available at any station, and you can buy tickets at any station, too. Note that there is no reduction for buying a round-trip *(aller-retour)* ticket rather than a one-way *(aller simple)* ticket with one exception: Rail travelers get a 25% discount for a return ticket (ask for a *billet de séjour*) between stations at least 500 kilometers apart, providing journeys do not take place at peak times and include at least part of a Sunday. For further information contact the SNCF (88 rue St-Lazare, 75009 Paris, tel. 45–82–50–50).

By Bus France's excellent train service means that long-distance buses are rare; regional buses, too, are found mainly where the train service is skimpy. Excursions and bus holidays are organized by the SNCF and other tourist organizations, such as **Horizons Européens.** Ask for the brochure at any major travel agent, or contact **France-Tourisme** (3 rue d'Alger, 75001 Paris, tel. 42–61–85–50).

By Car

Road Conditions Roads marked N *(Route Nationale)* and D *(Route Départementale)* are the best option for budget travelers. They are usually wide, unencumbered, and fast (you can average 80 kph [50 mph] with luck), and there are no tolls *(péages)*, as on expressways, which are designated as A *(Autoroutes)*. Rates vary and can be steep.

There are excellent links between Paris and most French cities, but poor ones between the provinces (principal exceptions: the A62 between Bordeaux and Toulouse, and the A9/A8 that runs the length of the Mediterranean).

It is often difficult to avoid Paris when crossing France; this need not cause too many problems if you steer clear of the rush hours (7–9:30 AM and 4:30–7:30 PM).

The cheap, informative, and well-presented regional yellow Michelin maps are an invaluable navigational aid.

Gas Gas prices vary enormously: anything from 5 to 6 francs per liter. You'll pay least outside supermarkets and hypermarkets, and the most in Paris, along expressways, and in isolated rural areas. Don't let your tank get too low (if you're unlucky, you can go for many miles in the country without hitting a gas station). At the pumps, opt for "super" (high-grade/four-star), recommended for most cars, rather than "essence" (low-grade/two-star).

Rules of the Road Drive on the right. Be aware of the erratically followed French tradition of giving way to drivers coming from the right, unless there is an international stop sign. Seat belts are obligatory for all passengers, and children under 12 may not travel in the front seat. Speed limits: 130 kph (81 mph) on expressways; 110 kph (68 mph) on major highways; 90 kph (56 mph) on minor rural roads; 50 kph (31 mph) in towns. French drivers break these limits and police dish out hefty on-the-spot fines with equal abandon.

Driver's licenses issued in the United States and Canada are valid in France, but you must be able to prove you have third-party insurance. You may also take out an International Driving Permit before you leave to smooth out difficulties if you have an accident or as an additional piece of identification. Permits are available for a small fee through local offices of the **American Automobile Association** (AAA) and the **Canadian Automobile Association** (CAA), or from their main offices (AAA, 1000 AAA Dr., Heathrow, FL 32746–0001, tel. 800/336–4357; CAA, 2 Carlton St., Toronto, Ont. M5B 1K4, tel. 416/964–3170).

Parking Parking is a nightmare in Paris and often difficult in large towns. Meters and ticket-machines (pay and display) are commonplace (be sure to have a supply of 1-franc coins). In smaller towns, parking may be permitted on one side of the street only, alternating every two weeks: Pay attention to signs. The French park as anarchically as they drive, but don't follow their example: If you're caught out of bounds, you could be due for a hefty fine and your vehicle may be unceremoniously towed away to the dreaded compound (500 francs to retrieve it).

Breakdowns If you break down on an expressway, go to the nearest roadside emergency telephone and call the breakdown service. If you break down anywhere else, find the nearest garage or, failing all else, contact the police (dial 17).

Car Rentals If you're flying into Paris or some other city in France and are planning to spend time there, save money by arranging to pick up your car in the city the day you depart; otherwise, arrange to pick up and return your car at the airport. You'll have to weigh the added expense of renting a car from a major company with an airport office against the savings on a car from a budget company with offices in town. You could waste precious hours trying to locate the budget company in return for only a small financial savings. If you're arriving and departing from different airports, look for a one-way car rental with no return fees.

Be prepared to pay more for cars with automatic transmissions. Since they are not as readily available as those with manual transmissions, reserve them well in advance.

To find the cheapest car rentals you will need to venture into the nearby suburbs. The best bet is **Eco Car** (83 av. Michelet, 93400 St-Ouen, tel. 40–10–23–28), about a 10-minute walk from the Porte de Clignancourt métro stop. Eco Car provides a Renault 5 for around $20 a day plus 20¢ per kilometer; a three-day rental (with 600 kilometers included) costs $130. **Rual** (94 av. Jean-Jaurès, 93500 Pantin, tel. 48–45–21–20), near the Porte de la Villette métro stop, offers a Peugeot 205 for around $40 a day plus 45¢ per kilometer. If you rent a car for at least a week, you pay about $70 a day for unlimited mileage.

The advantage of renting from the biggest firms, **Avis** and **Hertz**, is that their extensive nationwide networks enable you to pick up a car in one town and leave it in another at no extra charge. An unlimited-mileage rental of at least a week will cost roughly $600 a week plus $85 for each extra day. If you plan to rent for three weeks or more, consider Avis's 30-day $1,700 scheme (maximum 3,000 kilometers).

Avis (5 rue Bixio, 75007 Paris, tel. 45–50–32–31) and Hertz (27 rue St-Ferdinand, 75017 Paris, tel. 45–74–97–39) also offer three-day weekend deals (maximum 1,000 kilometers) for around $180. The cost is just $140 if you pick up and leave your car outside popular areas such as Paris or the Riviera. For daily car rentals, Avis, Hertz, and **National Interrent** (48 rue de Berri, 75008 Paris, tel. 45–63–04–27) all offer deals starting at around $55 a day plus 85¢ per kilometer ($16 a day extra for collision damage waiver). All prices quoted include taxes and are based on the cheapest models available: Ford Fiesta (Hertz); Opel Corsa, Volkswagen Polo, or Fiat Uno (Avis); Peugeot 205, Fiat Uno, or Renault 5 (National Interrent).

It's best to arrange a car rental before you leave. You won't save money by waiting until you arrive in France, and you may find that the type of car you want is not available at the last minute. Rental companies usually charge according to the exchange rate of the dollar at the time the car is returned or when the credit-card payment is processed. Three companies with special programs to help you hedge against the falling dollar, by guaranteeing advertised rates if you pay in advance, are **Budget Rent-a-Car** (3350 Boyington St., Carrollton, TX 75006, tel. 800/527–0700), **Connex Travel International** (983 Main St. Peekskill, NY 10566, tel. 800/333–3949), and **Cortell International,** 17310 Red Hill Ave., Suite 360, Irvine, CA 92714, tel. 800/228–2535). Other budget rental companies serving Europe include **Europe by Car** (1 Rockefeller Plaza, New York, NY 10020, tel. 212/245–1713, 800/223–1516, in 800/252–9401), **Auto Europe** (Box 1097 Sharps Wharf, Camden, ME 04843, tel. 800/223–5555, in Maine 800/342–5202, in Canada 800/237–2465), **Foremost Euro-Car** (5430 Van Nuys Blvd., Van Nuys, CA 91404, tel. 800/423–3111), and **Kemwel** (106 Calvert St. Harrison, NY 10528, tel. 800/678–0678). Others with European rentals include **Avis** (tel. 800/331–1212), **Hertz** (tel. 800/223–6472, in New York 800/654–3001), and **National Interrent** (tel. 800/CAR–RENT).

By Plane France's domestic airline service is called **Air Inter,** with flights from Paris to all major cities and many interregional flights. For long journeys—from Paris to the Riviera, for instance—air travel is a time saver, though train travel is always much cheaper. Most domestic flights from Paris leave from **Orly Airport**

(tel. 49–75–15–15). For details, check with the local airport or call Air Inter (tel. 45–46–90–00).

By Bicycle There is no shortage of wide, empty roads and flat or rolling countryside in France suitable for biking. The French themselves are great bicycling enthusiasts. The most popular areas for cycling include the Loire Valley, Charente, Burgundy, Normandy, Brittany, Provence, the Landes, and the Vosges. All but the hardiest riders will find the Alps and Pyrénées tough going.

Bikes can be hired at more than 250 train stations (ask for the SNCF *Guide du Train et du Vélo*) for 40 francs a day (30 francs a day from the third day, 20 francs a day from day 11); you need to leave a 500-franc deposit unless you have a Visa or MasterCard. You must usually return the bike to a station within the same département. Bikes may be sent as luggage on trains (cost: 75 francs packed, 100 francs unpacked), but many in rural areas will transport them free of charge.

For renting a bike in Paris try **Bicyclub** (8 pl. de la Porte-de-Champerret, 75017 Paris, el. 42–27–28–82). Rates are 60 francs per day or 350 francs per week. **Paris Vélo** (2 rue du Fer-à-Moulin, 75005 Paris, tel. 43–37–59–22) rents out bikes for 80 francs per day or 360 francs per week. Both stores require a 1,000-franc deposit, though may accept a credit card.

For further information contact the Fédération Française de Cyclotourisme (8 rue Jean-Marie-Jégo, 75013 Paris, tel. 45–80–30–21). The yellow Michelin maps (1:200,000 scale) are fine for roads, but the best large-scale maps are prepared by the Institut Géographique National (IGN, 107 rue La Boétie, 75008 Paris, tel. 42–25–87–90). Try their blue series (1:25,000) or orange series (1:50,000). Both indicate elevations and steep grades. Several good bike routes are described in detail in the chapters that follow.

On Foot France has a huge network of footpaths—some 40,000 kilometers (25,000 miles). The most popular are in such hilly regions as the Vosges, Massif Central, Pyrénées, Alps, Ardennes, Jura, Beaujolais, and Champagne. Other good bets include windswept Brittany, the picturesque Dordogne Valley, and forested areas of the Ile-de-France (Fontainebleau, St-Germain, Rambouillet). For details contact the **Club Alpin Français** (24 av. Laumière, 75019 Paris, tel. 42–02–68–64) or the **Fédération Française de la Randonnée Pédestre** (8 av. Marceau, 75008 Paris, tel. 47–23–62–32), which publishes good topographical maps and guides. The IGN maps sold in many bookshops are also invaluable (*see* Biking, *above*).

Telephones

Local Calls The French telephone system is modern and efficient. Telephone booths are plentiful; you will nearly always find them at post offices and often in cafés. A local call costs 73 centimes for the first minute plus 12 centimes per additional minute; half-price rates apply weekdays between 9:30 PM and 8 AM, from 1:30 PM Saturday, and all day Sunday.

Pay phones work principally with 50-centime, 1- and 5-franc coins (1 franc minimum). Lift the receiver, place the coin or coins in the appropriate slots, and dial. Unused coins are returned when you hang up. A vast number of French pay phones are now operated by cards *(télécartes)*, which you can buy from post offices and some tobacco shops, or *tabacs* (cost: 40 francs for 50 units; 96 francs for 120).

All French phone numbers have eight digits; a code is required only when calling the Paris region from the provinces (add 16–1 for Paris) and for calling the provinces from Paris (16 then the number). The number system was changed only in 1985; therefore, you may still come across some seven-digit numbers (in Paris) and some six-digit ones (elsewhere). Add 4 to the beginning of such Paris numbers, and the former two-figure area code to provincial ones.

International Calls Dial 19 and wait for the tone, then dial the country code (1 for the United States and Canada; 44 for the United Kingdom), area code (minus any initial 0) and number.

Calling at certain specified times lowers your per-minute cost: You'll pay 5.60 francs on calls made to the United States and Canada 2 AM–noon daily (French time), 6.30 francs noon–2 PM and 8 PM–2 AM weekdays, noon–2 AM Sunday; 3 francs per minute on calls to the United Kingdom 9:30 PM–8 AM and 2 AM–8 PM Saturday; all-day Sunday and holidays. These rates compare favorably to daytime per-minute costs: 7.70 francs to the United States and Canada, 4.50 francs to the United Kingdom. Three minutes from Paris to New York or Los Angeles costs 16.80–23.10 francs.

AT&T's USA Direct program allows callers to take advantage of AT&T rates by connecting directly with the AT&T system. To do so from France dial 0011. You can either dial direct (1 + area code + number), billing the call to a credit card, or make a collect call.

Operators and Information To find a number in France or to request other information, dial 12 (no charge). For international inquiries, dial 19–33 plus the country code.

Mail

Postal Rates Airmail letters to the United States and Canada cost 4 francs for 20 grams, 6.90 francs for 30 grams, 7.20 francs for 40 grams, and 7.50 francs for 50 grams. Letters to the United Kingdom cost 2.50 francs for up to 20 grams. Letters cost 2.50 francs within France; postcards cost 2.30 francs within France and if sent to Canada, the United States, the United Kingdom, and Common Market countries; 3.70 francs if sent airmail to North America. Stamps can be bought in post offices and cafés sporting a red *Tabac* sign outside.

Receiving Mail If you're uncertain where you'll be staying, have mail sent to **American Express** (tel. 800/543–4080 for a list of foreign offices) or to the local post office, addressed as **Poste Restante.** American Express has a $2 service charge per letter, and you must have either American Express traveler's checks or an account with American Express, plus proper I.D.

Tipping

You are under no obligation to leave tips in bars and restaurants, but if you are especially pleased with the service leave a few small coins from your change. Tip taxi drivers and hairdressers about 10%. Give ushers in theaters and movie theaters

1 or 2 francs. In some theaters and hotels, coat check attendants may expect nothing (if there is a sign saying *Pourboire Interdit*—Tips Forbidden); otherwise give them 5 francs. Washroom attendants usually get 5 francs, though the sum is often posted.

If you stay in a hotel for more than two or three days, it is customary to leave something for the chambermaid—about 10 francs per day. In expensive hotels you may well call on the services of a baggage porter (bell boy) and hotel porter and possibly the telephone receptionist. All expect a tip: Plan on about 10 francs per item for the baggage boy, but the other tips will depend on how much you've used their services—common sense must guide you here. In hotels that provide room service, give 5 francs to the waiter (this does not apply to breakfast served in your room). If the chambermaid does some pressing or laundering for you, give her 5 francs on top of the charge made.

Gas-station attendants get nothing for gas or oil, and 5 or 10 francs for checking tires. Train and airport porters get a fixed sum (6–10 francs) per bag, but you're better off getting your own baggage cart if you can (a 10-franc coin—refundable—is sometimes necessary). Museum guides should get 5–10 francs after a guided tour, and it is standard practice to tip tour guides (and bus drivers) 10 francs or more after an excursion, depending on its length.

Opening and Closing Times

Banks Banks are open weekdays but have no strict pattern regarding times. In general, though, hours are from 9:30 to 4:30. Most banks, but not all, take a one-hour, or even a 90-minute, lunch break. Banks in rural areas are often open Saturday instead of Monday.

Museums Most museums are closed one day a week (usually Tuesday) and on national holidays. Usual opening times are from 9:30 to 5 or 6. Many museums close for lunch (noon–2); many are open afternoons only on Sunday.

Shops Large stores in big towns are open from 9 or 9:30 until 6 or 7 (without a lunch break). Smaller shops often open earlier (8 AM) and close later (8 PM) but take a lengthy lunch break (1–4). This siesta-type schedule is routine in the south of France. Corner groceries, often run by immigrants (*"l'Arabe du coin"*), frequently stay open until around 10 PM.

Shopping

Though Paris is the fashion capital, good clothes can be bought everywhere and are invariably cheaper outside the capital; the presence of numerous clothing manufacturers just outside Troyes, in Burgundy, makes prices there up to 50% lower than elsewhere in France. Local wines and brandies such as cognac, armagnac, calvados, and marc come in great variety in France. Hand-crafted items are abundant: olive-wood bowls and utensils and the clay figurines known as *santons* in Provence, and local pottery, *faïence*, such as that found in Quimper, Brittany, for instance. Every region has its distinctive food products as well.

V.A.T. Refunds A number of shops, particularly large stores and shops in holiday resorts, offer V.A.T. refunds to foreign shoppers. You are entitled to an Export Discount of 13%, only applicable if your purchases in the same store reach a minimum 4,200 francs (for residents of EC countries) or 2,000 francs (residents of non-EC countries).

Bargaining Shop prices are clearly marked, and bargaining isn't a way of life. Still, at outdoor markets and flea markets and in antiques stores, you can try your luck. If you're thinking of buying several items, you've nothing to lose by cheerfully suggesting to the storeholder, *"Vous me faites un prix?"* ("How about a discount?").

Beaches

When your prime concern is inexpensive accommodations and perhaps a few quiet moments on the sand, you'll skip the beach scene in July and August in favor of June or September.

You'll also steer clear of the Riviera. It's as crowded as it is pricey, and, anyway, sand is in shorter supply than pebbles. Better beaches, with vast stretches of sand, face north toward the Channel and west toward the Atlantic. Prices are highest at the popular resorts such as Biarritz, Arcachon, Les Sables d'Olonne, La Baule, Dinard, St-Malo, Cabourg, Deauville, and Le Touquet—though even here the careful traveler can find good values. Price levels are lower at St-Raphael on the Mediterranean, at St-Georges de Didonne and St-Jean-de-Luz on the Atlantic, and Etretat, Trouville, and Houlgate on the Channel.

Between October and May, prices are rock bottom—at the sprinkling of hotels that remain open. But particularly at Breton beaches, the nation's most picturesque, there's a great deal to be said for the eerie solitude of a beach town in blustery weather, or in sunniest springtime just before the hordes descend.

Lodging

Hotels in France are among the cheapest in western Europe. They vary considerably in comfort and style, and are classed by the state in categories ranging from * through **** deluxe. One- and two-star hotels form the backbone of our recommendations, though some moderately priced three-star hotels are included, too. Because France's hotel infrastructure is so extensive and affordable, the rare alternative accommodation, such as a youth hostel, is a poor second choice.

A room with a shower (*douche*) is always cheaper than one with a bath (*baignoire*). The cheapest rooms have neither, though you'll pay up to an extra \$3–\$6 if you take a shower or bath. All rooms in French hotels should have a washbasin. Prices must, by law, be posted at the hotel entrance and should include taxes and service. Prices are always by room, not per person (ask for a *grand lit* if you want a double bed). Breakfast is not always included in this price, but you are usually expected to have it and are often charged for it regardless. In smaller rural hotels you may be expected to have your evening meal at the hotel, too.

Hotels France, luckily, is not dominated by big hotel chains, which, in any case, tend to lack atmosphere. Here are a few just in case: The **Ibis** and **Climat de France** are two of the more moderately priced chains; the new **Formula 1** chain provides basic comfort for up to three persons per room for a set 134 francs per night. The distinctive green-and-yellow signs of the **Logis de France** organization signal small, inexpensive hotels that can be relied on for minimum standards of comfort, character, and regional cuisine. The Logis de France paperback guide is widely available in bookshops (cost: 61 francs) or from Logis de France, 83 av. d'Italie, 75013 Paris. **France-Accueil** is another friendly low-cost chain (free booklet from France-Accueil, 85 rue Dessous-des-Berges, 75013 Paris).

Housekeeping and Self-catering Best bets are the **Gîtes Ruraux,** which offer a family or group the possibility of a low-cost, housekeeping/self-catering vacation in a furnished cottage, chalet, or apartment in the country; rentals are by the week or month. For details contact either the **Maison des Gîtes de France** (35 rue Godot-de-Mauroy, 75009 Paris, tel. 47–42–20–20), naming which region interests you, or the **French Government Tourist Office** in London (178 Piccadilly, W1V OAL, tel. 01/491–7622), which runs a special reservation service.

Bed-and-Breakfast B&Bs, known in France as **Chambres d'Hôte,** are becoming increasingly popular in rural areas. Check local tourist offices for details.

Youth Hostels Given that cheap hotel accommodations in France are so easy to find, there is scarcely any economic reason for staying in a youth hostel, especially since locations are often out-of-the-way and standards of comfort don't match those of hostels in neighboring countries. If you enjoy a hostel ambience, however, you may care to note the address of the French headquarters (**Fédération Unie des Auberges de Jeunesse,** 10 rue Notre-Dame-de-Lorette, 75009 Paris).

Camping French campsites, which cost from 10 to 150 francs a day depending on the facilities, have a high reputation for organization and amenities but tend to be jam-packed in July and August. More and more campsites now welcome advance reservations; if you're traveling in summer, it makes good sense to book ahead.

A guide to the country's campsites is published by the **Fédération Française de Camping et de Caravaning** (78 rue de Rivoli, 75004 Paris); the *Michelin Camping and Caravanning Guide* gives full details.

Ratings Highly recommended hotels are indicated by a star ★.

The following price categories are used throughout the book, based on a standard double room including tax and service charge:

Category	Paris and the Riviera	Less Expensive Regions
Moderate	under 550 frs. ($100)	under 350 frs. ($63)
Inexpensive	under 400 frs. ($75)	under 250 frs. ($45)
Budget	under 250 frs. ($45)	under 150 frs. ($27)

Dining

Few countries match France's reputation for good food, and eating in France can be a memorable experience whatever your budget. The simple pleasures of a picnic lunch with baguette, camembert, and local *jambon* (ham), purchased at local boulangeries, fromageries, and charcuteries, can be as enjoyable as haute cuisine in the formal splendor. But the prime feature of French dining is the plethora of restaurants where you can eat out without digging too far into your finances. Although takeout places are mushrooming in the larger towns, most locals balk at eating french fries with anything other than a juicy steak, and their notion of "fast food" is gobbling down a three-course lunch in a brasserie in less than 90 minutes.

Many French spend a lot of the evening eating, too, but unless your own appetite is equally gargantuan we suggest you make lunch the main meal of your day. For around $10–$20 you can enjoy a full, filling meal with soup, a main course of meat or sometimes fish, plus vegetables, salad, cheese, and/or dessert. Bread and often wine are included in the price. The best value can be had in bars or brasseries that specialize in drinks the rest of the day, and many "serious" restaurants also offer a good-value lunchtime menu. Go for the *plat du jour* if there is one: it will usually be the freshest and best prepared main course available, and often sells out quickly (often before 12:30). Note that you will be charged the full cost of the fixed-price menu whether or not you eat everything on it.

Many restaurants also offer fixed-price menus in the evening, although they are pricier than their lunchtime offerings. Be wary of ones that don't, since eating à la carte is nearly always massively more expensive. Remember that the cost of a fixed-price meal rises significantly as you add extras—aperitifs, coffee, bottled wine. Go for a carafe of house wine if possible, and if you want coffee to finish your meal, get it at the counter in a café, where it will cost you significantly less.

Watch out for restaurants specializing in couscous, pizza, and other foreign food. Though increasingly common in France, they tend to be expensive. And despite their traditional popularity, regional specialties such as *choucroute* (sauerkraut) in Alsace or *bouillabaisse* (fish stew) along the Mediterranean can also be costly. So can seafood—so if you are addicted to prawns or oysters, buy them at a market and eat them on your own. One last suggestion: Avoid snacks (if you can). Patisseries, candy, and the like do not come cheap.

French breakfasts are relatively skimpy: good coffee and croissants, and fruit juice if you request it. You can "breakfast" in cafés as well as in your hotel, where the meal is sometimes included with the price of the room. If you're in the mood for bacon and eggs, however, you'll have to do some searching.

Mealtimes Dinner is the main meal and usually begins at 8 PM. Lunch starts at 12:30 or 1.

Precautions Tap water is safe, though not always appetizing (least of all in Paris). Mineral water—there is a vast choice of both still (*eau plate*) and fizzy (*eau gazeuse*)—is a palatable alternative. Perhaps the biggest eating problem in France is saying no: If you're invited to a French family's home, you will be encouraged, if not expected, to take two or three servings of everything offered.

Ratings Highly recommended restaurants are indicated by a star ★.

The following price categories are used throughout the book, based on the cheapest fixed-price menu or on a main course, salad, and dessert chosen à la carte:

Category	Paris and the Riviera	Less Expensive Regions
Moderate	under 250 frs. ($45)	under 200 frs. ($36)
Inexpensive	under 175 frs. ($32)	under 125 frs. ($23)
Budget	under 100 frs. ($18)	under 75 frs. ($14)

Credit Cards

The following credit card abbreviations are used: AE, American Express; DC, Diners Club; MC, MasterCard; and V, Visa.

France at a Glance: A Chronology

Knowing the basic outline of French history will make your perambulations through the nation's cities, towns, and villages just that much more meaningful.

The Beginnings

c 3500 BC Megalithic stone complexes erected at Carnac, Brittany

c 1500 BC Lascaux cave paintings executed (Dordogne, southwest France)

c 600 BC Greek colonists found Marseille

after 500 BC Celts appear in France

58–51 BC Julius Caesar conquers Gaul; writes up the war in *De Bello Gallico*

52 BC Lutetia, later to become Paris, is built by the Gallo-Romans

46 BC Roman amphitheater built at Arles

14 BC The Pont du Gard, the aqueduct near Nîmes, is erected

AD 212 Roman citizenship conferred on all free inhabitants of Gaul

406 Invasion by the Vandals (Germanic tribes)

451 Attila invades, and is defeated at Châlons

The Merovingian Dynasty

486–511 Clovis, king of the Franks (481–511), defeats the Roman governor of Gaul and founds the Merovingian Dynasty. Great monasteries, such as those at Tours, Limoges, and Chartres, become centers of culture

497 Franks converted to Christianity

567 The Frankish kingdom is divided into three parts—the eastern countries (Austrasia), later to become Belgium and Germany; the western countries (Neustria), later to become France; and Burgundy

732 Arab expansion checked at the Battle of Poitiers

The Carolingian Dynasty

768–778 Charlemagne (768–814) becomes king of the Franks (768); conquers northern Italy (774); and is defeated by the Moors at Roncesvalles in Spain, after which he consolidates the Pyrénées border (778)

c 782 Carolingian renaissance in art, architecture, and education

800 The pope crowns Charlemagne Holy Roman Emperor in Rome. Charlemagne expands the kingdom of France far beyond its present borders and establishes a center for learning at his capital, Aix-la-Chapelle (Aachen, in present-day Germany)

814–987 Death of Charlemagne. The Carolingian line continues until 987 through a dozen or so monarchs, with a batch called Charles (the Bald, the Fat, the Simple) and a sprinkling of Louis. Under the Treaty of Verdun (843), the empire is divided in two—the eastern half becoming Germany, the western half France

The Capetian Dynasty

987 Hugh Capet (987–996) is elected king of France and establishes the principle of hereditary rule for his descendants. Settled conditions and the increased power of the Church see the flowering of the Romanesque style of architecture in the church of Notre-Dame la Grande in Poitiers and the basilica at Vézelay

1066 Norman conquest of England by William the Conqueror (1066–87)

1067 Work begins on the Bayeaux Tapestry, the Romanesque work of art celebrating the Norman Conquest

c 1100 First universities in Europe include Paris. Development of European vernacular verse: *Chanson de Roland*

1140 The Gothic style of architecture first appears at St-Denis and later becomes fully developed at the cathedrals of Chartres, Reims, Amiens, and Notre-Dame in Paris

c 1150 Struggle between the Anglo-Norman kings (Angevin Empire) and the French; when Eleanor of Aquitaine switches husbands (from Louis VII of France to Henry II of England), her extensive lands pass to English rule

1194 Chartres Cathedral is begun; Gothic architecture spreads throughout western Europe

1204 Fourth Crusade: Franks conquer Byzantium and found the Latin Empire

1257 The Sorbonne university is founded in Paris

1270 Louis IX (1226–70), the only French king to achieve sainthood, dies in Tunis on the seventh and last Crusade

1302–07 Philippe IV (1285–1314), the Fair, calls together the first States-General, predecessor to the French Parliament. He disbands the Knights Templars to gain their wealth (1307)

1309 Papacy escapes from a corrupt and disorderly Rome to Avignon in southern France, where it stays for nearly 70 years

The Valois Dynasty

1337–1453 Hundred Years' War between France and England: episodic fighting for control of those areas of France gained by the English crown following the marriage of Eleanor of Aquitaine and Henry II

1348–1350 The Black Death rages in France

1428–31 Joan of Arc (1412–31), the Maid of Orléans, sparks the revival of French fortunes in the Hundred Years' War but is captured by the English and burned at the stake at Rouen

1434 Johannes Gutenberg invents the printing press in Strasbourg, Alsace

1453 France finally defeats England, terminating the Hundred Years' War and the English claim to the French throne

1475 Burgundy at the height of its power under Charles the Bold

1494 Italian wars: beginning of Franco-Habsburg struggle for hegemony in Europe

1515–47 Reign of François I, who imports Italian artists, including Leonardo da Vinci (1452–1519), and brings the Renaissance to France. The palace of Fontainebleau is begun (1528)

1558 France captures Calais, England's last territory on French soil

1562–98 Wars of Religion (Catholics versus Protestants/Huguenots) within France

The Bourbon Dynasty

1589 The first Bourbon king, Henri IV (1589–1610), is a Huguenot who converts to Catholicism and achieves peace in France. He signs the Edict of Nantes, giving limited freedom of worship to Protestants. The development of Renaissance Paris gets under way

c 1610 Scientific revolution in Europe begins, marked by the discoveries of mathematician and philosopher René Descartes (1596–1650)

1643–1715 Reign of Louis XIV, the Sun King, an absolute monarch who builds the Baroque power base of Versailles and presents Europe with a glorious view of France. With his first minister, Colbert, Louis makes France, by force of arms, the most powerful nation-state in Europe. He persecutes the Huguenots, who emigrate in great numbers, nearly ruining the French economy

1660 Classical period of French culture: writers Molière (1622–73), Jean Racine (1639–99), Pierre Corneille (1606–84), and painter Nicolas Poussin (1594–1665)

c 1715 Rococo art and decoration develop in Parisian boudoirs and salons, typified by the painters Antoine Watteau (1684–1721) and, later, François Boucher (1703–70) and Jean-Honoré Fragonard (1732–1806)

1700 onward Writer and pedagogue Voltaire (1694–1778) is a central figure in the French Enlightenment, along with Jean-Jacques Rousseau (1712–78) and Denis Diderot (1713–84), who, in 1751, compiles the first modern encyclopedia. The ideals of the Enlightenment—for reason and scientific method and against social and political injustices—pave the way for the French Revolution. In the arts, painter Jacques-Louis David (1748–1825) reinforces revolutionary creeds in his severe neoclassical works

1756–63 The Seven Years' War results in France's losing most of her overseas possessions and in England's becoming a world power

1776 The French assist in the American War of Independence. Ideals of liberty cross the Atlantic with the returning troops to reinforce new social concepts

The French Revolution

1789–1804 The Bastille is stormed on July 14, 1789. Following upon early Republican ideals comes the Terror and the administration of the Directory under Robespierre. There are widespread political executions—Louis XVI and his queen, Marie Antoinette, are guillotined in 1793. Reaction sets in, and the instigators of the Terror are themselves executed (1794). Napoleon Bonaparte enters the scene as the champion of the Directory (1795–99) and is installed as First Consul during the Consulate (1799–1804)

The First Empire

1804 Napoleon crowns himself Emperor of France at Notre-Dame in the presence of the pope

1805–12 Napoleon conquers most of Europe. The Napoleonic Age is marked by a neoclassical style in the arts, called Empire, as well as by the rise of Romanticism—characterized by such writers as Chateaubriand (1768–1848) and Stendhal (1783–1842), and the painters Eugène Delacroix (1798–1863) and Théodore Géricault (1791–1824)—which is to dominate the arts of the 19th century

1812–14 Winter cold and Russian determination defeat Napoleon outside Moscow. The emperor abdicates and is transported to Elba in the Mediterranean (1814)

Restoration of the Bourbons

1814–15 Louis XVIII, brother of the executed Louis XVI, regains the throne after the Congress of Vienna is held to settle peace terms

1815 The Hundred Days: Napoleon returns from Elba and musters an army on his march to the capital, but lacks national support. He is defeated at Waterloo (June 18) and exiled to the island of St. Helena in the South Atlantic

1821 Napoleon dies in exile

1830 Bourbon king Charles X, locked into a prerevolutionary state of mind, abdicates. A brief upheaval (Three Glorious Days) brings Louis-Philippe, the Citizen King, to the throne

1840 Napoleon's remains are brought back to Paris

1846–48 Severe industrial and farming depression contribute to Louis-Philippe's abdication (1848)

Second Republic and Second Empire

1848–52 Louis-Napoleon (nephew and step-grandson of Napoleon I) is elected president of the short-lived Second Republic. He makes a successful attempt to assume supreme power and is declared Emperor of France, taking the title Napoleon III

c 1850 The ensuing period is characterized in the arts by the emergence of realist painters—Jean-François Millet (1814–75), Honoré Daumier (1808–79), Gustave Courbet (1819–77)—and late-Romantic writers—Victor Hugo (1802–85), Honoré de Balzac (1799–1850), and Charles Baudelaire (1821–87)

1853 Baron Haussmann (1809–91) re-creates the center of Paris, with great boulevards connecting important squares, or *places*

1863 Napoleon III inaugurates the Salon des Refusés in response to critical opinion. It includes work by Edouard Manet (1832–83), Claude Monet (1840–1926), and Paul Cézanne (1839–1906) and is commonly regarded as the birthplace of Impressionism and of modern art in general

The Third Republic

1870–71 The Franco-Prussian War sees Paris besieged, and Paris falls to the Germans. Napoleon III takes refuge in England. The Commune is established, an attempt by the extreme left to seize power. France loses Alsace and Lorraine to Prussia before the peace treaty is signed

1871–1914 Before World War I, France expands her industries and builds up a vast colonial empire in Northwest Africa and Southeast Asia. Sculptor Auguste Rodin (1840–1917), musicians Maurice Ravel (1875–1937) and Claude Debussy (1862–1918), and writers such as Stéphane Mallarmé (1842–98) and Paul Verlaine (1844–96) set the stage for Modernism

1874 Emergence of the Impressionist school of painting: Monet, Pierre-Auguste Renoir (1841–1919), and Edgar Degas (1834–1917)

1889 The Eiffel Tower is built for the Paris World Exhibition. Centennial of the French Revolution

1894–1906 Franco-Russian alliance (1894). Dreyfus affair: the spy trial and its anti-Semitic backlash shake France

1898 Pierre and Marie Curie (1859–1906, 1867–1934) observe radioactivity and isolate radium

1904 The Entente Cordiale: England and France become firm allies

1907 Exhibition of Cubist painting in Paris

1914–18 During World War I, France fights with the Allies, opposing Germany, Austria-Hungary, and Turkey. Germany invades France; most of the big battles (Vimy Ridge, Verdun, Somme, Marne) are fought in trenches in northern France. French casualties exceed 5 million. With the Treaty of Versailles (1919), France regains Alsace and Lorraine and attempts to exact financial and economic reparations from Germany

1918–39 Between wars, Paris attracts artists and writers, including Americans—Ernest Hemingway (1899–1961) and Gertrude Stein (1874–1946). France nourishes major artistic movements: Constructivism, Dadaism, Surrealism, and Existentialism

1923 France occupies the Ruhr, a major industrial area in Germany's Rhine valley

1939–45 At the beginning of World War II, France fights with the Allies until invaded and defeated by Germany in 1940. The French government, under Marshal Pétain (1856–1951), moves to Vichy and cooperates with the Nazis. French overseas colonies split between allegiance to the legal government of Vichy and declaration for the Free French Resistance, led (from London) by General Charles de Gaulle (1890–1970)

1944 D-day, June 6: The Allies land on the beaches of Normandy and successfully invade France. Additional Allied forces land in Provence. Paris is liberated in August 1944, and France declares full allegiance to the Allies

1944–46 A provisional government takes power under General de Gaulle; American aid assists French recovery

The Fourth Republic

1946 France adopts a new constitution; French women gain the right to vote

1946–54 In the Indochinese War, France is unable to regain control of her colonies in Southeast Asia. The 1954 Geneva Agreement establishes two governments in Vietnam: one in the north, under the Communist leader Ho Chi Minh, and one in the south, under the emperor Bao Dai. U.S. involvement eventually leads to French withdrawal

1954–62 The Algerian Revolution achieves Algeria's independence from France. Thereafter, other French African colonies gain independence

1957 The Treaty of Rome establishes the European Economic Community (now known as the European Community—EC), with France a founding member

The Fifth Republic

1958–68 De Gaulle is the first president under a new constitution; he resigns in 1968 after widespread disturbances begun by student riots in Paris

1976 The first supersonic transatlantic passenger service begins with the Anglo-French Concorde

1981 François Mitterrand is elected the first Socialist president of France since World War II

1988 Mitterrand is elected for a second term

1989 Bicentennial celebration of the French Revolution

1990 TGV train clocks a world record—515 kph (322 mph)—on a practice run. Channel Tunnel link-up between French and English workers

1992 Winter Olympics staged in and around Albertville, Savoie. EuroDisneyland opens east of Paris.

Popular Itineraries

A lean travel budget does not mean that you can't savor the best of France. Inexpensive public transportation makes it possible to sightsee in some of the country's most visitable areas without the expense of renting a car. The following tours take in favorite landmarks and popular attractions—and all can be done by bus and/or train.

Great Gothic Cathedrals

Medieval cathedrals are among France's most precious heritage, and some of the best ones are conveniently close to Paris.

After paying homage to Notre-Dame, take the métro (line 13) north to the dowdy suburb of **St-Denis,** where the kings of France are buried in a cathedral-size basilica with a majestic nave and the earliest Gothic choir (1140s). Catch the train at Paris's Gare du Nord and head north to **Beauvais**, whose 13th-century choir is the highest in the world—alas, the nave was never built! Then continue to **Amiens** (by train, via Creil): Its cathedral is almost as high and the largest completed one in France. Go east from Amiens to **Laon**, where the many-towered cathedral sits majestically atop a mighty hill known as the "crowned mountain." You can make a detour from Laon to **Soissons**—check out its cathedral and the ruined facade of the abbey of St-Jean-des-Vignes—before continuing southeast to **Reims**, where the kings of France were crowned. The richly sculpted facade is the glory of Reims. Disciplined Gothic is on display at the cathedral in nearby **Châlons-sur-Marne**, where the old church of Notre-Dame-en-Vaux also warrants scrutiny.

All these sites are just short distances apart by train. (If you are traveling by car, you can cut across the country—via the cathedral towns of Troyes and Sens—to **Orléans**.) If you are traveling by train, return to Paris (via Meaux, with its own cathedral) and head southwest to visit the majestic cathedrals at Orléans and **Tours**, whose intricate, recently cleaned facade contains delicate ornaments by Renaissance craftsmen at work on nearby châteaus. The stained glass at Tours is also outstanding. Head north to **Le Mans**, whose choir—almost as high as that at Beauvais—juts out spectacularly atop a steep mound, then head northeast to **Chartres** and its spires and glass of unparalleled splendor.

Length of Trip 7 days.

Getting Around
By Car Amiens is a 149-kilometer (92.5-mile) drive from Paris (north along the A1 and then northwest on D934). A car enables you to cut from Châlons-sur-Marne to Orléans via Troyes and Sens (265 kilometers/165 miles), without returning to Paris.

By Train Rail travelers will have to make separate trips from Paris to visit Sens and Troyes.

The Main Route **One night: Paris.** Visit Notre-Dame and the Basilica St-Denis.

One night: Amiens. Visit the cathedrals of Beauvais and Amiens.

One night: Laon. Explore the cathedrals of Laon, Soissons, and Reims.

One night: Châlons-sur-Marne. See the Châlons cathedral and the church of Notre-Dame-en-Vaux.

One night: Orléans. Visit Orléans cathedral (if traveling by car, stop at Troyes and Sens en route).

One night: Le Mans. Visit the cathedrals of Tours and Le Mans. Return to Paris via Chartres.

Information *See* chapters on the Ile-de-France, and Champagne and the North.

Burgundy

Burgundy is one of France's best-known wine-making regions. While the opportunity to try some of the world's most celebrated wines is a major drawing card, visitors will also enjoy the region's irresistible combination of rolling hills, picturesque towns, impressive churches, and outstanding restaurants.

The cathedral town of **Sens** is the gateway to Burgundy as you approach from Paris. The attractive Yonne Valley leads south toward old, pretty **Auxerre**, redolent of the unhurried flavor of Burgundian life. Continue to **Avallon** to admire the fine views from its ancient ramparts, and detour by local excursion bus or by car to nearby **Vézelay**, whose Romanesque basilica counts as one of Europe's leading early medieval buildings. The tiny surrounding village remains unspoiled by tourist crowds. So does the patchwork of meadowland that can be surveyed from the basilica's hilltop site. Veer south through the Morvan Forest to **Autun**, once a major Roman town—several monuments from that period still stand—and home to a powerful cathedral. Then cut east to stylish, historic **Beaune**, where you can sample Burgundy's famous wines and admire the medieval Hôtel Dieu, with its multicolored tile roof. Finally, head north through the vineyards to **Dijon**, Burgundy's capital and the opulent home of the once-mighty grand dukes (their palace now houses an exceptional art museum) and several superb restaurants.

Length of Trip 7 days.

Getting Around
By Car Sens is 110 kilometers (70 miles) southeast of Paris via A6/N6. Though Burgundy's towns can be visited by public transportations, its charming rural corners can best be appreciated by car.

By Train Trains run from Paris to Sens and Auxerre, where you can change for Avallon and Autun. To get from Autun to Beaune, change at Etang. Dijon, a 20-minute train trip from Beaune, is 90 minutes from Paris by TGV.

The Main Route **One night: Auxerre.** See Sens and visit the old town of Auxerre.

One night: Avallon. Make excursion to Vézelay.

One night: Autun. Admire Roman remnants and cathedral.

One night: Beaune. Sample wines at the Marché aux Vins.

One night: Dijon. Head through vineyards, then visit Dijon's museums, churches, and restaurants.

Information *See* chapter on Burgundy.

Châteaus of the Loire Valley

The Loire Valley provides a fascinating three-dimensional overview of French history, thanks to the hundreds of châteaus that dot its wooded terrain. A cathedral and museum make **Orléans** an interesting place from which to start your tour, but the first château you encounter is farther west at **Chambord**—the largest of all the Loire châteaus and surrounded by an extensive forest. Nearby **Cheverny** was one of the last Loire châteaus to be built, as its formal neoclassicism testifies. The attractive town of **Blois** makes an excellent base for visiting Chambord and Cheverny and has churches and narrow streets, as well as a château that was built over several periods. **Chaumont** and **Amboise** both offer terrific views across the Loire, and at Amboise, you may visit the Clos-Lucé and its display of models based on designs by Leonardo da Vinci (who died here in 1519). **Chenonceau,** built across the River Cher, has an unforgettable setting.

Tours is the principal city of the Loire Valley, and despite heavy bombing in 1944, it retains its picturesque old quarter and superb cathedral. It makes a sensible base for exploring such nearby châteaus as **Villandry** (with its formal Renaissance gardens and tree-lined avenues), fortresslike **Langeais,** romantic **Azay-le-Rideau,** and **Ussé** (said to have inspired Perrault's fairy tale *Sleeping Beauty*). **Chinon** is, or was, an authentic castle; its ruined walls tower high above a delightful town. A medieval abbey at **Fontevraud** and a famous riding school at **Saumur** (home of another opulent château) add variety to the tour. **Angers** has a castle and two fine museums—one with the colossal, vividly colored 14th-century *Apocalypse* tapestry, the other showcasing the sculpture of 19th-century local David d'Angers.

Length of Trip 10 days.

Getting Around

By Car Orléans is a 90-minute drive (120 kilometers/75 miles) south of Paris via A10. Picturesque roads run along both banks of the Loire.

By Train A respectable train service runs down the valley from Orléans to Angers, stopping at Blois, Chaumont, Amboise, Tours, Langeais, and Saumur. Branch lines connect Tours to Chenonceau and Azay-le-Rideau/Chinon. You will need to take a bus from Blois to reach Chambord and Cheverny, and from Saumur to reach Fontevraud. A bike is the best way to reach Villandry (from Azay) and Ussé (from Chinon).

The Main Route

One night: Orléans. See the cathedral.

Two nights: Blois. See Chaumont, and take a bus to Chambord and Cheverny.

One night: Amboise. See château and Clos-Lucé, then visit Chenonceau.

One night: Tours. You could stay three nights and see Azay and Chinon from here rather than changing hotels.

One night: Azay-le-Rideau. Make excursion to Villandry.

One night: Chinon. Make excursion to Ussé.

One night: Saumur. Stop off at Langeais en route; then see Fontevraud Abbey.

One night: Angers.

Information *See* chapter on the Loire Valley.

Eastern Brittany and Mont-St-Michel

Castles, ancient town walls, and spectacular coastal views await you as you venture into Brittany. Start your tour at **Vitré**, with its cobbled streets and venerable hilltop castle, and detour to **Fougères,** site of one of Europe's largest medieval castles (surrounded by a moat!). Lively **Rennes,** the capital of Brittany, provides the intriguing contrast of graceful neoclassical architecture and rickety half-timbered medieval houses.

Head north toward the **Mont-St-Michel**, a staggering medieval abbey atop a steep offshore crag that becomes inaccessible at high tide. A huge granite cathedral dominates historic **Dol-de-Bretagne,** where nearby Mont Dol emerges from marshy wasteland. With its tumbling alleyways and striped black-and-white timber houses, pretty **Dinan** seems straight out of a Hollywood movie set. A bracing seaside walk along the ramparts of **St-Malo** awaits you farther north, and a short boat trip will bring you to the elegant resort of **Dinard** and its own spectacular coastal promenades.

Length of Trip 6 days.

Getting Around
By Car The A11/A81 expressway is the fastest way to drive from Paris to Vitré and Rennes.

By Train Several mainland trains from Paris (Gare Montparnasse) stop at Vitré on their way to Rennes. All other towns visited are accessible by train except Fougères (take a bus from Vitré) and Mont-St-Michel (catch a bus or taxi from Pontorson station).

The Main Route **One night: Vitré.** Visit castle.

One night: Rennes. Visit Fougères castle and old Rennes.

One night: Mont-St-Michel. Explore Dol.

One night: Dinan.

One night: St-Malo. Make boat excursion to Dinard.

Information *See* chapters on Brittany and (for Mont-St-Michel) Normandy.

Provence

Roman remains and soft, sun-kissed landscapes of vines and olive groves provide the backdrop for a tour of Provence. Start at **Orange**, site of a majestic Roman theater and stately triumphal arch, before continuing on to the bustling nearby town of **Avignon**, famous for a now-decapitated medieval bridge and its role as the 14th-century home-in-exile of the popes, who built the colossal fortress-palace. A short trip west brings you to **Nîmes** and its well-preserved Roman arena, temple, and Maison Carrée; detour to the nearby three-tiered Pont de Gard aqueduct, a major feat of Roman engineering.

The sturdy castle at **Tarascon** sits proudly by the River Rhône. Farther south is the picturesque town of **Arles**, with its own Roman remains. Make excursions from Arles to the daring clifftop village of **Les Baux-de-Provence**, with its medieval ruins, and to **St-Rémy-de-Provence**, site of the well-preserved Roman arch and mausoleum. Continue south to the dowdy, vibrant port of **Marseille**, then head inland to the area's historic capital, **Aix-en-Provence**, an elegant mixture of narrow medieval streets and majestic 18th-century mansions.

Length of Trip 7 days.

Getting Around
By Car Orange is a six-hour drive (628 kilometers/390 miles) from Paris via the A6/A7 expressway. The expressway continues to Avignon and Marseille.

By Train The TGV runs from Paris (Gare de Lyon) to Avignon, continuing toward either Nîmes or Marseille. Trains serve all other points on this itinerary with two exceptions: You'll need to take a bus from Nîmes to the Pont du Gard and from Arles to Les Baux and St-Rémy.

The Main Route **One night: Avignon.** Visit theater and archway in Orange.

One night: Nîmes. Detour to the Pont du Gard.

Two nights: Arles. Visit Tarascon castle and make excursions to Les Baux and St-Rémy.

One night: Marseille.

One night: Aix-en-Provence.

Information *See* chapter on Provence.

2 Paris

The Historic Heart, the Left Bank, Montmartre

A city of vast, noble perspectives and winding, hidden streets, Paris remains a combination of the pompous and the intimate. Whether you've come looking for sheer physical beauty, cultural and artistic diversions, world-famous shopping, history, or simply local color, you will find it here in abundance.

The city's 20 districts, or *arrondissements,* have their own distinctive character, as do the two banks of the Seine, the river that weaves its way through the city's heart. The tone of the *Rive Droite* (Right Bank) is set by spacious boulevards and formal buildings, while the *Rive Gauche* (Left Bank) is more carefree and bohemian.

The French capital is also, for the tourist, a practical city: It's relatively small as capitals go, and its major sites and museums are within walking distance of one another. The city's principal tourist axis is less than 6 kilometers (4 miles) long, running parallel to the north bank of the Seine from the Arc de Triomphe to the Bastille.

There are several "musts" that any first-time visitor to Paris will be loath to miss: the Eiffel Tower, the Champs-Elysées, the Louvre, and Notre-Dame. It is only fair to say, however, that a visit to Paris will never be quite as simple as a quick look at a few landmarks. Every *quartier* has its own treasures, and travelers should adopt the process of discovery—a very pleasant prospect in this most elegant of French cities.

Essential Information

Important Addresses and Numbers

Tourist Information There are the main Paris tourist office (127 av. des Champs-Elysées, 75008 Paris, tel. 47–23–61–72; open daily 9 AM–8 PM; closed Christmas Day and New Year's Day) and branches at all mainline train stations, except Gare St-Lazare. Dial 47–20–88–98 for recorded information in English. At these offices—and in certain métro stations—you can buy a museum pass (*Carte Inter-Musées*) offering unlimited access to more than 60 museums and monuments over a one-, three-, or five-day period (price: 60, 120, or 180 francs).

Embassies **U.S.** (2 av. Gabriel, 8e, tel. 42–96–12–02), **Canada** (35 av. Montaigne, 8e, tel. 47–23–01–01), and **U.K.** (35 rue du Fbg. St-Honoré, 8e, tel. 42–66–91–42).

Emergencies **Police** (tel. 17), **ambulance** (tel. 15 or 45–67–50–50), **doctor** (tel. 43–37–77–77), and **dentist** (tel. 43–37–51–00).

Hospitals The **American Hospital** (63 blvd. Victor-Hugo, Neuilly, tel. 46–41–25–25 or 47–45–71–00) has a 24-hour emergency service.

The **Hertford British Hospital** (3 rue Barbès, Levallois-Perret, tel. 47–58–13–12) also offers a 24-hour service.

Pharmacies **Pharmacie des Champs-Elysées** (Galerie des Champs, 84 av. des Champs-Elysées, 8e, tel. 45–62–02–41), open 24 hours; **Drugstore** (corner of blvd. St-Germain and rue de Rennes, 6e), open daily until 2 AM; **Pharmacie des Arts** (106 blvd. Montparnasse, 14e), open daily until midnight.

English-Language Bookstores **W.H. Smith** (248 rue de Rivoli, 1er, tel. 42–60–37–97), **Galignani** (224 rue de Rivoli, 1er, tel. 42–60–76–07), **Brentano's** (37 av. de l'Opéra, 2e, tel. 42–61–52–50), and **Shakespeare and Co.** (rue de la Bûcherie, 5e).

Travel Agencies **American Express** (11 rue Scribe, 9e, tel. 47–77–70–00) and **Air France** (119 av. des Champs-Elysées, 8e, tel. 42–99–23–64).

Where to Change Money Exchange offices in most of the mainline Paris rail stations (Austerlitz, Lyon, Est, Nord, St-Lazare) are open 7 AM–8 PM. They are convenient but do not offer the best rates. A majority of the banks in central Paris provide exchange facilities at more competitive rates, usually with a fixed commission. Note also: The *Change Automatique* (66 av. des Champs-Elysées), open round the clock, accepts $5, $10, and $20 bills; and the *Change de Paris* bureau (2 rue de l'Amiral-Coligny) across from the Louvre.

Arriving and Departing by Plane

Airports and Airlines Paris is served by two international airports: **Charles de Gaulle,** also known as Roissy, 26 kilometers (16 miles) northeast of the downtown area, and **Orly,** 16 kilometers (10 miles) south. Major carriers, among them TWA, Delta, and Air France, fly daily from the United States, while Air France and British Airways between them offer hourly service from London.

Between the Airports and Downtown The easiest way to get into Paris from **Charles de Gaulle** (Roissy) airport is on the **RER-B** line, the suburban express train. A free shuttle bus runs between the two terminal buildings and the train station, taking about 10 minutes. Trains to central Paris (Les Halles, St-Michel, Luxembourg) leave every 15 minutes; the fare is 31 francs, and the journey time is 30 minutes. **Buses** run every 15 minutes from Charles de Gaulle to the Arc de Triomphe and the Air France air terminal at Porte Maillot. The fare is 38 francs, and the journey time is about 40 minutes, though rush-hour traffic often makes this a slow and frustrating trip.

From **Orly** airport, the simplest way to get into Paris is on the **RER-C** line; there's a free shuttle bus from the terminal building to the train station, and trains leave every 15 minutes. The fare is 24 francs, and the journey time is about 30 minutes. **Buses** run every 12 minutes between Orly airport and the Air France air terminal at Les Invalides on the Left Bank; the fare is 31 francs, and the trip can take from 30 minutes to an hour.

Arriving and Departing by Car, Train, and Bus

By Train Paris has six international train stations: **Gare du Nord** (northern France, northern Europe, and England via Calais or Boulogne); **Gare St-Lazare** (Normandy and England via Dieppe); **Gare de l'Est** (Strasbourg, Luxembourg, Basel, and central Europe); **Gare de Lyon** (Lyon, Marseille, the Riviera, Geneva, Italy); and **Gare d'Austerlitz** (Loire Valley, southwest France, Spain). **Gare Montparnasse** has taken over as the main terminus for Bordeaux- and southwest-bound trains since the introduction of the new TGV-Atlantique service. For information call 45–82–50–50.

By Bus Paris has no central bus depot. Long-distance bus journeys within France are rare compared with train travel. The leading Paris-based bus company is **Eurolines** (3 av. de la Porte de la Villette, 19e, tel. 40–38–93–93).

Getting Around

Paris is relatively small as capital cities go, and most of its prize monuments and museums are within easy walking distance of one another in any given area. To help you find your way around, we suggest that you buy a *Plan de Paris par arrondissement*, a city guide with separate maps of each district, including the whereabouts of métro stations and an index of street names.

Maps of the métro/RER network are available free from any métro station and many hotels. They are also posted on every platform, as are maps of the bus network. Bus routes are also marked at bus stops and on buses. Métro tickets, also valid for buses and the RER, are relatively cheap.

By Métro The métro is by far the quickest and most efficient way of getting around the city and runs from 5:30 AM until 1:15 AM. Stations are recognizable either by a large yellow "M" within a circle, or by their distinctive, curly, green art nouveau railings and archway bearing the full title (Métropolitain).

With 13 lines crisscrossing Paris and its environs, the métro is fairly easy to navigate. It is essential to know the name of the last station on the line you take, however, since this name appears on all signs. A connection (you can make as many as you like on one ticket) is called a *correspondance*. At junction sta-

Paris Métro

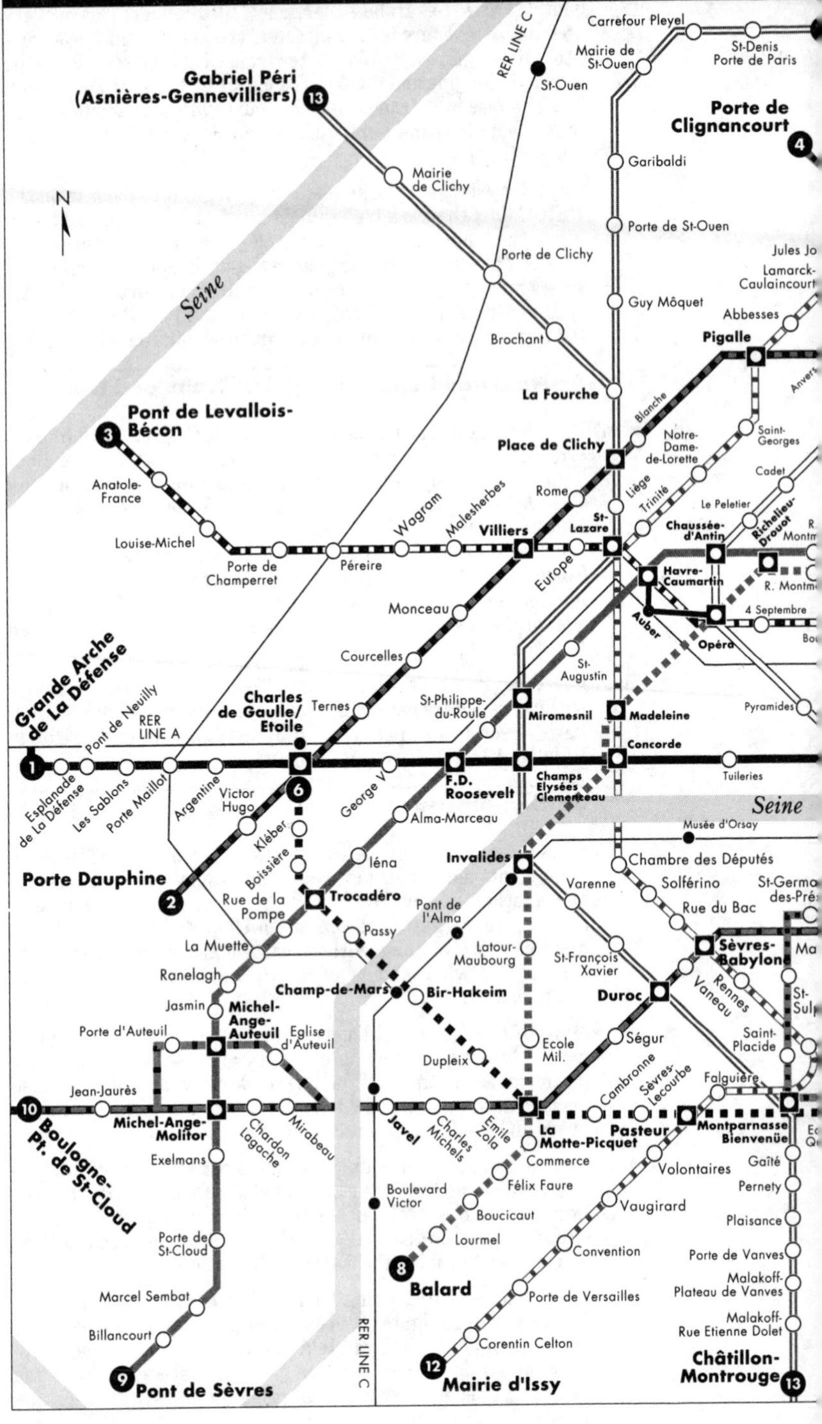
RER LINE C
Carrefour Pleyel
Mairie de St-Ouen
St-Denis Porte de Paris
St-Ouen
Gabriel Péri (Asnières-Gennevilliers)
13
Porte de Clignancourt
4
Garibaldi
Mairie de Clichy
N
Porte de St-Ouen
Porte de Clichy
Jules Jo
Lamarck-Caulaincourt
Seine
Guy Môquet
Abbesses
Brochant
Pigalle
Anvers
La Fourche
Blanche
Pont de Levallois-Bécon
3
Place de Clichy
Notre-Dame-de-Lorette
Saint-Georges
Anatole-France
Rome
Liège
Trinité
Cadet
Wagram
Malesherbes
St-Lazare
Le Peletier
Louise-Michel
Villiers
Chaussée-d'Antin
Richelieu-Drouot
Porte de Champerret
Péreire
Europe
Havre-Caumartin
R. Montm
Monceau
Auber
4 Septembre
Opéra
Courcelles
St-Augustin
Grande Arche de La Défense
Pont de Neuilly
Charles de Gaulle/ Etoile
Ternes
St-Philippe-du-Roule
Miromesnil
Madeleine
Pyramides
RER LINE A
Concorde
1
Esplanade de La Défense
Les Sablons
Porte Maillot
Argentine
Victor Hugo
6
George V
F.D. Roosevelt
Champs Elysées Clemenceau
Tuileries
Seine
Alma-Marceau
Musée d'Orsay
Kléber
Boissière
Invalides
Chambre des Députés
Porte Dauphine
Iéna
Varenne
Solférino
St-Germa des-Prés
2
Rue de la Pompe
Trocadéro
Pont de l'Alma
Rue du Bac
Passy
Latour-Maubourg
Sèvres-Babylone
La Muette
St-François Xavier
Ranelagh
Champ-de-Mars
Bir-Hakeim
Duroc
Rennes
Vaneau
St-Sulp
Jasmin
Michel-Ange-Auteuil
Porte d'Auteuil
Eglise d'Auteuil
Ecole Mil.
Ségur
Saint-Placide
Dupleix
Cambronne
Sèvres-Lecourbe
Falguière
Jean-Jaurès
10
Boulogne-Pt. de St-Cloud
Michel-Ange-Molitor
Chardon Lagache
Mirabeau
Javel
Charles Michels
Emile Zola
La Motte-Picquet
Pasteur
Montparnasse Bienvenüe
Exelmans
Commerce
Volontaires
Gaîté
Félix Faure
Pernety
Boulevard Victor
Boucicaut
Vaugirard
Plaisance
Porte de St-Cloud
Lourmel
Convention
Porte de Vanves
8
Balard
Malakoff-Plateau de Vanves
Marcel Sembat
Porte de Versailles
Malakoff-Rue Etienne Dolet
Billancourt
RER LINE C
Corentin Celton
Châtillon-Montrouge
9
Pont de Sèvres
12
Mairie d'Issy
13

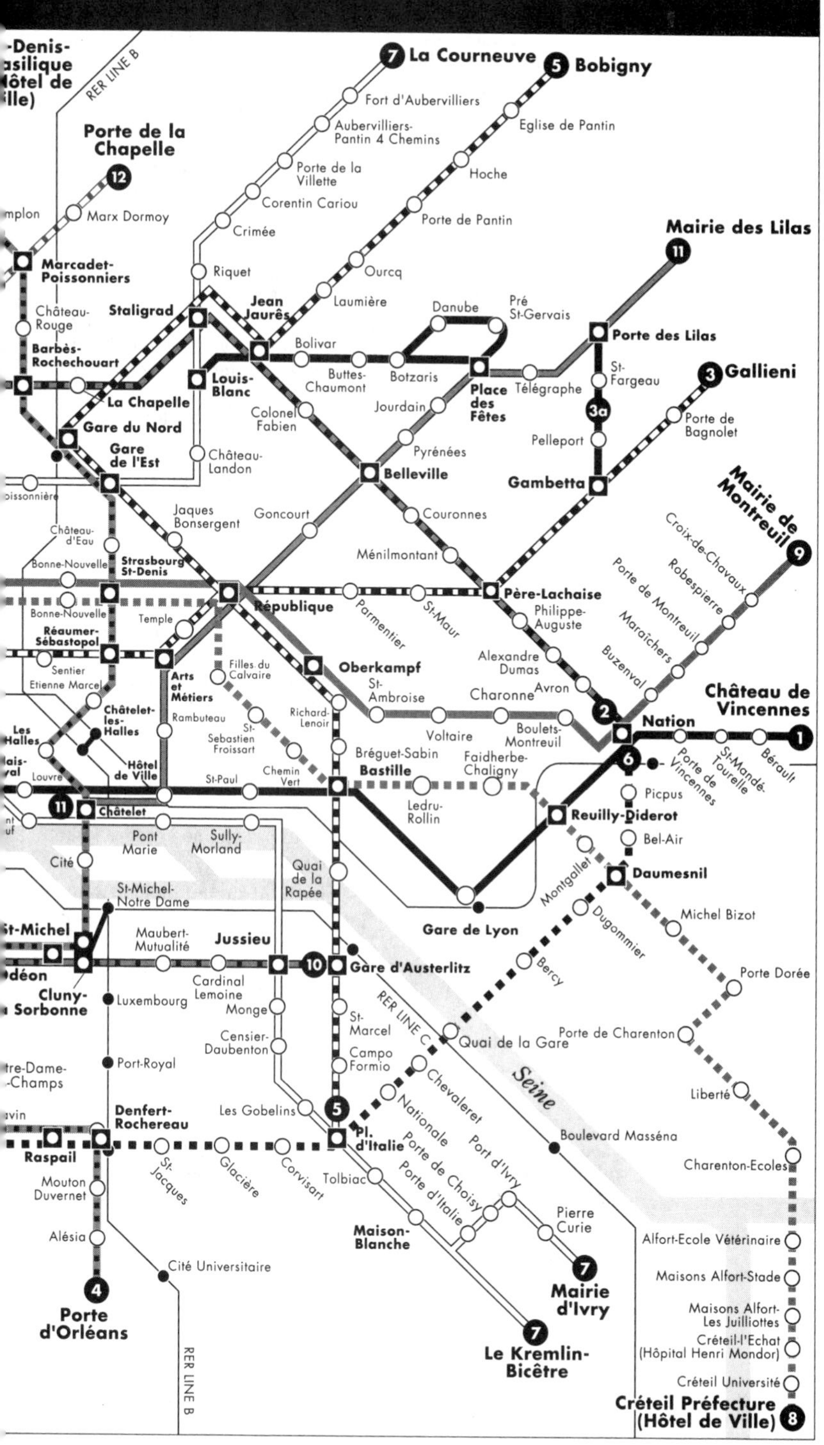
La Courneuve
Bobigny
Porte de la Chapelle
Fort d'Aubervilliers
Aubervilliers-Pantin 4 Chemins
Eglise de Pantin
Porte de la Villette
Hoche
Corentin Cariou
Marx Dormoy
Crimée
Porte de Pantin
Mairie des Lilas
Marcadet-Poissonniers
Riquet
Ourcq
Château-Rouge
Staligrad
Jean Jaurès
Laumière
Danube
Pré St-Gervais
Porte des Lilas
Barbès-Rochechouart
Bolivar
Louis-Blanc
Buttes-Chaumont
Botzaris
Place des Fêtes
Télégraphe
St-Fargeau
Gallieni
La Chapelle
Gare du Nord
Colonel Fabien
Jourdain
Porte de Bagnolet
Gare de l'Est
Château-Landon
Pyrénées
Pelleport
Belleville
Gambetta
Mairie de Montreuil
Jaques Bonsergent
Goncourt
Couronnes
Croix-de-Chavaux
Château-d'Eau
Bonne-Nouvelle
Strasbourg St-Denis
Ménilmontant
Robespierre
Porte de Montreuil
République
Père-Lachaise
Temple
Parmentier
St-Maur
Philippe-Auguste
Maraîchers
Réaumer-Sébastopol
Sentier
Etienne Marcel
Arts et Métiers
Filles du Calvaire
Oberkampf
Alexandre Dumas
Buzenval
Avron
Château de Vincennes
Charonne
St-Ambroise
Châtelet-les-Halles
Les Halles
Rambuteau
St-Sebastien Froissart
Richard-Lenoir
Nation
Voltaire
Boulets-Montreuil
Bréguet-Sabin
Faidherbe-Chaligny
Porte de Vincennes
St-Mandé-Tourelle
Bérault
Hôtel de Ville
Louvre
St-Paul
Chemin Vert
Bastille
Picpus
Châtelet
Ledru-Rollin
Reuilly-Diderot
Pont Marie
Sully-Morland
Bel-Air
Cité
Quai de la Rapée
Montgallet
Daumesnil
St-Michel-Notre Dame
Gare de Lyon
Michel Bizot
St-Michel
Maubert-Mutualité
Jussieu
Dugommier
Odéon
Gare d'Austerlitz
Bercy
Cluny-La Sorbonne
Cardinal Lemoine
Porte Dorée
Luxembourg
Monge
RER LINE C
Censier-Daubenton
St-Marcel
Quai de la Gare
Porte de Charenton
Port-Royal
Campo Formio
Chevaleret
Seine
Liberté
Notre-Dame-des-Champs
Nationale
Denfert-Rochereau
Les Gobelins
Pl. d'Italie
Port d'Ivry
Boulevard Masséna
Raspail
St-Jacques
Glacière
Corvisart
Porte de Choisy
Charenton-Ecoles
Mouton Duvernet
Tolbiac
Porte d'Italie
Pierre Curie
Alésia
Maison-Blanche
Alfort-Ecole Vétérinaire
Cité Universitaire
Maisons Alfort-Stade
Mairie d'Ivry
Porte d'Orléans
Maisons Alfort-Les Juilliottes
Créteil-l'Echat (Hôpital Henri Mondor)
Le Kremlin-Bicêtre
RER LINE B
Créteil Université
Créteil Préfecture (Hôtel de Ville)

tions, illuminated orange signs, bearing the name of the line terminus, appear over the correct corridors for *correspondance.* Illuminated blue signs, marked *sortie,* indicate the station exit. Some lines and stations in the less salubrious parts of Paris are a bit risky at night: lines 2 and 13 in particular. In general, however, the métro is relatively safe throughout.

The métro network connects with the RER network at several points in Paris. RER trains, which race across Paris from suburb to suburb, are a sort of supersonic métro and can be great time savers.

All métro tickets and passes are valid for RER and bus travel within Paris. Métro tickets cost 5.50 francs each, though a *carnet* (10 tickets for 34.50 francs) is a better value. If you plan to do a lot of traveling on the same day, buy a Formule 1 coupon (23 francs). If you are staying longer, opt for a two-zone *coupon jaune* (54 francs) valid Monday through the following Sunday, or a two-zone *carte orange* (190 francs), valid for a calendar month.

Access to métro and RER platforms is through an automatic ticket barrier. Slide your ticket in and pick it up as it pops up. Keep your ticket during your journey; you'll need it to leave the RER system.

By Bus Paris buses are green and are marked with the route number and destination in front and major stopping places along the sides. Most routes operate from 6 AM to 8:30 PM; some continue until midnight. Ten night buses operate hourly (1 to 6 AM) between Châtelet and various nearby suburbs. The brown bus shelters, topped by red-and-yellow circular signs, contain timetables and route maps.

Tickets are not available on buses; they must be bought in advance from métro stations or *tabac* shops. If you have individual yellow tickets (as opposed to weekly or monthly tickets), state your destination and be prepared to punch one or more tickets in the red-and-gray machines on board the bus.

By Taxi Paris taxis may not have the charm of their London counterparts—there is no standard vehicle or color—but they're cheaper. Daytime rates (7 AM till 7:30 PM) are a standard 2.80 francs per kilometer, and nighttime rates are around 4.20 francs. There is a basic charge of 10 francs for all rides. You are best off asking your hotel or restaurant to call for a taxi; cruising cabs can be hailed but are annoyingly difficult to spot. Otherwise, ask where to find the nearest taxi stand (*station de taxis*). Note that taxis seldom take more than three people at a time.

By Bicycle You can rent bikes in the Bois de Boulogne (Jardin d'Acclimatation), Bois de Vincennes, some RER stations, and from the Bateaux-Mouches embarkation point by place de l'Alma. Or try Paris-Vélo (2 rue du Fer-à-Moulin, 5e, tel. 43–37–59–22). Rental rates vary from about 80 to 140 francs per day, 140 to 220 francs per weekend, and 350 to 500 francs per week.

Lodging

At last count, the Paris tourist office's official (albeit incomplete) hotel guide listed 1,123 hotels in 20 inner-city districts, or *arrondissements*, alone. Despite this huge choice, you should always be sure to make reservations well in advance, except, paradoxically, during July and August, when the trade fairs, conventions, and conferences that crowd the city the rest of the year come to a halt.

Our listings have been compiled with the aim of identifying hotels that offer maximum atmosphere, convenience, and comfort. We do not include many chain hotels for the simple reason that those in Paris are little different from those in other major cities. We prefer to list special, one-of-a-kind hotels that will, in themselves, contribute greatly to the charm of your stay. For the most part, hotels on the Right Bank offer greater luxury, or at any rate formality, while those on the Left Bank are smaller and offer more in the way of a certain, old-fashioned Parisian charm. Remember that room prices are rarely affected by the number of occupants: single rooms invariably work out to be more expensive than doubles.

It is possible to find budget hotels even in central Paris, but don't expect spacious rooms or high standards of comfort. Luckily, those parts of Paris in top demand among fat-walleted business travelers (mainly the 7th, 8th, and 17th arrondissements to the west of the capital) do not correspond with the preferences of the average visitor, who can find better value in such central locations as the Marais and Quartier Latin. However, there is no reason to despair if you do not find a hotel in the heart of the city: Paris is relatively small, and public transportation so efficient that you are never far from the hub of things. The best way of reserving a hotel room is through the Paris tourist office (127 av. des Champs-Elysées, 8e, tel. 47–23–61–72). You can also book hotels through the tourist offices at Orly and Charles-de-Gaulle airports.

Other than in the largest and most expensive hotels, almost all Parisian hotels have certain idiosyncrasies. Plumbing can be erratic, though rarely to the point that it becomes a problem. Air-conditioning is relatively rare in budget hotels. This can cause difficulties chiefly because of noise in summer, when on stuffy, sultry nights you may have no choice but to open the windows. Ask for a room *sur cour*—overlooking the courtyard (almost all hotels have one)—or, even better, if there is one, *sur le jardin*—overlooking the garden.

Breakfast is usually included, sometimes at extra cost, and generally consists of coffee (with milk) and bread and/or croissant. If breakfast is not included at your hotel we suggest you buy your croissant at a boulangerie and eat it on the way to a café, where you can get coffee.

Under 550 francs

Central Paris

Collège de France. The Collège de France offers peace and quiet in the heart of the Latin Quarter. Rooms are simply decorated in pale greens and light browns. The prettiest have oak beams and are up on the seventh floor under the eaves. There's no restaurant or bar. *7 rue Thénard, 5e, tel. 43–26–78–36. 23*

Argenson, **3**
Ceramic, **1**
Choiseul-Opéra, **6**
Collège de France, **20**
Dhély's, **18**
Esméralda, **19**
Family, **4**
Jules-César, **27**
Kensington, **13**
Le Laumière, **22**
Lenox, **17**
Lille, **12**
London Palace, **7**
Londres Stockholm, **5**
Mayflower, **2**
Midi, **31**
Modern Hôtel-Lyon, **29**
Montpensier, **11**
Paris-Lyon Palace, **28**
Pavillon, **16**
Place des Vosges, **25**
Queen's Hotel, **15**
Régyn's Montmartre, **10**
Résidence Alhambra, **24**
St-Louis-Marais, **26**
Sévigné, **23**
Solférino, **13**
Sorbonne, **30**
Timhotel Montmartre, **9**
Utrillo, **8**
Vieux Marais, **21**

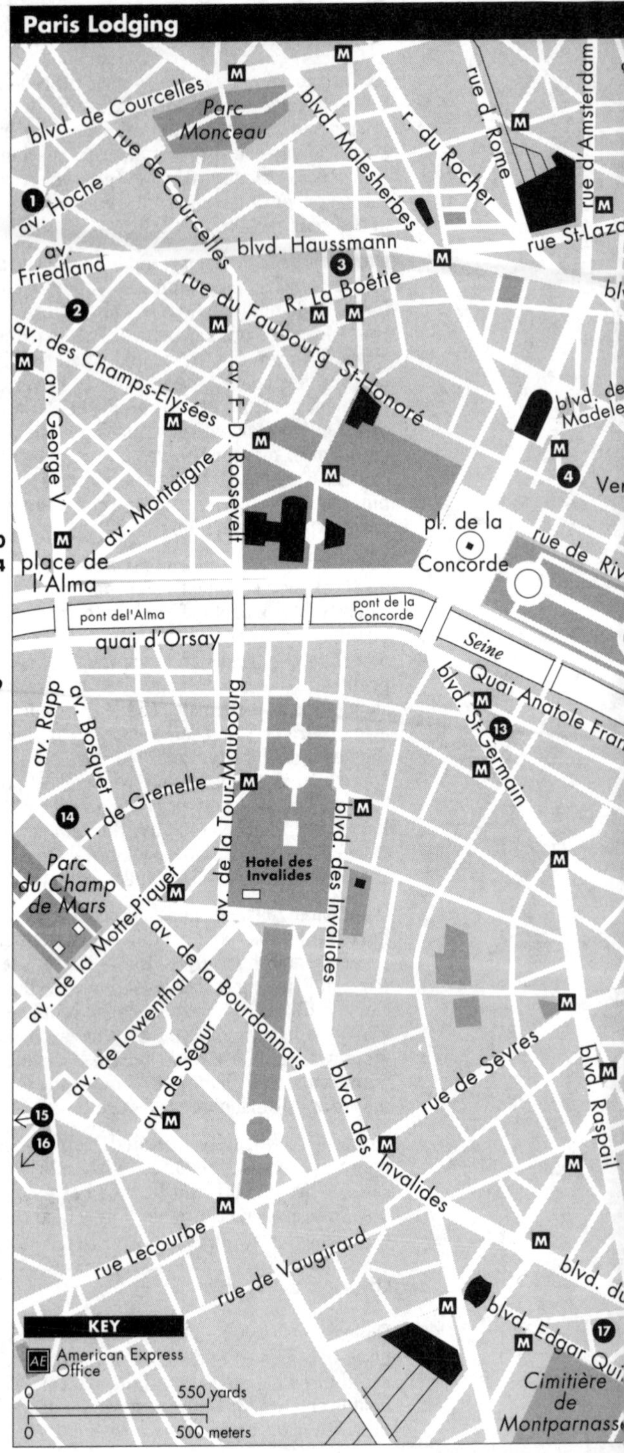

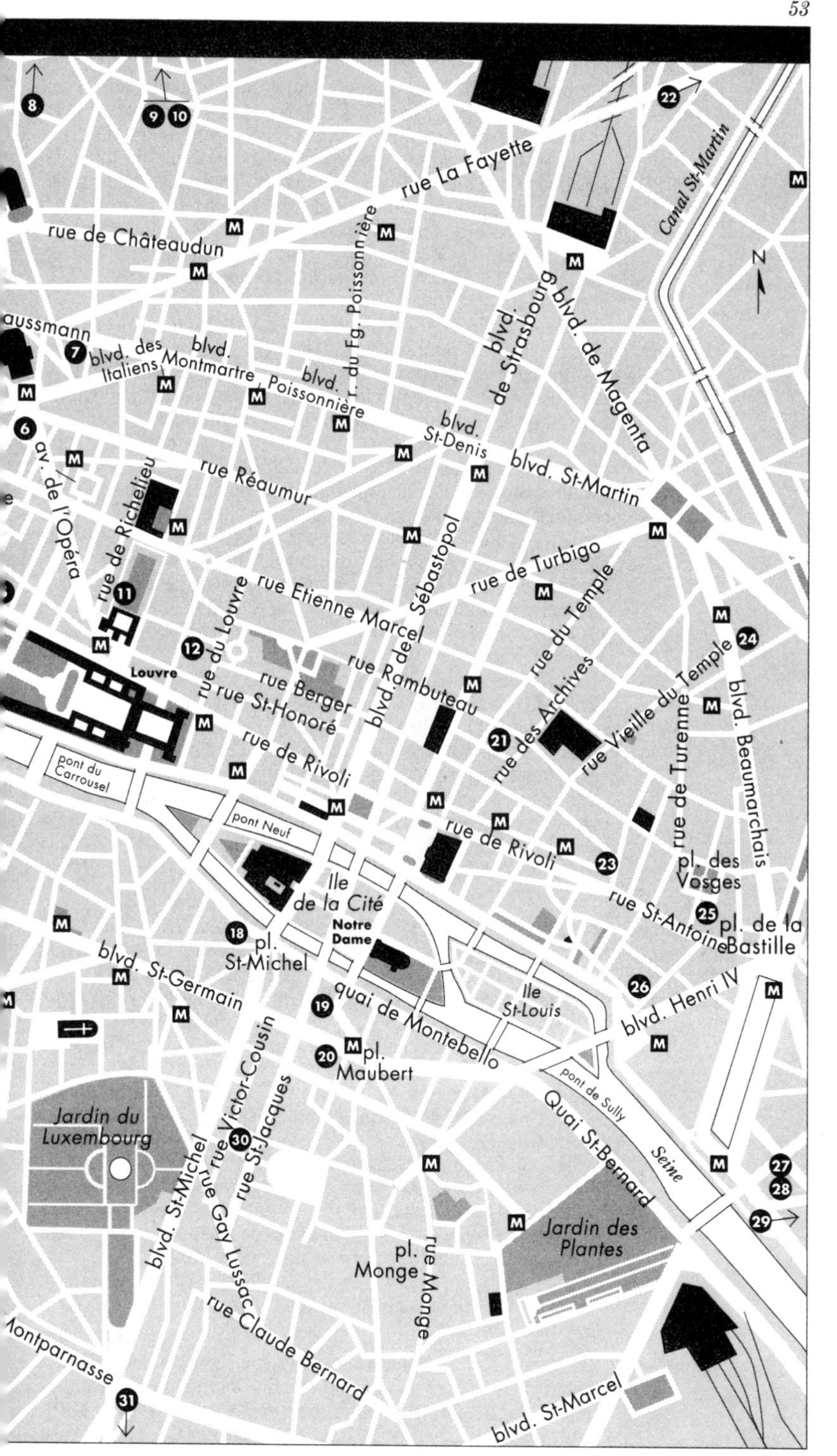
rue La Fayette
rue de Châteaudun
Canal St-Martin
r. du Fg. Poissonnière
blvd. de Strasbourg
blvd. de Magenta
aussmann
blvd. des Italiens
blvd. Montmartre
blvd. Poissonnière
blvd. St-Denis
blvd. St-Martin
av. de l'Opéra
rue de Richelieu
rue Réaumur
rue du Louvre
rue Etienne Marcel
blvd. de Sébastopol
rue de Turbigo
rue du Temple
Louvre
rue Berger
rue St-Honoré
rue Rambuteau
rue des Archives
rue Vieille du Temple
rue de Turenne
blvd. Beaumarchais
rue de Rivoli
pont du Carrousel
pont Neuf
rue de Rivoli
pl. des Vosges
Ile de la Cité
Notre Dame
rue St-Antoine
pl. de la Bastille
pl. St-Michel
blvd. St-Germain
quai de Montebello
Ile St-Louis
blvd. Henri IV
pl. Maubert
pont de Sully
Quai St-Bernard
Seine
rue Victor-Cousin
rue St-Jacques
Jardin du Luxembourg
blvd. St-Michel
rue Gay Lussac
Jardin des Plantes
pl. Monge
rue Monge
rue Claude Bernard
Montparnasse
blvd. St-Marcel
N
M
6 7 8 9 10 11 12 18 19 20 21 22 23 24 25 26 27 28 29 30 31

rooms with bath, 6 with shower. AE. Métro: Maubert-Mutualité.

Montpensier. This handsome 17th-century mansion was transformed into a hotel in 1874. It offers the kind of small-hotel charm and character for which Paris is known, as the clientele, many of them regulars, will testify. All the rooms are individually decorated and vary greatly in size. Those on the top floor, for example, are tiny and modern. The location, on an attractive street running parallel to the gardens of the Palais Royal, is ideal. There's no restaurant or bar. *12 rue de Richelieu, 1er, tel. 42–96–28–50. 37 rooms with bath, 6 without bath. MC, V. Métro: Palais Royal.*

Family. The Family is a small, two-star hotel near the Madeleine, just a few minutes' walk from the Tuileries Gardens. It was entirely renovated in 1988, but rooms have kept their stylish '30s look. There's no restaurant, but breakfast and snacks can be served in your room. Service is exceptionally friendly. *35 rue Cambon, 1er, tel. 42–61–54–84. 25 rooms and 1 suite, all with bath. AE, MC, V. Métro: Madeleine.*

Londres Stockholm. An appealing combination of character and comfort singles out the small Londres Stockholm. The lobby has exposed oak beams, statues in niches, and rustic-looking stone walls. The rough-cast white walls in the rooms are set off by deep red carpeting. There's no restaurant or bar, but limited room service is available. *13 rue St-Roch, 1er, tel. 42–60–15–62. 29 rooms with bath, 2 with shower only. AE, MC, V. Métro: Tuileries.*

St-Louis-Marais. The local grapevine has made this tiny, early 17th-century building a great favorite with those in the know. Its location in the south of the Marais, near the Seine, has much to do with it. But the hotel itself has other merits. Its small, oak-beamed rooms are all individually decorated; pretty rugs slide around on worn tile floors, and copies of Old Master paintings adorn the walls. There's no restaurant or bar; breakfast is served in your room. *1 rue Charles-V, 4e, tel. 48–87–87–04. 5 rooms with bath, 9 with shower. MC, V. Closed in Aug. Métro: Sully-Morland.*

South Paris (Montparnasse, Austerlitz, Gare de Lyon)

Modern Hôtel-Lyon. Despite its less than inspiring name, the Modern Hôtel-Lyon, located between place de la Bastille and the Gare de Lyon, has been run by the same family since 1910. They pride themselves on maintaining the hotel's reputation for personal service and have also lately inaugurated a floor-by-floor renovation program. Rooms are decorated in beige and cream shades. There's no restaurant, but there's a good bar. *3 rue Parrot, 12e, tel. 43–43–41–52. 51 rooms and 1 suite, 36 with bath, 15 with shower. Facilities: bar. AE, MC, V. Métro: Gare de Lyon.*

Paris-Lyon Palace. Located near the Gare de Lyon, this attractive three-star hotel has been extensively renovated. Rooms are modern and functional, but the large, plant-filled lobby has been decorated in an appealing art deco style. There's no restaurant, but the bar is open from lunch till 1 AM. Service is notably warm. *11 rue de Lyon, 12e, tel. 43–07–29–49. 64 rooms with bath, 64 with shower. Facilities: bar. AE, DC, MC, V. Métro: Gare de Lyon.*

West Paris

Pavillon. The entrance to the family-run Pavillon lies behind a garden at the end of an alley off rue St-Dominique, guaranteeing peace and quiet. Although some rooms in this former 19th-century convent are tiny, all have been redecorated and feature

Laura Ashley wallpaper and old prints. Breakfast is served in the little courtyard in summer. There's no restaurant or bar, but snacks can be served in your room. *54 rue St-Dominique, 7e, tel. 45–51–42–87. 18 rooms, most with shower. MC, V. Métro: Latour-Maubourg.*

Under 400 francs

Central Paris

Place des Vosges. A loyal American clientele swears by the small, historic Place des Vosges, which is located on a charming street just off the exquisite square of the same name. The entrance hall is imposingly grand and is decorated in Louis XIII style, but some of the rooms are little more than functional. There's no restaurant, but there is a welcoming little breakfast room. *12 rue de Birague, 4e, tel. 42–72–60–46. 11 rooms with bath, 5 with shower. AE, DC, MC, V. Métro: St-Paul-Le Marais.*

Vieux Marais. As its name implies, this charming, two-star hotel lies in the heart of the Marais. It dates to the 16th century; today an elevator takes the strain out of coping with six floors. The rooms and bathrooms are simply decorated in light, refreshing colors and are impeccably clean. Try to get a room overlooking the courtyard. Breakfast is served in a pretty, corn-colored lounge. The staff is exceptionally courteous. *8 rue de Plâtre, 4e, tel. 42–78–47–22. 22 rooms with bath, 8 with shower. MC, V. Métro: Rambuteau.*

Sorbonne. This pretty, early 18th-century hotel, located right by the Sorbonne, was transformed in 1988 when its handsome stone facade was cleaned. As part of the cleanup, fresh flowers are now put into every room, augmenting their existing simple elegance. There's no restaurant or bar, but the receptionist is English, so you'll have no trouble making dining and entertainment plans. Try for a room overlooking the little garden. *6 rue Victor-Cousin, 5e, tel. 43–54–58–08. 10 rooms with bath, 27 with shower. MC, V. Métro: Luxembourg.*

Choiseul-Opéra. The historic, classical facade of the Choiseul-Opéra, located between the Opéra and place Vendôme, belies the strictly functional interior. Service is relaxed but efficient, and the staff is happy to try out its English on guests. There's no restaurant or bar. *1 rue Daunou, 2e, tel. 42–61–70–41. 28 rooms with bath, 14 with shower. AE, DC, MC, V. Métro: Opéra.*

North and East Paris (St-Lazare, Gare du Nord, Gare de l'Est)

London Palace. You'll want to stay here for the location, near the Opéra, and for the straightforward, family-run ambience. The mood throughout is strictly functional but perfectly acceptable for a short stay. There's no restaurant or bar. Public parking lots are nearby. *32 blvd. des Italiens, 9e, tel. 48–24–54–64. 19 rooms with bath, 30 with shower. AE, MC, V. Métro: Opéra.*

Timhotel Montmartre. The reason for listing what is only one of eight Timhotels in Paris is simply the location of the Montmartre member of the chain—right in the leafy little square where Picasso lived at the turn of the century. Rooms are basic and functional, though the Montmartre theme is continued by the Toulouse-Lautrec posters. There's no restaurant, but breakfast is served in your room. *11 rue Ravignan, 18e, tel. 42–55–74–79. 6 rooms with bath, 58 with shower. AE, DC, MC, V. Métro: Abbesses.*

Régyn's Montmartre. Despite small rooms (all recently renovated), this small, owner-run hotel on Montmartre's place des Abbesses is rapidly gaining an enviable reputation for simple, stylish accommodations. A predominantly young clientele and a correspondingly relaxed atmosphere have made this an attractive choice for some. Try for one of the rooms on the upper floors, with great views over the city. *18 pl. des Abbesses, 18e, tel. 42–54–45–21. 14 rooms with bath, 8 with shower. MC, V. Métro: Abbesses.*

Utrillo. Newly renovated, the Utrillo is found on a quiet side street at the foot of Montmartre. The decor is appealing, with prints in every room and a marble-topped breakfast table. Because the color white is emphasized throughout, the hotel seems light, clean, and more spacious than it actually is. *7 rue Aristide-Bruant, 18e, tel. 42–58–13–44. 30 rooms with bath or shower. Facilities: sauna. AE, DC, MC, V. Métro: Blanche.*

South Paris (Montparnasse, Austerlitz, Gare de Lyon)

Jules-César. The address may be unfashionable, but the Bastille, Jardin des Plantes, and Ile St-Louis are just a short walk away, and the Gare de Lyon is just around the corner. The hotel, built in 1914, has been restored: The lobby is rather glitzy, but the guest rooms are more subdued. Rooms facing the street are larger than those in the back and have a somewhat better view. The largest is room 17, which can accommodate a third bed. *52 av. Ledru-Rollin, 12e, tel. 43–43–15–88. 4 rooms with bath, 44 with shower. MC, V. Métro: Gare de Lyon.*

Midi. This place is close to both Montparnasse and the Latin Quarter, and there are métro and RER stations nearby. Don't be put off by the nondescript facade and reception area; most of the rooms were renovated in 1987, and those facing the street are both large and quiet. Request room 32, if possible, and avoid the cheapest rooms, which are quite dingy and unattractive. *4 av. René-Coty, 14e, tel. 43–27–23–25. 50 rooms, 20 with bath, 21 with shower. No credit cards. Métro: Denfert-Rochereau.*

West Paris

Kensington. Perhaps the main reason for staying in this small two-star hotel is the superb view of the Eiffel Tower from the two top floors. Rooms are tiny but freshly decorated and always impeccably clean; all have double-glazed windows. Additional renovations during 1988 further improved facilities. There's no restaurant, but limited room service is available. *79 av. de la Bourdonnais, 7e, tel. 47–05–74–00. 26 rooms, 12 with bath, 14 with shower. AE, DC, MC, V. Métro: Ecole Militaire.*

Solférino. Located behind the Musée d'Orsay and a two-minute walk from the Seine, the Solférino is a favorite. There's no great luxury here, but for all-around good value, the hotel is hard to beat. Rooms are simply decorated in pastel colors, and there's a delightful little veranda-cum-lounge for breakfast or drinks. There's no restaurant. *91 rue de Lille, 7e, tel. 47–05–85–54. 32 rooms and 1 suite, all with bath or shower; 6 do not have a private toilet. MC, V. Closed Christmas through New Year's. Métro: Solférino.*

Ceramic. These are the lowest rates you'll ever pay this close to the Arc de Triomphe and Champs-Elysées. The hotel sports an impressive 1904 tiled facade that embodies Belle Epoque taste, and the reception area, replete with crystal chandeliers and velvet armchairs, is glamorous. Those guest rooms that face the street, such as rooms 412, 422, and 442, have huge bay windows and intricate plaster moldings. Rooms facing the courtyard are rather average. *34 av. de Wagram, 8e, tel. 42–*

27–20–30. 53 rooms with bath or shower. DC, MC, V. Métro: Etoile.

Queen's Hotel. One of only a handful of hotels located in the desirable residential district around rue la Fontaine, Queen's is within walking distance of the Seine and the Bois de Boulogne. The hotel is small and functional, but standards of comfort and service are high. Flowers on the facade add an appealing touch. *4 rue Bastien-Lepage, 16e, tel. 42–88–89–85. 7 rooms with bath, 15 with shower. MC, V. Métro: Michel-Ange-Auteuil.*

Under 250 francs

Central Paris

Lille. You won't find a less expensive base for exploring the Louvre than this hotel, located just a short distance from the Cour Carrée. The hotel hasn't received a face-lift in years, but then neither have the prices. The decor is somewhat shabby, but it's the epitome of Vieux Paris, and the money you save by staying here can come in handy if you indulge in a shopping spree along the nearby rue de Rivoli or Forum des Halles. *8 rue du Pélican, 1er, tel. 42–33–33–42. 14 rooms, some with shower. No credit cards. Métro: Palais Royal.*

Sévigné. Located in the up-and-coming Marais district and convenient to the métro and the place des Vosges, this hotel remains a good bet for quality low-budget accommodations. The hotel is clean and well run, and the staff is personable. Extensive renovation a few years back resulted in a mirror-lined lobby, new breakfast room, and a shower or bath in every room. Rooms facing rue Malher are quieter, but those facing busy rue St-Antoine offer a view of the church of St-Paul-St-Louis. *2 rue Malher, 4e, tel. 42–72–76–17. 30 rooms with shower or bath. No credit cards. Métro: St-Paul-Le Marais.*

Esméralda. Lovers of small, charming Parisian hotels—the rooms are a little dusty perhaps, but they positively exude Gallic charm—will want to stay at this simple hotel. It's set in a fine 17th-century building opposite Notre-Dame—request a room with a view—near Square Viviani. All the rooms are small—the cheapest are midget size—but all have the same feel of time-worn clutter and warmth. Many have copies of 17th-century furniture. *4 rue St-Julien-le-Pauvre, 5e, tel. 43–54–19–20. 15 rooms with bath, 4 with shower. No credit cards. Métro: St-Michel.*

Dhély's. Who would have thought that you could find such a reasonably priced hotel so close to the lively, bohemian place St-Michel? Tucked away behind a portico on the tiny rue de l'Hirondelle, the clean, white facade of this hotel is a pleasure to stumble upon. New showers were recently installed in small bathrooms. Be sure to reserve well in advance. *22 rue de l'Hirondelle, 5e, tel. 43–26–58–25. 14 rooms, some with shower. No credit cards. Métro: St-Michel.*

North and East Paris (St-Lazare, Gare du Nord, Gare de l'Est)

Résidence Alhambra. This hotel is on the edge of the historic Marais quarter and is conveniently close to five métro lines. The Alhambra's gleaming white exterior and flower-filled window boxes provide a bright spot in an otherwise drab neighborhood. The interior has been redecorated, and some improvements include fresh pastel shades in the smallish guest rooms, marble-topped breakfast tables, and a lobby filled with plants and leather armchairs. Most rooms have color TV, unusual for hotels in this price range. *13 rue de Malte, 11e, tel.*

47-00-35-52. 50 rooms, most with bath or shower. MC, V. Métro: Oberkampf.

Le Laumière. Though it's located some way from downtown, the low rates of this two-star hotel, close to the tumbling Buttes-Chaumont park, are hard to resist. Most rooms are functional only, but some of the larger ones overlook the garden. The staff is exceptionally helpful. There's no restaurant, but breakfast is available until midday. *4 rue Petit, 19e, tel. 42-06-10-77. 54 rooms, 39 with bath or shower. AE, DC, MC, V. Métro: Laumière.*

West Paris

Argenson. This friendly, family-run hotel provides what may well be the best value in the swanky 8th Arrondissement. Some of the city's greatest sights are just a 10-minute walk away. Old-time charm in the form of period furnishings, molded ceilings, and floral arrangements is not compromised by some modern touches, such as the new bathrooms that were installed in 1988. The best rooms are numbers 23, 33, 42, 43, and 53. *15 rue d'Argenson, 8e, tel. 42-65-16-87. 48 rooms with bath or shower. DC, MC, V. Métro: Miromesnil.*

Splurges

Deux-Iles. This cleverly converted 17th-century mansion on the residential Ile St-Louis has long won plaudits for charm and comfort. Flowers and plants are scattered around the stunning hall. The fabric-hung rooms, though small, have exposed beams and are fresh and airy. Ask for a room overlooking the little garden courtyard. There's no restaurant, but drinks are served in the cellar bar until 1 AM. The lounge is dominated by a fine chimneypiece and doubles as a second bar. You'll spend $110 to $140 for a double room. *59 rue St-Louis-en-Ile, 4e, tel. 43-26-13-35. 8 rooms with bath, 9 with shower. Facilities: bar (closed Sun.). No credit cards. Métro: Pont-Marie.*

Hôtel d'Angleterre. Some claim the Hôtel d'Angleterre is the ultimate Left Bank hotel—a little small and shabby, but elegant and perfectly managed. The 18th-century building was originally the British ambassador's residence; later, Hemingway made it his Paris home. Rooms vary greatly in size, price (the range is $125 to $200), and style: Some are imposingly formal, others are homey and plain. Ask for one overlooking the courtyard. There's no restaurant, but a small bar has been installed. *44 rue Jacob, 6e, tel. 42-60-34-72. 29 rooms with bath. Facilities: bar. AE, DC, MC, V. Métro: St-Germain-des-Prés.*

Exploring Paris

Guided Tours

A bus tour of Paris makes a fine introduction to the city but is expensive; we suggest you explore Paris on foot or by the green RATP buses used for public transportation (bus 69 passes a number of major sites on its way from Champ-de-Mars to Père Lachaise, via Invalides, the Louvre, and Bastille). Bateaux-Mouches boat tours provide a pleasant, reasonably priced overview of Paris.

Orientation Tours

The two largest bus-tour operators are **Cityrama** (3 pl. des Pyramides, 1er, tel. 42-60-30-14) and **Paris Vision** (214 rue de Rivoli, 1er, tel. 42-60-31-25). **American Express** (11 rue

Scribe, 9e, tel. 42–77–70–00) also organizes tours from its headquarters near the Opéra. Tours are generally in double-decker buses with either a live or a tape-recorded commentary (English is available) and last two hours. Expect to pay about 140 francs.

The **RATP** (Paris Transport Authority) has many guide-accompanied excursions in and around Paris. Inquire at its Tourist Service Board (pl. de la Madeleine, 8e) or at its office (53 quai des Grands-Augustins, 6e).

Special-Interest Tours **Cityrama, Paris Vision,** and **American Express** offer a variety of theme tours ("Historic Paris," "Modern Paris," "Paris-by-Night") lasting from 2½ hours to all day and costing 150 to 420 francs (more if admission to a cabaret show is included).

Hour-long **boat trips** along the Seine are a must for the first-time visitor. Some boats serve lunch and dinner; make reservations in advance. The following services operate regularly throughout the day and in the evening: **Bateaux-Mouches** has departures from Pont de l'Alma (Right Bank, 8e, tel. 42–25–96–10); **Vedettes du Pont-Neuf** has departures from Square du Vert-Galant (Ile de la Cité, 1er, tel. 46–33–98–38); **Bateaux Parisiens-Tour Eiffel** has departures from Pont d'Iéna (Left Bank, 15e, tel. 47–05–50–00), and **Canauxrama** (tel. 42–39–15–00) organizes half- and full-day canal tours in flat-bottomed barges along picturesque canals in Eastern Paris (departures from 5 bis quai de la Loire, 19e, or from Bassin de l'Arsenal, 12e, opposite 50 blvd. de la Bastille).

Walking Tours There are plenty of guided tours of specific areas of Paris, often concentrating on a historical or architectural topic—"Restored Mansions of the Marais," for instance, or "Private Walled Gardens in St-Germain." The guides are enthusiastic and dedicated, though not always English-speaking. Charges range from 35 francs to 50 francs, and tours last about two hours. Details are published in the weekly magazines *Pariscope* and *L'Officiel des Spectacles* under the heading "Conférences." You can sometimes make advance reservations for walking tours organized by the **Caisse Nationale des Monuments Historiques,** Bureau des Visites/Conférences (Hôtel de Sully, 62 rue St-Antoine, 4e, tel. 44–61–20–00).

Paris for Free—or Almost

Unfortunately, Paris doesn't offer many organized sights that can be enjoyed without first digging deep into your pockets. That said, the city is one of the world's most scenic and exciting capitals, and just strolling along, breathing in its rich, romantic atmosphere, is an occupation in which every visitor will want to indulge.

Museums A number of museums are free on Sunday, including the Petit Palais, the Paris Museum of Modern Art, the Musée Carnavalet, and the homes of Honoré de Balzac and Victor Hugo.

Except for its modern art museum and those galleries with temporary exhibitions, the vast halls of **Beaubourg** (Pompidou Center) are always open free of charge. Outside, on the plateau Beaubourg, you can be entertained for hours by the fire-eaters, Indian rope tricksters, musicians, mimes, and clowns who gather here during summer months. Similar entertainment can be found on the square in front of St-Germain-des-Prés, on the Left Bank.

Walks A walk along the **Seine** is at the top of the list; although roads have invaded some sections of quays, you can still stroll peacefully along the riverbank between place de la Concorde and the Louvre before crossing the Pont des Arts footbridge and continuing along the **Left Bank**, past Notre-Dame, as far as the Jardin des Plantes; the last section of this walk takes you through the avant-garde statuary of the **Musée de la Sculpture en Plein Air.** The northern banks of the **Ile St-Louis** also make for an idyllic saunter. Other great places to wander are the **Marais,** with its clash of ramshackle streets and stately mansions; **Montmartre,** with its tumbling alleyways and flights of steps; along the banks of the **Canal St-Martin,** with its locks, footbridges, and flavor of Amsterdam; and, of course, down the **Champs-Elysées,** continuing along the arcaded rue du Rivoli to the Louvre.

Parks Paris's many parks and gardens can be enjoyed free of charge. The **Tuileries, Jardin du Luxembourg,** and the **Palais-Royal** are the most central locations, and don't forget the lower reaches of the Champs-Elysées or the newly landscaped gardens at **Les Halles,** with their ivy-strewn archways and dramatic views of St-Eustache. A short métro ride will take you to **Parc Monceau** (mock ruins), the **Jardin des Plantes** (superb flowers), the **Arènes de Lutèce** (Roman remains), the **Buttes-Chaumont,** and **Parc Montsouris** (the last two have their own lake). The **Champ de Mars,** stretching away from the Eiffel Tower, has long, straight, uncrowded alleys that make it the best jogging venue in Paris. The **Bois de Boulogne** and **Bois de Vincennes** offer acres of woods and lakes. Gardening enthusiasts should consider paying the small admission charges to admire the outstanding floral displays at the **Serres d'Auteuil, Parc Bagatelle,** or **Parc Floral** at Vincennes. Melancholy charm lurks amid the lush foliage and bombastic sepulchres at the vast, lugubrious **Père Lachaise Cemetery.**

Views Everyone has a favorite Paris view, but here are some of the most dramatic: the **Sacré Coeur** as you emerge from rue de Steinkerque; the **Eiffel Tower** from Trocadéro; the **Arc de Triomphe** from avenue Foch; **Notre-Dame** from Pont de l'Archevêché; the columns at **place de la Nation** from cours de Vincennes. The best views of Paris are from high up the Eiffel Tower or Tour Montparnasse, but cheaper alternatives are from the dome of the Sacré Coeur, the towers of Notre-Dame, the elevator at the Pompidou Center or from high up rue de Ménilmontant in northeast Paris. Other picturesque views include **Ile de la Cité** from the Pont des Arts footbridge; **rue des Barres** and the back of St-Gervais church from quai de l'Hôtel de Ville; and the **Tuileries** and **Right Bank** from the café terrace at the Musée d'Orsay.

People Watching The best places include **St-Germain-des-Prés** and **place St-Sulpice** (6e), **boulevard Montparnasse** (14e), **place de l'Opéra** (9e), **place de la Contrescarpe** (5e), and **place Victor-Hugo** (16e).

And for the modest price of a cup of coffee, you're guaranteed a ringside seat in any of Paris's sidewalk cafés, where you can amuse yourself for hours watching the world go by.

Concerts A number of Paris churches give free concerts (especially on Sunday afternoons), including **St-Sulpice,** the **Madeleine, St-**

Germain-l'Auxerrois, St-Eustache, St-Merri, Notre-Dame, and the **American Church.** You can also attend concerts for free at the headquarters of **Radio-France** (116 av. du Président-Kennedy, 16e). Check details in *Pariscope* or *L'Officiel des Spectacles*.

Orientation

The best method of getting to know Paris is on foot. With this in mind, we've divided our coverage of Paris into six tours. Use our routes as a base; concentrate on the areas that are of particular interest to you; and, above all, enjoy to the full the sights, sounds, and smells of this exciting city.

Highlights for First-time Visitors

Arc de Triomphe and Champs-Elysées, Tour 3
Beaubourg (Pompidou Center), Tour 2
Eiffel Tower, Tour 4
The Louvre, Tour 1
Musée de Cluny, Tour 5
Musée d'Orsay, Tour 4
Notre-Dame, Tour 1
Place des Vosges, Tour 2
Place Vendôme, Tour 3
Sacré Coeur, Tour 6
Sainte-Chapelle, Tour 1

Tour 1: The Historic Heart

Numbers in the margin correspond to points of interest on the Paris map.

Of the two islands in the Seine—the Ile St-Louis and Ile de la Cité—it is the latter that forms the historic heart of Paris. It was here that the earliest inhabitants of Paris, the Gaulish tribe of the Parisii, settled around 250 BC. Whereas the Ile St-Louis is largely residential, the Ile de la Cité remains deeply historic: It is the site of the great, brooding cathedral of Notre-Dame. Few of the island's other medieval buildings have survived, most having fallen victim to Baron Haussmann's ambitious rebuilding of the city in the mid-19th century. Among the rare survivors are the jewellike Sainte-Chapelle, a vision of shimmering stained glass, and the Conciergerie, the grim former city prison.

The tour begins at the western tip of the Ile de la Cité, at the
1 sedate **Square du Vert Galant.** The statue of the *Vert Galant* himself, literally the "vigorous [by which was really meant the amorous] adventurer," shows Henri IV sitting sturdily on his horse. Henri, king of France from 1589 until his assassination in 1610, was something of a dashing figure as well as a canny statesman.

Crossing the Ile de la Cité, just behind the Vert Galant, is the oldest bridge in Paris, confusingly called the **Pont Neuf,** or New Bridge. Completed in the early 17th century, it was the first bridge in the city to be built without houses lining either side. Turn left onto it. Once across the river, turn left again and walk down to rue l'Amiral-de-Coligny, opposite the massive eastern facade of the Louvre. Before heading for the museum, howev-

Paris Arrondissements

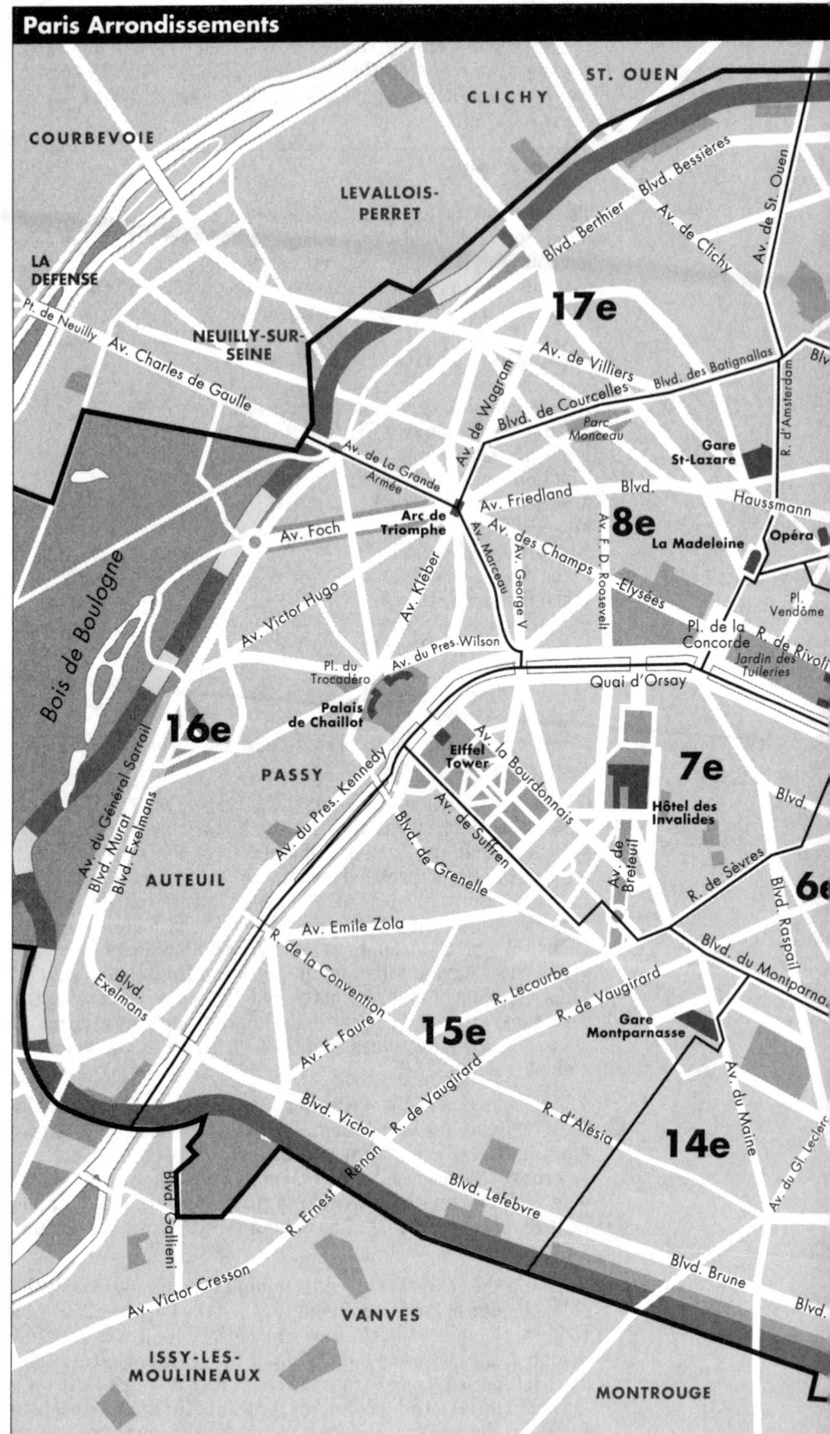

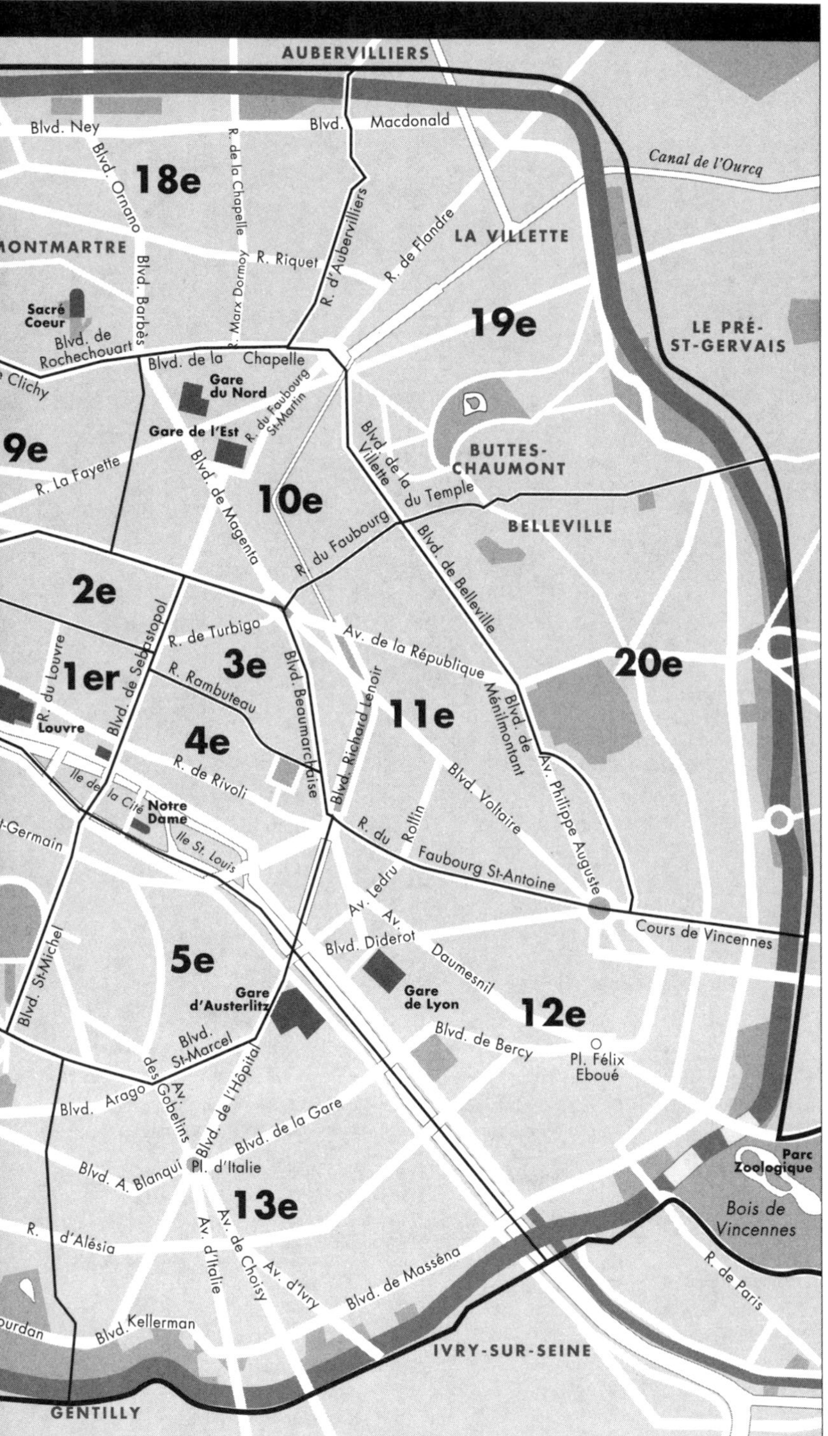
AUBERVILLIERS
Blvd. Ney
Blvd. Macdonald
Canal de l'Ourcq
18e
Blvd. Ornano
R. de la Chapelle
R. d'Aubervilliers
R. de Flandre
LA VILLETTE
MONTMARTRE
Blvd. Barbès
R. Marx Dormoy
R. Riquet
19e
LE PRÉ-ST-GERVAIS
Sacré Coeur
Blvd. de Rochechouart
Blvd. de la Chapelle
Clichy
Gare du Nord
R. du Faubourg St-Martin
Gare de l'Est
Blvd. de la Villette
BUTTES-CHAUMONT
9e
R. La Fayette
Blvd. de Magenta
10e
du Temple
R. du Faubourg
BELLEVILLE
2e
Blvd. de Belleville
R. de Turbigo
Av. de la République
20e
1er
3e
R. du Louvre
Blvd. de Sebastopol
R. Rambuteau
Blvd. Beaumarchaise
Blvd. Richard Lenoir
11e
Blvd. de Ménilmontant
Louvre
4e
Av. Philippe Auguste
R. de Rivoli
Blvd. Voltaire
Ile de la Cité
Notre Dame
Rollin
St-Germain
Ile St. Louis
R. du Faubourg St-Antoine
Av. Ledru
Av. Daumesnil
Cours de Vincennes
Blvd. Diderot
5e
Blvd. St-Michel
Gare d'Austerlitz
Gare de Lyon
12e
Blvd. de Bercy
Blvd. St-Marcel
Pl. Félix Eboué
Blvd. de l'Hôpital
Av. des Gobelins
Blvd. Arago
Blvd. de la Gare
Parc Zoologique
Blvd. A. Blanqui
Pl. d'Italie
13e
Bois de Vincennes
R. d'Alésia
Av. de Choisy
Av. d'Italie
Av. d'Ivry
Blvd. de Masséna
R. de Paris
Blvd. Kellerman
IVRY-SUR-SEINE
GENTILLY

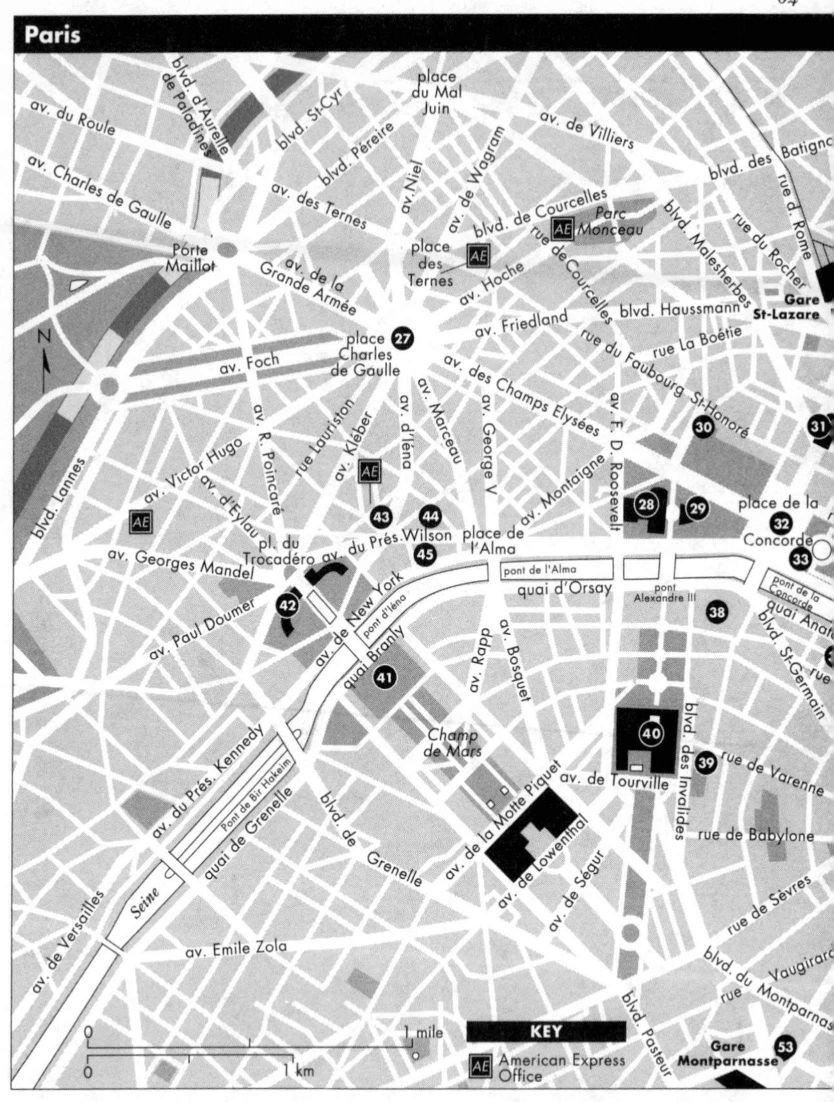

Arc de Triomphe, **27**
Archives Nationales, **17**
Beaubourg, **16**
Bibliothèque Nationale, **8**
Bourse du Commerce, **10**
Carrefour de Buci, **47**
Closerie des Lilas, **54**
Comédie-Française, **6**
Cour Carré, **3**
Ecole Nationale des Beaux-Arts, **50**
Eglise de la Madeleine, **31**
Eiffel Tower, **41**
Forum des Halles, **12**
Grand Palais, **28**
Hôtel Carnavalet, **21**
Hôtel des Invalides, **40**
Hôtel des Monnaies/ Institut de France, **49**
Hôtel de Sens, **25**
Hôtel de Ville, **15**
Hôtel et Musée de Cluny, **58**
Ile St-Louis, **26**
Jardin des Plantes, **61**
Jardin des Tuileries, **34**
Louvre, **4**
Musée Bricard de la Serrure, **18**
Musée Cognacq-Jay, **20**
Musée de l'Art Moderne de la Ville de Paris, **45**
Musée d'Orsay, **37**
Musée Eugène Delacroix, **51**
Musée Guimet, **43**

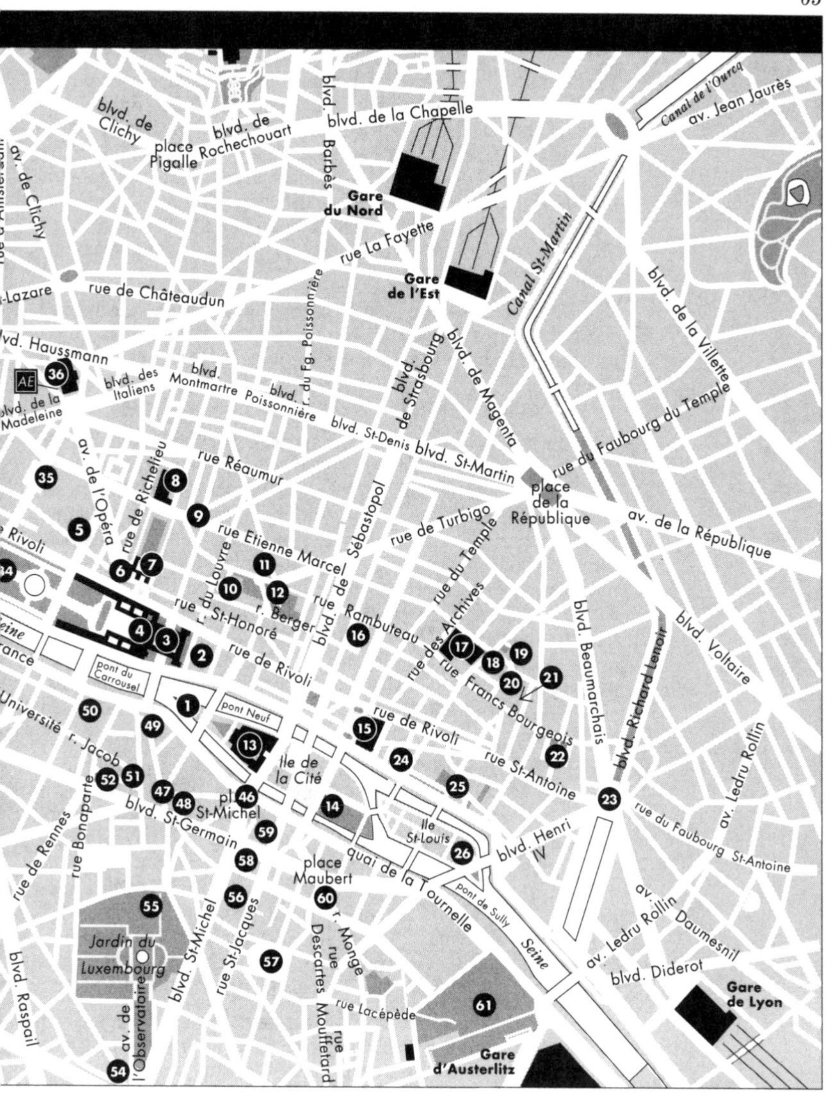

Musée Picasso, **19**
Musée Rodin, **39**
Notre-Dame, **14**
Opéra, **36**
Orangerie, **33**
Palais Bourbon, **38**
Palais de Chaillot, **42**
Palais de la Mutualité, **60**
Palais de l'Elysée, **30**
Palais de Justice, **13**
Palais du Luxembourg, **55**
Palais Galliera, **44**
Palais Royal, **7**
Panthéon, **57**
Petit Palais, **29**
Place de la Bastille, **23**
Place de la Concorde, **32**
Place des Victoires, **9**
Place des Vosges, **22**
Place St-Michel, **46**
Place Vendôme, **35**
Procope, **48**
St-Eustache, **11**
St-Germain-des-Prés, **52**
St-Germain-l'Auxerrois, **2**
St-Gervais-St-Protais, **24**
St-Roch, **5**
St-Séverin, **59**
Sorbonne, **56**
Square du Vert Galant, **1**
Tour Maine-Montparnasse, **53**

er, stay on the right-hand sidewalk and duck into the church of
2 **St-Germain-l'Auxerrois.** This was the French royal family's Paris church in the days before the Revolution, when the Louvre was a palace rather than a museum. The fluid stonework of the facade reveals the influence of 15th-century Flamboyant Gothic, the final, exuberant fling of the Gothic before the classical takeover of the Renaissance. Note the unusual double aisles and the exceptionally wide windows—typical of the style. The triumph of classicism is evident, however, in the 18th-century fluted columns around the choir, the area surrounding the altar.

The Louvre colonnade across the road screens one of Europe's
3 most dazzling courtyards, the **Cour Carré,** a breathtakingly monumental, harmonious, and superbly rhythmic ensemble. In the crypt below, excavated in 1984, sections of the defensive towers of the original, 13th-century fortress can be seen.

Saunter through the courtyard and pass under the **Pavillon de l'Horloge,** the Clock Tower, and you'll come face-to-face with I.M. Pei's **glass pyramid,** surrounded by three smaller pyramids. The pyramid marks the new entrance to the Louvre and houses a large museum shop, café, and restaurant. It is also the terminal point for the most celebrated city view in Europe—a majestic vista stretching through the Arc du Carrousel, the Tuileries Gardens, across place de la Concorde, up the Champs-Elysées to the towering Arc de Triomphe, and ending at the giant modern arch at La Tête Défense, a further 2½ miles away. Needless to say, the architectural collision between classical stone blocks and pseudo-Egyptian glass panels has caused a furor.

4 Today's **Louvre** is the end product of many generations of work. It began in the early 13th century, when Philippe-Auguste built it as a fortress to protect the city's western flank. The earliest parts of the current building date from the reign of François I at the beginning of the 16th century, and subsequent monarchs—Henri IV (1589–1610), Louis XIII (1610–43), Louis XIV (1643–1715), Napoleon (1802–14), and Napoleon III (1851–70)—all contributed to its construction. The open section facing the Tuileries Gardens was once the site of the Palais des Tuileries, the main residence of the royal family in Paris.

Over the centuries, the Louvre has been used as both a royal residence and a home for minor courtiers; at one point, it was taken over by a rabble of artists who set up shop and whose chimneys projected higgledy-piggledy from the otherwise severe lines of the facades. After a stint as headquarters of the French Revolution, the Louvre was finally established, in Napoleon's time, as a museum, though the country's last three monarchs continued to make it their home.

The number-one attraction for most visitors is Leonardo da Vinci's enigmatic *Mona Lisa,* "La Joconde" to the French; be forewarned that you will find it encased in glass and surrounded by a mob of tourists. The collections are divided into seven sections: Oriental antiquities; Egyptian antiquities; Greek and Roman antiquities; sculpture; paintings, prints, and drawings; furniture; and objets d'art. Unless you enjoy masochistic 10-hour slogs around museums, don't try to see it all at once. Try, instead, to make repeat visits—the Louvre is half-price on Sunday. Some highlights of paintings, in addition to the *Mona Lisa,* are *The Inspiration of the Poet,* by Nicolas Poussin (1594–1665); *The Oath of the Horatii,* by Jacques-Louis David (1748–1825); *The Raft of the Medusa,* by Théodore Géricault (1791–1824); and *La Grande Odalisque,* by Jean-Auguste Dominique Ingres (1780–1867). Probably the best-loved bit of sculpture is Michelangelo's pair of *Slaves,* intended for the tomb of Pope Julius II; the French crown jewels (in the objets d'art section) include the mind-boggling 186-carat Regent diamond. *Palais du Louvre. Admission: 31 frs. adults, 16 frs. ages 18–25 and on Sun. Open daily 9–6, Mon. and Wed. until 9:45; closed Tues.*

Stretching westward from the main entrance to the Louvre and the glass pyramid is an expanse of stately, formal gardens. These are the **Jardins des Tuileries** (*see* Tour 3: From the Arc de Triomphe to the Opéra, *below*).

Running the length of the Louvre's northern side is Napoleon's arcaded rue de Rivoli. Cross it and you're in **place des Pyramides,** face-to-face with its gilded statue of Joan of Arc on horseback. Walk up rue des Pyramides and take the first left,
5 rue St-Honoré, to the Baroque church of **St-Roch.** The church was completed in the 1730s, the date of the cool, classical facade. It's worth having a look inside to see the bombastically Baroque altarpiece in the circular Lady Chapel.

Return to rue des Pyramides and follow rue St-Honoré to **place André-Malraux,** with its exuberant fountains. The Opéra building is visible down the avenue of the same name, and on one cor-
6 ner of the square, at rue de Richelieu, is the **Comédie-Française,** the time-honored setting for performances of classical French drama. The building dates from 1790, but the Comédie-Française company was created by Louis XIV in 1680. If you understand French and have a taste for the mannered, declamatory style of French acting, you will appreciate an evening here (*see* The Arts and Nightlife, *below*).

To the right of the theater (as you face it from the Louvre) is the
7 unobtrusive entrance to the gardens of the **Palais Royal.** The buildings of this former palace date from the 1630s and are royal only in that the builder, Cardinal Richelieu (1585–1642), magnanimously bequeathed them to Louis XIII. Today the Palais Royal is home of the French Ministry of Culture and is not open to the public. But don't miss the **gardens,** divided by rows of perfectly trimmed little trees, a surprisingly little-known oasis in the gray heart of the city. There's not much chance that you'll miss the black-and-white striped columns in the courtyard or the revolving silver spheres that slither around in the two fountains at either end, the controversial early-1980s work of architect Daniel Buren. Walk to the end, away from the main palace, and peek into the opulent, Belle Epoque, glass-lined interior of **Le Grand Véfour,** one of the swankiest and most sumptuously appointed restaurants in the city.

Around the corner, on rue de Richelieu, stands France's na-
8 tional library, the **Bibliothèque Nationale,** containing over 7 million printed volumes. Visitors can admire Robert de Cotte's 18th-century courtyard and peep into the 19th-century reading room. *58 rue de Richelieu. Open daily noon–6.*

From the library, walk along rue des Petits-Champs to the cir-
9 cular **place des Victoires.** It was laid out by Mansart, a leading proponent of French 17th-century classicism, in 1685, in honor

of the military victories of Louis XIV. You'll find some of the city's most upscale fashion shops here and on the surrounding streets.

Head south down rue Croix-des-Petits-Champs. The second
10 street on the left leads to the circular 18th-century **Bourse du Commerce,** or Commercial Exchange. Alongside it is a 100-foot-high fluted column, all that remains of a mansion built here in 1572 for Catherine de Médicis. The column is said to have been used as a platform for stargazing by her astrologer, Ruggieri.

You can easily spot the bulky outline of the church of
11 **St-Eustache,** away to the left. It is a huge church, the "cathedral" of Les Halles, built, as it were, as the market people's Right Bank reply to Notre-Dame. Under construction from 1532 to 1637 and modified over the centuries, the church is a curious architectural hybrid. Its exterior flying buttresses, for example, are solidly Gothic, yet its column orders, rounded arches, and comparatively simple window tracery are unmistakably classical. Few buildings bear such eloquent witness to stylistic transition.

If Notre-Dame and the Louvre represent Church and State, respectively, Les Halles (pronounced "lay al") stands for the common man. For centuries, this was Paris's central market. Closed in 1969, it was replaced by a striking shopping mall, the
12 **Forum des Halles.** The surrounding streets have since undergone a radical transformation, much like the neighboring Marais, and the shops, cafés, restaurants, and chic apartment buildings make it an example of successful urban redevelopment.

From place du Châtelet cross back over the Seine on the Pont-au-Change to the Ile de la Cité. To your right looms the impos-
13 ing **Palais de Justice,** the Courts of Law, built by Baron Haussmann in his characteristically weighty classical style around 1860. The main buildings of interest on the Ile de la Cité, however, are the medieval parts of the complex, spared by Haussmann in his otherwise wholesale destruction.

The **Conciergerie,** the northernmost part of the complex, was originally part of the royal palace on the island. Most people know it, however, as a prison, the grim place of confinement for Danton, Robespierre, and Marie Antoinette during the French Revolution. Inside you'll see the guardroom (the Salle des Gens d'Armes), a striking example of Gothic monumentality; the cells, including the one in which Marie Antoinette was held; and the chapel, where objects connected with the ill-fated queen are displayed. *Admission: 24 frs. adults, 13 frs. children, students, and senior citizens. Joint ticket (with Ste-Chapelle): 40 frs. (20 frs.). Open daily 9–6 (10–5 in winter).*

The other perennial crowd-puller in the Palais de Justice is the **Sainte-Chapelle,** the Holy Chapel, one of the supreme achievements of the Middle Ages. It was built by the genial and pious Louis IX (1226–70) to house what he took to be the Crown of Thorns from Christ's crucifixion and fragments of the True Cross. Architecturally, for all its delicate and ornate exterior decoration, the design of the building is simplicity itself; in essence, no more than a thin, rectangular box much taller than it is wide. Some clumsy 19th-century work has added a deadening touch, but the glory of the chapel—the stained glass—is spectacularly intact: The walls consist of at least twice as much glass as masonry. Try to attend one of the regular, candlelit concerts given here. *Admission: 24 frs. adults, 13 frs. children under 17. Open daily 9:30–6 (10–5 in winter).*

Take rue de Lutèce opposite the Palais de Justice down to place
Louis-Lépine and the bustling **Marché aux Fleurs,** the flower
market. Around the corner is the most enduring symbol of Par-
14 is, the cathedral of **Notre-Dame.** The building was started in
1163, with an army of stonemasons, carpenters, and sculptors
working on a site that had previously seen a Roman temple, an
early Christian basilica, and a Romanesque church. The chancel and altar were consecrated in 1182, but the magnificent
sculptures surrounding the main doors were not put into position until 1240. The north tower was finished 10 years later. Despite various changes in the 17th century, principally the
removal of the rose windows, the cathedral remained substantially unaltered until the French Revolution, when much destruction was wrought, mainly to statuary.

Place du Parvis, in front of the cathedral, is the perfect place from which to gaze at the building's famous facade, divided neatly into three levels. At the first-floor level are the three main entrances, or portals, the Portal of the Virgin on the left; the Portal of the Last Judgment in the center; and the Portal of St. Anne on the right. Above this level are the restored statues of the kings of Israel, the Galerie des Rois (which took a beating during the French Revolution). Above the gallery is the great rose window and, on top of that, the Grande Galerie, at the base of the twin towers. The south tower houses the great bell of Notre-Dame, as tolled by Quasimodo, Victor Hugo's fictional hunchback.

The interior of the cathedral, with its vast proportions, soaring nave, and gentle, multicolored light filtering through the stained-glass windows, inspires awe, despite the inevitable throngs of tourists. On the south side of the chancel is the **Treasury,** with a collection of garments, reliquaries, and silver and gold plate. (Admission: 15 frs. adults, 10 frs. students and senior citizens, 5 frs. children. Open Mon.–Sat. 9:30–6, Sun. 2–6.) The 387-step climb to the top of the towers is worth the effort for the close-up view of the famous gargoyles and the expansive view over the city. (Entrance via the north tower. Admission: 30 frs. adults, 16 frs. students and senior citizens, 5 frs. children. Open daily 10–5.)

If your interest in the cathedral is not yet sated, duck into the **Musée Notre-Dame,** which displays artwork and documents tracing the cathedral's history. *10 rue du Cloître Notre-Dame. Admission: 10 frs. Open Wed. and weekends only, 2:30–6.*

Tour 2: The Marais and Ile St-Louis

The history of the Marais began when Charles V, king of France in the 14th century, moved the French court from the Ile de la Cité. However, it wasn't until Henri IV laid out the place Royale, today the place des Vosges, in the early 17th century that the Marais became *the* place to live. Following the French Revolution, however, the Marais rapidly became one of the most deprived, dissolute areas in Paris. It was spared the attentions of Baron Haussmann, the man who rebuilt so much of Paris in the mid-19th century, so that, though crumbling, its ancient golden-hued buildings and squares remained intact. Today's Marais once again has staked a convincing claim as the city's most desirable district.

15 Begin your tour at the **Hôtel de Ville** (City Hall), overlooking the Seine. It was in the square on the Hôtel de Ville's south side that Robespierre, fanatical leader during the period of the French Revolution known as the Reign of Terror, came to suffer the fate of his many victims when a furious mob sent him to the guillotine in 1794. Following the accession of Louis-Philippe in 1830, the building became the seat of the French government, a role that came to a sudden end with the uprisings in 1848. In the Commune of 1871, the Hôtel de Ville was burned to the ground. Today's exuberant building, based closely on the Renaissance original, went up between 1874 and 1884.

From the Hôtel de Ville, head north across rue de Rivoli and up rue du Temple. On your right, you'll pass one of the city's most popular department stores, the **Bazar de l'Hôtel de Ville,** or BHV as it's commonly known. The first street on your left, rue de la Verrerie, will take you to the stores, restaurants, and galleries of the rue St-Martin.

The Centre National d'Art et de Culture Georges Pompidou,
16 known as **Beaubourg,** is next. The center hosts an innovative and challenging series of exhibits, in addition to housing the world's largest collection of modern art. Its brash architectural style—it has been likened to a gaudily painted oil refinery—has caused much controversy, however. Many critics think it is beginning to show its age (it only opened in 1977) in a particularly cheap manner: Witness the cracked and grimy plastic tubing that encases the exterior elevators, and the peeling, skeletal interior supports. Probably the most popular thing to do at Beaubourg is to ride the escalator up to the roof to see the Parisian skyline unfolding as you are carried through its clear plastic piping. There's a sizable restaurant and café on the roof. Aside from the art collection (from which American painters and sculptors are conspicuously absent), the building houses a movie theater; a language laboratory; an extensive collection of tapes, videos, and slides; an industrial design center; and an acoustics and musical research center. *Plateau Beaubourg, tel. 42–77–12–33. Admission free. Admission to Modern Art museum: 27 frs. Open Wed.–Mon. noon–10 PM, weekends 10–10; closed Tues. Guided tours: weekdays 3:30, weekends 11.*

Don't leave the plateau without stopping for coffee at the **Café Beaubourg** on the corner of rue St-Merri. A staircase takes you up from the first floor to a *passerelle,* or foot bridge, linking the two sides of a mezzanine. The severe, high-tech design is lightened by the little glass-top tables, which are gradually being covered with artists' etchings.

Leave plateau Beaubourg by its southwestern corner and head down little rue Ste-Croix de la Bretonnerie to visit the Marais's Jewish quarter. You'll see the more obvious of the area's historical highlights if you take rue Rambuteau, which runs along the north side of the center (to your left as you face the building). The **Quartier de l'Horloge,** the Clock Quarter, opens off the plateau here. An entire city block has been rebuilt, and despite the shops and cafés, it retains a resolutely artificial quality. The mechanical clock around the corner on rue Clairvaux will amuse children, however: St. George defends Time against a dragon, an eagle-beaked bird, or a monstrous crab (symbolizing earth, air, and water, respectively) every hour, on the hour. At noon, 6 PM, and 10 PM, he takes on all three at once.

You are now poised to plunge into the elegant heart of the Marais. The historic homes here are now private residences, but don't be afraid to push through the heavy doors, or *portes-cochère*, to glimpse the discreet courtyards that lurk behind.

From the little market on rue Rambuteau, take the first left, up rue du Temple, to the 17th-century **Hôtel de Montmor,** at no. 79. It was once the scene of an influential literary salon—a part-social, part-literary group—that included the philosopher Descartes (1596–1650) and the playwright Molière (1622–73).

Take rue de Braque (opposite) down to the Hôtel de Soubise,
17 now the **Archives Nationales** (its collections form part of the Musée de l'Histoire de France). The museum's highlights are the papers dating from the revolutionary period, including Marie Antoinette's last letter, the pattern book from which she would select a new dress every morning, and Louis XVI's diary that contains his sadly ignorant entry for July 14, 1789, the day the Bastille was stormed at the start of the French Revolution: *Rien* (nothing), he wrote. You can also visit the apartments of the Prince and Princess de Soubise: Don't miss them if you have any interest in the lifestyles of 18th-century French aristocrats. The Archives buildings also include the elegant **Hôtel de Rohan,** built for the archbishops of Strasbourg in 1705 (open only during temporary exhibits). *60 rue des Francs-Bourgeois, tel. 40-27-62-18. Admission: 12 frs. adults, 8 frs. children. Open Wed.-Mon. 1:45-5:45; closed Tues.*

Turn right onto rue des Archives, then take the first right onto rue des Quatre-Fils, which becomes rue de la Perle. At no. 1 is
18 the **Musée Bricard de la Serrure,** the Lock Museum. The museum's sumptuous building is perhaps more interesting than the assembled locks and keys within; it was built in 1685 by Bruand, the architect of Les Invalides. If you have a taste for fine craftsmanship, you will appreciate the intricacy and ingenuity of many of the older locks. One represents an early security system—it would shoot anyone who tried to open it with the wrong key. *Hôtel Bruand, 1 rue de la Perle. Admission: 10 frs. Open Tues.-Sat. 10-noon and 2-5; closed Mon., Aug., and last week of Dec.*

From here it is but a step to the Hôtel Salé, built between 1656
19 and 1660, and today the popular **Musée Picasso;** be prepared for long lines. The collection encompasses pictures, sculptures, drawings, prints, ceramics, and other assorted works of art given to the French government after the painter's death, in 1973, in lieu of death duties. What's notable about it—other than its being the world's largest collection of works by Picasso—is that these were works that the artist himself owned and especially valued. There are works from every period of his life, as well as paintings by Paul Cézanne, Joan Miró, Pierre Auguste Renoir, Georges Braque, Edgar Degas, Henri Matisse, and others. The palatial surroundings add greatly to the visit. *5 rue de Thorigny, tel. 42-71-25-21. Admission: 21 frs. Open Wed. 9:15 AM-10 PM, Thurs.-Mon. 9:15-5:15; closed Tues.*

Cut across place Thorigny and take rue Elzévir. Halfway down
20 on the left is the **Musée Cognacq-Jay,** transferred here in 1990 from its original home near the Opéra. The museum is devoted to the arts of the 18th century: furniture, porcelain, and paintings (Watteau and Boucher notably). The Hôtel Donon, a 15th-century mansion, was virtually in ruins before its tasteful transformation by the City of Paris. *8 rue Elzévir, tel. 40–27–07–21. Admission: 12 frs. Open Tues.–Sun. 10–5:30.*

Continue down rue Elzévir to rue des Francs-Bourgeois,
21 where the substantial **Hôtel Carnavalet** became the scene, in the late-17th century, of the most brilliant salon in Paris, presided over by Madame de Sévigné. She is best known for the hundreds of letters she wrote to her daughter during her life; they've become one of the most enduring chronicles of French high society in the 17th century. In 1880, the hotel was transformed into the **Musée de l'Histoire de Paris;** its extraordinary exhibits of the Revolution, which have now moved to the neighboring Hôtel Peletier St-Fargeau, include some fascinating macabre models of guillotines. *23 rue de Sévigné, tel. 42–72–21–13. Admission: 30 frs. adults, 20 frs. children and senior citizens. Open Tues.–Sun. 10–5:30; closed Mon.*

22 Now walk along to **place des Vosges,** a minute or two farther along rue des Francs-Bourgeois. Place des Vosges, or place Royale as it was originally known, is the oldest square in Paris: Laid out by Henri IV at the beginning of the 17th century, it is the model for all the later city squares on which most French urban developments are based. The harmonious balance of the square, with its symmetrical town houses of pale pink stone, makes it a pleasant place to spend a hot summer's afternoon. At no. 6 is the **Maison de Victor Hugo,** which commemorates the workaholic French writer.

From place des Vosges, follow rue du Pas-de-la-Mule and turn
23 right down rue des Tournelles until you reach **place de la Bastille,** site of the infamous prison. Until 1988, there was little more to see at place de la Bastille than a huge traffic circle and the **Colonne de Juillet,** the July Column. As part of the country-wide celebrations held in July 1989, the bicentennial of the French Revolution, a 3,000-seat **opera house** boasting five moving stages and a gleaming curved-glass facade was put up on the south side of the square. Redevelopment projects have changed what was formerly a humdrum neighborhood into one of the city's most chic and attractive.

The **Bastille** was built by Charles V in the late-14th century and destroyed in 1789 during the French Revolution. The ground plan is marked by paving stones set into the modern square. The Bastille was originally intended not as a prison but as a fortress to guard the eastern entrance to the city. By the reign of Louis XIII (1610–43), however, it was used almost exclusively to house political prisoners, including, in the 18th century, Voltaire and the Marquis de Sade. This obviously political role led the "furious mob" (in all probability no more than a largely unarmed rabble) to break into the prison on July 14, 1789, kill the governor, steal what firearms they could find, and set free the seven remaining prisoners.

Return toward the Hôtel de Ville down rue St-Antoine, forking
24 off left down rue François-Miron to the church of **St-Gervais-St-Protais,** named after two Roman soldiers martyred

by the Emperor Nero in the 1st century AD. The original church—one of the earliest in Paris; no trace remains of it now—was built in the 7th century. The present building, a riot of Flamboyant decoration, went up between 1494 and 1598, making it one of the last Gothic constructions in the country. Before you go in, pause to look at the facade, put up between 1616 and 1621. While the interior is late Gothic, the exterior is one of the earliest examples of the classical, or Renaissance, style in France.

Don't cross the Seine to Ile St-Louis yet. Take rue de l'Hôtel de Ville to where it meets rue de Figuier. The painstakingly re-
25 stored **Hôtel de Sens** (1474) on the corner is one of a handful of Parisian homes to have survived since the Middle Ages. With its pointed corner towers, Gothic porch, and richly carved decorative details, it is a strange mixture, half defensive stronghold, half fairytale château. Built at the end of the 15th century for the archbishop of Sens, it was once the home of Henri IV and his queen, Marguerite, philanderers both. While Henri dallied with his mistresses—he is said to have had 56—at a series of royal palaces, Marguerite entertained her almost equally large number of lovers here. Today the building houses a fine arts library, the **Bibliothèque Forney** (admission free; open Tues.–Fri. 1:30–8:30, Sat. 10–8:30).

26 Cross pont Marie to the residential **Ile St-Louis,** the smaller of the two islands in the heart of Paris, linked to the Ile de la Cité by pont St-Louis. There are no standouts here and no great sights, but for idle strolling, window shopping, or simply sitting on one of the little quays and drinking in the views, the Ile St-Louis exudes a quintessentially Parisian air.

Berthillon has become a byword for delicious ice cream. Cafés all over Ile St-Louis sell its glamorous products, but the place to try them is still the little shop on rue St-Louis-en-l'Ile. Expect to wait in line. *31 rue St-Louis-en-l'Ile. Closed Mon. and Tues.*

Tour 3: From the Arc de Triomphe to the Opéra

This tour takes in grand, opulent Paris; the Paris of imposing vistas; long, arrow-straight streets; and plush hotels and jewelers. It begins at the Arc de Triomphe, standing sturdily at the top of the most famous street in the city, the Champs-Elysées.

Place Charles-de-Gaulle is known by Parisians as **l'Etoile,** the star—a reference to the streets that fan out from it. It is one of Europe's most chaotic traffic circles, and short of a death-defying dash, your only way of getting to the Arc de Triomphe in the middle is to take an underground passage from the Champs-Elysées or avenue de la Grande-Armée.

27 The colossal, 164-foot **Arc de Triomphe** was planned by Napoleon to celebrate his military successes. Unfortunately, the great man's strategic and architectural visions were not entirely on the same plane: When it was required for the triumphal entry of his new empress, Marie Louise, into Paris in 1810, it was still only a few feet high. To save face, he ordered a dummy arch of painted canvas to be put up. (The real thing wasn't finished until 1836.) After recent, extensive cleaning, its elaborate relief sculptures are magnificent. The highlight is the scene by François Rude, illustrated to the right of the arch when viewed from

the Champs-Elysées. Called *Departure of the Volunteers in 1792*, it's commonly known as *La Marseillaise* and depicts *La Patrie*, or the Fatherland, with outspread wings exhorting the volunteers to fight for France.

If you like views, go up to the viewing platform at the top of the monument, from which you can admire the vista down the Champs-Elysées toward place de la Concorde and the distant Louvre. A small museum halfway up the arch is devoted to its history. France's *Unknown Soldier* is buried beneath the archway; the flame is rekindled every evening at 6:30. *Pl. Charles-de-Gaulle. Admission: 30 frs. adults, 16 frs. children and senior citizens. Open daily except public holidays 10–6; 10–5:30 in winter.*

Laid out by landscape gardener Le Nôtre in the 1660s as a garden sweeping away from the Tuileries, the cosmopolitan **Champs-Elysées** occupies a central role in French national celebrations. It witnesses the finish of the Tour de France cycle race on the last Sunday of July and is the site of vast ceremonies on Bastille Day, July 14 (France's national holiday), and November 11, Armistice Day. Start by walking down from l'Etoile on the left, where 300 yards down, at no. 116-B, is the famous **Lido** nightclub: Foot-stomping melodies in French and English, and champagne-soaked, topless razzmatazz pack in the crowds every night. Opposite, avenue George-V leads down to the **Prince de Galles** (Prince of Wales) at no. 33 (with the red awning) and the **George V** (with the blue awning), two of the city's top hotels. Continue down avenue George-V, and turn right down Pierre-Ier-de-Serbie to the church of **St-Pierre de Chaillot** on avenue Marceau. The monumental frieze above the entrance, depicting scenes from the life of St. Peter, is the work of Henri Bouchard and dates from 1937. Returning to avenue George-V, continue toward the slender spire of the **American Cathedral of the Holy Trinity,** built by G. S. Street between 1885 and 1888. *Open weekdays 9–12:30 and 2–5, Sat. 9–noon. Services: weekdays noon, Sun. 9 AM and 11 AM; Sun. School and nursery.*

At the bottom of avenue George-V is the place de l'Alma and the Seine. Just across the Alma bridge, on the left, is the entrance to **Les Egouts,** the Paris sewers (admission: 22 frs; open Sat.–Wed. 11–5). If you prefer a less malodorous tour of the city, stay on the Right Bank and head down the sloping side road to the left of the bridge, for the embarkation point of the **Bâteaux-Mouches** motorboat tours of the Seine.

Stylish avenue Montaigne leads from the Seine back toward the Champs-Elysées.

Two blocks east along the Champs-Elysées on avenue Winston-
28 Churchill sit the **Grand Palais** and the Petit Palais, erected before the Paris World Fair of 1900. As with the Eiffel Tower, there was never any intention that these two buildings would be anything other than temporary additions to the city. Together they recapture the opulence and frivolity of the Belle Epoque. Today the atmospheric iron-and-glass interior of the Grand Palais plays regular host to major exhibitions. *Av. Winston-Churchill. Admission varies according to exhibition. Usually open 10:30–6:30, often until 10 PM on Wed.*

29 The **Petit Palais** has a beautifully presented permanent collection of lavish, 17th-century furniture and French 19th-century

paintings, with splendid canvases by Courbet and Bouguereau. Temporary exhibits are often held here, too. The sprawling entrance gallery contains several enormous turn-of-the-century paintings on its walls and ceiling. *Av. Winston-Churchill. Admission: 12 frs. adults, 6 frs. children. Open Tues.–Sun. 10–5:30.*

Cross the Champs-Elysées and head down avenue de Marigny to **rue du Faubourg St-Honoré,** a prestigious address in the world of luxury fashion and art galleries. High security sur-
30 rounds the French president in the **Palais de l'Elysée.** This "palace," where the head of state works and receives official visitors, was originally constructed as a private mansion in 1718. It has known presidential occupants only since 1873; before then, Madame de Pompadour (Louis XV's influential mistress), Napoleon, Josephine, and Queen Victoria all stayed here. Today the French government, the Conseil des Ministres, meets here each Wednesday. *Not open to the public.*

Continue down to rue Royale. This classy street, lined with
31 jewelry stores, links place de la Concorde to the **Eglise de la Madeleine.** With its rows of uncompromising columns, the Madeleine's sturdy neoclassical edifice looks more like a Greek temple than a Christian church. The only natural indoor light comes from three shallow domes. The inside walls are richly and harmoniously decorated, and gold glints through the murk. The church was designed in 1814 but not consecrated until 1842. The portico's majestic Corinthian colonnade—cleaned and renovated in 1991–92—supports a gigantic pediment with a sculptured frieze of *The Last Judgment.* From the top of the steps, stop to admire the view down rue Royale across the Seine.

At the far end of the rue Royale, on the right (as you look from La Madeleine), is the legendary **Maxim's** restaurant. Unless you choose to eat here—an expensive and not always rewarding experience—you won't be able to see the interior decor, a riot of crimson velvet and florid art nouveau furniture.

There is a striking contrast between the gloomy locked-in feel
32 of the high-walled rue Royale and the broad, airy **place de la Concorde.** This huge square is best approached from the Champs-Elysées: The flower beds, chestnut trees, and sandy sidewalks of the avenue's lower section are reminders of its original leafy elegance. Place de la Concorde was built in the 1770s, but there was nothing in the way of peace or concord about its early years. From 1793 to 1795, it was the scene of over a thousand deaths by guillotine; victims included Louis XVI, Marie Antoinette, and Danton. The obelisk, a present from the viceroy of Egypt, was erected in 1833. The handsome, symmetrical, 18th-century buildings facing the square include the deluxe **Hôtel Crillon** (far left), though there's nothing so vulgar as a sign to identify it—just an inscribed marble plaque. Facing one side of place de la Concorde are the Tuileries Gardens. Two smallish buildings stand sentinel here. To the left, nearer rue de Rivoli, is the **Jeu de Paume,** fondly known to many as the former home of the Impressionists (now in the Musée d'Orsay). It underwent extensive renovation in 1990–91 before reopening as a gallery for temporary exhibitions of contemporary art. The other identical building nearer the Seine is the
33 recently restored **Orangerie,** containing some early 20th-century paintings by Monet (*Waterlilies*) and Renoir, among oth-

ers. *Pl. de la Concorde. Admission: 23 frs. (12 frs. Sun.). Open Wed.–Mon. 9:45–5:15; closed Tues.*

34 As gardens go, the formal and wonderfully patterned **Jardin des Tuileries** is typically French, a charming place to stroll and survey the surrounding cityscape. Leave the Tuileries by the rue de Rivoli gateway across from rue de Castiglione and the hefty bronze column of place Vendôme.

35 **Place Vendôme** is one of the world's most opulent squares, a perfectly proportioned example of 17th-century urban architecture (by Mansart), now holding numerous upscale jewelers and the **Ritz.** Napoleon had the square's central column made from the melted bronze of 1,200 cannons captured at the battle of Austerlitz in 1805. That's him standing vigilantly at the top.

Cross the square and continue down rue de la Paix to place de
36 l'Opéra. The **Opéra,** begun at the behest of Napoleon III and completed in 1875 to the design of Charles Garnier, typifies the pompous Second Empire style of architecture. The monumental foyer and staircase are a stage in their own right where, on first nights, celebrities preen and prance. If the lavishly upholstered auditorium (ceiling painted by Marc Chagall in 1964) seems small, it is only because the stage is the largest in the world—more than 11,000 square yards. The **Opéra museum,** containing a few paintings and theatrical mementos, is unremarkable. *Admission: 17 frs. Open daily 11–4:30; closed occasionally. Tel. 47–42–57–50.*

Tour 4: From Orsay to Trocadéro

The Left Bank has two faces: the cozy, ramshackle Latin Quarter (*see* Tour 5: The Left Bank, *below*) and the spacious, stately 7th Arrondissement, covered in this tour. The latest addition
37 to this area is already the most popular: the **Musée d'Orsay,** a stylishly converted train station housing key Impressionist works, as well as important examples of other 19th- and 20th-century schools. The chief artistic attraction here is the collection of Impressionist works, featured on the top floor. Highlights include Monet's *Waterlilies* and Renoir's *Le Moulin de la Galette.* The Post-Impressionists—Paul Cézanne, Vincent van Gogh, Paul Gauguin, and Henri de Toulouse-Lautrec—are all also represented on this floor.

On the first floor, you'll find the work of Edouard Manet and the delicate nuances of Edgar Degas. Pride of place, at least in art-history terms, goes to Manet's *Déjeuner sur l'Herbe,* the painting that scandalized Paris in 1863. If you prefer modern developments, head for the exhibit of paintings by the early 20th-century group known as the *Fauves* (meaning wild beasts, as they were dubbed by an outraged critic in 1905)—particularly Henri Matisse, André Derain, and Maurice de Vlaminck. Sculpture at the Orsay means, first and foremost, Auguste Rodin. Two further highlights are the faithfully restored Belle Epoque restaurant and the model of the entire Opéra quarter, displayed beneath a glass floor. Prepare for huge crowds: The best times for relatively painless viewing are at lunchtime or on Thursday evening. *1 rue de Bellechasse. Admission: 31 frs. adults, 16 frs. students and on Sun. Open Tues.–Sun. 10–6 (Thurs. 10–9:15); closed Mon.*

Continue along the left bank of the Seine to the 18th-century
38 **Palais Bourbon** (directly across from place de la Concorde), home of the Assemblée Nationale (French Parliament). The colonnaded facade was commissioned by Napoleon. Though it's not open to the public, there is a fine view from the steps across to place de la Concorde and the church of the Madeleine.

Head south to rue de Varenne and the Hôtel Biron, better
39 known as the **Musée Rodin.** The splendid house, with its spacious vestibule and light, airy rooms, retains much of its 18th-century atmosphere and makes a handsome setting for the sculpture of Rodin (1840–1917), including the famous *Thinker* (*le Penseur*) and *Kiss* (*le Baiser*). Don't leave without visiting the garden: It is exceptional, both for its rosebushes (over 2,000) and its sculptures. *77 rue de Varenne, tel. 47-05-01-34. Admission: 20 frs., 10 frs. Sun. Open Tues.–Sun. 10–6, 10–5 in winter; closed Mon.*

40 From the Rodin Museum, you can see the **Hôtel des Invalides** along rue de Varenne, founded by Louis XIV in 1674 to house wounded (or "invalid") veterans. Only a handful of old soldiers live there today, but the building houses one of the world's foremost military museums, **Musée de l'Armée,** with a vast collection of arms, armor, uniforms, banners, and military pictures. The **Musée des Plans-Reliefs,** housed on the fifth floor of the right-hand wing, contains a fascinating collection of scale models of French towns made to illustrate the fortifications planned by the 17th-century military engineer Sébastien de Vauban. The largest and most impressive is Strasbourg, which takes up an entire room.

The museums are not the only reason for visiting the Invalides, however. The building itself is an outstanding monumental ensemble in late-17th-century Baroque, designed by Libéral Bruant (1635–97) and Jules Hardouin-Mansart (1646–1708). The main, cobbled courtyard is a fitting scene for the parades and ceremonies still occasionally held here. The most impressive dome in Paris towers over the **Eglise du Dôme** (Church of the Dome). The Dôme church was designed by Mansart and built between 1677 and 1735. The remains of Napoleon are here, in a series of six coffins, one inside the next, within a bombastic tomb of red porphyry. Among others commemorated in the church are French World War I hero Marshal Foch and fortification builder Vauban, whose heart was brought to the Invalides at Napoleon's behest. *Hôtel des Invalides. Admission: 30 frs. adults, 20 frs. children. Open daily 10–6, 10–4:45 winter. A* son-et-lumière *(sound-and-light show) in English is held in the main courtyard on evenings throughout the summer.*

Turn right out of the Dôme church and follow avenue de Tourville to the Champ de Mars. At the far end looms Paris's
41 best-known landmark, the **Eiffel Tower.** Built by Gustave Eiffel for the World Exhibition of 1889, the centennial of the French Revolution, it was still in good shape to celebrate its own 100th birthday. Such was Eiffel's engineering wizardry that even in the strongest winds, his tower never sways more than 4½ inches. Today it exudes a feeling of mighty permanence. As you stand beneath its huge legs, you may have trouble believing that it nearly became 7,000 tons of scrap iron when its concession expired in 1909. Only its potential use as a radio antenna saved the day; it now bristles with a forest of radio and televi-

sion transmitters. The energetic can stride up the stairs as far as the third deck. If you want to go to the top, 1,000 feet up, you'll have to take the elevator. It's expensive, but on a clear day, the view is definitely worth it. *Pont d'Iéna. Cost by elevator: 2nd floor, 17 frs.; 3rd floor, 34 frs.; 4th floor, 51 frs. Cost by foot: 8 frs. (2nd and 3rd floors only). Open daily 9:30 AM–11 PM (midnight July–Aug.).*

Visible just across the Seine from the Eiffel Tower, on the
42 heights of Trocadéro, is the massive, sandy-colored **Palais de Chaillot,** a cultural center built in the 1930s. The gardens between the Palais de Chaillot and the Seine contain an aquarium and some dramatic fountains, and the terrace between the two wings of the palace offers a wonderful view of the Eiffel Tower.

The Palais de Chaillot contains four large museums, two in each wing. In the left wing (as you approach from the Seine) are the **Musée de l'Homme,** an anthropological museum, with primitive and prehistoric artifacts from throughout the world (admission: 25 frs. adults, 15 frs. children; open Wed.–Mon. 10–5), and the **Musée de la Marine,** a maritime museum with exhibits on French naval history right up to the age of the nuclear submarine (admission: 40 frs. adults, 20 frs. children and senior citizens; open Wed.–Mon. 10–6).

The other wing is dominated by the **Musée des Monuments Français,** without question the best introduction to French medieval architecture. Its long first-floor gallery pays tribute to French buildings, mainly of the Romanesque and Gothic periods (roughly AD 1000–1500), in the form of painstaking copies of statues, columns, archways, and frescoes. Substantial sections of a number of French churches and cathedrals are represented here, notably Chartres and Vézelay. Murals and ceiling paintings—copies of works in churches around the country—dominate the other three floors. *Admission: 16 frs., 8 frs. on Sun. Open Wed.–Mon. 9:45–5:15.*

The **Musée du Cinéma,** tracing the history of motion pictures from the 1880s, is located in the basement. *Admission: 22 frs. adults, 14 frs. children and senior citizens. Open Wed.–Mon., guided tours only, on the hour at 10, 11, 2, 3, and 4.*

The area around the Palais de Chaillot offers a feast for muse-
43 um lovers. The **Musée Guimet** has three floors of Indo-Chinese and Far Eastern art, including stone Buddhas, Chinese bronzes, ceramics, and painted screens. *6 pl. d'Iéna. Admission: 25 frs., 15 frs. students, senior citizens, and on Sun. Open Wed.–Mon. 9:45–5:10; closed Tues.*

44 Nearby is the **Palais Galliera,** home of the **Musée de la Mode et Costume** (Museum of Fashion and Costume), a late-19th-century town house that hosts revolving exhibits. The admission price is steep; step in only if the exhibit really appeals. *10 av. Pierre-Ier-de-Serbie. Admission: 25 frs. Open Tues.–Sun. 10–5:40.*

45 The **Musée de l'Art Moderne de la Ville de Paris** has both temporary exhibits and a permanent collection of modern art. Among the earliest works in the vast galleries are Fauvist paintings by Vlaminck and Derain, followed by Picasso's early experiments in Cubism. Other highlights include works by Robert Delaunay, Georges Braque, and Amedeo Modigliani. There is also a large room devoted to art deco furniture and screens; a pleas-

ant, if expensive, museum café; and an excellent bookshop with many books in English. *11 av. du Président-Wilson. Admission: 15 frs., free Sun. for permanent exhibitions only. Open Tues.–Sun. 10–5:40, Wed. 10–8:30.*

Tour 5: The Left Bank

References to the Left Bank have never lost their power to evoke the most piquant images of Paris. Although the bohemian strain the area once nurtured has lost much of its vigor, people who choose to live and work here today are, in effect, turning their backs on the formality and staidness of the Right Bank. As a matter of fact, President Mitterrand himself lives here.

The Left Bank's geographic and cerebral hub is the Latin Quarter, which takes its name from the university tradition of studying and speaking in Latin, a practice that disappeared at the time of the French Revolution. The area is populated mainly by students and academics from the Sorbonne, the headquarters of the University of Paris.

46 **Place St-Michel** is a good starting point for exploring the rich slice of Parisian life that the Left Bank offers. Leave your itineraries at home and wander along the neighboring streets lined with restaurants, cafés, galleries, old bookshops, and all sorts of clothing stores, from tiny boutiques to haute-couture showrooms. If you follow quai des Grands Augustins and then quai de Conti west from St-Michel, you will be in full view of the Ile de la Cité and the Louvre.

For an alternative route crowded more with humanity than with traffic, pick up the pedestrian rue St-André des Arts at the southwest corner of place St-Michel. Just before you reach the carrefour de Buci crossroads at the end of the street, turn onto the cour du Commerce St-André. Jean-Paul Marat printed his revolutionary newspaper, *L'Ami du Peuple*, at no. 8, and it was here that Dr. Guillotin conceived the idea for a new "humane" method of execution that, apparently to his horror, was used during the French Revolution.

47 Continue to the **carrefour de Buci,** once a notorious Left Bank landmark. By the 18th century, it contained a gallows, an execution stake, and an iron collar for punishing troublemakers. Many Royalists and priests lost their heads here during the bloody course of the French Revolution. Nearby rue de Buci has one of the best markets in Paris. The stands close by 1 PM and do not open at all on Monday.

Several interesting, smaller streets of some historical significance radiate from the carrefour de Buci. Rue de l'Ancienne-Comédie, which cuts through to the busy place de l'Odéon, is so named because no. 14 was the first home of the now legendary French theater company, the Comédie-Française. Across the
48 street sits the oldest café in Paris, the **Procope** (now a classy restaurant). Opened in 1686, it has been a watering hole for many of Paris's literati, including Voltaire, Victor Hugo, and Oscar Wilde. Ben Franklin was a patron, as were the fomenters of the French Revolution—Marat, Danton, Desmoulins, and Robespierre. Napoleon's hat, forgotten here, was encased in a glass dome.

Stretching north toward the Seine is the rue Dauphine, the street that singer Juliet Greco put on the map when she opened the **Tabou jazz club** here in the '50s. The club attracted a group of young intellectuals who were to become known as the Zazous, a St-Germain movement prompting the jazz culture, complete with all-night parties and "free love."

The next street that shoots out of the carrefour (moving coun-
49 terclockwise) is rue Mazarine, housing the **Hôtel des Monnaies,** the national mint. Louis XVI transferred the Royal Mint to this imposing mansion in the late-18th century. Although the mint was moved in 1973, weights and measures, and limited-edition coins are still made here. You can see the vast collection of coins, documents, engravings, and paintings at the **Musée Monétaire.** *11 quai Conti. Admission: 15 frs. adults, 10 frs. students and senior citizens; free on Sun. Open Tues., Thurs.–Sun. 1–6, Wed. 1–9.*

Next door is the **Institut de France,** one of France's most revered cultural institutions and one of the Left Bank's most impressive waterside sights, with its distinctive dome and commanding position overlooking the quai. It was built as a college in 1661; in the early 19th century, Napoleon stipulated that the Institut de France be transferred here from the Louvre. The **Académie Française,** the oldest of the five academies that compose the Institut de France, was created by Cardinal Richelieu in 1635. Its first major task was to edit the French dictionary; today, among other functions, it is still charged with safeguarding the purity of the French language. Membership is the highest literary honor in France. Not until 1986 was a woman, author Marguerite Yourcenar, elected to its ranks. *Guided visits are reserved for cultural associations only.*

Just west along the waterfront, on quai Malaquais, stands the
50 **Ecole Nationale des Beaux-Arts,** whose students can usually be seen painting and sketching on the nearby quais and bridges. The school, once the site of a convent, was established in 1816. Allow yourself time to wander into its courtyard and galleries to see the casts and copies of the statues that were once stored here, or stop in at one of the temporary exhibitions of professors' and students' works. *14 rue Bonaparte. Open daily 1–7.*

Tiny **rue Visconti,** running east–west off rue Bonaparte (across from the entrance to the Beaux-Arts), has a lot of history packed into its short length. In the 16th century, it was known as Paris's "Little Geneva"—named after Europe's foremost Protestant city—because of the Protestant ghetto that formed here. Jean Racine, one of France's greatest playwrights and tragic poets, lived at no. 24 until his death in 1699. Honoré Balzac set up a printing shop at no. 17 in 1826, and the fiery Romantic artist Eugène Delacroix (1798–1863) worked here from 1836 to 1844.

Farther down the gallery-lined rue de Seine, swing right onto the pretty rue Jacob, where both Wagner and Stendhal once lived. Then turn left onto rue de Fürstemberg, which broadens out into one of Paris's most delightful and secluded little squares. Delacroix's studio here has been turned into the
51 charmingly tiny **Musée Eugène Delacroix;** it contains a small collection of sketches and drawings, while the garden at the rear is almost as interesting. *6 rue Fürstemberg. Admission:*

11 frs. adults, 6 frs. youths 18–25 and senior citizens over 60. Open Wed.–Mon. 9:15–12:30 and 2–5:15; closed Tues.

52 **St-Germain-des-Prés,** Paris's oldest church, began as a shelter for a relic of the True Cross brought back from Spain in AD 542. Behind it, rue de l'Abbaye runs alongside the former **Abbey Palace,** dating from AD 990. Interesting interior details include the colorful 19th-century frescoes in the nave by Hippolyte Flandrin, a pupil of the classical painter Ingres. The church stages superb organ concerts and recitals; programs are displayed outside and in the weekly periodicals *Officiel des Spectacles* and *Pariscope*.

Across the cobbled place St-Germain-des-Prés stands the celebrated **Deux Magots** café, still thriving on its '50s reputation as one of the Left Bank's prime meeting places for the intelligentsia. These days, you're more likely to rub shoulders with tourists than with philosophers, but a sidewalk table still affords a perfect view of Left Bank life.

In the years after World War II, Jean-Paul Sartre and Simone de Beauvoir would meet "The Family"—their intellectual clique—two doors down at the **Café de Flore,** on the boulevard St-Germain. Today the Flore has become more of a gay hangout, but it is a scenic spot that never lacks for action, often in the form of the street entertainers performing in front of the church.

If you now pick up the long rue de Rennes and follow it south, you'll soon arrive in the heart of Montparnasse. The opening of
53 the **Tour Maine-Montparnasse** in 1973 forever changed the face of this former painters' and poets' haunt. The tower, containing offices and a branch of the Galeries Lafayette department store, was part of a vast redevelopment plan that aimed to make the area one of Paris's premier business and shopping districts. As Europe's tallest high rise, it claims to have the fastest elevator in Europe and affords stupendous views of Paris, and you pay dearly to enjoy them. *Admission: 35 frs. adults, 21 frs. students and senior citizens, 14 frs. children 5–14. Open daily 10 AM–11 PM, weekdays 10–10 in winter.*

Up boulevard du Montparnasse and across from the Vavin métro station are two of the better-known gathering places of Montparnasse's bohemian heyday, the **Dôme** and **La Coupole** brasseries. La Coupole opened in 1927 and soon became a home away from home for some of the area's most famous residents, such as Guillaume Apollinaire, Max Jacob, Jean Cocteau, Erik Satie, Igor Stravinsky, and the inevitable Ernest Hemingway.

Continue along boulevard du Montparnasse to the intersection with boulevard St-Michel, where the verdant avenue de l'Observatoire sweeps down to the Luxembourg Gardens. Here you'll find perhaps the most famous bastion of the Left Bank
54 café culture, the **Closerie des Lilas.** Now a pricey but pretty bar-restaurant, the Closerie remains a staple on all literary tours of Paris, not least because of the commemorative plaques fastened onto the bar, marking the places where renowned writers used to sit. Charles Baudelaire, Paul Verlaine, Ernest Hemingway, and Guillaume Apollinaire are just a few of the names.

Walk down avenue de l'Observatoire to the **Jardin du Luxembourg** (the Luxembourg Gardens), one of the city's few large

parks. Its fountains, ponds, trim hedges, precisely planted rows of trees, and gravel walks are typical of the French fond-
55 ness for formal gardens. At the far end is the **Palais du Luxembourg** itself, gray and formal, built, like the park, for Maria de Médicis, widow of Henri IV, at the beginning of the 17th century. The palace remained royal property until the French Revolution, when the state took it over and used it as a prison. Danton, the painter Jacques-Louis David, and American political philosopher and author Tom Paine (1737–1809) were all detained here. Today it is the site of the French Senate and is not open to the public.

If you follow rue Vaugirard (the longest street in Paris) one block east to boulevard St-Michel, you will soon be at the place de la Sorbonne, nerve center of the Left Bank's student population. The square is dominated by the **Eglise de la Sorbonne,** whose outstanding exterior features are its 10 Corinthian columns and cupola. Inside is the white marble tomb of Cardinal Richelieu. (The church is open to the public only during exhibitions and cultural events.) The university buildings of La Sorbonne spread out around the church from rue Cujas down to the visitor's entrance on rue des Ecoles.

56 The **Sorbonne** is the oldest university in France—indeed, one of the oldest in Europe—and has for centuries been one of France's principal institutions of higher learning. It is named after Robert de Sorbon, a medieval canon who founded a theological college here in 1253 for 16 students. By the 17th century, the church and university buildings were becoming dilapidated, so Cardinal Richelieu undertook to have them restored; the present-day Sorbonne campus is largely a result of that restoration. For a glimpse of a more recent relic of Sorbonne history, look for Puvis de Chavannes's painting of the *Sacred Wood* in the main lecture hall, a major meeting point during the tumultuous student upheavals of 1968.

Behind the Sorbonne, bordering its eastern reach, is the rue St-Jacques. The street climbs toward the rue Soufflot, named
57 in honor of the man who built the vast, domed **Panthéon,** set atop place du Panthéon. One of Paris's most physically overwhelming sites—it was commissioned by Louis XV as a mark of gratitude for his recovery from a grave illness in 1744—the Panthéon is now a memorial to the famous, with monumental frescoes by Puvis de Chavannes and a crypt that holds the remains of such national heroes as Voltaire, Emile Zola, and Jean-Jacques Rousseau. *Admission: 24 frs. adults, 13 frs. youths 18–24, 5 frs. ages 17 and under. Open daily 10–5:30 (summer), 10–noon and 2–5 (winter).*

Up rue St-Jacques and left on the rue des Ecoles is the square Paul-Painlevé; behind it lies the entrance to the inimitable
58 **Hôtel et Musée de Cluny.** Built on the site of the city's enormous Roman baths, the Musée de Cluny is housed in a 15th-century mansion that originally belonged to the monks of Cluny Abbey in Burgundy. But the real reason anyone comes to the Cluny is to see its superb tapestry collection. The most famous series is the graceful *Dame à la Licorne* (the *Lady and the Unicorn*), woven in the 15th or 16th century, probably in the southern Netherlands. There is also an exhibition of decorative arts from the Middle Ages; a vaulted chapel; and a deep, cloistered courtyard with mullioned windows, set off by the *Boatmen's Pillar,*

Paris's oldest sculpture, at its center. *Admission: 15 frs. Open Wed.–Mon. 9:45–5:15; closed Tues.*

Above boulevard St-Germain, rue St-Jacques reaches toward the Seine, bringing you past the elegant proportions of the
59 church of **St-Séverin,** the parish church of the entire Left Bank during the 11th century. Rebuilt in the 16th century and noted for its width and its Flamboyant Gothic architecture, the church dominates a close-knit neighborhood filled with quiet squares and pedestrian streets. Note the splendidly deviant spiraling column in the forest of pillars behind the altar. *Open weekdays 11–5:30, Sat. 11–10.*

Running riot around the relative quiet of St-Séverin are streets filled with restaurants of every description and serving everything from take-out souvlaki to five-course haute cuisine. Rue de la Huchette is the most heavily trafficked of the restaurant streets and is especially good for its selection of cheaper Greek food houses and Tunisian pâtisseries.

Cross to the other side of rue St-Jacques. In square René-Viviani, which surrounds the 12th-century church of **St-Julien-le-Pauvre,** stands an acacia that is supposedly the oldest tree in Paris (although it has a rival claim from another acacia at the Jardin des Plantes). This tree-filled square also gives you one of the more spectacular views of Notre-Dame.

Behind the church, to the east, are the tiny, elegant streets of the recently renovated Maubert district, bordered by quai de Montebello and boulevard St-Germain. Rue de Bièvre, once filled with tanneries, is now guarded at both ends to protect President Mitterrand's private residence.

Public meetings and demonstrations have been held in place Maubert ever since the Middle Ages. Nowadays, most gather-
60 ings are held inside or in front of the **Palais de la Mutualité** on the corner of the square, also a venue for jazz, pop, and rock concerts. On Tuesday, Thursday, and Saturday, it is transformed into a colorful outdoor food market.

61 The **Jardin des Plantes,** several blocks southeast, is an enormous swath of greenery containing spacious botanical gardens and a number of natural-history museums. It is stocked with plants dating back to the first collections of the 17th century and has since been enhanced by subsequent generations of devoted French botanists. The garden claims to shelter Paris's oldest tree, an *Acacia robinia,* planted in 1636. It also contains a small, old-fashioned zoo, an alpine garden, an aquarium, a maze, and a number of hothouses. *Admission: 12–25 frs. adults, 8–15 frs. children. Open Wed.–Sun. 2–5; closed Mon. and Tues.*

At the back of the gardens, in place du Puits-de-l'Hermite, you can drink a restorative cup of sweet mint tea in **La Mosquée,** a beautifully kept white mosque, complete with minaret. The Moslem restaurant here serves copious quantities of couscous. The sunken garden and tiled patios are open to the public—the prayer rooms are not—and so are the luxurious *hammams,* or Turkish baths (open Fri. and Sat. 11–7 men only; Mon., Wed., and Thurs. 11–7 women only). *Admission: 15 frs. adults, 10 frs. students and senior citizens. Open Sat.–Thurs., guided tours 9–12 and 2–6.*

Tour 6: Montmartre

Numbers in the margin correspond to points of interest on the Montmartre map.

On a dramatic rise above the city is **Montmartre,** site of the basilica of Sacré-Coeur—Paris's best-known landmark after the Eiffel Tower—and home to a once-thriving artistic community, now reduced to gangs of third-rate painters clustered in the area's most famous square, the place du Tertre. Despite their presence, and the fact that the fabled nightlife of old Montmartre has fizzled down to some glitzy nightclubs and porn shows, the area still exudes a sense of history.

62 Begin your tour at **place Blanche,** site of the Moulin Rouge. Place Blanche (White Square) takes its name from the clouds of chalky dust churned up by the windmills that once dotted Montmartre. The windmills were set up here not just because the hill was a good place to catch the wind—at over 300 feet, it's the highest point in the city—but because Montmartre was covered with cornfields and quarries right up to the end of the 19th century. Today only two of the original 20 windmills are intact. The most famous, immortalized by painter Toulouse-Lautrec, is the **Moulin Rouge,** or Red Windmill, built in 1885 and turned into a dance hall in 1900; the place is still trading shamelessly on the notion of Paris as a city of sin (*see* Arts and Nightlife, *below*).

For a taste of something more authentically French than the Moulin Rouge's computerized light shows, walk up rue Lepic, site of one of the most colorful and tempting **food markets** in Paris (closed Mon.).

Turn left onto rue des Abbesses and walk along to the small **Montmartre cemetery.** It contains the graves of many prominent French men and women, including Edgar Degas and Adolphe Sax, inventor of the saxophone. The Russian ballet dancer Vaslav Nijinsky is buried here as well.

Walk along rue des Abbesses, then turn onto rue Tholoze,
63 which leads to the **Moulin de la Galette,** one of the two remaining windmills in Montmartre, now unromantically rebuilt. To reach it you pass **Studio 28:** This seems no more than a scruffy little movie theater, but when it opened in 1928, it was the first *art et essai,* or experimental theater, in the world, and has shown the works of such directors as Jean Cocteau, François Truffaut, and Orson Welles before the films' official premieres.

64 Return to rue des Abbesses, turn left, and walk to **place des Abbesses.** Though commercial, the little square has the kind of picturesque and slightly countrified architecture that has made Montmartre famous.

There are two competing attractions just off the square. Theater buffs should head down the tiny rue André-Antoine. At no. 37, you'll see what was originally the **Théâtre Libre,** the Free Theater, which was influential in popularizing the groundbreaking works of naturalist playwrights Henrik Ibsen and August Strindberg. The other attraction is **rue Yvonne-le-Tac,** scene of a vital event in Montmartre's early history and linked to the disputed story of how this quarter got its name. Some say the name Montmartre comes from the Roman temple to Mercury that was once here, called the Mound of Mercury, or

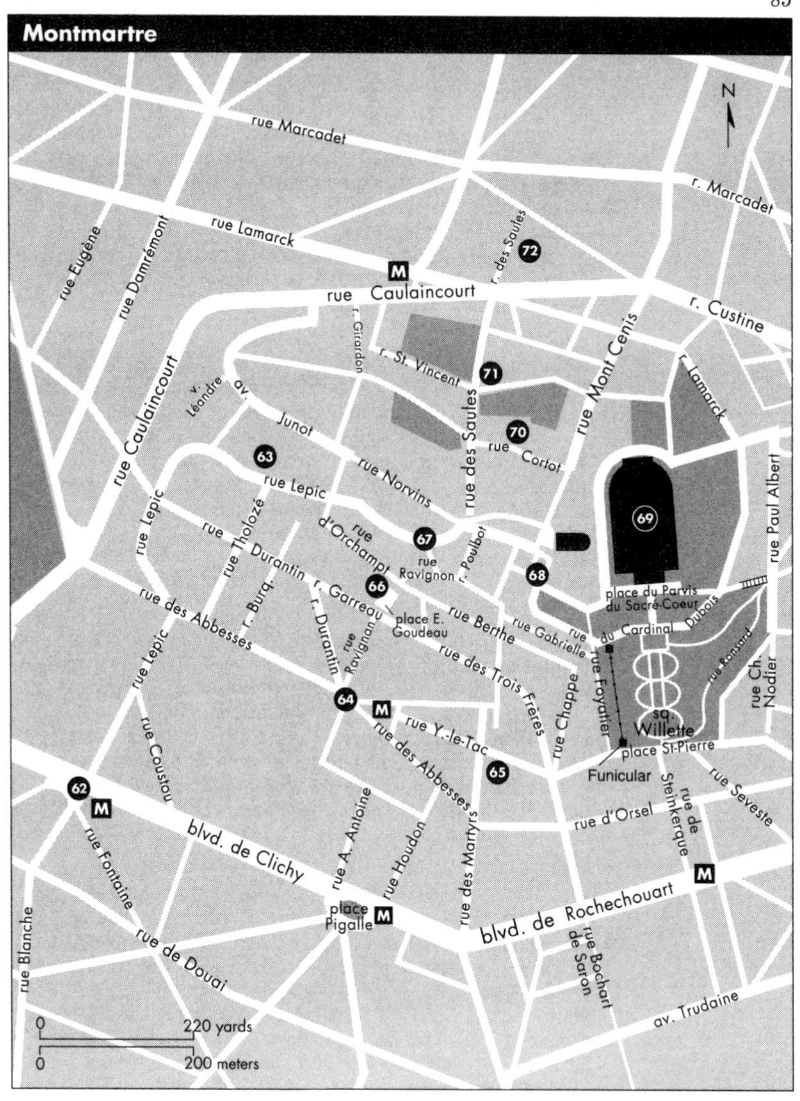

Basilique du Sacré-Coeur, **69**

Bâteau-Lavoir, **66**

Chapelle du Martyre, **65**

Lapin Agile, **71**

Moulin de la Galette, **63**

Musée de l'Art Juif, **72**

Musée du Vieux Montmartre, **70**

Place Blanche, **62**

Place des Abbesses, **64**

Place du Tertre, **68**

Place Jean-Baptiste Clément, **67**

Mons Mercurii. Others contend that it was an adaptation of
Mons Martyrum, a name inspired by the burial here of Paris's
first bishop, St-Denis. (The popular yet implausible version of
his martyrdom is that he was beheaded by the Romans in AD
250 but arose to carry his severed head from rue Yvonne-le-Tac
to an area 6 kilometers [4 miles] north, now known as St-
Denis.) St-Denis is commemorated by the 19th-century
65 **Chapelle du Martyre** at no. 9. It was in the crypt of the original
chapel that the Italian priest Francis Xavier founded the Jesuit
order in 1534, a decisive step in the efforts of the Catholic
Church to reassert its authority in the face of the Protestant
Reformation.

From rue Yvonne-le-Tac, retrace your steps through place des
Abbesses. Take rue Ravignon on the right, climbing to the
summit via place Emile-Goudeau, an enchanting little cobbled
66 square. Your goal is the **Bâteau-Lavoir,** or Boat Wash House, at
its northern edge. Montmartre poet Max Jacob coined the
name for the old building on this site, which burned down in
1970: Not only did it look like a boat, he said, but the warren of
artists' studios within were always paint-spattered and in need
of a good hosing down. The drab, present-day concrete building
also contains art studios, though none so illustrious as those of
Cubist painters Picasso and Braque, which were housed here in
years gone by.

67 Continue up the hill to **place Jean-Baptiste Clément.** The Italian painter and sculptor Modigliani (1884–1920) had a studio here at no. 7. Some people have claimed that he is the greatest Italian artist of the 20th century, the man who fused the genius of the Italian Renaissance with the modernity of Cézanne and Picasso. Modigliani claimed he would drink himself to death—he eventually did—and chose the wildest part of town in which to do it. Most of the old-time cabarets are gone now, though, and only the Moulin Rouge still reflects a glimmer of the old atmosphere.

Rue Norvins, formerly rue des Moulins, runs behind and parallel to the north end of the square. Turn right, walk past the
68 bars and tourist shops, and you'll reach **place du Tertre.** At most
times of the year, you'll have to fight your way through the
crowds to the southern end of the square and the breathtaking
view over the city. The real drawback here, though, is the
swarm of artists clamoring to dash off your portrait. Most are
licensed, but there is a fair share of con men. If one produces a
picture of you without having asked first, you're under no obligation to buy it!

La Mère Catherine, the restaurant at the north end of the square, was a favorite with the Russian cossacks who occupied Paris after Napoleon's 1814 exile to the island of Elba. Little did the cossacks know that when they banged on the tables and shouted "bistro," the Russian word for "quick," they were inventing a new breed of French restaurant. Now fairly touristic, La Mère Catherine is surprisingly good, though prices are high.

It was in place du Tertre that one of the most violent episodes in French history began, one that colored French political life for generations. Despite popular images of later 19th-century France—and Paris especially—as a time of freedom and prosperity, the country was desperately divided into two camps for much of this period: a militant underclass, motivated by resentment of what they considered an elitist government, and a reactionary and fearful bourgeoisie and ruling class. In March 1871, the antimonarchist Communards clashed with soldiers of the French government leader, Adolphe Thiers. The Communards formed the Commune, which ruled Paris for three months. Then Thiers ordered his troops to take the city, and upwards of 10,000 Communards were executed after the Commune's collapse.

Looming behind the church of St-Pierre on the east side of the
69 square, the **Basilique du Sacré-Coeur** was erected in 1873 (after Thiers's death) as a kind of guilt offering for the ruthless killing of the Communards. Even so, the building was to some extent a reflection of political divisions within the country, financed by French Catholics fearful of an anticlerical backlash and determined to make a grand statement on behalf of the Church. Stylistically, the Sacré-Coeur borrows elements from Romanesque and Byzantine models, fusing them under its distinctive Oriental dome. The gloomy, cavernous interior is worth visiting for its golden mosaics; climb to the top of the dome for the view over Paris.

More of Montmartre beckons north and west of the Sacré-Coeur. Take rue du Mont-Cenis down to rue Cortot, site of the
70 **Musée du Vieux Montmartre.** Like the Bateau-Lavoir, the building that is now the museum sheltered an illustrious group of painters, writers, and assorted cabaret artists in its heyday toward the end of the 19th century. Foremost among them were Pierre-Auguste Renoir and Maurice Utrillo, who was the Montmartre painter par excellence. Taking the gray, crumbling streets of Montmartre as his subject matter, Utrillo discovered that he worked much more effectively from cheap postcards than from the streets themselves. Look carefully at the pictures in the museum here and you will see the plaster and sand he mixed with his paints to help convey the decaying buildings of the area. The next best thing about the museum is the view over the tiny vineyard on neighboring rue des Saules. *12 rue Cortot. Admission: 25 frs. adults, 15 frs. children and senior citizens. Open Tues.–Sun. 11–6.*

There's an equally famous Montmartre landmark on the corner
71 of rue St-Vincent, just down the road: the **Lapin Agile,** or the Nimble Rabbit. It's a bar-cabaret, originally one of the raunchiest haunts in Montmartre. Today it manages against all odds to preserve at least something of its earlier flavor, unlike the Moulin Rouge.

Behind the Lapin Agile is the **St-Vincent Cemetery,** whose entrance is off little rue Lucien Gaulard. It's a tiny graveyard, but serious students of Montmartre might want to visit to see Utrillo's burial place. Continue north on rue des Saules, across
72 busy rue Caulaincourt, and you'll come to the **Musée de l'Art Juif,** the Museum of Jewish Art, containing devotional items, models of synagogues, and works by Camille Pissarro and Marc Chagall. *42 rue des Saules. Admission: 15 frs. adults, 10 frs. students and children. Open Sun.–Thurs. 3–6; closed Aug., Fri., and Sat.*

Day Trips from Paris

Beauvais. Visit the world's tallest cathedral choir and the neighboring tapestry and local history museums. It's a 75-minute train journey from Paris (Gare du Nord). *See* Chapter 7, Champagne and the North.

Chantilly. Peruse the lakeside château's superb art collection, then inspect the luxurious stables next to the famous race course or wander through the forest. It's just a 30-minute train ride from Paris (Gare du Nord). *See* Chapter 7, Champagne and the North.

Chartres. Spires and stained glass are the twin glories of this picturesque old town. It's just a one-hour train ride from Paris (Gare Montparnasse). *See* Chapter 3, Ile-de-France.

Compiègne. This haughty town hosts a former royal palace—favored for wild weekends by Napoléon III—and museums devoted to cars and toy soldiers. It's a one-hour train ride from Paris (Gare du Nord). *See* Chapter 7, Champagne and the North.

Fontainebleau. The Rennaissance château here, forerunner to Versailles, has superb 19th-century furniture and an exquisite park. It's just a 50-minute train ride from Paris (Gare de Lyon). *See* Chapter 3, Ile-de-France.

Maisons-Laffitte. One of France's most majestic Baroque mansions is a mere 20-minute train journey from Paris (Gare St-Lazare). *See* Chapter 3, Ile-de-France.

Malmaison. The memory of star-crossed lovers Josephine and Napoleon still haunts this small, elegant château in a western suburb. The journey from central Paris takes about 30 minutes (take RER-A to La Défense, then bus 158-A). *See* Chapter 3, Ile-de-France.

Rambouillet. A lake, rambling parkland, and an informal château, boasting additions over many centuries, have made Rambouillet a favorite occasional home for many French presidents. It's just a 45-minute train journey from Paris (Gare Montparnasse). *See* Chapter 3, Ile-de-France.

Reims. The capital of Champagne is best known for its distinctive sparkling wines, available for the sampling in one of the city's many firms. But it also boasts a glorious cathedral and a Roman arch. It's a 90-minute train journey from Paris (Gare de l'Est). *See* Chapter 7, Champagne and the North.

Rouen. Timbered houses, cobbled streets, and an abundance of superb old churches make Rouen—where Joan of Arc was burned at the stake—one of France's most attractive cities. It's a 70-minute train ride up the Seine Valley from Paris (Gare St-Lazare). *See* Chapter 6, Normandy.

St-Germain-en-Laye. This smart suburban town stands on the edge of a vast forest; its château has formal gardens and contains a large collection of prehistoric artifacts. It's a 30-minute RER ride (Line A) from central Paris. *See* Chapter 3, Ile-de-France.

Thoiry. There is something for everyone here: culture at the Renaissance château with its magnificent tapestries and works of art; and adventure in the gardens and the safari park, filled with elephants, wolves, bears, and ligrons (a cross between a lion and a tiger). It's a 50-minute combined train and bus trip from Gare Montparnasse in Paris (access is difficult except on summer weekends, unless you have a car). *See* Chapter 3, Ile-de-France.

Tours. The new TGV train has put the Loire Valley's major town within an hour of Paris. Visit the well-restored old sector and the mighty cathedral. Trains leave from Montparnasse. *See* Chapter 4, The Loire Valley.

Troyes. A number of fine churches, a top modern art museum, and an unspoiled town center justify a 90-minute train journey from Paris (Gare de l'Est). *See* Chapter 9, Burgundy.

Vendôme. Medieval shopping streets, a stately church and hilltop ruined castle, and the splitting of the Loir River into "canals" makes Vendôme one of France's most picturesque towns. It's just 42 minutes from Paris (Gare Montparnasse) by TGV. *See* Chapter 4, The Loire Valley.

Versailles. If you make just one trip from Paris, come and admire the Sun King's huge château and Marie Antoinette's delightful mock hamlet. It's just a 25-minute RER ride (Line C) from Paris. *See* Chapter 3, Ile-de-France.

Shopping

Paris's reputation as an international capital of such luxury industries as fashion and perfume makes it a great place for window shopping but offers little comfort to the budget traveler; Chanel and Yves Saint-Laurent come no cheaper in Paris than elsewhere. If you are prepared to stray off the tourist path to such somewhat uninviting localities as the Sentier district on the northern edge of the Marais, or the grid of grimy streets at the foot of Montmartre, you can find cheap—and sometimes stylish—clothes without much difficulty. There is a wide choice of affordable souvenirs along the rue de Rivoli, ranging from porcelain boxes, imitation Sèvres china, and miniature Eiffel Towers to printed scarves, tea towels, and busts of Napoleon. Any number of stalls in the métro sell zany jewelry and wool scarves at cheap prices, while the *bouquinistes* (secondhand bookstores) along the Seine offer browsing and bargaining if you're after old books, posters, photos, or maps.

Shopping Districts

A general rule of thumb is that the Left Bank is geared more to small, specialty shops and boutiques, while the Right Bank is home to the high-fashion houses, the most ostentatious shops, and the large department stores.

On the Left Bank, **St-Germain-des-Prés** has long been a center for bookshops, ready-to-wear fashion stores, and specialty shops. Shoe and fabric shops crowd the **rue des Saints-Pères**, while the **rue de Rennes**, running from St-Germain to Montparnasse, is packed with a variety of clothing stores, many quite inexpensive. The **Montparnasse Tower** contains several department stores.

On the Right Bank, the modern, three-tiered **Forum des Halles** has recently become a popular shopping spot. The area around the mall contains numerous shops with knick-knacks and clothes. **Place des Victoires** is one of the leading centers of avant-garde Parisian fashion.

The **Opéra** district contains landmark department stores.

Shopping Arcades The various shopping arcades scattered around Paris often date to the 19th century. Many have been splendidly restored, with arching glass roofs, marble flooring, and brass lamps set off to full advantage. Most are conveniently located in the 1st and 2nd arrondissements on the Right Bank.

The **Galerie Vivienne** (4 rue des Petits Champs, 2e), between the Bourse (Stock Exchange) and Palais Royal, is a delightful place in which to amble.

Galerie Véro-Dodat (19 rue Jean-Jacques Rousseau, 1er) has painted ceilings and slender copper pillars.

Passage des Panoramas (11 blvd. Montmartre, 2e) is the granddaddy of them all, opened in 1800. You can window-shop here until about 9 PM, when the ornamental gates at either end are closed.

Department Stores Paris has a good selection of department stores, several of which are conveniently grouped on the Right Bank around the Opéra. **Printemps** (64 blvd. Haussmann, 9e) claims to be the "most Parisian department store." Its main rival is **Galeries Lafayette** (40 blvd. Haussmann, 9e), and competition is fierce. Both go out of their way to cater to foreign visitors, and each offers excellent services, including multilingual hostesses, *bureaux de change* (exchange bureaus), and sales. For visitors in a hurry, both stores have the added attraction of a series of designer boutiques.

The budget **Monoprix** and **Prisunic** stores are cheap and cheerful. The largest Prisunic outlets are at 109 Champs-Elysées, on the corner of rue La Boétie, 8e; and 25 avenue des Ternes. Monoprix's handiest outlet for tourists is at 21 avenue de l'Opéra, 1er.

Markets Every *quartier* in Paris boasts an open-air food market, if only for a few days a week. Sunday morning, until 1 PM, is usually a good time to go; Monday is the most likely closing day. The local markets usually concentrate on food, but they always have a few brightly colored flower stalls. Some markets have stalls that sell antiques, clothing, household goods, and secondhand books. Their lively—sometimes chaotic—atmosphere makes them a sight worth seeing even if you don't want to buy anything.

Many of the better-known markets are located in areas you'd visit for sightseeing. Our favorites are on **rue de Buci,** 6e (open daily); **rue Mouffetard,** 5e; and **rue Lepic** in Montmartre. (The last two are best on weekends.) The **Marché d'Aligre** (open Saturday, Sunday, and Monday mornings) is located beyond the Bastille on rue d'Aligre in the 12th Arrondissement. It's not very touristic, but Parisians from all over the city know and love it.

Paris's main **flower market** is located right in the heart of the city on Ile de la Cité, between Notre-Dame and the Palais de Justice. It's open every day except Monday. On Sunday, it becomes a bird market.

The huge **Marché aux Puces** on Paris's northern boundary (métro: Porte de Clignancourt) is the city's largest flea market. It's not as cheap as it was in days of yore, but it remains a great place to barter, browse, and maybe even buy. The century-old labyrinth of alleyways is packed with antiques dealers and junk stalls. *Open weekends and Mon.*

Specialty Stores
Gift Ideas

Those wishing to take home china and crockery should head for the **rue du Paradis,** 10e; it's lined with china shops selling goods at a wide range of prices.

Shoppers looking for fabrics should try **Dreyfus** (2 rue Charles-Nodier, 18e).

For children, try **Le Monde en Marché** (34 rue Dauphine, 6e), which has a great selection of wooden toys, puppets, and miniatures.

Clothing

Lolita Lempicka (corner of rue des Rosiers and rue Paveé, 4e) is one of the newest stars of French ready-to-wear, with a junior collection, **Lolita Bis,** located on the opposite corner.

Pierlot (4 rue du Jour, 1er) is a favorite shopping spot for young French career girls, while **Naf Naf** (10 rue du Jour) and **Chipie** (31 rue de la Ferronerie, 1er) offer sporty, trendy clothes.

For the city's cheapest threads, try **Tati,** a Parisian institution (140 rue de Rennes, 6e).

Perfume

This tried-and-true Parisian gift is available at **Annick Goutal's** exquisite boutique (14 rue de Castiglione, 1er) or at the chain **Sephora** (outlets at 66 rue Chaussée d'Antin, 9e; 30 av. de l'Italie, 13e; 46 av. Général-Leclerc, 14e; and 50 rue de Passy, 16e). **Jean Laporte** has two highly original boutiques (5 rue des Capucines, 1er, and 84 bis rue Grenelle, 7e).

Dining

Eating out is one of the perennial delights of this most civilized of cities. Some complain that the French capital is overrated gastronomically and that the Parisian restaurateur is resting complacently on his or her laurels. Of course, not every restaurant offers a gastronomic adventure, and bad meals at unconscionable prices are no more unknown in Paris than at home. The important point to remember is that the city's restaurants exist principally to cater to the demanding needs of the Parisians themselves, and any restaurant that fails to meet their high standards is unlikely to stay in business long.

Dining on a budget in Paris means, first and foremost, the bustling bistros and brasseries where white-aproned waiters scribble your order on paper tablecloths before returning almost immediately with *plats du jour* (plates of the day) and carafes of *vin du patron* (house wine). Steak and *andouillette* (chitterling sausage), served with french fries, are typical main courses. Fast-food chains (McDonald's, Burger King, Quick) are catching on—but more for their novelty impact than quality or value. Grabbing quick things to eat in Paris on a regular basis is hard on the budget—a sandwich in a bar will set you back $3 and even a street-corner crêpe costs at least $1.50 (usually more)—while a simple, yet wonderfully gratifying, picnic of baguette, ham, and cheese split between a couple of people is a great deal. And if you find the right setting—say the Luxembourg Gardens or the Square Viviani on the Left Bank opposite Notre-Dame—it can be memorable.

Almost all restaurants offer two basic types of menu: à la carte and fixed-price (*un menu* to the French). The fixed-price menu will almost always offer the best value, though you will have to eat three or sometimes four courses, and choices will be limited.

Lunch is usually served from noon to 2. You shouldn't have difficulty getting a table if you arrive by 12:30; after 1, however, you may have problems, especially if you want a full three-course meal. Dinner is rarely served before 8, and 9:30 is not considered unduly late.

Highly recommended restaurants are indicated by a star ★.

Under 250 francs

Central Paris

★ **Auberge des Deux Signes.** Dining at the Auberge des Deux Signes, opposite Notre-Dame, is quite an experience. The medieval decor in this converted 13th-century chapel is enchanting, and the atmosphere is enhanced by *your* choice of classical music! The cuisine is traditional, with a hint of southwestern richness. Try either of the fixed-price menus. *46 rue Galande, 5e, tel. 43–25–46–56. Reservations advised. AE, DC, MC, V. Closed Sat. lunch, Sun., and Aug. Métro: St-Michel.*

Chez Paul. Lovers of the authentic Parisian bistro—and they don't come much more authentic than this—rejoice at the survival of Chez Paul. It's located on the Ile de la Cité, between the Pont Neuf and the Palais du Justice, on one of the prettiest squares in Paris. Dining on the terrace is an experience to remember. The food is sturdily traditional, with snails, and calf's head in shallot sauce as long-time favorites. Readers recommend this restaurant. *15 pl. Dauphine, 1er, tel. 43–54–21–48. Reservations required. No credit cards. Closed Mon., Tues., and Aug. Métro: Pont-Neuf.*

La Colombe. "The Dove" lives up to its name and is home to 14 white doves. It also offers one of the most charming dining experiences in Paris. The restaurant is set in a beautiful 13th-century house on the Seine, right near Notre-Dame. Try to secure a table on the leafy terrace. The food is predominantly classic, but with nouvelle touches. The good-value, fixed-price lunch menu is also available for dinner before 9 PM. *4 rue de la Colombe, 4e, tel. 46–33–37–08. Reservations advised. AE, DC, MC, V. Closed Sun. and Mon. lunch. Métro: Cité.*

Chez Papa. The refreshing open-plan decor of Chez Papa makes a pleasant change from the bustle and tightly packed tables of most St-Germain restaurants. A shiny-black baby-grand piano, surrounded by a host of plants, stands out against the white walls and high ceiling. There's soft music from 9 every evening. The cuisine is surprisingly light, considering that the dishes themselves are usually associated with the sturdiest French traditional food: snails, cassoulet, and pot-au-feu. A good fixed-price lunch menu makes Chez Papa an ideal lunch spot. *3 rue St.-Benoît, 6e, tel. 42–86–99–63. Reservations advised. AE, DC, MC, V. Closed Sun. Moderate. Métro: St-Germain-des-Prés.*

★ **L'Escargot Montorgueil.** This is one of the best-known restaurants in Paris, in business since 1832 and boasting wonderful period decor. The new owners—proprietors of the classy Tour d'Argent—have promised to maintain both the look and the classic food. As the name implies, snails served in every way are the specialty. A fixed-price lunch menu helps keep costs low. *38 rue Montorgueil, 1er, tel. 42–36–83–51. Reservations* *advised for dinner. AE, DC, MC, V. Closed Mon. and most of Aug. Métro: Etienne-Marcel.*

Louis XIV. Try to get a table on the terrace by one of the windows; the restaurant is on place des Victoires and has a terrific view of the statue of the Sun King in the center. Decor is traditional, and waiters pad around in long white aprons. Specialties include rabbit *à la moutarde* (with mustard) and duck with olives. *1 bis pl. des Victoires, 1er, tel. 40–26–20–81. Reservations advised for lunch. MC, V. Closed weekends and Aug. Métro: Sentier.*

Au Petit Coin de la Bourse. The proximity of the Paris stock exchange explains the number of businesspeople who flock here. They come to enjoy both the robust, semi-classical cuisine—there's a terrific-value fixed-price dinner menu (lunching here is expensive)—and the authentic '20s decor. Try the bouillabaisse and the unusual seafood sauerkraut. *16 rue Feydeau, 2e, tel. 45–08–00–08. Reservations for lunch essential. AE, DC, MC, V. Closed weekends. Métro: Bourse.*

★ **Brasserie Bofinger.** Head here to eat in one of the oldest and most genuine brasseries in town, with a dark interior, complete with waiters in black jackets and white aprons, and unbeatable atmosphere. Seafood and sauerkraut are the traditional favorites, but there's the expected variety of hearty brasserie fare, too, all served until late in the evening, year-round. *3 rue de la Bastille, 4e, tel. 42–72–87–82. Reservations advised. AE, DC, V. Métro: Bastille.*

Au Pactole. Owner and chef Roland Magne offers a range of imaginative nouvelle and traditional cuisine, including some mouth-watering fish dishes and creative desserts. The decor is in striking orange and yellow, and the fixed-price lunch menu offers good value. *44 blvd. St-Germain, 5e, tel. 43–26–92–28. Reservations advised. AE, MC, V. Closed Sat. lunch and Sun. Métro: Maubert-Mutualité.*

Chez Toutoune. This restaurant has always been convivially crowded, but these days, Chez Toutoune and her little boutique next door are bursting at the seams. The food is unmistakably *bourgeois*, a little heavy for some tastes but much appreciated by those with a weakness for solid, everyday fare. There's an excellent fixed-price menu and terrific desserts—try the apple tart. *5 rue de Pontoise, 5e, tel. 43–26–56–81. Reservations for dinner essential. MC, V. Closed Sun., Mon. lunch, and Aug. Métro: Maubert-Mutualité.*

Echaudé St-Germain. The intimacy of this pretty little restaurant, shielded from the busy world outside by lace curtains, has won the enthusiastic approval of Left Bank high-lifers. The food is classic and simple. The fixed-price menu is an unusually good value. *21 rue de l'Echaudé, 6e, tel. 43–54–79–02. Reservations essential. AE, DC, MC, V. Métro: Mabillon.*

Le Muniche. Despite its name, there's nothing German about the cuisine featured in this St-Germain brasserie, apart, that is, from the excellent sauerkraut. Otherwise, the accent is typically French, with seafood predominating. Try the good-value, fixed-price menu. The restaurant is open till very late. *22 rue Guillaume-Apollinaire, 6e, tel. 46–33–62–09. Reservations advised. AE, DC, MC, V. Métro: St-Germain-des-Prés.*

Le Petit Zinc. This is the smaller, more intimate cousin of the neighboring Muniche, operated by the same group. A friendly team of waiters bustles around providing magnificent seafood. Open till very late. *11 rue St-Benoît, 6e, tel. 46–33–51–66. Res-*

ervations essential. AE, DC, MC, V. Métro: St-Germain-des-Prés.

North and East Paris (St-Lazare, Gare du Nord, Gare de l'Est)

Da Graziano. Located right under one of the neighborhood's remaining windmills, Da Graziano offers an exquisite taste of Italy in the heart of Montmartre. Owner Federighi Graziano is as chic as his restaurant—chandeliers, mirrors, and flowers proliferate—and as Tuscan as the cuisine. His fresh pasta is memorable. He also offers a range of French dishes, some named after stars who have dined here. Try the smoked beef *à la* Jean Marais. The inexpensive fixed-price lunch menu makes the climb up the hill well worthwhile. *83 rue Lepic, 18e, tel. 46–06–84–77. Reservations required. MC, V. Closed Feb. Métro: Blanche.*

South Paris (Montparnasse, Austerlitz, Gare de Lyon)

Aux Senteurs de Provence. The name says it all. You come here for pungent, south-of-France specialties, all very much in the traditional mold of *cuisine bourgeoise* (simple, good food). The decor and the house specialty—bouillabaisse—help evoke the sun-lit mood of Provence. *295 rue Lecourbe, 15e, tel. 45–57–11–98. Reservations advised. AE, DC, MC, V. Closed Sun., Mon., and Aug. Métro: Lourmel.*

West Paris

La Petite Chaise. What was once a coaching inn, opened in 1680, has since become one of the most popular restaurants in the city. While the decor may be on the musty side, the simple, good-value food, with such specialties as seafood pancakes and avocado mousse, is the important factor here. *36 rue de Grenelle, 7e, tel. 42–22–13–35. Reservations advised. Dress: casual. MC, V. Métro: Rue de Bac.*

Au Clocher du Village. The simple, country-villagelike interior of the Clocher du Village, with old posters on the walls, wine presses hanging from the ceiling, lace curtains, and a gleaming brass coffee machine on the bar, provides the perfect complement to simple, well-prepared classic French cuisine. Service is straightforward and friendly. It's a place like this that can make eating out in Paris special. There's nothing very fancy here, yet the whole place exudes that inimitable Gallic culinary flair. *8 bis rue Verderet, tel. 42–88–35–87. Reservations advised. Dress: casual. MC, V. Closed weekends and Aug. Métro: Eglise d'Auteuil.*

Under 175 francs

Central Paris

Willi's. British wine fanatic Mark Williamson runs this renowned haunt for Anglophiles and other French bons vivants. Wine takes preference over food, but the meals are high quality, too—light and fresh, much like the lively modern decor. The staff will happily advise you on what to drink, but bear in mind that most of the wines here will push your check appreciably higher. *13 rue des Petits-Champs, 1er, tel. 42–61–05–09. Reservations advised lunchtime. MC, V. Closed Sun. Métro: Bourse.*

Coconnas. With its warm Italian decor and early 18th-century paintings of beautiful place des Vosges, the little Coconnas has won plaudits from critics and humble diners alike. Depending on your mood, you can choose either nouvelle dishes or cuisine *à l'ancienne,* solid 19th-century fare with not so much as a hint of nouvelle innovation. Owned and run by the proprietors of the celebrated Tour d'Argent, the Coconnas has a considerable reputation to live up to. If the overbooking is anything to go by, it obviously does. *2 bis pl. des Vosges, tel. 42–78–58–16. Reservations required. AE, DC, MC, V. Closed Mon., Tues., and mid-Dec.–mid-Jan. Métro: St-Paul-Le Marais.*

Grizzli. A dancing-bear sign hangs in this old restaurant, built in 1902. Some of the dishes concocted by Bernard Arény, however, are resolutely modern: cold ratatouille with poached egg, or rabbit with raisins. Arény's southwest origins are reflected in the pitchers of Marmandais wine and the grilled lamb served Pyrenean-style—on a slate. *7 rue St-Martin, 4e, tel. 48–87–77–56. Reservations advised. Closed Sun. lunch, Mon., and Christmas–New Year's. MC, V. Métro: Châtelet.*

Saumoneraie. This is reason enough for fish lovers to make for rue Descartes, halfway up the Montagne Ste-Geneviève. A traditional bistro-style haunt, with bare stone walls, it specializes in salmon but offers a wide range of fish and seafood dishes. There's also a good-value fixed-price menu. *6 rue Descartes, 5e, tel. 46–34–08–76. Reservations required. AE, DC, MC, V. Métro: Cardinal-Lemoine.*

Vagénende. Dark wood, gleaming mirrors, and superprofessional waiters—perfect in their black jackets and white aprons—take the Vagénende dangerously close to turn-of-the-century pastiche. Nonetheless, the superior brasserie food—seafood and hearty *cuisine bourgeoise*—and the busy atmosphere make this a restaurant to take seriously. The homemade fois gras and the chocolate-based desserts are outstanding. *142 blvd. St-Germain, 5e, tel. 43–26–68–18. Reservations advised. Dress: casual. AE, MC, V. Métro: St-Germain-des-Prés.*

Jo Goldenberg. This is a New York–style deli, buried deep in the heart of the Marais's Jewish quarter. It's no upstart, however; it's been in business since the beginning of the century and has long since become a Parisian institution, homey and bustling, with an atmosphere you won't find anywhere else in the city. Jewish, Hungarian, and Russian specialties are featured, together with live music most evenings. Try the stuffed carp. *7 rue des Rosiers, 4e, tel. 48–87–20–16. Reservations advised. AE, DC, MC, V. Métro: St-Paul-Le Marais.*

Petit St-Benoît. This is a wonderful place—small, amazingly inexpensive, always crowded, and with decor that's plain to the point of barely existing. The food is correspondingly basic, but quite good for the price. Expect to share a table. *4 rue St-Benoît, 6e. No reservations or credit cards. Closed weekends. Métro: St-Germain-des-Prés.*

North and East Paris (St-Lazare, Gare du Nord, Gare de l'Est)

Mansouria. Despite its off-the-beaten-track location, to the west of place de la Bastille, Mansouria is worth the trip if you have any interest in Moroccan food—it's in a class of its own. The decor is fresh and modern, and the service is friendly and relaxed. Try any of the *tagines*, a range of sophisticated spicy Moroccan "stews," and the pigeon "pie" with sugar. *11 rue Faidherbe, 11e, tel. 43–71–00–16. Reservations required. MC, V. Closed Aug., Tues., and Wed. lunch. Moderate. Métro: Faidherbe-Chaligny.*

South Paris (Montparnasse, Austerlitz, Gare de Lyon)

★ **Bistrot d'André.** This classic bistro stands close to the former site of the Citroën automobile factory, and car mementos—mainly plaques and old photos—line the walls. The wooden chairs and maroon-velvet benches conjure up a mood of prewar Paris. Bistro cooking at its sturdiest and most reliable includes snails, *andouillette* (pork sausage), and *confit de canard* (duck preserved in its fat). An aperitif and four courses plus coffee comes to under 150 francs, while a decent bottle of Burgundy won't push your check skyward either. *232 rue St-Charles, 15e, tel. 45–57–89–14. Reservations advised. MC, V. Closed Sat. lunch and Sun. Métro: Balard.*

Au Boeuf Gros Sel. Salt beef is the undisputed champion of the menu here. The food, like the simple decor, is plain and ultra-traditional. Save room for the *tarte Tatin*, the French version of apple pie. *299 rue Lecourbe, 15e, tel. 45–57–36–53. Reservations advised. MC, V. Closed Sun., Mon. lunch, and Aug. Métro: Lourmel.*

West Paris **L'Ecluse.** In this select, wood-paneled wine bar, you can order a whole range of Bordeaux by the glass. Stylish snacks, such as foie gras or carpaccio, make this a great place for a light lunch. *15 pl. de la Madeleine, 8e, tel. 42–65–34–69. Reservations not required. Closed Sun. MC, V. Métro: Madeleine.*

Under 100 francs

Central Paris **Self-service Tuileries.** Snacks and meals easy on a budget are hard to come by in this upbeat area of Paris, so this clean, pleasant spot recommended by readers is a good bet. *206 rue de Rivoli, 1er, tel. 42–60–68–74. No reservations or credit cards. Métro: Tuileries.*

Le Trappiste. A few blocks south of Les Halles and just north of place du Châtelet, 20 different international beers are available on draught, along with well over 180 bottled. Mussels and french fries are the traditional accompaniment, although various other snacks (hot dogs and sandwiches) are also available. There are tables upstairs and on the pavement. *4 rue St-Denis, 1er, tel. 42–21–37–96. Reservations not required. MC, V. Métro: Châtelet.*

★ **Trumilou.** Overlooking the Seine opposite the Ile St-Louis, this very French little bistro is a real find. Despite the harsh lighting, the mood is boisterous and welcoming, with many regulars among the diners. Bright and splashy paintings line the walls. The food is resolutely traditional, with such time-honored favorites as *boeuf bourguignon* and sweetbreads. *84 quai de l'Hôtel-de-Ville, 4e, tel. 42–77–63–98. Reservations accepted. MC, V. Closed Mon. Métro: Pont Marie.*

Polidor. The Polidor is another of the Left Bank's time-honored bistros, little changed from the days when James Joyce and Hemingway came here to spend long, drunken evenings. The typical bistro fare is offered in generous portions. Try the fixed-price menus for maximum value at lunchtime on weekdays. *41 rue Monsieur-le-Prince, 6e, tel. 43–26–95–34. No phone reservations or credit cards. Métro: Odéon.*

Fast Food. The leading fast-food chains in Paris include McDonald's, Burger King, Freetime, Loveburger, and Picpain (a slightly Frenchified version). Oh Poivrier!, with its distinctive, cool-gray interior-designer decor, specializes in inventive salads with peppery dressings. You can be sure of a good choice of fast-food outlets at Les Halles (especially around Square des Innocents) and along the lower reaches of boulevard St-Michel. Rue de la Harpe and rue de la Huchette, which leads off the boulevard close to the Seine, are choked with cheap Greek restaurants and Tunisian pastry shops.

North and East Paris (St-Lazare, Gare du Nord, Gare de l'Est)

Chartier. Low prices, simple decor, and classic fare have earned Chartier an enviable reputation as one of the best restaurant values in Paris. The choice isn't wide, but the food is always hearty and filling. Try the steak tartare if it's on the menu and you're feeling adventurous. *7 rue du Fbg.-Montmartre, 9e, tel. 47–70–86–29. No reservations or credit cards. Métro: Rue Montmartre.*

Le Pupillin. This unpretentious bistro is a handy address in the heart of Paris, midway between Montmartre and the Grands Boulevards. On the ground floor: a bar serving snacks and a plat du jour (often steak or ham). Upstairs: an airy dining room and more inventive cuisine, with a three-course set menu at 70 francs. *19 rue Notre-Dame-de-Lorette, 9e, tel. 42–85–46–06. Reservations advised. MC, V. Closed for lunch on weekends. Metro: Saint-Georges.*

★ **Le Maquis.** Visitors often miss this spot on the little-traveled north side of Montmartre. But locals know it and come often. They appreciate the warm, friendly atmosphere created by owner-chef Claude Lesage, as well as his excellent, traditional French cuisine. The superb 63-franc lunchtime menu, which changes daily, usually has the place packed at midday, so it's best to book a table before you head for Montmartre. *69 rue Caulaincourt, 18e, tel. 42–59–76–07. Reservations advised. MC, V. Métro: Lamarck-Caulaincourt.*

Fast Food. If you're craving a burger, you'll find a reasonable choice in the following localities: along the Grands Boulevards east of Opéra (especially near the Richelieu-Drouot métro); at place de Clichy; and opposite Gare du Nord.

South Paris (Montparnasse, Austerlitz, Gare de Lyon)

Bistro de la Gare. The 6th Arrondissement boasts two members of this popular chain. Of them, the one on boulevard Montparnasse is the better, not because the food is noticeably finer—it's much the same in all the restaurants—but because of the decor. It's crowded with art nouveau trimmings, and the expansive glass window is classified as a historic monument. *59 blvd. du Montparnasse, 6e, tel. 45–48–38–01. Reservations not required. MC, V. Métro: Montparnasse-Bienvenüe.*

★ **Chez Grand-Mère.** Homey, grandma-style cooking here means filling French favorites such as rabbit in mustard sauce or duck with mushrooms. The dining room's clutter of eccentric bric-a-brac doesn't prevent locals from piling in to sample the 70-franc lunchtime menu or dining à la carte for around 130 francs. *92 rue Broca, 13e, tel. 47–07–13–65. Reservations advised. No credit cards. Métro: Gobelins.*

Fast Food. The streets around the Tour Montparnasse—notably boulevard du Montparnasse itself—offer a wide choice.

West Paris

Fontaine de Mars. The Fontaine de Mars is a simple little family-style restaurant located in the otherwise expensive area around the Eiffel Tower. The low-priced lunch menu is popular with the local residents—always a good sign. Alternatively, take your pick from a wide choice of traditional country-style dishes, like beef in sea salt or beef casserole. Eat outside by the little fountain in the summer. *129 rue St-Dominique, 7e, tel. 47–05–46–44. Reservations recommended. MC, V. Closed Sat. evening, Sun., and Aug. Métro: Ecole Militaire.*

Thoumieux. This large, 1920s-style restaurant, not far from the Eiffel Tower, has been in the same family for three generations. The cuisine comes exclusively from the southwest of France (meaning that rich duck dishes predominate). Try the fixed-price menu for maximum value. *79 rue St-Dominique, 7e, tel. 47–05–49–75. Reservations advised. MC, V. Closed Mon. Métro: Latour-Maubourg.*

Fast Food. Most leading chains are represented along the northern half of the Champs-Elysées.

Splurges

L'Assommoir. L'Assommoir is known not just for its subtle cuisine—there's a superb range of sophisticated fish dishes—but for the personality of owner and chef Philippe Larue, who speaks English to perfection and has a tremendous sense of humor. He has covered the walls of his charming little bistro with samples from his vast collection of paintings. L'Assommoir also has the advantage of being on a peaceful little street away from crowded place du Tertre. *12 rue Girardon, 18e, tel. 42–64–55–01. Reservations advised. MC, V. Closed Sun., Mon., Aug., and Christmas. Métro: Lamarck-Caulaincourt. 250–300 francs.*

The Arts and Nightlife

The Arts

The weekly magazines *Pariscope* and *L'Officiel des Spectacles*, published on Wednesday, give detailed entertainment listings, as does *Figaroscope*, a free supplement to the Wednesday edition of the daily newspaper *Le Figaro*. *Paris Free Voice* gives monthly listings in English—you can find it in bilingual bookstores or at the American Church (65 quai d'Orsay). The best place to buy tickets is at the venue itself; otherwise, try your hotel or a travel agency such as **Paris-Vision** (214 rue de Rivoli). Tickets for some events can be bought at the **FNAC** stores (there are special ticket counters in branches at 26 av. des Ternes, near the Arc de Triomphe; and at the Forum des Halles). Half-price tickets for many same-day theater performances are available at the booth next to the Madeleine church.

Theater A number of theaters line the grand boulevards between Opéra and République, but there is no Paris equivalent to Broadway or London's West End. Shows are mostly in French. Classical drama is performed at the **Comédie-Française** (Palais-Royal, tel. 40–15–00–15). You can reserve seats in person about two weeks in advance or turn up an hour beforehand and wait in line for cheap returned tickets.

A completely different sort of pleasure is to be found near place St-Michel at the tiny **Théâtre de la Huchette** (23 rue de la Huchette, 5e, tel. 43–26–38–99), where Ionesco's short plays make a deliberate mess of the French language.

Concerts The **Salle Pleyel** (252 rue du Fbg. St-Honoré, tel. 45–63–07–96), near the Arc de Triomphe, remains Paris's principal home of classical music. Paris isn't as richly endowed as New York or London when it comes to orchestral music, but the city compensates with a never-ending stream of inexpensive lunchtime and evening concerts in churches. The candlelit concerts held in the **Sainte-Chapelle** are outstanding—make reservations well in advance. **Notre-Dame** is another church where you can combine sightseeing with good music.

Opera The **Opéra** itself (tel. 47–42–53–71) is a dramatically flamboyant hall, and after Rudolf Nureyev's stint as artistic director, its ballet choreography has reached new heights. But getting tickets is not always easy. The **Opéra Comique** (the French term for opera with spoken dialogue), close by (5 rue Favart, 2e, tel. 42–86–88–83), is more accessible.

The **Théâtre Musical de Paris** (2 pl. du Châtelet, tel. 40–28–28–28) offers opera and ballet for a wider audience at more reasonable prices. The **Opéra-Bastille** (Place de la Bastille, tel. 40–01–16–16), which opened in early 1990, stages both traditional opera and symphony concerts under its dynamic young Korean director Myung-Whun Chung.

Dance Apart from the traditional ballets sometimes on the bill at the Opéra, the highlights of the Paris dance year are the visits of major foreign troupes, usually to the **Palais des Congrès** at Porte Maillot (tel. 40–68–22–22) or the **Palais des Sports** at the Porte de Versailles (tel. 48–28–40–48). The annual **Festival de la Danse** is staged at the **Théâtre des Champs-Elysées** on avenue Montaigne (tel. 47–20–36–37) in October.

Films There are hundreds of movie theaters in the city, and a number of them show English films. Look for the initials "V.O."—they mean original version (not dubbed). Cinema admission runs from 35 to 45 francs. There are reduced rates on Monday; programs change Wednesday. Old and rare films are often screened at the **Pompidou Center** and **Musée du Cinéma** at Trocadéro.

Nightlife

Paris's nightclubs are household names, at least among foreign tourists. But except for the Folies-Bergère, which is a straightforward theater, Paris cabaret does not come cheap.

Cabaret The **Crazy Horse** (12 av. George-V, 8e, tel. 47–23–32–32) is one of the best known for pretty girls and risqué dance routines, lots of humor and little clothing. Cheapest ticket: 195 francs (standing).

The **Moulin Rouge** (pl. Blanche, 18e, tel. 46–06–00–19) is an old favorite at the foot of Montmartre. Cheapest ticket: 395 francs (seat and champagne).

Nearby is the **Folies-Bergère** (32 rue Richer, 9e, tel. 42–46–77–11), not as "in" as it once was, but still renowned for its glitter and its vocal numbers. Cheapest seats: 75 francs.

The **Lido** (116 bis av. des Champs-Elysées, 8e, tel. 40–76–56–10) stars the famous Bluebell Girls and tries to win you over through sheer exuberance. Cheapest ticket: 395 francs (seat and champagne).

Bars and Nightclubs The more upscale Paris nightclubs tend to be both expensive (1,000 francs for a bottle of gin or whiskey) and private—in other words, you'll usually need to know someone who's a member to get through the door. **Club 79** (79 av. des Champs-Elysées, 8e) is probably the handiest bet for dancing the night away.

Other places for a fun evening out include:

Caveau des Oubliettes. Traditional folk singing and ballads are performed in a medieval cellar with Gothic arches and heavy beams. It's very popular with tourists, but still full of energetic charm. *Admission (with drink): 110 francs. 1 rue St-Julien-le-Pauvre, 5e. Open 9 PM–2 AM. Closed Sun.*

Le Lapin Agile. This is a touristy but picturesque Montmartre setting: hard wooden benches, brandied cherries, and thumping great golden French oldies. *22 rue des Saules, 18e. Admission (with drink): 90 frs. Open 9 PM–2 AM.*

La Rôtisserie de l'Abbaye. French, English, and American folk songs are sung to the accompaniment of a guitar in a medieval setting. The action starts around 8 PM; come early or you won't get in. You can dine here, too. *22 rue Jacob, 6e. Admission (including dinner): 200–400 frs. Closed Sun.*

Jazz Clubs

Paris is one of the great jazz cities of the world, with plenty of variety, including some fine, distinctive local coloring. For nightly schedules, consult the magazines *Jazz Hot* or *Jazz Magazine.* Remember that nothing gets going until 10 or 11 PM and that entry prices can vary widely from about 30 francs to over 100 francs.

The Latin Quarter is a good place to track down Paris jazz. The **Caveau de la Huchette** (5 rue de la Huchette, 5e) offers Dixieland in a hectic, smoke-filled atmosphere.

Le Petit Opportun (15 rue des Lavandières-Ste-Opportune, 1er) is a converted Latin Quarter bistro with a cramped, atmospheric basement that sometimes features top-flight American soloists with French rhythm sections. At street level, there is a pleasant bar with recorded music and less-expensive drinks.

On the Right Bank is **New Morning** (7 rue des Petites-Ecuries, 10e), a premier venue for visiting American musicians and top French bands.

Discos

Club Zed (2 rue des Anglais, 5e) boasts lively dancing and some rock-only evenings.

The long-established **Balajo** (9 rue de Lappe, 11e) is crowded and lots of fun, with plenty of nostalgic '60s sounds some nights.

Les Bains (7 rue du Bourg-l'Abbé, 3e), once a public bathhouse, now specializes in new-wave music and features live music on Wednesday.

3 Ile-de-France

Versailles, Chartres, Fontainebleau

Far from being a sprawl of faceless gray suburbia, the region surrounding Paris—poetically known as the Ile-de-France—has as much history and beauty as the capital itself. Thanks to a comprehensive rail network, its profusion of cathedrals, châteaus, and picturesque old towns are all within an hour of central Paris. Most visitors are surprised to find such vast forests and swards of lush meadowland so close to the capital.

Ile-de-France never lost favor with the powerful, partly because its many forests—large chunks of which still stand—harbored sufficient game for even bloated, cosseted monarchs to achieve a regular kill. First Fontainebleau, in humane Renaissance proportions, then Versailles, on a minion-crushing, Baroque scale, reflected the royal desire to transform hunting lodges into palatial residences.

The 17th century was a time of prodigious building in the Ile-de-France—a period that bequeathed a vast array of important sights to admire and explore. The château, gardens, and well-preserved town of Versailles should not be overlooked. But do not neglect Versailles's slightly lesser neighbors; Vaux-le-Vicomte, Thoiry, Rambouillet, and Chartres would bask in superstar status anywhere else. And, after the crowds of Versailles in midsummer, you will welcome the relative tranquillity of these smaller châteaus.

By way of contrast, April 1992 saw the opening of Euro Disneyland near Marne-la-Vallée, 32 kilometers (20 miles) east of Paris. The allure of Mickey Mouse and Donald Duck is attracting visitors from all over Western Europe, and a massive complex

Ile-de-France

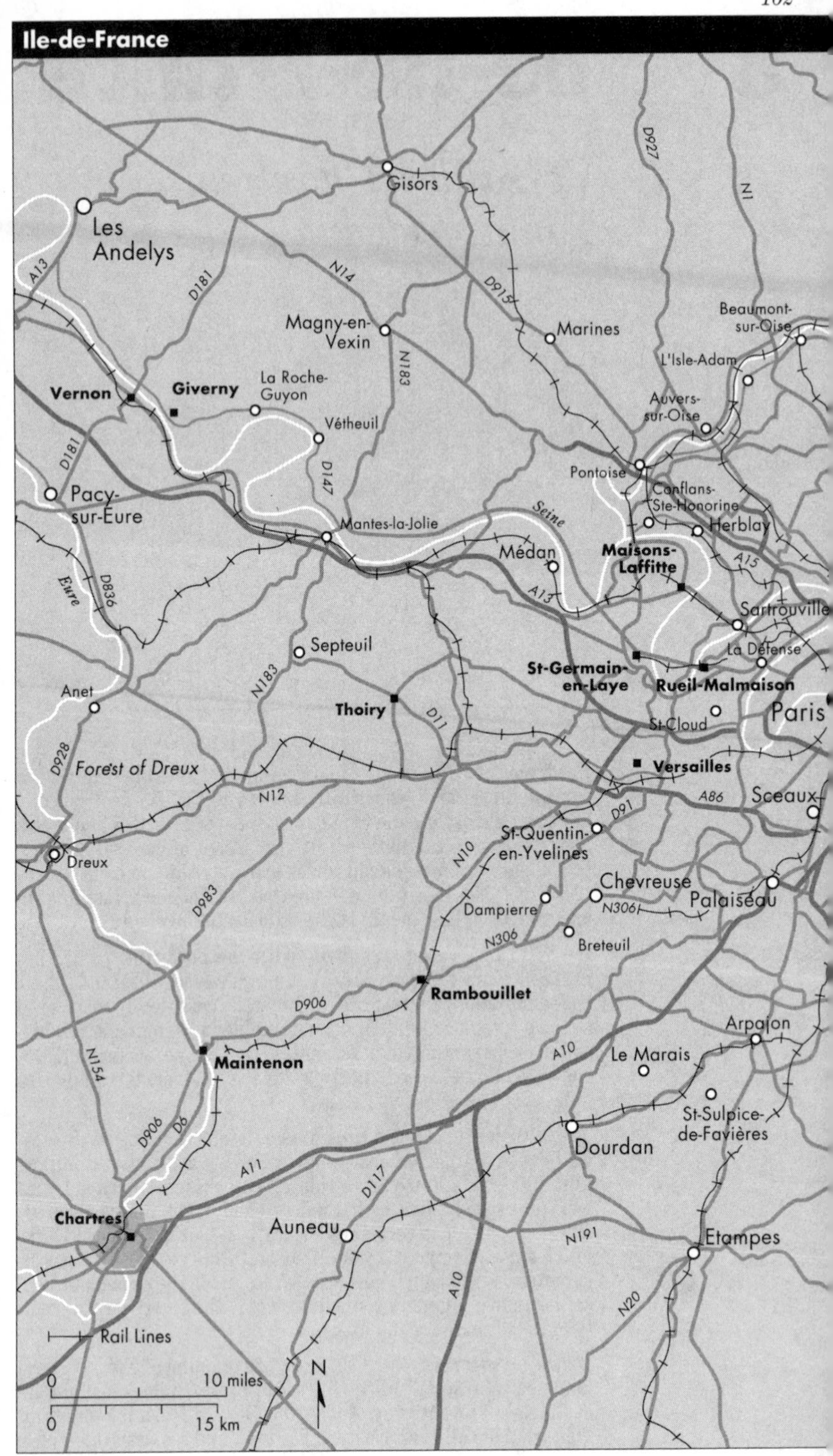

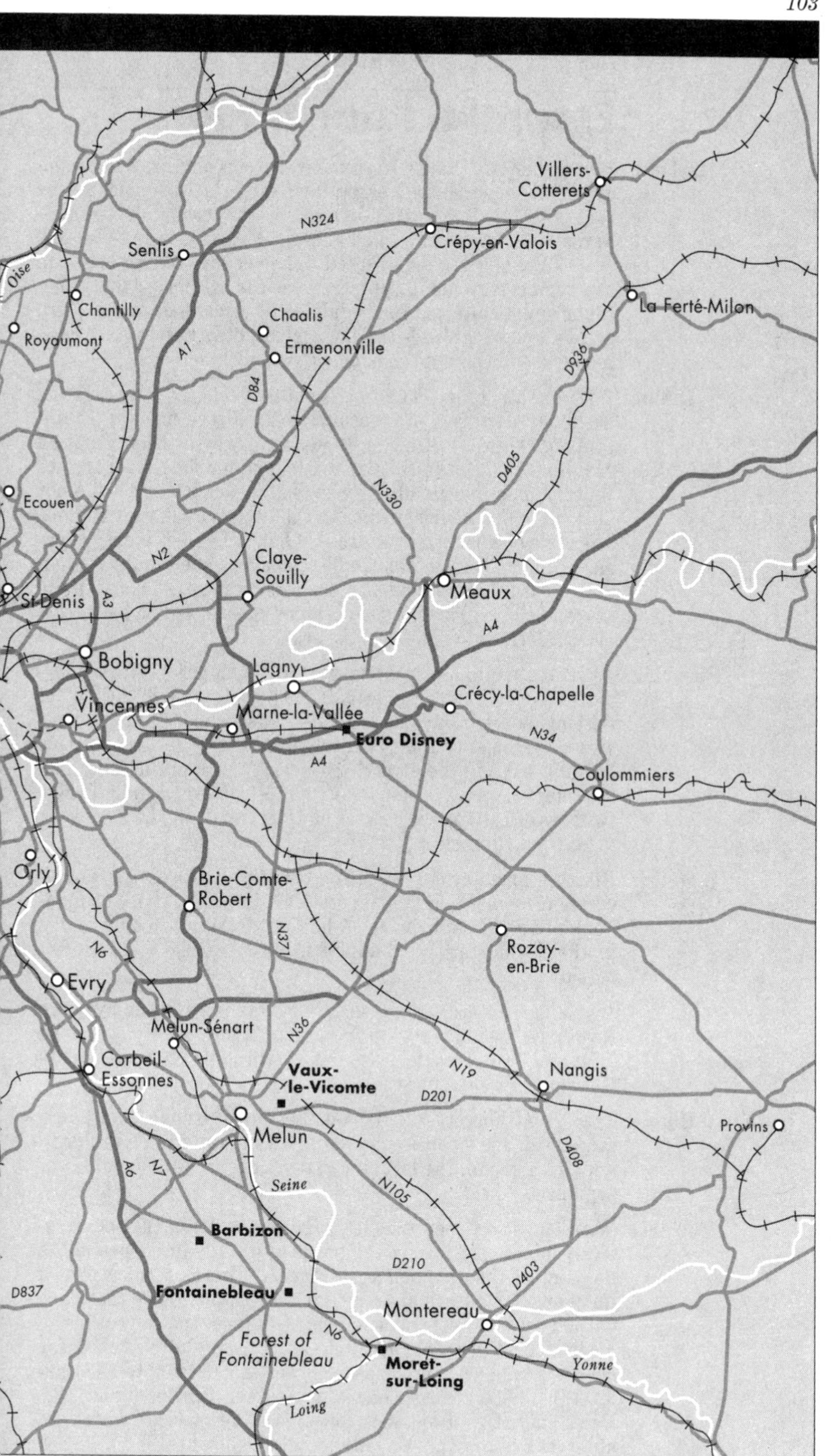
Villers-
Cotterets
N324
Crépy-en-Valois
Senlis
Oise
Chantilly
Royaumont
Chaalis
Ermenonville
La Ferté-Milon
A1
D84
D936
D405
N330
Ecouen
N2
Claye-
Souilly
Meaux
St-Denis
A3
A4
Bobigny
Lagny
Crécy-la-Chapelle
Vincennes
Marne-la-Vallée
Euro Disney
A4
N34
Coulommiers
Orly
Brie-Comte-
Robert
N371
Rozay-
en-Brie
N6
Evry
Melun-Sénart
N36
Corbeil-
Essonnes
Vaux-
le-Vicomte
N19
Nangis
D201
Melun
Provins
A6
N7
D408
Seine
N105
Barbizon
D210
D837
Fontainebleau
D403
Montereau
N6
Forest of
Fontainebleau
Moret-
sur-Loing
Yonne
Loing

of hotels and restaurants has been built alongside the new leisure park to accommodate them.

Essential Information

Lodging Remember two things: In summer, hotel rooms are at a premium and reservations are essential; relative lack of choice means that almost all accommodations in the swankier towns—Versailles, Rambouillet, and Fontainebleau—are on the costly side. Take nothing for granted. Some of the smaller hotels in the region may not accept credit cards, although the Carte Bleue and its international equivalents (MasterCard and Visa) are widely recognized—unlike American Express, which is often refused in all but the plushest establishments.

Dining With wealthy tourists and weekending Parisians providing the backbone of the region's seasonal clientele, the smarter restaurants of Ile-de-France can be just as pricey as their Parisian counterparts. But in smaller towns, and for those prepared to venture only marginally off the beaten tourist track, it's not difficult to find nourishing meals that won't break your budget. The style of cuisine mirrors that of Paris: There is plenty of variety but few things that can be considered specifically regional. In season, sumptuous game and asparagus are found in the south of the region; the soft, creamy cheese of Brie hails from Meaux and Coulommiers to the east.

Shopping Most of the Ile-de-France's working population either commutes to Paris or plows farmland. There is little in the way of regional specialties, and, with Paris never more than an hour away, serious shopping—particularly for clothes—means heading back to the capital. However, there are notably fine souvenir shops at Vaux-le-Vicomte, Giverny, and Thoiry (where you can sample cookies and jams made by the American viscountess herself).

Bicycling Biking is an enjoyable way to explore the area; you can rent bicycles from many local train stations, including those of Rambouillet and Fontainebleau. A booklet detailing 16 bike routes in the region can be obtained from the **SNCF** (tel. 42–61–50–50).

If you like to watch people pedaling more than you enjoy doing it yourself, be in the region on the last Sunday of July, when the **Tour de France** cycle race passes through en route to its Champs-Elysées climax.

Hiking The great forests of Rambouillet, St-Germain, and Fontainebleau are much frequented by walkers; if you'd prefer to go with a group, the local tourist offices can furnish details of organized hikes.

The Arts With Paris so close, it seems pointless to detail the comparatively minor offerings of the towns of the Ile-de-France in the domains of theater, music, or cinema. There are, however, a number of arts festivals staged in the Ile-de-France that have earned esteem in their own right. Of these, the largest is the **Festival de l'Ile-de-France** (mid-May–early July), famed for concerts held at châteaus themselves (for details, tel. 42–96–02–32). There are also music festivals in **Provins** (June), **St-Denis** (mid-May–June, with concerts in the basilica), and at the abbey of **Royaumont** (May–June, tel. 30–35–40–18).

An invaluable list of monthly regional events is the *Tourisme Loisirs* brochure produced by the **Comité Régional du Tourisme Ile-de-France** (73 rue Cambronne, 75015 Paris, tel. 45–67–89–41).

Highlights for First-time Visitors

Chartres Cathedral, Tour 1
Château of Fontainebleau, Tour 2
Claude Monet's house and gardens at Giverny, Tour 3
Château of Vaux-le-Vicomte, Tour 2
Château and gardens of Versailles, Tour 1
Thoiry—château and safari park, Tour 1

Tour 1: From Versailles to Chartres

No visit to Paris is complete without an excursion to Versailles, the starting point for this tour, which takes in the châteaus of Rambouillet and Maintenon, conveniently situated along the Versailles–Chartres rail line.

If, after days of museum lines and crowded métros, you feel a sense of escape as you leave Paris, you won't be the first. Back in the 17th century, Louis XIV, the Sun King, was barely out of his teens when he began to cast his cantankerous royal eye over the Ile-de-France in search of a new power base. Marshy, inhospitable Versailles, 24 kilometers (15 miles) to the west of Paris, was the place of his dreams. Down came its modest royal hunting lodge and up, up, and along went the new château.

From Paris
By Train Suburban trains (RER-C) to Versailles's Rive Gauche station leave central Paris (St-Michel, Musée d'Orsay, Invalides, Eiffel Tower) every ¼ hour. The trip takes 20–25 minutes.

By Car The drive from Paris (Porte d'Auteuil) to Versailles along A13 takes 20 minutes (longer during the evening rush hour).

Versailles

Tourist office: 7 rue des Réservoirs, to the right of the château close to the park entrance, tel. 39–50–36–22.

Numbers in the margin correspond to points of interest on the Versailles map.

Just 400 yards down avenue de Sceaux from the RER station
1 stands the **château of Versailles.** Today it seems outrageously big—but it wasn't nearly big enough for the sycophantic army of 20,000 noblemen, servants, and hangers-on who moved in with Louis. A new capital had to be constructed from scratch. Tough-thinking town planners dreamed up vast Baroque mansions and avenues broader than the Champs-Elysées.

It is hardly surprising that Louis XIV's successors soon felt out of sync with their architectural inheritance. Louis XV, who inherited the throne from the Sun King in 1715, transformed the royal apartments into places to live rather than pose in. The unfortunate Louis XVI—reigning monarch at the time of the French Revolution—cowered at the Petit Trianon in the leafy depths of Versailles park, well out of the mighty château's shad-

Cathédrale St-Louis, **6**
Château, **1**
Eglise Notre-Dame, **7**
Grand Trianon, **2**
Hameau, **4**
Musée Lambinet, **8**
Petit Trianon, **3**
Royal Stables, **5**

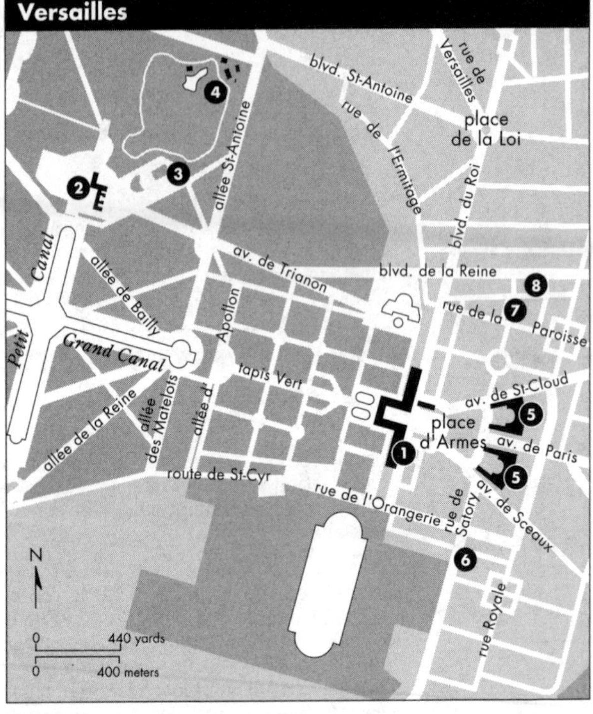

ow. His queen, Marie Antoinette, lost her head well before her trip to the guillotine in 1793, pretending to be a peasant shepherdess amid the ersatz rusticity of her cute hamlet.

The château was built by French architects Louis Le Vau and François Mansart between 1662 and 1690. Enter through the gilt iron gates from the huge place d'Armes. On the first floor of the château, right in the middle as you approach across the sprawling cobbled forecourt, is Louis XIV's bedchamber. The two wings were occupied by the royal children and princes of the blood, with courtiers making do in the attics.

The highlight for many on the guided tour of the palace is the **Galerie des Glaces** (Hall of Mirrors), fully restored to sparkling glory. It was here, after France's capitulation, that Prince Otto von Bismarck proclaimed the unified German Empire in 1871, and here, too, that the controversial Treaty of Versailles, asserting Germany's responsibility for World War I, was signed in 1919.

The **Grands Apartements** (State Rooms) that flank the Hall of Mirrors retain much of their original Baroque decoration: gilt stucco, painted ceilings, and marble sculpture. Perhaps the most extravagant of these rooms is the **Salon d'Apollon,** the former throne room, dedicated to the sun god Apollo, Louis XIV's mythical hero. Equally interesting are the **Petits Apartements,** where the royal family and friends lived in (relative) intimacy.

In the north wing of the château can be found the solemn white-and-gold **chapel,** designed by François Mansart and completed in 1710; the miniature **opera house,** built by J. A. Gabriel for Louis XV in 1770; and, connecting the two, the **17th-century Galleries,** with exhibits retracing the château's history. The south wing contains the wide, lengthy **Galerie des Batailles** (Gallery of Battles), lined with gigantic canvases extolling French military glory. *Admission: 30 frs. adults, 15 frs. students and senior citizens. Open Tues.–Sun. 9–7, 9–5:30 in winter; closed Mon.*

After the awesome feast of interior decor, the **park** outside is an ideal place to catch your breath. The gardens were designed by the French landscape architect Le Nôtre, whose work here represents formal French landscaping at its most rigid and sophisticated. The 250-acre grounds include woods, lawns, flower beds, statues, artificial lakes, and fountains galore. They are at their golden-leafed best in the fall but are also enticing in summer—especially on those Sundays when the fountains are in full flow. They become a spectacle of rare grandeur during the **Fêtes de Nuit** floodlighting and fireworks shows held in July and September. *The grounds are free and open daily. Tel. 39–50–36–22 for details of the fountains and Fêtes de Nuit.*

If you wander too far into the park woods you can easily get lost. Follow signs to skirt the numerous basins (or ponds) until you reach the **Grand Canal.** Move down the right bank, along gravelly paths beneath high-plinthed statues, until you discover that the canal is in the form of a cross—with two smaller arms known as the **Petit Canal.** At the crossing, bear right toward the Grand Trianon (in all, about a mile from the château).

2 The **Grand Trianon,** built by Mansart in 1687, is a scaled-down, pink-marble pleasure palace, now used to entertain visiting heads of state. When it is not in use, the palace is opened so that visitors can admire its lavish interior and early 19th-century furniture. *Admission: 16 frs. adults, 8 frs. students and senior citizens; joint ticket for the two Trianons 20 frs. adults, 10 frs. students and senior citizens. Open Tues.–Sun. 11–12:30 and 2–5:30; closed Mon.*

3 The **Petit Trianon,** close by, was built by architect Gabriel in the mid-18th century. It is a mansion, not a palace, and is modest by Versailles standards—though still sumptuously furnished. It contains mementos of its most illustrious inhabitant, Marie Antoinette. Look for her initials wrought into the iron railings of the main staircase.

Beyond the Petit Trianon and across the Petit Lac, which looks
more like a stream as it describes a wriggly semicircle, is the
4 queen's so-called hamlet **(Hameau).** With its watermill, genu-
ine lake (Grand Lac), and pigeon loft, this phony village is outrageously pretty; it was here that Marie Antoinette lived out her romanticized dreams of peasant life. *Admission: 11 frs. adults, 6 frs. students and senior citizens; joint ticket for the two Trianons 20 frs. adults, 10 frs. students and senior citizens. Open Tues.–Sun. 2–5:30; closed Mon.*

The town of Versailles is attractive, and its spacious, leafy boulevards make agreeable places to stroll. Facing the château are
5 the **royal stables,** buildings of regal dimensions and appearance.
Take avenue de Sceaux, to the right, and turn right again along
6 rue de Satory, which leads to the **Cathédrale St-Louis,** an aus-

tere edifice built between 1743 and 1754 by Mansart's grandson, with notable paintings and an organ loft.

Turn right out of the cathedral, then left down avenue Thiers, which cuts through the town's three major boulevards—avenues de Sceaux, de Paris, and de St-Cloud—to the ancient mar-
7 ket square, where rue de la Paroisse heads left to the **Eglise Notre-Dame.** This sturdy Baroque monument was built from 1684 to 1686 by Mansart (and is therefore older than the cathedral) as parish church for the Sun King's new town. Louis XIV himself laid the foundation stone.

Behind the church, in an imposing 18th-century mansion on
8 boulevard de la Reine, is the **Musée Lambinet,** a museum with a wide-ranging collection—a maze of cozy, finely furnished rooms replete with paintings, weapons, fans, and porcelain. *54 blvd. de la Reine. Admission free. Open Tues.–Sun. 2–6; closed Mon.*

Lodging
Under 350 frs.

Bellevue. This intimate hotel could hardly be handier, just 200 yards from the château on the avenue that leads to the RER station. Rooms are soundproofed and comfortable, if somewhat faded, and most have 18th-century-style furniture. *12 av. de Sceaux, 78000, tel. 39–50–13–41. 24 rooms with bath or shower. Facilities: bar. AE, DC, MC, V.*

Under 250 frs.

Home St-Louis. The small, recently modernized Home St-Louis is a good, cheap, quiet bet—close to the cathedral and not too far from the château. There's no restaurant. *28 rue St-Louis, 78000, tel. 39–50–23–55. 27 rooms, some with bath. MC, V.*

Dining
Under 125 frs.

Potager du Roy. There is excellent value in this restaurant run by Philippe Letourneur, a protégé of Gérard Vié. The cuisine improves constantly, yet prices stay moderate. The bistro and its adjoining terrace become crowded in summer because visitors find the 115- and 160-franc menus hard to resist. *1 rue Maréchal-Joffre, tel. 39–50–35–34. Reservations required. Jacket and tie required. MC, V. Closed Sun., Mon.*

Quai No 1. Fish and seafood rule supreme amid the sails, barometers, and model ships of this quaintly decked out restaurant. Home-smoked salmon and sauerkraut with fish are specialties. Eating à la carte isn't too expensive, and there are lower-priced set menus. *1 av. de St-Cloud, tel. 39–50–42–26. Reservations advised. MC, V. Closed Sun. lunch, Mon.*

Shopping

Versailles is perhaps the region's most commercial town. After visiting the château, you might want to stop in at **Aux Colonnes,** a highly rated *confiserie* (confectioner's shop) with an astounding array of chocolates and candies (14 rue Hoche; closed Mon.). A huge choice of cheeses—including one of France's widest selection of goat cheeses—can be smelled, admired, and eventually purchased from **Eugène Le Gall** (15 rue Ducis; closed Sun. afternoon and Mon.). Stuffed olives, dried fruits, and more exotic spices and teas than you thought existed can be had from **Arts Populaires** (15 rue des Deux-Portes; closed Sun. afternoon and Mon. morning). Anyone in the mood for antiques hunting should visit Versailles's passage de la Geôle, site of a good thrice-weekly flea market (10 rue Rameau; open Fri.–Sun. 9–7).

Thoiry

Hourly trains from Versailles's mainline Chantiers station take 25 minutes to Montfort-l'Amaury. From here, take a taxi to reach Thoiry, 10 km (6 mi) away.

Owner Vicomte de La Panouse and his American wife, Annabelle, have restored the **château of Thoiry** and its park to their former glory, opening both to the public. The result is a splendid combination of history, culture, and adventure. The superbly furnished 16th-century château has archive and gastronomy museums and overlooks a safari park, where you can picnic with the bears and lions.

The château was built in 1564. Its handsome Renaissance facade is set off by gardens landscaped in typically disciplined French fashion by Le Nôtre. The discipline has unexpected justification: The château is positioned to be directly in line with the sun as it rises in the east at the summer solstice (June 21) and as it sets in the west at the winter solstice (December 21). To heighten the effect, the central part of the château appears to be a transparent arch of light, thanks to its huge glass doors and windows.

The viscountess is a keen gardener and enjoys experimenting in the less formal **Jardin à l'Anglaise** (English Garden), which also contains a cricket ground, and in her late-flowering **Autumn Garden.** Visitors are allowed to wander at leisure, although few dare stray from the official footpath through the **animal reserve!** Note that those parts of the reserve containing the wilder beasts—deer, zebra, camels, hippos, bears, elephants, and lions—can be visited only by car.

The reserve hit the headlines when the first-ever ligrons—a cross between a lion and a tiger—were born here a few years ago. These new-look beasts (bigger than either a lion or a tiger) are now into their second generation and can be seen from the safety of a raised footbridge in the **Tiger Park.** Nearby, as emus and flamingos stalk in search of tidbits, there is a **children's play area** that features an Enchanted Burrow to wriggle through and a huge netted Cobweb to bounce around in.

Highlights of the château's interior include the **Grand Staircase,** with its 18th-century Gobelin tapestries, and the **Green and White Salons,** with their old, painted harpsichord, portraits, and tapestries. There is an authentic, homey, faintly faded charm to these rooms, especially when log fires crackle in their enormous hearths on damp afternoons.

The distinguished history of the Panouse family—a Comte César even fought in the American Revolutionary War—is retraced in the **Archive Museum,** where papal bulls, Napoleonic letters, and Chopin manuscripts (discovered in the attic in 1973) mingle with missives from Thomas Jefferson and Benjamin Franklin.

The château pantries house a **Museum of Gastronomy,** whose tempting display of *pièces montées*—virtuoso banquet showpieces—re-create the designs of ace 19th-century chef Antoine Carême. Early recipe books, engravings, and old copper pots are also displayed. *Admission: château 26 frs.; animal reserve plus gardens 78 frs. adults, 64 frs. children. Open weekdays*

10–6, weekends 10–6:30, 10–5 winter. Château interior closed mornings.

Lodging and Dining
Under 250 frs.

Etoile. Handily situated for visitors to Thoiry château and safari park, the Etoile offers a special low-priced tourist menu, as well as a wide choice of à la carte dishes. A garden and a ping-pong table add to the hotel's homey appeal. *38 rue de la Porte St-Martin, tel. 34–87–40–21. 12 rooms with bath. AE, DC, MC, V. Closed Mon. and Jan.*

Rambouillet

Trains leave hourly from Versailles–Chantiers and take 35 minutes to reach Rambouillet. Tourist office: Place de la Libération, tel. 34–83–21–21.

Surrounded by a huge forest, **Rambouillet** is a haughty town once favored by kings and dukes. Today it is home to affluent gentry and, occasionally, President Mitterrand. When the president is not entertaining visiting bigwigs, the château and its grounds are open to all.

Make for the **Hôtel de Ville** (town hall), an imposing Classical building in red brick, and wander around the corner to the **château.** Most of the buildings you see date from the early 18th century, but the muscular **Tour François I** (Tower of François I), named after the king who breathed his last therein in 1547, once belonged to a 14th-century castle. *Admission: grounds free; château (guided tours only), 25 frs. Open Wed.–Mon. 10–noon and 2–6; closed Tues.*

If your appetite for château interiors has already been satisfied, you'll be able to forego Rambouillet's without feeling too guilty. The château's exterior charms are hidden as you arrive, but if you head to the left of the buildings—and if nature is in bloom—you are in for two pleasant surprises. A splendid lake, with several enticing islands, spreads out for you, beckoning you to explore the extensive grounds beyond. Before you do, however, turn around: There, behind you, across trim flower beds awash with color, is the facade of the château—a sight of unsuspected serenity, asymmetry, and, as more flowers spill from its balconies, cheerful informality.

If time allows, veer left around the lake and carry on until you reach two interesting groups of outbuildings: the **Laiterie de la Reine** (built as a dairy for Marie Antoinette), with its small temple, grotto, and shell-lined **Chaumière des Coquillages** (Shell Pavilion); and the **Bergerie Nationale** (National Sheepfold), site of a more serious agricultural venture; the merino sheep reared here, prized for the quality and yield of their wool, are descendants of beasts imported from Spain by Louis XVI in 1786. *Admission: 15 frs. (Laiterie), 12 frs. (Bergerie). Laiterie open Jan.–Apr., Thurs.–Mon. 10–noon and 2–6; May–Nov., 10–noon and 2–4; closed Dec. and Tues., Wed. The Bergerie can be visited Fri.–Sun. 2:30–5:30 (Sun. only in winter).*

Dining
Under 125 frs.

La Poste. You can bank on traditional, unpretentious cooking at this former coaching inn right in the center of town. Until recently, it could seat only 36 diners, but a new room was opened upstairs, doubling the capacity. Service is good, as is the selection of fixed-price menus, weekends included. *101 rue du Gén-*

éral-de-Gaulle, tel. 34–83–03–01. Reservations advised. Jacket and tie required. AE, MC, V.

Maintenon

Trains run from Versailles–Chantiers, via Rambouillet, to Maintenon every 1½ hours; journey time is 40 minutes from Versailles and about 15 minutes from Rambouillet.

The Renaissance **château of Maintenon** once belonged to Louis XIV's mistress, Madame de Maintenon, whose private apartments form the hub of the short interior visit. A round brick tower (14th century) and a 12th-century keep are all that remain of the buildings on the site. The formal gardens ease their way back from the château to the unlikely ivy-covered arches of a ruined aqueduct, one of the Sun King's most outrageous projects. His aim: to provide Versailles (some 50 kilometers, or 30 miles away) with water from the River Eure. In 1684, 30,000 men were signed up to construct a three-tiered, 3-mile aqueduct as part of the project. Many died of fever in the process, and construction was called off in 1688. *Admission: 26 frs. Open Easter–Oct., Wed.–Sat. 2:30–6, Sun. 10–noon and 2:30–6; Nov.–Easter, Sat. 2:30–6, Sun. 10–noon and 2:30–6, closed weekdays.*

Chartres

Trains run from Versailles to Chartres, via Maintenon, every 1½ hours. Journey time is 55 minutes from Versailles and 18 minutes from Maintenon, which is 19 km (12 mi) away. Chartres tourist office: Place de la Cathédrale, tel. 37–21–50–00.

As you snake along the River Eure from Maintenon, try to spot the noble, soaring spires of **Chartres Cathedral** before you reach the town; they form one of the most famous sights in western Europe.

Worship on the site of the cathedral goes back to before the Gallo-Roman period; the crypt contains a well that was the focus of Druid ceremonies. In the late-9th century, Charles II (known as the Bald) presented Chartres with what was believed to be the tunic of the Virgin, a precious relic that attracted hordes of pilgrims. Chartres swiftly became a prime destination for the Christian faithful; pilgrims trek here from Paris to this day.

Today's cathedral dates primarily from the 12th and 13th centuries, having been built after the previous, 11th-century edifice burned down in 1194. A well-chronicled outburst of religious fervor followed the discovery that the Virgin's relic had miraculously survived unsinged, and reconstruction moved ahead at a breathtaking pace: Just 25 years were needed for the cathedral to rise from the rubble.

The lower half of the facade is a survivor of the earlier Romanesque church: This can be seen most clearly in the use of round arches rather than the pointed Gothic type. The main door (**Portail Royal**) is richly sculpted with scenes from the Life of Christ, and the flanking towers are also Romanesque. The taller of the two spires (380 feet versus 350 feet) dates from the start of the 16th century; its fanciful Flamboyant intricacy contrasts sharply with the stumpy solemnity of its Romanesque counterpart across the way.

The **rose window** above the main portal dates from the 13th century, and the three windows below it contain some of the finest examples of 12th-century stained glass in France.

The interior is somber, and your eyes will need time to adjust to the murk. The reward: the gemlike richness of the stained glass, with the famous deep "Chartres blue" predominating. The oldest window is arguably the most beautiful: **Notre Dame de la Belle Verrière,** in the south choir. *Pl. Notre-Dame.*

Just behind the cathedral stands the **Musée des Beaux-Arts** (Museum of Fine Arts), a handsome 18th-century building that used to be the Bishop's Palace. Its varied collection includes Renaissance enamels; a portrait of the Dutch scholar Erasmus by German painter Hans Holbein; tapestries; armor; and some fine, mainly French paintings dating from the 17th to the 19th century. There is also an entire room devoted to the forceful 20th-century land- and snowscapes of Maurice de Vlaminck, who lived in the region. *29 rue Cloître Notre-Dame. Admission: 10 frs. adults, 5 frs. students and senior citizens. Open Wed.–Mon. 10–11:45 and 2–5:45; closed Tues.*

The **museum gardens** overlook the old streets that tumble down to the River Eure. Take rue Chantault down to the river, cross over, and head right along rue de la Tannerie (which, in turn, becomes rue de la Foulerie) as far as rue du Pont St-Hilaire. From here, there is a picturesque view of the roofs of old Chartres nestling beneath the cathedral. Cross over the bridge and head up to the **Eglise St-Pierre,** whose magnificent windows date to the early 14th century. There is more stained glass (17th century) to admire at the **Eglise St-Aignan** nearby, just off rue St-Pierre. Wander at will among the steep, narrow surrounding streets, using the spires of the cathedral as your guiding landmark.

Lodging
Under 250 frs.
★

Poste. Prices in downtown Chartres tend to reflect the town's appeal to tourists and affluent commuters working in Paris. The Hôtel de la Poste, five minutes' walk from both station and cathedral, is a notable exception. Rooms are comfortable if a little small, and the restaurant offers two set menus under 100 francs. *3 rue du Gal-Koenig, 28000, tel. 37–21–04–27. 60 rooms, some with bath or shower. Facilities: restaurant. AE, DC, MC, V.*

Dining
Under 125 frs.

Le Buisson Ardent. A wood-beamed, second-floor restaurant, Le Buisson Ardent offers filling, low-priced menus, imaginative nouvelle food, and a view of Chartres cathedral (it's just down the street opposite the south portal). Service is gratifyingly attentive. Try the fruity Gamay de Touraine, an ideal wine for lunchtime. *10 rue au Lait, tel. 16/37–34–04–66. Reservations accepted. AE, DC, V. Closed Sun. and Tues. evening, Wed.*

Shopping

Stained glass being the key to Chartres's fame, enthusiasts may want to visit the **Galerie du Vitrail** (17 rue Cloître Notre-Dame), which specializes in the noble art. Pieces range from small plaques to entire windows, and there are books on the subject in English and French.

Tour 2: Fontainebleau and Environs

Elegant Fontainebleau, home to the finest château in the Ile-de-France after Versailles, is the home base for a short tour that also takes in pretty Moret-sur-Loing (a short train ride away), Barbizon, and Vaux-le-Vicomte.

From Paris

By Train Trains to Fontainebleau leave Paris (Gare de Lyon) every 1¼ hours. The trip takes about 40 minutes.

By Car The 64-kilometer (40-mile) drive from Paris along A6 and N7 takes about an hour.

Fontainebleau

Tourist office: 31 pl. Napoléon-Bonaparte, behind the château, tel. 64–22–25–68.

Numbers in the margin correspond to points of interest on the Fontainebleau map.

Like Chambord in the Loire Valley or Compiègne to the north, **Fontainebleau** earned royal esteem as a hunting base. Indeed, a hunting lodge once stood on the site of the current château, along with a chapel built in 1169 and consecrated during exile by Thomas à Becket (1118–70), the now-canonized archbishop of Canterbury. Today's château was begun under the flamboyant Renaissance prince François I, the French contemporary of England's Henry VIII.

Although Sun King Louis XIV's architectural energies were concentrated on Versailles, he nonetheless commissioned architect François Mansart to design new pavilions at Fontainebleau and had Le Nôtre replant the gardens. But it was Napoleon who spent lavishly to make a Versailles, as it were, out of Fontainebleau.

When you come to Fontainebleau by train, you'll actually disembark in neighboring Avon, then catch the half-hourly bus at the station for the 1½-mile trip to the château. The bus will let you off near its gardens.

Walk past the parterres to the left of the Etang des Carpes
1 (Carp Pond) and turn left into an alley that leads to the **Cour
Ovale**—a courtyard shaped like a flattened oval with, at the
2 straight end, the domed **Porte du Baptistère**, an imposing
gateway designed by court architect Francesco Primaticcio (1504–70). The gateway's name commemorates the fact that the Dauphin—the male heir to the throne, later to become Louis XIII—was baptized under its arch in 1606. Opposite is the
3 **Cour des Offices**, a large, severe square built at the same time
as the place des Vosges in Paris (1609).

The hedge-lined alley continues to the Jardin de Diane (Garden of Diana), with its peacocks and statue of the hunting goddess surrounded by mournful hounds. Cross this informal garden
4 and enter the palace's most majestic courtyard, the **Cour du
5 Cheval-Blanc**, dominated by the famous **horseshoe staircase**
built by Jean Androuet du Cerceau in the early 17th century. Climb the steps to the château entrance.

Cour des Offices, **3**
Cour du Cheval-Blanc, **4**
Cour Ovale, **1**
Galerie de Diane, **8**
Horseshoe staircase, **5**
Napoleon's apartments, **6**
Porte du Baptistère, **2**
Salle de Bal, **9**
Throne room/Queen's Bedroom, **7**

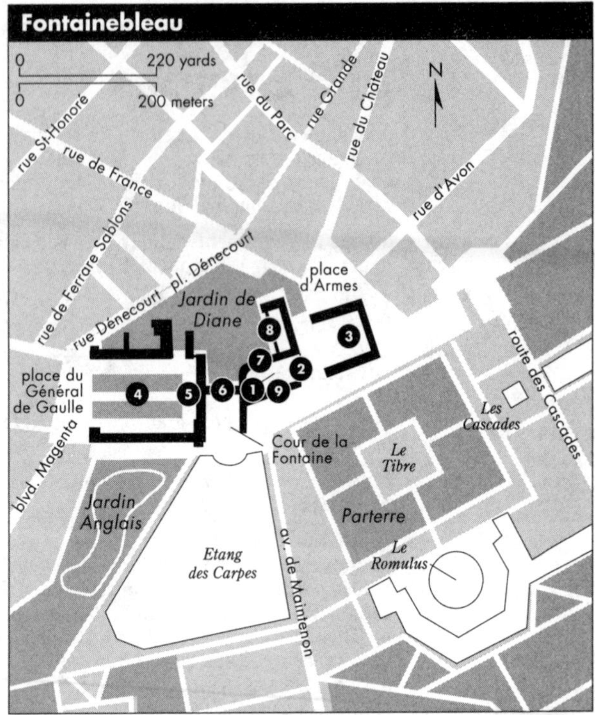

6 In **Napoleon's apartments** on the second floor, you can ogle a lock of his hair, his Légion d'Honneur medal, his imperial uniform, the hat he wore on his return from Elba in 1815, and the bed in which he used to sleep.

7 There is also a **throne room**—one of Napoleon's foibles, since the kings themselves were content with the one at Versailles—and the **Queen's Bedroom,** known as the Room of the Six
8 Maries. The seemingly endless **Galerie de Diane,** built during the reign of Henri IV (1589–1610), was used as a library. Other salons boast 17th-century tapestries, marble reliefs by Jacquet de Grenoble, and paintings and frescoes by the versatile Italian Francesco Primaticcio (besides being court architect to François I, he was also a top-rate painter, sculptor, and interior designer).

Jewel of the interior, though, is the ceremonial ballroom—the
9 **Salle de Bal**—nearly 100 feet long, with wood paneling and a gleaming parquet floor whose pattern matches that of the ceiling.

If time permits, complete your visit with a stroll around the leafy **Jardin Anglais** (English Garden) to the right of the Etang des Carpes. *Admission: 25 frs. adults, 12 frs. children. Open Wed.–Mon. 9:30–12:30 and 2–5; closed Tues. Gardens open 9–dusk; admission free.*

Lodging
Under 250 frs.

Hôtel de Londres. The balconies of this tranquil, family-style hotel overlook the château and the Cour des Adieux, where Napoleon bid his troops a fond farewell; the austere 19th-century facade is preserved by government order. Inside, the decor is dominated by Louis XV–style gilt furniture. *1 pl. Général-de-Gaulle, 77300, tel. 64–22–20–21. 22 rooms, most with bath. Facilities: restaurant, bar, outdoor dining. AE, DC, MC, V. Closed Dec. 20–Jan. 31.*

Ile de France. This old-fashioned mansion has been extensively renovated, and there are some modern rooms in the garden annexes, well away from the bustle of one of Fontainebleau's main thoroughfares. The restaurant—you can eat outdoors in summer—offers four set menus for under 100 francs, with a surprising mix of French and Chinese-style dishes. *128 rue de France, 77300, tel. 64–22–21–17. 25 rooms, most with bath or shower. Facilities: restaurant. AE, DC, MC, V.*

Dining
Under 125 frs.

Le Dauphin. The homey, rustic Dauphin is located near the Hôtel de Ville (Town Hall), just a five-minute walk from the château. Prices are reasonable, and specialties include snails, *confit de canard* (conserve of duck), and a variety of homemade desserts. *24 rue Grande, tel. 64–22–27–04. Reservations advised, especially on Sun. Closed Tues. dinner, Wed., Feb., and Sept. 1–8.*

Barbizon

Buses travel the 10 km (6 mi) to Barbizon from Fontainebleau 3 times daily. The trip takes 30 minutes. Tourist offices: 41 rue Grande, tel. 60–66–41–87.

Barbizon, on the western edge of the 42,000-acre Forest of Fontainebleau, retains the atmosphere of a small village, despite the intrusion of expensive art galleries, tacky souvenir shops, and weekending Parisians.

Its fame derives from the colony of landscape painters—Camille Corot, Jean-François Millet, and Théodore Rousseau, among others—who lived here from the 1830s on. Their innovative commitment to working outdoors paved the way for the Impressionists, as did their willingness to accept nature on its own terms rather than use it as an idealized base for carefully structured compositions.

After working hours, the Barbizon painters repaired to the **Auberge du Père Ganne.** The inn is still standing—it's now a museum—and you can soak up the arty mood here or at the houses of Millet and Rousseau farther along the single main street (Grande-Rue). *Musée-Auberge du Père Ganne, 92 Grande-Rue. Admission free. Open Easter–Oct., Wed.–Mon. 10–5:30, closed Tues.; Nov.–Easter, Wed., Fri., and Sun. only, 10–5:30.*

Lodging
Under 250 frs.

Auberge des Alouettes. This delightful, family-run 19th-century inn is set on two acres of grounds (which the better rooms overlook). The interior has been redecorated in '30s style, but many rooms still have their original oak beams. The popular restaurant (reservations are essential), with its large open terrace, features light cuisine (no heavy sauces) and barbecued beef in summer. *4 rue Antoine-Barye, 77630, tel. 60–66–41–98. 23 rooms with bath. Jacket and tie required in restaurant. Facilities: tennis. AE, DC, MC, V. Moderate.*

Dining
Under 125 frs.

Le Relais. Delicious country-French specialties are served here in large portions, and there is a good choice of fixed-price menus. The restaurant is spacious, with a big open fire, and paintings and hunting trophies decorate the walls. The owner is rightly proud of the large terrace where diners can eat in the shade of lime and chestnut trees. *2 av. Charles-de-Gaulle, tel. 60–66–40–28. Reservations required weekends. Jacket and tie advised. MC, V. Closed Tues., Wed., second half Aug., most of Jan. Moderate.*

Vaux-le-Vicomte

To reach Vaux-le-Vicomte you will need a bike or taxi for the trip from Melun station, 8 km (5 mi) away. Trains make the 13-minute trip from Fontainebleau to Melun every 1½ hours.

The château of **Vaux-le-Vicomte** was built between 1656 and 1661 for court financier Nicolas Fouquet. The construction process was monstrous even for those days: Entire villages were razed, 18,000 workmen called in, and ace designers Louis Le Vau, Charles Le Brun, and esteemed landscape architect André Le Nôtre hired to prove that Fouquet's sense of aesthetics matched his business acumen. Unfortunately, his housewarming party was too lavish for the likings of star guest Louis XIV. King Louis threw a fit of jealousy, hurled the tactless Fouquet in jail, and promptly began building Versailles to prove just who was boss.

The high-roofed château, partially surrounded by a moat, is set well back from the roadside behind iron railings topped with sculpted heads. A cobbled avenue winds its way up to the entrance. Stone steps lead to the vestibule, which, given the noble scale of the exterior, seems small. There is no grand staircase, either—the stairs are tucked away in the left wing and lead to a set of rooms that could almost be described as pokey.

Painter Charles Le Brun's lush interior decoration partly compensates: His major achievement is the ceiling of the **Chambre du Roi** (Royal Bedchamber), depicting Time Bearing Truth Heavenwards, framed by stucco work by sculptors François Girardon and Legendre. Along the frieze you can make out small squirrels—known as *fouquets* in local dialect.

But the château's most impressive room is the **Grand Salon** on the ground floor. With its unusual oval form and 16 caryatid pillars symbolizing the months and seasons, it possesses harmony and style despite its unfinished state (the cupola remains depressingly blank).

An astute exhibition, complete with life-size wax figures, explains the rise and fall of Nicolas Fouquet. The version is, not surprisingly, favorable to the château's founder—accused by Louis XIV and subsequent historians of megalomania and shady financial dealings, but apparently condemned on little evidence by a court eager to please the jealous, irascible monarch. The exhibition continues in the basement, whose narrow corridors and stone vaults have, in parts, a suitably dungeonlike feel. The **kitchens** are also down here, a more cheerful sight, with their gleaming copperware and old menus.

Although the château's interior lacks majesty, there is no mistaking the grandeur of Le Nôtre's **gardens,** which have been carefully restored. Visit the **Musée des Equipages** (Carriage Museum) in the stables and inspect a host of lovingly restored carriages and coaches. *Admission: 42 frs. adults, 34 frs. students and senior citizens (gardens only, 20 frs.). Open daily*

10–6, 10–5 in winter; closed Dec.–Jan. (except Christmas–New Year's). Candlelight visits May–Sept., Sat. 8:30–11 PM; admission: 50 frs.

To the right of the château entrance is an imposing barn that has been transformed into a self-serve **cafeteria.** Here, beneath the ancient rafters of a stout wood-beam roof, you can enjoy coffee, cheap pitchers of wine, and good steaks. Insist on *bien cuit* (well done) if you don't want your meat too bloodily rare.

Moret-sur-Loing

Trains make the 8-minute journey from Fontainebleau, 10 km (6 mi) away, every 1¼ hours.

Close to the confluence of the Rivers Seine and Yonne, the charming village of **Moret-sur-Loing** was immortalized by Impressionist painter Alfred Sisley, who lived here for 20 years at 19 rue Montmartre (not open to the public), around the corner from the church of Notre-Dame. Close by, across the river, is the thatched **house-museum** of another illustrious former inhabitant: truculent World War I leader Georges Clemenceau (1841–1929), known as the Tiger. His taste for Oriental art and his friendship with Impressionist Claude Monet are evoked. *Follow signs to the Grange Batelière. Guided tours only: 35 frs. Open Easter–Oct., weekends 2:30–6; closed Nov.–Easter.*

The best view of Moret is from the far banks of the Loing. Cross the narrow bridge (one of the oldest in France and invariably clogged with traffic) to gaze back at the walls, rooftops, and church tower. A good time to visit Moret is on a summer evening when locals stage *son-et-lumière* (sound-and-light) pageants illustrating the village's history.

Tour 3: Excursions from Paris

This is not so much a tour as a series of excursions from Paris. A train trip to Vernon brings you within striking distance of Claude Monet's house and garden at Giverny, although a bike or taxi ride is required to complete the trip. Suburban trains whisk you to the superb châteaus of Maisons-Laffitte and St-Germain-en-Laye, and a combination of RER and bus brings you to the Malmaison home of Josephine and Napoleon. The RER also takes you east to the doors of Euro Disneyland.

Vernon and Giverny

Trains leave Paris (Gare St-Lazare) every 2 hours for the 50-minute ride to Vernon. You will need a bike or a taxi to complete the journey to Giverny. Vernon tourist office: Rue Carnot, tel. 32–51–39–60.

The village of **Giverny**, a place of pilgrimage for art lovers, was where Claude Monet lived for the second half of his life and died in 1926 at age 86. After decades of neglect, his pretty pink-washed house, with its green shutters, studios, and, above all, the wonderful garden with its famous lily pond, have been lovingly restored.

Monet was brought up in Normandy, in northwestern France, and, like many of the Impressionists, was stimulated by the soft light of the Seine Valley. After several years at Argenteuil, just north of Paris, he moved downriver to Giverny in 1883, along with his two sons, mistress Alice Hoschedé (whom he later married), and her own six children. By 1890, a prospering Monet was able to buy the house outright; three years later, he purchased another plot of land across the road to continue his gardening experiments, diverting the little River Epte to make a pond.

Soon the much-loved and oft-painted waterlilies and Japanese bridges were special features of Monet's garden. They readily conjure up the image of the grizzle-bearded brushman dabbing cheerfully at his canvas—pioneering a breakup of form that was to have a major impact on 20th-century art.

Provided you steer clear of the tourist battalions that tramp through Giverny on weekends and hot summer days, Monet's house—which you enter from the modest country lane that masquerades as Giverny's major thoroughfare—feels refreshingly like a family home after the formal French châteaus. The rooms have been restored to Monet's original designs: the kitchen with its blue tiles, the buttercup-yellow dining room, Monet's bedroom containing his bed and desk. Walls are lined with the Japanese prints Monet avidly collected, as well as with reproductions of his works.

The exuberant **garden** breaks totally with French tradition, with flowers spilling over the paths. You can reach the enchanting **water garden,** with its lilies, bridges, mighty willow, and rhododendrons, via an attractively decorated tunnel. *84 rue Claude-Monet. Admission: 30 frs. (garden only, 16 frs.). Open Apr.–Oct., Tues.–Sun. 10–noon and 2–6 (garden open 10–6); closed Mon. and Nov.–Mar.*

Most people visit **Vernon** simply because it's en route to Giverny. However, there are several reasons to stop by when you're in the area, quite apart from its pleasant riverside location on the Seine. There are medieval timber-frame houses; the best of these has been chosen by local authorities to house the Tourist Office, on rue Carnot. Alongside is the arresting rose-windowed facade of **Notre-Dame** church. The facade, like the high nave, dates from the 15th century, but the rounded Romanesque arches in the choir attest to the building's 12th-century origins. The church is a fine sight when viewed from behind—Claude Monet painted it several times from across the Seine.

A few minor Monet canvases, along with other late-19th-century paintings, can be admired in the **Musée Poulain** (Town Museum) at the other end of rue Carnot. This rambling old mansion is seldom crowded, and the helpful curators are happy to explain local history to visitors who are intrigued by the town's English-sounding name. *Rue du Pont. Admission: 9 frs. (free Wed.). Open Tues.–Sun. 2–5:30; closed Mon.*

Maisons-Laffitte

Two trains per hour make the 21-minute trip from Paris (Gare St-Lazare) to Maisons-Laffitte.

The early Baroque **château of Maisons**, constructed by architect François Mansart from 1642 to 1651, is one of the least known châteaus in the Ile-de-France. This was not always the case: Sun King Louis XIV came to the housewarming party, and Louis XV (1715–74), Louis XVI (Marie Antoinette's husband, 1774–93), the 18th-century writer Voltaire, and Napoleon all stayed here. The interior clearly met their exacting standards, thanks to the well-proportioned entrance vestibule with its rich sculpture; the winding **Escalier d'Honneur,** a majestic staircase adorned with paintings and statues; and the royal apartments, above, with their parquet floors and elegant wall paneling. *Admission: 24 frs. adults, 13 frs. students and senior citizens. Open daily 9–5.*

Rueil-Malmaison

Take the RER-A from Paris to La Défense, then switch to bus 158-A.

Rueil-Malmaison is today a faceless, if pleasant, western suburb of Paris, but the memory of star-crossed lovers Napoleon and Josephine still haunts its Malmaison château on avenue Napoléon-Bonaparte.

Built in 1622, **La Malmaison** was bought by the future Empress Josephine in 1799 as a love nest for Napoleon and herself (they had married three years earlier). After the childless Josephine was divorced by the heir-hungry emperor in 1809, she retired to La Malmaison and died here on May 29, 1814.

The château has 24 rooms furnished with exquisite tables, chairs, and sofas of the Napoleonic period; of special note are the library, game room, and dining room. The walls are adorned with works by artists of the day, such as Jacques-Louis David, Pierre-Paul Prud'hon, and Baron Gérard. Take time to admire the clothes and hats belonging to Napoleon and Josephine, particularly the display of the empress's gowns. Their carriage can be seen in one of the garden pavilions, and another pavilion contains a unique collection of snuffboxes donated by Prince George of Greece. The gardens themselves are delightful, especially the regimented rows of spring tulips. *15 av. du Château. Admission: 26 frs. adults, 16 frs. students, senior citizens, and on Sun. Open Wed.–Mon. 10–noon and 1:30–5; closed Tues.*

The **Bois Préau,** which stands close to La Malmaison, is a smaller mansion dating back to the 17th century. It was acquired by Josephine in 1810, after her divorce, but subsequently reconstructed in the 1850s. Today its 10 rooms, complete with furniture and objects from the Empire period, are devoted mainly to souvenirs of Napoleon's exile on the island of St. Helena. *Entrance from av. de l'Impératrice. Admission: 23 frs. Open Wed.–Mon. 10–noon and 1:30–5; closed Tues.*

St-Germain-en-Laye

The RER-A makes the 30-minute journey from central Paris every 15 minutes. Tourist office: 38 rue au Pain, tel. 34–51–05–12.

The elegant town of **St-Germain-en-Laye**, perched on a hill above the Seine and encircled by forest, has lost little of its original cachet, despite the invasion of wealthy Parisians who commute to work on the RER. Next to the train station, at the heart of St-Germain, is the town's chief attraction—its stone-and-brick **château.**

Most of the defensive-looking château, with its dry moat and intimidating circular towers, dates from the 16th and 17th centuries. Yet a royal palace has existed here since the early 12th century, when Louis VI—known as *Le Gros* (The Fat)—exploited St-Germain's defensive potential in his bid to pacify the Ile-de-France. A hundred years later, Louis IX (St-Louis) added the elegant **Sainte-Chapelle,** which is the château's oldest remaining section. The figures on the tympanum (the inset triangular area over the main door) are believed to be the first known representations of French royalty, portraying Louis with his mother, Blanche de Castille, and other members of his family.

Charles V (1364–80) built a powerful defensive keep in the mid-14th century, but from the 1540s, François I and his successors transformed St-Germain into a palace of more domestic, and less warlike, vocation. Until 1682—when the court moved to Versailles—it remained the country's foremost royal residence outside Paris. Since 1867, the château has housed a major **Musée des Antiquités Nationales** (Museum of Ancient History), holding a trove of artifacts, figurines, brooches, and weapons from the Stone Age through to the 8th century. *Admission: 15 frs. (8 frs. on Sun.). Open Wed.–Mon. 9–5:15; closed Tues.*

Another place to visit in St-Germain is the tranquil **Musée du Prieuré** (Priory Museum), some 600 yards from the château (follow rue au Pain from the church). This museum is devoted to the work of the artist Maurice Denis (1870–1943) and his fellow Nabis—painters opposed to the naturalism of their 19th-century Impressionist contemporaries. Denis found the calm of the former Jesuit priory suited to his spiritual themes, which he expressed in stained glass, ceramics, and mosaics, as well as oils. *2 bis rue Maurice-Denis. Admission: 20 frs. adults, 10 frs. children and senior citizens. Open Wed.–Fri. 10–5:30, weekends 10–6:30; closed Mon. and Tues.*

Dining
Under 200 frs.

La Petite Auberge. The specialty here is farmhouse-style cooking from the Aveyron region of southwest France. Fresh meat is cooked over an open fire throughout the year, and cheerful red wine (Chinon, from the Loire Valley) is drawn straight from the barrel. Game is served in season. *119-bis rue L. Desnoyer, tel. 34–51–03–99. Reservations accepted. Jacket required. MC, V. Closed Tues. dinner, Wed., part of Jan., and mid-July–mid-Aug.*

Under 125 frs.

La Feuillantine. Friendly service and an imaginative, well-priced set menu have rapidly made this restaurant a success with locals as well as tourists. Gizzard salad, salmon with endive, and pullet with herbs are among the specialties. *10 rue des Louviers, tel. 34–51–04–24. Reservations advised. MC, V. Closed Christmas.*

Euro Disneyland

The RER-A makes the 40-minute journey from central Paris 3 times an hour (more often at peak periods) to Marne-la-Vallée-Chessy. Tourist office: Festival Disney, tel. 60–43–33–33.

Now you can get a dose of American pop culture in between visits to the Louvre and the Left Bank. On April 12, 1992, the Euro Disney complex opened in Marne-la-Vallée, just 32 kilometers (20 miles) east of Paris. The complex is divided into several areas, including Euro Disneyland, the pay-as-you-enter theme park that is the main reason for coming here. Occupying 136 acres, Euro Disneyland is less than half a mile across and ringed by a railroad with whistling steam engines. Smack in the middle of the park is the soaring Sleeping Beauty Castle, which is surrounded by a plaza from which you can enter the four "lands" of Disney: Frontierland, Adventureland, Fantasyland, and Discoveryland. In addition, Main Street U.S.A. connects the castle to Euro Disneyland's entrance, under the pointed pink domes of the Disneyland Hotel. *Admission to Euro Disneyland: 225 frs. adults, 150 frs. children under 12; 2-day Passport, 425 frs. adults, 285 frs. children; 3-day Passport, 565 frs. adults, 375 frs. children. Open Apr.–mid-June, weekdays 9–7, weekends 9–midnight; mid-June–Aug., daily, 9–midnight; Sept.–Oct., weekdays 9–7, weekends 9–9; Nov.–Mar., weekdays 10–6, weekends 10–7.*

There are, in fact, six hotels in the 4,800-acre Euro Disney complex, all part of a section called the Euro Disney Resort, just outside the theme park. The resort also comprises parking lots, a train station, and the Festival Disney entertainment center, with restaurants, a theater, dance clubs, shops, a post office, and a tourist office. Cheaper accommodations—log cabins and campsites—are available at Camp Davy Crockett, but it is located farther away from the theme park.

Future plans at Euro Disney call for a second theme park, a convention center, a new golf course, a new campsite, more hotels, and film studios.

Dining Euro Disneyland is peppered with places to eat, ranging from snack bars and fast-food joints to full-service restaurants—all with a distinguishing theme. In addition, all Disney hotels have restaurants that are open to the public. But since these are outside the theme park, it is not recommended that you waste time traveling to them for lunch. Be aware that only the hotel restaurants serve alcoholic beverages; Disney's no-alcohol standard is maintained throughout the theme park. Eateries serve nonstop as long as the park is open. *Reservations advised for sit-down restaurants. AE, DC, MC, V at sit-down restaurants; no credit cards at others. 70 frs.–100 frs. at counter-service restaurants; 150 frs.–250 frs. at sit-down restaurants.*

4 The Loire Valley

Châteaus and Citadels

Few areas of Europe possess the magic of the Loire Valley, renowned for its constellation of enticing châteaus spanning an architectural range between medieval fortress (Langeais, Angers) and Renaissance pleasure palace (Chenonceau, Cheverny). The whole area exudes a sedate charm barely dispelled by the hordes of midsummer tourists. Woods, vineyards, and venerable towns of white stone line the softly lit valley christened the Garden of France, once the playground of kings and princes. Although trains speed between the valley's major towns, it takes a chugalong country bus—or a bike—to track down the more secluded sites, such as Ussé with its fairy-tale turrets, or Chambord, lurking in the heart of a forbidding forest infested with timid deer and ferocious boar.

The Loire Valley was hotly disputed by France and England during the Middle Ages, belonging to England (under the Anjou Plantagenet family) between 1154 and 1216 and again during the Hundred Years' War (1337–1453). It took the example of Joan of Arc, called the "Maid of Orléans" after the scene of her most rousing military successes, for the French finally to expel the English.

In addition to its abundant châteaus, the Loire Valley offers visitors a host of opportunities for outdoor recreation. Horseback riding, fishing, canoeing, and swimming facilities abound. In the summer, tourists and natives alike flock to concerts, music festivals, fairs, and the celebrated *son-et-lumière* (sound-and-light) extravaganzas held on the grounds of many châteaus. Simply wandering the banks of the placid river and exploring her gentle hills, dotted with woods and castles, provides a welcome break for tired city dwellers.

Essential Information

Lodging Even before the age of the train, the Loire Valley drew visitors from far and wide, eager to see the great châteaus and sample the sweetness of rural life. Hundreds of hotels of all kinds have sprung up to accommodate today's travelers. Three smaller groups, the **Château-Accueil, La Castellerie,** and **Bienvenue au Château,** offer pleasant accommodations for a limited number of guests. Illustrated lists of these groups are available from French Government Tourist Offices abroad, as well as in France. At the lower end of the price scale are the **Logis de France** hotels. These small, traditional hotels are located in towns and villages throughout the region and usually offer terrific value for the money. The Logis de France handbook is available free from French Tourist Offices abroad and for 65 francs in French bookshops, or it can be ordered directly from Logis de France Services (83 av. d'Italie, Paris 75013, tel. 45–84–83–84). The Loire Valley is one of the country's most popular vacation destinations, so always make reservations well in advance.

Dining The region known as the "garden of France" produces a cornucopia of farm-fresh products—from beef, poultry, game, and fish to butter, cream, wine, fruit, and vegetables. It sends its early crops to the best Parisian tables, yet keeps more than enough for local use. Loire wines can be extremely good—and varied. Among the best: Savennières and Cheverny (dry white); Coteaux du Layon (sweet white); Cabernet d'Anjou (rosé); Bourgueil and Chinon (red); and Saumur and Vouvray (sparkling white).

Shopping The region's extraspecial produce is Loire wine. It's not a practical buy for tourists—except for instant consumption—but if wine-tasting tours of vineyards inspire you, enterprising wine makers will arrange shipment to the United States; think in terms of hundreds rather than dozens. Try the **Maison du Vin** in Angers (pl. Président-Kennedy, next to the tourist office), and **Maison des Vins de Touraine** in Tours (19 sq. Prosper Mérimée). Loire food specialties include barley sugar *(sucre d'orge)* and prunes stuffed with marzipan *(pruneux fourrés);* both are widely available at food shops throughout the valley.

Bicycling This is excellent country for biking—not too hilly, not too flat. Bikes can be rented at most train stations and at dozens of other outlets (try **Au Col de Cygne,** 46 bis rue du Dr-Fournier, Tours; and **Leprovost,** 13 rue Carnot, Azay-le-Rideau). **Loisirs Accueil** offices in Blois and Orléans offer organized trips; these often include luggage transportation and camp or youth hostel accommodations (8 rue d'Escures, Orléans, tel. 38–62–04–88; or 11 pl. du Château, Blois, tel. 54–78–55–50).

Hiking Scenic footpaths abound. Long-distance walking paths *(sentiers de grande randonnée)* pass through the Loire Valley and are marked on Michelin maps with broken lines and route numbers. Tourist offices will supply sketch maps of interesting paths in their area.

The Arts and Nightlife The Loire Valley's favorite form of cultural entertainment is the *son-et-lumière* (sound-and-light show), a dramatic spectacle that takes place after dark on summer evenings on the grounds of major châteaus. Programs sometimes take the form of historical pageants, with huge casts of people in period costume and caparisoned horses, the whole floodlit and backed by music and commentary, a few with earphone translations in English. They may also take the form of spectacular lighting and sound shows, with spoken commentary and dialogue but no visible figures, as at **Chenonceau.** The most magnificent *son-et-lumière* occurs at **Le Lude,** on the River Loir (not the Loire), 48 kilometers (29 miles) northeast of Saumur and 50 kilometers (30 miles) northwest of Tours. (It's an 85-minute bus ride from Le Mans.) Here more than 200 performers present a pageant chronicling the history of the château and region from the Hundred Years' War on. The spectacle is enhanced by fountains and fireworks.

Festivals For four weeks, usually beginning in early July, the **Festival d'Anjou** enlivens the area around Angers with music, theater, and dance. In July, the château grounds at **Loches** are the setting for a series of open-air concerts. And in the medieval **Grange du Meslay** near Tours, top-class international musicians gather in late June and July for the **Fêtes Musicales de Touraine.**

Highlights for First-time Visitors

Amboise, Tour 2
Blois, Tour 2
Château de Chambord, Tour 2
Château d'Ussé, Tour 1
Château de Chenonceau, Tour 1
Chinon, Tour 1
Saumur, Tour 1
The gardens at Villandry, Tour 1

Tour 1: The Western Loire Valley—Angers to Tours

Angers, with its sturdy castle and apocalypse tapestry, is the starting point for this tour. The main rail line from Angers east to Tours goes through Saumur—whence you can take a bus to the medieval abbey at Fontevraud—and through Langeais, a good base for bike excursions to Ussé and Villandry. Several rail excursions are possible from Tours, the largest city on the Loire—to the châteaus of Azay, Chinon, Chenonceau, Loches, or the captivating old towns of Bourges and Vendôme.

From Paris *By Train* TGV bullet trains to Angers leave Paris (Gare Montparnasse) 12 times daily. The trip takes 1½ hours.

By Car The 295-kilometer (185-mile) drive from Paris along A11 takes 3 hours.

Angers

Tourist office: Place Kennedy, opposite the castle, tel. 41–88–69–93.

The former capital of the Anjou region, **Angers** lies on the banks of the River Maine, just north of the Loire, about 105 kilometers (65 miles) west of Tours and 215 kilometers (135 miles) from Orléans. In addition to a towering medieval fortress filled with extraordinary tapestries, the town has a fine Gothic cathedral, a choice of art galleries, and a network of pleasant, traffic-free shopping streets. Well served by public transportation, Angers is the starting point for numerous bus, riverboat, hiking, biking, horseback, and ballooning excursions.

The town's principal sights all lie within a compact square formed by the three main boulevards and the River Maine. The castle is a five-minute walk from the station. Take rue de la Gare, turn left onto rue Hoche, then next right at place de l'Académie: The castle greets you across boulevard de Gaulle. Before you go in, stop at the **Maison du Vin** (5 bis pl. Kennedy), the organization that represents Anjou's wine producers. It can provide lots of leaflets about wines, suggestions about which vineyards to visit, and even a free sample or two.

The **Château,** a massive shale-and-limestone castle-fortress dating from the 13th century, glowers over the town from behind its turreted moats. The moats are now laid out as gardens, overrun with deer and blooming flowers. As you explore the grounds, note the startling contrast between the thick, defensive walls and the formal garden, with its delicate, white tufastone chapel, erected in the 16th century. For a sweeping view of the city and surrounding countryside, climb one of the castle towers.

A new gallery within the castle grounds houses the great **Tapestry of the Apocalypse,** completed in 1390. Measuring 16 feet high and 120 yards long, it shows a series of 70 horrifying and humorous scenes from the Book of Revelation. In one, mountains of fire fall from heaven while boats capsize and men struggle in the water; another shows an intriguing, seven-headed beast. *Pl. Kennedy. Admission: 31 frs. adults, 17 frs. students and senior citizens, 6 frs. children. Open daily, mid-Sept.–May 9–12:30 and 2–6; June–mid-Sept. 9–7.*

Just east of the château is the **Cathédrale St-Maurice** (pl. Freppel), a 12th- and 13th-century Gothic cathedral noted for its curious Romanesque facade and original stained-glass windows; you'll need binoculars to appreciate both fully. A few steps north, practically in the cathedral's shadow, lies Angers's large covered food market, **Les Halles** (pl. Mondain; open Tues.–Sat. 9–7; Sun. 9–1). Treat it as a gourmet museum, or stop in for an exotic lunch. A modern shopping mall sits right above it.

Just south of the cathedral, in a house that once sheltered Cesare Borgia and Mary, Queen of Scots, is the **Musée des Beaux-Arts** picture gallery. Among the museum's attractions is an impressive collection of Old Masters from the 17th and 18th centuries, including paintings by Raphael, Watteau, Fragonard, and Boucher. *10 rue du Musée. Admission: 5 frs. Open mid-Sept.–May, Tues.–Sun. 10–noon and 2–6; June–mid-Sept., daily 9:30–12:30 and 2–7.*

Around the corner, in the refurbished Eglise Toussaint, is the **Musée David d'Angers,** housing a collection of dramatic sculptures by Jean-Pierre David (1788–1859), the city's favorite son. *33 rue Toussaint. Admission: 10 frs. adults, children free. Open mid-Sept.–May, Tues.–Sun. 10–noon and 2–6; June–mid-Sept., daily 9:30–12:30 and 2–7.*

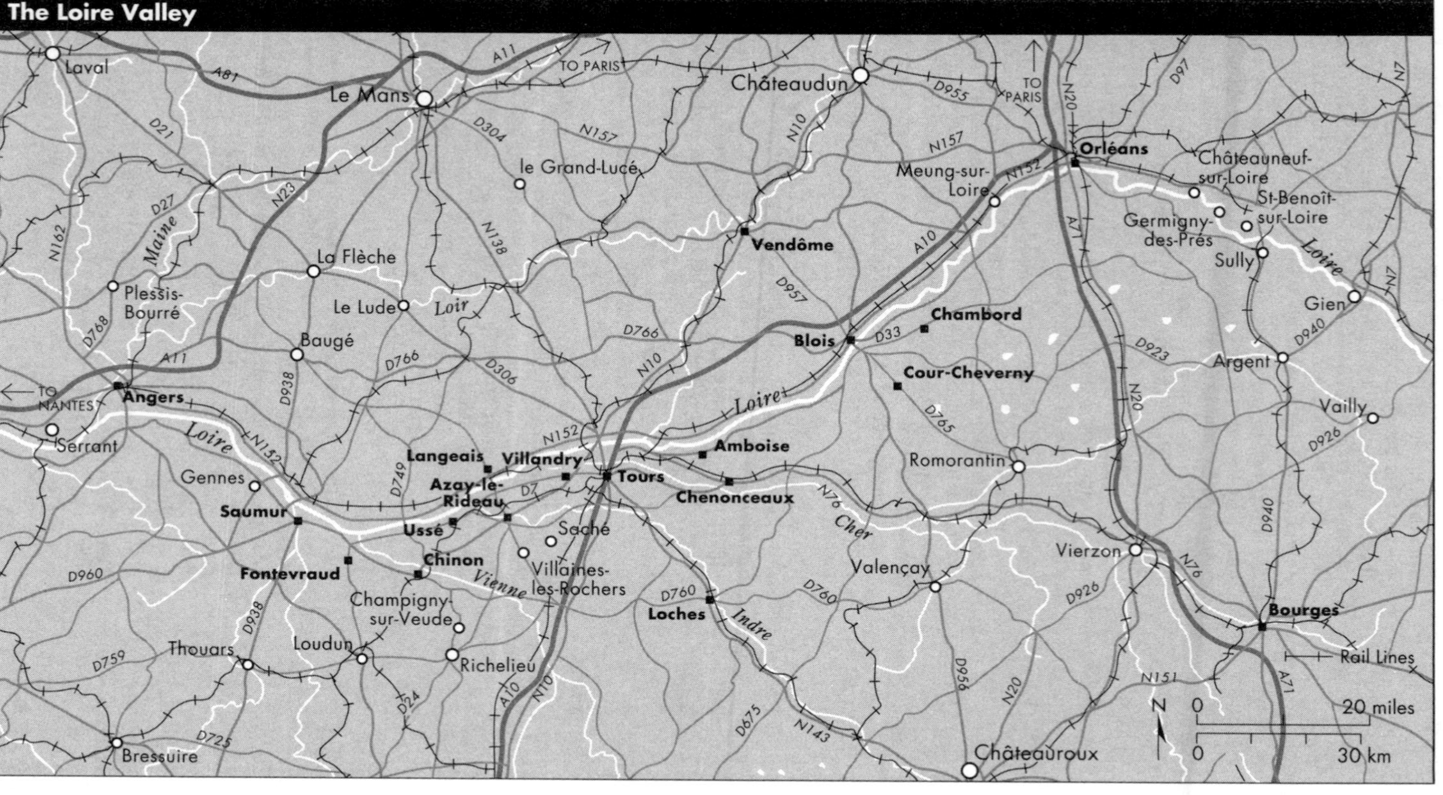
The Loire Valley
Laval
Le Mans
Châteaudun
Orléans
Châteauneuf-sur-Loire
St-Benoît-sur-Loire
Germigny-des-Prés
Sully
Gien
Argent
Vailly
Meung-sur-Loire
le Grand-Lucé
Vendôme
Blois
Chambord
Cour-Cheverny
Romorantin
Vierzon
Bourges
La Flèche
Le Lude
Baugé
Plessis-Bourré
Angers
Serrant
Gennes
Saumur
Fontevraud
Langeais
Villandry
Azay-le-Rideau
Ussé
Chinon
Tours
Amboise
Chenonceaux
Saché
Villaines-les-Rochers
Champigny-sur-Veude
Loudun
Richelieu
Thouars
Bressuire
Loches
Valençay
Châteauroux
Loire
Loir
Maine
Cher
Indre
Vienne
TO PARIS
TO NANTES
A11
A81
A10
A71
N20
N7
N10
N23
N138
N152
N157
N162
N76
N143
N151
D21
D27
D97
D768
D938
D766
D306
D304
D955
D957
D33
D765
D923
D940
D926
D956
D760
D675
D725
D759
D960
D749
D7
D24
Rail Lines
N
0
20 miles
0
30 km

Lodging and Dining
Under 350 frs.

Anjou. In business since 1850, Anjou has recently been redecorated in a vaguely 18th-century style. Each room is individually styled, though all are spacious and feature double-glazed windows. The restaurant, Salamandre, is an affordable place to sample local fare (try the duck with turnips) and has a fine wine list. *1 blvd. Foch, 49100, tel. 41–88–24–82. 53 rooms with bath. Facilities: restaurant. AE, DC, MC, V.*

Dining
Under 125 frs.
★

Toussaint. Chef Michel Bignon dishes up nouvelle versions of traditional local dishes, plus fine wines and tasty desserts, in a cozy, 400-year-old dining room. Loire River fish with *beurre blanc* (white butter sauce) is a particular specialty. *7 pl. Kennedy, tel. 41–87–46–20. Reservations required. Jacket required. AE, MC, V. Closed Sun. evening, Mon., part of Feb.*

Under 75 frs.

Jean Foucher. If you're visiting Angers's food market, Les Halles, during the summer, look out for the fish stall of Jean Foucher, who will prepare you a platter of *fruits de mer* (shellfish) to go. The prices are very reasonable. *Les Halles, pl. Mondain, tel. 41–86–06–32. No credit cards. Closed Sun. and Mon.*

Maître Kanter. This chain restaurant, located at the covered market, provides simple food and swift service. It's a convenient refueling spot, and the firm's own beer is available on tap. Try the steak and french fries, or the sauerkraut with sausages and ham. *Les Halles, tel. 41–87–93–30. No reservations. V.*

Saumur

Trains make the 25-minute trip from Angers every 2½ hours. Saumur tourist office: Place Bilange, tel. 41–51–03–06.

Saumur is known for a flourishing mushroom industry, which produces 100,000 tons per year. The same cool tunnels in which the mushrooms grow also provide an ideal storage place for the local *vins mousseux* (sparkling wines).

Next door to the tourist office, at the **Maison du Vin de Saumur,** local wine producers show off their products and provide information about visits to local vineyards. *25 rue Beaurepaire. Open summer, Mon.–Sat. 9–12:30 and 2–6:30. Closed Mon. in winter.*

Towering high above town and river is Saumur's elegant, white 14th-century **château,** a 10-minute walk from the tourist office. The route takes you through the pretty, old town and place St-Pierre, with its lively Saturday market.

If the château looks familiar, it's probably because you've seen it in countless reproductions from the famous *Très Riches Heures* (*Book of Hours*) painted for the duc de Berri in 1416, now in the Musée Condé at Château de Chantilly (*see* Tour 3 in Chapter 7). Inside it's bright and cheerful, with fairy-tale gateway and plentiful potted flowers. The **Musée des Arts Décoratifs** and the **Musée du Cheval** (Horse Museum) are housed here. The former offers a fine collection of medieval objets d'art and 18th- and 19th-century porcelain, and the latter covers the history of the horse, with exhibits ranging from saddles to skeletons. Both are included in the guided tour. Afterward, climb the **Tour de Guet** (Watchtower) for an impressive view. *Admission: 28 frs. adults, 18 frs. children, students, and* *senior citizens. Open June–Sept., daily 9–7; Oct.–May, Mon.–Sat. 9:15–12:30 and 2–6.*

Fontevraud

Three buses daily make the 16-km (10-mi) trip from Saumur to Fontevraud.

Fontevraud is famous for its large abbey, which played a key role in the medieval history of France and England. Founded in 1099, the abbey offered separate churches and living quarters for nuns, monks, lepers, "repentant" female sinners, and the sick. Between 1115 and the French Revolution in 1789, 39 different abbesses—among them a granddaughter of William the Conqueror—directed its operations. The abbey church contains the tombs of Henry II of England; his wife, Eleanor of Aquitaine; and their son, Richard Coeur de Lion—Richard the Lionhearted. Though their bones were scattered during the Revolution, the effigies remain. Napoleon turned the abbey church into a prison, and so it remained until 1963, when historic restoration—still under way—began.

The great 12th-century abbey church is one of the most eclectic structures in France. The medieval section is built of simple stone and topped with a series of domes; the chapter-house, with its collection of 16th-century religious wall paintings (prominent abbesses served as models), is unmistakably Renaissance; and the paving stones bear the salamander emblems of François I. Next to the long refectory, you will find the unusual octagonal kitchen, its tall spire, the **Tour d'Evrault,** serving as one of the abbey's 20 faceted stone chimneys. *Admission: 25 frs. adults, 14 frs. senior citizens, 6 frs. children. Open June–mid-Sept., daily 9–7; mid-Sept.–Oct. 9:30–12:30 and 2–6; Nov.–mid-Apr. 9:30–12:30 and 2–5:30; mid-Apr.–May 9:30–12:30 and 2–6:30.*

Lodging and Dining
Under 350 frs.

Domaine de Mestré. A secluded working farm and home of the charming Dauge family, this ancient, rectangular enclave of creamy stone buildings has cozy guest rooms and a cheerful dining room for breakfast and good, simple family-style meals. *Fontevraud-l'Abbaye, 49590, tel. 41–51–75–87. 10 rooms. Lunch and dinner (110 frs.) by reservation.*

Langeais

Five trains daily make the 25-minute trip from Saumur. Three run daily from Angers (journey time 50–70 minutes). Langeais tourist office: 2 pl. de la Mairie, tel. 47–96–58–22.

Towering over tiny **Langeais** (pop. 3,960) is the uncompromising bulk of **Langeais Castle.** Chunky turrets and a drawbridge guard the entrance at the far end of the main street. But the intimidation mellows inside. A tiered garden sweeps away behind the castle, and the tour of the interior makes it abundantly clear that past inhabitants lived comfortably: This is one of the few Loire châteaus to retain medieval furniture and decoration, perhaps because it was one of the last fortified castles to be built (in the 1460s) prior to the return of peace and the onset of Renaissance prosperity. The upper castle walls are pierced with holes from which boiling oil was never, apparently, poured. *Admission: 30 frs. adults, 23 frs. senior citizens, 17* *frs. children. Open mid-Mar.–Oct., daily 9–6:30; Nov.–mid-Mar., Tues.–Sun. 9–noon and 2–5.*

Lodging and Dining
Under 250 frs.

Duchesse Anne. There is something of a dearth of accommodation in tiny Langeais, but this friendly, unpretentious old hotel is fine for a short stay, despite its smallish rooms. The restaurant serves up traditional French cuisine with menus at 55, 97, and 170 francs, and there is a large terrace for outdoor meals. *10 rue de Tours, 37130, tel. 47–96–82–03. 9 rooms, some with shower. Facilities: restaurant (closed Wed. and Sun. evening). MC, V. Call for winter closing dates.*

Ussé

Inaccessible by public transportation, Ussé can be reached from Langeais, 14 km (8½ mi) away by bicycle. Rentals are available at the Langeais train station.

Ussé is the archetypal fairy-tale château, with its astonishing array of delicate towers and turrets. Tourist literature describes it as the original Sleeping Beauty castle—the inspiration for Charles Perrault's beloved 17th-century story. Though parts of the castle date from the 1400s, most of it was completed two centuries later. It is a flamboyant mix of Gothic and Renaissance styles—stylish and romantic, built for fun, not fighting. Its history supports its playful image: It suffered no bloodbaths—no political conquests or conflicts. And a tablet in the chapel indicates that even the French Revolution passed it by.

After admiring the château's luxurious furnishings and 19th-century French fashion exhibit, climb the spiral stairway to the tower to view the River Indre through the battlements. Here you will also find a waxwork effigy of Sleeping Beauty herself. Before you leave, visit the 16th-century chapel in the garden; its door is decorated with pleasingly sinister skull-and-crossbone carvings. *Admission: 59 frs. adults, 19 frs. children. Open daily 9–noon and 2–6.*

Villandry

Inaccessible by public transportation, Villandry can be reached by bike from Langeais, 12 km (7½ mi) away, or from Ussé, 21 km (13 mi) away.

The **château of Villandry** is renowned for its extravagant, terraced gardens. Both the château and gardens date from the 16th century, but, over the years, they fell into disrepair. In 1906, Spanish doctor Joachim Carvalla and his wife, American heiress Ann Coleman, bought the property and began a long process of restoration. The gardens were replanted according to a rigorous, geometrical design, with zigzagging hedges enclosing flower beds, vegetable plots, and gravel walks. The result is an aristocratic 16th-century *jardin à la française* (French garden). Below an avenue of 1,500 precisely pruned lime trees lies an ornamental lake, filled with swans: Not a ripple is out of place. The aromatic and medicinal garden, with plots neatly labeled in three languages, is especially appealing.

The château itself has a remarkable gilded ceiling—imported from Toledo, Spain—and a collection of fine Spanish paintings. However, the garden is unquestionably the main attraction, and since it is usually open during the two-hour French lunch break, you can have it to yourself for a good part of the afternoon. *Admission: château and gardens, 35 frs. adults, 31 frs. students and senior citizens; gardens only, 23 frs. adults, 20 frs. students and senior citizens. Château open mid-Feb.–mid-Nov., daily 9–6; garden is open all year, daily 9–sunset (or 8, whichever is earlier).*

Lodging and Dining
Under 350 frs.

Cheval Rouge. This is a fine, old-fashioned hotel whose restaurant is popular with the locals. It boasts an excellent Loire wine list and surprisingly good food, considering its touristy location right next to the château. Good bets are the terrine of foie gras, the calf sweetbreads, and the wood-fired grills. The 20 guest rooms are tidy, and all have bath or shower. *37510 Villandry, tel. 47–50–02–07. Reservations advised. MC, V. Closed Sun. evening and Mon., except in summer, and Jan.–Feb.*

Tours

Six daily trains make the 20-minute trip to Tours from Langeais. The Angers–Tours express runs every 2½ hours and takes an hour. Tourist office: Place du Maréchal-Leclerc, opposite the train station, tel. 47–05–58–08.

Numbers in the margin correspond to points of interest on the Tours map.

Tours, the largest town along the Loire Valley, makes a fine base for excursions to numerous châteaus. Though high-rise blocks pepper the city outskirts, the historic center has been lovingly restored and preserved.

Start your tour at place du Maréchal-Leclerc, usually called the
1 **place de la Gare.** Here you'll find the fine Belle Epoque train station, with its cast-iron curlicues, the bus station, and the tourist office. Many of the most convenient hotels are situated here or just around the corner.

The city plan is fairly simple. Turn left from place du Maréchal-Leclerc, down boulevard Heurteloup, to reach place Jean-Jaurès; then turn right onto rue Nationale. This street holds many of the city's major shops, and if you continue along it for just over a half mile, you'll reach the River Loire. Turn right a couple of blocks before the river, and you'll soon reach the cathedral, the château, and the Musée des Beaux-Arts. If you turn left, you'll come to the place Plumereau and a quaint pedestrian precinct.

What is left of the château is of minor interest, but, within it,
2 you will find the **Historial de la Touraine**—a group of more than 150 waxwork models representing historic figures, such as St. Martin and Joan of Arc, whose deeds helped shape this region over 15 centuries. There's also a small aquarium. *Quai d'Orléans. Admission: wax museum, 29 frs. adults, 14 frs. students and children; aquarium, 22 frs. adults, 14 frs. students and children. Open daily 9–11:30 and 2–6:30. Closed mornings Jan.–mid-Mar.*

3 The **Cathédrale St-Gatien,** built between 1239 and 1484, reveals a mixture of architectural styles. Its majestic two-towered facade was cleaned and restored in 1990. The stained glass, in particular, deserves binoculars, and you will want to visit the

Cathédrale St-Gatien, **3**
Historial de la Touraine, **2**
Musée des Beaux-Arts, **4**
Musée des Vins/ Musée du Compagnonnage, **5**
Musée du Gemmail, **6**
Place de la Gare, **1**

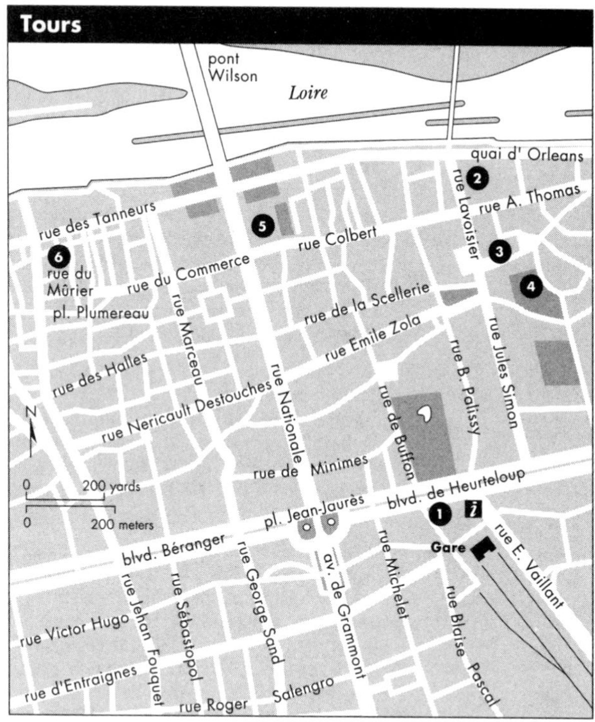

little children's tomb with its kneeling angels, built in memory of the two children of Charles VIII and Anne of Brittany. *Rue Lavoisier. Open daily 9–noon and 2–6.*

4 Next door, in what was once the archbishop's palace, is the **Musée des Beaux-Arts** (Fine Arts Museum). It houses an eclectic selection of treasures: works by Rubens, Rembrandt, Boucher, Degas, and sculptor Alexander Calder. There's even Fritz the Elephant, stuffed in 1902. *18 pl. François Sieard. Admission: 30 frs. adults; students, children, and senior citizens free. Open Wed.–Mon. 9–12:45 and 2–6; closed Tues.*

5 Two small museums stand at the river end of rue Nationale: the **Musée des Vins** (Wine Museum) and the **Musée du Compagnonnage** (Guild Museum). You may wish to see the latter, at least. *Compagnonnage* is a sort of apprenticeship-trade-union system, and here you see the masterpieces of the candidates for guild membership: virtuoso craftwork, some of it eccentric (an Eiffel Tower made of slate, for instance, or a varnished-noodle château). These stand as evidence of the devotion to craftsmanship that is still an important feature of French life. Both the guild and the wine museum are set in and around the cloisters of an old church—a pleasant setting, and you are free to visit them at your own pace. *Musée des Vins, 16 rue Nationale. Admission: 10 frs. adults, 5 frs. students. Open Wed.–Mon. 9–11:30 and 2–4:30; closed Tues. Musée du Compagnonnage, 8 rue Nationale. Admission: 20 frs. adults, 10 frs. students and children. Open Wed.–Mon. 9–11:30 and 2–4:30; closed Tues.*

From rue Nationale, narrow rue du Commerce leads you to the oldest and most attractive part of Tours, the area around **place Plumereau.** It's a great area for strolling, largely traffic-free, and full of little squares, open-air cafés, and pricey antiques shops. From place Plumereau, head one block along rue Briconnet, and take the first left onto rue du Mûrier. The
6 **Musée du Gemmail,** halfway down on the right in the imposing 19th-century Hôtel Raimbault, houses an unusual collection of three-dimensional colored-glass window panels. Depicting patterns, figures, and even portraits, the panels are both beautiful and intriguing, since most of the gemlike fragments of glass come from broken bottles. *7 rue du Mûrier. Admission: 25 frs. adults, 15 frs. students and children. Open Mar. 1–Sept. 15, Tues.–Sun. 10–11:30 and 2–6.*

Lodging
Under 250 frs.

Hotel du Cygne. There's a simple, old-fashioned charm to this quiet, centrally located hotel. Window boxes overflow with flowers, a fire is often crackling in the lounge, and the owners are helpful and kind. These touches and the reasonable price are enough to compensate for a slightly tattered decor. *6 rue du Cygne, 37000, tel. 47–66–66–41. 20 rooms, some with bath. AE, MC, V.*

Lodging and Dining
Under 250 frs.

Moderne. This old mansion in a quiet street near the Palais des Congrès provides good value in a traditional atmosphere that pleases both tourists and businessmen. Room sizes vary, with the largest topping 300 francs. French cooking can be sampled via set menus priced at 80 and 100 francs. *1 rue Victor-Laloux, 37000, tel. 47–05–32–81. 23 rooms, some with bath. Facilities: restaurant (closed lunch, Sun. evening, and Jan.). AE, MC, V.*

Dining
Under 200 frs.

Les Tuffeaux. Though it has recently changed hands, this restaurant retains its place as one of Tours's best. Chef Gildas Marsollier has been winning customers with his delicious fennel-perfumed salmon and remarkable desserts. Gentle lighting and a warm, understated decor provide a soothing background. *19 rue Lavoisier, tel. 47–47–19–89. Reservations advised. MC, V. Closed Sun., Mon. lunch, and part of July.*

Shopping

In addition to its wines, **Maison des Vins de Touraine** in Tours (19 sq. Prosper Mérimée; closed Sun. and Mon. mornings) offers a wide selection of local products and crafts, including ceramics.

Azay-le-Rideau

The 6 daily trains from Tours take 33 minutes to Azay.

Nestled in a sylvan setting on the banks of the River Indre, the white, 16th-century château of **Azay-le-Rideau** was—like Ussé—a Renaissance pleasure palace rather than a serious fortress.

A financial scandal forced its builder, royal financier Gilles Berthelot, to flee France shortly after its construction in 1520. For centuries, it passed from one private owner to another and was finally bought by the state in 1905. Though the interior offers an interesting blend of furniture and artwork, you may wish to spend most of your time exploring the enchanting private park. During the summer, visitors can enjoy delightful *son-et-lumière* shows on the castle grounds. *Admission: 25 frs. adults, 14 frs. students, 6 frs. children. Open daily, July–Aug.*

9–7; Apr.–June and Sept. 9:30–6; Oct.–Mar. 10–12:30 and 2–5.

Lodging and Dining
Under 350 frs.

Grand Monarque. Just yards from the château, this mildly eccentric, popular hotel draws hundreds of visitors. It has played host to celebrities, royals, and tourists alike. Guest rooms are tastefully, individually decorated. The restaurant has a pleasant, shaded dining garden where good, traditional food is served with an extensive selection of Loire wines. *3 pl. de la République, 37190, tel. 47–45–40–08. 28 rooms with bath. AE, DC, MC, V. Facilities: restaurant (closed mid-Nov.–mid-Mar.).*

Chinon

Five trains a day arrive in Chinon from Tours, 65 minutes away, and 7 trains from Azay. Bicycles can be rented at Chinon station.

Located in the fertile countryside between the Loire and the Vienne rivers, **Chinon** is the birthplace of author François Rabelais (1494–1553). Today it is dominated by the towering ruins of its medieval **fortress-castle,** perched high above the River Vienne. Though the main tourist office is in the town below, in summer a special annex operates from the castle grounds. Both the village and the château stand among steep, cobbled slopes, so wear comfortable walking shoes.

The vast fortress dates from the time of Henry II of England, who died here in 1189 and was buried at Fontevraud. Two centuries later, the castle witnessed an important historic moment: Joan of Arc's recognition of the disguised dauphin, later Charles VII. In the early 17th century, the castle was partially dismantled by its then-owner, Cardinal Richelieu (1585–1642), who used many of its stones to build a new palace 21 kilometers (13 miles) away. (That palace no longer exists.)

At Chinon, all but the royal chambers—which house a small museum—is open to the elements. For a fine view of the region, climb the **Coudray Tower,** where, in 1302, leading members of the crusading Knights Templar were imprisoned before being taken to Paris, tried, and burned at the stake. The **Tour de l'Horloge,** whose bell has been sounding the hours since 1399, houses a small **Joan of Arc museum.** *Admission: 21 frs. adults, 15 frs. students. Open daily, July–mid-Sept. 9–7; mid-Sept.–Oct. and mid-Mar.–June 9–6; Nov.–Feb. 9–noon and 2–5. Closed Tues. Dec. and Jan.*

Follow the signposted steps down into the old town, or drive your car to the River Vienne pathway. **Place de l'Hôtel**—the main square—is the best place to begin exploring. Stop by the tourist office and pick up a plan of the town's fine medieval streets and alleys. While you are there, visit **Le Musée du Vin** (Wine Museum) in the vaulted cellars. This is a fascinating exhibit, full of information on vine growing and wine- and barrel-making. An English commentary is available, and the admission charge entitles you to a sample of the local product. *Admission: 20 frs. Open May–Sept., Fri.–Wed. 10–noon and 2–6.*

Lodging and Dining
Under 250 frs.

Hostellerie Gargantua. In the 15th century, the building housing the Gargantua was a bailiff's palace. Today this small, quiet hotel offers an array of rooms in various sizes and styles. Simple good taste prevails throughout. The restaurant, with its charming old dining room and outside tables for summer, serves delicious local specialties. *73 rue Haute-St-Maurice, 37500, tel. 47–93–04–71. 9 rooms, most with bath. AE, DC, MC, V. Closed mid-Nov.–Mar.*

Dining
Under 200 frs.
★ **Au Plaisir Gourmand.** Gourmets from all around come here to celebrate, and lucky tourists will get a table only if they make reservations (the dining room in this charming old house seats 30). Chef Jean-Claude Rigollet makes inventive use of fresh, local produce. For a real treat, try the Vienne River trout. Au Plaisir Gourmand gives top quality without frills and features exceptional local wines, and if you order carefully, you can dine well for less than you'd expect. *Quai Charles VII, tel. 47–93–20–48. Reservations required. Jacket and tie required. MC, V. Closed Sun. dinner, Mon., last 3 weeks in Feb., and second half of Nov.*

Under 75 frs. **Jeanne de France.** Local families and swarms of young people patronize this lively little pizzeria in the town's main square. But it's a far cry from an American pizza joint: Here you can also buy jugfuls of local wine, steaks, and french fries. *12 pl. Général-de-Gaulle, tel. 47–93–20–12. Reservations accepted. Closed Jan., and Wed. Oct.–May.*

Chenonceaux

The 4 daily trains from Tours take 40 minutes to Chenonceaux.

You could happily spend a day in the village of **Chenonceaux**, visiting its château (whose name is for some reason spelled without the final *x*). From long-ago historic figures, such as Diane de Poitiers, Catherine de Médicis, and Mary, Queen of Scots, to a host of modern travel writers, many have called it the "most exciting" and the "most romantic" of all the Loire châteaus. You are free to wander about (there are attendants to answer questions). For most of the year, the château is open—unlike many others—all day. The only drawback is its popularity: If you want to avoid a roomful of English schoolchildren, take a stroll on the grounds and come back when they stop for lunch.

More pleasure palace than fortress, Chenonceau was built in 1520 by Thomas Bohier, a wealthy tax collector. When he went bankrupt, it passed to François I. Later, Henri II gave it to his mistress, Diane de Poitiers. After his death, Henri's not-so-understanding widow, Catherine de Médicis, expelled Diane to nearby Chaumont and took back the château. It is to Catherine that we owe the lovely gardens and the handsome three-story extension whose arches span the river.

Before you go inside, pick up an English leaflet at the gate. Then walk around to the right of the main building and admire the peaceful, delicate architecture; the formal garden; and the river gliding under the arches. The romantically inclined may want to rent a rowboat and spend an hour drifting. Inside the château are splendid ceilings, colossal fireplaces, and authentic furnishings. Paintings include works by Rubens, Andrea del Sarto, and Correggio. And as you tour the rooms, be sure to pay your respects to former owner Madame Dupin, whose face is captured in Nattier's charming portrait. Thanks to the great affection Madame Dupin inspired among her proletarian neighbors, the château and its treasures survived the Revolution intact.

A waxworks exhibition (**Musée des Cires**), housed in one of the outbuildings, illustrates four centuries of French history. There are also excellent *son-et-lumière* shows throughout the summer. *Admission: château 35 frs. adults, 25 frs. children; wax museum 10 frs. Open mid-Feb.–Nov., daily 9–5, 6, or 6:30, depending on the season; mid-Nov.–mid-Feb., daily 9–4:30.*

Lodging and Dining
Under 350 frs.

Bon Laboureur. In 1882, it won Henry James's praise as a simple, rustic inn. Since then, the Bon Laboureur has come up in the world: It's elegantly modern, with a few old oak beams surviving, and a pretty garden where you can eat in summer. The food—especially the fresh fish and the hotel's own garden vegetables—is commendable. *6 rue du Dr-Bretonneau, 37150, tel. 47–23–90–02. 36 rooms with bath. Facilities: restaurant, garden. AE, DC, MC, V. Closed Dec.–mid-Feb.*

Loches

The 5 daily trains from Tours take 80 minutes to get to Loches, which is 18 km (11 mi) due south of Chenonceaux.

Loches, set on a rocky spur just beside the River Indre, is a walled citadel dominating a small, medieval village, like Chinon. But although Chinon's citadel is a ruined shell, much of Loches's is well preserved and stands as a living part of the town.

As you approach the citadel, the first building you will come across is the church of **St-Ours:** Note its striking roof formed of octagonal pyramids, dating from the 12th century; the doorway sculpted with owls, monkeys, and mythical beasts; and the baptismal font converted from a Roman altar.

The **Logis Royaux**—the château—has a terrace that provides a fine view of the roofs and river below and the towers and swallows' nests above. Inside, keep an eye out for the vicious, two-man crossbow that could pierce an oak door at 200 yards. There are some interesting pictures, too, including a copy of the well-known portrait that shows an extremely disgruntled Charles VII and one of his mistresses, Agnes Sorel, posed as a virtuous Virgin Mary (though semitopless). Her alabaster image decorates her tomb, guarded by angels and lambs. Agnes died in 1450, at age 28, probably the result of poisoning by Charles's son, the future Louis XI. The little chapel was built by Charles VIII for his queen, Anne of Brittany, and is lavishly decorated with sculpted ermine tails, the lady's emblem.

After the tour, amble over to the *donjon,* or tower keep. One 11th-century tower, half-ruined and roofless, is open for individual exploration, though the others require guided supervision. These towers contain dungeons and will delight anyone who revels in prison cells and torture chambers. *Admission: château and keep, 23 frs. adults, 6 frs. students. Open Feb.–mid-Mar., Thurs.–Tues. 9–noon and 2–5; mid-Mar.–June, daily 9–noon and 2–6; July and Aug., daily 9–6; Sept. and Oct., Thurs.–Tues. 9–noon and 2–5; closed Dec.–Jan.*

Vendôme

The daily trains from Tours to Vendôme take 1 hour (26 minutes via TGV).

Charming **Vendôme** is not on most tourists' itineraries, but its picturesque appeal amply merits a visit. Vendôme's château is in ruins, but the **gardens** surrounding it offer knockout views of the town center. From place du Château, head down to admire the Flamboyant Gothic abbey church of **La Trinité,** with its unusual 12th-century clock tower and fine stained glass. Take time to stroll through the narrow streets of this enchanting little town.

Lodging and Dining
Under 150 frs.

Auberge de la Madeleine. This venerable hotel lies on a small square by the Madeleine church, just around the corner from the banks of the Loire and a delightful five-minute walk from the town center. The pleasant setting attracts discerning international visitors throughout the summer—as does the splendid 75-franc menu in the hotel restaurant, Le Jardin du Loir. *6 pl. de la Madeleine, 41100, tel. 54–77–20–79. 9 rooms with bath or shower. Facilities: restaurant (closed Wed.). MC, V. Closed part of Feb.*

Dining
Under 125 frs.

Paris. Don't be put off by the drab postwar exterior of this restaurant close to the train station: It serves generous portions of seasonal produce, with veal and chicken fricassee, as well as grilled boar in autumn, among the specialties. Menus at 90 and 128 francs (also at 200 and 240 francs) represent excellent value. *1 rue Darreau, tel. 54–77–02–71. Reservations recommended. MC, V. Closed Sun. evening, Mon., last week of Jan., and first 3 weeks Aug.*

Bourges

Four trains daily make the 95-minute journey to Bourges from Tours. Bourges tourist office: 21 rue Victor-Hugo, tel. 48–24–75–33.

The towers of the august 13th-century cathedral of **Bourges** can be seen on the horizon as you draw near. Ironically, though, **Cathédrale St-Etienne** is less easy to spot once you've arrived in the town itself; its asymmetrical facade is hidden away down a narrow street and is impossible to photograph. The central portal is a masterpiece of medieval sculpture: Cherubim, angels, saints, and prophets cluster in the archway above the tympanum, which contains an elaborate representation of *The Last Judgment.*

The interior is unlike that of any other Gothic cathedral. The forest of tall, slender pillars rising from floor to vaults is remarkable enough, but the unique feature is the height of the side aisles flanking the nave: 65 feet, high enough to allow windows to be pierced above the level of the second side aisle. The cathedral contains exquisite stained glass, some dating to its construction. *Off rue du Guichet.*

The center of Bourges, downhill from the cathedral, has been restored to medieval glory. Rue Mirebeau and rue Coursalon, pedestrian-only streets full of timber-framed houses, are charming places for browsing and shopping. At one end of rue Coursalon, over rue Moyenne—Bourges's busy but less-distinguished main street—is the **Palais Jacques-Coeur,** one of the most sumptuous Gothic dwellings in France. Interior highlights are the vaulted chapel, wooden ceilings covered with original paintings, and the dining room with its wall tapestries and massive fireplace. *Rue Jacques-Coeur. Admission: 20 frs. adults. Guided tours daily, Easter–Oct. 9–11 and 2–5; Nov.–Easter 9–11 and 2–4.*

Lodging and Dining
Under 250 frs.

D'Artagnan. This comfortably renovated hotel on spacious place Séraucourt, just 500 yards south of the cathedral, provides sizable rooms with chunky wooden fittings. The dependable French restaurant boasts menus at 100 and 130 francs. *19 pl. Séraucourt, 18000, tel. 48–21–51–51. 74 rooms with bath or shower. Facilities: restaurant, piano bar. AE, MC, V.*

Tour 2: The Eastern Loire Valley—Blois to Orléans

From homely Blois, our first base, you can visit Amboise (by train) and the châteaus of Cheverny and Chambord (by bus), before heading upriver to Orléans, the nearest Loire city to Paris.

From Paris
By Train

Express trains to Blois leave Paris (Gare d'Austerlitz) about every 2 hours. The trip takes between 1½ and 2 hours depending on the train.

By Car

The 169-kilometer (105-mile) drive from Paris along A10 takes 2 hours.

Blois

Tourist office: 3 av. Jean-Laigret, just up from the château, tel. 54–74–06–49.

Perched on a steep hillside overlooking the Loire, about midway between Tours and Orléans, **Blois** is a quaint town, with its white facades, redbrick chimneys, and blue-slate roofs. It is also convenient, thanks to few traffic problems and direct train links not only to Paris but also to all the major towns along the Loire.

Avenue Jean-Laigret leads down from the station to the **château**, ¼ mile away. This splendid structure is among the valley's finest. Your ticket entitles you to a guided tour—in English when there are enough visitors who can't understand French—but you are more than welcome to roam around without a guide if you visit between mid-March and August. Before you enter the building, stand in the courtyard and admire four centuries of architecture. On one side stands the 13th-century hall and tower, the latter offering a stunning view of town and countryside. The Renaissance begins to flower in the Louis XII wing (built between 1498 and 1503), through which you enter, and comes to full bloom in the François I wing (1515–24). The masterpiece here is the openwork spiral staircase, painstakingly restored. The fourth side is the classical Gaston d'Orléans wing (1635–38).

At the bottom of the staircase there's a *diaporama*, an audiovisual display tracing the château's history. Upstairs you'll find a series of enormous rooms with tremendous fireplaces decorated with the gilded porcupine, emblem of Louis XII; the ermine of Anne of Brittany; and, of course, François I's salamander, breathing fire and surrounded by flickering flames. There are intricate ceilings, carved and gilded paneling, and a sad little picture of Mary, Queen of Scots. In the great council room, the duc de Guise was murdered on the orders of Henri III in 1588. Don't miss the **Musée des Beaux-Arts,** the art gallery, in the Louis XII wing. The miscellaneous collection of paintings from the 16th to the 19th century is interesting and often amusing. The château also offers a *son-et-lumière* (sound-and-light) display most summer evenings. *Admission: 30 frs. adults, 15 frs. students and senior citizens. Open mid-Mar.–Oct. 9–6; Nov.–mid-Mar. 9–12 and 2–5.*

Lodging
Under 250 frs.

Anne de Bretagne. A storybook-style French pension decked out with flowers, the Anne de Bretagne offers clean, simple rooms featuring bright bedspreads and curtains. It's a quaint and quiet place in which to spend a night. *31 av. du Dr-Jean-Laigret, 41000, tel. 54–78–05–38. 29 rooms, most with bath. AE, DC, MC, V. Closed one week in Feb. and most of Mar.*

Dining
Under 200 frs.
★

La Bocca d'Or. Original dishes such as succulent pigeons and *chaud-froid* (cooked but served cold) of oysters and asparagus are the order of the day in this stylish, vaulted 14th-century cellar restaurant, presided over by chef Patrice Galland and his genial American wife, Francine. La Bocca d'Or is a small place with a growing reputation, so be sure to reserve a table. *15 rue Haute, tel. 54–78–04–74. AE, MC, V. Closed Sun., Mon. lunch, and late Jan.–early Mar.*

La Péniche. This innovative restaurant is actually a luxurious barge moored along the banks of the Loire. Charming chef Germain Bosque serves up beautifully presented fresh seafood specialties (notably lobsters and oysters). *Promenade du Mail, tel. 57–74–37–23. Reservations advised. AE, DC, MC, V.*

Noë. It's a good sign that locals crowd the pastel dining room at the "Noah," half a mile uptown from the château, and you won't be disappointed. They come along to enjoy inexpensive house specialties such as chicken liver, duckling, and carp in a wine sauce—and to enjoy the set menus, priced at 100 and 150 francs. *10 bis av. de Vendôme, tel. 54–74–22–26. Reservations recommended. MC, V. Closed Sat. lunch, Tues. and Sun. evening, and Mon.*

Amboise

Trains from Blois to Amboise take 20 minutes and run early morning, lunchtime, and twice in the afternoon.

Amboise is a picturesque little town with bustling markets, plentiful hotels and restaurants, and a historic **château.**

A Stone Age fortress stood here, and an early bridge gave the stronghold strategic importance. In AD 503, Clovis, king of the Franks, met with Alaric, king of the Visigoths, on an island (now the site of an excellent campground). In the years that followed, the Normans attacked the fortress repeatedly. The 15th and 16th centuries were Amboise's golden age, and during this time, the château, enlarged and embellished, became a royal palace. Charles VII stayed here, as did the unfortunate Charles VIII, best remembered for banging his head on a low doorway (you will be shown it) and dying as a result. François I, whose long nose appears in so many château paintings, based his court here. In 1560, his son, young François II, settled here with his wife, Mary Stuart (otherwise known as Mary, Queen of Scots), and his mother, Catherine de Médicis. The castle was also the setting for the Amboise Conspiracy, an ill-fated Protestant plot organized against François II; visitors are shown where the corpses of 1,200 conspirators dangled from the castle walls. In later years, a decline set in, and demolition occurred both before and after the Revolution. Today only about a third of the original building remains standing.

The château's interior is partly furnished, though not with the original objects; these vanished when the building was converted to a barracks and then a button factory. The great round tower is reached by a spiral ramp rather than by a staircase; designed for horsemen, it is wide enough to accommodate a small car. You are free to explore the grounds at your own pace, including the little chapel of St-Hubert, with its carvings of the Virgin and Child, Charles VIII, and Anne of Brittany. There are frequent *son-et-lumière* pageants on summer evenings. *Admission: 28 frs. adults. Open daily Jan.–mid-Apr. 9–11:55 and 2–5; mid-Apr.–June 9–11:55 and 2–6:25; July and Aug. 9–6:25.*

Up rue Victor-Hugo, five minutes from the château, is the **Clos Lucé,** a handsome Renaissance manor house. François I lent the house to Leonardo da Vinci, who spent the last four years of his life here, dying in 1519. You can wander from room to room at will. The basement houses an extraordinary exhibition: working models of some of Leonardo's inventions. Though impractical in his own time, perhaps, when technology was limited, they were built recently by engineers from IBM, using the detailed sketches contained in the artist's notebooks. Mechanisms on display include three-speed gearboxes, a military tank, a clockwork car, and even a flying machine. *At the eastern end of rue Victor-Hugo. Admission: 31 frs. adults. Open daily, Feb.–mid-Mar. and mid-Nov.–Dec. 9–6; mid-Mar.–mid-Nov. 9–7. Closed Jan.*

Lodging and Dining
Splurge

Choiseul. Amboise's top hotel also offers a superb restaurant. Choiseul sits on the banks of the Loire, just below the château. Though the guest rooms have recently been modernized, they retain an old and distinctive charm. *36 quai Charles-Guinot, 37400, tel. 47–30–45–45. 35 rooms with bath. Facilities: restaurant, garden, pool. MC, V. Closed Dec.–mid-Jan. 500 frs and up.*

Dining
Under 125 frs.

Auberge du Mail. Set in a cozy, rustic, 14-room inn on the banks of the Loire River, this restaurant offers good food at a fair price (there's a 90-franc set menu) and plenty of atmosphere; try the fish stew with baby eels. *32 Quai Général de Gaulle, tel. 47–57–60–39. Reservations advised. Dress: casual. AE, DC, MC, V. Closed Fri. in winter and 1st 2 wks in Dec.*

Cour-Cheverny

Three daily buses make the 20-minute journey from Blois to Cour-Cheverny (as the château village is officially called).

The main attraction here is the classical **château of Cheverny,** finished in 1634. The interior, with its painted and gilded rooms, splendid furniture, and rich tapestries depicting the labors of Hercules, is one of the grandest in the Loire region. American visitors will admire the bronze of George Washington in the gallery, alongside a document bearing his signature. Together, Louis XVI and Washington founded the Society of the Cincinnati, reserved for officers who fought in the War of Independence. Three of the present owner's ancestors were members of the group.

One of the chief delights of Cheverny is that you can wander freely at your own pace. Unfortunately, the gardens are off-limits, as is the Orangery, where the *Mona Lisa* and other masterpieces were hidden during World War II. But you are free to contemplate the antlers of 2,000 stags in a nearby Trophy Room. Hunting, called "venery" in the leaflets, continues vigorously here, red coats, bugles, and all. In the kennels next-door, dozens of hounds lounge about dreaming of their next kill. Feeding times—*la soupe aux chiens*—are posted on a noticeboard, and visitors are welcome to watch the dogs gulp down their dinner. *Admission: 28 frs. adults, 16 frs. students. Open daily, mid-June–mid-Sept., 9:15–6:30; mid-Sept.–mid-June, 9:30–noon and 2:30–5.*

Chambord

Three buses daily travel to Chambord from Blois, 18 km (11 mi) away.

The largest of the Loire châteaus, the **château of Chambord** is also one of the valley's two most popular touring destinations (Chenonceau being the other). But although everyone thinks Chenonceau is extravagantly beautiful, reactions are mixed as to the qualities of Chambord. Set in the middle of a royal game forest, Chambord is the kind of place William Randolph Hearst would have built if he had had more money: It's been described as "megalomaniac," "an enormous film-set extravaganza," and, in its favor, "the most outstanding experience of the Loire Valley."

A few facts set the tone: The facade is 420 feet long, there are 440 rooms and 365 chimneys, and a wall 32 kilometers (20 miles) long encloses the 13,000-acre forest (you can wander in 3,000 of these, the rest being reserved for wild boar and other game). François I started building in 1519; the job took 12 years and required 1,800 workmen. His original grandiose idea was to divert the Loire to form a moat, but someone (probably his adviser, Leonardo da Vinci) persuaded him to make do with the River Cosson. François used the château only for short stays; yet when he first arrived, 12,000 horses were required to transport his luggage, servants, and hangers-on! Later kings also used Chambord as an occasional retreat, and Sun King Louis XIV had Molière perform here. In the 18th century, Louis XV gave the château to Maréchal de Saxe as a reward for his victory over the English and Dutch at Fontenoy in 1745. When not besporting himself with wine, women, and song, the marshal stood on the roof overseeing the exercises of his own regiment of 1,000 cavalry.

Now, after long neglect—all the original furnishings vanished during the French Revolution—Chambord belongs to the state. Vast rooms are open to visitors (you can wander freely), and have been filled with a variety of exhibits—not all concerned with Chambord, but interesting nonetheless. Children will enjoy repeated trips up and down the enormous **double-helix staircase:** It looks like a single staircase, but an entire regiment could march up one spiral while a second came down the other, and they would never meet. Also be sure to visit the roof terrace, whose forest of towers, turrets, cupolas, gables, and chimneys was described by 19th-century novelist Henry James as "more like the spires of a city than the salient points of a single building."

Chambord also offers a short *son-et-lumière* show, in French, English, and German, successively, on many evenings from mid-May to mid-October. *Admission: 31 frs. adults, 17 frs. students. Open daily, June 15–Sept. 15 9:30–6:45; mid-Sept.–mid-June 9:30–11:45 and 2–4:45 or 5:45, depending on season. Guided tours available Oct.–Apr.*

Lodging
Under 350 frs.

St-Michel. Guests enjoy simple and comfortable living in this revamped country house at the edge of the woods across from Chambord château. A few of the more expensive rooms boast spectacular views, and there's a pleasant café-terrace for contemplative drinks. *103 pl. St-Michel, 41250, tel. 54–20–31–31. 39 rooms, 31 with bath. Facilities: restaurant, tennis, terrace. MC, V. Closed mid-Nov.–Dec. 20.*

Orléans

Ten direct trains make the 40-minute run from Blois to Orléans each day. Orleans tourist office: Place Albert-Ier, tel. 38–53–05–95.

Numbers in the margin correspond to points of interest on the Orléans map.

The strategic position of **Orléans** as a natural bridgehead over the Loire has long made it the target of hostile confrontations and invasions. Julius Caesar slaughtered its inhabitants and burned it to the ground. Five centuries later, Attila and his Huns did much the same. Next came the Normans; then the Valois kings turned it into a secondary capital. The story of the Hundred Years' War, Joan of Arc, and the siege of Orléans is widely known. During the Wars of Religion (1562–98), much of the cathedral was destroyed, and a century ago, ham-fisted town planners razed many of the city's fine old buildings. During World War II, both German and Allied bombs continued the job. Nevertheless, there is much of interest left, and, in recent years, dedicated and sensitive planners have done much to bring the city back to life.

The tourist office is on boulevard de Verdun, just in front of the train station. From here, rue de la République takes you 400 yards south to the main square—the **place du Martroi,** with its statue of Joan of Arc. A block farther south, turn left down rue Jeanne-d'Arc for the cathedral, or continue south down **rue Royale;** the latter is lined with excellent shops of all descriptions. Rue Royale brings you to the quai du Châtelet and the banks of the Loire. Make a left turn here to arrive at the
1 **Nouvelle Halle,** the covered market, with its tempting food displays. (Drivers would do best to park at the Campo Santo, by the cathedral, where there's a large underground parking lot.)

2 **Cathédrale Ste-Croix** is a riot of pinnacles and gargoyles, both Gothic and pseudo-Gothic, the whole embellished with 18th-century wedding-cake towers. Novelist Marcel Proust (1871–1922) called it France's ugliest church, but most people find it impressive. Inside you'll see vast quantities of stained glass

Cathédrale Ste-Croix, **2**
La Maison de Jeanne d'Arc, **5**
Musée des Beaux-Arts, **3**
Musée Historique, **4**
Nouvelle Halle, **1**

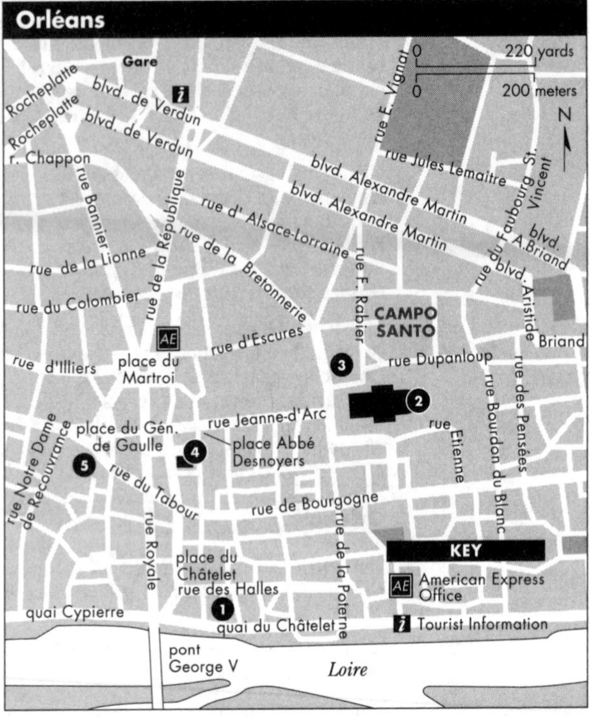

and 18th-century woodcarving, plus the modern **Chapel of Joan of Arc,** with plaques in memory of the British and American war dead. *Pl. Ste-Croix. Open daily 9–noon and 2–6.*

3 The modern **Musée des Beaux-Arts** (the art gallery) is just across the street from the cathedral. Take the elevator to the top and work your way down, viewing works by such artists as Tintoretto, Velázquez, Watteau, Boucher, Rodin, and Gauguin. *1 rue Ferdinand Rabier. Admission: 13 frs. adults, 6.50 frs. students. Open Wed.–Mon. 10–noon and 2–6; closed Tues.*

Retrace your steps along the rue Jeanne-d'Arc and turn left
4 onto place Abbé Desnoyers to visit the **Musée Historique.** This Renaissance town house contains both "fine" and "popular" works of art connected with the town's history and a remarkable collection of pagan bronzes of animals and dancers. These last were hidden from zealous Christian missionaries in the 4th century and discovered in a sand pit near St-Benoît in 1861. *Hôtel Cabu, pl. Abbé Desnoyers. Admission: 8 frs. adults, 4 frs. students. Open Wed.–Mon. 10–noon and 2–6.*

Another block west on rue Jeanne-d'Arc, in place du Général-
5 de-Gaulle, is **La Maison de Jeanne-d'Arc.** Seventeen-year-old Joan stayed on the site during the 10-day siege of Orléans in 1429, in a house that underwent many changes before it was bombed flat in 1940. This reconstruction contains exhibits about her life, costumes of her time, and models of siege engines. *Pl. du Général-de-Gaulle. Admission: 8 frs. adults, 4 frs. students. Open May–Oct., Tues.–Sun. 10–noon and 2–6; Nov.–Apr., Tues.–Sun. 2–6.*

Lodging
Under 350 frs.

Urbis. This modern 66-room hotel is part of a nationwide chain of simple, reasonably priced hotels. What it lacks in ambience, it makes up for in cleanliness and reliability. *17 rue Paris, 45000, tel. 38–62–40–40. 66 rooms. Facilities: parking. AE, MC.*

Dining
Under 125 frs.

L'Assiette. This is a brisk but comfortable place, right on place du Martroi. Choose your main course (simple grilled meats, mostly), and while it's cooking, help yourself to a wide variety of hors d'oeuvres and table wine from the barrel. You're entitled to as much of both as you want—and desserts are "free," too: The price of your meal depends on the main dish (menus run from 98 francs to 350 francs). *12 pl. du Martroi, tel. 38–53–46–69. Reservations advised. AE, MC, V.*

Shopping

Travelers with a sweet tooth will appreciate the Orléans specialty known as *cotignac*—an orangey-red molded jelly made from quinces. It can be bought from most local pâtisseries and is produced almost exclusively by **Gilbert Jumeau** (1 rue Voisinas, St-Ay), 8 kilometers (5 miles) west of Orléans. For fine chocolates, try the **Chocolaterie Royale** in Orléans (53 rue Royale).

5 Brittany

Land of the Sea, Land of the Forest

Rugged Brittany, jutting out into the Atlantic, gazes across the English Channel at Cornwall. The two regions share a Celtic heritage and a wild, untamed feel. Though Brittany became part of France in 1532, Bretons have never felt true kinship with their fellow Frenchmen; many still speak their own language, especially in the remoter parts of the interior, and regional folklore is still very much alive. An annual village *pardon* (a religious festival) will give you a good idea of what these are all about. At these, banners and statues of saints are borne in colorful parades accompanied by hymns; the whole event is rounded off by food of all kinds. Finistère (from *Finis Terrae*, or Land's End) département, Brittany's westernmost district, is renowned for the costumes worn on such occasions—notably the starched lace bonnets, or *coiffes*, which can tower 15 inches above the wearer's head.

Although Brittany's towns took a mighty hammering from the retreating Nazis in 1944, most have been tastefully restored, the large, concrete-cluttered naval base at Brest being an exception. Rennes, the only Breton city with more than 200,000 inhabitants, retains its traditional charm, as do the towns of Dinan, Quimper, and Vannes. Many ancient man-made delights are found in the region's villages, often in the form of *calvaires* (ornate burial chapels). Other architectural highlights include castles and cathedrals, the most outstanding examples being those of Fougères and Dol, respectively.

Geographically, Brittany is divided in two: maritime Armor ("land of the sea") and hinterland Argoat ("land of the forest"). The north of Brittany tends to be wilder than the south, where the countryside becomes softer as it descends toward Nantes and the Loire. Wherever you go, the coast is close by; the frenzied, cliff-bashing Atlantic surf alternates with sprawling beaches and bustling harbors. Getting around by public transportation is a challenge, and bicycling is the best way to get to remote coastal spots away from towns and villages.

Our tours cover a representative selection of the windswept Brittany that's accessible by train and bus. The first covers the northeastern part of the province, noted for its massive castles and impressive fortifications, and the second takes in highlights of the southern coast.

Essential Information

Lodging Although Brittany's economy is somewhat dependent on tourism, the region remains an unspoiled, unhurried spot for visitors on all kinds of budgets. Recent TGV links make the area easily accessible from Paris, bringing larger crowds in the summer, so it is always best to make reservations far in advance. There are an increasing number of luxury hotels (many of which are former châteaus), but the majority of Brittany's lodgings are comfortable and moderately priced. Dinard, on the English Channel, and La Baule, on the Atlantic, are the two most exclusive resorts; Quiberon, also on the Atlantic, is more run-down. All three areas have larger hotels and offer a greater choice of restaurants. Off-season, many hotels close in coastal areas, but prices drop at those that don't.

Dining Breton cuisine is dominated by fish and seafood. Shrimp, crayfish, crabs, oysters, and scallops are found throughout the region, but the linchpin of Breton menus is often lobster, prepared in sauce or cream or grilled. Popular meats include ham and lamb, frequently served with kidney beans. Fried eel is a traditional dish in the Nantes district. Brittany is particularly famous for its *galettes* and *crêpes*, thin pancakes served with sweet or savory fillings; these are a specialty at the distinctively Breton cafés known as *crêperies*. Accompanied by a glass of local cider, they are ideal for a light, inexpensive meal.

Shopping Keep an eye out for such typical Breton products as brass and wooden goods, faïence pottery, puppets, dolls, and locally designed jewelry, woven or embroidered cloth. Woolens are a specialty, notably thick marine sweaters.

Bicycling Bikes can be rented at several train stations, including the one in Quimper (tel. 98–98–31–60), and at shops in St-Malo (**Diazo,** 47 quai Duguay-Trouin, tel. 99–40–31–63), Dol (**Cycles Gondange,** 64 rue de Rennes, tel. 99–48–03–20), and Dinard (**Duval Cycles,** 53 rue Gardiner, tel. 99–46–19–63).

Hiking There are three types of long-distance footpaths in Brittany: coastal paths (*sentiers de douanier*), towpaths (*chemins de halage*) along canals between Nantes and Brest, and traditional hiking paths (GR, or *sentiers de grande randonnée*), found throughout France. For more information and detailed guides, contact **L'Association Bretonne des Relais & Itinéraires** (9 rue des Portes-Mordelaises, 35200 Rennes, tel. 99–31–59–44).

Beaches From St-Malo to Brest as far as the Côte d'Emeraude, then south to Nantes, the Brittany coast has any number of clean, sandy beaches—the best are found at Dinard, Perros-Guirec, Trégastel-Plage, Douarnenez, Carnac, and La Baule.

Festivals **Pardons**—traditional religious parades-cum-pilgrimages that invariably showcase age-old local costumes—are the backbone of Breton culture. The pardon held at windswept Ste-Anne-la-Palud on the last Sunday in August is the most spectacular. There are further manifestations of local folklore, often including dancers and folk singers, at the various Celtic festivals held in summer, of which the **Festival de Cornouaille** in Quimper, in late July, is the biggest.

Highlights for First-time Visitors

Menhirs and dolmens at Carnac, Tour 2
Ville Close, Concarneau, Tour 2
Dinan (Old Town), Tour 1
Nantes, Tour 2
Rennes, Tour 1
Vitré (Old Town), Tour 1
St-Malo (ramparts), Tour 1

Tour 1: From Rennes to St-Malo

From Rennes and St-Malo, your two base towns on this tour, short train journeys take you to Vitré, Dol, and Dinan. From Vitré, a bus trip brings you to Fougères Castle, and the elegant resort of Dinard lies a short boat ride across the Rance Estuary from St-Malo.

From Paris
By Train TGV bullet trains to Rennes leave Paris (Gare Montparnasse) 12 times daily, several continuing to Quimper. The trip to Rennes takes 2–2½ hours.

By Car The 345-kilometer (215-mile) drive from Paris along A11 and A81 takes 3½ hours.

Rennes

Tourist office: Pont de Nemours, in the middle of the main boulevard south of the cathedral, tel. 99–79–01–98.

Rennes (pronounced "wren"), the traditional capital of Brittany, has a different flavor from other towns in the region, mainly because of a terrible fire in 1720, which lasted a week and destroyed half the city. The remaining cobbled streets and half-timbered, 15th-century houses make an interesting contrast with the classicism of Jacques Gabriel's disciplined granite buildings, broad avenues, and spacious squares.

Head down avenue Janvier from the station and turn left after 600 yards onto quai Emile-Zola. A further 700 yards along, some 200 yards past the tourist office, take the fifth right up into the old town. The **Cathédrale St-Pierre,** a 19th-century building in classical style that took 57 years to construct, looms above rue de la Monnaie. Stop in to admire its richly decorated interior and outstanding 16th-century Flemish altarpiece. *Pl. St-Pierre. Open Sept.–June, daily 8:30–noon and 2–5; July–Aug., Mon.–Sat. 8:30–noon and 2–5, Sun. 8:30–noon.*

The pedestrian rue Lafayette and rue Nationale lead to the **Palais de Justice** (Law Courts). This palatial building, originally home to the Breton Parliament, was designed in 1618 by Salomon de Brosse, architect of the Luxembourg Palace in Paris, and was the most important building in Rennes to escape the 1720 fire. After admiring its white stone-and-granite facade, venture inside to view the splendid interior. Among its various magnificent halls is the richly carved and painted **Grand' Chambre,** a former parliamentary chamber whose walls are covered with Gobelin tapestries that retrace the history of Brittany. *Pl. du Parlement de Bretagne. Admission: 15 frs. Open Wed.–Mon. 10–noon and 2–6; closed Tues.*

Head down from the Palais de Justice and left across quai Emile-Zola to the **Palais des Musées,** a huge building containing two museums—the **Musée des Beaux-Arts** and **Musée de Bretagne.** The Fine Arts Museum on the second floor houses one of the country's best collections of paintings outside Paris, featuring works by Georges de la Tour, Jean-Baptiste Chardin, Camille Corot, Paul Gauguin, and Maurice Utrillo, to name only a few. The ground-floor Museum of Brittany retraces the region's history, period by period, by way of costumes, models, porcelain, furniture, coins, statues, and shiny push-button visual displays. *20 quai Emile-Zola. Admission: joint ticket 18 frs. adults, 9 frs. children under 14. Open Wed.–Mon. 10–noon and 2–6. Closed holidays.*

Northeast of the museum building, a five-minute walk via rue Gambetta and rue Victor-Hugo, is the **Jardin du Thabor,** a large, formal French garden with regimented rows of trees, shrubs, and flowers. Even the lawns are manicured—not often the case in France. There is a notable view of the church of **Notre-Dame-en-St-Mélaine** in one corner.

Lodging

Under 350 frs.

Central. This stately, late-19th-century hotel lives up to its name and sits close to Rennes Cathedral. The individually decorated guest rooms look out over the street or courtyard; ask for one of the latter, as they're quieter. English-speaking guests are frequent. There's no restaurant. *6 rue Lanjuinais, 35000, tel. 99–79–12–36. 43 rooms, most with bath. AE, DC, MC, V.*

Under 250 frs.

Angélina. This little charmer wins on sheer unpretentiousness: friendly welcome, clean rooms, robust breakfasts, and windows double-glazed to keep out the noise (it is on Rennes's principal boulevard, within a five-minute walk of the old town). Don't be put off by the fact that the hotel begins on the third floor of an ordinary-looking street block. *1 quai Lamennais, 35100, tel. 99–79–29–66. 26 rooms, with shower or bath. AE, DC, MC, V.*

Dining

Under 200 frs. ★

Palais. The best, though not the most expensive, restaurant in Rennes must thank its highly inventive team of young chefs for its considerable reputation. Specialties include roast rabbit and, during winter, fried oysters in crab sauce. The lightish cuisine varies according to season and is offered via two menus. The decor is sharp-edged contemporary, the site conveniently central. *6 pl. du Parlement de Bretagne, tel. 99–79–45–01. Dinner reservations required. Jacket required. AE, DC, MC, V. Closed Sun. dinner, Mon., and Aug.*

Under 125 frs. ★

Le Grain de Sable. Situated at the bottom of rue des Dames leading to the cathedral is a thoroughly unusual restaurant.

Brittany

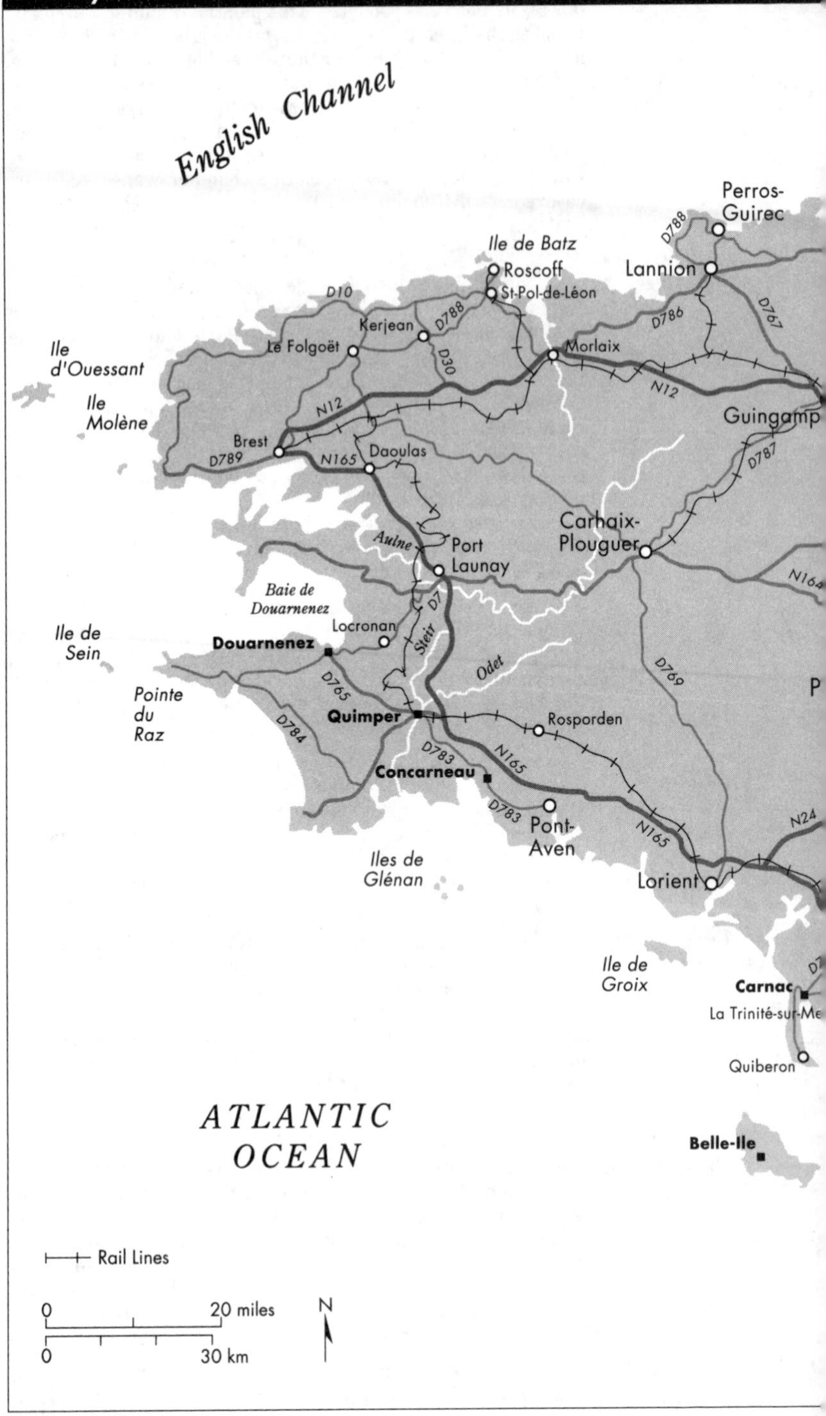

English Channel
Ile de Batz
Roscoff
St-Pol-de-Léon
Perros-Guirec
Lannion
D788
D10
Kerjean
D788
D786
D767
Le Folgoët
D30
Morlaix
Ile d'Ouessant
Ile Molène
N12
N12
Guingamp
Brest
D789
N165
Daoulas
D787
Carhaix-Plouguer
Aulne
Port Launay
N164
Baie de Douarnenez
D7
Ile de Sein
Locronan
Douarnenez
Steir
Odet
D769
Pointe du Raz
D765
D784
Quimper
Rosporden
D783
N165
Concarneau
D783
Pont-Aven
N165
N24
Iles de Glénan
Lorient
Ile de Groix
Carnac
La Trinité-sur-Me
Quiberon
ATLANTIC OCEAN
Belle-Ile
Rail Lines
0
20 miles
0
30 km
N

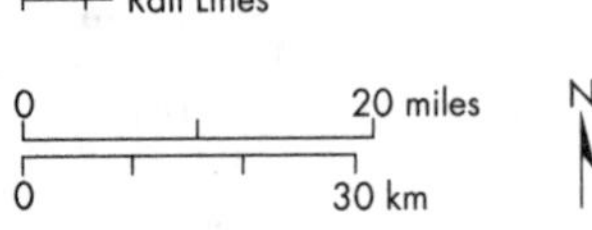

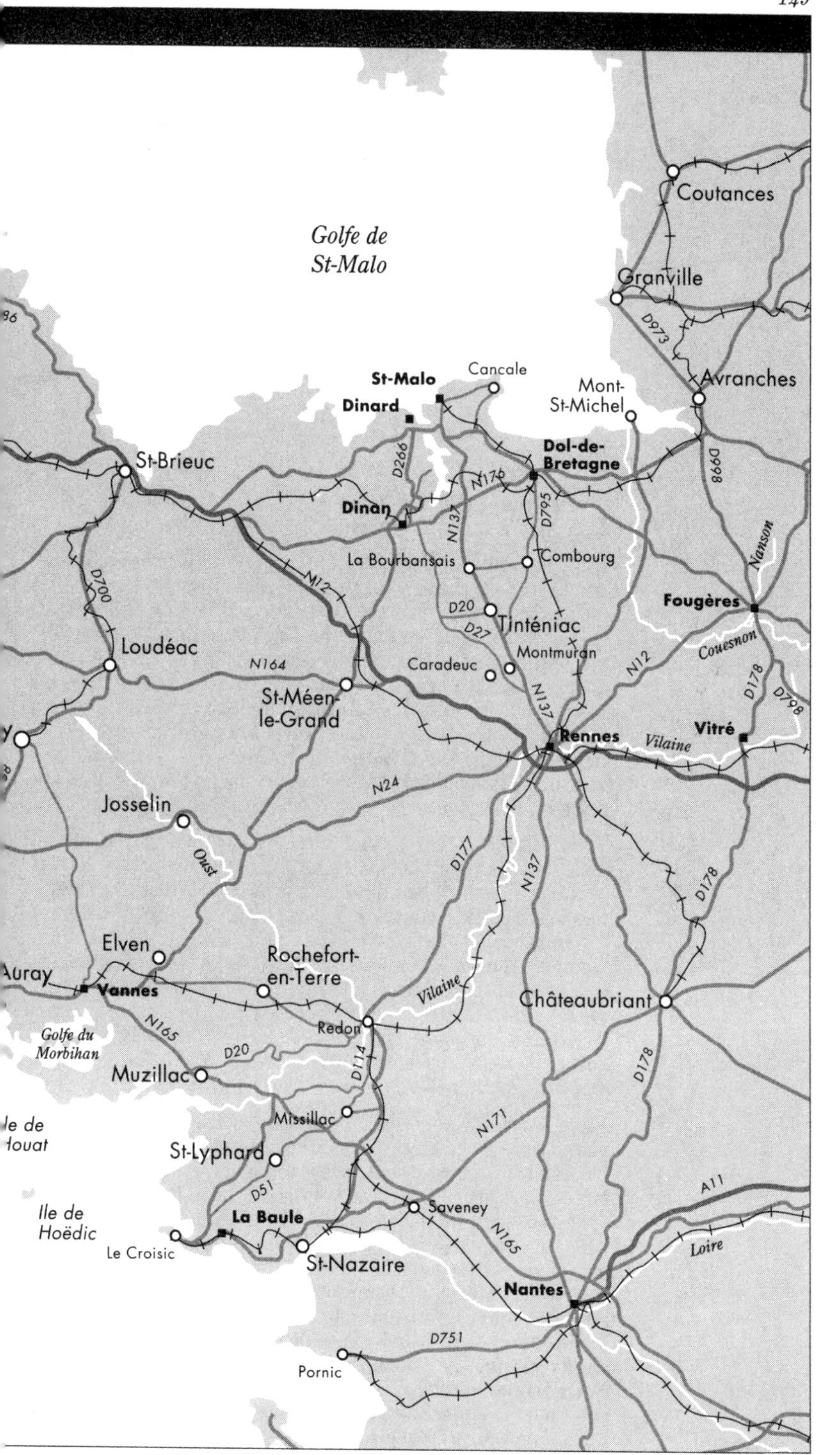
Golfe de St-Malo
Coutances
Granville
D973
Avranches
Cancale
St-Malo
Dinard
Mont-St-Michel
Dol-de-Bretagne
D998
St-Brieuc
D266
N176
Dinan
N137
D795
La Bourbansais
Combourg
Nanson
D700
N12
D20
Tinténiac
Fougères
D27
Couesnon
Loudéac
N164
Caradeuc
Montmuran
N12
St-Méen-le-Grand
N137
D178
D798
Vitré
Rennes
Vilaine
N24
Josselin
Oust
D177
N137
D178
Elven
Rochefort-en-Terre
Auray
Vannes
Vilaine
Châteaubriant
Redon
N165
Golfe du Morbihan
D20
D114
Muzillac
D178
Missillac
N171
le de
Houat
St-Lyphard
D51
A11
Ile de Hoëdic
La Baule
Saveney
N165
Le Croisic
St-Nazaire
Loire
Nantes
D751
Pornic

Plants, candelabra, faded photos, and a settee in the middle of the dining room create an ambience that escapes tackiness only by sheer eccentricity (a rocking horse sways in one corner). The cuisine is equally offbeat; expect garlic puree or endive with melted cheese to accompany the grilled meats that dominate the menu. Piped music warbles from opera to Louis Armstrong as the playful waitresses receive noisy reprimands from Hervé in the kitchen. *2 rue des Dames, tel. 99–30–78–18. Reservations advised. MC, V. Closed Sun., Mon. dinner.*

Shopping The streets surrounding the cathedral are full of 15th- and 16th-century houses in both medieval and Renaissance styles. Many have been converted for use as shops, boutiques, restaurants, and crêperies; a lively **street market** is held in and around place des Lices on Saturday morning. Places for good textiles are **Tidreiz** (pl. du Palais) and **Au Roy d'Ys** (29 blvd. de Magenta).

Vitré

Seven trains make the 30-minute trip from Rennes every day. Tourist office: Place St-Yves, tel. 99–75–04–46.

Built high above the Vilaine Valley, **Vitré** (pronounced "vee-tray") is one of the age-old gateways to Brittany: There's still a feel of the Middle Ages about its dark, narrow alleys and tightly packed houses. The town's leading attraction is its formidable **castle,** shaped in an imposing triangle with fat, round towers. An 11th-century creation, it was first rebuilt in the 14th and 15th centuries to protect Brittany against invasion and was to prove one of the province's most successful fortresses: During the Hundred Years' War (1337–1453) the English repeatedly failed to take it, even though they occupied the rest of the town.

Time, not foreigners, came closest to ravaging the castle, which was heavily, though tastefully, restored during the past century. The town hall, however, is an unfortunate 1913 addition to the castle courtyard. You can visit the wing to the left of the entrance, beginning with the Tour St-Laurent and continuing along the walls via Tour de l'Argenterie, with its macabre collection of stuffed frogs and reptiles preserved in glass jars, to Tour de l'Oratoire. *Admission: 8 frs. Open Apr.–June, Wed.–Mon. 10–noon and 2:30–5:30, closed Tues.; July–Sept., daily 10–noon and 1:30–6; Oct.–Mar., Wed.–Fri. 10–noon and 2–5:30, Mon. 2–5:30, closed Tues. and weekends.*

Vitré's castle makes a splendid sight, especially from a vantage point on rue de Fougères across the river valley below. The castle stands at the west end of town, facing the narrow, cobbled streets of the remarkably preserved old town. Rue Poterie, rue d'En-Bas, and rue Beaudrairie, originally the home of tanners (the name comes from *baudoyers*—leather workers), make up a web of medieval streets as picturesque as any in Brittany; take time to stroll through them, soaking up the atmosphere. Fragments of the town's medieval ramparts remain, including the 15th-century **Tour de la Bridolle** on place de la République, five blocks up from the castle. Built in the 15th and 16th centuries, **Notre-Dame** church has a fine, pinnacled south front and dominates a large square of the same name (you'll have passed it on the left on your way to place de la République).

Lodging
Under 150 frs.

Chêne Vert. Vitré is badly placed in the hotel stakes, but since this old town makes such a pleasant overnight stop we feel obliged to suggest this establishment, which is conveniently accessible from the road (D857, which links Rennes and Laval), just opposite the train station and a 10-minute stroll through cobbled streets from Vitré Castle. It is the epitome of a French provincial hotel: creaky stairs, fraying carpets, oversoft mattresses, and less-than-enthusiastic service—all, including a copious dinner, for next to nothing. Look carefully, however, and you will notice some intriguing touches—an enormous model ship on the second floor, for example, or the zinc-plated walls that submerge the dining room in art deco/ocean-liner pastiche. *2 pl. de la Gare, 35500, tel. 99–75–00–58. 22 rooms, a few with bath. Closed mid-Sept.–mid-Oct.; restaurant closed Fri. dinner and Sat., Oct.–May.*

Fougères

Buses run 4 times per day from Vitré to Fougères. The trip lasts about 40 minutes.

Fougères, a traditional cobbling and cider-making center, was for many centuries a frontier town, valiantly attempting to guard Brittany against attack. Perhaps one of the reasons for its conspicuous lack of success is the site of the **castle:** Instead of sitting high up on the hill, it spreads out down in the valley, though the sinuous River Nançon does make an admirable moat. The 13-towered castle covers over five acres, making it one of the largest in Europe. Although largely in ruins, the castle is an excellent example of the military architecture of the Middle Ages, and it is impressive both inside and out. The thick walls—up to 20 feet across in places—were intended to resist 15th-century artillery fire, but the castle was to prove vulnerable to surprise attacks and sieges. A visit inside the castle walls reveals three lines of fortification, with the cosseted keep at their heart. There are charming views over Fougères from the Tour Mélusine and, in the Tour Raoul, a small shoe museum. The second and third stories of the Tour de Coigny were transformed into a chapel during the 16th century. *East end of town on pl. Raoul II. Admission: 12 frs. Open Apr.–Oct., daily 10–noon and 2–5; closed Nov.–Mar.*

The oldest streets of Fougères are alongside the castle, clustered around the elegant slate spire of **St-Sulpice** (rue de Lusignan), a Flamboyant Gothic church holding several fine altarpieces. A number of medieval houses line rue de la Pinterie, leading directly from the castle up to the undistinguished heart of town.

In the 1790s, Fougères was a center of Royalist resistance to the French Revolution. Much of the action in 19th-century novelist Honoré de Balzac's bloodcurdling novel *Les Chouans* takes place hereabouts; the novel's heroine, Marie de Verneuil, had rooms close to the church of **St-Léonard** (follow the river left from the castle), which overlooks the Nançon Valley. Both path and church, with its ornate facade and 17th-century tower, have changed little; the garden through which the path leads is known today as the **Jardin Public.**

Another man who was inspired by the scenery of Fougères was locally born Emmanuel de La Villéon (1858–1944), a little-known Impressionist painter. His works are displayed in the

Musée La Villéon, in one of the oldest surviving houses (dating to the 16th century) in hilltop Fougères; to reach it from the Jardin Public, head left past St-Léonard, and cross the square onto the adjacent rue Nationale. The more than 100 paintings, pastels, watercolors, and drawings suggest serene, underestimated talent. The artist's work ranges from compassionate studies of toiling peasants to pretty landscapes in which soft shades of green melt into hazy blue horizons. *51 rue Nationale. Admission: 8 frs. Open Easter–mid-June, weekends only, 11–12:30 and 2:30–5; mid-June–mid-Sept., weekdays 10:30–12:30 and 2:30–5:30, weekends and holidays 11–12:30 and 2:30–5.*

Dol-de-Bretagne

Trains make the 35-minute trip to Dol from Rennes 14 times daily. Dol tourist office: 3 Grande-Rue, tel. 99–48–15–37.

The ancient town of **Dol** looks out from its 60-foot cliffs over Le Marais, a marshy plain stretching across to Mont St-Michel, 21 kilometers (13 miles) northeast. The **Promenade des Douves,** laid out along the northern part of the original ramparts, offers extensive views of Le Marais and Mont Dol, a 200-foot granite mound, 3 kilometers (2 miles) north, legendary scene of combat between St. Michael and the devil. Unfortunately, the stately trees that line the promenade suffered heavily in a 1987 hurricane.

At the end of the promenade, note the **Cathédrale St-Samson** (pl. de la Cathédrale), a damp, soaring, fortresslike bulk of granite dating mainly from the 12th to the 14th century. This mighty building shows just how influential the bishopric of Dol was in days gone by. The richly sculpted Great Porch, carved wooden choir stalls, and stained glass in the chancel all deserve close scrutiny.

Turn down rue des Ecoles to the small **Musée Historique d'Art Populaire** (Museum of Folk Art). During a short, cheerful guided tour, you'll see costumes, weapons, and a series of scale models retracing life in Dol since prehistoric times. The glory of the museum, though, is its assembly of colored wooden religious statues. *Rue des Ecoles. Admission: 14 frs. Open Apr.–Sept., Wed.–Mon. 10–5; closed Tues.*

Rue des Ecoles leads to Dol's picturesque main street, Grande-Rue-des-Stuarts, lined with medieval houses. The oldest, at no. 17, boasts a chunky row of Romanesque arches.

Lodging and Dining
Under 250 frs.

Logis de la Bresche Arthur. With its crisp outlines, white walls, and ample glass frontage, the hotel may not be quite as historic as it sounds, but it remains the coziest lodging place in Dol. Rooms are functional; local character is reserved for the restaurant, where smoked salmon, seafish, and home-prepared foie gras top the menu. *36 blvd. Deminiac, 35120, tel. 99–48–01–44. 24 rooms with bath. Facilities: restaurant. AE, DC, MC, V.*

Dinan

Six trains make the ½-hour journey from Dol each day, and 7 make the 70-minute trip from Rennes (all but 1 require a change in Dol). Dinan tourist office: 6 rue de l'Horloge, tel. 96–39–75–40.

Dinan has close links with Brittany's 14th-century anti-English warrior-hero Bertrand du Guesclin, whose name is commemorated in countless squares and hostelries across the province. Du Guesclin won a famous victory here in 1359 and promptly married a local girl, Tiphaine Raguenel. When he died in the siege of Auvergne (central France) in 1380, his body was dispatched home to Dinan. Owing to the great man's popularity, however, only his heart completed the journey—the rest of him having been confiscated by devoted followers in towns along the route.

Begin your stroll around the old town at the tourist office, housed in a charming 16th-century building on rue de l'Horloge. For a superb view of the town, climb to the top of the nearby belfry, the **Tour de l'Horloge.** *Admission: 5 frs. Open July–Aug., Mon.–Sat. 10–noon and 2–6.*

Turn left and head half a block along to admire the triangular-gabled wooden houses in **place des Merciers, rue de l'Apport,** and **rue de la Poissonnerie.** With their overhanging balconies and black-and-white half-timbered houses, these cobbled streets are so pretty you may think you've stumbled onto a Hollywood movie set. Restore your faith with a visit to the nearby church, the **Basilique St-Sauveur** (turn right out of place des Merciers along rue Haute-Voie, then take the second left into the church square). The church is a mixture of styles, ranging from the Romanesque south front to the Flamboyant Gothic facade and Renaissance side chapels. Du Guesclin's heart lies in the north transept.

The **Jardin Anglais** (English Garden) is just behind the church; it's not really much of a garden, but its old trees nicely frame the east end of St-Sauveur. More spectacular views are found at the bottom of the garden, which looks down the plummeting Rance Valley to the river 250 feet below.

Leading down to the harbor, cobbled, sloping rue du Jerzual—a beautifully preserved medieval street—is full of boutiques and crafts shops purveying woodcarvings, jewelry, leather work, glass, painted silk, and other craft items. It is divided halfway down by the town walls and massive Porte du Jerzual gateway.

Dinan's harbor seems somewhat forlorn; although there are sailings in summer up the River Rance to Dinard and St-Malo, abandoned warehouses bear witness to vanished commercial activity, with only an occasional restaurant to brighten up the place.

Stagger back up the hill (it's steep) and turn right, well after the Porte du Jerzual, onto rue de l'Ecole. This street leads down to another gateway, the Porte St-Malo, from which the leafy Promenade des Grands Fossés heads left on a tour of the best-preserved section of the town walls. Follow these walls around as far as the **castle.** Here you can visit the two-story Coëtquen Tower and 100-foot, 14th-century keep, containing varied displays of medieval effigies and statues, Breton furniture, and local *coiffes* (lace headdresses). *Porte de Guichet. Admission: 14 frs. Open June–Aug., 9–noon and 2–7, Sept.–Oct. and Mar.–May, 9–noon and 2–6, Nov.–Feb., 2–5; closed Tues.*

Lodging and Dining
Under 350 frs.

D'Avagour. This hotel is splendidly situated opposite Dinan Castle's Tour du Connétable and has its own flower garden to boot; most of the cozy guest rooms look out onto either the garden or the castle. You can be sure of a warm welcome from the affable owner, Madame Quinton. The hotel attracts numerous foreign guests—American, English, and Italian, in particular. The restaurant offers traditional cuisine (shellfish, duck, apple tart) at prices that remain reasonable, even as they shoot up from lunch to dinner. The chance to dine in the garden in warm weather is a plus. *1 pl. du Champ-Clos, 22100, tel. 96–39–07–49. 27 rooms with bath. Facilities: restaurant, garden. AE, DC, MC, V.*

Dining
Under 125 frs.

Relais des Corsaires. The old hilltop town of Dinan is full of restaurants and cafés specializing in *galettes*, Brittany's distinctive crêpes. But we suggest that you wander down to the old port on the banks of the Rance to dine at this casual spot, named after the pirates who apparently raided the wharves of Dinan. The mid-range prix-fixe menu provides an ample four-course meal, with alternative menus at higher and lower prices. The costlier à la carte choices are not as good for the money. There are two separate, oak-beamed dining rooms; the lush main room with aquarium and attentive, rather unctuous service, communicates by way of a hatch with a smaller room with an impressively long bar, patrolled by Madame Ternisien, the attractive *patronne* who likes to give herself the airs and graces of a grande dame. *7 rue du Quai, tel. 96–39–40–17. Reservations accepted. AE, DC, MC, V.*

Shopping

Wool yarn by the yard and English cakes and scones by the dozen: That's the unlikely combination you'll find at this strange little American-run outfit, **La Toison d'Or** (rue du Jerzual). Long wooden benches add to the atmosphere, if not the comfort, as you settle down for a cup of coffee and a snack.

St-Malo

Five trains make the 1-hour trip from Dinan each day (with a change at Dol), and 11 trains make the 50-minute journey from Rennes. St-Malo tourist office: Esplanade St-Vincent, tel. 99–56–64–48.

The ancient walled town of **St-Malo** is a one-time pirate base whose stone ramparts have stood firm against the Atlantic since the 13th century. The town itself has proved less resistant: A week-long fire in 1944, kindled by retreating Nazis, wiped out nearly all the old buildings. Restoration work was more painstaking than brilliant, but the narrow streets and granite houses of the old town, known as *Intra Muros* ("within the walls") have been satisfactorily re-created, enabling St-Malo to regain its role as a busy fishing port and seaside resort.

North American visitors can pay homage here to Jacques Cartier, who set sail from St-Malo in 1535 to discover the St. Lawrence River and found Québec. Cartier's tomb is in the church of **St-Vincent** (off Grande-Rue), and his statue looks out over the town ramparts, four blocks away—along with that of swashbuckling corsair Robert Surcouf, hero of many daring 18th-century raids on the British Navy (he's the one pointing an accusing finger over the waves at *l'Angleterre*). The ramparts themselves date from the 12th century but were considerably enlarged and modified in the 18th. They extend from the castle in St-Malo's northeast corner and ring the old town, with a total length of over a mile. The views from the ramparts are stupendous, especially at high tide. Five hundred yards offshore is the **Ile du Grand Bé,** a small island housing the somber military tomb of Viscount Chateaubriand, who was born in St-Malo. The islet can be reached by a causeway at low tide, as can the **Fort National,** a massive fortress with a dungeon constructed in 1689 by that military-engineering genius, Sébastien de Vauban. *By the castle. Admission: 8 frs. Open Apr.–Sept., daily 9:30–noon and 2:30–6.*

At the edge of the ramparts, overlooking the Fort National, is **St-Malo Castle,** whose great keep and watchtowers command an impressive view of the harbor and coastline. The castle houses two museums: the **Musée de la Ville,** devoted to local history, and the **Quic-en-Grogne,** a tower where various episodes and celebrities from St-Malo's past are recalled by way of waxwork reconstruction. *Porte St-Vincent. Admission: 10 frs. (Musée de la Ville), 15 frs. (Quic-en-Grogne). Open May–Sept., daily 9:30–noon and 2–6:30; Apr. and Oct., daily 10–noon and 2–6; closed Tues. Oct.–Mar.*

Lodging
Under 250 frs.

Jean-Bart. This clean, quiet hotel next to the ramparts, whose decor makes liberal use of cool blue, bears the stamp of diligent renovation: The beds are comfortable and the bathrooms shiny-modern. Though rooms are on the small side, some boast exhilarating sea views. *12 rue de Chartres, 35400, tel. 99–40–33–88. 17 rooms, most with bath. MC, V. Closed mid-Nov.–mid-Feb.*

Dining
Under 125 frs.

Café de la Bourse. Wherever you search for a restaurant in the old town of St-Malo, you will feel you are being hemmed into an overcommercialized tourist trap. This restaurant, where prawns and oysters are downed by the shovel, is no exception. However, though its wooden seats and some tacky navigational paraphernalia—ships' wheels and posters of grizzled old sea dogs—are hardly artistic, the large, L-shaped dining room makes amends with genuinely friendly service and a bountiful seafood platter for two. It includes at least three tanklike crabs and an army of cockles, whelks, and periwinkles. *1 rue de Dinan, tel. 99–56–47–17. Reservations accepted. AE, V.*

Shopping

The market held in the streets of old St-Malo on Tuesday and Friday is one of the most colorful in the province.

Dinard

Boats plow frequently across the strait between St-Malo and Dinard.

Dinard, a stylish, slightly snobbish vacation resort, may be fraying on the edges these days, but its picture-book setting on the Rance Estuary opposite St-Malo makes up for any shabbiness. Until the middle of the last century, Dinard was a minor fishing village. It became all the rage, thanks to propaganda from a rich American named Coppinger; avenues were baptized Edward VII and George V as English royalty jumped on the bandwagon. Grand hotels and luxurious villas are still plentiful.

It's not hard to see why uppercrust Edwardians loved the place, with its dramatic cliffs, lush vegetation, bracing coastal walks, and three sandy beaches. To make the most of Dinard's exhilarating setting, head down to the town's southern tip, the

Pointe de la Vicomté, where cliffs offer panoramic views across the Baie du Prieuré and Rance Estuary. The **Plage du Prieuré,** named after a priory that once stood here, is a sandy beach ringed by yachts, dinghies, and motorboats. The **Clair de Lune Promenade** hugs the seacoast on its way toward the English Channel, passing in front of the small jetty used by boats crossing to St-Malo. Shortly after, the street reaches the **Musée de la Mer** (Marine Museum and Aquarium). Virtually every known species of Breton bird and sea creature is on display here, in two rooms and 24 pools. Another room is devoted to the polar expeditions of explorer Jean Charcot, one of the first men to chart the Antarctic; there are poignant souvenirs of his last voyage, in 1936, from which he never returned. *Claire de Lune Promenade. Admission: 10 frs. Open Pentecost Sun.–Sept., daily 10–noon and 2–6.*

The Clair de Lune Promenade, lined with luxuriant semitropical vegetation, really hits its stride as it rounds the Pointe du Moulinet to the Prieuré Beach. River meets sea in a foaming mass of rock-pounding surf, and caution is needed as you walk along the slippery path. Your reward: the calm and shelter of the **Plage de l'Ecluse,** an inviting sandy beach, bordered by a casino and numerous stylish hotels. The coastal path picks up again on the far side, ringing the Pointe de la Malouine and Pointe des Etêtés before arriving at Dinard's final beach, the **Plage de St-Enogat.**

Lodging and Dining
Under 250 frs.

La Vallée. Prices at this traditional late-19th-century hotel vary according to the room. The best—the most expensive in the house—have a sea view: The Clair de Lune Promenade and Prieuré Beach are within shouting distance. The hotel itself is decorated in a stockily elegant *fin-de-siècle* (turn-of-the-century) style, with an authentic French feel. The restaurant's seafood comes on the moderate and expensive menus. *6 av. George-V, 35800, tel. 99–46–94–00. 26 rooms with bath. Facilities: restaurant (closed Tues. Oct.–Apr.). V. Closed mid-Nov.–mid-Dec., second half of Jan.*

Tour 2: From Quimper to Nantes

This tour takes in some of Brittany's most distinctive countryside as it follows the main train route down the coast from Quimper to Nantes. Douarnenez, Concarneau, and Carnac require a bus ride from the nearest station, and boats cross to the pretty island of Belle-Ile from sea-swept Quiberon several times daily.

From Paris
By Train

Express trains to Quimper leave Paris (Gare Montparnasse) 9 times daily. The trip takes 5–5½ hours.

By Car

The 560-kilometer (350-mile) drive from Paris to Quimper takes about 6 hours. Leave A81 at Rennes and follow N24.

Quimper

Tourist office: rue de l'Amiral-de-la-Grandière, across the river from the old town, tel. 98–53–04–05.

Today a lively commercial town, **Quimper** (pronounced "campair") was the ancient capital of the Cornouaille province and was founded, it is said, by King Gradlon 1,500 years ago. It owes its strange-looking name to its site at the confluence *(kemper* in Breton) of the Odet and Steir rivers. The banks of the Odet make a charming place to stroll. Highlights of the old town include **rue Kéréon,** a lively shopping street, and the stately **Jardin de l'Evêché** (Bishop's Gardens) behind the cathedral in the center of the old town.

From the station turn right onto avenue de la Gare and continue along the banks of the Odet River (blvd. de Kerguelen) to the **Cathédrale St-Corentin.** This masterpiece of Gothic architecture is the second-largest cathedral in Brittany (after that of Dol). Legendary King Gradlon is represented on horseback just below the base of the spires, harmonious mid-19th-century additions to the medieval ensemble. The luminous 15th-century stained glass is particularly striking. *Pl. St-Corentin.*

Two museums flank the cathedral. Works by major masters, such as Rubens, Corot, and Picasso, mingle with pretty landscapes from the local Gauguin-inspired Pont-Aven school in the **Musée des Beaux-Arts** (Fine Arts Museum), and local furniture, ceramics, and folklore top the bill in the **Musée Départemental** (Regional Museum) on adjacent rue du Roi-Gradlon. *Musée des Beaux-Arts: Admission 20 frs.; open Wed.–Mon. 9:30–noon and 1–5. Musée Départemental: Admission 10 frs.; open mid-Sept.–Apr., Wed.–Sun. 9–noon and 2–5, May–mid-Sept., Wed.–Mon. 9–noon and 2–5.*

Quimper sprang to nationwide attention as an earthenware center in the mid-18th century, when it started producing second-rate imitations of the Rouen ceramics known as faïence, featuring blue Oriental motifs. Today's more colorful designs, based on floral arrangements and marine fauna, are still often hand-painted. There are guided visits to the main pottery, the **Faïencerie Henriot,** and its museum, situated on the banks of the Odet south of the old town. *Allée de Locmaria. Admission: 12 frs. Open Mon.–Thurs. 9:30–11 and 1:30–4:30; Fri. 9:30–11 and 1:30–3.*

Lodging
Under 150 frs.

Terminus. There are plenty of French hotels with this unappealing name, nearly all of them unremarkable buildings near train stations. This one is no exception. But it's cheap, convenient, clean, and cheerful, and in summer, it throbs with students and foreigners (and gets a bit noisy). *14 av. de la Gare, 29000, tel. 98-90-00-63. 25 rooms, some with bath or shower. AE, MC, V.*

Dining
Under 75 frs.

Cariatides. Crêpes are a Brittany specialty, and the best place to sample them in Quimper—with an obligatory bottle of the local cider—is in this bustling crêperie housed in an atmospheric medieval building a stone's throw from the cathedral. The wide choice of traditional sweet crêpes, plus savory versions made from *froment* (white flour) or *blé noir* (buckwheat), pulls in a lively, youthful crowd throughout the year. *4 rue Guéodet, tel. 98-95-15-14. MC, V. Closed Sun.*

Shopping

The streets around the cathedral (especially **rue du Parc**) are full of shops, several selling the woolen goods and thick fisherman's sweaters for which Brittany is known. Quimper's hand-painted earthenware can be bought at the **Kéraluc**

Faïencerie (14 rue de la Troménie on the Bénodet road) or at **Henriot** (12 pl. St-Corentin).

Douarnenez

Four buses make the 30-minute run daily from Quimper, 22 km (14 mi) away.

Douarnenez is a charming old fishing town of quayside paths and narrow streets. Sailing enthusiasts will be interested in the town's biennial classic boat rally in mid-August (the next event will take place in 1994), when traditionally rigged sailing boats of every description ply the waters of the picturesque Bay of Douarnenez.

Concarneau

A dozen trains make the 14-minute run daily from Quimper to Rosporden, where you connect with a bus that takes a further 20 minutes to Concarneau. Tourist office: Quai d'Aiguillon, tel. 98–97–01–44.

Located 21 kilometers (13 miles) from Quimper at the mouth of the Baie de la Forêt, **Concarneau** looks south across the Atlantic toward the desolate Islands of Glénan. Concarneau is the third-largest fishing port in France. During its *criée*, an early-morning auction held from Monday to Thursday, local fishwives can be heard in full cry as they sell off the recent catch.

The **Ville Close,** the fortified islet in the middle of the harbor, is Concarneau's main attraction. To reach it, you must cross a drawbridge. The islet's narrow streets and huge granite ramparts make for an enjoyable afternoon's roam, though rue Vauban—the main street—contains a lot of tacky souvenir shops; ignore them and concentrate on the fantastic views of the bay. From early medieval times, Concarneau was regarded as impregnable, and the fortifications were further strengthened by the English under John de Montfort during the War of Succession (1341–64). This enabled the English-controlled Concarneau to withstand two sieges by Breton hero Bertrand du Guesclin; the third siege was successful for the plucky du Guesclin, who drove out the English in 1373. Three hundred years later, Sébastien de Vauban remodeled the ramparts into what you see today: half a mile long and highly scenic, offering views across the two harbors on either side of the Ville Close. *Admission to ramparts: 5 frs. Open Easter–Sept., daily 9–7; winter 10–5.*

At the end of rue Vauban closest to the drawbridge is the **Musée de la Pêche** (Fishing Museum), occupying an enormous hall in the former arsenal. Here you will encounter historical explanations of fishing techniques from around the world, plus such displays as an antiwhale harpoon gun and a giant Japanese crab. Turtles and fish may be seen in the museum's many aquariums. *Admission: 25 frs. Open Sept.–June, daily 10–12:30 and 2–7; July–Aug., daily 10–6.*

If you're in Concarneau in the second half of August, you will be able to enjoy the **Fête des Filets Bleus** (Blue Net Festival) in the Ville Close. This festival is a week-long folk celebration during which Bretons in costume swirl and dance to the wail of bagpipes.

Lodging
Under 250 frs.

Sables Blancs. A great advantage of this old-fashioned hotel is that all guest rooms feature soul-satisfying views of the sea: The name is derived from the hotel's location near the *Sables Blancs* (White Sands) beach. Be sure to request a room in a lower price range, because not all are truly inexpensive. The hotel restaurant is adequate, with set menus at reasonable prices. *Plage des Sables Blancs, 29110 Concarneau, tel. 98–97–01–39. 48 rooms with bath. Facilities: restaurant. AE, DC, MC, V. Closed Nov.–mid-Mar.*

Dining
Under 200 frs.

Le Galion. Flowers, wooden beams, silver candlesticks, old stones, and a roaring hearth form a pleasant backdrop to Henri Gaonach's marine tours de force at this, one of Concarneau's best fish restaurants. There are three set menus, priced to suit those looking for an inexpensive meal as well as famished gourmets. *15 rue St-Guénolé, Ville-Close, tel. 98–97–30–16. AE, DC, MC, V. Closed Sun. evening and Mon. in winter and mid-Jan.–mid-Feb.*

Belle-Ile

Trains from Quimper (via Rosporden) continue to Auray (70 minutes from Quimper), where 7 buses make the 90-minute trip to Quiberon each day. Belle-Ile tourist office: Quai Bonnelle, tel. 97–31–81–93.

The spa town of Quiberon is famed for its soothing waters and fine beaches. But the best reason to visit is its proximity to 18-kilometer-long (11-mile-long) **Belle-Ile**, Brittany's largest island. Boats leave from the cheerful harbor of Port-Maria, and bikes can be rented on the island at Joël Banet Garage in St-Palais (quai Gambetta, tel. 97–31–50–70).

Despite being a mere 45-minute boat trip from Quiberon, Belle-Ile is much less commercialized, and the scenery is truly exhilarating. Near Sauzon, the island's prettiest settlement, is a staggering view across to the Quiberon Peninsula and Gulf of Morbihan from the **Pointe des Poulains,** erstwhile home of the Belle Epoque's femme fatale, actress Sarah Bernhardt. The nearby **Grotte de l'Apothicairerie** is a grotto whose name derives from the local cormorants' nests, said to resemble pharmacy bottles. Farther south, near Port Goulphar, is another dramatic sight—the **Grand Phare** (lighthouse), built in 1835 and rising 275 feet above sea level. Its light is one of the most powerful in Europe, visible from 75 miles across the Atlantic. If the keeper is available, you may be able to climb to the top and admire the view.

Lodging and Dining
Under 150 frs.

Bretagne. Staying on Belle-Ile can be pricey. But at this old dockside house by the harbor at Le Palais, the island's liveliest town, the cheapest rooms, the ones without shower or toilet, start at around 100 francs. Better appointed, more spacious accommodations cost 300 francs. Seafood reigns in the dining room, which looks out to sea, and you can net a set menu for 60 or 100 francs. *Quai Macé, 56360 Le Palais, tel. 97–31–80–14. 29 rooms, some with bath or shower. Facilities: bar, restaurant. MC, V.*

Dining
Under 200 frs.

La Forge. A sure bet for lunch or dinner, La Forge specializes in traditional cuisine, based on seafood and fish, at affordable prices. Old wooden beams and remnants of the building's original purpose—blacksmithing—contribute to the pleasant, rustic atmosphere. *Rte. de Port-Goulphar, Bangor, tel. 91–31–51–76. Reservations required in summer. AE, DC, MC, V. Closed Wed. and Jan.–Feb.*

Shopping **Henri Le Roux** (18 rue du Port-Maria, near the harbor in Quiberon) has taken the art of chocolateering to dizzying heights.

Carnac

Seven buses daily make the 60-minute run from Quiberon to Carnac. Tourist office: 74 av. des Druides, tel. 97–52–13–52.

Carnac has its beaches, but it's famed for its **megalithic monuments** dating from the Neolithic and Early Bronze ages (3500–1800 BC). The whys and wherefores of their construction remain as obscure as those of their English contemporary, Stonehenge, although religious beliefs and astrology were doubtless an influence. The 2,395 menhirs that make up the three *Alignements* (Kermario, Kerlescan, and Ménec) are positioned with astounding astronomical accuracy in semicircles and parallel lines over half a mile long. There are also smaller-scale dolmen ensembles and three tumuli (mounds or barrows), including the 130-yard-long **Tumulus de St-Michel,** topped by a small chapel affording fine views of the rock-strewn countryside. *Guided tours of the tumulus daily Apr.–Sept. Cost: 5 frs.*

Lodging and Dining
Under 350 frs.

La Marine. This comfortable, intimate old-timer nestling in the old town beside the church is quieter than hotels nearer the beaches. Rooms are fully modernized, though on the small side, and the restaurant purveys seafood prepared with French flair, with menus starting at 100 francs. (Watch out: Eating à la carte doesn't represent the same good value.) *4 pl. de la Chapelle, 56340, tel. 97–52–07–33. 28 rooms with bath. Facilities: restaurant (closed Sun. evening and Mon.). AE, DC, MC, V. Closed mid-Nov.–mid-Mar.*

Lann-Roz. This large mansion on avenue de la Poste, the main street connecting the old town to Carnac-Plage, the beach, is a good find in pricey Carnac, although the largest rooms top 300 francs. A veranda overlooks an attractive garden, and bubbly patronne Anne Le Calvez plays host to a mix of businessmen and international tourists. Unless you opt for the 120-franc menu, the cost of your meal may seem steep. The seafood is a good bet. *12 av. de la Poste, 56340, tel. 97–52–11–01. 14 rooms with bath or shower. Facilities: restaurant. AE, DC, MC, V. Closed Jan. and Wed. out of season.*

Vannes

Eight trains run from Quimper to Vannes during the day. The trip averages 90 minutes. Trains make the 15-minute trip from Auray to Vannes every 2 hours or so. Vannes tourist office: 1 rue Thiers, tel. 97–47–24–34.

Vannes (pronounced "vahn"), scene of the declaration of unity between France and Brittany in 1532, is one of the few towns in Brittany to have been spared damage during World War II, so its authentic regional charm remains intact. Be sure to visit the **Cohue** (medieval market hall—now a temporary exhibition center) and the picturesque **place Henri IV** and browse in the small boutiques and antiques shops in the surrounding pedestrian streets. The ramparts, Promenade de la Garenne, and medieval washhouses are all set against the backdrop of the much-restored **Cathédrale St-Pierre,** with its 1537 Renaissance chapel, Flamboyant Gothic transept portal, and treasury in the old chapterhouse. *Pl. du Cathédrale. Admission: 3 frs. Treasury open mid-June–mid-Sept., Mon.–Sat. 10–noon and 2–6.*

Lodging and Dining
Under 350 frs.

Image Ste-Anne. This charming hotel is housed in a suitably old, rustic building in the center of historic Vannes. The warm welcome and comfortable guest rooms make the price of a night here seem more than acceptable, as a varied foreign clientele has realized. Mussels, sole in cider, and duck are featured on the restaurant's menus; set menus are all very reasonably priced. *8 pl. de la Libération, 56000, tel. 97-63-27-36. 35 rooms with bath or shower. Facilities: restaurant (closed Sun. dinner Nov.–Mar.). MC, V.*

Dining
Under 200 frs.

Lys. Intricate nouvelle cuisine, based on fresh local produce, makes this restaurant a pleasant dinner spot close to the agreeable Promenade de la Garenne. The setting, in a late-18th-century Louis XVI style, is at its best by candlelight, with piano music in the background. *51 rue du Maréchal-Leclerc, tel. 97-47-29-30. Reservations required. Jacket and tie required. AE, DC, MC, V. Closed Mon., mid-Nov.–mid-Dec., and Sun. dinner.*

Nantes

There are 3 direct trains daily to Nantes from Quimper (3 hours) and from Vannes (1½ hours away); others require a change at Redon. Nantes tourist office: Place du Commerce, tel. 40-47-04-51.

Numbers in the margin correspond to points of interest on the Nantes map.

Nantes is a tranquil, prosperous city that seems to pursue its existence without too much concern for what's going on elsewhere in France. Although it is not really part of Brittany—it officially belongs to the Pays de la Loire—the dukes of Brittany were in no doubt that Nantes belonged to their domain, and the castle they built is the city's principal tourist attraction.

Turn left out of the station onto cours J.-F. Kennedy, a busy
1 highway that leads to the **Château des Ducs de Bretagne**, 400 yards away. This massive, well-preserved 15th-century fortress with a neatly grassed moat was largely built by François II, who led a hedonistic existence here, surrounded by ministers, chamberlains, and an army of servants. Numerous monarchs later stayed in the castle, where, in 1598, Henri IV signed the famous Edict of Nantes advocating religious tolerance.

Within the Harnachement—a separate building inside the castle walls—you'll find the **Musée des Salorges** (Naval Museum), devoted principally to the history of seafaring; a separate section outlines the triangular trade that involved transportation of African blacks to America to be sold as slaves. As you cross the courtyard to the Grand Gouvernement wing, home to the **Musée d'Art Populaire Régional** (Regional Folk Art Museum), look for the old well, where the ducal coat of arms is entwined in some magnificent wrought-iron decoration. The Musée d'Art Populaire features an array of armor, furniture, 19th-century Breton costumes, and reconstituted interiors illustrating the former life in the Vendée region to the south. *Just off rue du*

Cathédrale St-Pierre, **2**
Château des Ducs de Bretagne, **1**
Grand Théâtre, **5**
Manoir de la Touche, **6**
Musée des Beaux-Arts, **3**
Palais Dobrée, **7**
Passage Pommeraye, **4**

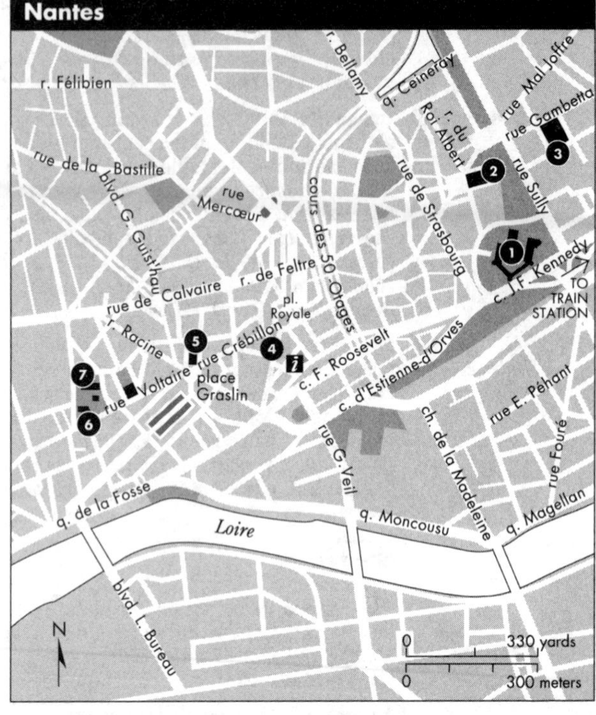

Château. Admission: 15 frs., free Sun. Castle and museums open Sept.–June, Wed.–Mon. 10–noon and 2–6, closed Tues.; July–Aug., daily 10–noon and 2–6.

2 Opposite the castle is the **Cathédrale St-Pierre,** one of France's latest Gothic cathedrals; building began only in 1434, well after most other medieval cathedrals had been completed. The facade is ponderous and austere, in contrast to the light, wide, superbly renovated interior, whose vaults rise higher (120 feet) than those of Notre-Dame in Paris. In the transept, notice Michel Colombe's early 16th-century tomb of François II and his wife, Marguerite de Foix, which is one of France's finest examples of funerary sculpture. *Pl. St-Pierre.*

Behind the cathedral, past the 15th-century Porte St-Pierre, is
3 the **Musée des Beaux-Arts** (Fine Arts Museum), with a fine collection of paintings from the Renaissance on, featuring works by Jacopo Tintoretto, Georges de la Tour, Jean-Auguste Ingres, and Gustave Courbet. *10 rue Georges-Clemenceau. Admission: 10 frs., free Sun. Open Wed.–Mon. 10–noon and 1–5:15.*

The cobbled streets around the castle and cathedral make up the town's medieval sector. Across cours des 50-Otages, a broad boulevard, is the 19th-century city. From place Royale stroll and window-shop down busy rue Crébillon. Halfway
4 down on the left is the **Passage Pommeraye,** an elegant shopping gallery erected in 1843. At the far end of rue Crébillon is place
5 Graslin and its 1783 **Grand Théâtre.**

Just along rue Voltaire from place Graslin is the 15th-century
6 **Manoir de la Touche,** once home to the bishops of Nantes. Its
7 medieval silhouette is offset by the mock-Romanesque **Palais Dobrée,** next door, built by arts connoisseur Thomas Dobrée during the last century. Among the treasures within are miniatures, tapestries, medieval manuscripts, and enamels, and one room is devoted to the Revolutionary Wars in Vendée. *Pl. Jean V. Admission: 10 frs., free Sun. Open Wed.–Mon. 10–noon and 2–5; closed Tues.*

Lodging
Under 350 frs.

Astoria. A conveniently central and unpretentious hotel in a quiet street near both the train station and the castle, the Astoria has prices that are as comfortable as its modern-looking rooms. There's no restaurant. *11 rue Richebourg, 44000, tel. 40–74–39–90. 45 rooms with bath or shower. MC, V. Closed Aug.*

Dining
Under 200 frs.
★

Colvert. This small, modern bistro serves interesting dishes based on seafood or game, according to season. Chef Didier Macoin is an expert at original sauces (lentils and honey to accompany roast pigeon), and the charming waitresses are delighted to explain the intricate differences among the five prix-fixe menus. The inexpensive lunchtime menu, including aperitif, is an excellent value. *14 rue Armand-Brossard, tel. 40–48–20–02. Reservations advised. MC, V. Closed Sat. lunch, Sun., and Sept.*

Mon Rêve. Fine food and a delectable parkland setting are offered at this cozy little restaurant about 8 kilometers (5 miles) east of town. Chef Gérard Ryngel concocts elegantly inventive regional fare (the duck or rabbit in muscadet are good choices), while his wife, Cécile, presides over the dining room with aplomb. Allow $40 for your round-trip cab fare. *Rte. des Bords de Loire, Basse-Goulaine, tel. 40–03–55–50. Reservations advised. AE, DC, MC, V. Closed 2 weeks in Feb., and Wed. Oct.–Mar.*

Under 125 frs.

La Cigale. Miniature palm trees, gleaming woodwork, colorful enamel tiles, and painted ceilings are why this café is officially recognized as a *monument historique.* You can savor its Belle Epoque ambience without spending a fortune: The 69- and 120-franc menus are just right for a quick lunch, although the banks of fresh oysters and the well-stacked dessert cart may tempt you to go for a leisurely meal à la carte. *4 pl. Graslin, tel. 40–69–76–41. Reservations suggested. V.*

Shopping

The commercial quarter stretches from place Royale to place Graslin. For antiques, try **Cibot** (7 rue Voltaire). Don't miss chocolate specialist **Georges Gautier** (9 rue de la Fosse), with his *Muscadets Nantais*—grapes dipped in brandy and covered in chocolate.

La Baule

Trains make the 1-hour trip from Nantes every couple of hours. La Baule tourist office: 9 pl. de la Victoire, tel. 40–24–34–44.

La Baule is one of the most fashionable resorts in France. Like Le Touquet and Dinard, it is a 19th-century creation, founded in 1879 to make the most of the excellent sandy beaches that extend for some 10 kilometers (about 6 miles) around the broad, sheltered bay between Pornichet and Le Pouliguen. A pine forest, planted in 1840, keeps the shifting sand dunes firmly at bay.

An air of old-fashioned chic still pervades La Baule's palatial hotels, villas, and gardens, but there's nothing old-fashioned about the prices: Hotels and restaurants should be chosen with care. Nightclubbers will be in their element here, and the resort's summer season buzzes with prestigious events, such as horse shows and classic car contests. The elegant promenade, overlooking the huge beach, is lined with luxury hotels and features a casino.

Lodging
Under 350 frs.

Concorde. This establishment numbers among the least expensive good hotels in pricey La Baule. It's calm, comfortable, recently modernized, and close to the beach (ask for a room with a sea view). There's no restaurant. *1 av. de la Concorde, 44500, tel. 40–60–23–09. 47 rooms with bath or shower. Closed Oct.–Easter.*

Dining
Under 125 frs.

La Pergola. The inventive finesse of its haute cuisine and the warmth of its welcome have given La Pergola a substantial reputation. The restaurant is conveniently situated in the center of La Baule, next to the casino and a stone's throw from the beach. Meat and fish are prepared with aplomb in a variety of subtle sauces. Ordering à la carte is expensive, so stick with the moderately priced set menu. *147 av. des Lilas, tel. 40–24–57–61. Reservations advised. Jacket required. MC, V. Closed for lunch Mon., Wed., and Fri.*

6 Normandy

Rouen, Mont-St-Michel

Mont-St-Michel, an offshore outcrop crowned by a giant and daring medieval abbey, is the most visited site in France outside Paris. But that isn't the only reason to visit Normandy. Its countryside charms, from the wild, granite cliffs in the west to the long sandy beaches along the Channel coast, from the wooded valleys of the south to the lush green meadows and apple orchards in the center, make it well worth exploring.

It was from Normandy that William the Conqueror set sail for Hastings in 1066, going down in history as Britain's last invader. The Bayeux Tapestry weaves a timeless tale. In Rouen in 1431, Joan of Arc was burned at the stake, marking a turning point in the Hundred Years' War, the last major medieval conflict between the French and the English. And it was in Normandy that Allied forces landed in 1944; memories still linger for pilgrims flocking to the desolate D-day sands. You can also visit Rouen, where Claude Monet spent days painting the mighty cathedral, and the spectacular cliffs at Etretat that he so admired; other Impressionists captured images of the intimate harbor at Honfleur, as pretty as ever. Normandy is also one of the country's finest gastronomic regions, producing excellent cheeses such as Camembert, and Calvados, a powerful apple brandy.

Etretat, Cabourg, the D-day beaches, and Mont-St-Michel require bus journeys to complement the erratic regional train service. We doubt you'll mind the extra hassle.

Essential Information

Lodging There are accommodations to suit every taste in Normandy. In the beach resorts, the season is very short, July and August only, but weekends are busy for much of the year; in June and September, accommodations are usually available at short notice. If you're staying on the coast, beware of Deauville and Cabourg, two swanky, outrageously expensive resorts.

Dining Normandy is the land of butter, cream, cheese, and Calvados. Many dishes are cooked with rich sauces; the description *à la normande* usually means "with a cream sauce." The richness of the milk makes for excellent cheese: *Pont-l'Évêque* (known since the 13th century) is made in the Pays d'Auge with milk that is still warm and creamy, and *Livarot* (also produced for centuries) uses milk that has stood for a while; don't be put off by its strong smell. Then there are the excellent *Pavé d'Auge* and the best known of them all, *Camembert,* a relative newcomer, invented by a farmer's wife in the late-18th century. There are many local specialties. Rouen is famous for its *canard à la Rouennaise* (duck in blood sauce); Caen for its *tripes à la mode de Caen* (tripe cooked with carrots in a seasoned cider stock); and Mont-St-Michel for *omelette Mère Poulard* (hearty omelet made by a local hotel manager in the late-19th century for travelers to Mont-St-Michel). Then there are *sole dieppoise* (sole poached in a sauce with cream and mussels), excellent chicken from the Vallée d'Auge, and lamb from the salt marshes. Those who like *boudin noir* (blood sausage) have come to the right region, and for seafood lovers, the coast provides oysters, lobster, and shrimp. Normandy is not a wine-growing area but produces excellent cider. The best comes from the Vallée d'Auge and is 100% apple juice; when poured into the glass, it should fizz a bit but not froth.

Shopping Handmade lace is a great rarity, and admirers will certainly think it's worth spending some time searching it out. Prices are high, but then, this kind of labor-intensive, high-quality creation never comes cheap. In Bayeux, try the **Conservatoire de la Dentelle de Bayeux,** Hotel de Doyen, on rue Leforestier, near the cathedral.

Normandy is a food lover's region, and some of the best buying is to be done in food markets and charcuteries. Calvados is hard to find outside France, and although it's generally available in wine shops around the country, you'll find a wider choice of good-quality Calvados in Normandy itself.

Bicycling Roads along the coast and inland along the Seine valley and through the Suisse Normande area around Caen make for pleasant pedaling. Bicycles are available for rent from train stations in Bayeux, Caen, Dieppe, and Le Tréport for about 50 francs per day. Or try **Family Home** in Bayeux (39 rue du Gal-de-Dais, tel. 31–92–15–22).

Hiking There are 10 long-distance, signposted itineraries and countless well-indicated footpaths for shorter walks; overnight hostels are found at many points. Contact the **Comité Départemental de la Randonnée Pedestre de Seine-Maritime** (B.P. 680, 76008 Rouen).

Beaches Wherever you go on the Normandy coast, you'll look at the chilly waters of the English Channel: Those used to warmer climes may need all their resolve to take the plunge, even on hot, sunny days. The most fashionable Norman resorts lie along the Floral Coast, the eastern end of the Calvados Coast between Deauville/Trouville and Cabourg; it's virtually one long, sandy beach, with the different towns overlapping. The rest of the Calvados Coast is also a succession of seaside resorts, though the beaches that saw the Normandy landings have not been so developed as those farther east. While the resort towns of the western Calvados Coast don't lack for charm, they don't have the character of Honfleur or the unspoiled and rugged beauty of the pebbly Alabaster Coast, stretching from Le Havre to beyond Dieppe. The resorts here are more widely spaced, separated by craggy cliffs, and even in the summer months, beaches are relatively uncrowded.

The Arts Normandy's cultural activities revolve around music, both classical and modern. Many churches host evening concerts, with organ recitals drawing an especially large number of enthusiasts. Jazz aficionados will be interested in the **European Traditional Jazz Festival** held in mid-June at Luneray, 8 kilometers (5 miles) southwest of Dieppe. One of the biggest cultural events on the Norman calendar is the **American Film Festival,** held in Deauville during the first week of September.

Festivals A **Joan of Arc Commemoration** takes place in Rouen at the end of May, featuring a variety of parades, street plays, concerts, and exhibitions that recall the life—and death—of France's patron saint.

Highlights for First-time Visitors

Abbaye aux Hommes, Caen, Tour 2
Bayeux Tapestry, Tour 2
Cathédrale Notre-Dame and Old Town, Rouen, Tour 1
D-day landing beaches, Tour 2
Deauville/Trouville, Tour 2
Honfleur, Tour 2
Musée des Beaux-Arts, Le Havre, Tour 1
Mont-St-Michel, Tour 2

Tour 1: Rouen and Upper Normandy

Rouen forms the hub of this tour and is an ideal base for exploring Upper Normandy: by bus toward Le Havre, or by train toward the pretty harbor towns of Dieppe and Fécamp. Traveling along the coast—notably to Etretat—is possible only by bus.

From Paris
By Train Express trains to Rouen leave Paris (Gare St-Lazare) hourly. The trip takes 70–90 minutes.

By Car The 135-kilometer (85-mile) drive from Paris along A13 takes 1½ hours.

Rouen

Tourist office: 25 pl. de la Cathédrale, opposite the cathedral front, tel. 35–71–41–77.

Normandy

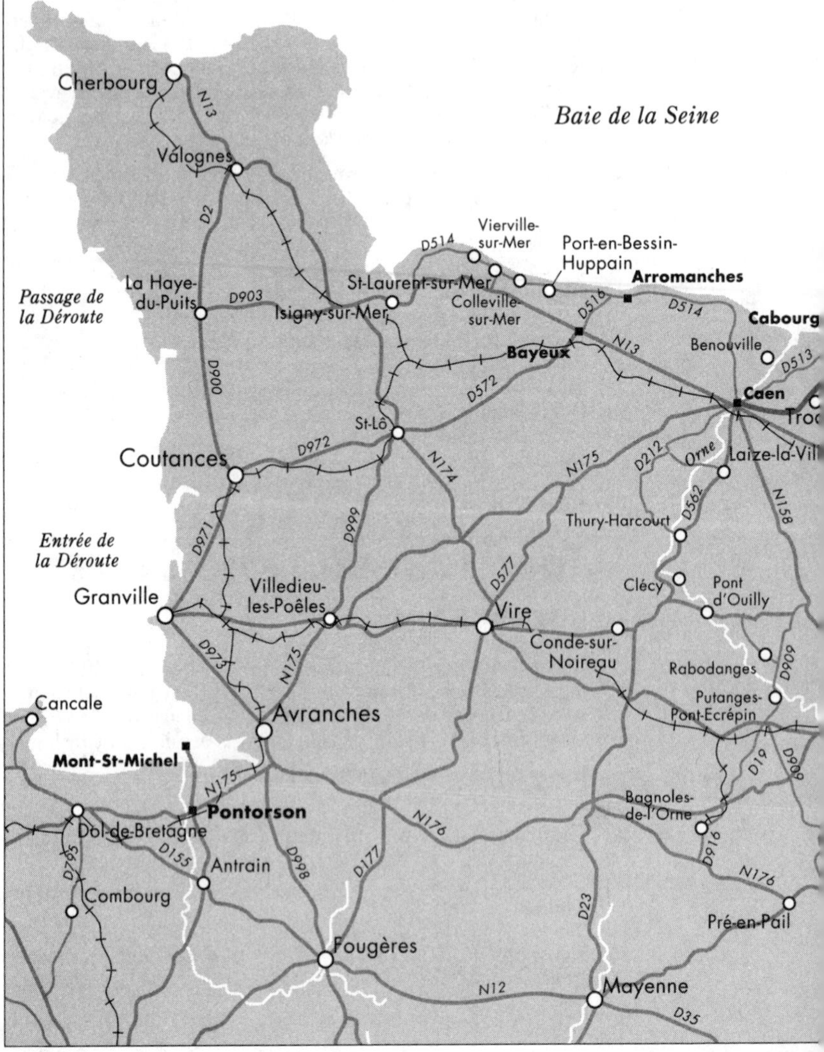

Cherbourg
N13
Baie de la Seine
Valognes
D2
D514
Vierville-sur-Mer
Port-en-Bessin-Huppain
Arromanches
La Haye-du-Puits
Passage de la Déroute
D903
St-Laurent-sur-Mer
Isigny-sur-Mer
Colleville-sur-Mer
D516
D514
Cabourg
Benouville
D513
N13
Bayeux
D900
D572
Caen
St-Lô
D972
Coutances
N174
N175
D212
Orne
Laize-la-Vil
Thury-Harcourt
D562
N158
Entrée de la Déroute
D971
D999
D577
Villedieu-les-Poêles
Clécy
Pont d'Ouilly
Granville
Vire
Conde-sur-Noireau
D973
N175
Rabodanges
D909
Putanges-Pont-Ecrépin
Cancale
Avranches
Mont-St-Michel
D19
D909
N175
Pontorson
Bagnoles-de-l'Orne
Dol-de-Bretagne
N176
D795
D155
Antrain
D998
D177
D916
N176
Combourg
D23
Pré-en-Pail
Fougères
N12
Mayenne
D35

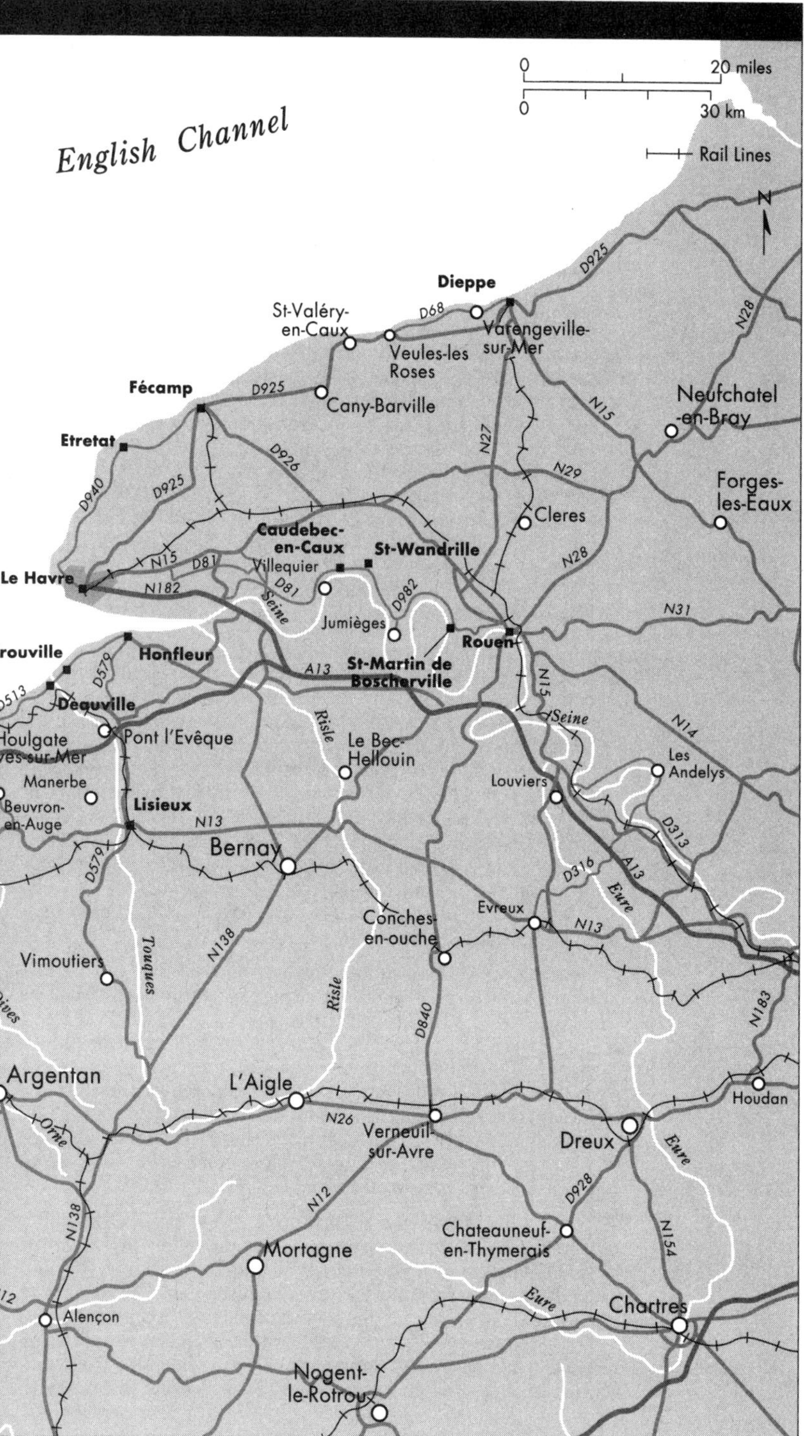

English Channel
0
20 miles
0
30 km
Rail Lines
N
Dieppe
St-Valéry-en-Caux
Veules-les Roses
Varengeville-sur-Mer
Fécamp
Cany-Barville
Etretat
Neufchatel-en-Bray
Forges-les-Eaux
Cleres
Caudebec-en-Caux
St-Wandrille
Villequier
Le Havre
Jumièges
Rouen
Trouville
Honfleur
St-Martin de Boscherville
Deauville
Houlgate
Pont l'Evêque
Le Bec-Hellouin
Les Andelys
Louviers
Manerbe
Beuvron-en-Auge
Lisieux
Bernay
Evreux
Conches-en-ouche
Vimoutiers
Argentan
L'Aigle
Houdan
Verneuil-sur-Avre
Dreux
Chateauneuf-en-Thymerais
Mortagne
Chartres
Alençon
Nogent-le-Rotrou
Seine
Risle
Eure
Touques
Dives
Orne
D925
D68
N28
N15
N27
N29
D926
D940
N182
D81
D982
N31
A13
D579
D513
N14
N13
D313
D316
N138
D840
N183
N26
N12
D928
N154

Numbers in the margin correspond to points of interest on the Rouen map.

The city of **Rouen** is a blend of ancient and modern, a large part having been destroyed during World War II. Even before its massive postwar reconstruction, the city had expanded outward during the 20th century with the development of industries spawned by its increasingly busy port, now the fifth largest in France. In its more distant past, Rouen gained celebrity when Joan of Arc was burned at the stake here in 1431. Now it is known as the City of a Hundred Spires, and many of its important edifices are churches.

Head down rue Jeanne d'Arc from the station and turn left after 700 yards onto rue du Gros-Horloge, which leads directly to
1 the magnificent **Cathédrale Notre-Dame.** Dominating the place du Cathédrale, it is one of the masterpieces of French Gothic architecture, immediately recognizable to anyone familiar with the works of Impressionist Claude Monet, who rendered its west facade in an increasingly misty, yet always beautiful, series, "Cathédrales de Rouen." The original 12th-century construction was replaced after a terrible fire in 1200; only the left-hand spire, the Tour St-Romain, survived the flames. The imposing 250-foot tower on the right, known as the "Butter Tower," was added in the 15th and 16th centuries and completed in the 17th, when a group of wealthy citizens donated large sums of money—for the privilege of eating butter during Lent.

Interior highlights include the 13th-century choir, with its pointed arcades; vibrant stained glass depicting the crucified Christ (restored after heavy damage during World War II); and massive stone columns topped by some intriguing carved faces. The first flight of the famous Escalier de la Librairie (Booksellers' Staircase) rises up from a tiny balcony just to the left of the transept and is attributed to Guillaume Pontifs, who is also responsible for most of the 15th-century work seen in the cathedral. *Pl. de la Cathédrale. Open mid-Mar.–Oct., daily 7:30–noon and 2–7 (Sun. 7:30–6); Nov.–Dec. 14 and Jan. 16–mid-Mar., Wed. and weekends 10–12:30 and 2–4:30. Closed mid-Dec.–mid-Jan.*

Leaving the cathedral, head right, and cross rue de la République to place St-Maclou, an attractive square surrounded by picturesque half-timbered houses with steeply pointed roofs.
2 The square's **Eglise St-Maclou** bears testimony to the wild excesses of Flamboyant architecture; take time to examine the central and left-hand portals under the porchway on the main facade, covered with little bronze lion heads and pagan engravings. Inside, note the 16th-century organ, with its Renaissance wood carving, and the fine marble columns. *Pl. St-Maclou. Opening times same as Cathédrale Notre-Dame, above.*

3 To the right is the **Aître St-Maclou** (184–186 rue Martainville), a former ossuary that is one of the last reminders of the plague that devastated Europe during the Middle Ages; these days, it holds Rouen's School of Art and Architecture. The ossuary (a charnel house used for the bodies of plague victims) is said to have inspired the French composer Camille Saint-Saëns (1835–1921) when he was working on his *Danse Macabre.* The building's massive double frieze is especially riveting, carved with

Aître St-Maclou, **3**
Cathédrale Notre-Dame, **1**
Eglise Jeanne d'Arc, **8**
Eglise St-Maclou, **2**
Eglise St-Ouen, **4**
Gros-Horloge, **9**
Musée de Ferronerie Le Secq des Tournelles, **7**
Musée de la Céramique, **6**
Musée des Beaux-Arts, **5**

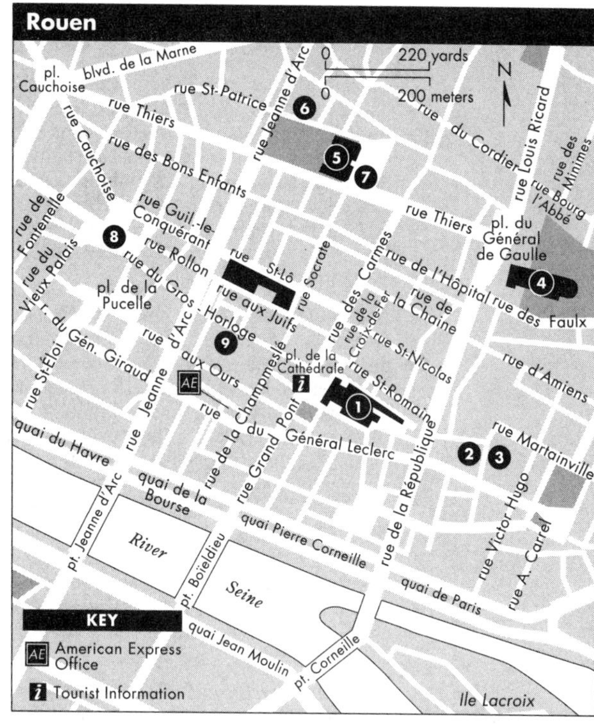

some graphic skulls, bones, and grave diggers' tools. *Open daily 9:30–8.*

Turn right up rue de la République to place du Général-de-
4 Gaulle, site of the **Eglise St-Ouen,** a fine example of later Gothic architecture. The stained-glass windows, dating from the 14th to the 16th century, are the most spectacular features of the otherwise spare structure. The church's 19th-century pipe organs have few equals in France. *Pl. du Général-de-Gaulle. Open mid-Jan.–mid-Mar. and Nov.–mid-Dec., Wed., Sat., and Sun. 10–12:30 and 2–4:30; mid-Mar.–Oct., Wed.–Mon. 10–12:30 and 2–6. Closed mid-Dec.–mid-Jan.*

Walk west on rue Thiers to get to a cluster of Rouen's fine mu-
5 seums, the most important of which is the **Musée des Beaux-Arts** (Fine Arts Museum), on square Vedral. It contains a fine collection of French paintings from the 17th and 19th centuries, including works by Claude Monet, Alfred Sisley, and Auguste Renoir. An entire room is devoted to Rouen-born Théodore Gericault, and there are impressive works by Delacroix and Chassériau. The museum once showcased a superb collection of Norman ceramics, but these are now housed
6 separately in the **Musée de la Céramique** (Ceramic Museum), a
7 few steps down the road. The **Musée de Ferronerie Le Secq des Tournelles** is located right behind the Musée des Beaux-Arts. This museum claims to possess the world's finest collection of wrought iron, with exhibits spanning the 3rd through the 19th century. Displays include a range of items used in daily life, accessories, and professional instruments used by surgeons, barbers, carpenters, clockmakers, and gardeners. *Admission: 11*

frs. for each of 3 museums. All 3 museums are open Thurs.–Mon. 10–noon and 2–6, Wed. 2–6; closed Tues.

Continue down rue Thiers, then turn left onto rue Jeanne-
d'Arc and head toward place du Vieux-Marché, dominated by
8 the thoroughly modern **Eglise Jeanne d'Arc.** Dedicated to the
saint, the church was built on the spot where she was burned to
death in 1431. Not all is spanking new, however; the church is
graced with some remarkable 16th-century glass windows tak-
en from the former Eglise St-Vincent, destroyed in 1944. *Pl. du
Vieux-Marché. Open Sat.–Thurs. 10–12:15 and 2–6, Fri. 2–6;
closed during services.*

Leading out of place du Vieux-Marché is Rouen's most popular
attraction, the rue du Gros-Horloge. The name of this little pe-
9 destrian street comes from the **Gros-Horloge** itself, a giant
Renaissance clock; in 1527, the Rouennais had a splendid arch
built especially for it, and today its golden face looks out over
the street (the ticket to the Musée des Beaux-Arts includes admission to the ornate belfry). Though the ancient thoroughfare
is crammed with boutiques and fast-food joints, a few old
houses, dating from the 16th century, remain. Wander through
the surrounding old town, a warren of tiny streets lined with
over 700 half-timbered houses. Instead of standing simply as
monuments to the past, these cobbled streets have been successfully transformed into a lively pedestrian shopping precinct, and the old buildings now contain the most fashionable
shops in the city.

Lodging
Under 250 frs.

Québec. There are no frills here. But this straightforward hotel is both inexpensive and central, just five minutes from the cathedral as you head toward the Seine. Rooms are small. *18 rue de Québec, 76000, tel. 35–70–09–38. 38 rooms, some with bath or shower. AE, MC, V. Closed Christmas and New Year's.*

Dining
Under 125 frs.

Les Maraîchers. Also called Bistrot d'Adrian, this simple bistro offers such dependable classics as fish soup and tête de veau. Daily set menus at 87 francs and 135 francs are available. *37 pl. du Vieux-Marché, tel. 35–71–57–73. Reservations advised. Dress: casual. AE, DC, MC, V.*

Under 75 frs.

La Petite Auberge. This homey inn tucked away on a quiet street serves up typical bistro fare—steamed mussels, chunky pâtés—in generous portions. The crowd is local, the service friendly. There are set menus at 69 francs, 96 francs, 129 francs, and 180 francs. *164 rue Martainville, tel. 35–70–80–18. Reservations advised on weekends. Dress: casual. MC, V. Closed Mon. evening.*

Under 75 frs.

Vieux Logis. This tiny restaurant near the Hôtel de Ville, elegantly fitted out with 18th-century-style furnishings, is the pride and joy of jolly Joseph Guillou. He treats visitors to a 65-franc menu that includes wine and coffee and goes down as the best dining value in Rouen. *5 rue Joyeuse, tel. 35–71–55–30. Reservations essential. No credit cards.*

St-Wandrille

Buses leave Rouen hourly for Le Havre, stopping at St-Martin, St-Wandrille, and Caudebec. The river is just a short walk from the bus stops. The journey time from Rouen to St-Wandrille is about 45 minutes.

The Seine valley between Rouen and Le Havre is full of interesting sights, old and new, dotted amid some lovely scenery.

Within 10 minutes of Rouen is the 11th-century abbey church of St-George in **St-Martin de Boscherville**. About 16 kilometers (10 miles) farther along the right bank of the Seine, in **St-Wandrille,** is another Benedictine abbey. The **Abbaye de St-Wandrille** survives as an active monastery to this day; it was founded in the 7th century, sacked (by the Normans), and rebuilt in the 10th century. You can still hear the monks sing their Gregorian chants at morning Mass if you're here early in the day (9:25 weekdays and 10 Sunday and holidays). *Guided tours at 3 and 4 weekdays and at 11:30 AM Sun. and holidays; cost: 15 frs. adults.*

From St-Wandrille, it's only a couple of miles to the charming little village of **Caudebec-en-Caux**; if the day is sunny, you should be sure to take a stroll along the banks of the Seine. The village's 15th-century Eglise Notre-Dame was described by French monarch Henri IV (1589–1610) as "the most beautiful chapel in the kingdom."

Le Havre

Trains leave Rouen 16 times daily for Le Havre, 55 minutes away. The journey takes 3 hours by bus. Le Havre tourist office: 1 pl. de l'Hotel-de-Ville, tel. 35–21–22–88.

Le Havre is a bustling modern town, France's second-largest port (after Marseille). Largely rebuilt after 1945, it was bombarded no fewer than 146 times during World War II, and reinforced concrete and bleak open spaces have not done much for the town's atmosphere. The old seafaring quarter of Sainte-Adresse is worth a visit, however. From its fortress, you have panoramic views of the port and the Seine estuary.

At the opposite end of the seafront, at the tip of boulevard François-Ier, sits the metal-and-glass **Musée des Beaux-Arts.** On the ground floor there's a remarkable collection of Raoul Dufy's work, including oils, watercolors, and sketches. Dufy (1877–1953) was born in Le Havre and devoted a lot of time to his native region: views of Norman beaches and of Le Havre itself. If you can't spend much time in Normandy, go upstairs to have a look at works by one of the forerunners of Impressionism—Eugène Boudin. Boudin's compelling beach scenes and Norman countrysides will give you a taste of what you're missing. *Blvd. Clemenceau. Admission free. Open Wed.–Mon. 10–noon and 2–6; closed Tues.*

Lodging
Under 250 frs.

Astoria. Local charm isn't a characteristic of Le Havre lodging establishments, and this hotel just opposite the train station is no exception. But if you want a practical, friendly, well-equipped stopping place, try it. Quiet and popular with traveling salesmen, it offers half-pension terms at 175-275 francs per head. *13 cours de la République, 76600, tel. 35–25–00–03. 37 rooms with bath or shower. AE, DC, MC, V.*

Fécamp

Trains run 9 times daily from Rouen (journey time 65 minutes, with a change at Bréauté-Beuzeville). Tourist office: Place Bellet, tel. 35–28–20–51.

Fécamp, an ancient fishing port, was Normandy's primary place of pilgrimage before Mont-St-Michel stole all the glory. Fécamp no longer has a commercial fishing fleet, but you will still see lots of boats in the private yachting marina. The magnificent **Eglise de La Trinité** (just off boulevard de la République) bears witness to the town's religious past. The Benedictine abbey was founded by the Duke of Normandy in the 11th century and became the home of the monastic order of the Précieux Sang et de la Trinité (referring to Christ's blood, which supposedly arrived here in the 7th century). Fécamp is also the home of the liqueur Benedictine. The **Musée de la Bénédictine,** seven blocks across town on rue Boufart, was rebuilt in 1892 in a florid mixture of neo-Gothic and Renaissance styles and remains one of Normandy's most popular attractions. *110 rue Alexandre-le-Grand. Admission: 24 frs. adults, 12 frs. children 10–17 (including a tasting). Open Easter–mid-Nov., daily 9:30–noon and 2–5:30; mid-Nov.–Easter, 2 guided tours daily at 10:30 and 3:30.*

Dining
Under 125 frs.
★

L'Escalier. This delightfully simple little restaurant overlooks the harbor and serves traditional Norman cuisine. The several inexpensive fixed-price menus (80 francs, 130 francs, and 160 francs) offer mainly fish and seafood. *101 quai Bérigny, tel. 35–28–26–79. Reservations essential in summer. AE, MC, V. Closed Oct.*

Etretat

Eight buses run daily from Fécamp to Etretat. Tourist office: Place de la Mairie, tel. 35–27–05–21.

The coast between Le Havre and Dieppe is known as the Alabaster Coast, and its most attractive resort is **Etretat.** The town's soaring white cliffs, an inspiration to Monet and many other painters, are almost as famous in France as Dover's are in England. Although the promenade running the length of Etretat's pebble beach has been spoiled by a proliferation of seedy cafés and french-fry stands, the town retains its vivacity and charm. Its landmarks are two arched cliff formations, the **Falaise d'Amont** and the **Falaise d'Aval,** which jut out over the sea on either side of the bay, and a 300-foot needle of rock, the **Aiguille,** which thrusts up from the sea near the Falaise d'Amont. Through the huge archways carved by the sea into the cliffs, you can walk to neighboring beaches at low tide. For a breathtaking view of the whole bay, take the path up to the Falaise d'Aval on the southern side, from which you can hike for miles across the Manneporte hills.

Lodging
Splurge

Dormy House. Thanks to its location halfway up the southern cliff, Dormy House provides dramatic views of the bay. Four buildings, dating from different periods and in a variety of architectural styles, make up the hotel. The large rooms are furnished in oak and sport cheerful floral drapes. Most guests stay on half-board (this plan includes breakfast plus lunch or dinner); the restaurant specializes in fish and seafood. *Rte. du Havre, 76790, tel. 35–27–07–88. 51 rooms. Facilities: restaurant. AE, DC, MC, V. Closed weekdays mid-Nov.–mid-Mar. 350 frs.–560 frs.; 335 frs.–445 frs. per person for half-board.*

Dining
Under 125 frs.

Les Roches Blanches. Expect a warm welcome at this cozily unpretentious family-run restaurant near the sea, which has three good-value menus. The house specialty is veal escalope with mushrooms, flambéed in Calvados, and there is a good range of fish and seafood dishes. *Rue Abbé-Cochet, tel. 35-27-07-34. Reservations advised, especially for Sun. lunch. MC, V. Closed Tues., Wed., and Thurs. (Wed. only July–early Sept.) and Jan. and Oct.*

Dieppe

Eleven trains make the daily trip into Rouen, 50–65 minutes away. Tourist office: Pont Jehan Ango, tel. 35-84-11-77.

Dieppe is a charming blend of a fishing and commercial port and a Norman seaside town. The boulevard du Maréchal-Foch, a seafront promenade, separates an immense lawn from an unspoiled pebble beach where, in 1942, many Canadian soldiers were killed during the so-called Jubilee raid. Overlooking the Channel, at the western end of the bay, stands the 15th-century **Château de Dieppe,** which dominates the town from its clifftop position. It contains the town museum, well known for its collection of ivories. In the 17th century, Dieppe imported vast quantities of elephant tusks from Africa and Asia, and as many as 350 craftsmen settled here to work the ivory; their efforts can be seen in the form of ship models, nautical accessories, or, upstairs, in religious and day-to-day objects. The museum also has a room devoted to sketches by Georges Braque. *Rue de Chaste. Admission: 10 frs. adults, 7 frs. students and children. Open June–Sept., daily 10–noon and 2–6; Oct.–June, Wed.–Mon. 10–noon and 2–5.*

Lodging and Dining
Under 350 frs.

La Présidence. The modern Présidence overlooks the sea and offers airy, well-appointed guest rooms and an "English" bar, Le Verrazane. In the delightful fourth-floor restaurant, Le Panoramic, the cooking is classic, unpretentious, and tasty. *1 blvd. de Verdun, 76200, tel. 35-84-31-31. 88 rooms, 79 with bath. Facilities: restaurant. AE, DC, MC, V.*

Tour 2: Caen and Lower Normandy

This tour uses the historic city of Caen as a base, heading east along the coast by bus (since there are no trains) to Deauville and Honfleur, and west to Mont-St-Michel via Bayeux, home to the famous tapestry and a launching pad for bus excursions to the D-day landing beaches.

From Paris
By Train

Express trains to Caen leave Paris (Gare St-Lazare) every 1½ hours. The trip takes 2 to 2½ hours.

By Car

The 240 kilometer (150-mile) drive from Paris along A13 takes 2½ hours.

Caen

Tourist office: Place St-Pierre, opposite St-Pierre church, tel. 31-86-27-65.

William of Normandy ruled from **Caen,** the capital of lower Normandy, in the 11th century before he conquered England. Nine hundred years later, the two-month Battle of Caen devastated the town in 1944. Much of the city burned in a fire that raged for 11 days, and the downtown area was almost entirely rebuilt after the war.

Turn right out of the station and take rue de la Gare across the River Orne. This long, straight street becomes avenue du Maréchal Juin and leads down to the castle. Turn left here and continue half a mile to the town's main tourist attraction, the **Abbaye aux Hommes,** a monastery built by William the Conqueror. "The Men's Abbey" was begun in Romanesque style in 1066 and was added to during the 18th century. Note the magnificent facade of the Eglise St-Etienne, whose spareness is enhanced by two 11th-century towers topped by octagonal spires. Inside, what had been William the Conqueror's tomb was destroyed by 16th-century Huguenots during the Wars of Religion, but the choir still stands; it was the first to be built in Norman Gothic style, and many subsequent choirs were modeled after it. *Pl. Louis-Guillouard. Guided tours of the abbey cost 10 frs. and begin daily at 9:30, 11, 2:30, and 4 and last 1–1 ½ hours.*

Head right up Fosses St-Julien to the Esplanade du Château. The ruins of William the Conqueror's **fortress,** built in 1060 and sensitively restored after the war, glower down on all who approach. The castle gardens are a perfect spot for strolling, and the ramparts afford good views of the city. Within the rampart walls lies the **Musée des Beaux-Arts,** a fine-arts museum whose impressive collection includes Rembrandts and Titians; it is closed for renovations and is not scheduled to reopen until 1994. Also within the castle are the **Musée de Normandie,** displaying regional arts, and the chapel of St-George. *Entrance by the Enceinte du Château. Admission to each: 6 frs. Open Wed.–Mon. 10–1 and 2–5; closed Tues.*

Take rue des Chanoines right to the **Abbaye aux Dames,** the "Ladies' Abbey," built by William the Conqueror's wife, Matilda, in 1062. Its Eglise de la Trinité, a squat church, is a good example of 11th-century Romanesque architecture, though its original spires were replaced by bulky balustrades in the early 18th century. The 11th-century crypt once held Matilda's tomb, which was destroyed during the French Revolution. Note the intricate carvings on columns and arches in the chapel. *Pl. Reine-Mathilde. Admission free. Guided tours daily at 2:30 and 4.*

Head back down rue des Chanoines and continue on rue Montoir-Poissonnerie. Turning left onto place St-Pierre, you'll come face-to-face with the Caen Tourist Office. It merits a visit not only for its excellent information resources but also for its splendid site in the **Hôtel d'Escoville,** a 16th-century mansion built by a wealthy town merchant, Nicolas le Valois d'Escoville. The building was badly damaged during the war but has since been restored; the rather austere facade conceals an elaborate inner courtyard, reflecting the Italian influence on early Renaissance Norman architecture.

A good introduction to the Normandy landings of 1944 can be had at the **Mémorial,** a museum opened in the north of the city in 1988. Videos, photos, arms, paintings, and prints detail the Battle of Normandy and the French Liberation. *Esplanade Général-Eisenhower. Admission: 45 frs. Open Jan. 15–Dec. 31, daily 9–7 (ask about evening hours in summer).*

Lodging and Dining
Under 350 frs.

Le Relais des Gourmets. One of the best hotels in town also has a terrific restaurant. The luxurious modern guest rooms are spacious and airy, and an Old World atmosphere reigns in the public rooms, which are dotted with some charming antiques. The plush restaurant offers a sophisticated level of service and classic local cuisine. The gratinéed lobster with crayfish and turbot with *cèpe* mushrooms are memorable. Meals are served in the garden during summer months. *15 rue de Geôle, 14300, tel. 31–86–06–01. 32 rooms with bath. Facilities: restaurant (closed Sun. dinner), garden. AE, DC, MC, V.*

★ **Le Dauphin.** Despite its downtown location, Le Dauphin offers peace and quiet. The building is a former priory dating from the 12th century, though the smallish guest rooms are briskly modern. Those overlooking the street are soundproofed, and the rooms in back have views of the serene garden courtyard. The wood-beam breakfast room is a delightful place to start the day. The service is especially friendly and efficient, both in the hotel and in the excellent, though rather expensive, restaurant that specializes in traditional Norman cooking (but can be notably inventive). Fish is featured on the menu, though the veal sweetbreads in a mushroom sauce is a good choice as well. The copious 165-franc set menu is an especially good value (there are also set menus at 95, 220 and 320 francs). *29 rue Gémare, 14000, tel. 31–86–22–26. 22 rooms with bath. Facilities: restaurant (closed Sat.), garden. AE, DC, MC, V. Closed mid-July–mid-Aug.*

Dining
Under 125 frs.

Paquebot. A young, trendy clientele enjoys the kitschy art deco interior of this establishment near the castle, not to mention its 90-franc weekday menu. If you spend a little more to eat à la carte, such delicacies as pigeon and foie gras in puff pastry and a tartare of oysters and scallops await—which is the operative word, since service tends to be unhurried. There are also menus at 100, 145, and 240 francs. *7 rue des Croisiers, tel. 31–85–10–10. AE, DC, MC, V. Closed Sat. lunch and Sun.*

Shopping

Caen has a morning **market** on Sunday in place Courtonne (where food and some clothing is sold) and a larger one on Friday in place St-Sauveur. It also hosts a bric-a-brac and antiques fair in June.

Cabourg

Buses run from Caen to Cabourg every 2 hours. Cabourg tourist office: Jardin du Casino, tel. 31–91–01–09.

Cabourg retains a certain frowsy 19th-century elegance. Its streets fan out from a central hub near the seafront where the casino and the Grand Hôtel are situated. The early 20th-century novelist Marcel Proust, author of *In Search of a Lost Time,* was a great admirer of the town's pleasant seaside atmosphere and spent much of his time here. One of the volumes in his epic paints a perfect picture of life in the resort, to which the town responded by naming its magnificent seafront promenade after him.

Lodging and Dining
Under 250 frs.

Auberge du Parc. Situated just opposite the public garden to which its name refers, the Parc hotel is small and unpretentious—which is saying something in swanky Cabourg. Its white walls and flower-decked facade offer a cheerful welcome at a price you'll find hard to beat here, and the bus from Caen stops close by. The 75-franc menu is a good bet. *31 av. du Gé* *néral-Leclerc, 14390, tel. 31–91–00–82. 10 rooms, some with shower. Facilities: restaurant (closed Tues. and Wed. [except July–Aug.]); hotel closed Oct.–Easter. MC, V.*

Deauville and Trouville

The Caen–Le Havre bus runs from Cabourg to Deauville every 2 hours. Two trains per day make the 25-minute run to Trouville-Deauville station from Cabourg-Dives (summer only). Deauville tourist office: Place de la Mairie, tel. 31–88–21–43.

The twin but contrasting resorts of **Deauville** and **Trouville** are separated only by the estuary of the River Touques. Although Trouville is now considered an overflow town for its more prestigious neighbor, it became one of France's first seaside resorts when Parisians began flocking here in the mid-19th century.

Deauville is a chic watering hole for the French bourgeoisie and would-be fashionable personalities from further afield, who are attracted by its racecourse, casino, marina and regattas, palaces and gardens, and, of course, its sandy beach. The **Promenade des Planches**—the boardwalk extending along the seafront and lined with deck chairs, bars, and striped cabanas—is the place for celebrity spotting. Nevertheless, it's Trouville that stands out for authenticity rather than glamour. It, too, has a casino and boardwalk as well as a bustling fishing port and a native population that makes it a livelier place out of season than Deauville. Both tend to be expensive, but it's possible to get by on a budget if you watch it.

Lodging
Under 350 frs.

Le Continental. One of Deauville's oldest buildings is home to this provincial seaside hotel. The owner, Madame Perrot, is brisk and efficient, as is the service. The guest rooms are small and somewhat Spartan—but this is Deauville, after all, and for the price you can't do much better. The Continental is handily placed between the port and the casino, but it doesn't have a restaurant. *1 rue Désiré-Le-Hoc, 14800, tel. 31–88–21–06. 48 rooms, most with bath. AE, DC, MC, V.*

Under 250 frs.

Carmen. This straightforward, unpretentious little hotel is just around the corner from the casino in Trouville. The rooms range from the plain and inexpensive to the comfortable and moderate. The restaurant offers good home cooking at value-for-the-money prices. *24 rue Carnot, 14360, tel. 31–88–35–43. 14 rooms, 12 with bath. Facilities: restaurant (closed Mon. dinner and Tues.). AE, DC, MC, V. Closed 1 week in Feb., 1 week in Apr., and 1 week in Oct.*

Dining
Under 125 frs.

Les Vapeurs. This friendly, animated brasserie with neon-lit '50s decor, one of the most popular places in Trouville, serves good, fresh food at any time, day or night, and both the famous and not-so-famous like to meet here after dark. *160 blvd. Fernand-Moureaux, tel. 31–88–51–24. Closed Tues. dinner and Wed. Reservations advised. DC, MC, V.*

Honfleur

The Caen–Le Havre bus runs from Deauville to Honfleur every 2 hours. Tourist office: 33 cours des Fossés, tel. 31–89–23–30.

Honfleur, a colorful port on the Seine estuary, epitomizes Normandy for many people. It was once an important departure point for maritime expeditions, and the first voyages to Canada in the 15th and 16th centuries embarked from here. Its 17th-century harbor is fronted on one side by two-story stone houses with low, sloping roofs and on the other by tall, narrow houses whose wooden facades are topped by slate roofs. The whole town is a museum piece, full of half-timbered houses and cobbled streets.

Honfleur was colonized by French and foreign painters in the 19th century, and the group later known as the Impressionists used to meet in the **Ferme St-Siméon,** now a luxurious hotel. Honfleur has also inspired artists of other hues: Charles Baudelaire, the 19th-century poet and champion of Romanticism, wrote his poem *L'Invitation au Voyage* here, and the French composer Erik Satie was born in Honfleur in 1866.

Today Honfleur is one of the most popular vacation spots in northern France. During the summer, its hotels rarely have vacancies and its cafés and restaurants are always packed. Soak up the seafaring atmosphere by strolling around the old harbor, and pay a visit to the **Eglise Ste-Catherine,** which dominates the harbor's northern corner (rue des Logettes). The wooden church was built by townspeople to show their gratitude for the departure of the English at the end of the Hundred Years' War (1453), when masons and architects were occupied with national reconstruction.

Lodging and Dining
Splurge

Le Cheval Blanc. Occupying a renovated, 15th-century building on the harborfront, this hotel has 33 guest rooms, many of them recently redecorated and all offering views of the port across the main road through town. The restaurant is under separate management, though it is also called the Cheval Blanc, and it serves homey food for a reasonable price. *2 quai des Passagers, 14600, tel. 31–89–13–49. 33 rooms, 14 with bath. MC, V. Closed Jan. 360 frs. and up.*

Under 350 frs.

Hostellerie Lechat. One of the best-known and -loved establishments in Honfleur stands in a pretty square just behind the harbor in a typical 18th-century Norman building. The spacious guest rooms have recently been renovated in pretty French-provincial decor that makes good use of cheerful prints and colors. Foreign guests are given a warm welcome, especially in The American bar. The rustic, beamed restaurant serves top-notch Norman cuisine; lobster features prominently on the menu. *3 pl. Ste-Catherine, 14600, tel. 31–89–23–85. 24 rooms with bath. Facilities: restaurant (closed Jan., Wed., and Thurs. lunch mid-Sept.–early June), bar. AE, DC, MC, V.*

Dining
Under 125 frs.

L'Ancrage. Massive seafood platters top the bill at this casual delight occupying a two-story 17th-century building overlooking the harbor. The cuisine is authentically Norman—simple but good. If you want a change from fish and seafood, try the succulent calf sweetbreads. *16 rue Montpensier, tel. 31–89–00–70. Reservations advised, especially in summer. MC, V. Closed Tues. dinner mid-Sept.–mid-June, Wed., and Jan.*

Lisieux

Trains leave Caen for Lisieux, 30 minutes away, at least every 2 hours. Lisieux tourist office: 11 rue d'Alençon, tel. 31–62–08–41.

Lisieux is the main market town of the prosperous Pays d'Auge, an agricultural region famous for cheeses named after such towns as Camembert, Pont l'Evêque, and Livarot. It is also a land of apple orchards from which the finest Calvados brandy comes. Lisieux emerged relatively unscathed from World War II, though it boasts few historical monuments beyond the **Cathédrale St-Pierre,** built in the 12th and 13th centuries. It is also famous for its patron saint, Ste-Thérèse, who was born and died in the last quarter of the 19th century, having spent the last 10 of her 25 years as a Carmelite nun. Thérèse was canonized in 1925, and in 1954 a basilica—one of the world's largest 20th-century churches—was dedicated to her; to get there from the cathedral, walk down avenue Victor-Hugo and branch left onto avenue Ste-Thérèse.

Dining
Under 125 frs.

France. Lisieux is better known for providing spiritual sustenance than gastronomic pleasure, but this old-fashioned restaurant in the town center, just two minutes' walk from the cathedral, offers a wide choice of good seafood, salads, and homemade pasta, and there are set menus at 78, 108, and 145 francs. *5 rue au Char, tel. 31–62–03–37. Reservations recommended. MC, V. Closed first week in June, 3 weeks in Jan., and Mon.*

Shopping

The **Distillerie du Père Jules** (rte. des Dives) offers first-rate Calvados.

Bayeux

Trains make the 15-minute journey from Caen to Bayeux every 2 hours at least. Tourist office: 1 rue des Cuisiniers, tel. 31–92–16–26.

Charming **Bayeux** was the first town to be liberated during the Battle of Normandy in 1944, but its long history stretches back many centuries before World War II.

We begin our tour at the **Musée de la Tapisserie,** located in an 18th-century building on rue de Nesmond and showcasing the world's most celebrated piece of needlework, the **Bayeux Tapestry.** The medieval work of art—stitched in 1067—is really a 225-foot-long embroidered scroll, which depicts, in 58 separate scenes, the epic story of William of Normandy's conquest of England in 1066, a watershed in European history. The tapestry's origins remain obscure, though it was probably commissioned from Saxon embroiderers by the count of Kent—also the bishop of Bayeux—to be displayed in his newly built cathedral. Despite its age, the tapestry is in remarkably good condition; the extremely detailed scenes provide an unequaled record of the clothes, weapons, ships, and lifestyles of the day. *Centre Guillaume le Conquerant, rue de Nesmond. Admission: 25 frs. adults, 12 frs. students and children (5 frs. for a cassette translation). Open mid-May–mid-Sept., daily 9–7; mid-Sept.–mid-Oct. and mid-Mar.–mid-May, 9–12:30 and 2–6:30; mid-Oct.–mid-Mar., 9:30–12:30 and 2–6.*

To reach the **Musée Baron Gérard,** head up rue de Nesmond to rue Larchet, turning left into lovely place des Tribuneaux. The museum contains fine collections of Bayeux porcelain and lace, ceramics from Rouen, and 16th- to 19th-century furniture and paintings. *Pl. des Tribuneaux. Admission: 15 frs. adults, 8 frs. students and children. Open daily, June–Aug., 9–7; Sept.–mid-Oct. and mid-Mar.–May, 9:30–12:30 and 2–6:30; mid-Oct.–mid-Mar., 10–12:30 and 2–6.*

Behind the museum, with an entrance on rue du Bienvenu, sits Bayeux's most important historic building, the **Cathédrale Notre-Dame.** The cathedral is a harmonious mixture of Norman and Gothic architecture. Note the portal on the south side of the transept, which depicts the assassination of English Archbishop Thomas à Becket in Canterbury Cathedral in 1170, following his opposition to King Henry II's attempts to control the church. Note the whimsical paintings in the nave. *Open July–Aug., Mon.–Sat. 8–7, Sun. 9–7; Sept.–June, Mon.–Sat. 8:30–noon and 2:30–7, Sun. 9–12:15 and 2:30–7.*

Return to the 20th century by turning left, walking to place au Blois, and continuing down rue St-Loup. Turn right on boulevard du Général-Fabian-Ware, site of the **Musée de la Bataille de Normandie,** whose detailed exhibits trace the story of the Battle of Normandy from June 7 to August 22, 1944. The ultramodern museum contains an impressive array of war paraphernalia, including uniforms, weapons, and equipment. *Blvd. Général-Fabian-Ware. Admission: 20 frs. adults, 10 frs. students and children. Open daily June–Aug., 9–7; Sept.–mid-Oct. and mid-Mar.–June, 9:30–12:30 and 2–6:30; mid-Oct.–mid-Mar., 10–12:30 and 2–6.*

Lodging
Under 350 frs.

Churchill. This small, stylish, friendly hotel opened in the town center in 1986 and has already made a mark with foreign visitors. There are good-value menus, and solid breakfasts (ham and eggs available on request) are served in the airy veranda. *14 rue St-Jean, 14400, tel. 31–21–32–80. 32 rooms with bath or shower. AE, DC, MC, V. Closed mid-Nov.–mid-Mar.*

★ **Hôtel d'Argouges.** This lovely 18th-century hotel is an oasis of calm in the city center, and many rooms offer views of the well-tended flower garden. The rooms are superb, tastefully furnished in French-provincial chic and featuring rustic beamed ceilings. There's no restaurant. *21 rue St-Patrice, 14400, tel. 31–92–88–86. 25 rooms with bath. Facilities: garden. AE, DC, MC, V.*

Lodging and Dining
Splurge

Le Lion d'Or. The Lion d'Or is a handsome '30s creation, conveniently situated in the center of town. Palm trees arch over the garden courtyard, and flowers cascade from balcony window boxes. Rooms are comfortable and well furnished with pretty fabrics. Fine Norman cuisine is served in the chic wood-beamed restaurant, decorated in shades of apricot. Specialties include *andouille chaud Bovary*, no doubt Madame Bovary's own recipe for hot sausages, and fillet of sole in a creamy lobster sauce. *71 rue St-Jean, 14400, tel. 31–92–06–90. 28 rooms with bath. Facilities: restaurant. AE, DC, MC, V. Closed Christmas–mid-Jan. 380 frs.–440 frs.*

Under 150 frs.

Notre-Dame. It's difficult to find a better setting for a night in Bayeux than the Notre-Dame, located on a charming cobbled street leading to the west front of the cathedral. You can sit outside on the terrace and drink in the scene with your evening aperitif. Accommodations and cuisine are average, and the place attracts the occasional horde of coach-bound tourists. But with room rates starting at 130 francs, and set menus at 82, 110, 118, and 155 francs, you can't complain. *44 rue des Cuisiniers, tel. 31–92–87–24. 24 rooms, some with shower. Facilities: restaurant (closed Sun. evening and Mon. in winter). MC, V. Closed Mon. mid-Oct.–mid-Apr.*

Arromanches

Three buses daily make the 20-minute run from Bayeux to Arromanches, 3.7 km (6 mi) north; the first leaves just after midday.

Operation Overlord, the code name for the Invasion of Normandy, called for five beachheads—dubbed Utah, Omaha, Gold, Juno, and Sword—to be established along the Calvados Coast, to either side of **Arromanches**. Preparations started in mid-1943, and British shipyards worked furiously through the following winter and spring building two artificial harbors (called Mulberries), boats, and landing equipment. The operation was originally scheduled to take place on June 5, but poor weather caused it to be postponed for a day.

The British troops that landed on Sword, Juno, and Gold quickly pushed inland and joined with parachute regiments that had been dropped behind the German lines. U.S. forces met with far tougher opposition on Omaha and Utah beaches, however, and it took them six days to secure their positions and meet the other Allied forces. From there, they pushed south and west, cutting off the Cotentin Peninsula on June 10 and taking Cherbourg on June 26. Meanwhile, British forces were encountering fierce resistance at Caen and did not take it until July 9. By then, U.S. forces had turned their attention southward, but it took two weeks of bitter fighting to dislodge the Germans from the area around St-Lô; the town was finally liberated on July 19.

After having boned up on the full story of the Normandy invasion, you'll want to go and see the area where it all took place. The beaches are within walking distance of Arromanches and its bus stop. There's little point in visiting all five sites, since not much remains to mark the furious fighting waged hereabouts. In the bay of Arromanches, however, some elements of the floating harbor are still visible. Linger here a while, contemplating those seemingly insignificant hunks of concrete protruding from the water, and try to imagine the extraordinary technical feat involved in towing the two floating harbors across the Channel from England. (The other was moored at Omaha Beach but was destroyed on June 19, 1944, by an exceptionally violent storm.)

If you're interested in yet more battle documentation, visit the **Musée du Débarquement,** right on the seafront, whose exhibits include models, mock-ups, and photographs depicting the invasion. *Admission: 25 frs. adults, 18 frs. senior citizens, 12 frs. students and children. Open July–Aug., daily 9–6:30; Sept., daily 10–6; Oct.–Apr., daily 10–11:30 and 2–5:30 or 6:30 depending on season; May–June, daily 10–6:30. Closed 2–3 wks in Jan.*

Pontorson and Mont-St-Michel

Two trains daily leave for Pontorson from Caen and Bayeux, 1 in the early morning, the other in the late afternoon. The journey lasts around 2 hours. A bus (or taxi) is needed to reach Mont-St-Michel from Pontorson station. Tourist office: Corps de Garde des Bourgeois, tel. 33–60–14–30.

You can glimpse the spire-topped **Mont-St-Michel**, known as the Merveille de l'Occident (Wonder of the West), long before you reach the causeway that links it with the mainland. Its dramatic silhouette may well be your most lasting image of Normandy. The wonder of the abbey stems not only from its rocky perch a few hundred yards off the coast (it's cut off from the mainland at high tide), but from its legendary origins in the 8th century and the sheer exploit of its construction, which took more than 500 years, from 1017 to 1521. The abbey stands at the top of a 264-foot mound of rock, and the granite used to build it was transported from the Isles of Chausey (just beyond Mont-St-Michel Bay) and Brittany and laboriously hauled up to the site.

Legend has it that the Archangel Michael appeared to Aubert, bishop of Avranches, inspiring him to build an oratory on what was then called Mont Tombe. The original church was completed in 1144, but new buildings were added in the 13th century to accommodate the monks, as well as the hordes of pilgrims who flocked here even during the Hundred Years' War, when the region was in English hands. The Romanesque choir was rebuilt in an ornate Gothic style during the 15th and 16th centuries. The abbey's monastic vocation was undermined during the 17th century, when the monks began to flout the strict rules and discipline of their order, a drift into decadence that culminated in the monks' dispersal and the abbey's conversion into a prison well before the French Revolution. In 1874, the former abbey was handed over to a governmental agency responsible for the preservation of historical monuments; only within the past 20 years have monks been able to live and work here once more.

A highlight of the abbey is the collection of 13th-century buildings on the north side of the mount. The exterior of the buildings is grimly fortresslike, but inside are some of Normandy's best examples of the evolution of Gothic architecture, ranging from the sober Romanesque style of the lower halls to the masterly refinement of the cloisters and the elegance of the refectory.

The climb to the abbey is hard going, but it's worth it. Head first for the Grand Degré, the steep, narrow staircase on the north side. Once past the ramparts, you'll come to the pink-and-gray granite towers of the Châtelet and then to the Salle des Gardes, the central point of the abbey. Guided tours start from the Saut Gautier terrace (named after a prisoner who jumped to his death from it)—you must join one of these groups if you want to see the beautifully wrought Escalier de Dentelle (Lace Staircase) inside the church. *Admission: 32 frs. adults, 18 frs. students and senior citizens, 6 frs. children under 12. Open mid-May–mid-Sept., daily 9:30–6; mid-Sept.–mid-May, daily 9:30–11:45 and 1:45–5 or 4:15; depending on month.*

The island village, with its steep, narrow street, is best visited out of season, from September to May. The hordes of souvenir sellers and tourists can be stifling in summer months, but you can always take refuge in the abbey's gardens. The ramparts in general and the North Tower in particular offer dramatic views of the bay.

Be warned: Before you visit this awe-inspiring monument, note that the sea that separates the rock from the mainland is extremely dangerous. It's subject to tidal movements that produce a difference of up to 45 feet between low and high tides, and because of the extremely flat bay bed, the water rushes in at an incredible speed. Also, there are nasty patches of quicksand, so tread with care!

Lodging and Dining
Under 350 frs.

Terrasses Poulard. The hotel is a recent addition to this popular restaurant, a result of the proprietor's buying up and renovating the neighboring houses to create an ensemble of buildings that exude great charm and character, clustered around a small garden in the middle of the mount. The large restaurant attracts hordes of tourists; if you don't mind being surrounded by fellow Americans, Canadians, and Britons, you'll no doubt enjoy the traditional cuisine. *On the main road opposite the parish church, 50116, tel. 33–60–14–09. 29 rooms with bath. Facilities: restaurant, library, billiards room. AE, DC, MC, V.*

7 Champagne and the North

Reims, Chantilly, Lille

British tourists have traditionally zipped right through the North en route to Paris and Switzerland. This may change with the 1993 opening of the new Channel Tunnel, and with it the new Paris–London TGV line. (Already, businesses are scrambling for premises in the area, and wealthy British citizens are snapping up well-priced property with an eye toward commuting from France.) But for now, it's easy to budget food and lodging costs here, while the dense rail network connecting the region's numerous towns and cities keeps transportation costs low.

It's generally a green and pleasant land where serene, wooded landscapes predominate. To the east, the plains give way to hills. The grapes of Champagne flourish on the steep slopes of the Marne Valley and on the so-called Mountain of Reims. There are no mountains, of course, even though the mighty mound of Laon is known as the Crowned Mountain because of the bristling silhouette of its many-towered cathedral. Reims is the only city in Champagne, and one of France's richest tourist venues. The kings of France were crowned in its cathedral until 1825, and every age since the Roman has left an architectural mark. The small nearby towns of Ay and Epernay play an equally important role in the thriving champagne business, which has conferred wealth and, sometimes, an arrogant reserve on the region's inhabitants. The down-to-earth folk of the north provide a warmer welcome.

This chapter explores the vast region of Champagne and the North in three tours. The first covers the North of France proper, with a look at some windswept Channel beaches, the second stops at towns in the Champagne area, and the third takes in châteaux and a cathedral in the Oise département just a short distance from Paris.

Essential Information

Lodging Northern France is loaded with old hotels, often rambling and simple, seldom pretentious. Good value is easy to come by.

Dining The cuisine of northern France is robust and hearty, like that of neighboring Belgium. Beer predominates and is often used as a base for sauces (notably for chicken). French fries and mussels are featured on most menus, and vans selling fries and hot dogs are common sights. Great quantities of fish, notably herring, are eaten along the coast, while inland delicacies include *andouillettes* (chitterling sausages), tripe, and pâté made from duck, partridge, or woodcock. Anyone with a sweet tooth will enjoy the region's ubiquitous macaroons and minty Cambrai *bêtises* (boiled sweets made of sugar, glucose, and mint). Ham, pigs' feet, gingerbread, and a champagne-based mustard are specialties of the Reims area, as is *ratafia*, a sweet aperitif made from grape juice and brandy. To the north, a glass of *genièvre* (a brandy made from juniper berries and sometimes added to black coffee to make a drink called a *bistoul)* is the typical way to conclude a good meal.

Shopping Northern France and shopping are intimately associated in the minds of many visitors, especially the English. The cross-Channel ferry trip to Calais and Boulogne has become something of an institution, with one rather ignoble aim: to stock up on as much tax-free wine and beer as is legally and physically possible. Supermarkets along the coast are admirably large and well stocked, though you may want to consider local juniper-based *genièvre* brandy, which is a more original choice. Boulogne, France's premier fishing port, is famous for its kippers (smoked herring). Calais has long been renowned as a lace-making center. Wooden puppets are a specialty at Amiens, and glazed earthenware is part of St-Omer's historical heritage. Antiques dealers are legion; some of the best buys can be made at the busy auction houses *(commissaires-priseurs)* at Lille and Calais, among other towns. Note that while Reims owes its prestige to champagne, a number of its central shops duly charge sky-high prices. You'll find the best buys at small producers in the villages along the Montagne de Reims between Reims and Epernay (not Bouzy, though).

Bicycling Bicycles can be rented from many train stations for around 40 francs a day. Get details of special routes from the **Comité Départemental de Cyclotourisme** (75 rue Louis-Drouart, Les Ageux, 60700 Pont-Ste-Maxence). Mountain biking is also popular in the Noyon area; get in touch with **Patrick Drocourt** (48 rue du Maréchal-Joffre, 60150 Montmacq, tel. 44–76–40–49).

Hiking Favored areas for hiking include the Forêt de Compiègne, the Montagne de Reims, and the Channel coast. For further details contact the regional tourist office (Place Rihour, 59002 Lille).

Beaches The northern French coast, from Calais to Le Touquet, is one long, sandy beach, known as the Côte d'Opale. Apart from swimming in the ocean and in indoor and outdoor pools throughout the region, you may care to try your hand at speed sailing or handling a sand buggy, those windsurf boards on wheels that race along the sands at up to 70 mph. Known as *char à voile*, the sport can be practiced at Le Touquet, Hardelot, Dunkerque, Bray-Dunes, and Berck-sur-Mer; the craft are readily available for rent. For details, contact amiable Claude Wantier at the **Drakkars** club in Hardelot, south of Boulogne (tel. 21–91–81–96); the cost is 60–80 francs per hour.

The Arts The hub of cultural activity in northern France is **Lille**—a lively museum and concert center where exotic happenings can take place at any time (a recital of traditional music by Tibetan monks, for example).

Festivals The various local carnivals include the **Dunkerque Carnival** in February and March, the **Roses Festival** in Arras in May, and the **Kermesse de la Bêtise** festival in Cambrai in early September.

Highlights for First-time Visitors

Cathédrale Notre-Dame, Reims, Tour 2
Cathédrale St-Pierre, Beauvais, Tour 3
Cathedral and ramparts of Laon's old town, Tour 2
Château of Chantilly, Tour 3
The resort town of Le Touquet, Tour 1
Castle of Pierrefonds, Tour 3
Musée Matisse, Le Cateau-Cambrésis, Tour 1

Tour 1: Lille and The North

Although Lille makes a good base for visiting such interesting towns as Arras, Le Cateau, and St-Omer, this tour has an itinerant flavor. It starts at Amiens and, after Lille, loops around the Channel coast from Calais down to Montreuil. Except for Le Touquet, which is accessible by bus from nearby Etaples, all towns can be reached by train.

From Paris *By Train* Express trains to Amiens, Arras, and Lille leave Paris (Gare du Nord) every 2 hours. The trip takes 70 minutes to Amiens (sometimes with a change at Longueau), 1½ hours to Arras, and about 2¼ hours to Lille.

By Car The 225-kilometer (140-mile) drive from Paris along A1 takes 2½ hours to Lille. Allow 1½ hours to Amiens (take the D934 turnoff from Roye) and 2 hours to Arras.

Amiens

Tourist office: 20 pl. Notre-Dame, by the cathedral, tel. 22–91–16–16.

Amiens, the capital of Picardy, is a catastrophic example of postwar reconstruction. Yet this stolid brick city has a couple of worthwhile attractions, most notably the **Cathédrale Notre-Dame**, the largest church in France. Cross the square in front of the train station, turn right into boulevard d'Alsace-Lorraine, then down rue Gloriette. Go straight for 500 yards until you reach the cathedral.

Although the cathedral lacks the stained glass of Chartres or the sculpture of Reims, for architectural harmony, engineering proficiency, and sheer size, it has no peer. The soaring, asym-

Champagne and the North
BELGIUM
Brussels
Scheldе
Tournai
Mons
Dunkerque
N1
Calais
Sangatte
D940
Cap Gris-Nez
A26
D916
A25
Steenvorde
N43
St-Omer
N42
Hazebrouck
Boulogne-sur-Mer
Hardelot
D341
Samer
Lille
Le Touquet
D126
Fruges
Béthune
A26
A1
N39
Montreuil-sur-Mer
D916
N41
St-Amand-les-Eaux
Lens
Vimy Ridge
Douai
Hesdin
St-Pol-sur-Ternoise
N39
Mont St-Eloi
Neuville
N50
D943
Lewarde
Valenciennes
Rue
D928
Arras
St-Valery-sur-Somme
D938
N25
D939
Aulnoye
Cambrai
Avesnes-sur-Helpe
N2
D932
D940
D925
Doullens
N30
N43
D925
Abbeville
N1
Bapaume
A2
D960
Le Cateau-Cambrésis
Somme
D919
Thiepval
N25
Busigny
D917
La Capelle
Albert
D929
A26
N29
Blangy-St-Bresle
Amiens
Péronne

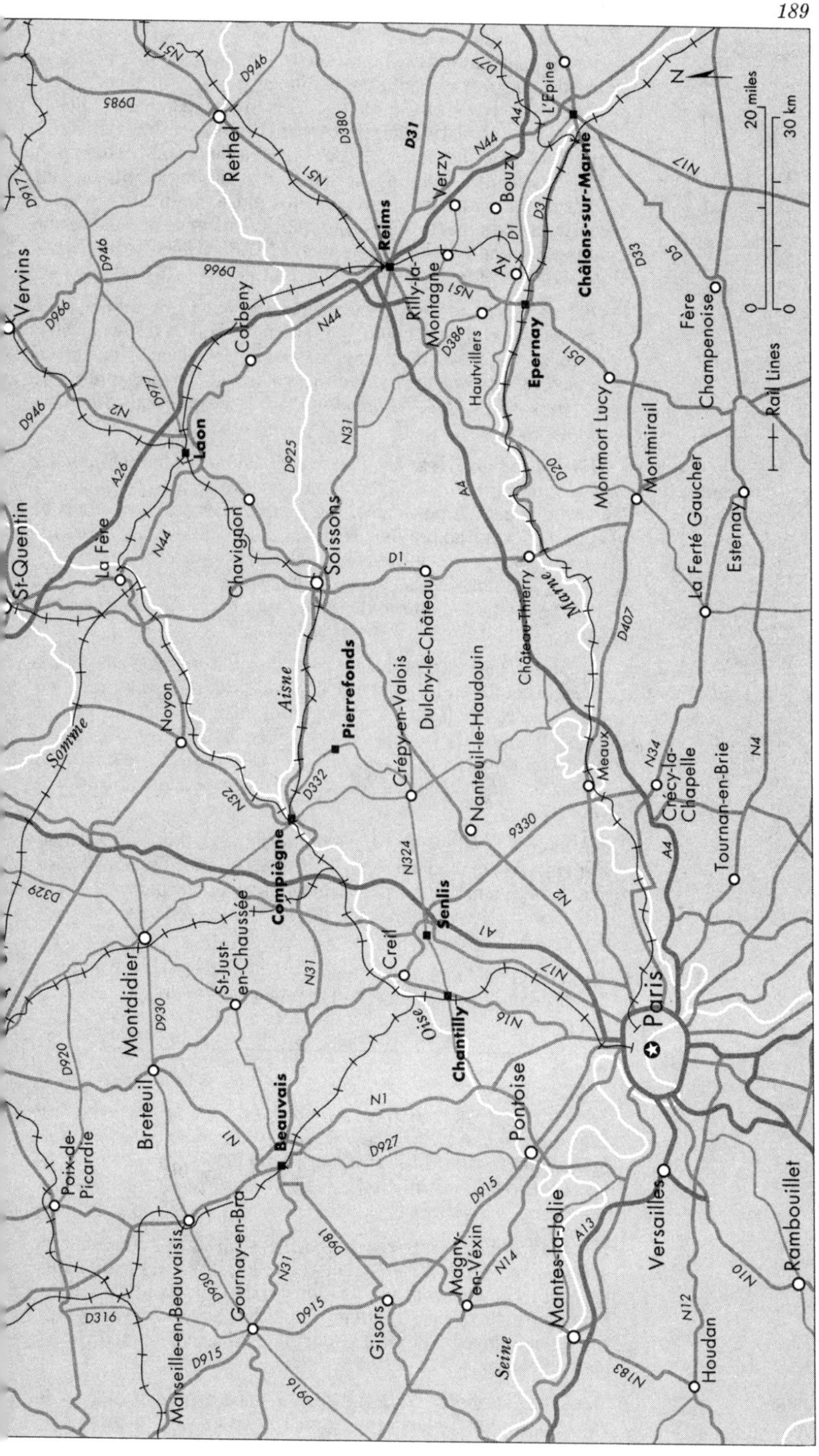
Vervins
St-Quentin
La Fère
Laon
Corbeny
Chavignon
Soissons
Reims
Rethel
Rilly-la-Montagne
Verzy
Bouzy
Ay
Hautvillers
Epernay
Châlons-sur-Marne
L'Epine
Fère Champenoise
Montmort Lucy
Montmirail
La Ferté Gaucher
Esternay
Château-Thierry
Dulchy-le-Château
Crépy-en-Valois
Nanteuil-le-Haudouin
Pierrefonds
Noyon
Compiègne
Senlis
Creil
Chantilly
Meaux
Crécy-la-Chapelle
Tournan-en-Brie
Paris
Versailles
Rambouillet
Houdan
Mantes-la-Jolie
Magny-en-Véxin
Pontoise
Gisors
Beauvais
Gournay-en-Bray
Marseille-en-Beauvaisis
Poix-de-Picardie
Breteuil
Montdidier
St-Just-en-Chaussée
Somme
Aisne
Oise
Marne
Seine
N
20 miles
30 km
0
Rail Lines
A1
A4
A13
A26
N1
N2
N4
N10
N12
N14
N16
N17
N31
N32
N34
N44
N51
N183
N324
D1
D3
D5
D20
D31
D33
D51
D77
D380
D386
D407
D915
D916
D917
D920
D925
D927
D930
D946
D966
D981
D985
D316
D329
D332
9330

metrical facade boasts a notable Flamboyant Gothic rose window and dominates the nondescript surrounding brick streets. Inside, the overwhelming sensation of space is enhanced by the absence of pews in the nave, a return to medieval tradition. There is no stylistic disunity to mar the perspective: Construction took place between 1220 and 1264, a remarkably short period in cathedral-building terms. One of the highlights of your visit is hidden from the eye, at least until you lift up the choir stalls and admire the humorous, skillful misericord (seat) carvings executed between 1508 and 1518. *Pl. Notre-Dame. Open all day except noon–2.*

On leaving the cathedral, turn left along rue Cormant and take the second right onto rue Victor-Hugo. Midway down, you'll discover the **Hôtel de Berny,** an elegant 1634 mansion full of period furniture and devoted to local art and regional history. *34 rue Victor-Hugo. Admission: 15 frs. Open Tues.–Sun. 10–noon and 2–6.*

Lodging
Under 250 frs.

Hôtel de la Paix. Near the Picardy Museum, the hotel is housed in a building reconstructed after World War II. The view of a nearby church from some of the rooms offsets a certain lack of personality, although the breakfast room tries valiantly to suggest an 18th-century Louis XV salon. Foreign visitors are frequent, and English is spoken. *8 rue de la République, 80000, tel. 22–91–39–21. 26 rooms, some with bath. No credit cards. Closed Sun. and mid-Dec.–mid-Jan.*

Dining
Under 125 frs.

Joséphine. This unpretentious restaurant in central Amiens is a reliable choice and a good value. Solid fare, decent wines, and rustic decor (a bit on the stodgy side, like the sauces) pull in many foreign customers, notably the British. *20 rue Sire-Firmin-Leroux, tel. 22–91–47–38. Reservations advised in summer. AE, MC, V. Closed Sun. evening, Mon., and 3rd week of Aug.*

Mermoz. Nouvelle and traditional cuisine are skillfully blended here in a fresh, modern setting close to the train station. There are three menus, and the choice changes according to the season. *7 rue Jean-Mermoz, tel. 22–91–50–63. Reservations advised. AE, V. Closed Sat., Sun., and mid-July–mid-Aug.*

The Arts

The **Théâtre d'Animation Picard** (51 rue de Prague, tel. 22–46–29–09) partly overcomes the language barrier with its use of puppets.

Arras

Trains run frequently from Amiens to Arras, but at irregular intervals; journey time varies from 45 to 70 minutes. Trains between Arras and Lille run every hour or so. The trip takes 36 minutes. Arras tourist office: Place des Héros, tel. 21–51–26–95.

If you have time before reaching Lille, stop off at **Arras,** capital of the historic Artois region between Flanders and Picardy and now something of a sprawling industrial town. Its historic core bears witness to the grandeur of another age, however, when the town enjoyed medieval importance as a trading and cloth-making center.

Take rue Gambetta from the station and turn right after 500 yards onto rue Delansorne, which winds down to **place des**

Héros, separated from **Grand' Place** by a short block. These two main squares are harmonious examples of 17th- and 18th-century Flemish civil architecture, with gabled facades that recall those in Belgium and Holland and testify to the unifying influence of the Spanish colonizers of the "Low Lands" during the 17th century. The smaller, arcaded place des Héros is dominated by the richly worked—and much restored—**Hôtel de Ville,** capped by a 240-foot belfry.

Turn left out of the square, then right onto rue Paul-Doumer. Walking a block along brings you to the imposing 18th-century premises of a former abbey, now the **Musée des Beaux-Arts** (Fine Arts Museum), which houses a rich collection of porcelain and, especially, painting, with several major 19th-century French works. *22 rue Paul-Doumer. Admission: 16 frs. adults, 8 frs. children and senior citizens. Open Wed.–Fri. and Mon. 10–noon and 2–5, Sat. 10–noon and 2–6, Sun. 2–5; closed Tues. and Sun. morning.*

The 19th-century **Cathédrale St-Vaast,** a short block farther on, is a white-stone Classical building, every bit as vast as its name (pronounced "va") suggests. It replaced the previous Gothic cathedral destroyed in 1799; though it was half-razed during World War I, restoration was so skillfully done you'd never know.

At first glance you might not guess that Arras was badly mauled during World War I. Not far off, though, are parks and memorials recalling the fierce battles. Arras is a convenient base for visiting the area's numerous superbly cared-for cemeteries and memorials, which number among the most poignant sights in northern France.

Lodging
Under 350 frs.
★

Univers. This stylish hotel occupies a converted 18th-century monastery and has a pretty garden and a charming restaurant. Its central position and views of the courtyard and garden make it a favorite stopover with vacationers heading south. The interior has recently been modernized, but it retains its rustic provincial furniture. *5 pl. de la Croix-Rouge, 62000, tel. 21–71–34–01. 36 rooms, most with bath. Facilities: restaurant (closed Sun. in Aug.), garden. AE, MC, V.*

Lodging and Dining
Under 250 frs.

Le Chanzy. Huge and popular, this casual spot offers three set menus and as many dining rooms. The restaurant specializes in ambitious gastronomy, based on the grills in which the chef is expert, though standard brasserie fare is available at lunch. There are more than 100,000 bottles in the cellar, and the main room is decked out in a luxuriously flashy '50s-style decor (renovation overdue). Le Chanzy also has 20 guest rooms. *8 rue Chanzy, tel. 21–71–02–02. Reservations advised. AE, DC, MC, V.*

Dining
Under 125 frs.

L'Antoniolus. Large portions of fresh ingredients are dished out here, amid cheerful greenery that spills onto a veranda. Though eating à la carte may nudge your tab upward, there is good value to be had here. *2 rue Eugène-Pottier, tel. 21–51–66–99. Reservations advised on weekends and in summer. AE, MC, V.*

Lille

Trains run from Arras to Lille every hour or so; the journey takes 36 minutes. Lille tourist office: Place Rihour, just down rue des Manneliers from the Vieille Bourse, tel. 20–30–81–00.

For a big city supposedly reeling beneath the problems of its main industry, textiles, **Lille** is a remarkably dynamic, attractive place. The city has had a checkered history, experiencing Flemish, Austrian, and Spanish rule before passing into French hands for good in 1667. Today it is thoroughly French, though with a Belgian penchant for beer and french fries. Although the downtown area contains several narrow streets full of old buildings, Lille does not boast any outstanding tourist sights. Yet with its choice of shops, restaurants, and museums, it makes an enjoyable overnight rest stop.

Head down rue Faidherbe from the station, cross place du Théâtre, and turn right onto rue de la Grande Chaussée. This narrow street rapidly becomes rue des Chats-Bossus, then rue de la Monnaie and leads to the **Hospice Comtesse** in the heart of the old town. Founded by Jeanne de Constantinople, countess of Flanders, as a hospital in 1237, it was rebuilt in the 15th century after a fire destroyed most of the original building. Local artifacts from the 17th and 18th centuries form the backbone of the museum now housed here, but its star attraction is the Salle des Malades (Sick Room), featuring a majestic wooden ceiling. *32 rue de la Monnaie. Admission: 10 frs. adults. Open Wed.–Mon. 10–12:30 and 2–6; closed Tues.*

Follow rue de la Monnaie as it curves right and branch off at rue de la Grande Chaussée. The Grand' Place (or, to give it its full name, place du Général-de-Gaulle) is a fitting site for the **Vieille Bourse** (former stock exchange), one of the most charming buildings in central Lille. The quadrangle of elegant, richly worked buildings was erected by Julien Destrée in the 1650s as a commercial exchange to rival those already existing in Belgium and Holland. Just two short blocks down rue de Paris brings you to the sumptuous **Eglise St-Maurice** (on the right), a large, five-aisled church built between the 15th and 19th centuries.

A block farther along, turn right onto rue du Molinel and continue until you hit the frenzied traffic of boulevard de la Liberté, a vast street that roars through central Lille. Half a block down, on the left, is the **Musée des Beaux-Arts,** the largest fine arts museum in France outside of Paris, and extensively renovated in 1991–92. It houses a noteworthy collection of Dutch and Flemish paintings by Anthony Van Dyck, Peter Paul Rubens, Flemish Primitives, and Dutch landscapists, as well as some charmingly understated still lifes by Chardin, works by the Impressionists, a few bombastic 19th-century French painters, and dramatic canvases by El Greco, Goya, Tintoretto, and Paolo Veronese. An extensive ceramics section displays some fine examples of Lille faïence, which uses opaque glazing techniques to achieve some remarkable effects. *Pl. de la République. The museum was closed at press time, and the date of reopening uncertain; call 20–57–01–84 for details.*

Head left out of the art gallery, making for the gigantic **citadel,** which glowers down on the old town from its perch on the west end of the boulevard. Construction started shortly after that of the Vieille Bourse in the mid-17th century; of course that military marvel, Sébastien de Vauban, got the commission. Some 60 million bricks were used, and the result is a fortified town in its own right, with monumental towers and walls. These days, the citadel is used as a barracks. *Visits on Sun. during summer months.*

Lodging
Under 250 frs.

Paix. Probably the best hotel in central Lille for price and location, the Paix is close to the Vieille Bourse and 200 yards from the train station. Most rooms are large and recently decorated, and have new bathrooms. *46 bis rue de Paris, 59800, tel. 20–54–63–93. 35 rooms, most with bath or shower. AE, DC, MC, V.*

Dining
Under 200 frs.
★

Devinière. Chef Willy Waterlot has created one of Lille's most fashionable eating places: The welcome is warm, the dining room embellished with cheerful flowers, and the produce used in his nouvelle cuisine fresh and changed according to the season. Since these pleasures come at merely moderate tabs by those who order carefully, and since the restaurant is small, it's frequently packed; plan ahead. *61 blvd. Louis-XIV, tel. 20–52–74–64. Reservations required. Jacket required. AE, DC, MC, V. Closed part of Aug.*

Under 125 frs.

La Coquille. The wood beams and pink bricks of this venerable restaurant in a building dating from 1727 set a delightful scene for a quiet, light, fish meal—with delicious chocolate and caramel desserts as a finale. *60 rue St-Etienne, tel. 20–54–29–82. Reservations advised. MC, V. Closed Sat. lunch, Sun., and Aug.*

The Arts

The **Orchestre National de Lille** is a well-respected symphony orchestra (3 pl. Mendès-France, tel. 20–54–67–00), and Lille boasts one of France's few regional opera houses, the **Opéra du Nord** (pl. du Théâtre, tel. 20–55–48–61).

Le Cateau-Cambrésis

Two trains in the morning and 2 in the afternoon leave Lille for Le Cateau; change at Aulnoye and allow at least 1½ hours for the journey.

There is one good reason for making the arduous rail excursion from Lille to **Le Cateau**: to visit the **Palais Fénelon,** former home to the archbishops of Cambrai and today the **Musée Matisse,** devoted to the work of artist Henri Matisse (1869–1954), who was born in Le Cateau. Along with a number of early oil paintings and sculptures, there is a superb collection of 50 drawings selected by Matisse himself and arranged in a carefully lit room on the second floor. The enthusiastic curator, Dominique Szymusiak, will show you around (her English is excellent). Reserve a guided tour by calling 27–84–13–15 at least a week before your visit. *Admission: 15 frs. adults, 3.50 frs. children. Open Wed.–Sun. 10–noon and 2–6 (5 in winter).*

St-Omer

Trains run from Lille to St-Omer every hour (except midmorning and early afternoon). Express trains take 50 minutes, local trains up to 1½ hours. St-Omer tourist office: Pl. du Pain-Levé, tel. 21–98–70–00.

St-Omer is a delightful small town, too often neglected by hasty motorists on their way south. It is not the archetypal northern industrial town; with its yellow-brick buildings, it even looks different from its neighbors, and a distinct air of 18th-century prosperity hovers about the place. Stroll through the narrow streets surrounding the Basilique Notre-Dame and, if time allows, visit the **Hôtel Sandelin** on rue Carnot (open Wed.–Sun. 10–noon and 2–5). Now the town museum, the 1777 mansion is furnished with 18th-century furniture and paintings and contains an exceptional collection of porcelain and faïence.

Dining
Under 125 frs.

Le Cygne. Duck breast *(magret de canard)* tops the menu at Le Cygne—not swan, as the name suggests. It's in the old sector of St-Omer near the cathedral and offers two set menus—one three-course, the other four-course. Traditional regional cooking holds sway. *8 rue Caventou, tel. 21–98–20–52. Reservations accepted. MC, V. Closed Tues., Sat. lunch, and Dec. 10–31.*

Calais

All trains from Lille to St-Omer continue to Calais, 35 minutes and 40 km (25 mi) to the northeast. Calais tourist office: 12 blvd. Clemenceau, tel. 21–96–62–40.

Few vestiges remain of old **Calais**, the pretty port town that owed its wealth to the lace industry rather than to day-trippers making the Channel crossing from Dover, 38 kilometers (24 miles) away, by the million every year. You won't want to stay here long, but there are a few sights to see before you dash off.

You don't need to be a sculpture fanatic to appreciate Auguste Rodin's bronze **Monument des Bourgeois de Calais,** which lords it over the east end of the Parc St-Pierre next to place du Soldat-Inconnu. The bourgeois in question were townspeople who, in 1347, offered their lives to English king Edward III in a bid to save fellow citizens from merciless reprisals after Calais's abortive attempts to withstand an eight-month siege (Calais was an English possession until 1558 and was the last English toehold in France). Edward's queen, Philippa, intervened on their behalf and the courageous men were spared; Calais, on the other hand, remained in English hands for another 200 years.

Head up traffic-clogged boulevard Jacquard, turning right onto rue Richelieu. Three blocks along, at no. 25, is the **Musée des Beaux-Arts et de la Dentelle** (Fine Arts and Lace Museum, admission: 10 frs., free Wed.; open Wed.–Mon. 10–noon and 2–5:30), which contains some fine 19th- and 20th-century pictures, local historical displays, and exhibits documenting the Calais lace industry. Turn left at the next block, making for the much-restored **Eglise Notre-Dame,** where Général de Gaulle was married in 1921. Take time to admire the simple, vertical elegance of the windows and the ornate fan vaulting inside.

Lodging and Dining
Under 150 frs.

George V. This clean, pleasant hotel is on rue Royale, the main street through the old town. The restaurant can seem heavy-handed, both for its pseudo-rustic decor and an overambitious cuisine that improbably pairs salmon and beef with endive and wine butter. With its two-course 65-franc menu, the Petit George bistro alongside offers a better deal. *36 rue Royale, 62100, tel. 21–97–68–00. 45 rooms with bath or shower. Facilities: restaurant (closed Sat. lunch and Sun. evening). AE, DC, MC, V.*

Dining
Under 75 frs.

Sole Meunière. As its name ("sole fried in butter") suggests, the intimate Sole Meunière is a temple of fish and seafood. Not that anything else could be expected from a restaurant next to Calais harbor! The menus start at a very low price and top out on a moderate level. *1 blvd. de la Résistance, tel. 21–34–43–01. Reservations advised. AE, DC, MC, V. Closed Mon. and mid-Dec.–mid-Jan.*

Shopping

Lace shops still abound in Calais, with its long tradition of lace-making; try **La Dentellière** (30 blvd. de l'Egalité).

Boulogne-sur-Mer

Trains from Calais to Boulogne run every 1½ hours; journey time varies from 32 to 45 minutes, depending on whether you go via express or local train. Boulogne tourist office: Pont Maquet, by the port, tel. 21–31–68–38.

The contrast between the lower and upper sections of **Boulogne** is startling. The rebuilt concrete streets around the port are gruesome and sinister, but the Ville Haute—the old town on the hill—is a different world, and you can begin to understand why Napoleon chose Boulogne as his base while preparing to cross the channel. The Ville Haute is dominated by the formidable **Notre-Dame** basilica, its distinctive elongated dome visible from far out at sea. Surrounding the basilica are charming cobbled streets and tower-flanked ramparts, dating from the 13th century and offering excellent views. The four main streets of the old town intersect at place Bouillon, where you can see the 18th-century brick town hall, and the Hôtel Desandrouins, where Napoleon spent many long nights pondering how to invade Britain.

Some 1½ miles north of Boulogne just off the main Calais road (N1)—a brisk half-hour walk—you can visit **Colonne de la Grande Armée.** Work began on this 160-foot marble column in 1804 to commemorate Napoleon's soon-to-be-abandoned plans to invade England, but it was finished 30 years later under Louis-Philippe. The 263 steps take you to the top and a wide-reaching view. If the weather is clear and you're blessed with Napoleonic vision, you may be able to make out the distant cliffs of Dover. *Admission free. Open daily 10–noon and 2–5.*

Lodging
Under 250 frs.

Métropole. This small hotel is handy for ferry passengers but, like most of the Ville Basse (lower town), no great architectural shakes. While no exciting views are to be had from this rather faceless '50s building, the guest rooms are adequately furnished and individually decorated. There is no restaurant. *51 rue Thiers, 62200, tel. 21–31–54–30. 27 rooms, some with bath. Facilities: garden. AE, DC, MC, V. Closed Christmas and New Year's.*

Dining
Under 200 frs.
★

Brasserie Liégeoise. Good food spiced with delicious nouvelle touches helps this old, established restaurant remain at the forefront of the Boulogne eating scene. The decor is modern—an eccentric contrast of black and yellow—and so are the prices for both à la carte and set-menu meals. Yet the delicate sauces and interesting combinations, such as duck liver with mushrooms, are well worth the extra expense. *10 rue Monsigny, tel. 21–31–61–15. Reservations required on weekends. Jacket required. AE, DC, MC, V. Closed Wed., and Sun. dinner.*

Le Touquet

Trains make the 18-minute journey from Boulogne to Etaples every 2 hours (at least). A shuttle bus completes the trip to Le Touquet, about 5 km (3 mi) distant. Two direct trains a day make the 2-hour trip from Lille to Etaples. Le Touquet tourist office: Pl. de l'Hermitage, tel. 21–05–21–65.

Le Touquet, though just a short distance down the coast from Boulogne, is a total contrast. An elegant Victorian seaside resort, it sprang out of nowhere in the 19th century, adopting the name Paris-Plage. Mainly because gambling laws were stricter in Victorian England than in France, Englishmen were the town's mainstay, not Parisians. A cosmopolitan atmosphere remains, although many Frenchmen, attracted by the airy, elegant avenues and invigorating climate, have moved here for good. To one side lies a fine sandy beach; to the other, an artificial forest planted in the 1850s. A casino, golf courses, and racetrack cater to fashionable pleasure.

Lodging and Dining
Under 250 frs.

Chaumière. Le Touquet's determined attachment to its Victorian style and swank often means a lean deal for those with thin wallets. The Chaumière is a good option. Its restaurant is one of the few in town with realistic prices—honest seafood menus run 90 and 150 francs, with lobster a specialty—and rooms start at 200 francs. And the location, close to the beach on the same street as the casino, couldn't be better. Out of season, you'll find business seminars and TV programs in English to enliven rainy days. *80 rue St-Jean, 62520, tel. 21–05–12–11. 21 rooms, some with bath or shower. Facilities: restaurant. AE, DC, MC, V.*

Splurge ★

Westminster. With its redbrick facade, this giant—one of the finest hotels in the country—looks as if it were built just a few years ago; in fact, it dates from the 1930s and, like the rest of the hotel, has been extensively restored by its new owners, the personable Flament brothers. The hotel offers a modestly priced coffee bar (serving lunch and dinner), a swanky dining room (offering classic but well-prepared French cuisine), and an "American bar" that serves cocktails for under 50 francs. Try the Westminster Special, a lethal concoction of vodka, blue curaçao, Grand Marnier, and orange juice. The enormous double rooms, which start at $80, represent good value, and the bridal suite is the last word in thick-carpeted extravagance. *Av. du Verger, 62520, tel. 21–05–48–48. 115 rooms with bath. Facilities: restaurants, bar, squash court, indoor pool, Jacuzzi, sauna, solarium. AE, DC, MC, V. 480 frs. and up.*

Montreuil-sur-Mer

Six trains daily make the 10-minute run from Etaples to Montreuil, which lies 16 km (10 mi) inland from Le Touquet. Montreuil tourist office: Place Darnétal, tel. 21–06–04–27.

Ancient **Montreuil-sur-Mer** features majestic walls and ramparts, as well as faded, nostalgic charm to which various authors, notably Victor Hugo, have succumbed; an important episode of his epic work *Les Misérables* is set here.

Whenever citadels and city walls loom on the French horizon, it's a fair bet that Vauban had a hand in their construction. Montreuil is no exception. In about 1690, he supplemented the existing 16th-century towers of the **citadel** with an imposing wall, whose grassy banks and mossy flagstones can be explored at leisure. There are extensive views on all sides. *Admission: 7 frs. Open daily 10–noon and 2–5.*

The old cobbled streets of the town make equally agreeable places to stroll. The **Eglise St-Saulve** (just off rue Carnot; open summer only) boasts some fine paintings and a facade dating, in part, from the 11th century.

Lodging and Dining
Under 250 frs.

Bellevue. This small, old-fashioned hotel is conveniently situated close to the train station. Room prices start at 90 francs, and the restaurant offers set menus at 80 and 155 francs. *6 av. du 11-novembre, 62170, tel. 21–06–04–19. 13 rooms with bath or shower. Facilities: restaurant. MC, V. Closed second half of Dec.*

Tour 2: Reims and Champagne Country

Using venerable Reims as a hub, this tour makes rail excursions north to Laon and south through the champagne vineyards to Epernay and Châlons-sur-Marne.

From Paris
By Train

Express trains to Reims leave Paris (Gare de l'Est) 8 times daily. The trip takes 1½ hours.

By Car

The 150-kilometer (95-mile) drive from Paris along the A4 expressway also takes about 1½ hours.

Reims

Tourist office: 1 rue Jadart, off to the left as you view the cathedral facade, tel. 26–47–25–69.

Numbers in the margin correspond to points of interest on the Reims map.

Several major producers are headquartered in **Reims**, the spiritual capital of the champagne industry, and you won't want to miss the chance to visit the chalky maze of cellars that tunnel under the city center.

Cross the garden opposite the train station, take rue Thiers, and turn right after 150 yards onto Cours Langlet, which cuts
1 through the city's shopping district to the **Cathédrale Notre-Dame,** one of the most famous in France and the age-old setting for the coronations of the French kings (Charles X's was the last, in 1825). Its glory is its facade, which is so skillfully proportioned that initially you have little idea of the building's monumental size. Above the north (left) door hovers the *Laughing Angel*, a delightful statue whose famous smile threatens to melt into an acid-rain scowl. Pollution has succeeded war as the ravager of the building's fabric. Restoration is an ongoing process; take a look in the postcard shops opposite to get an idea of the pounding the cathedral took between 1914 and 1918.

The high, solemn nave is at its best in summer, when the plain lower walls are adorned by 16th-century tapestries relating the life of the Virgin. The east-end windows boast stained glass by

Basilique St-Rémi, **4**
Cathédral Notre-Dame, **1**
Mumm, **6**
Musée St-Denis, **3**
Palais du Tau, **2**
Porte Mars, **8**
Salle de Guerre, **7**
Taittinger, **5**

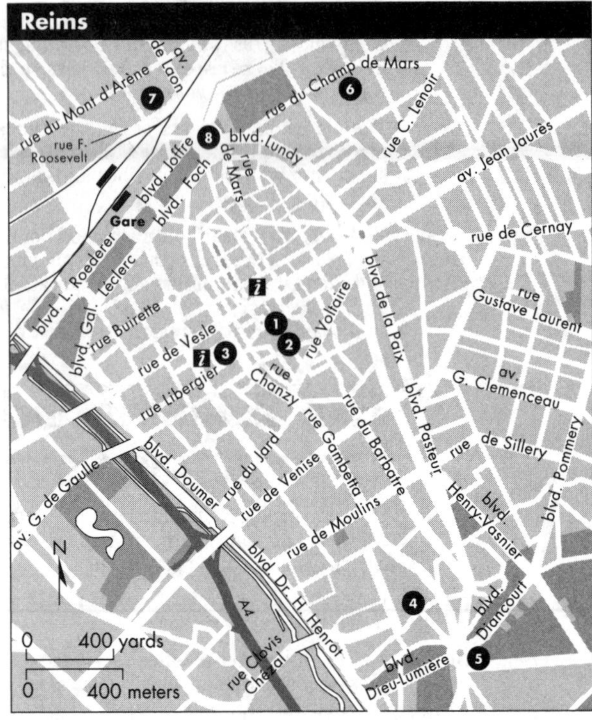

Marc Chagall. Admire the vista toward the west end, with an interplay of narrow pointed arches of different sizes.

With the exception of the 15th-century towers, most of the original building went up in the 100 years after 1211. A stroll around the outside will reinforce the impression of harmony, discipline, and decorative richness. The east end presents an idyllic sight across well-tended lawns. There are spectacular light shows both inside (40 francs) and outside the cathedral (free) in July and August. *Pl. du Cardinal-Luçon.*

2 Next door, the **Palais du Tau** (former archbishop's palace) houses an impressive display of tapestries and coronation robes, as well as several statues "rescued" from the cathedral facade. The second-floor views of Notre-Dame are terrific. *2 pl. du Cardinal-Luçon. Admission: 24 frs. adults, 13 frs. senior citizens, 6 frs. children. Open Tues.–Sun. 10–noon and 2–6 (2–5 in winter).*

3 Two blocks from the cathedral, on the right, is the **Musée St-Denis,** featuring an outstanding collection of paintings spearheaded by no fewer than 27 Corots and Jacques-Louis David's celebrated portrait of Revolutionary leader Jean-Paul Marat, stabbed to death in his bath by a disillusioned female supporter. *8 rue Chanzy. Admission: 10 frs. Open Wed.–Mon. 10–noon and 2–6.*

As you leave the museum, turn right and continue along rue
4 Chanzy and rue Gambetta to the 11th-century **Basilique St-Rémi,** honoring the 5th-century saint who gave his name to the city. St-Rémi is nearly as long as the cathedral, and its interior

seems to stretch into the endless distance, an impression created by the nave's relative murk and lowness. The airy, four-story Gothic choir contains some fine original 12th-century stained glass.

Several champagne producers organize visits to their cellars, combining video presentations with guided tours of their cav-
5 ernous, chalk-hewn underground warehouses. **Taittinger** (9 pl. St-Nicaise; closed weekends Dec.–Feb.) has the most spectacular cellars. Few show much generosity when it comes to pouring samples, though, so we recommend you double back across
6 town to **Mumm,** which does. (If the 1½ miles from Taittinger is too much, either take a taxi from the station or skip St-Rémi and Taittinger and concentrate on the cathedral and Mumm.) *34 rue du Champ-de-Mars. Open Mar.–Nov., Thurs.–Tues. 9:30–noon and 2–5:30; closed Wed.*

From Mumm, head down rue du Champ-de-Mars toward the train station, turn right onto avenue de Laon, then left onto rue
7 Franklin-Roosevelt. A short way along is the **Salle de Guerre,** where General Eisenhower established Allied headquarters at the end of World War II. It was here, in a well-preserved, map-covered room, that the German surrender was signed in May 1945. *12 rue Franklin-Roosevelt. Admission: 10 frs. adults, 5 frs. children. Open Wed.–Mon. 10–noon and 2–6; closed Tues.*

8 The **Porte Mars,** an unlikely but impressive Roman arch adorned by faded bas-reliefs depicting Jupiter, Romulus, and Remus, looms up just across from the train station.

Lodging
Under 350 frs.

Hôtel de la Paix. A modern, eight-story hotel, 10 minutes' walk from the cathedral, La Paix boasts admirably equipped, stylish rooms, plus a pretty garden, swimming pool, and a rather incongruous chapel. Its brasserie-style restaurant, Drouet, serves generous breakfasts and good, though not inexpensive, cuisine (mainly grilled meats and seafood). *9 rue de Buirette, 51000, tel. 26–40–04–08. 105 rooms with bath. Facilities: restaurant (closed Sun.), pool, patio bar. AE, DC, MC, V. Moderate.*

Under 250 frs.

Gambetta. The Gambetta experience is not what you'd call out of this world, but then, the prices are reassuringly down to earth. A location close by Reims's venerable cathedral is the hotel's main claim to fame. Guest rooms are small and somewhat featureless but clean and acceptable for the price. *9 rue Gambetta, 51000, tel. 26–47–41–64. 14 rooms with bath. Facilities: restaurant (closed Sun. dinner and Mon. lunch). V.*

Dining
Under 200 frs.
★

Le Vigneron. This friendly little brasserie in a 17th-century mansion is cozy and cheerful, with two tiny dining rooms that display a jumble of champagne-related paraphernalia—from old advertising posters to venerable barrels and tools of the trade. The food is delightful as well: distinctly hearty, prepared with finesse—and relatively cheap. Try the *andouillettes* (chitterling sausages) slathered with Reims's delicious champagne-spiked mustard. *Pl. Paul-Jamot, tel. 26–47–00–71. Reservations strongly advised. MC, V. Closed Sat. lunch, Sun., Christmas–New Year's, and most of Aug.*

Splurge
★

Boyer–Les Crayères. Gérard Boyer is one of the country's most highly rated chefs. Duck, foie gras in pastry, and truffles figure among his specialties and are complemented by an extensive wine list that pays homage to Reims's champagne heritage. The setting, not far from the Basilique St-Rémi, is magnificent, too: a 19th-century château surrounded by an extensive, well-tended park. The decor is opulent, typified by ornate chandeliers, towering ceilings, gilt mirrors, intricate cornices, and glossy paneling. There are 22 luxurious suites as well. *64 blvd. Henry-Vasnier, tel. 26–82–80–80. Reservations required. Jacket and tie required. AE, DC, MC, V. Closed Mon., Tues. lunch, and Christmas–New Year's. 450–700 frs.*

Laon

Six trains daily make the 50-minute journey from Reims to Laon. Tourist office: Place du Parvis, in front of the cathedral, tel. 23–20–28–62.

With its splendid hilltop site, **Laon** is sometimes called the "crowned mountain"—a reference to the forest of towers sprouting from its ancient cathedral. The site, cathedral, and enchanting old town are worth seeing. Strangely, not many people do; few Parisians, for instance, have ever heard of the place.

In the middle of the old town, just off place Aubry, is **Cathédrale Notre-Dame,** constructed between 1160 and 1235 and a superb example of early Gothic. The recently cleaned, light interior gives the impression of order and immense length (120 yards in total). The flat east end, an English-inspired feature, is unusual in France. The upper galleries that extend around the building are typical of early Gothic; what isn't typical is that you can actually visit them (and the towers) with a guide from the tourist office on the cathedral square. The filigreed elegance of the five remaining towers is audacious by any standards and rare: Medieval architects preferred to concentrate on soaring interiors, with just two towers at the west end. Even those not usually affected by architecture will appreciate the sense of movement about Laon's majestic west front; compare it with the more placid, two-dimensional feel of Notre-Dame in Paris. Look, too, for the stone bulls protruding from the towers, a tribute to the stalwart, 12th-century beasts that carted up blocks of stone from quarries far below.

The medieval **ramparts,** virtually undisturbed by passing traffic, provide a ready-made itinerary for a tour of old Laon. Panoramic views, sturdy gateways, and intriguing glimpses of the cathedral lurk around every bend. Another notable survivor from medieval times is the **Chapelle des Templiers,** a small, well-preserved octagonal 12th-century chapel on the grounds of the town museum. *Porte d'Ardon. Admission: 7 frs. Open Apr.–Oct., Wed.–Mon. 10–noon and 2–6; Nov.–Mar. until 5.*

Lodging and Dining
Under 150 frs.

Bannière de France. In business since 1685, the old-fashioned, uneven-floored Bannière de France is just five minutes' walk from Laon's picturesque cathedral and the medieval Ville Haute (upper town). Madame Lefèvre, the *patronne,* speaks fluent German and English. Guest rooms are cozy and quaintly decorated, and the restaurant's venerable dining room features sturdy cuisine (trout, guinea fowl) and well-priced set menus. *11 rue Franklin-Roosevelt, 02000, tel. 23–23–21–44. 18 rooms, a few with bath. Facilities: restaurant. AE, DC, MC, V. Closed Christmas and New Year's.*

Dining
Under 200 frs.

La Petite Auberge. Young chef Willy-Marc Zorn dishes up modern, imaginative cuisine at this 18th-century-style restaurant close to the train station in Laon's Ville Basse. The 150-franc menu is a good bet. *45 blvd. Pierre-Brossolette, tel. 23–23–02–38. Reservations advised. AE, DC, MC, V.*

Epernay

There are no trains between Reims and Epernay between 8:15 AM and noon; they make the 20-minute journey every hour or so at other times. Tourist office: 7 av. de Champagne, tel. 26–55–33–00.

Unlike Reims with its numerous treasures, **Epernay**, on the banks of the River Marne, appears to live only for champagne; there seems little relation between the fabulous wealth of Epernay's illustrious inhabitants and the drab, dreary appearance of the town as a whole. Most of the champagne houses are spaced out along the long, straight avenue de Champagne, and although their names may provoke sighs of wonder, their functional or overdressy facades are a disappointment.

The attractions are underground, in the cellars. Of the various houses open to the public, **Mercier** offers the best deal; its sculpted, labyrinthine caves contain one of the world's largest wooden barrels (with a capacity of over 200,000 bottles) and can be visited in the speed and comfort of a small train. A generous glass of champagne is your posttrip reward. *75 av. de Champagne. Admission free. Open 10–noon and 2–5.*

Dining
Under 75 frs.

Terrasse. Local champagne executives jostle with discerning tourists for tables at this friendly spot on the banks of the Marne. There are four set menus—those at 75 and 125 francs are particularly good bets. *7 quai de la Marne, tel. 26–55–26–05. Reservations recommended. AE, MC, V. Closed Sun. evening, Mon., and Feb.*

Shopping

Champagne is not the only Epernay specialty. At **La Chocolaterie,** Monsieur Thibaut performs confectionary miracles before your eyes—and you can take a seat in the adjoining Salon de Thé if you feel the urge to indulge on the spot (9 rue Gallice, tel. 26–51–58–04; closed Sun. and Mon.).

Châlons-sur-Marne

Two trains in the early morning and 1 in the afternoon make the trip from Epernay, which is 16 minutes and 35 km (22 mi) away. Three trains daily cover the 38-minute run from Reims. Tourist office: 3 quai des Arts, tel. 26–65–17–89.

Strangely enough, the official administrative center of the champagne industry is not Reims or Epernay but **Châlons-sur-Marne.** Yet the principal interest of this large town is to fans of medieval architecture. The **Cathédrale St-Etienne** is a pure, harmonious 13th-century construction with large nave windows and tidy flying buttresses; the overall effect is marred only by the bulky 17th-century Baroque west front. Of equal merit is the church of **Notre-Dame des Vaux,** with its twin spires, Romanesque nave, and early Gothic choir and vaults. The small **museum** beside the excavated cloister contains outstanding medieval statuary. *Rue Nicolas-Durand. Admission: 15 frs. Open Tues.–Sun. 10–noon and 2–6.*

Lodging and Dining
Under 350 frs.
Angleterre. This stylish venue in central Châlons, close to the church of Notre-Dame-en-Vaux, has fully renovated rooms (most with marble bathrooms) and rates that start in the moderate range. In the airy, modern restaurant, Jacky Michel uses champagne as a base for sauces. *19 pl. Monseigneur-Tissier, 51000, tel. 26–68–21–51. 18 rooms with bath or shower. AE, DC, MC, V. Closed Sun., Christmas, and second half of July.*

Tour 3: The Oise Département

Haughty Chantilly, worth visiting to see its château and forest, forms the base for two excursions. Antique Senlis is accessible by bus, and Beauvais, home to France's highest cathedral, is a short journey by rail. The tour then continues by train to Compiègne, site of another château and base for bus trips to splendidly restored Pierrefonds Castle.

From Paris
By Train
Express trains to Chantilly leave Paris (Gare du Nord) every 30 minutes during the early morning and evening, and 3 times during the rest of the day. The trip takes 30 minutes.

By Car
The 51-kilometer (32-mile) drive from Paris to Senlis along A1 takes about ½ hour. Chantilly is another 9½ kilometers (6 miles) away.

Chantilly

Tourist office: 23 av. du Maréchal-Joffre, down a short street opposite the station, tel. 44–57–08–58.

To reach the **château of Chantilly,** about a mile from the station, head down to avenue du Maréchal-Joffre, turn left, then go right onto rue du Connétable, Chantilly's main street. This leads past the stables, then veers right, affording the first glimpse of the imposing, golden-hued château, sitting snugly behind an artificial, carp-filled lake.

Despite appearances, much of the current building is not old but is 19th-century Renaissance pastiche, rebuilt in the 1870s. The lavish interior contains the outstanding **Condé Collection** of illuminated medieval manuscripts, tapestries, furniture, and paintings. The most famous room, the **Santuario,** boasts two celebrated works by Italian painter Raphael (1483–1520)—the *Three Ages of Woman* and *The Orleans Virgin*—plus an exquisite ensemble of 15th-century miniatures by the most illustrious French painter of his time, Jean Fouquet (1420–81). Farther on, in the Cabinet des Livres, is the **Book of Hours** of the Duc de Berri, one of the finest medieval manuscripts.

Other highlights of this unusual museum are the **Galérie de Psyché,** with 16th-century stained glass and portrait drawings by Flemish artist Jean Clouet II; the **chapel,** with sculptures by Jean Goujon and Jacques Sarrazin; and the extensive **collection of paintings** by 19th-century French artists, headed by Jean Auguste Ingres. *Admission: 30 frs. adults, 7 frs. children; 12 frs. park only. Open Easter–Oct., Wed.–Mon. 10–6; Nov.–Easter, 10:30–12:30 and 2–5; closed Tues.*

Behind the château is a large **park,** based on that familiar combination of formal bombast and romantic eccentricity. The neatly planned parterres and mighty straight-banked canal contrast pleasantly with the Jardin Anglais (English Garden), with its waterfall, and the make-believe village that inspired Marie Antoinette's version at Versailles.

Across the lake from the château is the Chantilly racecourse, inaugurated in 1834 by the prestigious French Jockey Club. In one corner (to the right as you leave the château) are the majestic 18th-century stables **(Grandes Ecuries)**, where up to 240 horses and 400 hounds for stag and boar hunts could be accommodated in straw-lined comfort. Today the stables host the **Musée du Cheval** (Horse Museum) and a glittering array of carriages. *Admission: 40 frs. adults, 35 frs. students and senior citizens, 30 frs. children. Open daily 10:30–5:30 (6 on weekends).*

Lodging
Under 250 frs.

Etoile. This small, underwhelming hotel is conveniently placed on the avenue leading from the train station to the château. It's cheap and acceptable for a night's stopover, though your reception may be somewhat lacking in warmth. *3 av. du Maréchal-Joffre, 60500, tel. 44–57–02–55. 10 rooms with bath. MC, V.*

Dining
Under 200 frs.
★

Relais Condé. What is probably the classiest restaurant in Chantilly is pleasantly situated opposite the racecourse, in a building that originally served as an Anglican chapel. A reasonably priced menu makes it a suitable lunch spot. An extensive wine list and several filling recipes—*burbet* (freshwater cod) with peppers, veal kidneys in mustard sauce—warrant a lengthier (if more expensive) visit in the evening. *42 av. du Maréchal-Joffre, tel. 44–57–05–75. Reservations required. Jacket and tie required for dinner. AE, DC, V. Closed Mon. and Sun. evening.*

Under 125 frs.

Relais du Coq Chantant. The discreet, upmarket style of this well-established restaurant attracts a classy clientele of golfers and horse fanciers. They may be willing to splash out à la carte, but we suggest that you opt for a set menu to sample a traditional meal based on fowl or rabbit. *21 rte. de Creil, tel. 44–57–01–28. Reservations advised. Jacket required. AE, DC, MC, V.*

Under 75 frs.

Capitainerie. As the château of Chantilly is a fair walk from the town's main street, it makes sense to have a quick lunch on the spot at this self-service restaurant. Situated in the château's medieval basement and adorned with old kitchen utensils, it offers a buffet of salads, cheeses, and desserts, complemented by the occasional hot dish—and service is nonstop from about 10:30 to 6:30. *Château, tel. 44–57–15–89. No reservations or credit cards. Closed Tues.*

Senlis

Buses meet most trains at Chantilly for the drive to Senlis, which is 25 minutes and about 10 km (6 mi) away. Tourist office: Place du Parvis, tel. 44–53–06–40.

The crooked, mazelike streets of **Senlis** are dominated by the svelte soaring spire of the Gothic cathedral of **Notre-Dame.** This is prime hunting country. On the grounds of the ruined royal castle opposite the west front of the cathedral is the **Musée de la Vénerie,** which claims to be Europe's only full-fledged hunting museum. Suitable artifacts, prints, and paintings rekindle the atmosphere of the kingly pursuit. *Château*

Royal. Admission: 15 frs. adults, 8 frs. children. Open for guided visits on the hour, Mon. 10–noon and 2–3, Tues. and Wed. 2–5, Thurs.–Sun. 10–noon and 2–5.

Down the lane behind the cathedral is the former church of **St-Pierre,** with its Flamboyant facade; across place Notre-Dame, the large square beside the cathedral, is the **Fondation Cziffra,** the former church of St-Frambourg, converted into an exhibition center by Hungarian-born pianist Gyorgy Cziffra in 1977, with a small adjoining museum devoted to regional architectural finds. *1 pl. St-Frambourg. Admission: 10 frs. adults, 6 frs. students. Open weekends only 3–6.*

Lodging
Under 150 frs.

Hostellerie Porte-Bellon. This is the closest you'll get to spending a night in the historic center of Senlis. A modest yet efficient hotel, the Porte-Bellon is just a five-minute walk from the cathedral and is close to the bus station. *35 rue Bellon, 60300, tel. 44–53–03–05. 20 rooms, most with bath. Facilities: restaurant. V. Closed mid-Dec.–mid-Jan., Fri. (except in summer).*

Dining
Under 125 frs.
★

Les Gourmandins. This cozy, two-floored, recently opened restaurant in old Senlis serves some interesting dishes—try the salad with duck and truffles—and offers a fine wine list. The fixed-price menu is a bargain for a weekday lunch; dining à la carte can nudge the expensive range. *3 pl. de la Halle, tel. 16/44–60–94–01. Reservations advised. MC, V.*

Beauvais

Five trains daily make the 8-minute trip from Chantilly to nearby Creil, where you can change for Beauvais, 35 minutes away. Beauvais tourist office: 1 rue Beauregard, tel. 44–45–08–18.

Like Reims, **Beauvais** still bears the painful scars of two world wars. It was savagely bombed in June 1940, and the ramshackle streets of the old town have resurfaced as characterless modern blocks. One survivor is the beautiful old Bishop's Palace, now the **Musée des Beaux-Arts** (Fine Arts Museum). Within its chambered recesses, you'll find a varied collection of art, embracing paintings, ceramics, and regional furniture. Highlights include an epic canvas of the French Revolution by 19th-century master Thomas Couture, complete with preparatory sketches (all tastefully assembled in a large room once used as the district law court), and the charming attic under the sloping roofs, which qualifies as one of the loveliest rooms in all France. *1 rue du Musée. Admission: 16 frs. Open Wed.–Mon. 10–noon and 2–6; closed Tues.*

The town's showpiece is unquestionably the **Cathédrale St-Pierre,** adjacent to the art museum (pl. St-Pierre). You may have an attack of vertigo just gazing up at its vaults, which, at 153 feet, are the highest in France. Such daring engineering was not without risk: The choir collapsed in 1284, shortly after completion. The transept, an outstanding example of Flamboyant Gothic, was not attempted until the 16th century. It was crowned by an improbable 450-foot spire that promptly came crashing down. With funds rapidly dwindling, the nave was never begun, delivering the final coup de grâce to Beauvais's ambition of becoming the largest church in Christendom. The 10th-century church, known as the **Basse Oeuvre** (closed to the public), juts out impertinently where the nave should have been.

From 1664 to 1939, Beauvais was one of France's leading tapestry centers; it reached its zenith in the mid-18th century under the direction of renowned artist Jean-Baptiste Oudry. The **Galérie Nationale de la Tapisserie,** a modern museum next to the cathedral, has examples from all periods of the town's tapestry history. *24 rue Henri-Brispot. Admission: 18 frs. Open Mar.–Oct., Tues.–Sun. 9:30–11:30 and 2–6; Nov.–Feb., Tues.–Sun. 10–11:30 and 2:30–4:30.*

Lodging
Under 150 frs.

Palais. This small, family-run hotel is no palace. But it's quiet, cheap, and central—just three minutes' walk from the cathedral. *9 rue St-Nicolas, 60000, tel. 44–45–12–58. 15 rooms, some with shower or bath. AE.*

Dining
Under 125 frs.

Marignan. Sturdy French dishes such as duck with orange and trout with almonds are the mainstay at the Marignan, located near St-Etienne church just off place Hachette. Go for the filling 105-franc menu, as eating à la carte will cost well over 200 francs. If you're in a hurry or want a cheaper meal, try the bustling ground-floor brasserie, where sauerkraut and andouillette stand out. *1 rue Malherbe, tel. 44–48–15–15. Reservations suggested. AE, MC, V. Closed Sun. evening, Mon., and two weeks in Aug.*

Compiègne

From Beauvais, change at Creil for Compiègne. From Chantilly there are 6 trains to Compiègne during the day. The trip takes 45 minutes. Compiègne tourist office: Place de l'Hôtel-de-Ville, tel. 44–40–01–00.

Compiègne, a bustling town of some 40,000 people, stands at the northern limit of the Ile de France forest, on the edge of the misty plains of Picardy: prime hunting country, a sure sign that there's a former royal palace in the vicinity. The one here enjoyed its heyday in the mid-19th century under Napoleon III. But the town's place in history looks both further back—Joan of Arc was held prisoner here—and further forward: The World War I armistice was signed in Compiègne Forest on November 11, 1918.

The 18th-century **palace** was restored by Napoleon I and favored for wild weekends by his nephew Napoleon III, emperor from 1851 to 1870. The entrance ticket includes access to apartments, the Musée du Second Empire, Musée de la Voiture (Car Museum), and the attractive palace park. *Pl. du Palais. Admission: 25 frs. Open Wed.–Mon. 9:30–4:30; closed Tues.*

One of the central highlights of Compiègne is the late-15th-century town hall, or **Hôtel de Ville,** possessing an exceptional Flamboyant Gothic facade with fine statuary. Make time to visit the **Musée de la Figurine** for its amazing collection of 85,000 lead soldiers depicting military uniforms through the ages. *28 pl. de l'Hôtel de Ville. Admission: 11 frs. Open Apr.–Oct., Tues.–Sun. 9–noon and 2–6.*

Lodging and Dining
Under 250 frs.

France. This 17th-century house, on a narrow street in the old town near the ornate Hôtel de Ville, is calm, comfortable, and inexpensive; rates start at 120 francs for its rooms, many of which have period furniture. Though service in the restaurant sometimes lacks enthusiasm, it does have style—lace tablecloths, wooden beams, and Louis XVI furniture—and its wide selection of half bottles is welcome. *17 rue Eugène-Floquet, 60200, tel. 44-40-02-74. 21 rooms, some with bath or shower. Facilities: bar, restaurant. MC, V.*

Dining
Under 125 frs.
Picotin. Its three inexpensive menus make the old-fashioned Picotin a good choice for lunch or dinner after you've visited the nearby château. The traditional cuisine (salads, steaks, and chocolate desserts) offers few surprises—or disappointments. *22 pl. de l'Hôtel-de-Ville, tel. 44-40-04-06. Reservations strongly advised. V. Closed Tues.*

Pierrefonds

There are 3 daily buses from Compiègne to Pierrefonds, 14 km (9 mi) to the southeast.

Attractive, lakeside **Pierrefonds** is dominated by its huge 12th-century **château,** comprehensively restored to imagined former glory by the noted architect Viollet-le-Duc at the behest of upstart Emperor Napoleon III in the 1860s. What he left is a crenellated fortress with a fairy-tale silhouette. A visit takes in the chapel, barracks, and the majestic keep holding the lord's bedchamber and reception hall. *Admission: 24 frs. Guided tours only, Apr.–Oct., Wed.–Mon. 9:30–11:15 and 1:30–5:15; Nov.–Mar., Wed.–Sun. 10–noon and 2–4:30.*

Lodging
Under 250 frs.
Etrangers. A small restaurant, serving game in season, and an attractive lakeside terrace make this an ideal halting place beneath the mighty castle of Pierrefonds. The three-story hotel was recently modernized, although it still lacks an elevator; American and Japanese visitors are frequent. *10 rue Beaudon, 60350, tel. 44-42-80-18. 32 rooms, many with bath. Facilities: restaurant (closed Sun. dinner and Mon. Sept.–mid-Jan.). MC, V. Closed mid-Jan.–mid-Feb.*

8 Alsace-Lorraine and the Jura–Franche-Comté Region

Strasbourg, Nancy

Nancy is one of France's most attractive cities, and Metz merits a visit, but the real reason for coming to eastern France is to see Alsace. With the Vosges Mountains looming to the west and the River Rhine flowing to the east, Alsace seems caught between France and Germany. Its flower-strewn villages are maintained with spotless Germanic efficiency. Their names and those of most inhabitants sound German, as does the local dialect. Local dishes such as sauerkraut and sausage taste German, and the regional daily newspaper is printed in German as well as in French. Nonetheless, the people of Alsace are definitely not German, and they growl at any suggestion that their lifestyle, character, and love of the good life are not determinedly French. It's entirely typical that rich foie gras, a regional product that's a favorite of French chefs, tops restaurant menus all over the area.

Strasbourg, the capital of Alsace, is also the unofficial "capital" of Europe. Home to European political institutions and a symbol of Franco-German reconciliation, it is a city of immense cultural, historic, and architectural interest. Colmar, farther south, is equally picturesque; Mulhouse less so, but its outstanding car and train museums compensate. The Route du Vin winds its way down Alsace through vineyards and villages of breathtaking beauty, which you can glimpse—but only glimpse—through the windows of the Strasbourg–Colmar train. There is a good case here for renting a bike in, say, Colmar, and wending your way from town to town—or abandoning budgetary caution and renting a car.

To the south of Alsace-Lorraine is the Jura-Franche-Comté region. Better known to Europeans than Americans, the Jura Mountains form a natural border some 242 kilometers (150 miles) long that curves between France and Switzerland. The birthplace of Louis Pasteur and Victor Hugo, and home to the celebrated aperitif Pernod, the Jura is dotted with picturesque little towns where local craftsmen still make wooden toys, clocks, and pipes. The area is renowned for its wines and cheese, and a cuisine that draws on the plentiful local lake and river fish—especially trout.

Nowhere in France is farther from the sea, so the climate in Alsace-Lorraine is continental: Winters can be extremely cold and summers mighty hot. The Vosges Mountains, which often act as a cloud buffer, ensure that rain is less frequent in Alsace than in Lorraine.

Essential Information

Lodging Hotel accommodations are easier to find in Lorraine than in Alsace, where advance reservations are essential during summer months (especially in Strasbourg and Colmar). Glamorous Strasbourg, a leading tourist venue and home to a multitude of Eurocrats, is one of France's most expensive cities.

Dining Alsatian cooking is distinctive in its marriage of German and French tastes. It tends to be heavy: *Choucroute* (sauerkraut), served with ham and sausages, or *Baeckoffe* (a type of potato pie), washed down with a mug of local beer or a pitcher of wine, is a filling means of combating the cold of winter or fueling up during long walks through the Vosges. But there is some sophistication, too. The local foie gras is admirably accompanied by a glass of Gewürztraminer, preferably late-harvested *(vendanges tardives)* for extra sweetness. Riesling, the classic wine of Alsace, is often used to make a sauce that goes exceptionally well with trout or chicken. Snails and seasonal game (pheasant, partridge, hare, venison, and boar) are other favorites, as are Munster cheese, salty *Bretzel* loaves, and flaky, briochelike *Kouglof* bread.

Salmon, pike, eel, and trout can be found in rivers throughout Alsace and Lorraine. Carp fried in breadcrumbs is a specialty of southern Alsace. Lorraine, renowned for its famous quiches, is also known for its dumplings, Madeleines, almond candies *(dragées)*, and macaroons. Lorraine shares the Alsatian love of pastry and fruit tarts, often made with mirabelle plums, but only in German-influenced Alsace will you find *winstubs* (down-to-earth café-wine bars serving wine by the jug and snacks and meals heavy on local specialties such as sauerkraut, sausage, and snails). Restaurant prices tend to be lower in Lorraine than in Alsace.

Shopping Among the specialties of Alsace are the handwoven checkered napkins and tablecloths known as **kelches** and the hand-painted **earthenware molds** for *Kouglof* bread. These goods can be found throughout this tourist-oriented province, where every pretty village has a souvenir shop of greater or lesser standing. Glass and crystal are produced by skilled artisans at **Baccarat,** 60 kilometers (37 miles) east of Nancy; its town center is dominated by attractive crystal shops. And the lively city centers of

Strasbourg and Colmar are crammed with specialized shops and boutiques.

Bicycling A guide for biking in Lorraine is available from the **Comité Départemental de Cyclotourisme** (33 rue de la République, 54950 Laronxe). Bikes can be rented at many local train stations—including those in Verdun and Gérardmer in Lorraine, and Strasbourg, Saverne, Sélestat, and Colmar.

Hiking Hiking in the Vosges foothills is a rewarding pastime; for a list of signposted trails, contact the **Sélestat** tourist office (10 blvd. Leclerc, tel. 88–92–02–66).

The Arts Strasbourg is a lively cultural center. Not only does it have its own orchestra, the **Strasbourg Philharmonic Orchestra** (Palais des Congrès, tel. 88–37–67–77), but it also hosts a variety of seasonal arts events. The annual **Festival de Musique** is held in Strasbourg from June to early July at the modern Palais des Congrès and at the cathedral (tel. 88–32–43–10 for details). There is a rock festival in June, organized by Strasbourg's Centre Culturel (13 pl. André-Maurois), and the city offers summer concerts at the Pavillon Joséphine in the Orangerie. A monthly handbook, *Strasbourg Actualités*, is a mine of information on local cultural events.

Festivals Many regional towns and villages, especially the wine villages of Alsace, stage festivals in summer. Note the spectacular, pagan-inspired burning of the three pine trees at **Thann** (late June) and the Flower Carnival at **Sélestat** (mid-August). There are impressive *son-et-lumière* (sound-and-light) performances at the château of **Saverne** and the cathedral of **Strasbourg** (check dates and times locally).

Highlights for First-time Visitors

Cathédrale Notre-Dame, Strasbourg, Tour 1
Château des Rohan, Strasbourg, Tour 1
Haut-Koenigsbourg, Tour 1
Issenheim Altarpiece, Musée d'Unterlinden, Colmar, Tour 1
Cathédrale, Metz, Tour 2
Nancy, Tour 2
Toul, Tour 2
Chapel, Ronchamp, Tour 3

Tour 1: Alsace

Elegant Strasbourg, sitting proudly by the German frontier, is the star of Alsace. Trains head south through this narrow province to the towns of Obernai, Sélestat, and Colmar, whose churches, museums and old streets deserve scrutiny. Use Colmar as a base for an excursion to Mulhouse, home to outstanding rail and automobile museums.

From Paris
By Train Express trains to Strasbourg leave Paris (Gare de l'Est) 10 times daily. The trip takes 3 hours 50 minutes.

By Car The 490-kilometer (305-mile) drive along A4 from Paris to Strasbourg takes 5 hours.

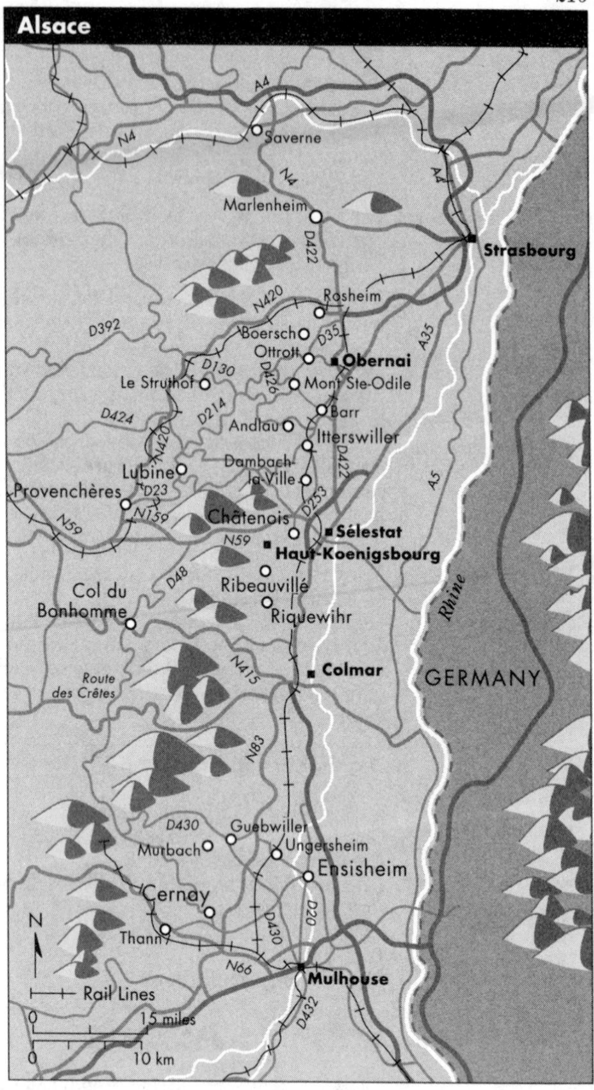

Strasbourg

Tourist office: 10 pl. Gutenberg, down rue Mercière from the cathedral, tel. 88–32–57–07.

Numbers in the margin correspond to points of interest on the Strasbourg map.

Perhaps the most interesting and attractive French city after Paris, **Strasbourg** is an irresistible mixture of old houses, waterways, and museums; looming above them all is the colossal single spire of the cathedral.

The Romans knew Strasbourg as Argentoratum. After a spell as part of the Holy Roman Empire, the city was united with

France in 1681 but retained independence regarding legislation, education, and religion under the honorific title Free Royal City. Since World War II, Strasbourg has become a symbol city, embodying Franco-German reconciliation and the wider idea of a united Europe. It plays host to the European Parliament and Council of Europe and acts as a neutral stomping ground for such controversial political figures as Yasser Arafat, leader of the Palestinian Liberation Organization.

1 The **Cathédrale Notre-Dame** is a tortuous ¾-mile walk from the station. To get there, take rue du Maire-Küss, which becomes rue du 22-novembre after the canal and arrives at the bottom corner of place Kléber; skirt the square and turn right at the far end onto rue des Grandes-Arcades, then turn left after 250 yards up pedestrian rue des Hallebardes. The cathedral itself, with its splendid openwork spire, is at the hub of Strasbourg, on place de la Cathédrale.

Pink masonry covers the facade. Not content with the outlines of the walls themselves, medieval builders stuck huge, slender, rodlike shafts of stone everywhere: You feel as if you can reach up and snap one off. The spire, finished in 1439, looks absurdly fragile as it tapers skyward like some elongated, 466-foot wedding cake; only the 528-foot spire of Ulm, in Germany, climbs higher.

The interior presents a stark contrast to the facade. For a start, it is older, virtually finished by 1275. Then, at 105 feet, the nave does not create the same impression of soaring height: Its broad windows emphasize the horizontal rather than the vertical. In the nave, note Hans Hammer's ornately sculpted pulpit (1484–86), with its 50 statuettes, and the richly painted 14th- to 15th-century organ loft that rises from pillar to ceiling.

Another contrast is apparent within—that between the choir and the nave. The choir is not ablaze with stained glass but is framed by chunky masonry. The original brickwork of the cupola is visible, as if no one had ever gotten around to decorating it. The fact that the choir is raised above the level of the rest of the church heightens the contrast and reinforces an aura of murky, mystical sanctity.

The elaborate 16th-century **Chapelle St-Laurent,** to the left of the choir, merits a visit, but most visitors turn to the right to admire the **Angels' Column,** an intricate pillar dating from 1230, formed by clustering, tubelike colonnettes harboring three tiers of delicate statues. Nearby, the daring Renaissance machinery of the 16th-century **Astronomical Clock** whirs into action at 12:30 PM daily: Macabre clockwork figures—including a skeletal Father Time and the screeching rooster that reminds the Apostle Peter of his broken promise—enact the story of Christ's Passion. *Admission to clock: 8 frs.*

There is a *son-et-lumière* (sound-and-light) performance in the cathedral every evening from April through the end of September. The text is in French or German, but virtuoso lighting effects translate into any language. *Admission: 30 frs. adults, 15 frs. children under 18. Performances at 8:15 and 9:15 PM.*

2 A worthy complement to the cathedral is the **Musée de l'Oeuvre Notre-Dame,** opposite the south front. There is more to this museum than the usual assembly of dilapidated statues rescued from the local cathedral before they fell off. A conscious effort

Strasbourg

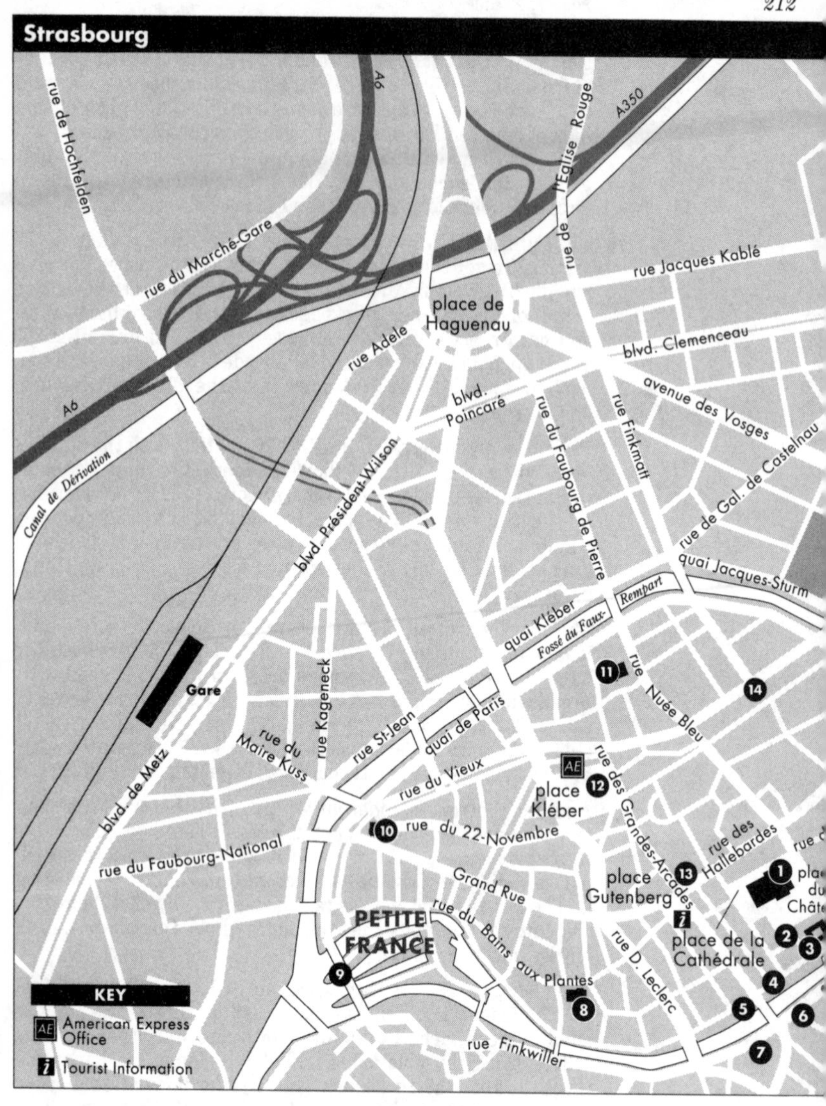

Ancienne Douane, **5**
Cathédrale Notre-Dame, **1**
Château des Rohan, **3**
Cour du Courbeau, **6**
Musée Alsacien, **7**
Musée de l'Oeuvre Notre-Dame, **2**
Musée Historique, **4**
Orangerie, **19**
Palais de l'Europe, **18**
Palais de l'Université, **17**
Place Broglie, **14**
Place de la République, **15**
Place du Marché-Neuf, **13**
Place Kléber, **12**
Ponts Couverts, **9**
St-Paul, **16**
St-Pierre-le-Jeune, **11**
St-Pierre-le-Vieux, **10**
St-Thomas, **8**

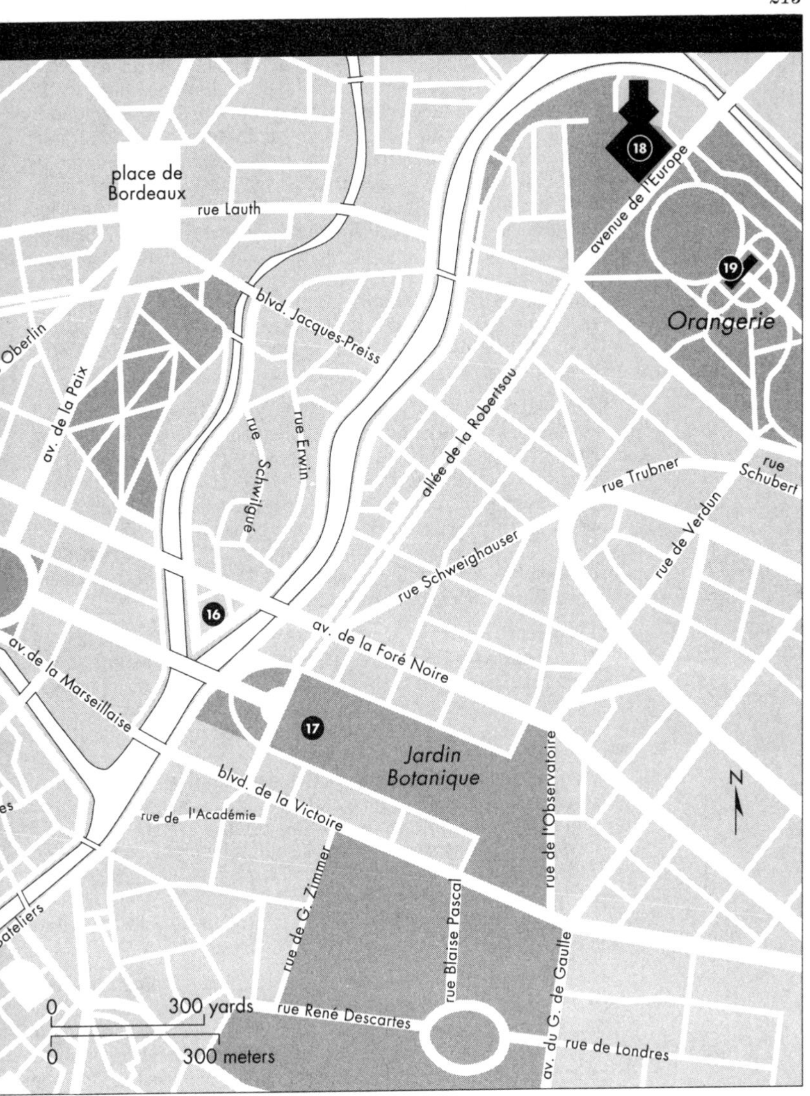

place de Bordeaux
rue Lauth
blvd. Jacques-Preiss
Oberlin
av. de la Paix
rue Schwilgué
rue Erwin
allée de la Robertsau
avenue de l'Europe
Orangerie
rue Trubner
rue Schubert
rue de Verdun
rue Schweighauser
av. de la Foré Noire
av. de la Marseillaise
Jardin Botanique
rue de l'Observatoire
blvd. de la Victoire
rue de l'Académie
rue de G. Zimmer
rue Blaise Pascal
av. du G. de Gaulle
rue René Descartes
rue de Londres
N
0
300 yards
0
300 meters
16
17
18
19

has been made to create a church atmosphere and provide an appropriate setting for the works of art. Part of one room evokes a narrow, low-roofed cloister. A dimly lit, high-walled chamber, reached through a creaky wooden door, is ringed by stone screens with pinnacles and pointed gables. Soon you'll find yourself in the stonemasons' workshop. A polished wooden staircase leads to a suite of small passages and large rooms, with drawings, stained glass, and gold objects. All the architectural elements of the Renaissance—pediments, spiral pillars, and cornices—can be found on the bulky wardrobes and cupboards produced by local cabinetmakers. There are some fine Old Master paintings as well. *Pl. du Château. Admission: 14 frs. adults, 7 frs. students and children. Open Apr.–Sept., Wed.–Mon. 10–noon and 2–6; Oct.–Mar., Wed.–Sat., Mon. 2–6, Sun. 10–noon; closed Tues.*

Alongside the Musée de l'Oeuvre Notre-Dame, between the
3 cathedral and the river, is the **Château des Rohan,** onetime palace of the powerful Rohans, a dynasty of prince-bishops who held both political and spiritual sway over the city and region. The exterior of Robert de Cotte's neoclassical building (1732–42) is starkly austere. The glamour is inside, in Robert le Lorrain's magnificent ground-floor rooms, led by the great **Salon d'Assemblée** (Assembly Room) and the book- and tapestry-lined **Bibliothèque des Cardinaux** (Cardinals' Library).

The library leads to a series of less august rooms that house the **Musée des Arts Décoratifs** (Decorative Arts Museum) and its elaborate display of ceramics. Works by Hannong, a porcelain manufacturer active in Strasbourg from 1721 to 1782, are comprehensively represented; dinner services by other local kilns reveal the influence of Chinese porcelain in their delicate patterns. Equally interesting are the dishes and terrines in animal form (turkeys' and hogs' heads), or table decorations imitating plums and cauliflowers—of doubtful taste but technical tours de force. Furniture, tapestries, and silver-gilt complete the collection. *Pl. du Château. Admission: 18 frs. adults, 9 frs. students and children. Open Apr.–Sept., Wed.–Mon. 10–noon and 2–6; Oct.–Mar., Wed.–Sat., Mon. 2–6, Sun. 10–noon; closed Tues.*

About 50 yards north of the cathedral, and running parallel to it, is rue des Hallebardes, Strasbourg's most stylish pedestrian-only shopping street. It leads to **place Gutenberg,** dominated by an elegant three-story building with large windows, constructed between 1582 and 1585, now used as the Chamber of Commerce and city tourist office. Johannes Gutenberg (1400–68), after whom the square is named, invented the printing press in Strasbourg in 1434. On one side of his statue, executed in 1840 by sculptor David d'Angers, is a plaque bearing the U.S. Declaration of Independence, in acknowledgment of its influence on French revolutionary soldiers from Alsace.

4 The **Musée Historique** (Local History Museum) stands between place Gutenberg and the river. Wooden floors and beam roofs create a suitably historic atmosphere in which to admire maps, armor, arms, bells, uniforms, printing paraphernalia, cardboard toy soldiers, and two huge relief models of Strasbourg, one made in 1727, the other in 1836. *3 rue de la Grande-Boucherie. Admission: 18 frs. adults, 9 frs. students and senior citizens. Open Oct.–Mar., Wed.–Mon. 2–6; Apr.–Sept., Wed.–Mon. 10–noon and 2–6; closed Tues.*

5 The **Ancienne Douane,** opposite, was constructed in 1358 to serve as a customs house. It now houses a brasserie and temporary exhibitions. *Admission: 20 frs. adults, 10 frs. students and children. Open Wed.–Mon. 11–6; closed Tues.*

6 Across the river is the **cour du Courbeau,** a ramshackle 14th-century courtyard whose hostelry once welcomed kings and
7 emperors. Facing the Ancienne Douane is the **Musée Alsacien.** If you want a glimpse of how Alsace families used to live, this is the place to visit. Local interiors—kitchens, bedrooms, and sitting rooms (the last two often combined)—have been faithfully reconstituted. The diverse activities of blacksmiths, clog makers, saddlers, and makers of artificial flowers are explained with the help of old-time artisans' tools and equipment. *23 quai St-Nicolas. Admission: 12 frs. adults, 6 frs. students and children. Open Oct.–Mar., Wed.–Sat., Mon. 2–6, Sun. 10–noon and 2–6; Apr.–Sept., Wed.–Mon. 10–noon and 2–6; closed Tues.*

Cross the river two bridges farther down to admire the church
8 of **St-Thomas** (quai Finkwiller), particularly the mausoleum of Marshal Maurice of Saxony (1696–1750), a key figure in the 1740–48 War of Austrian Succession. Follow the banks of the River Ill toward the picturesque quarter of **La Petite France,** whose cobbled streets are lined with richly carved, half-timbered Renaissance houses. The Ill, which branches into several
9 canals, is spanned by the **Ponts Couverts,** three connected 14th-century covered bridges, each with its tall, stern, stone tower.

10 Quai Turckheim leads to the church of **St-Pierre-le-Vieux,** whose choir is decorated with scenes from the Passion (circa 1500) by local painter Henri Lutzelmann. Follow the quay
11 around to **St-Pierre-le-Jeune,** consecrated in 1320, to admire its painted rood screen, immense choir, and 14th-century frescoes.

Alsace provided the French Revolution with 64 generals and marshals. One of the most famous was Jean-Baptiste Kléber (1753–1800), assassinated in Cairo after being left in charge of Egypt by Napoleon in 1799. Kléber's statue lords it over
12 Strasbourg's busiest square, **place Kléber,** situated up rue des Grandes-Arcades from St-Pierre-le-Jeune.

Rue des Orfèvres, one of the lively pedestrian streets leading off from rue des Hallebardes, is connected to the noisy, commercial rue des Grandes-Arcades by a cobbled, leafy square—the
13 **place du Marché-Neuf**—seldom discovered by visitors. This peaceful oasis is a fine place to stop for a drink, and its two open-air cafés are open till late at night.

14 Rue de l'Outre heads down to another large square, **place Broglie,** home of the city hall, the 18th-century Municipal Theater, and the Banque de France. The bank occupies the site of the house where the *Marseillaise* (composed by Rouget de Lisle, and originally entitled *Battlesong of the Rhine Army)* was sung for the first time in 1792.

15 The spacious layout and ponderous architecture of **place de la République** have nothing in common with the old town across the river, except the local red sandstone. A different hand was at work here—that of occupying Germans, who erected the former Ministry (1902); the Academy of Music (1882–92), ex-Re-

gional Parliament; and the Palais du Rhin (1883–88), destined to be the German imperial palace.

Much of northern Strasbourg bears the German stamp. Head right out of place de la République, past the neo-Gothic church
16 17 of **St-Paul,** to the pseudo-Renaissance **Palais de l'Université**—constructed between 1875 and 1885 (though Strasbourg University itself dates from 1621). Heavy, turn-of-the-century houses, some betraying the whimsical curves of the art-nouveau style, frame allée de la Robertsau, a tree-lined boulevard that would not look out of place in Berlin; follow its length to
18 reach the modern **Palais de l'Europe,** designed by Paris architect Henri Bernard in 1977. The Palais houses the European Court of Human Rights and the Council of Europe, founded in 1949 and independent of the European Community (founded in 1957), whose 12 members are joined here by representatives from the traditionally nonaligned countries—Austria, Norway, Sweden, and Switzerland—plus Cyprus, Iceland, Liechtenstein, Malta, and Turkey. The European flag that flutters in front of the Palais—a circle of 12 gold stars on a blue background—was created for the Council of Europe in 1955 and adopted by the European Community in 1986. *Av. de l'Europe. Visits weekdays at 9, 10, 3, 4, and 5.*

Just across the street from the Palais de l'Europe, the
19 **Orangerie** is a delightful park laden with flowers and punctuated by imperious copper beeches. It contains a lake and, close by, a small reserve of rare birds, including flamingos and noisy local storks.

Lodging
Under 250 frs.

Gutenberg. A 200-year-old mansion is the setting of this charming hotel, just off place Gutenberg and only a few hundred yards from the cathedral. Several rooms, and the reception and breakfast area, have kept their original furniture, underlining a picturesque appeal that once enjoyed the dubious favors of Hitler's Wehrmacht. There's no restaurant. Be sure to ask for one of the lower-priced rooms, since some are more expensive than others. *31 rue des Serruriers, 67000, tel. 88–32–17–15. 50 rooms, some with bath. MC, V. Closed first week Jan.*

Under 150 frs.

Michelet. First impressions of the Michelet may be a shade gloomy, but students and foreign tourists flock here. Rooms are clean, if small, and offer unbeatable value given the location near the cathedral, off place Gutenberg. *48 rue du Vieux-Marché-aux-Poissons, 67000, tel. 88–32–47–38. 20 rooms, some with shower. No credit cards.*

Dining
Under 200 frs.
★

Au Gourmet Sans Chiqué. A cheerful welcome can be expected at this intimate bistro *sans chiqué* (without pretentions) down one of Old Strasbourg's many narrow streets, where herbs and spices are tellingly used by young chef Daniel Klein. The cheapest set menu represents fine value and is best accompanied by a bottle of the house Gewürztraminer. *15 rue Sainte-Barbe, tel. 88–32–04–07. Reservations advised. AE, DC, MC, V. Closed Mon., part of Jan., and most of Aug.*

Under 75 frs.

Zum Strissel. With its wooden floor, stained-glass windows, and exposed beams, this is a typical *winstub,* Alsace's distinctive pub–cum–wine bar. The three set menus under 100 francs, the selection of regional favorites such as snails and sauerkraut, and the local white wine sold by the jug attract a lively crowd, especially since the location is conveniently between the cathedral and the river. *5 pl. de la Grande-Boucherie, tel. 88–*

32–14–73. Reservations recommended on weekends. MC, V. Closed Sun., Mon., and the second half of July.

Shopping **Rue des Hallebardes** next to the cathedral, adjacent **rue des Grandes-Arcades** (with its shopping mall), and **place Kléber** form the commercial heart of Strasbourg; chocolate shops and delicatessens selling local foie gras are delicious places for browsing.

Obernai

Local trains make the 30-minute journey from Strasbourg in the early morning, at lunchtime, and in the late afternoon. Obernai tourist office: Chapelle du Beffroi, pl. du Marché, tel. 88–85–64–13.

At the heart of **Obernai**, one of the most attractive towns in Alsace, is the medieval place du Marché, dominated by the stout, square 13th-century **Kappellturm** Belfry, topped by a pointed steeple flanked at each corner by frilly openwork turrets added in 1597. The nearby **Puits à Six-Seaux,** constructed in the 1570s, is an elaborate Renaissance well whose name recalls the six buckets suspended from its metal chains. Just behind the belfry is Obernai's **Hôtel de Ville,** rebuilt in 1848 but incorporating much of the original Renaissance building, notably its richly carved balcony.

North of the town hall, the twin spires of the parish church of **St-Pierre-et-St-Paul** compete with the belfry for skyline preeminence. They date, as does the rest of the church, from the 1860s, although the 1504 Holy Sepulcher altarpiece in the north transept is a survivor from the previous church, along with some 15th-century stained glass.

Sélestat

Seven trains a day from Obernai make the 30-minute trip to Sélestat. There are hourly trains from Strasbourg, a 20- to 40-minute trip. Sélestat tourist office: 10 blvd. Leclerc, tel. 88–92–02–66.

Sélestat is a busy town with two impressive churches. **St-Foy** dates from between 1155 and 1190; its Romanesque facade remains largely intact (the spires were added in the 19th century), as does the 140-foot octagonal tower over the crossing. Sadly, the interior was mangled during the centuries, chiefly by the Jesuits; their most inspired legacy is the Baroque pulpit of 1733 illustrating the life of the founder of their movement, St. Francis Xavier. Note the Romanesque bas-relief next to the baptistery, originally the lid of a sarcophagus. *Just off rue du Marché Vert.*

Take rue de Babil one block south to the later, Gothic church of **St-Georges.** It, too, has a fine tower, built in 1490 and some 200 feet tall. There is medieval stained glass in the rose window above the south door and in the windows of the choir, telling the tales of saints Catherine, Helen, and Agnes.

Head left down rue du Sel to the **Bibliothèque Humaniste,** a major library founded in 1452 and installed in the former Halle aux Blés. Among the precious manuscripts on display are a 7th-century lectionary and a 12th-century Book of Miracles. Altarpieces, jewelry, sculpture, and earthenware are also exhibited.

1 rue de la Bibliothèque. Admission: 8 frs. Open weekdays 9–noon and 2–5, Sat. 9–noon.

Dining *Under 125 frs.* **Vieille Tour.** Rustic decor and waiters decked out in local costume entice diners to the far side of place d'Armes from St-Foy church, to enjoy the healthy contrast of traditional dishes and more unexpected fare such as leek and mushroom salad. The best value is the 90-franc menu, as à la carte dining can push your check up to 200 francs. *8 rue Jauge, tel. 88–92–15–02. Reservations recommended. MC, V. Closed Sun. evening, Mon., and two weeks in July.*

Haut-Koenigsbourg

Haut-Koenigsbourg is inaccessible by public transportation, so you'll need to take a taxi from Sélestat, 5 mi away, or rent a bike at the train station.

The romantic, crag-top castle of **Haut-Koenigsbourg** looks just as a kaiser thought it should: In 1901, German emperor Wilhelm II was presented with the 13th-century ruins by the town of Sélestat (or Schelestadt, the German name used then) and restored them with some diligence and no lack of imagination—squaring the main tower's original circle, for instance. Today Haut-Koenigsbourg is besieged by tourists and should be avoided on sunny summer days. At other times, the site, panorama, drawbridge, and amply furnished imperial chambers merit a visit. *Admission: 30 frs. Open Apr.–Oct., daily 10–noon and 2–6; Nov.–Dec., Feb.–Mar., daily 10–noon and 2–5; closed Jan.*

Colmar

Trains make the 15-minute run from Sélestat every 1½ hours or so. There are hourly trains from Strasbourg, 35 minutes away. Colmar tourist office: 4 rue Unterlinden, tel. 89–41–02–29.

The heart of the proud merchant town of **Colmar** remains intact: A web of pedestrian streets fans out from the beefy-towered church of **St-Martin.** To the east lies Grand'Rue, with its 15th-century **Ancienne Douane** (Customs House) and twin-turreted **Maison aux Arcades** (1609). To the south is the pretty, water-crossed district known as **Petite Venise.**

Alongside St. Martin's, on rue Mercière (no. 11), is the **Maison Pfister** (1537), which, with its decorative frescoes and medallions, counts as one of the most impressive dwellings in town. On the other side of rue des Marchands is the **Musée Bartholdi,** former home of Frédéric Auguste Bartholdi (1834–1904), the local sculptor who designed the Statue of Liberty. *30 rue des Marchands. Admission: 12 frs. Open Apr.–Oct., daily 10–noon and 2–6; Nov.–Mar., weekends 10–noon and 2–5; closed weekdays.*

In the nearby **Dominican Church** (pl. des Dominicains) can be seen the Flemish-influenced *Madonna of the Rosebush* (1473) by Martin Schongauer (1445–91), a talented engraver as well as a painter. This work, stolen from St. Martin's in 1972 and later recovered and hung here, has almost certainly been reduced in size from its original state. Realistic birds, buds, thorns, and flowers add life to the gold-background solemnity. *Admission: 8 frs.*

Take rue des Têtes past the Maison des Têtes (1608)—so called because of the carved heads proliferating on its facade—to the **Musée d'Unterlinden,** France's best-attended provincial museum. The star attraction of this former medieval convent is the **Issenheim Altarpiece** (1512–16) by Martin Grünewald, majestically displayed in the convent's Gothic chapel. The altarpiece was originally painted for the Antoine convent at Issenheim, 32 kilometers (20 miles) south of Colmar, and was believed to have miraculous healing powers over ergot, a widespread disease in the Middle Ages caused by poisonous fungus found in moldy grain. The altarpiece's emotional drama moves away from the stilted restraint of earlier paintings toward the humanistic realism of the Renaissance: The blanched despair of the Virgin, clutched by a weeping St. John, is balanced, on the other side of the cross, by the grave expression of John the Baptist. The blood of the crucified Christ gushes forth, and his face is racked with pain. A dark, simple background heightens the composition's stark grandeur.

The altarpiece was closed and folded according to the religious calendar and contains several other scenes apart from the *Crucifixion:* The *Incarnation* features angelic musicians playing celestial melodies as a white-bearded God, the Father, patrols the heavens; to the left, an incredulous Mary receives the Angel Gabriel; to the right, Christ rises from his tomb amid a bold halo of orange and blue. The third arrangement portrays, to the left, St. Anthony in conversation with St. Paul in a wild, overgrown landscape, while to the right, nightmarish beasts, reminiscent of Hieronymous Bosch, make up the torturous *Temptation of St. Anthony.*

Modern art, stone sculpture, and local crafts cluster around the 13th-century cloisters to complete Unterlinden's folksy charm. *Rue Unterlinden. Admission: 25 frs. adults, 12 frs. students. Open Apr.–Oct., daily 9–noon and 2–6; Nov.–Mar., Wed.–Mon. 9–noon and 2–5; closed Tues.*

Lodging
Under 250 frs.
★

Colbert. The plus here is a convenient location, halfway between the train station and the ancient town center. Ask for one of the quieter rooms along rue des Taillandiers. Guest rooms are well equipped and air-conditioned, though the decor is a little loud. *2 rue des Trois-Epis, 68000, tel. 89–41–31–05. 50 rooms with bath or shower. Facilities: bar. MC, V.*

Dining
Under 125 frs.
★

Buffet de la Gare. Not all train-station buffets can claim gastronomic fame, but hungry travelers will enjoy this one. With its stained-glass windows, Buffet de la Gare looks more like a church than a station. And the waiters exude pastoral concern rather than ticket-collecting officiousness: They will happily advise you how best to connect between platters of crayfish or pâté *en croute* (in pastry) and duck in red-wine sauce. Order carefully and the low tab will surprise you. *9 pl. de la Gare, tel. 89–41–21–26. Reservations accepted. MC, V.*

Splurge

Schillinger. Genial Jean Schillinger lords it over one of the smoothest-run restaurants in Alsace. Impeccable service, velvet upholstery, and gleaming silver cutlery complement an exhaustive wine list and meticulously prepared fish, veal, and salt-cooked pigeon. *16 rue Stanislas, tel. 89–41–43–17. Reser-*

vations required. Jacket and tie required. AE, DC, V. Closed Sun. dinner, Mon. 250–350 frs.

Mulhouse

Trains from Colmar run every ½ hour and take 25 minutes. Trains run from Strasbourg every 1½ hours and take an hour. Mulhouse tourist office: 9 av. Foch, tel. 89–45–68–31.

Mulhouse, a pleasant if unremarkable industrial town, is worth visiting for its museums. Dutch and Flemish masters of the 17th to 18th centuries top the bill at the **Musée des Beaux-Arts** (Fine Arts Museum, 14 pl. Guillaume Tell; closed Tues). But it is cars and trains that attract most visitors. Some 500 vintage and modern cars, dating from the steam-powered Jacquot of 1878 and spanning 100 different makes, are featured in the **Musée National de l'Automobile.** The highlights are the two Bugatti Royales. Only a handful of these stately cars was ever made; one was auctioned in 1987 for $8 million. *192 av. de Colmar. Admission: 34 frs. adults, 22 frs. students. Open Wed.–Mon. 10–6.*

A reconstructed Stephenson locomotive of 1846 sets the wheels rolling at the **Musée Français du Chemin de Fer** (National Train Museum), a 10-minute walk west down rue J.-Hofer. Rolling stock is spread over 12 tracks, including a vast array of steam trains and the BB 9004 electric train that held the rail speed record of 207 mph from 1955 to 1981. A section of the museum also houses a display of firefighters' equipment. *2 rue de Glenn. Admission: 34 frs. adults, 22 frs. students. Open Apr.–Sept., daily 9–6; Oct.–Mar., daily 10–5.*

Tour 2: Lorraine

If you visit just one place in Lorraine, it should be Nancy, a city of ducal splendor with a mix of medieval and neoclassical architecture. Historic Toul and Metz—each with venerable cathedrals and many old buildings—make rewarding excursions by train.

From Paris *By Train* Express trains to Nancy leave Paris (Gare de l'Est) every 2 hours. The trip takes 2 hours 40 minutes.

By Car The 335-kilometer (210-mile) drive to Nancy from Paris via A4 (branching off onto A31 at Metz) takes 3½ hours.

Nancy

Tourist office: 14 pl. Stanislas, opposite the Hôtel de Ville, tel. 83–35–22–41.

Numbers in the margin correspond to points of interest on the Nancy map.

Nancy is one of France's richest cities in architectural terms. Medieval ornament, 18th-century grandeur, and Belle Epoque fluidity rub shoulders in a town center that combines commercial bustle with stately elegance.

Turn left out of the station, then right down rue Stanislas, which leads down to **place Stanislas**, the symbolic heart of Nancy. The severe, gleaming-white Classical facades of this stylish

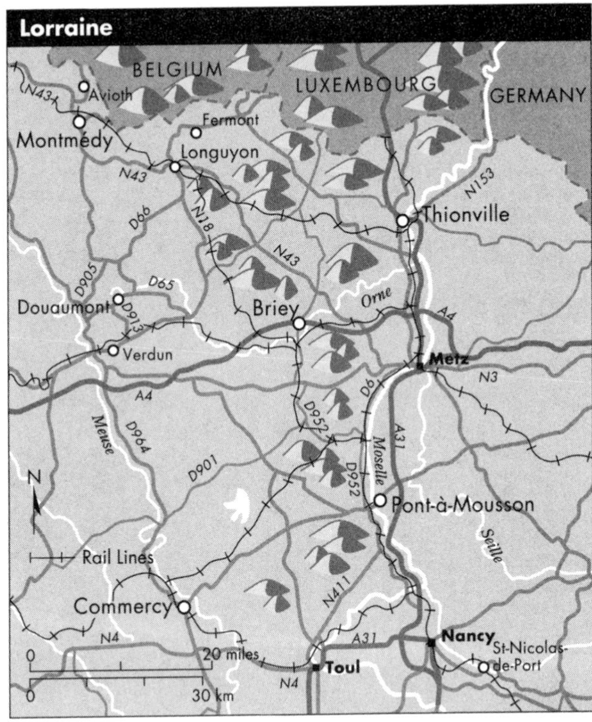

square are given a touch of rococo jollity by fancifully wrought gilt-iron railings. King Stanislas had a bit of a rococo history himself. He was offered the throne of Lorraine by his French son-in-law Louis XV, after managing to lose the crown of Poland—twice (once in 1709 and again in 1736).

1 One side of place Stanislas is occupied by the **Hôtel de Ville**
2 (Town Hall); another houses the **Musée des Beaux-Arts** (Fine
Arts Museum). On the ground floor, 19th- and 20th-century pictures by Claude Monet, Edouard Manet, Maurice Utrillo, and the Italian painter Amedeo Modigliani mingle with 150 works in glass and crystal by local art nouveau master Antonin Daum. A hefty *Transfiguration* by Rubens adorns the staircase that leads to the second floor and its wealth of Old Masters from the Italian, Dutch, Flemish, and French schools. *Pl. Stanislas. Admission: 16 frs. adults, 10 frs. children; free Wed. for children and students. Open Wed.–Sun. 10:15–12:30 and 1:30–5:45, Mon. 1:30–5:45; closed Tues.*

Before leaving place Stanislas, take a look down rue Maurice-Barrès (to the left of the Hôtel de Ville) at the twin towers of
3 the **cathedral.** This vast, frigid edifice was built in the 1740s in a
chunky Baroque style that has none of the ease and grace of the 18th-century place Stanislas. Its most notable interior feature is a murky 19th-century fresco in the dome; restoration is promised and sorely needed.

From place Stanislas, the tree-lined place de la Carrière leads
4 down to the colonnaded facade of the **Palais du Gouvernement,**
former home to the governors of Lorraine. To the right are

Avenue Foch, **17**
Boulevard Charles-V, **9**
Cathedral, **3**
Cours Léopold, **10**
Eglise des Cordeliers, **8**
Hôtel de Ville, **1**
Musée de l'Ecole de Nancy, **19**
Musée des Arts et Traditions Populaires, **7**
Musée des Beaux-Arts, **2**
Musée Historique Lorrain, **6**
Palais du Gouvernement, **4**
Rue Bénit, **13**
Rue Chanzy, **14**
Rue Henri-Poincaré, **15**
Rue Louis-Majorelle, **18**
Rue Mazagran, **16**
Rue Raugraff, **12**
Rue St-Dizier, **11**
St-Epvre, **5**

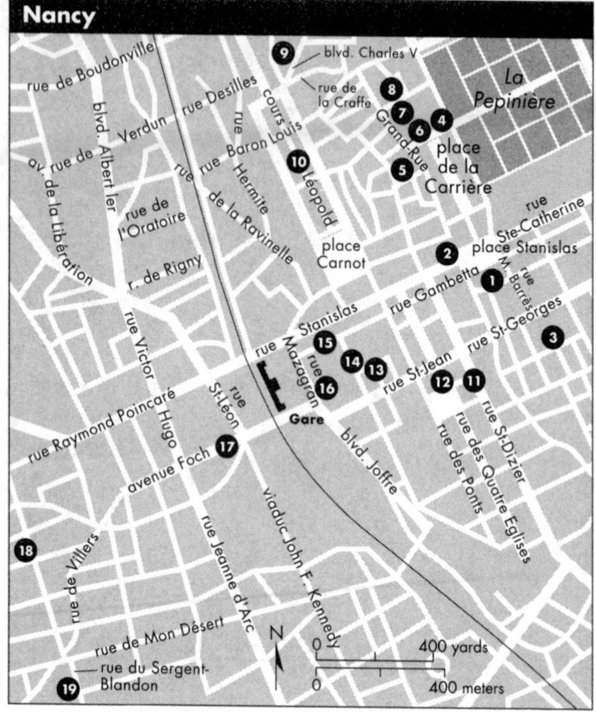

some spacious formal gardens known as **La Pépinière;** to the left
5 is the 275-foot spire of **St-Epvre,** a splendid neo-Gothic church rebuilt in the 1860s. Thanks to the efforts of Monsignor Trouillet, an entrepreneurial builder-priest, St-Epvre embodies craftsmanship of a cosmopolitan kind. Most of the 2,800 square yards of stained glass were created by the Geyling workshop in Vienna, Austria; the chandeliers were made in Liège, Belgium; many carvings are the work of Margraff of Munich, Germany; the heaviest of the eight bells was cast in Budapest, Hungary; and the organ, though manufactured by Merklin of Paris, was inaugurated in 1869 by Austrian composer Anton Bruckner.

Opposite St-Epvre is Nancy's principal medieval thoroughfare, Grande-Rue. Note the equestrian statue of Duke Antoine (1512) above the elaborate doorway of the Palais Ducal (Ducal Palace) to the right. The main entrance to the palace, and the Lorraine History Museum, which it now houses, is 80 yards farther down the street.

6 The **Musée Historique Lorrain** has a delightfully far-flung assembly of exhibits. Your visit begins in a low terracelike building across the palace lawn, with several showcases of archaeological finds ranging from Stone Age implements and ancient pottery to Roman coins and sculpture. Across the courtyard is the poorly indicated entrance to the main building, which welcomes visitors into a long, narrow room lined with medieval statues.

A spiral stone staircase leads up to the palace's most impressive room, the **Galerie des Cerfs;** exhibits here (including pictures, armor, and books) recapture the Renaissance mood of the 16th and 17th centuries—one of elegance and jollity, though not devoid of stern morality, as an elaborate series of huge tapestries, *La Condamnation du Banquet,* expounds on the evils of drink and gluttony with their allegorical sermon.

The rest of the museum is taken up mainly with paintings, furniture, and an extensive display of porcelain and earthenware. In a series of attic rooms, posters, proclamations, and the inevitable *tricolor* banners retrace local history from Napoleon up to World War I. *64 Grande-Rue. Admission: 18 frs. adults, 12 frs. children. Open mid-June–Sept., Wed.–Mon. 10–noon and 2–6; Oct.–mid-June, Wed.–Mon. 10–noon and 2–5; closed Tues.*

Continue along Grande-Rue to the Couvent des Cordeliers, a
7 former convent that contains the **Musée des Arts et Traditions
Populaires.** Its treatment of local preindustrial society is based
on reconstituted rural interiors equipped with domestic tools
and implements. The dukes of Lorraine are buried in the crypt
8 of the adjoining **Eglise des Cordeliers,** a Flamboyant Gothic
church; the intricately sculpted limestone tombs of René II and
his wife Philippa de Gueldra are impressive. The octagonal Ducal Chapel was begun in 1607 in the classical style, modeled on the Chapel of the Médicis in Florence. *Grande-Rue. Admission to chapel: 14 frs. adults, 9 frs. children. Open Easter–Oct., Tues.–Sun. 10–noon and 2–6; Nov.–Easter, Tues.–Sun. 10–noon and 2–5; closed Mon.*

From the medieval to the modern, head down rue de la Craffe to begin an **art nouveau tour** of Nancy. Art nouveau caught fire here at the end of the 19th century, representing a breakaway from decorative stereotype toward an innovative, fluid style of design based on motifs taken from nature.

9 Around the corner from rue de la Craffe, at 1 **boulevard
Charles-V,** is a house by Lucien Weissenburger (1904) whose
windows, by Jacques Gruber, include one in the form of the
10 double-armed cross of Lorraine. The adjacent **cours Léopold**
has another Weissenburger creation (1905) at no. 52, and you'll see more Gruber windows at no. 40.

Continue to the end of cours Léopold, cross place Carnot, turn
11 left onto rue Stanislas, then take a second right onto **rue
St-Dizier.** At no. 42 is a bank designed in 1903 by French architects Biet and Vallin; its interior can be inspected during working hours (9–5 weekdays). Make the next left onto rue St-Jean,
12 then a left onto **rue Raugraff.** At no. 86 is a house by Vallin
13 (1906). Return to rue St-Jean and continue to **Rue Bénit.** At no.
2 is the first building in Nancy with a metallic structure: not
just iron girders, either, but intricately wrought metal pillars,
the work of Schertzer to the design of Gutton. There is more
stained glass by Gruber, while the exterior decoration tells us
that the building began life as a seed shop. The next street
14 along, parallel to rue Bénit, is **rue Chanzy;** at no. 9 is another
bank, designed by Emile André, with interior furnishings by
Majorelle and yet more Gruber windows.

15 At 40 **rue Henri-Poincaré,** a street running parallel to rue Stanislas, is a commercial building of 1908 by Toussaint and Marchal, with metal structure by Schertzer, glass by Gruber,

and wrought iron by Majorelle. The facade is adorned with the
Lorraine thistle, and hops—used to make beer—symbolize lo-
16 cal breweries. **Rue Mazagran** greets you at the far end of the
street with, at no. 5, the Excelsior Brasserie; its rhythmic facade, severe by art nouveau standards, is illuminated at night.

17 At the far end of rue Mazagran is **avenue Foch,** a busy boulevard that heads past the train station into a district lined with solid, serious mansions clearly built for Nancy's affluent 19th-century middle class. At no. 41, more ironwork by Majorelle can be admired; yet another architect, Paul Charbonnier, was responsible for the overall design in 1905. At no. 69, the occasional pinnacle suggests Gothic influence on a house built in 1902 by Emile André, who designed the neighboring no. 71 two years later.

18 On the right, past rue de Villers, is **rue Louis-Majorelle.** At no. 1 stands a villa built in 1902 by Paris architect Henri Sauvage for Majorelle himself. Sinuous metal supports seem to sneak up on the unsuspecting balcony like swaying cobras, scrutinizing the spacious windows and reckoning them to be yet further productions of that in-demand glazier Jacques Gruber.

19 End your art nouveau survey at the **Musée de l'Ecole de Nancy,** at 36 rue du Sergent-Blandan. This airy, turn-of-the-century town house was built by Eugène Corbin, an early patron of the School of Nancy. His personal collection forms the basis of this, the only museum in France devoted to art nouveau, and underlines the fact that architecture was not the only vehicle for the expression of art nouveau: Lamps, chairs, beds, stained glass, paintings, tables, and silverware are arrayed over two creaky stories. *36 rue Sergent-Blandon. Admission: 15 frs. adults, 10 frs. children. Open Nov.–Mar., Wed.–Mon. 10–noon and 2–6; Apr.–Oct. until 5; closed Tues.*

Lodging
Under 250 frs.

Central. Located next to the train station, the Central makes a less expensive but equally convenient alternative to the Grand Hôtel de la Reine. It is fully modernized, with double glazing to keep out the noise, and has a charming courtyard garden. There's no restaurant. *6 rue Raymond-Poincaré, 54000, tel. 83–32–21–24. 68 rooms with bath. AE, MC, V.*

Splurge
★

Grand Hôtel de la Reine. Definitely worth a splurge, this hotel is every bit as swanky as the place Stanislas on which it stands; the magnificent 18th-century building it occupies is officially classified as a historic monument. The guest rooms are decorated in a suitably grand Louis XV style, and the most luxurious look out onto the square. The classic-nouvelle restaurant, Le Stanislas, is costly, although the set menu at weekday lunch is a good value. Try the briochelike *kouglof,* a local delicacy made with mirabelle plums. *2 pl. Stanislas, 54000, tel. 83–35–03–01. 51 rooms with bath. Facilities: restaurant, bar, TV. Restaurant reservations required. Jacket and tie required. AE, DC, MC, V. 550 frs and up.*

Dining
Under 125 frs.

Petit Gastrolâtre. Admirers of nouvelle cuisine shouldn't pass up a visit to Nancy's most famous purveyor of the art, under the direction of chef Patrick Tanesy. Recommended dishes include salmon—try it any way it's offered—and a delectable fricassee of snails. *7 rue des Maréchaux, tel. 83–35–51–94. Reservations required. Jacket and tie required. No credit cards. Closed Sun., Mon., Christmas–New Year's, May, and first half Sept.*

Under 75 frs. **L' Entracte.** New owners have toned down the former razzmatazz (this used to be called the Manhattan Grill!) to concentrate on earnest French country cooking (quiche, steaks, salads). Ask for a table in the atmospheric candlelit cellar. Prices can be downright inexpensive providing you don't get carried away when you order. *123 Grande-Rue, tel. 83–36–62–71. Reservations accepted. V.*

Shopping Nancy has less regional cachet for shoppers than Strasbourg, though the streets next to the cathedral are full of life. At 9 place Stanislas is the Dickensian **La Cave du Roy,** where old wines, champagne, and spirits are arranged in endearing confusion as mustachioed Monsieur Henné chuckles his way around with Gallic courtesy. His rare red Côtes de Toul is highly recommended.

Toul

One train in the early morning, 1 at lunchtime, and 2 in the early afternoon make the 20-minute trip from Nancy to Toul. Tourist office: Parvis de la Cathédrale, tel. 83–64–11–69.

The charming old town of **Toul** nestles behind mossy, star-shaped ramparts. The ramshackle streets of the central part of the town can't have changed much for centuries—not since the embroidered, twin-towered facade, a Flamboyant Gothic masterpiece, was woven onto the **cathedral** in the second half of the 15th century. The cathedral's interior, begun in 1204, is long (321 feet), airy (105 feet high), and more restrained than the exuberant facade. The tall, slender windows of the unusually shallow choir sparkle in the morning sunshine.

The cathedral is flanked on one side by 14th-century **cloisters** and on the other by a pleasant garden behind the **Hôtel de Ville** (Town Hall), built in 1740 as the Bishop's Palace. Continue down rue de Rigny, turn right onto rue Michâtel, and then take a second right onto rue de Ménin, which winds its way down to the Porte de Metz. Veer left at the gateway, then left again onto rue Gouvion St-Cyr; at no. 25 is the **Musée Municipal** (Town Museum), housed in a former medieval hospital. The museum's well-preserved Salle des Malades (Patients' Ward) dates from the 13th century and displays archaeological finds, ceramics, tapestries, and medieval sculpture. *25 rue Gouvion St-Cyr. Admission: 12 frs. adults, 6 frs. children. Open Wed.–Mon. 10–noon and 2–6; closed Tues. and mornings in winter.*

Fork right onto rue de la Boucherie, which, over a 300-yard stretch lined with old houses, becomes successively rue du Collège, rue Pont de Vaux, and rue Gengoult. Eventually rue Sonaire leads off (right) to the attractive church of **St-Gengoult,** whose choir boasts some of the finest 13th-century stained glass in eastern France. The Flamboyant Gothic cloisters are later than those of the cathedral but equally picturesque. Owing to vandalism, St-Gengoult is open at certain times only. Inquire at the tourist office for details.

Dining
Under 125 frs. **Belle Epoque.** Except for the odd, seedy bar selling steak and french fries at lunchtime, historic downtown Toul is woefully short on places to eat. The homey, intimate Belle Epoque, situated on the road leading from the train station to the old town, is an exception. Its French cuisine is reliable, and there's a set menu for 90 francs. *31 av. Victor-Hugo, tel. 83–43–23–71. Res-*

ervations essential. MC, V. Closed Sat. lunch, Sun., and the first three weeks in July.

Metz

Hourly trains from Nancy make the 40-minute trip to Metz. Tourist office: Place d'Armes, tel. 87–75–65–21.

Despite its industrial background, **Metz** is officially classed as one of France's greenest cities: Parks, gardens, and leafy squares crop up everywhere. At its heart, towering above the Hôtel de Ville (Town Hall) and the 18th-century place d'Armes, is the **Cathédrale St-Etienne.**

At 137 feet from floor to roof, Metz Cathedral is one of the highest in France. It is also one of the lightest, thanks to nearly 1½ acres of window space. The narrow, 13th- to 14th-century nave channels the eye toward the dramatically raised 16th-century choir, whose walls have given way to huge sheets of gemlike glass by masters old and modern, including Russian-born artist Marc Chagall (1887–1985). A pair of symmetrical 290-foot towers flank the nave, marking the medieval division between two churches that were merged to form the cathedral. The tower with a fussy 15th-century pinnacle houses **Dame Mutte,** an enormous bell cast in 1605 and tolled on momentous occasions. The Grand Portal beneath the large rose window was reconstructed by the Germans at the turn of the century. The statues of the prophets include, on the right, *Daniel* sycophantically sculpted to resemble Kaiser Wilhelm II (his unmistakable upturned mustachios were shaved off in 1940). *Pl. d'Armes.*

Close by, in a 17th-century former convent, is the **Musée d'Art et d'Histoire** (Art and History Museum); turn left out of the cathedral and take rue des Jardins. The museum's wide-ranging collections encompass French and German paintings from the 18th century on, military arms and uniforms, and archaeology; local finds evoke the city's Gallo-Roman, Carolingian, and medieval past. Religious works of art are stored in the **Grenier de Chèvremont,** a granary built in 1457, with a many-windowed facade and stone-arcade decoration. *2 rue du Haut-Poirier. Admission: 15 frs., free Wed. Open Wed.–Mon. 10–noon and 2–5; closed Tues.*

Now walk back past the cathedral, continuing for another two blocks. At one end of the **Esplanade,** an agreeable terraced park overlooking the Moselle, is the 18th-century **Palais de Justice,** noted for the sculpted bas-reliefs in the courtyard (the one on the right portrays the 1783 Peace Treaty between France, England, Holland, and the United States) and its ceremonial staircase with wrought-iron banisters. Farther down the Esplanade is the small, heavily restored church of **St-Pierre-aux-Nonnains** (rue Poncelet). Parts are thought to date from the 4th century, making it the oldest church in France. Neighboring 13th-century **Chapelle des Templiers** (blvd. Poincaré) is also rare: It's the only octagonal church in Lorraine.

Lodging
Under 150 frs.

Métropole. This large, tastefully modernized station hotel is clean, comfortable, and well run. Rooms vary considerably in size and price. The brasserie alongside, under the same ownership, provides quick, straightforward meals. *5 pl. du Gal-de-Gaulle, 57000, tel. 87–66–26–22. 80 rooms, most with bath or shower. AE, MC, V.*

Dining
Under 200 frs.

La Dinanderie. In this intimate restaurant just across the River Moselle from the Metz Cathedral, chef Claude Piegiorgi serves cuisine you'll think clever—salmon cooked in mustard and chives or kiwi with lime and banana sorbet—at prices you'll call modest. Just watch your tab, because it's easy to let it go into a more expensive range. *2 rue de Paris, tel. 87–30–14–40. Reservations advised. AE, MC, V. Closed Sun., Mon., Christmas–New Year's, mid-Feb., and last 3 weeks Aug.*

Under 125 frs.

A La Ville de Lyon. Just behind the cathedral is this new venture in a venerable vaulted structure. It's well worth checking out for its fabulous wine list (30,000 bottles in stock) and inventive menu. Dishes range from fowl to curried fish. *7 rue des Piques, tel. 87–36–07–01. Reservations advised. AE, DC, MC, V. Closed Sun. dinner, Mon., end of July and most of Aug.*

Tour 3: Jura–Franche-Comté Region

This tour takes in the hilly Jura region south of Alsace—France's "Switzerland," known for its leafy valleys and towering rock formations. Picturesque Besançon, the wine town of Arbois (boyhood home of Pasteur), and the royal salt works at Arc-et-Senans number among the highlights.

From Paris
By Train

Eight TGVs daily make the 2½-hour trip from Paris (Gare de Lyon) to Besançon; several require a change at Dijon. A change at Besançon is usually necessary for the 70-minute ride to Belfort.

By Car

The 400-kilometer (250-mile) drive from Paris to Besançon along the A6/A36 takes 3½–4 hours. Belfort is 75 kilometers (47 miles) further along the A36.

Belfort

Tourist office: Rue Jules-Vallès, tel. 84–28–12–23.

Leave the station via rue Thiers and turn left after crossing the Savoureuse River. On place des Bourgeois, the celebrated 36-foot-high **Lion of Belfort,** sculpted in red sandstone by Félix-Auguste Bartholdi (best known as the sculptor of the Statue of Liberty in New York) towers over the heart of Belfort. The lion was commissioned to celebrate Belfort's heroic resistance during the Franco-Prussian war of 1870–71.

As the Prussians slashed through French defenses at Sedan (in the Ardennes), forcing Emperor Napoleon III to abdicate and making short shrift of French efforts to stop their advance on Paris, the town of Belfort, under the leadership of General Denfert-Rochereau, withstood a 103-day siege and only surrendered after the rest of France had capitulated. The Prussian leader Otto van Bismarck was so impressed by Belfort's plucky resistance that he declined to incorporate it into the German Empire along with neighboring Alsace, granting Belfort independent status. Although Alsace was returned to France in 1918, Belfort maintained its special status—making the *Territoire de Belfort* by far the smallest département in France. (A smaller replica of the Lion of Belfort can be found on Place Denfert-Rochereau in Paris.)

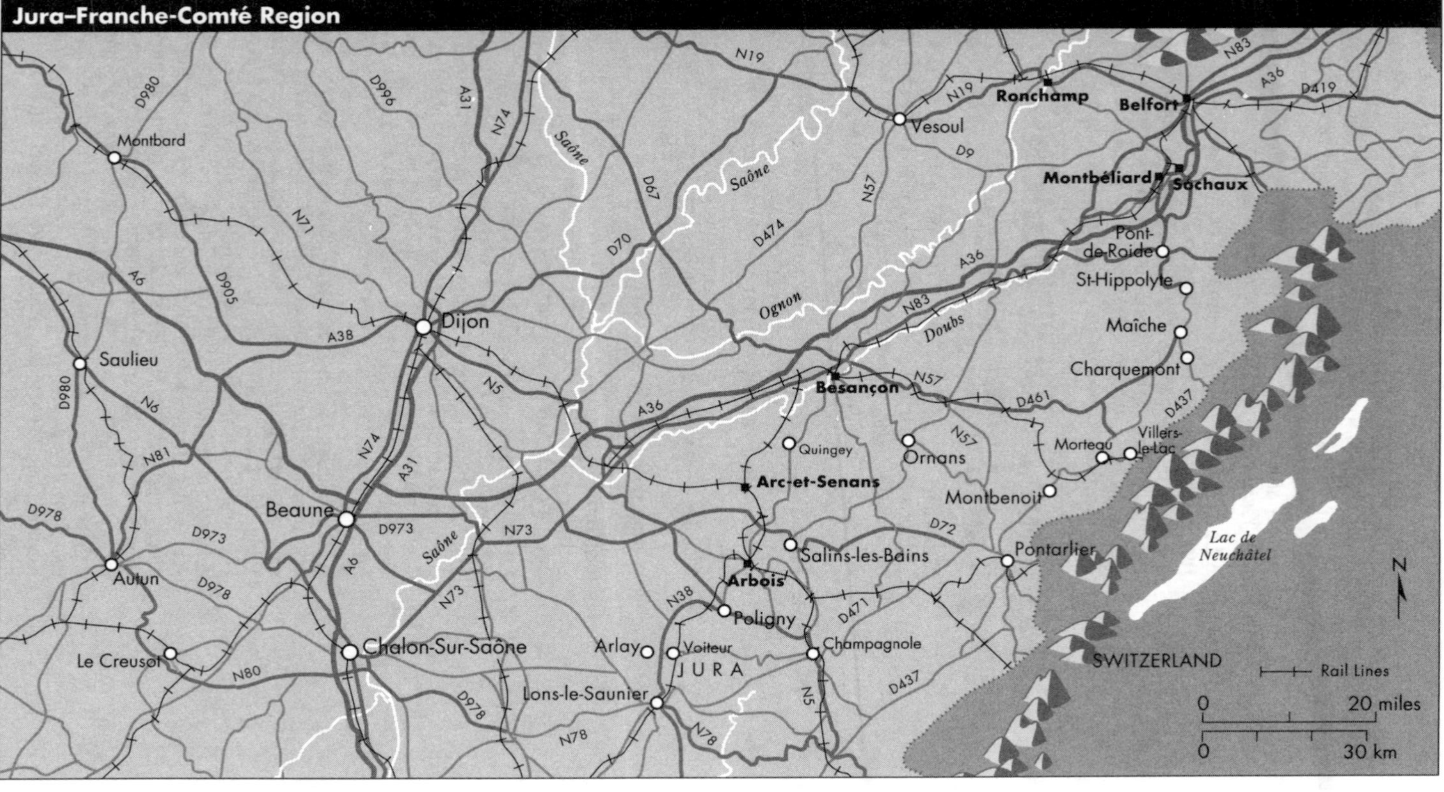
Jura–Franche-Comté Region
Montbard
Saulieu
Autun
Le Creusot
Dijon
Beaune
Chalon-Sur-Saône
Vesoul
Ronchamp
Belfort
Montbéliard
Sochaux
Pont-de-Roide
St-Hippolyte
Maîche
Charquemont
Besançon
Quingey
Ornans
Morteau
Villers-le-Lac
Montbenoit
Arc-et-Senans
Salins-les-Bains
Pontarlier
Arbois
Poligny
Champagnole
Arlay
Voiteur
JURA
Lons-le-Saunier
Saône
Ognon
Doubs
Lac de Neuchâtel
SWITZERLAND
N
Rail Lines
0
20 miles
0
30 km
D980
D996
A31
N74
D67
D70
N19
D9
N57
D474
N83
A36
D419
N71
A6
D905
A38
N5
N6
N81
D978
D973
N73
D461
D437
D72
N38
D471
N80
N78

Belfort's lion sits proudly at the foot of Vauban's impregnable hilltop château, now home to the **Musée d'Art et d'Histoire** (Art and History Museum), containing Vauban's 1687 scale model of the town, plus a detailed section on military history. From the castle you can look out over the old town toward the Vosges Mountains to the north and the Jura to the south. *Admission to château free. Admission to museum: 10 frs. Château open May–Sept., daily 8–noon and 2–7; Oct.–Apr., Wed.–Mon. 10–noon and 2–5. Museum open Wed.–Mon. 10–noon and 2–5.*

Lodging and Dining
Under 350 frs.

Château Servin. No surprises at this quiet, traditional hotel, set amid expansive grounds; rooms are comfortable and fully modernized, although some are small, and the dining room has plush carpeting and gleaming silverware. Chef Dominique Mathy prepares such dishes as spicy duck soup, caramelized spider crab, and foie gras with raspberry vinegar. *9 rue du Gal-Négrier, 90000, tel. 84–21–41–85. 9 rooms with bath or shower. Facilities: restaurant. AE, DC, MC, V. Closed Sun. evening, Fri., and Aug.*

Dining
Under 125 frs.

Pot au Feu. This rustic, red-sandstone bistro at the foot of the citadel offers tasty salads and roast turbot. *27 bis Grande Rue, tel. 84–28–57–84. Reservations advised. Dress: casual. MC, V. Closed Sun., Mon., and most of Aug.*

Ronchamp

Three trains daily (1 in the early morning, 2 more in the early evening) make the 25-minute run from Belfort.

The little town of Ronchamp, 21 kilometers (13 miles) northwest of Belfort, constitutes our sole excursion into the windswept département of Haute-Saône. Small it may be—containing a population of just 3,139—but Ronchamp has one of Europe's most famous postwar buildings, the hilltop chapel of **Notre-Dame-du-Haut,** designed by Swiss-born French architect Le Corbusier to replace the church destroyed here during World War II. The chapel's curved, sloping white walls, small, irregularly placed windows, and unadorned, slug-shaped gray concrete roof have no architectural equivalent. Many consider it Le Corbusier's masterpiece—utterly individual, yet imbued with peace and calm. *Open mid-Mar.–Oct., daily 9–7.*

Montbéliard

Trains run every 1 or 2 hours from Belfort to Montbéliard; the trip takes 13 minutes. Montbéliard tourist office: 1 rue Henri-Mouhot, tel. 81–94–45–60.

Industrial Montbéliard, base for the giant Peugeot automobile company, is redeemed by a stately, round-towered **château** a stone's throw from the train station. Its museum is devoted to zoology (with a special section on insects), geology, archaeology, and traditional local industries (clocks and music boxes). Etienne Oehmichen studied in Montbéliard before inventing the helicopter back in 1924. *Tel. 81–99–23–45. Admission free. Open Wed.–Mon. 2–5:30.*

Across the rail line in the neighboring suburb of Sochaux, Peugeot's production methods and colorful history can be explored at the **Musée de l'Aventure Peugeot,** and you can tour the factory. Peugeot produces some of Europe's most reliable cars and has made a big name in such cross-country rallies as the Paris–Dakar across the Sahara. The company originally concentrated on steel before producing its first bicycles, in 1886, and its first automobiles, in 1891. *Carrefour de l'Europe, Sochaux, tel. 81–94–48–21. Admission: 25 frs. adults, 15 frs. children. Open daily 9–noon and 2–5. Free guided tours of automobile factory leave museum weekdays at 8:30 AM.*

Besançon

Trains run most hours from Montbéliard to Besançon; the trip takes 50–65 minutes. Besançon tourist office: 2 pl. de la Première-Armée-Française, tel. 81–80–92–55.

The capital of Franche-Comté, Besançon nestles in a vast bend of the River Doubs. Its defensive potential was quickly spotted by Vauban, whose imposing citadel remains the town's architectural highlight. Besançon has long been a clock-making center and is the more recent birthplace of the synthetic silk (rayon) industry. The town's famous offsprings include Auguste and Louis Lumière, the inventors of a motion-picture camera, and poet Victor Hugo, born while his father was garrisoned here in 1802. Hugo is no local hero, though, having dismissed Besançon as an "old Spanish town," a disparaging reference to its medieval lip service to the Austro-Spanish Habsburgs.

From the station, follow signs for Centre Ville (Town Center). Ignore the first bridge across the River Doubs and continue another 200 yards to the Pont de la République, where you can get a good introduction to the town by taking a 75-minute trip on a 110-seater *vedette* motorboat. The trip takes in a lock and a 400-yard tunnel underneath the citadel. *Tel. 81–68–13–25. Ticket: 50 frs. Boats run summer afternoons (also 10:30 AM July–mid-Sept.).*

Wander around the quayside to the **Musée des Beaux-Arts** (Fine Arts Museum) and stop in to see its collection of tapestries, ceramics, and paintings by Bonnard, Renoir, and Courbet. There's also a section devoted to clocks and watches through the ages. *1 pl. de la Révolution, tel. 81–81–44–47. Admission: 16 frs. adults, free Wed. and Sun. Open Wed.–Mon. 9:30–11:45 and 2–6.*

Continue to the nearby Pont Battant and the start of Grande-Rue, Besançon's oldest street. This leads to the citadel, past fountains, wrought-iron railings, and stately 16th- to 18th-century mansions, the most stunning of which is the Renaissance Palais Granvelle (1540). Hugo was born at no. 140, the Lumière brothers just opposite. At the foot of the citadel, notice the **Horloge Astronomique,** a stupendous, 19th-century astronomical clock with 62 dials, 30,000 working parts, and an array of automations that spurt into action just before the hour. *2 rue du Chapitre, tel. 81–81–12–76. Admission: 20 frs. Open Wed.–Mon. 9:45–11:45 and 2:45–5:45; closed Wed. in winter.*

The **Citadelle** is perched on a rocky spur 350 feet above the town. Its triple ring of ramparts, now laid out as promenades and peppered with Vauban's original watch towers, offers extensive views of the city and countryside. The buildings contain a series of museums devoted to natural history, regional folklore, agricultural tools, and the French Resistance during

World War II. *Tel. 81–82–16–22. Admission to citadel and museums: 23 frs. adults, 16 frs. students and senior citizens. Open Wed.–Mon. 9:15–6:15 in summer, 9:45–4:45 in winter.*

Lodging
Under 250 frs.
Paris. With few decent hotels in the attractive heart of Besançon, this one is the best; it's well run, unpretentious, old-fashioned, and brightened by a tree-lined garden courtyard. *33 rue des Granges, 25000, tel. 81–81–36–56. 60 rooms, some with bath or shower. Facilities: parking lot. MC, V.*

Dining
Under 200 frs.
Mungo Park. This former warehouse on the banks of the River Doubs has been transformed into a welcoming, two-story restaurant that combines Old World beams and stonework with exotic African wall-hangings and empty tortoise shells. Locals pile in to sample the cuisine of Jocelyne Lotz, one of France's top female chefs, as she dishes up scallops fried in celery butter or caramelized rabbit with nettle leaves. Subtle herbs and spices add exotic grandeur to all her dishes; her husband, Gérard, looks after the extensive local wine list. *11 rue Jean-Petit, tel. 81–81–28–01. Reservations required. Dress: elegant casual. MC, V. Closed Sat. lunch, Sun., and first half of Aug.*

Under 125 frs.
Poker d'As. Wood carvings and gleaming brasswork lend an alpine chalet feel to this popular restaurant, but judging from his adventurous cuisine, we suspect that Benoît Ferreux is more of a city slicker—witness such delicacies as mussels in kirsch or pheasant with foie gras. Try the fillet of *rascasse* (scorpion fish) in a wine sauce, followed by homemade rhubarb tart. *14 rue du Clos St-Amour, tel. 81–81–42–49. Reservations advised. Dress: elegant casual. AE, DC, MC, V. Closed Sun. dinner, Mon., and most of July.*

Arc-et-Senans

Four trains daily (none in the morning) make the 35-minute journey from Besançon.

The **royal saltworks** at Arc-et-Senans, built 1774–79 by Claude-Nicolas Ledoux, are an extraordinary example of neoclassical industrial architecture. With their Palladian porticoes, rustication, and towering columns, the buildings—arranged in a gracious semicircle around sweeping lawns—have an almost palatial grandeur. Originally they were meant to form part of a rationally planned, circular *ville idéale* (ideal town), visions of which are conjured up by the Musée Ledoux's exhibition of scale models. Wander around the various buildings, admire their intricate wood-beam roofs, and learn about the long-gone salt industry. The caucuses of chatting foreign students that pour in to attend the conferences and training courses held here lend an international atmosphere to the tiny town with a population of 1,303. *Saline Royale, tel. 81–54–45–45. Admission: 27 frs. Open daily 9–noon and 2–6 (9–7 June–Sept.).*

Arbois

Two trains each afternoon make the 20-minute trip from Arc-et-Senans to Arbois; the early-morning train from Besançon, which does not stop at Arc, reaches Arbois in 45 minutes. Arbois tourist office: Rue de l'Hôtel-de-Ville, tel. 84–37–47–37.

Arbois is a pretty wine village, worth an overnight stop at its fine hotel-restaurant, Jean-Paul Jeunet (*see* Lodging and Dining, *below*). The famous bacteriologist Louis Pasteur (1822–95) grew up here and returned each year on holiday. His family home, still housing many of his possessions—his inkstand, school prizes, science books, and laboratory—has been lovingly preserved. *83 rue de Courcelles, tel. 84–66–11–72. Admission: 14 frs. Open Wed.–Mon. 10–noon and 2–4:30.*

The vines owned by Pasteur (he used grapes for his experiments on fermentation) have also been preserved and can be viewed just north of the town at the intersection of the main highway and the road to Montigny-lès-Arsures. The Arbois vineyard is one of the finest in eastern France; to learn more about it, visit the town-hall museum and peruse its collection of tools and documents. *Hôtel de Ville, tel. 84–66–07–45. Admission: 7 frs. Open July–Aug., Wed.–Mon. 10–noon and 3–7; Sept.–mid-Oct., Wed.–Mon. 3–7; closed mid-Oct.–June.*

Lodging and Dining
Under 350 frs.

Jean-Paul Jeunet. This former convent has become the Jura's most memorable hotel-restaurant. Ancient stone walls and massive wooden beams testify to the dining room's illustrious past, and they're brilliantly thrown into relief by Jeunet's subtle lighting and bold modern decor, which mixes assertive, contemporary art with sober, sackcloth wall-hangings. Start your evening with a glass of vintage Vin Jaune (say, 1969), the distinctive local wine that lingers on the palate like a good sherry. Then try such dishes as snails in a liquorice sauce or chicken with mushrooms cooked in Vin Jaune. The hotel rooms have up-to-date fittings and light, pinewood furniture. *9 rue de l'Hôtel-de-Ville, 39600, tel. 84–66–05–67. 18 rooms with bath or shower. Facilities: restaurant (closed Wed. lunch). DC, MC, V. Closed Tues. and Dec.–Jan.*

9 Burgundy

Vézelay, Beaune, Cluny

It's no coincidence that the emblem of Burgundy is a snail. The people of Burgundy eat snails regularly and often seem to move at a snail's pace. So do the area's sluggish cross-country trains—and so will you. Not that you'd want to do otherwise: This is a region for relaxing, for lingering over rich food and wines, ambling around ancient towns, strolling through verdant meadows, and taking in antique pilgrimage sites. Tiny Vézelay is topped by the most important church in medieval Christendom, whence pilgrims set out on the 900-mile journey to Spain's Santiago de Compostela; the now ruined Abbey of Cluny was once equally important.

There is just one city in Burgundy: Dijon, the former capital of the all-powerful Dukes of Burgundy. Today, their elegant palace houses one of France's finest provincial museums, and the city challenges Lyon as France's capital of gastronomy. Its principle industries are wine, mustard, and cassis (black currant liqueur).

The famous vineyards south of Dijon—the Côte de Nuits and Côte de Beaune—are among the world's most distinguished and picturesque. You need a car to visit the growers, and in any case you can't expect to unearth many bargains here. But there is plenty of wine to be had in Dijon and in Beaune, a charming old town clustered around the elaborately tile-roofed Hôtel-Dieu, the town's medieval hospital; its Marché aux Vins is a particularly good place for sampling.

Essential Information

Lodging For all its charms, Burgundy is seldom deluged by tourists, and finding accommodations is not hard. But there are few towns with so many hotels that you can be sure to find something, so always make advance reservations, especially in the wine country (from Dijon to Beaune). If you intend to visit Beaune for the Trois Glorieuses wine festival in November, make your hotel reservation several months in advance. Note that nearly all country hotels have restaurants, and you are usually expected to eat in them.

Dining The Burgundians are hearty eaters; whatever the class of restaurant, you are unlikely to go hungry—and even wealthy towns such as Dijon and Beaune offer an abundance of restaurants where you get plenty of value for your restaurant dollar.

Game, freshwater trout, ham, goat cheese, coq au vin, snails, mustard, and mushrooms number among the region's specialties. Meat is often served in rich, wine-based sauces. There is wine of all types and prices; whites range from cheapish Aligoté and classy Chablis to legendary Meursault, and red, from unpretentious Mâcon to indescribable Gevrey-Chambertin and Romanée-Conti.

Shopping Shopping is not one of life's major activities in sleepy Burgundy, where eating and drinking are most important. Mustard, snails, and all manner of candies (including chocolate snails—*escargots de Bourgogne)* may be found without difficulty, especially in the commercial heart of Dijon, with its numerous pedestrian streets. You can get the famous Burgundy wine at a relatively good price if you buy it from an individual producer. Note: Cassis, the local black currant liqueur, can be found easily enough anywhere else in France for much the same price.

Bicycling Attractive scenery, light traffic, and terrain that is seldom more than gently rolling make this a good area for bicycling; most tourist offices can give details about recommended routes. Bikes are available for rent at train stations in Autun, Auxerre, Avallon, Beaune, Chalon-sur-Sâone, Clamecy, Dijon, Mâcon, Saulieu, and Tonnerre. Cycle tours are organized by **Service Quatre Chemins** (33 Grande Rue Chauchien, 71400 Autun, tel. 85–52–07–91).

Hiking Enthusiastic hikers should consult the **Comité Départemental de la Randonnée Pédestre** (B.P.1601, 21000 Dijon cedex, tel. 80–73–81–81) or **La Peurtantaine** (Accueil Morvan Environnement, Ecole du Bourg, 71550 Anost, tel. 85–82–77–74) for information on paths and circuits. The Morvan Forest and vineyards between Dijon and Beaune make fine itineraries.

The Arts Cultural activity is best represented by music. The august ruined abbey of Cluny is one of the backdrops for the **Festival des Grands Crus,** held in August and September (tel. 85–59–05–34 for details). Autun Cathedral is the main venue for the **Musique en Morvan** festival in the second half of July, and Nevers the base for **Musique en Nivernais** during September and October. Dijon stages its own **Eté Musical** in June and July. Check local tourist offices for details of the programs.

Festivals Wine lovers from all over the world pour into Burgundy in the third week of November to celebrate the **Trois Glorieuses,** three days of bucolic festivities culminating in a monster wine auction at the Hospices de Beaune.

Highlights for First-time Visitors

Beaune (and wine-tasting at the Marché aux Vins), Tour 2
Palais des Ducs (Ducal Palace), Dijon, Tour 2
Ruins of Cluny Abbey, Tour 2
Troyes, Tour 1
Vézelay, Tour 1

Tour 1: Troyes and Northern Burgundy

This tour makes extensive use of slow-moving regional train lines. It heads south by train from Troyes to Auxerre, then travels through the wooded Morvan region of nothern Burgundy to the old Roman town of Autun. A bus excursion from Avallon is required to reach secluded Vézelay.

From Paris *By Train* Express trains to Troyes leave Paris (Gare de l'Est) 9 times daily. The trip takes 1½ hours.

By Car The 160-kilometer (100-mile) drive to Troyes from Paris takes 2¼ hours via N19.

Troyes

Tourist office: 16 blvd. Carnot, opposite the station, tel. 25–73–00–36.

Numbers in the margin correspond to points of interest on the Troyes map.

The inhabitants of **Troyes** would be seriously insulted if you mistook them for Burgundians. This old town is the capital of southern Champagne; as if to prove the point, its historic town center is shaped like a champagne cork. Visitors will be struck by the town's phenomenal number of old buildings, magnificent churches, and fine museums: Few, if any, French town centers contain so much to see and do. A wide choice of restaurants and a web of enchanting pedestrian streets with timber-framed houses add even more to Troyes's appeal.

Follow broad, leafy boulevard Gambetta from the station and swing right at the far end into quai Dampierre, which divides the center of Troyes. A good place to begin exploring is **place de la Libération,** where quai Dampierre meets the rectangular artificial lake known as the Bassin de la Préfecture. Although Troyes stands on the Seine, it is the capital of the département named after the River Aube, administered from the elegant
1 **Préfecture** that gazes across both the lake and place de la Libération from behind its gleaming gilt-iron railings.

But the most charming view from place de la Libération is undoubtedly that of the cathedral, whose 200-foot tower peeps through the trees above the statue and old lamps of the square's
2 central flower garden. The **Cathédrale St-Pierre St-Paul** is just a five-minute walk, in a tumbledown square that, like the narrow surrounding streets, has not changed for centuries.

Burgundy

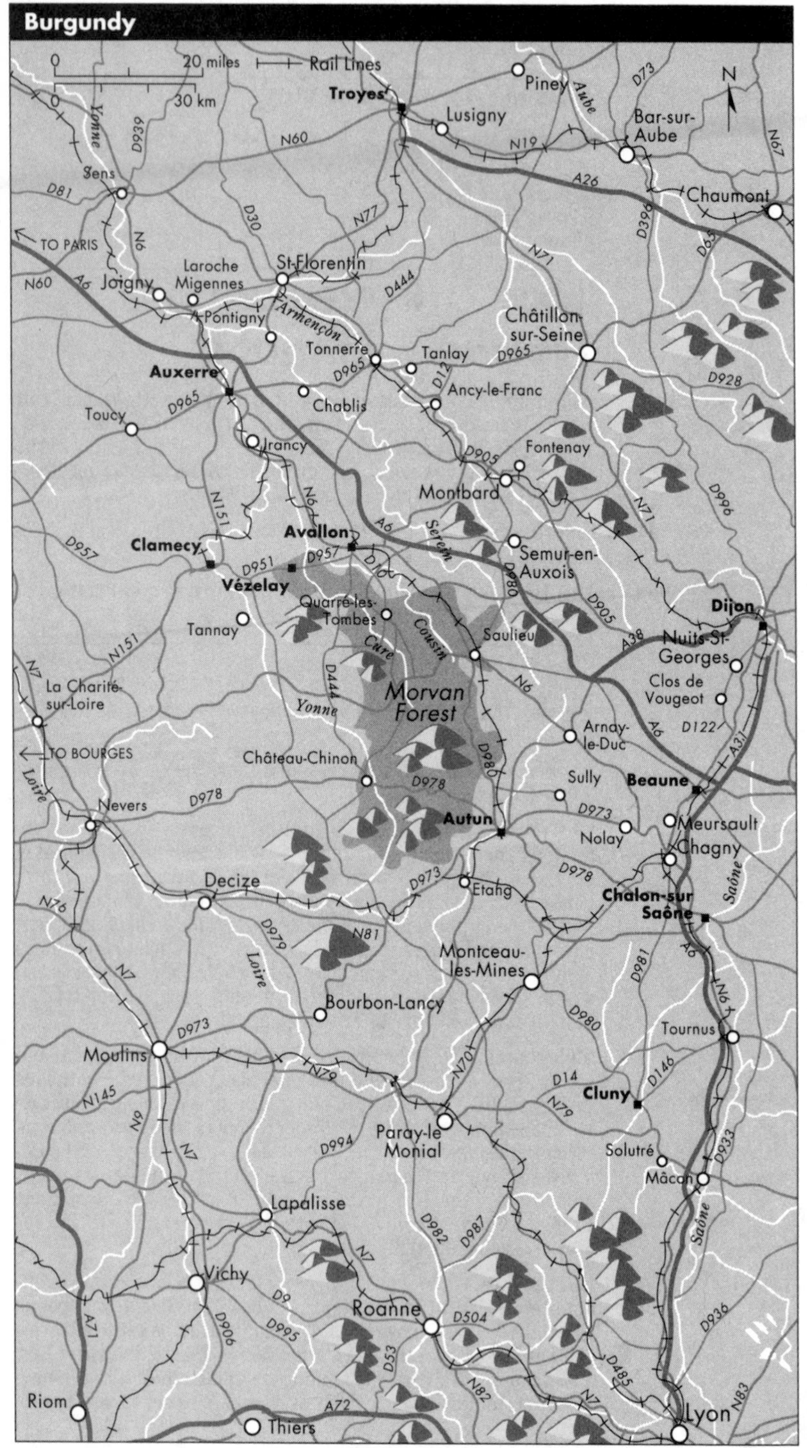

0
20 miles
0
30 km
Rail Lines
N
TO PARIS
TO BOURGES
Troyes
Piney
Lusigny
Bar-sur-Aube
Chaumont
Sens
Joigny
Laroche Migennes
St-Florentin
Pontigny
Armençon
Tonnerre
Tanlay
Châtillon-sur-Seine
Auxerre
Chablis
Ancy-le-Franc
Toucy
Irancy
Fontenay
Montbard
Clamecy
Avallon
Vézelay
Semur-en-Auxois
Quarré-les-Tombes
Tannay
Saulieu
Dijon
Nuits-St-Georges
Clos de Vougeot
Morvan Forest
La Charité-sur-Loire
Arnay-le-Duc
Château-Chinon
Sully
Beaune
Nevers
Autun
Nolay
Meursault
Chagny
Decize
Etang
Chalon-sur Saône
Montceau-les-Mines
Bourbon-Lancy
Tournus
Moulins
Cluny
Paray-le Monial
Solutré
Mâcon
Lapalisse
Vichy
Roanne
Riom
Thiers
Lyon
Yonne
Aube
Serein
Cure
Cousin
Loire
Saône
N60
N19
A26
D81
D939
D30
N77
N6
A6
D396
D65
N67
D73
D444
N71
D965
D12
D928
D905
D996
N151
D957
D951
D10
D980
A38
A31
D122
D978
D973
N7
N76
D979
N81
D981
D980
N70
N79
D14
D146
N145
N9
D994
D933
D982
D987
D9
D995
D906
A71
D504
D53
N82
D485
D936
N83
A72

Abbaye St-Loup, **4**
Basilique St-Urbain, **6**
Cathédrale St-Pierre St-Paul, **2**
Hôtel-Dieu, **5**
Hôtel de Ville, **7**
Maison de l'Outil, **10**
Musée d'Art Moderne, **3**
Musée Historique/ Musée de la Bonneterie, **12**
Préfecture, **1**
St-Jean, **8**
St-Nicolas, **13**
St-Pantaléon, **11**
Ste-Madeleine, **9**

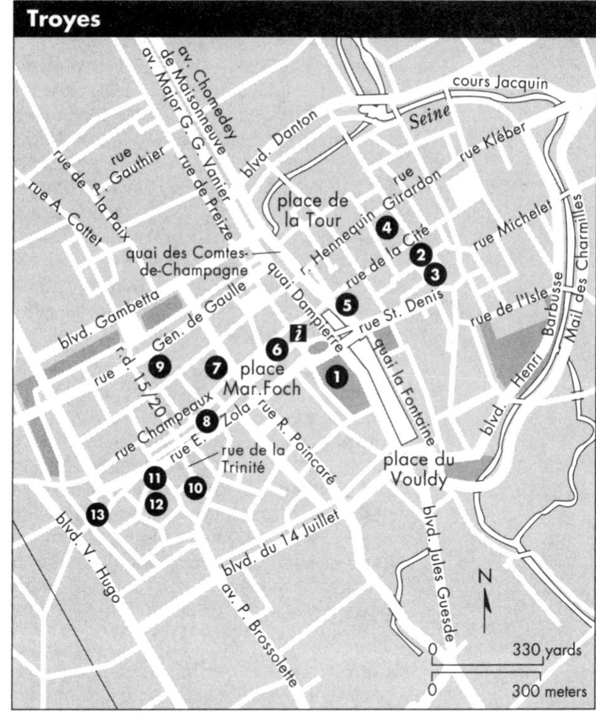

The cathedral is most striking for its incomplete one-towered facade; the small Renaissance campaniles on top of the tower; and the artistry of Martin Chambiges, who worked on the facade (note the large rose window). Try to see it at night, when its floodlit features are thrown into dramatic relief.

The cathedral's vast five-aisled interior, refreshingly light thanks to large windows and the near-whiteness of the local stone, dates mainly from the 13th century. Its renowned stained glass includes the fine examples of primitive 13th-century glass in the choir as well as the richly colored 16th-century glass of the nave and rose window on the facade. Note the arcaded triforium above the pillars of the choir: It was one of the first in France to be glazed rather than filled with stone. *Pl. St-Pierre. Open daily 8–6 or 7 in summer, 9–noon and 2–5 in winter. Free* son-et-lumière *(sound-and-light) show held in cathedral early July–late Aug., Fri. and Sat., 10:30 PM.*

3 To the right of the cathedral is the **Musée d'Art Moderne** (Modern Art Museum), housed in the 16th- to 17th-century former Bishop's Palace. Its magnificent interior, with huge fireplaces, carved wood-beamed ceilings, and a Renaissance staircase, plays host to the Levy Collection of modern art, featuring drawings, sculpture, and nearly 400 paintings. The assembly of Fauve works—a short-lived style that succeeded Impressionism at the start of the 20th century—is exceptional, notably the frenzied, hotly colored canvases by Maurice de Vlaminck, Georges Braque, and André Derain. *Pl. St-Pierre. Joint ticket covering all town museums: 20 frs. Open Wed.–Mon. 11–6; closed Tues.*

On the other side of the cathedral square are the former abbey
4 buildings of the **Abbaye St-Loup,** containing two museums. The ground-floor display is devoted to natural history, with impressive collections of birds and meteorites; the Musée des Beaux-Arts et Archéologie (Fine Arts and Archaeology Museum) is confusingly spread over two floors. In the former abbey cellars are local archaeological finds, especially gold-mounted 5th-century jewelry and a Gallo-Roman bronze statue of Apollo. There is also a section devoted to medieval statuary and gargoyles. Paintings from the 15th to the 19th centuries are exhibited on the second floor and include works by Rubens, Anthony Van Dyck, Antoine Watteau, François Boucher, and Jacques-Louis David. *21 rue Chrétien-de-Troyes. Joint ticket: 20 frs. Open Wed.–Mon. 10–noon and 2–6; closed Tues.*

From the Musée St-Loup, the rue de la Cité, packed with restaurants, leads back to quai Dampierre, passing in front of the
5 superb wrought-iron gates of the 18th-century **Hôtel-Dieu** (hospital), topped with the blue-and-gold fleurs-de-lis emblems of the French monarchy. Around the corner is the entrance to the **Musée de la Pharmacie,** the only part of the Hôtel-Dieu open to visitors. Take time to inspect the former medical laboratory, with its quaint assortment of pewter dishes and jugs, earthenware jars, and painted wooden boxes designed to contain herbs and medicines. *Quai Dampierre. Joint ticket: 20 frs. Open Wed.–Mon. 10–noon and 2–6; closed Tues.*

The cathedral sector north of quai Dampierre seems quiet and drowsy compared with the more upbeat, commercial southern part of Troyes. Cross over from the Hôtel-Dieu and continue
6 down rue Clemenceau to the **Basilique St-Urbain,** built between 1262 and 1286 by Pope Urban IV, who was born in Troyes. St-Urbain is one of the most remarkable churches in France, a perfect culmination of Gothic's quest to replace stone walls with stained glass. Huge windows, containing much of their original glass, ring the church, while the exterior bristles with the thrust-bearing flying buttresses that made this daring structure possible. Inquire at the tourist office (*see above*) about summer hours of this and other area churches.

Follow rue Urbain-IV down to **place du Maréchal-Foch,** the main square of central Troyes, flanked by cafés, shops, and the
7 delightful early 17th-century facade of the **Hôtel de Ville** (Town Hall). In summer, the square throbs from morning to night as residents and tourists swarm in to drink coffee or eat crêpes in the various cheap restaurants that spill into the rue Champeaux, Troyes's liveliest pedestrian street. Rue Champeaux
8 runs parallel to **St-Jean,** a lengthy church where England's warrior king, Henry V, married Catherine of France in 1420. The church's tall 16th-century choir contrasts with the low, earlier nave; the clock tower is an unmistakable landmark of downtown Troyes.

A little farther along rue Champeaux, the **ruelle des Chats** wanders off toward the church of Ste-Madeleine. The *ruelle,* or alley, is the town's narrowest thoroughfare: Its overhanging dwellings practically bump attics. Halfway down is the tastefully restored cour du Mortier d'Or, a tiny medieval courtyard.

9 The church of **Ste-Madeleine** (rue du Général-de-Gaulle), the oldest in Troyes, is best known for its elaborate triple-arched stone rood screen separating the nave and the choir. Only six

It's easy to recognize a good place when you see one.

American Express Cardmembers have been doing it for years.

The secret? Instead of just relying on what they see in the window, they look at the door. If there's an American Express Blue Box on it, they know they've found an establishment that cares about high standards.

Whether it's a place to eat, to sleep, to shop, or simply meet, they know they will be warmly welcomed.

So much so, they're rarely taken in by anything else.

Always a good sign.

other such screens still remain in France—most were dismantled during the French Revolution—and this one was carved with panache by Jean Gailde between 1508 and 1517. The church's west tower and main door also date from the early 16th century.

Take rue des Quinze-Vingts, which runs parallel to the ruelle des Chats, as far as rue Emile-Zola. Turn right, then second
10 left, onto rue de la Trinité. The museum known as **Maison de l'Outil** stands at no. 7 in the 16th-century Hôtel de Mauroy. Upstairs is a collection of pictures, models, and tools relevant to such traditional wood-related trades as carpentry, clog making, and barrel making. *7 rue de la Trinité. Joint ticket: 20 frs. Open daily 9–noon and 2–6.*

Close to the Maison de l'Outil, via rue Bordet, is another 16th-
11 century building: the church of **St-Pantaléon.** A number of fine stone statues, surmounted by canopies, cluster around its pillars. The tall, narrow walls are topped not by stone vaults but by a wooden roof, unusual for such a late church. Just as unexpected are the red-and-white streamers and *Solidarnosc* (Solidarity) banners sometimes found next to the altar: St-Pantaléon is used for services by the Polish community. *Rue de Turenne. Open 10–noon and 2–6 in summer months only; at other times apply to the tourist office.*

The Renaissance Hôtel de Vauluisant, opposite, houses two
12 museums. The **Musée Historique** (History Museum) traces the development of Troyes and southern Champagne, with a section devoted to religious art. The **Musée de la Bonneterie** (Textile Museum) outlines the history and manufacturing process of the town's traditional bonnet-making industry; some of the bonnets on display are over 200 years old. *Rue de Turenne. Joint ticket: 20 frs. Open Wed.–Mon. 10–noon and 2–6; closed Tues.*

Close by, beyond place Jean-Jaurès, is yet another church: that
13 of **St-Nicolas.** You may not be tempted by its grimy exterior, but undaunted souls will be rewarded by the chance to scale a wide stone staircase up to an exuberantly decorated chapel and an unexpected view over the nave. Notice the funny little spiral staircase on the left of the nave that appears to vanish into midwall. Open daily 3–6.

Lodging
Under 250 frs.

Le Marigny. Churches, crêpes, and pizzas dominate the cobbled, half-timbered core of Troyes. Le Marigny sits in their midst, on a quiet street adjacent to the narrow ruelle des Chats. With its tottering gables, the hotel looks pretty shaky from the outside; creaking floorboards confirm that it's shaky inside, too. The guest rooms are few, small, and faintly rundown—but prices are suitably old-fashioned. There is no restaurant. *3 rue Charbonnet, 10000, tel. 25–73–10–67. 15 rooms, 6 with bath or shower. V.*

Dining
Under 200 frs.

Bouchon Champenois. Large mirrors in this wood-beamed dining room reflect the striped, timbered patterns of the cour du Mortier d'Or, a tiny restored courtyard just outside, and make the restaurant an ideal place to savor Troyes's medieval ambience. Lunches are savory and light, and evening meals are plentiful, despite the low cost. *1 cour du Mortier d'Or, tel. 25–73–69–24. MC, V. Closed Sun. evening and Mon.*

Le Chanoine Gourmand. Tucked away on a charming old street behind the cathedral and not far from some of the town's best museums, this tiny restaurant offers creative cuisine at reasonable prices, and there's a 165-franc set menu. In summer, choose a table in the back garden from which to enjoy an appetizer of sweet langoustines in a limey vinaigrette sauce followed by any of the young chef's delicately prepared fish dishes. *32 rue de la cité, tel. 25–80–42–06. Reservations advised on weekends. Dress: casual but neat. AE, DC, MC, V. Closed Sun. dinner and Mon.; last 2 wks in Mar., 1 wk in early Aug., and late Dec.–early Jan.*

Shopping Numerous clothing manufacturers are established just outside the town, with the result that clothes prices in stores can be up to 50% cheaper than elsewhere in France. Rue des Bas-Trévois, rue Bégand (leather goods also), and rue Cartalon are good places to look; the best buys on jeans can be had at the **Jeans Shop** (64 rue Emile-Zola).

Auxerre

There are 2 trains daily from Troyes to Auxerre, 1 in late morning, 1 in late afternoon. Both take 2½–3 hours and require changes at St-Florentin and Laroche-Migennes. Auxerre tourist office: 1 quai de la République, tel. 86–51–06–19.

Auxerre is a small, peaceful town dominated by its **Cathédrale St-Etienne,** perched on a steep hill overlooking the River Yonne. The 13th-century choir, the oldest part of the edifice, contains its original stained glass, dominated by dazzling reds and blues. Beneath the choir is the frescoed 11th-century Romanesque crypt; alongside is the Treasury, featuring medieval enamels, manuscripts, and miniatures. *Pl. St-Etienne. Admission to crypt and treasury: 5 frs. each. Open daily 9–noon and 2–6, 2–5 on Sun.*

Fanning out from Auxerre's main square, place des Cordeliers (just up from the cathedral), are a number of venerable streets lined by 16th-century houses. Explore these before heading north toward the town's most interesting church, the former abbey of **St-Germain,** which stands parallel to the cathedral some 300 yards away. The church's earliest section aboveground is the 11th-century Romanesque bell tower, but the extensive underground crypt dates from the 9th century and preserves its original frescoes, some of the oldest in France. *Pl. St-Germain. Admission: 16 frs., free Wed. Guided tours of the crypt every half hour mid-June–mid-Sept., Wed.–Thurs. and Sat.–Mon. 9–noon and 2–6:30, Fri. 9–7:30; mid-Sept.–mid-June, Wed.–Mon. 9–11 and 2–5. Closed Tues.*

Lodging *Under 350 frs.* **Le Normandie.** The picturesque, vine-covered Normandie occupies a grand-looking building conveniently set in the center of Auxerre, a short walk from the cathedral. The guest rooms are unpretentious but of good value and are spanking clean. You can relax in the charming garden, but there is no restaurant on the premises. *41 blvd. Vauban, 89000, tel. 86–52–57–80. 48 rooms, with bath or shower. Facilities: garden, garage, sauna, gym, bar. AE, DC, MC, V.*

Dining *Under 200 frs.* **Jardin Gourmand.** As its name implies, this restaurant features a pretty garden where you can eat *en terrasse* during summer months; the interior, dominated by light-colored oak, is equally congenial. The cuisine is innovative—try the ravioli and foie gras or the duck with black currants—and the service is discreet. *56 blvd. Vauban, tel. 86–51–53–52. Reservations advised. MC, V. Closed Dec. and Mon. Sept.–June.*

Clamecy

Six daily trains travel from Auxerre to Clamecy. The trip takes 65 minutes. Clamecy tourist office: Rue du Grand-Marché, tel. 86–27–02–51.

Slow-moving **Clamecy** is not on many tourist itineraries, but its tumbling alleyways and untouched, ancient houses epitomize *La France Profonde* (the sleepy heartland of France). Clamecy's multishaped roofs, dominated by the majestic square tower of St-Martin's collegiate church, are best viewed from the banks of the Yonne. The river played a crucial role in Clamecy's development; trees from the nearby Morvan Forest were chopped down and floated in huge convoys to Paris. The history of this form of transport *(flottage)*, which lasted until 1923, is detailed in the **town museum.** *Av. de la République. Admission: 3 frs. Open Wed.–Mon. 10–noon and 2–6; closed Sun. Nov.–Easter.*

Lodging and Dining
Under 150 frs.

Boule d'Or. This down-to-earth country hotel (not particularly comfortable but oh-so-cheap) boasts a delightful setting by the River Yonne. Ask for a room facing the river—there are lovely views of Old Clamecy. The restaurant is housed in a former medieval chapel, which, together with absurdly inexpensive set menus, more than compensates for the often apathetic service. *5 pl. Bethléem, 58500, tel. 86–27–11–55. 25 rooms, many with bath. Closed Sun. evening and Christmas.*

Dining
Under 200 frs.

L'Angélus. The cuisine in this restaurant is as charming as the setting opposite the collegiate church, in a wood-beamed medieval landmark. The young chef, under the supervision of owners Madame and Monsieur Etienne, turns out a fine, lighter version of the region's traditional cuisine. *11 pl. St-Jean, tel. 86–27–23–25. Reservations advised. AE, DC, MC, V. Closed Wed. evening and Thurs. mid-Sept.–mid-June.*

Shopping

In homage to the logs that used to be floated downriver from Clamecy to Paris, a log-shaped, sugared-almond candy has long been chewed by *Clamecyçois*, as the local inhabitants are known. You can find your *bûchettes* at **Avignon** (22 rue de la Monnaie), a pastry shop–cum–tearoom close to the steps leading up to the church square.

Avallon

Six trains daily make the 60–70-minute trip from Auxerre to Avallon. Tourist office: 6 rue Bocquillot, tel. 86–34–09–12.

Avallon is spectacularly situated on a promontory jutting over the Cousin Valley. Its old streets and ramparts are pleasant places to stroll, before or after viewing the works of medieval stone carvers whose imaginations ran riot on the portals of the venerable church of **St-Lazarus.**

Lodging and Dining
Under 350 frs.
★

Les Capucins. This intimate hotel offers rooms in a wide range of prices, but is better known for its restaurant, which features four set menus dominated by regional cooking. Dishes of especially good value are the duck and the trout in flaky pastry. The desserts are excellent. *6 av. Paul-Doumer, 89200, tel. 86–34–06–52. 8 rooms with bath. AE, MC, V. Facilities: restaurant* *(closed Wed., Tues. dinner out of season Nov.–Mar.). Closed mid-Nov.–mid-Jan.*

Dining
Under 200 frs.

Morvan. Solid, filling dishes are offered at this folksy eatery just outside town; fish terrine, rabbit, and chocolate cake number among the menu's best. There is an adjoining rock garden. *7 rte. de Paris, tel. 86–34–18–20. Reservations accepted. AE, DC, V. Closed Sun. evening, Mon., most of Jan. and Feb., and second half of Nov.*

Vézelay

A bus for Vézelay leaves daily at 8 AM from place Vauban in Avallon, which is about 6 km (10 mi) away. The return bus departs at 5 PM. Tourist office: rue St-Pierre, tel. 86–33–23–69.

In the 11th and 12th centuries, the crag-top basilica in picturesque old **Vézelay** was one of the focal points of Christendom. Pilgrims poured in to gasp at the relics of St. Mary Magdalene before setting off on the great medieval trek to the shrine of St. James at Santiago de Compostela in northwest Spain.

By the mid-13th century, the authenticity of St. Mary's relics was in doubt; others had been discovered in Provence. The decline continued until the French Revolution, when the basilica and adjoining monastery buildings were sold by the state. Only the basilica escaped demolition and was itself falling into ruin when ace restorer Viollet-le-Duc rode to the rescue in 1840 (he also restored the cathedrals of Laon and Amiens, and Paris's Notre-Dame).

Today the basilica at Vézelay has recaptured its onetime glory and is considered France's most prestigious Romanesque showcase. Nowhere is this more evident than in the nave, whose carved column capitals are imaginatively designed and superbly executed, representing miniature medieval men in all manner of situations—working in the fields, wielding battle swords, or undergoing the tortures of hell.

The basilica's exterior is best seen from the leafy terrace to the right of the facade. Opposite is a vast, verdant panorama encompassing lush valleys and rolling hills. In the forefront is the Flamboyant Gothic spire of St-Père-sous-Vézelay, a tiny village a couple of miles away. *Open daily 7–7.*

Lodging
Under 250 frs.

Relais du Morvan. With its delightful setting, Vézelay makes a great place to stay. But it is, after all, a mere village (500 inhabitants) and contains just four hotels. Don't opt for the large, unfriendly, and astronomically expensive Lion d'Or; try instead to reserve a room at the cozy, budgetwise Relais du Morvan. There is a choice of three very affordable set menus in the restaurant. The welcome is cheerful, the rooms functional and unpretentious. *89450 Vézelay, tel. 86–33–25–33. 13 rooms, most with bath. Facilities: restaurant (closed Tues. evening and Wed.). MC, V. Closed early Jan.–mid-Feb.*

Autun

The rail trip takes 1¾–2¼ hours from Avallon to Autun (2¾–3½ hours from Auxerre). There are 3 trains daily. Autun tourist office: 3 av. Charles-de-Galle, tel. 85–52–20–34.

Julius Caesar referred to **Autun** as the "sister and rival of Rome itself." Its importance since Roman times is immediately apparent at the well-preserved archways, Porte St-André and Porte d'Arroux, and at the Théâtre Romain, once the largest arena in Gaul. Another famous warrior, Napoleon, studied here in 1779 at the military academy (now the Lycée Bonaparte).

Autun's principal monument, however, is its **cathedral,** built from 1120 to 1146 to house the relics of St. Lazarus; the main tower, spire, and upper reaches of the chancel were added in the late-15th century. The influx of medieval pilgrims accounts for the building's size (35 yards wide and nearly 80 yards long). Lazarus's tomb was dismantled in 1766 by canons who were believers in the rationalist credo of the Enlightenment. These clergy did their best to transform the Romanesque-Gothic cathedral into a classical temple at the same time, adding pilasters and classical ornament willy-nilly. Fortunately, some of the best medieval stonework, including the nave capitals and the tympanum above the main door—a *Last Judgment* sculpted by Gislebertus in the 1130s—emerged unscathed. Jean Auguste Ingres's painting depicting the *Martyrdom of St-Symphorien* has been relegated to a dingy chapel in the north aisle of the nave. *Pl. St-Louis. Open daily 8–5.*

Across from the cathedral, the **Musée Rolin** boasts several fine paintings from the Middle Ages and good examples of Burgundian sculpture, including another Gislebertus masterpiece, the *Temptation of Eve,* which originally topped one of the side doors of the cathedral. *Pl. St-Louis. Admission: 10 frs. Open Apr.–Sept., Wed.–Mon. 9:30–noon and 1:30–6, Sun. 10–noon and 2:30–5; Oct.–Mar., Wed.–Mon. 10–noon and 2–4 or 5, Sun. 10–noon and 2:30–5. Closed Tues.*

Lodging
Under 350 frs.

St-Louis. This comfortable hotel dates from the 17th century; legend has it that Napoleon once slept here. Guest rooms are cozily decorated and have a slightly faded charm. The hotel boasts a pleasant patio-garden and its own restaurant, La Rotonde. *6 rue de l'Arbalète, 71400, tel. 85-52-21-03. 52 rooms, some with bath. Facilities: restaurant, garden. AE, DC, MC, V. Closed Dec. 20–Feb 2.*

Dining
Under 125 frs.

Chalet Bleu. Recently opened in the center of Autun, this restaurant serves solid traditional French cuisine at prices that can be refreshingly inexpensive if you order carefully. The setting, complemented by spruce white furniture, is fresh and green and resembles a converted conservatory. Foie gras and beef with shallots are trustworthy choices. *3 rue Jeannin, tel. 85–86–27–30. Reservations advised. AE, DC, MC, V. Closed Mon. dinner, Tues., and Feb.*

Tour 2: From Dijon to Cluny

Dijon, the capital of Burgundy and a major cultural and gastronomic venue, is the base of this tour, which heads south through the wine town of Beaune to Chalon-sur-Saône, where buses leave for the delightful old town of Cluny, whose ruined abbey was once the most powerful religious center of western Europe.

From Paris *By Train* TGV bullet trains to Dijon leave Paris (Gare de Lyon) 8 times daily. The trip takes 1 hour 40 minutes.

By Car The 312-kilometer (190-mile) drive to Dijon from Paris along A6/A38 takes 3 hours.

Dijon

Tourist office: Place Darcy, down avenue Foch from the station, tel. 80–43–42–12.

Numbers in the margin correspond to points of interest on the Dijon map.

Dijon is the age-old capital of Burgundy. Throughout the Middle Ages, Burgundy was a duchy that led a separate existence from the rest of France, culminating in the rule of the four "Grand Dukes of the West" between 1364 and 1477. A number of monuments date from this period, such as the Palais des Ducs (Ducal Palace), now largely converted into an art museum.

Dijon's fame and fortune outlasted its dukes, and the city continued to flourish under French rule from the 17th century on. It has remained the major city of Burgundy—the only one, in fact, with more than 100,000 inhabitants. Its site, on the major European north–south trade route and within striking distance of the Swiss and German borders, has helped maintain its economic importance. The same can be said of its numerous gastronomic specialties: snails, mustard, and cassis, which is often mixed with white wine—preferably Burgundy Aligoté—to make Kir, one of France's most popular aperitifs.

From the station take avenue Foch down to place Darcy and head off right along pedestrian rue de la Liberté to the Palais des Ducs.

1 The **Palais des Ducs** is Dijon's leading testimony to bygone splendor. These days, it's home to one of France's major arts museums, the **Musée des Beaux-Arts,** where tombs of two of the aforementioned dukes—Philip the Bold and John the Fearless—spearhead a rich collection of medieval objects and Renaissance furniture. Among the paintings are works by Italian Old Masters, and French 19th-century artists, such as Théodore Géricault and Gustave Courbet, and their Impressionist successors, notably Édouard Manet and Claude Monet. The **ducal kitchens** (circa 1435) with their six huge fireplaces, and the 14th-century chapter house catch the eye, as does the 15th-century **Salle des Gardes** (Guard Room), with its richly carved and colored tombs and late-14th-century altarpieces. The elegant, classical exterior of the former palace can best be admired from place de la Libération and cour d'Honneur. *Pl. de la Libération. Admission: 10 frs., free Sun. Open Wed.–Sat. and Mon. 10–6, Sun. 10–12:30 and 2–6; closed Tues.*

Further links with Dijon's medieval past are found west of the town center, just off the avenue Albert Ier beyond the train station. Keep an eye out for the exuberant 15th-century gateway to the Chartreuse de Champmol—all that remains of a former charterhouse—and the adjoining **Puits de Moïse,** the so-called Well of Moses, with six large, compellingly realistic medieval statues on a hexagonal base (1395–1405).

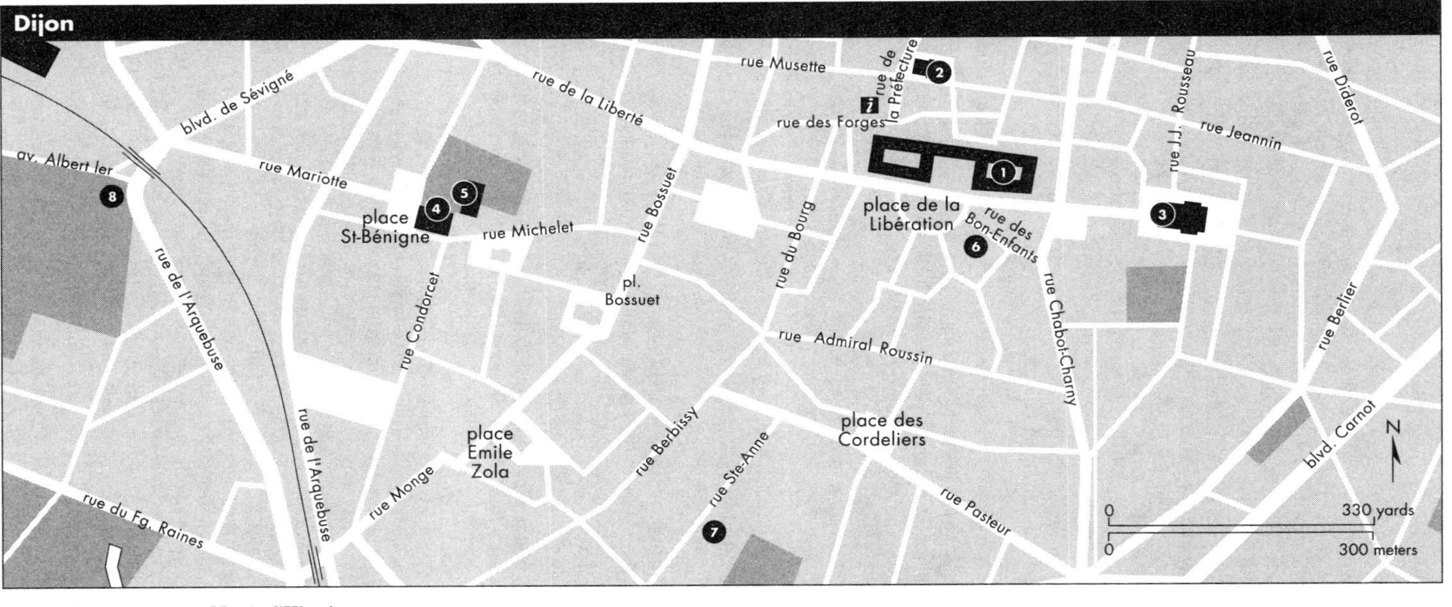

Cathédrale Ste-Bénigne, **4**
Musée Archéologique, **5**
Musée d'Art Sacré, **7**
Musée d'Histoire Naturelle et Jardin Botanique, **8**
Musée Magnin, **6**
Notre-Dame, **2**
Palais des Ducs, **1**
St-Michel, **3**

2 Among the city's outstanding old churches is **Notre-Dame** (rue
de la Préfécture), with its elegant towers, delicate nave stonework, 13th-century stained glass, and soaring chancel. The
3 church of **St-Michel** (rue Rameau) takes us forward 300 years
4 with its chunky Renaissance facade. **Cathédrale Ste-Bénigne**
(off rue Mariotte) is comparatively austere; its chief glory is
the 10th-century crypt—a forest of pillars surmounted by a rotunda.

Dijon is rich in museums, which all can be visited on a single
5 13-franc ticket. The **Musée Archéologique** (Archaeological Museum), housed in the former abbey buildings of Ste-Bénigne, traces the history of the region through archaeological discoveries. *5 rue du Docteur-Maret. Open Sept.–May, Wed.–Mon. 9–noon and 2–6; June–Aug., 9:30–6; closed Tues.*

6 The **Musée Magnin** is a 17th-century mansion showcasing original furnishings and a variety of paintings from the 16th to the 19th centuries. *4 rue des Bons-Enfants. Open Sept.–May, Tues.–Sun. 10–noon and 2–6; June–Aug., 10–6; closed Mon.*

7 The **Musée d'Art Sacré,** devoted to religious art, has a collection of sculpture and altarpieces in the appropriate setting of a former church. *15 rue Ste-Anne. Open Wed.–Mon. 9–noon and 2–6; closed Tues.*

8 The **Musée d'Histoire Naturelle et Jardin Botanique** encompasses a natural-history museum and impressive botanical gardens, with a wide variety of trees and tropical flowers. *1 av. Albert Ier. Museum open Wed.–Mon. 2–5; closed Tues.*

Lodging and Dining
Under 350 frs.

Central Urbis. This central, old-established hotel has benefited from recent modernization: Its sound-proofed, air-conditioned rooms offer a degree of comfort in excess of their price. The adjoining grill room, the Central Grill Rôtisserie, offers a good alternative to the gastronomic sophistication that is difficult to avoid elsewhere in Dijon. *3 pl. Grangier, 21000, tel. 80–30–44–00. 90 rooms, most with bath. Facilities: restaurant (closed Sun.). AE, DC, MC, V.*

Dining
Under 200 frs.

★ **Thibert.** Chef Jean-Paul Thibert has no need to give his restaurant a fancy name. The art-deco setting is perhaps a trifle severe, but the cuisine is refined and imaginative. The menu changes regularly. Cabbage stuffed with snails and prawns with peas and truffles figure among the *tours de force;* sorbets encased in black-and-white mixed chocolate will tempt you to indulge in dessert. Thibert also represents remarkable value for the money—for the moment at least—though it's possible to run up quite a tab if you feel like a splurge. *10 pl. Wilson, tel. 80–67–74–64. Reservations required. Jacket and tie required. AE, MC, V. Closed Sun., Mon. lunch, and 2 weeks in Aug.*

★ **Toison d'Or.** A collection of superbly restored 16th-century buildings belonging to the Burgundian Company of Winetasters forms the backdrop to this fine restaurant, which features a small wine museum in the cellar. Toison d'Or is lavishly furnished and quaint (candlelight *de rigueur* in the evening). The food is increasingly sophisticated. Try the langoustines with ginger and the nougat and honey dessert. *18 rue Ste-Anne, tel. 80–30–73–52. Reservations accepted. Jacket required. AE, DC, MC, V. Closed Sun. evening.*

Pré aux Clercs & Trois Faisans. Situated on the pretty, semicircular square opposite the ducal palace, this venerable eating institution has recently been salvaged after years of indifference. The all-too-classic cuisine (sometimes heavy and dull) is offset by an extensive wine cellar, deferential service, and the wood-beamed, stone-walled setting. According to local legend, it was here that Canon Kir invented the famous aperitif that bears his name, made with cassis and white wine. *13 pl. de la Libération, tel. 80–67–11–33. Reservations required. Jacket required. AE, DC, MC, V. Closed Sun. evening, Mon., and last week in Feb.*

Beaune

Hourly trains from Dijon take 20 minutes to Beaune. Tourist office: Rue de l'Hôtel-Dieu, tel. 80–22–24–51.

Wine has been made in nearby **Nuits-St-Georges** since Roman times; its "dry, tonic, and generous qualities" were recommended to Louis XIV for medicinal use. It is appropriate, then, that some of the region's finest vineyards should be owned by the **Hospices de Beaune,** founded in 1443 as a hospital, which carried on its medical activities until 1971, its nurses still sporting their strange medieval uniform.

A visit to the Hospices is one of the highlights of a stay in **Beaune**. The hospital's medical history is retraced in a museum whose wide-ranging collections feature some of the weird and wonderful instruments used by doctors back in the 15th century. You can also see Roger Van der Weyden's medieval Flemish masterpiece, *The Last Judgment*, plus a collection of tapestries (though a better series from the late-15th century, relating the life of the Virgin, can be admired in Beaune's main church, the 12th-century **Collégiale Notre-Dame,** just off avenue de la République). Each year, as part of the Trois Glorieuses, an auction of wines is held at the Hospices on the third Sunday of November; it's attended by connoisseurs and dealers from around the world. *Rue de l'Hôtel-Dieu. Museum admission: 25 frs. Open Dec.–Mar., daily 9–11:30 and 2–5:30; Apr.–Nov., daily 9–6.*

Despite the hordes of tourists, Beaune remains one of the most charming and attractive French provincial towns. There are few more delightful experiences than a visit to the candlelit cellars of the **Marché aux Vins** (rue Nicolas Rolin). Here you can taste as many of the regional wines as you wish—beginning with whites and fruity Beaujolais and ending with big reds like Gevrey-Chambertin—for around 40 francs.

Lodging
Under 350 frs.

Central. A well-run establishment with several enlarged and modernized rooms, the Central lives up to its name: It's just around the corner from the Hôtel-Dieu in downtown Beaune. The stone-walled restaurant is cozy—some might say cramped—and the cuisine is reliable. The service is efficient, if a little hurried. The evening meal is obligatory in season (July and August). *2 rue Victor-Millot, 21200, tel. 80–24–77–24. 20 rooms, most with bath. Facilities: restaurant (closed Sun. dinner Nov.–Apr., and Wed. Nov.–June). MC, V. Closed much of Dec. and Jan., and Sun. evening and Wed. Nov.–Apr.*

Dining
Under 200 frs.

Auberge St-Vincent. Perhaps the best thing about this restaurant is its admirable setting opposite the Hospices de Beaune. Not surprisingly, it pulls in plenty of tourists, and, consequently, the cuisine and ambience can seem bland. Service, though, is attentive, and the wine list is appropriately lengthy.

Prices are inexpensive if you order carefully, never more than moderate, with kidneys and marinated mullet among the top attractions. *Pl. Halle, tel. 80–22–42–34. Reservations advised. AE, DC, MC, V.*

L'Ecusson. Don't be put off by its unprepossessing exterior. This is a comfortable, friendly, thick-carpeted restaurant whose four variously priced set menus offer outstanding value. Rabbit terrine with tarragon followed by leg of duck in oxtail sauce, cheese, and dessert is a typical offering. *2 rue du Lieutenant-Dupuis, tel. 80–22–83–08. Reservations advised. AE, DC, MC, V. Closed Sun. (open for Sun. lunch Easter–mid-Nov.) and most of Feb.*

Chalon-sur-Saône

Trains from Beaune take 20–25 minutes to Chalon-sur-Saône; note that there are none in the early afternoon. Tourist office: Blvd. de la République, tel. 85–48–37–97.

Chalon-sur-Saône has its medieval heart near the **Eglise St-Vincent**—a former cathedral displaying a jumble of styles—close to the banks of the River Saône. Chalon is the birthplace of Nicéphore Niepce (1765–1833), whose early experiments, developed further by Jacques Daguerre, qualify him as the father of photography. The **Musée Nicéphore Niepce,** a fine museum occupying an 18th-century house overlooking the Saône, retraces the early history of photography and motion pictures with the help of some pioneering equipment. It also includes a selection of contemporary photographic work and a lunar camera used during the U.S. Apollo program. But the star of the museum must be the primitive camera used to take the first photographs in 1816. *Hôtel des Messageries, 28 quai des Messageries. Admission: 10 frs. Open Wed.–Mon. 9:30–11:30 and 2:30–5:30; closed Tues.*

Lodging and Dining
Splurge

St-Georges. Situated close to the train station, a few hundred yards from the town center, the friendly, white-walled St-Georges hotel has been tastefully modernized and possesses many spacious rooms. Its cozy restaurant is known locally for its efficient service and set menus of outstanding value. You can't go wrong with the duck in white pepper, foie gras with truffles, or roast pigeon. *32 av. Jean-Jaurès, 71100, tel. 85–48–27–05. 48 rooms, most with bath. Facilities: restaurant (closed Sat. lunch). AE, DC, MC, V. 350 frs.–440 frs.*

Cluny

Six buses daily make the pretty 90-minute run to Cluny from Chalon-sur-Saône. Cluny tourist office: 6 rue Mercière, tel. 85–59–05–34.

Though the old town of **Cluny** is charming in its own right, most visitors come to admire the magnificent ruins of the medieval **Abbey of Cluny.** Founded in the 10th century, it was the biggest church in Europe until the 16th century, when Michelangelo built St. Peter's in Rome. Cluny's medieval abbots were as powerful as popes. In 1098, Pope Urban II (himself a Cluniac) assured the head of his old abbey that Cluny was the "light of the world." That assertion, of dubious religious validity, has not stood the test of time, and Cluny's remains today stand as a reminder of the limits of human grandeur.

The ruins nonetheless suggest the size and glory of Cluny Abbey at its zenith. Only the Clocher de l'Eau-Bénite (a majestic bell tower) and the right arms of the two transepts, climbing 100 feet above ground, remain. The 13th-century *farinier* (flour mill), with its fine chestnut roof and collection of statues, can also be seen. The gardens contain an ancient lime tree, several hundred years old, named Abélard after the controversial philosopher who sought shelter at the abbey in 1142. No one is sure the tree is quite that old, though! *Admission: 25 frs. Guided visits Easter–Oct., daily 9–noon and 2–5; late morning and early afternoon only the rest of the year.*

Lodging and Dining
Under 350 frs.
★

Bourgogne. There's no better place to get into Cluny's medieval mood than the Bourgogne. What remains of the famous abbey is just next door, and the old-fashioned hotel building, which dates from 1817, stands where other parts of the abbey used to be. There is a small garden and a splendid restaurant with sober pink decor and refined cuisine: foie gras, snails, and the more exotic fish with ginger. There are also 14 hotel rooms; these start at 420 francs but are well worth a bit of a splurge. *Pl. de l'Abbaye, 71250, tel. 85–59–00–58. 14 rooms with bath. AE, DC, V. Closed mid-Nov.–late Feb., Tues. lunch, and Mon. mid-July–mid-Oct.*

Dining
Under 200 Frs

Potin Gourmand. Original dishes prepared with superfresh, seasonal ingredients make this simple spot a favorite with townspeople as well as visitors. The reasonable prices make it even more appealing. *Pl. Champ de Foire, tel. 85–59–02–06. AE, MC, V. Closed early Jan.–early Feb., Sun. evening, and Mon.*

10 Lyon and the Alps

The Rhône, Grenoble

In the heavily industrialized countries of northern Europe, big cities mean grimy factories, snarling traffic, and blocks of postwar concrete. Most French cities are different, and none more so than Lyon, where the silk weavers who made the city's fame beavered away in house attics before scuttling along narrow passages to transport their precious cloth. Much of central Lyon remains curiously intimate, especially the medieval streets around the cathedral. Museums, restaurants, Roman remains, lively pedestrian shopping streets, and not one, but two rivers—the Saône and the Rhône—complete the scene.

The TGV bullet train has put Lyon within just two hours of Paris and made it the obvious gateway to the French Alps. The boom in winter sports has hurtled the once-backward Alpine region into the 20th century, and rail and bus lines were further extended for the 1992 Winter Olympics in Albertville. Nonetheless, reaching many high-up villages remains an arduous proposition, but in both winter and summer, these journeys are definitely worthwhile. Though expensive for skiing, compared to the Pyrenees or the Vosges, the Alps usually offer good snow. In summer, they're unparalleled for hiking—and you don't have to be a mountain goat to enjoy their pleasures.

The character of the countryside away from Lyon and the mountains is determined by the Saône and Rhône rivers. Before reaching Lyon, the Saône flows between the lush hillside of the Beaujolais vineyards and the flat marshland of the Dombes. The Rhône, the great river of southern France, actually trickles to life high up in the Swiss mountains, then comes to life at Lyon, where it merges with the Saône and plummets due south in search of the Mediterranean. Its progress south from Lyon is often spectacular, as steep-climbing vineyards conjure up vistas that are more readily associated with the river's Germanic cousin, the Rhine.

Essential Information

Lodging The entire region is filled with hotels and country inns; at many, you'll be expected to take your evening meal there (especially in summer), but this tends to be more a pleasure than an obligation. The Alps' extensive hotel infrastructure is geared primarily to winter visitors, who are invariably expected to take *demi-pension* or *pension complète* (with two or three meals a day in the hotel).

Dining Lyon is a renowned capital of good cuisine. Both gourmets and gourmands will enjoy the robust local specialties, such as *saveloy* (sausage) and *quenelles* (fish dumplings). The *marrons glacés* (chestnuts poached in syrup and glazed) of Privas and the nougats of Montélimar delight a sweet tooth. The rivers and lakes of the Alps teem with pike and trout, and the hills are a riot of wild raspberries and black currants during summer months. *Raclette* is a warming Alpine winter specialty: melted cheese served with boiled potatoes, inch-long sour pickles called *cornichons*, and salami or ham. Mountain herbs form the basis of traditional drinks—try a tangy, dark **Suédois** or a bittersweet **Suze** (made from gentian), and round off your meal with a green Chartreuse.

Hiking Spectacular scenery and an invigorating mountain climate make the Alps a perfect base for a summer hiking holiday—and chair lifts can frequently help you negotiate the more daunting slopes. The Beaujolais hills north of Lyon are a gentler proposition.

Skiing In this region, whose ski season begins in December and lasts through April, the most famous ski resort is **Chamonix** (6,063 feet), beloved of experts. **Val d'Isère** (6,068 feet) ranks as one of Europe's swankiest resorts, with lots of cross-country runs as well as downhill slopes. Nearby **Tignes,** the highest of the Savoie resorts (6,930 feet), offers slopes to suit skiers of all abilities.Family groups favor **Morzine** (3,280 feet), a popular small resort with gentle slopes geared to the inexperienced. Chic, expensive **Megève** (3,650 feet) offers a lively nightlife and a particularly impressive network of *téléfériques* (cable cars) and helicopter services. **Courchevel** (6,068 feet) is renowned for its après-ski, while across the mountain, fashionable **Méribel** (5,428 feet) boasts lots of difficult runs.

The Arts and Nightlife Lyon is the region's liveliest arts center, with dozens of discos, piano bars, and nightclubs, and a full calender of concerts, theater, and arts events.

Festivals September in Lyon sees the internationally renowned **Festival Berlioz** (odd years) and the **Biennale de la Danse** (even years), as well as the **International Puppet Festival.** October brings the **Festival Bach** (tel. 78–72–75–31) and the Contemporary Arts Festival, **Octobre des Arts** (tel. 78–30–50–66). Jazz enthusiasts will want to catch Grenoble's popular **Cinq Jours de Jazz** (Five Days of Jazz) in February or March, and those with classical tastes are catered to during the **Session Internationale de Grenoble-Isère** in June and July.

Highlights for First-time Visitors

Cable-car ascent from Chamonix, Tour 2
Grenoble, Tour 2
"Trabouling" in Lyon, Tour 1
Fine Arts Museum, Lyon, Tour 1
Vienne, Tour 1

Tour 1: Lyon and the Northern Rhône

There is enough to see and visit in Lyon to warrant a stay of several days. Frequent trains whistle down the Rhône Valley to the towns of Vienne, Tournon, and Valence, which make for pleasant day trips.

From Paris *By Train* TGV bullet trains to Lyon leave Paris (Gare de Lyon) every hour. The trip takes 2–2¼ hours.

By Car Allow 4½ hours for the 465-kilometer (290-mile) drive to Lyon from Paris along the A6 expressway.

Lyon

Tourist offices: in a freestanding building in place Bellecour, tel. 78–42–25–75; and in the Perrache train station, tel. 78–42–22–07.

Numbers in the margin correspond to points of interest on the Lyon map.

Lyon and Marseille both like to claim they are France's "second city." In terms of size and commercial importance, Marseille probably grabs that title. But when it comes to tourist appeal, Lyon's a clear winner.

Lyon's development owes much to the city's exceptional site: halfway between Paris and the Mediterranean and within striking distance of Switzerland, Italy, and the Alps. The site is physically impressive, with steep cliffs dominating the River Saône, which flows parallel to the Rhône before the two converge south of the city center.

Because Lyon has never really had to endure hard times, a mood of untroubled complacency, rather than big-city bustle, prevails. The Lyonnais bask in the knowledge that their city has been important for over 2,000 years, ever since the Romans made it the capital of the occupied province of Gaul, shortly after founding the city in 43 BC. Even the name sounds appropriately proud—until you learn that it derives from the Roman Lugdunum, or "Hill of the Crow."

Few, if any, crows, rooks, or ravens are found these days on
1 **place Bellecour**, midway between the Saône and the Rhône. (To get there from La Part Dieu station, take the métro to Bellecour.) This imposing tree-shaded square, the largest in the city and one of the largest in France, derives its architectural distinction from the classical facades erected along its narrower sides in 1800. The large bronze statue of Louis XIV on horseback is the work of local sculptor Jean Lemot, installed

in 1828 to replace the original, which failed to survive the French Revolution.

Stop in at the tourist office in the southeast corner for a city map, information leaflets, and a 30-franc day-pass that enables you to visit all the city's museums. Then cross the square and head 500 yards north along lively rue du Président-Herriot before turning left onto rue Grenette. Take the Pont du Maréchal-Juin over the Saône to the old town at the foot of Fourvière Hill, crowned by the imposing silhouette of **Notre-Dame** basilica.

On the right bank of the Saône lies **Vieux Lyon** (Old Lyon), an atmospheric warren of streets and alleys. Turn right after the
2 bridge, then take the first left down a little alley to **place de la Baleine,** a small square lined with 17th-century houses. At the far end of place de la Baleine lies **rue St-Jean,** one of the many streets that weave their way around the banks of the Saône. Many of the area's elegant houses were built for the town's most illustrious denizens—bankers and silk merchants—during the French Renaissance under the 16th-century king François I. Originally, they had four stories; the upper floors were added in the last century. Look for the intricate old iron signs hanging over the shop doorways, many of which gave the streets their names.

A peculiarity of the streets of old Lyon are the *traboules,* quaint little passageways that cut under the houses from one street to another. Don't hesitate to venture in; they aren't private. There's a fine example at 24 rue St-Jean, just off place de la Baleine (to the left), which leads through to rue du Boeuf via an airy, restored courtyard.

Rue St-Jean was old Lyon's major thoroughfare. Stop in the elegant courtyard of no. 27 on your way north from place de la Baleine to place du Change, where money changers would op-
3 erate during Lyon's medieval trade fairs. The **Loge du Change** church, on one side of the square, was built by Germain Soufflot (best known as architect of the Panthéon in Paris) in 1747.

Take rue Soufflot to one side of the church and turn left onto rue de Gadagne, where the largest Renaissance ensemble in Lyon is located: the Hôtel de Gadagne, built between the 14th
4 and the 16th centuries and now home to the **Musée Historique de Lyon.** The first floor of this history museum contains medieval sculpture from long-gone local churches and abbeys, while other floors showcase local furniture, pottery, paintings, engravings, and antique playing cards. On the second floor is the **Musée de la Marionnette** (Puppet Museum), which traces the history of marionnettes from Guignol and Madelon (Lyon's local equivalent of Punch and Judy, created by Laurent Mourguet in 1795) through to contemporary hand and string puppets from across the globe. *10 rue de Gadagne. Admission to both museums free. Open Wed.–Mon. 10:45–6; closed Tues.*

Continue through tiny place du Petit-Collège to rue du Boeuf. One of old Lyon's finest mansions lies farther down rue
5 du Boeuf, at no. 16: the 17th-century **Maison du Crible,** a romantic, luxurious, and pricey nouvelle cuisine restaurant called Tour Rose. Venture into its courtyard to glimpse the Tour Rose itself—an elegant, pink-washed tower—and the charming terraced garden. Close by, at the corner of place Neuve St-Jean, is one of the most famous hanging signs in old

Lyon and the Alps

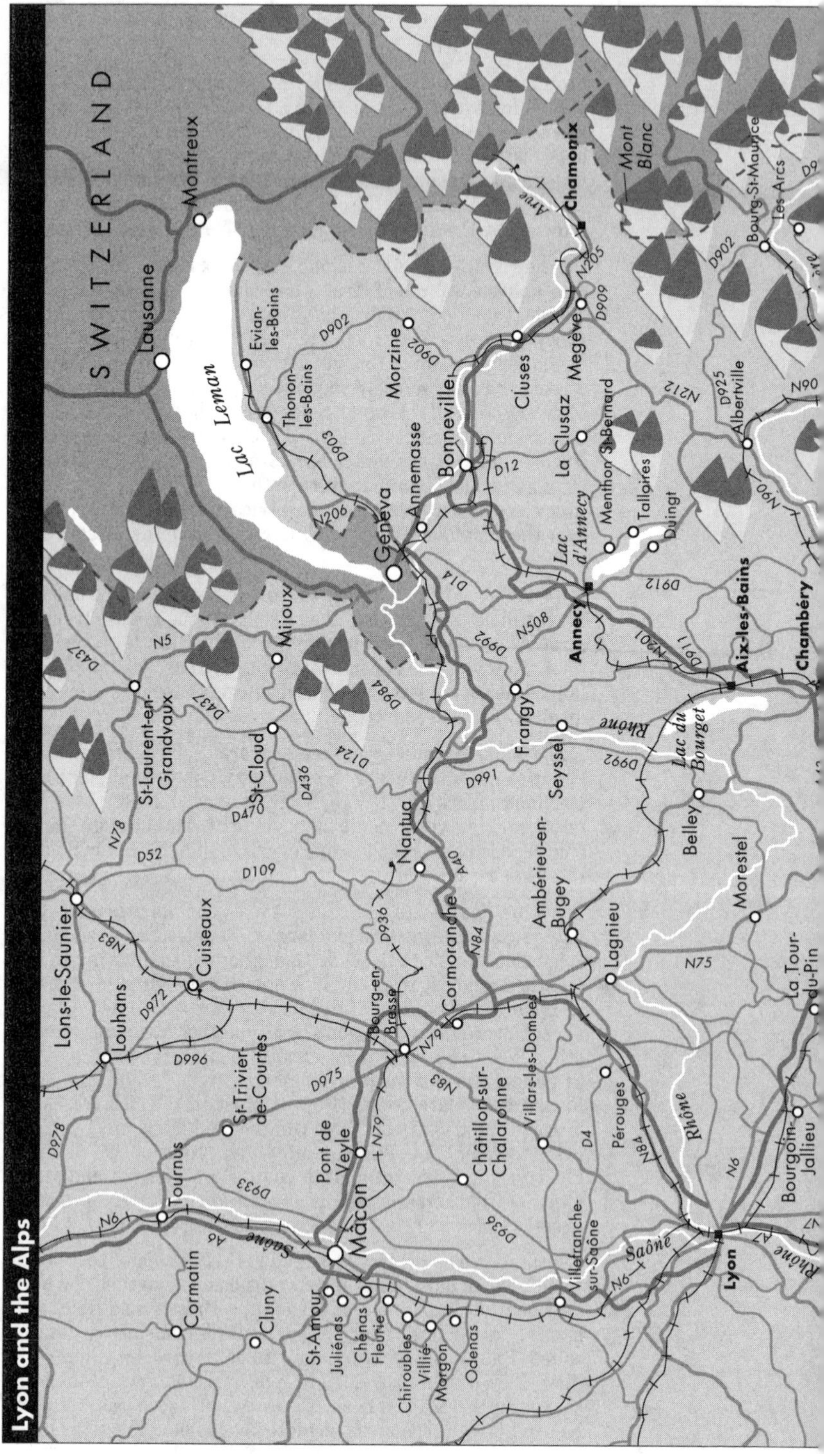

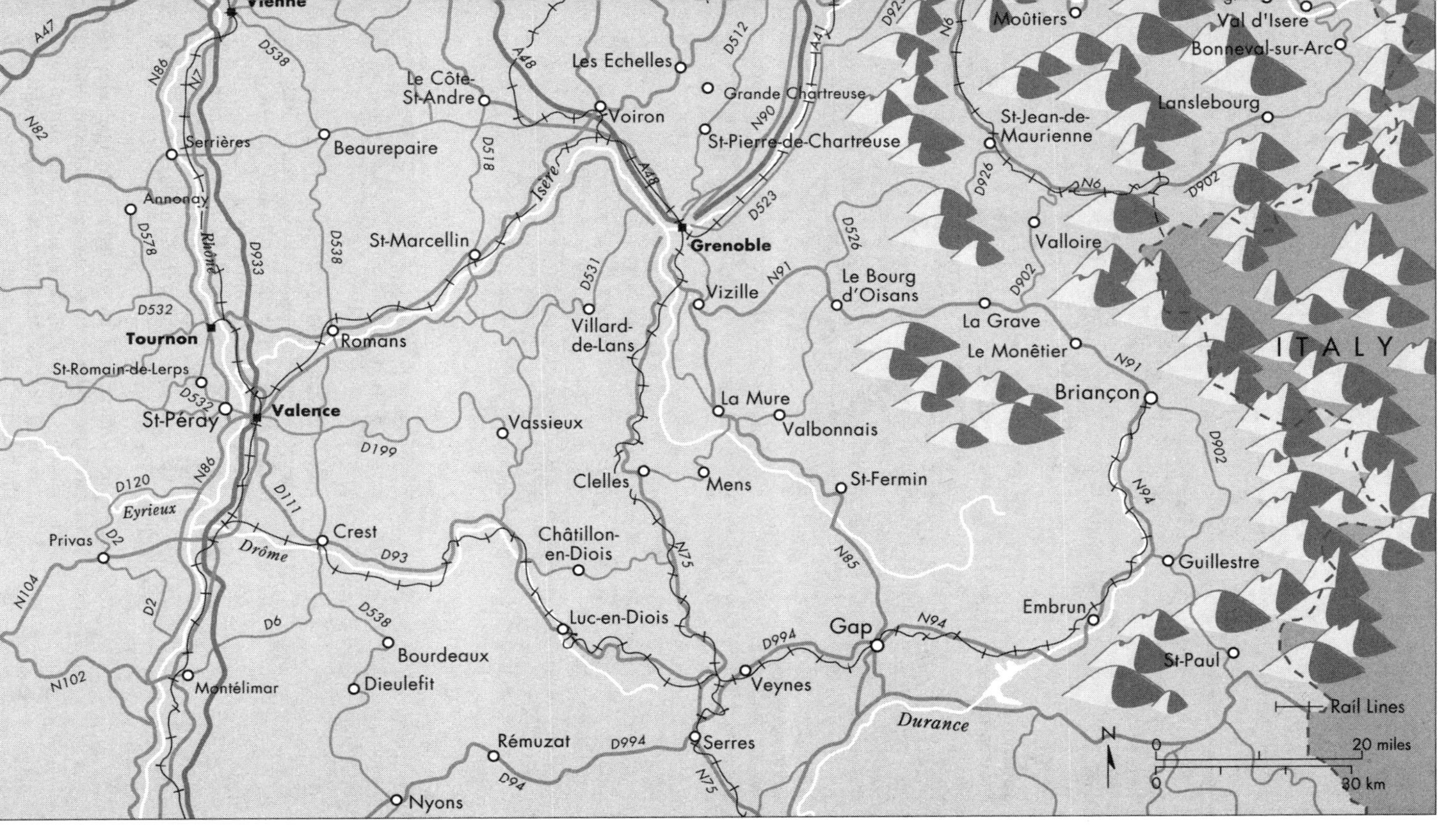
Vienne
Moûtiers
Val d'Isere
Bonneval-sur-Arc
Les Echelles
Le Côte-St-Andre
Grande Chartreuse
Voiron
St-Pierre-de-Chartreuse
Lanslebourg
St-Jean-de-Maurienne
Serrières
Beaurepaire
Annonay
Rhône
Isère
St-Marcellin
Grenoble
Valloire
Le Bourg d'Oisans
Vizille
La Grave
Le Monêtier
ITALY
Tournon
Romans
Villard-de-Lans
St-Romain-de-Lerps
Valence
St-Péray
La Mure
Valbonnais
Briançon
Vassieux
Clelles
Mens
St-Fermin
Eyrieux
Crest
Privas
Drôme
Châtillon-en-Diois
Guillestre
Luc-en-Diois
Embrun
Gap
Bourdeaux
St-Paul
Veynes
Montélimar
Dieulefit
Rail Lines
Durance
Rémuzat
Serres
N
0
20 miles
30 km
Nyons
A47
N86
N7
D538
A48
D512
A41
D92
N6
N82
N90
D518
D926
D902
D523
D578
D933
D526
D531
N91
D532
D199
D120
D111
N94
D2
D93
N75
N85
N104
D6
D994
N102
D94

Hôtel Paterin, **12**
Hôtel de Ville, **18**
Jardin Archéologique, **6**
Jardin des Chartreux, **14**
Jardin des Plantes, **15**
Loge du Change, **3**
Maison des Canuts, **17**
Maison du Crible, **5**
Musée de la Civilisation Gallo-Romaine, **9**
Musée des Arts Décoratifs, **20**
Musée des Beaux-Arts, **19**
Musée Historique de Lyon/Musée de la Marionnette, **4**
Musée Historique des Tissus, **21**
Notre-Dame-de-Fourvière, **10**
Place de la Baleine, **2**
Place Bellecour, **1**
Primatiale St-Jean, **7**
St-Paul, **13**
St-Polycarpe, **16**
Théâtres Romains, **8**
Tour Métallique, **11**

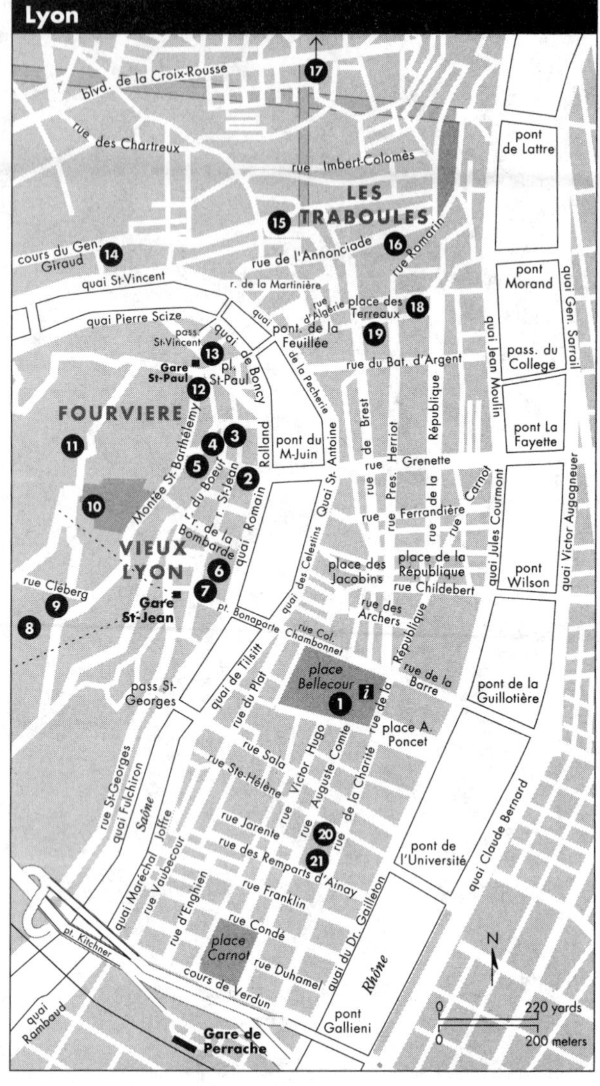

Lyon, the work of Giambologna (1529–1608), a renowned French sculptor who honed his skills in Renaissance Italy; the sign portrays the bull for which rue du Boeuf is named. Head down place Neuve and turn right onto rue St-Jean. A hundred yards farther, turn right onto rue de la Bombarde, which leads
6 to the peaceful **Jardin Archéologique** (Archaeological Gardens), with its excavated remains of the four churches that succeeded one another on the spot.

Alongside is one church that has withstood the onslaught of
7 time: the **Primatiale St-Jean,** Lyon's somewhat disappointing cathedral. You won't find any soaring roof or lofty spires here. Instead, a stumpy facade is stuck almost bashfully onto the nave, while the interior mishmash has its moments—the 13th-

century stained-glass windows in the choir or the variety of window tracery and vaulting in the side chapels—but lacks drama and a sense of harmony. The cathedral dates from the 12th century, and the chancel is Romanesque, but construction continued over three centuries and most of the building is Gothic (note the high pointed windows). Pope John XXII was consecrated here in 1316, and Henri IV married Marie de Médicis here in 1600. The 14th-century astronomical clock, in the north transept, chimes a hymn to St-Jean on the hour from noon to 3 PM as a screeching rooster and other automatons enact the Annunciation.

To the right of the cathedral facade stands the venerable 12th-century **Manécanterie** (choir school); upstairs you'll find a small Treasury museum housing medieval Limoges enamels, fine ivories, and embroidered robes. *70 rue St-Jean. Admission: 10 frs. Open weekdays 7:30–noon and 2–7:30; weekends 2–5.*

To the left of the cathedral as you leave is the **Gare St-Jean;** to continue our tour, take the *ficelle* (funicular railway) that leaves from here on its way to the top of Fourvière Hill. At the top, head along the Montée de Fourvière to the ruins of the
8 **Théâtres Romains** nearby. There are two semicircular theaters here: the **Grand Théâtre,** the oldest Roman theater in France, built in 15 BC to seat 10,000 spectators, and the smaller **Odéon,** with its geometric-patterned tiled flooring. The best time to appreciate the theaters is September, when they are used to stage events during the Lyon International Arts Festival. *Fourvière Hill. Admission free. Open Easter–Oct., weekdays 8–noon and 2–6, Sat. 9–noon and 3–6, Sun. 3–6; Nov.–Easter, weekdays 8–noon and 2–5, Sat. 9–noon and 3–5, Sun. 3–5.*

Since 1933, systematic excavations have unearthed many vestiges of the opulent Roman city of Lugdunum. These remains
9 can be viewed in the **Musée de la Civilisation Gallo-Romaine** (Gallo-Roman Museum), which overlooks the theaters. The museum's semisubterranean open-plan design is an unusual showcase for the collection of statues, mosaics, vases, coins, and tombstones. One of the museum's highlights is a large bronze plaque, the **Table Claudienne,** upon which is inscribed part of Emperor Claudius's speech to the Roman Senate in AD 48, conferring senatorial rights on the Roman citizens of Gaul. *Rue Radisson. Admission: 20 frs. adults, 15 frs. students and senior citizens. Open Wed.–Sun. 9:30–noon and 2–6; closed Mon. and Tues.*

Head back to the spot where the *ficelle* dropped you off. You won't be able to miss the pompous, late-19th-century basilica of
10 **Notre-Dame-de-Fourvière,** which has unfortunately become one of the symbols of Lyon. In terms of its mock-Byzantine architecture and hilltop site, it's a close cousin of Paris's Sacré-Coeur. Both were built for a similar reason: to underline the might of the Roman Catholic Church after the Prussian defeat of France in 1870 gave rise to the birth of the anticlerical Third Republic. The riot of interior decoration—an overkill of gilt, marble, and colorful mosaics—reveals that the Church had mind-boggling wealth to compensate for its waning political clout. *Fourvière Hill. Open daily 8–noon and 2–6.*

One of the few places in Lyon from which you can't see the Fourvière basilica is the terrace alongside it. The plummeting panorama reveals the city laid out on either side of the Saône and Rhône rivers, with the St-Jean cathedral facade in the foreground and the huge glass towers of the reconstructed Part-Dieu business complex glistening behind. For an even more sweeping view—encompassing the surrounding hills—climb the 287 steps of the basilica's **observatory.** *Admission: 6 frs. Open Easter–Oct., daily 10–noon and 2–6; Nov.–Easter, weekends 10–noon and 2–5.*

11 Looming beyond the basilica is a skeletal metal tower, **Tour Métallique,** built in 1893 and now used as a television transmitter. Take the stone staircase, **Montée Nicolas-de-Lange,** at the foot of the tower; this sneaks back down to old Lyon, emerging alongside the St-Paul train station at place St-Paul. Venture
12 briefly onto rue Juiverie, to the right; the **Hôtel Paterin** at no. 4 is a splendid Renaissance mansion, and the Hôtel Bullioud (no. 8) has a courtyard with an ingenious gallery constructed in 1536 by Philibert Delorme, one of France's earliest and most accomplished exponents of Classical architecture (he worked at the châteaus of Fontainebleau and Chenonceau in the Loire Valley).

To the left of place St-Paul is the 12th-century church of
13 **St-Paul;** the octagonal lantern, the frieze of animal heads in the chancel, and the Flamboyant Gothic chapel are all worth a look. Head around the church, take the St-Vincent footbridge over the Saône, and turn left along quai St-Vincent. Two hundred
14 yards along, to the right, is the **Jardin des Chartreux,** a small, leafy park. Cut through the park up to cours du Général Giraud, then turn right onto place Rouville, pausing to admire the splendid view of the river and Fourvière Hill.

15 Rue de l'Annonciade leads from place Rouville to the **Jardin des Plantes,** 250 yards away, a haven of peace in this otherwise busy quarter. These luxurious botanical gardens contain remnants of the **Amphithéâtre des Trois Gauls,** a once-huge circular amphitheater built in AD 19. From the gardens, you'll be able to survey the hilly, surrounding **Croix Rousse** district, which once resounded to the clanking of weaving looms that churned out yards of the silk and cloth for which Lyon became famous. By the 19th century, over 30,000 *canuts* (weavers) were working in Lyon; they set up their looms on the upper floors—the brightest—of the tightly packed houses. The houses were so tightly packed, in fact, that the only way to transport the finished fabrics was through the *traboules* (long narrow corridors leading through buildings and providing public access to other streets), which had the additional advantage of protecting the fabrics from bad weather.

For an impromptu tour of the Croix Rousse, leave the gardens and head along rue Imbert-Colomès as far as no. 20. Here, turn right through the *traboule* that leads to rue des Tables Claudiennes, then veer right across place Chardonnet. Take
16 the passage Mermet alongside **St-Polycarpe** church, then turn left into rue Leynaud. A *traboule* at no. 32 leads to montée St-Sébastien. Keep right, cross place Croix-Paquet, and take rue Romarin down to place des Terreaux. Armed with a detailed map, you could spend hours "trabouling" your way across the Croix Rousse, still a hive of activity despite the industrialization of silk and textile production and the ensuing demise of most of the original workshops. Old-time "Jacquard" looms can
17 still be seen in action at the **Maison des Canuts;** the weavers—many surprisingly young—are happy to show children how to

operate a miniature loom. *12 rue d'Ivry. Admission: 10 frs. Open weekdays 8:30–noon and 2–6:30, Sat. 9–noon and 2–6.*

The north side of the sizable place des Terreaux is lined with
18 cafés, from which you can survey the facade of the **Hôtel de Ville** (Town Hall), redesigned by architects Jules Hardouin-Mansart and Robert de Cotte after a serious fire in 1674 (the rest of the building dates to the early 17th century). In the middle of the square, four majestic horses rear up from a monumental 19th-century fountain by Frédéric Auguste Bartholdi, whose most famous creation is New York's Statue of Liberty. On the south side of the square is the elegant 17th-century front of the former Benedictine abbey **Palais St-Pierre,** now the city's art museum.

19 The **Musée des Beaux-Arts** (Fine Arts Museum) showcases the country's largest collection of art after the Louvre. The cloister gardens are studded with various worthy statues, including three works by Rodin: *The Walker, The Shadow,* and *The Bronze Age.* Inside, the wide-ranging collections include enamels, Byzantine ivories, Etruscan statuettes, 4,000-year-old Cypriot ceramics, and a plethora of Egyptian archaeological finds. Amid the usual wealth of Old Master, Impressionist, and modern paintings is a unique collection of works by the tight-knit Lyon School, whose twin characteristics are exquisitely painted flowers and an overbearing religious sentimentality. An entire room is devoted to one of the school's 19th-century luminaries, Louis Janmot, and his mystical cycle *The Poem of the Soul.* Janmot's own tortured soul emerges as you follow his hero's spiritual evolution in a series of immaculately painted visions that seesaw between the heavenly, the hellish, and the downright spooky. *Pl. des Terreaux. Admission: 20 frs. Open Wed.–Sun. 10:30–6; closed Mon. and Tues.*

From behind the Hôtel de Ville, head south by way of shop-lined rue de la République, which becomes rue de la Charité after place Bellecoeur. Some 300 yards down are two major muse-
20 ums. The **Musée des Arts Décoratifs** (Decorative Arts Museum) occupies an 18th-century mansion, with fine displays of silverware, furniture, objets d'art, ceramics, and tapestries. Take time to admire the outstanding array of Italian Renaissance porcelain. *30 rue de la Charité. Admission: 15 frs. (joint ticket with Fabrics Museum). Open Tues.–Sun. 9:30–noon and 2–6.*

21 The **Musée Historique des Tissus** (Fabrics Museum) contains a stream of intricate carpets, tapestries, and silks. You'll see Oriental tapestries dating as far back as the 4th century and a fabulous assembly of Turkish and Persian carpets from the 16th to the 18th centuries. European highlights include Italian Renaissance fabrics, Hispano-Moorish cloth from Spain, and 18th-century Lyon silks. A thorough description of the history of cloth down the ages is provided by a "genealogical tree," which covers one wall on the ground floor. *34 rue de la Charité. Admission: 15 frs. (joint ticket with Arts Musuem). Open Tues.–Sun. 10–noon and 2–5:30.*

Lodging
Under 250 frs.
★

Bellecordière. This clean and pleasant no-frills hotel is wonderfully located right in the heart of the city. Rooms are small, with simple, modern furniture and gray, industrial carpeting, but all have televisions, direct-dial telephones, and modern bathrooms. The management is friendly and serves a good and copious breakfast, and the neighborhood is quiet. *18 rue*

Bellecordière, 69001, tel. 78–42–27–28. 25 rooms with bath. AE, MC, V.

Bristol. This large, well-kept hotel, midway between the city-center Perrache station, has recently been modernized and soundproofed. It counts as one of the best-priced and most convenient bases for exploring Lyon. *28 cours de Verdun, 69002, tel. 78–37–56–55. 134 rooms, most with bath or shower. Facilities: sauna, workout room. Closed Christmas through New Year's. AE, DC, MC, V.*

Morand. This quiet and delightfully idiosyncratic hotel is located in a residential area of the city, a 10-minute taxi ride from the station. Flowers abound in the pretty inner courtyard that doubles as a breakfast veranda, and the smiles at the front desk foster a mood of good cheer and friendliness. Guest rooms are on the small side but feature lots of homey knickknacks. There's no restaurant. *99 rue de Créqui, 69006, tel. 78–52–29–96. 33 rooms, 27 with bath. AE.*

Dining
Under 125 frs.

★ **Brasserie Georges.** One of the city's oldest and largest brasseries, this inexpensive spot still retains its original mid-19th-century paneled ceiling. At any hour of the day or evening, you can relax over hearty dishes such as veal stew or sauerkraut, or go for more refined fare. *30 cours de Verdun, tel. 78–37–15–78. Reservations not necessary. AE, DC, MC, V.*

Café des Fédérations. For the past 80 years, this café has reigned as one of the city's friendliest eating spots, and even newcomers are treated as one of the gang. Jocular Raymond Fulchiron not only serves up deftly prepared Lyonnaise classics such as hearty *boudin blanc* (white-meat sausage), but he also comes out to chat with guests and make sure everyone feels at home. The decor is a homey mix of red-checked tablecloths, wood paneling, and sawdust on the floor, with old-fashioned bench seating. *8 rue du Major-Martin, tel. 78–28–26–00. Reservations advised. AE, DC, MC, V. Closed weekends, and Aug.*

Chez Sylvain. The old-fashioned decor of Chez Sylvain is a delightful reminder of its days as a favorite neighborhood beanery. Little has changed since, and the huge wooden counter, turn-of-the-century wall decorations, and original spiral staircase are the ideal backdrop for Sylvain's robust Lyonnaise cuisine; the tripe and *andouillettes* are especially good. *4 rue Tupin, tel. 78–42–11–98. Reservations accepted. V. Closed Sun., Mon., and Aug.*

★ **Le Vivarais.** This simple, tidy restaurant is run by Roger Duffaud, a former colleague of the superstar chef Alain Chapel, and it is one of the city's outstanding gourmet good buys. Don't expect napkins folded into flower shapes here—all the excitement happens on your plate. The menu offers a perfect contemporary take on the classics of the Lyonnais kitchen. Try the *lièvre royale* (hare cooked with onions, red wine, and cinnammon and then rolled and stuffed with truffles and pâté), the superb cheese tray, and the daily dessert, maybe a pear tart. The à la carte menu is fairly priced, and the 110-franc prix-fixe menu is a lip-smacking bargain. *1 pl. Gailleton, tel. 78–37–85–15. Reservations advised. Dress: casual. MC, V. Closed Sun.*

Splurge

★ **Paul Bocuse.** One of the country's most celebrated gourmet temples, this restaurant is no budget standby, and it's easy to get to only with a car, since it lies 12 kilometers (7 miles) north of town in Collonges-au-Mont-d'Or. But if you want to splurge, this is the place. The grandiose decor is perfectly matched by the excellence of the cuisine from the kitchen of the larger-than-life chef Paul Bocuse. Bocuse is often away on the lecture-tour trail, but his restaurant continues to please its elegantly dressed diners, who feast on such house specialties as truffle soup and succulent sea bass. The restaurant's reputation means you'll have to reserve a table long in advance. *50 quai de la Plage, tel. 78-22-01-40. Reservations required. Jacket and tie required. AE, DC, MC, V.*

Shopping **Lyon** makes for the region's best shopping for chic clothing; try the stores on **rue du Président Edouard-Herriot** and **rue de la République** in the center of town. Lyon has maintained its reputation as the French silks-and-textile capital, and all the big-name French and international designers have shops here; Lyonnais designer **Clémentine** (18 rue Emile-Zola) is a good bet for well-cut clothes, or, for trendy outfits for youngsters, try **Etincelle** (34 rue St-Jean) in the old town. If it's antiques you're after, wander down **rue Auguste-Comte** (from place Bellecour to Perrache); you'll find superb engravings at **Image en Cours** (26 rue du Boeuf) and authentic Lyonnais puppets on **place du Change,** both in the old town. Two excellent Lyon charcuteries are **Reynon** (13 rue des Archers) and **Vital Pignol** (17 rue Emile-Zola). For chocolates, try **Bernachon** (42 cours Franklin-Roosevelt), which many people consider to be the best chocolaterie in France. **La Boîte à Dessert** (rue de l'Ancienne Préfecture) is an innovative patisserie with tarts, cakes, and luscious, red peach turnovers.

The Arts *Lyon-Poche,* a weekly guide published on Wednesday and sold at any newsstand, will give details. The café-theater, a Lyonnais specialty, fuses art with café society: **Espace Gerson** (1 pl. Gerson, tel. 78-27-96-99) or **Café-Théâtre Accessoire** (26 rue de L'Annonciande, tel. 78-27-84-84). Lyon's Société de Musique de Chambre (Chamber Music Society) performs at **Salle Molière** (18 quai Bondy, tel. 78-28-03-11).

Nightlife As for nightlife, laser beams and video screens make **L'Aquarius** (43 quai Pierre-Scize) a frenetic place for dancing the night away in Lyon. **Comoëdia** (4 rue Charles-Dullin) is more low-key, with a downstairs disco and an old-fashioned piano bar upstairs. Expect anything from the tango to rock-and-roll at **Place Mobile** (2 rue Rene-Leynaud). Caribbean and African music are featured at **Le Club des Iles** (1 grande rue des Feuillants). The **Hot Club** (26 rue Lanterne) has been going strong for 40 years in a vaulted stone basement that features live jazz. **Le Melhor** (20 quai Dr-Gailleton) is a more restrained cocktail bar catering to the city's intellectual set. If you'd like a casual game of darts and a pint of bitter, head to the **Albion Public House** (12 rue Ste-Catherine). The **Bouchon aux Vins** wine bar (62 rue Mercière) has over 30 vintages for you to choose from; for a more romantic evening, make it a champagne toast in the intimate, wood-paneled **Metroclub** (2 rue Stella). Fifties fans should try the **Navire Bar** (3 rue Terme).

Vienne

Trains make the ½-hour journey from Lyon to Vienne every hour or so. Tourist office: Cours Briller, tel. 74-85-12-62.

Vienne was one of the most important towns of Roman Gaul and a religious and cultural center under its count-archbishops in the Middle Ages, and despite its role today as a major road and train junction, it retains abundant historic charm.

The tourist office stands in the leafy shadow of the **Jardin Public** (Public Gardens). Begin your tour here, turning right along quai Jean-Jaurès, beside the Rhône, to the nearby church of **St-Pierre.** Note the rectangular 12th-century Romanesque bell tower with its arcaded tiers. The lower parts of the church walls date from the 6th century.

Head down the left-hand side of the church and turn left again onto rue Boson, which leads to the cathedral of **St-Maurice.** Although the religious wars deprived this cathedral of many statues, much of the original decoration is intact; the arches of the portals on the 15th-century facade are carved with Old Testament scenes. The cathedral was built between the 12th and 16th centuries, with later interior additions, such as the splendid 18th-century mausoleum to the right of the altar, which contains the tombs of two of Vienne's archbishops. The entrance to the vaulted passage that once led to the cloisters, but now opens onto place St-Paul, is adorned with a frieze of the zodiac.

Place St-Paul and rue Clémentine bring you to place du Palais and the remains of the **Temple d'Auguste et de Livie** (Temple of Augustus and Livia), thought to date, in part, to the earliest Roman settlements in Vienne (1st century BC). The slender Corinthian columns that ring the temple were filled in with a wall during the 11th century, when the temple was used as a church; today, however, the temple has been restored to its original appearance.

Take rue Brenier to rue Chantelouve, site of a **Roman gateway** decorated with delicate friezes (the last vestige of the city's sizable Roman baths), then continue to rue de la Charité and the **Théâtre Romain.** This was one of the largest Roman theaters in Gaul (143 yards in diameter) and is only slightly smaller than Rome's famed Theater of Marcellus. Vienne's theater was buried under tons of rubble until 1922, but since then, the 46 rows of seating and parts of the marble flooring and frieze on the original stage have been excavated and renovated. Shows and concerts are staged here on summer evenings. *Admission: 16 frs. Open Apr.–mid-Oct., Wed.–Mon. 9–noon and 2–5:30; mid-Oct.–Mar., Wed.–Sat. 10–noon and 2–5, Sun. 1:30–5:30.*

Take rue de la Charité back down to rue des Orfèvres, lined with Renaissance facades, and continue on to the church of **St-André-le-Bas,** once part of a powerful abbey. Extensive restoration is in progress, but, if possible, venture inside to see the finely sculpted 12th-century capitals and the 17th-century wooden statue of St. Andrew. The adjacent cloisters are at their best during the summer music festival held here (and at the cathedral) from June to August.

Take the nearby bridge across the Rhône to inspect the excavated Cité Gallo-Romaine, where the Romans built most of their sumptuous private villas. *Admission: 16 frs. Open Apr.–Sept., daily 9–12:30 and 2:30–9; Oct.–Apr., daily 9–noon and 2–5.*

Lodging
Under 250 frs.

Central. Of Vienne's few good, inexpensive hotels, this house in the old town, close to the cathedral, is the most convenient. Medium-size rooms start at 210 francs. *3 rue de l'Archevêché,*

38200, tel. 74–85–18–38. 27 rooms with bath or shower. AE, MC, V. Closed Christmas through New Year's.

Dining
Under 125 frs.

Le Bec Fin. An inexpensive weekday menu makes the Bec Fin a good lunch spot, and it's a serious dinner venue as well. The well-run, unpretentious eatery is just opposite the cathedral; its main dishes—steak and freshwater fish—seldom disappoint and occasionally display a deft touch (as with the *burbot*, or cod, cooked with saffron). The gray-and-white dining room has an understated elegance. *7 pl. St-Maurice, tel. 74–85–76–72. Reservations accepted. Jacket required. MC, V. Closed Sun. dinner and Mon.*

Tournon

Trains run from Vienne to Tournon every 2 hours or so (journey time 35–50 minutes).

A hefty 15th- to 16th-century **château** is the chief attraction in **Tournon**, which stands on the banks of the Rhône at the foot of some impressive granite hills. From the château's two terraces, there are sumptuous views of the old town, river, and—towering above the village of Tain-l'Hermitage across the Rhône—the steep-climbing vineyards that produce Hermitage wine, one of the Rhône Valley's most refined (and costly) reds. The château houses a museum of local history, the **Musée Rhodanien,** which features an account of the life of locally born Marc Seguin (1786–1875), the engineer who built the first suspension bridge over the Rhône at Tournon in 1825 (the bridge was demolished in 1965). *Admission: 10 frs. adults, 5 frs. children. Open June–Aug., Wed.–Mon. 10–noon and 2–6; Apr.–May and Sept.–Oct., Wed.–Mon. 2–6; closed Tues.*

Lodging and Dining
Under 350 frs.

Château. This fine old hotel stands just across the Rhône from the wine village of Tain-l'Hermitage, and the restaurant, where set menus start at 100 francs, looks out on the famous, steeply terraced Hermitage vineyard. Most accommodations have been recently modernized and fitted with double-glazed windows; ask for a room that overlooks the river, although the best nudge 400 francs. *12 quai Marc-Séguin, 07300, tel. 75–08–60–22. 14 rooms with bath or shower. Facilities: restaurant (closed Sat. lunch). AE, DC, MC, V. Closed Nov. and weekends out of season.*

Valence

Trains make the 15-minute run from Tournon to Valence every 1½ hours. Tourist office: Blvd. Maurice-Clerc, tel. 75–43–04–88.

Valence, capital of the Drôme département, is the principal fruit-and-vegetable market for the surrounding region. Steep-curbed alleyways—known as *côtes*—extend from the banks of the Rhône to the heart of the old town around the cathedral of **St-Apollinaire.** Although the cathedral was begun in the 12th century in the Romanesque style, it's not altogether as old as it looks: Parts were rebuilt in the 17th century, and the belfry in the 19th. Alongside the cathedral, in the former 18th-century Bishops' Palace, is the **Musée des Beaux-Arts** (Fine Arts Museum), featuring local sculpture and furniture and a collection of 96 red-chalk drawings by deft landscapist Hubert Robert (1733–1808), a master of the picturesque. *Just off rue*

Saunière. Admission: 10 frs. adults, children free. Open daily 2–6; also 9–noon on Wed., Sat., and Sun.

Turn left out of the museum and cross hectic avenue Gambetta to the Champ-de-Mars, a broad terraced garden overlooking the Rhône, where there are fine views across to Crussol Castle. Just below the Champ-de-Mars is the **Parc Jouvet,** with 14 acres of pool and gardens.

Lodging and Dining
Under 150 frs.

Chaumont. A warm, friendly welcome and reliable home cooking make this small hotel-restaurant, a 10-minute walk up avenue Carnot from the tourist office, a hit with travelers. Service in the restaurant is speedy, and there is an extensive choice of set menus (four for under 120 francs); you can choose among pâtés, coq au vin, and *andouillette* (pork sausage) in white wine sauce. *79 av. Sadi-Carnot, 26000, tel. 75–43–10–12. 11 rooms, some with shower. Facilities: restaurant (closed Fri. evening and Sat.). MC, V. Closed the first three weeks of Aug. and part of Dec.*

Tour 2: Grenoble and the Alps

The Alps are captivating whatever the season. In winter, the dramatic, snow-carpeted slopes offer some of the best skiing in the world; in summer, chic spas, shimmering lakes, and breathtaking hilltop trails come into their own.

Grenoble, within sight of the peaks, forms a natural gateway to this mountain range, Europe's mightiest. Trains wind their way through the valleys to such attractive towns as Chambéry and Annecy. Reaching many of the high mountain ski resorts, among them Chamonix and Val d'Isère, requires a bus ride from the valley villages along narrow, twisting alpine highways—an experience that's exhilarating or terrifying, depending on how distracting you find the stupendous vistas en route.

From Paris
By Train

TGV trains to Grenoble leave Paris (Gare de Lyon) 6 times daily. The trip takes 3 hours 20 minutes.

By Car

Allow up to 6 hours for the 560-kilometer (350-mile) drive from Paris to Grenoble via A6, A43, and A48.

Grenoble

Tourist office: 14 rue de la République, opposite the covered market and close to the art museum, tel. 76–54–34–36.

Located 104 kilometers (65 miles) southeast of Lyon, **Grenoble** is a large, cosmopolitan city. Its skyscrapers and forbidding gray buildings—intimidating by homey French standards—bear witness to Grenoble's fierce desire to move with the times, as does the city's nuclear research plant. The city is also home to a large university and is the birthplace of Stendhal, perhaps the most famous French novelist of the 17th century.

Head down avenue Viallet from the station and cross the Jardin de la Ville at the far end to reach the banks of the Isère River. A cable car (25 francs round-trip) starting at quai St-Stéphane-Jay whisks you up to the hilltop and its **Fort de la Bastille** (open

Apr.–Oct., 9–midnight; Nov.–Dec. and Feb.–Mar., 10–7:30), offering splendid views of the city and River Isère. Walk down rue Maurice-Gignoux, past gardens, cafés, and stone mansions, to the **Musée Dauphinois,** a lively regional museum in a 17th-century convent, featuring displays of local folk arts and crafts. *30 rue Maurice-Gignoux. Admission: 10 frs. Open Wed.–Mon. 9–noon and 2–6; closed Tues.*

Heading left from the museum, make for the church of **St-Laurent,** which contains an atmospherically murky 6th-century crypt (one of the country's oldest Christian monuments) supported by a row of formidable marble pillars. *Rue St-Laurent. Open June–Sept., Wed.–Mon. 10–noon and 2:30–6:30; Oct.–May, by appointment only; closed Tues.*

Art buffs will want to cross the river and pick up rue Bayard, which runs four blocks down to the **Musée de Peinture et de Sculpture** (Painting and Sculpture Museum). The museum showcases an excellent series of 17th-century French and Spanish paintings, plus one of the most exciting modern collections outside Paris, starring Paul Gauguin, Henri Matisse, Amedeo Modigliani, and Pablo Picasso. *Pl. Verdun. Admission: 10 frs. Open Wed.–Mon. 10–noon and 2–6.*

Leave place Verdun by rue Blanchard and follow it five blocks to **place Grenette,** a lively pedestrian mall abloom with flowers and lined with sidewalk cafés. It makes a great place to relax and enjoy a *pastis*—an anise-flavored aperitif—while admiring the city's majestic mountain setting.

Dining
Under 125 frs.

Berlioz. Located 200 yards from the museum across place Verdun, this restaurant is a favorite with Grenoble food-lovers thanks to its light, airy decor, and its imaginative ways with French cuisine—exemplified by dishes such as marinated halibut with ginger. Best bets are set menus at 85 francs (lunch) and 115 francs. *4 rue de Strasbourg, tel. 76–56–22–39. Reservations recommended. AE, MC, V. Closed Sat. lunch, Sun., and mid-July–mid-Aug.*

Chambéry

Trains make the 40-minute trip from Grenoble to Chambéry every 2 hours or so. Chambéry tourist office: 24 blvd. de la Colonne, tel. 79–33–42–47.

Tasteful restorations have helped lively **Chambéry** recapture some of its past glory as capital of Savoy. Stop for coffee on the pedestrian **place St-Léger** before heading two blocks to visit the 14th-century **Château des Ducs de Savoie.** The château's Gothic Sainte-Chapelle contains some good stained glass and houses a replica of the notorious Turin Shroud, once thought to have been used to wrap up the crucified Christ (but probably, according to recent scientific analysis, a medieval hoax). *Rue Basse du Château. Admission: 15 frs. Guided tours daily Sept.–June at 2:15, four times daily July and Aug.*

Dining
Under 125 frs.

Trois Voûtes. A sense of spaciousness and the view of the street outside create an informal mood at this large, lively restaurant near the cathedral. Fondue is one of the local specialties on the long, varied menu, and there are several set menus (three for under 100 francs). *110 rue de la Croix-d'Or, tel. 79–33–38–56. Reservations not required. MC, V.*

Aix-les-Bains

Hourly trains take 10–15 minutes for the trip from Chambéry to Aix-les-Bains. Tourist office: Place Mollard, tel. 79-35-05-92.

The gracious spa town of **Aix-les-Bains** lies on the eastern shore of Lac du Bourget. Although swimming in the lake is not advised (it's freezing cold), you can sail, fish, play golf and tennis, or picnic on the 25 acres of parkland that stretches along the lakefront. Visit the ruins of the original Roman baths, under the present **Thermes Nationaux** (Thermal Baths), built in 1934 and renovated in 1972 (guided tours only; Apr.–Oct., Mon.–Sat. 3 PM; Nov.–Mar., Wed. 3 PM). The Roman Temple of Diana (2nd–3rd century AD) now houses an **archaeology museum** (entered via the tourist office on place Mollard).

There are half-hour boat trips from Aix-les-Bains across Lac du Bourget to the **Abbaye de Hautecombe,** where mass is celebrated with Gregorian chant. *Cost: 35 frs. Departures from the Grand Pont, Mar.–June and Sept.–Oct., daily 2:30; July–Aug. 9:30, 2, 2:30, 3, 3:30, and 4:30.*

Dining
Under 125 frs.

Dauphinois. The long dining room of this large, cheerful hotel-restaurant, 300 yards south of the train station, has an adjacent garden where you can enjoy alfresco meals in summer. Local ham and freshwater fish usually figure on the 110- and 140-franc set menus. *14 av. de Tresserve, tel. 79-61-22-56. Reservations recommended. AE, DC, MC, V. Closed mid-Dec.–mid-Feb.*

Annecy

Trains run every 1½ hours from Aix-les-Bains to Annecy. The trip takes 35 minutes. Tourist office: Clos Bonlieu, 1 rue Jean-Jaurès, tel. 50-45-00-33.

Annecy stands on the shores of a crystal-clear mountain lake—Lac d'Annecy—and is surrounded by rugged snow-tipped peaks. The canals, flower-covered bridges, and cobbled pedestrian streets of old Annecy are at their liveliest on market days, Tuesday and Friday, though the town park and the tree-lined boulevard have tranquil, invigorating appeal any day of the week. There are views over the lake from the towers of the 12th-century **castle,** set high on a hill above the town.

Dining
Under 125 francs

Le Petit Zinc. This reasonably priced bistro is the perfect place for a delicious lunch after you've finished wandering around the old quarter of Annecy. The cozy, beamed dining room is very popular with locals, who come for the cheese croquettes and salad, roast pork, and good carafe wines. There are also a wonderful cheese tray and home-baked desserts. *11 rue de Mont-Porens, tel. 50-51-12-93. MC, V. Closed Sun.*

Chamonix

Trains make the 2½-hour run from Annecy to Chamonix every 3 hours. You'll make a change at St-Gervais. Chamonix tourist office: 85 pl. Triangle-de-l'Amitié, tel. 50-53-00-24.

Chamonix, the oldest and perhaps most prestigious French winter sports resort, is a charmer of an alpine mountain town, despite its size, so it's not surprising that it was a favorite of

European vacationers long before it hosted the first Winter Olympics in 1924. Here, you don't have to be a skier or mountain climber to penetrate the lonely mountain fastnesses. In an incredible, spine-tingling trip, the world's highest cable car soars 12,000 feet from Chamonix up the Aiguille du Midi, from which there are staggering views of Europe's loftiest peak, the 15,700-foot **Mont-Blanc.** *Cost: 120 frs. round-trip. Open daily, May–Sept. 8–4:45, Oct.–Apr. 8–3:45.*

Lodging and Dining
Splurge

Albert I & Milan. Though some of the prices are high at this welcoming chalet-style hotel, it does offer the best value among Chamonix's quality lodging establishments. Many guest rooms have balconies, and all are furnished with elegant period reproductions. The dining room offers stupendous views of Mont-Blanc, and the cuisine scales heights of invention and enthusiasm; try the oysters fried with asparagus. There are set menus at 165 and 180 francs. *119 impasse du Montenvers, 74400, tel. 50–53–05–09. 30 rooms with bath. Facilities: restaurant (closed Wed. lunch), pool, tennis, sauna, Jacuzzi. AE, DC, MC, V. Closed middle 2 weeks of May and Oct. 23–Dec. 9.*

11 Provence

Roman Ruins, Avignon, Marseille

Away from the Riviera, the coastal part of the province described in Chapter 12, Provence offers ideal possibilities for memorable travel on a tight budget. Quite apart from the vineyards, olive groves, Roman remains, and near-permanent sunshine that form a backcloth accessible to all, it is a very practical region to visit: Excellent rail service (supplemented by regular buses) links major towns to country villages, and the distances involved are relatively minor. Marseille provides big-city bustle in a breathtaking setting between rocky hills and the Mediterranean, and Avignon, Arles, and Aix, along with Nîmes nearby in Languedoc, all have plenty to see yet are small enough to visit on foot.

Located in the south of France, bordered by Italy to the east and the blue waters of the Mediterranean, the area was known by the Romans as Provincia—The Province—for it was the first part of Gaul they occupied. Roman remains litter the ground in well-preserved profusion. The theater and triumphal arch at Orange, the amphitheater at Nîmes, the aqueduct at Pont-du-Gard, and the mausoleum at St-Rémy-de-Provence are considered the best of their kind in existence.

Provençal life continues at an old-fashioned pace. Hot afternoons tend to mean siestas, with signs of life discernible only as the shadows under the *platanes* (plane trees) start to lengthen and lethargic locals saunter out to play *boules* (the French version of bocce) and drink long, cooling *pastis*, an anise-based aperitif.

Essential Information

Lodging Accommodations are varied in this much-visited part of France, ranging from luxurious *mas* (converted farmhouses) to modest downtown hotels convenient for sightseeing. Service is often less than prompt, a casualty of the sweltering summer heat. Reservations are essential for much of the year, and many hotels are closed during winter.

Dining There's a lot to be said for simple Provençal food on a vine-shaded terrace. Have a pale green *pastis* as an aperitif with savory local black olives, or try the *tapenade*, a delicious paste of capers, anchovies, olives, oil, and lemon juice, best smeared on chunks of garlic-rubbed bread. Follow it up with *crudités* (raw vegetables) served with *aïoli* (a garlicky mayonnaise), and a simple dish of grilled lamb or beef, accompanied by a bottle of chilled rosé. Locals like to end their meal with a round of goat cheese and fruit.

A trip to the fish market at Marseille will reveal the astronomical price of the fresh local catch; in the Mediterranean there are too few fish chased by too many boats. Steer clear of the multitude of cheap Marseille fish restaurants, many with brisk ladies out front who deliver throaty sales pitches; any inexpensive fish menu must use frozen imports. The Marseille specialty of *bouillabaisse* is a case in point: Once a fisherman's cheap stew of spanking-fresh specimens too small or bony to put on sale, it has now become a celebration dish, with such heretical additions as lobster. The high-priced versions can be delicious, but avoid the cheaper ones, undoubtedly concocted with canned, frozen, and even powdered ingredients.

Shopping *Santons*, colorful painted clay figures traditionally placed around a Christmas crèche, make excellent gifts or souvenirs and can be found throughout the region. The hundreds of characters range from Mary, Joseph, and the Wise Men to fictional characters and notable personalities, both historic and contemporary. Two specialties of Aix-en-Provence are deliciously fragrant soaps with natural floral scents and *calissons d'Aix*, ingeniously sculpted high-quality marzipan made of almonds and eggs. Delicately patterned Provençal print fabrics made by Souleiado are beautiful and can be bought in lengths or already fashioned into dresses, scarves, and other items. You can find the prints in better-quality shops throughout the region, though Arles and Aix-en-Provence seem to have cornered most of the market.

Bicycling Bikes can be rented from train stations at Aix-en-Provence, Arles, Avignon, Marseille, Montpellier, Nîmes, and Orange; the cost is about 40 francs per day. Contact the **Comité Départemental de la Fédération Française de Cyclo** (2 rue Lavoisier, Avignon) for a list of the area's more scenic bike paths.

Hiking Trails are blazed (marked by discreet paint splashes) on the best routes. Contact the **Comité Départemental** (63 av. César-Franck, Avignon) for a detailed list of trails and outfitters.

Beaches Marseille has a large artificial beach with good facilities, and there are narrow sandy beaches either side of Toulon (west at Bandol and Sanary, east at Hyères). Cliffs dominate the coastline east of Marseille, and access to the sea is often difficult.

The Arts The summer music and drama festivals at Aix-en-Provence, Arles, Avignon, and Orange attract top performers. At Aix, the **International Arts and Music Festival,** with first-class opera, symphonic concerts, and chamber music, flourishes from mid-July to mid-August; its principal venue is the Théâtre de l'Archevêché in the courtyard of the Archbishop's Palace (pl. des Martyrs de la Résistance). At Arles, the **Music and Drama Festival** takes place in July in the Théâtre Antique (rue de la Calade/rue du Cloître). Avignon's prestigious **International Music and Drama Festival,** held during the last three weeks of July, is centered on the Grand Courtyard of the Palais des Papes (pl. du Palais, tel. 90–82–67–08). The **International Opera Festival** in Orange, during the last two weeks of July, takes place in the best-preserved Roman theater in existence, the Théâtre Antique (pl. des Frères-Mounet).

Highlights for First-time Visitors

Aix-en-Provence, Tour 2
Roman remains at Arles, Tour 1
Palais des Papes (Papal Palace), Avignon, Tour 1
Roman remains at Nîmes, Tour 1
Pont du Gard, Tour 1
Vieux-Port, Marseille, Tour 2
Théâtre Antique, Orange, Tour 1
Les Baux-de-Provence, Tour 1

Tour 1: Roman Provence

This tour takes the form of a triangle, with three base towns. From Avignon, you'll take a short rail trip to Orange; from Nîmes, ride the bus to the Pont du Gard aqueduct and to Tarascon; and from Arles, travel by bus to Les Baux and St-Rémy.

From Paris
By Train TGV bullet trains to Avignon leave Paris (Gare de Lyon) 6 times daily. The trip takes just under 4 hours.

By Car The 690-kilometer (430-mile) drive to Avignon from Paris via A6 and A7 takes about 6½ hours.

Avignon

Tourist office: 41 cours Jean-Jaurès, 400 yards down from the station, tel. 90–82–65–11.

Numbers in the margin correspond to points of interest on the Avignon map.

A warren of medieval alleys nestling behind a protective ring of chunky towers, **Avignon** is possibly best known for its Pont St-Bénezet, the Avignon bridge that many will remember singing about during their nursery-rhyme days. No one dances across the bridge these days, however—it's amputated in midstream, and has been ever since the 17th century, when a cataclysmic storm washed half of it away. Still, Avignon has lots to offer, starting with the Palais des Papes (Papal Palace), where seven exiled popes camped between 1309 and 1377 after fleeing from the corruption of Rome. Avignon remained papal property until 1791, and elegant mansions and a late 18th–century popu-

Provence
Vaison-la-Romaine
MONT VENTOUX
Malaucène
D975
D974
D938
Orange
Alès
D6
D68
D981
Châteauneuf-du-Pape
D17
Carpentras
Digne
N85
Anduze
Uzès
D981
N86
N7
L'Isle-sur-la-Sorgue
D25
Fontaine-de-Vaucluse
Roussillon
Gordes
Bonnieux
MONTAGNE DU LUBERON
Forcalquier
N100
Manosque
Castellane
Riez
D952
D999
N110
Pont du Gard
Avignon
Gardon
Rhône
A9
D979
N86
Nîmes
St-Rémy de Provence
D99
D5
Tarascon
Les Baux-de-Provence
St-Martin-de-Londres
D986
N113
A9
N570
Fontvieille
Arles
Durance
Salon-de-Provence
N113
Montpellier
La Grande Motte
Aigues-Mortes
D58
Petit Rhône
Camargue
Grand Rhône
Etang de Vaccarès
D570
Stes-Maries-de-la-Mer
D21
N568
Istres
Etang de Berre
N13
A7
Fos-sur-Mer
A51
Aix-en-Provence
Barjols
D562
Draguignan
A8
D560
Brignoles
Porte du St-Louis du Rhône
Golfe de fos
Ste-Maxime
N97
St-Tropez
Golfe du Lion
Rail Lines
N
Marseille
D2
Aubagne
D554
N98
N559
Cassis
D559
A50
N8
Ollioules
Evenos
La Ciotat
Sanary
Six-Fours-les-Plages
Hyères
Toulon
D559
D97
La Tour-Fondue
Ile de Port-Cros
Ile du Levant
Ile de Porquerolles
Mediterranean Sea
0
20 miles
0
30 km

lation of 80,000 bear witness to the town's 18th-century prosperity.

Avignon's main street, rue de la République, leads from the station and tourist office past shops and cafés to place de
1 l'Horloge and place du Palais, site of the colossal **Palais des Papes.** This "palace" creates a disconcertingly fortresslike impression, underlined by the austerity of its interior decor; most of the furnishings were dispersed during the French Revolution. Some imagination is required to picture it in medieval splendor, awash with color and worldly clerics enjoying what the 14th-century Italian poet Petrarch called "licentious banquets."

On close inspection, two different styles of building emerge: the severe **Palais Vieux** (Old Palace), built between 1334 and 1342 by Pope Benedict XII, a member of the Cistercian order, which frowned on frivolity, and the more decorative **Palais Nouveau** (New Palace), built in the following decade by the arty, extravagant Pope Clement VI. The Great Court, where visitors arrive, forms a link between the two.

The main rooms of the Palais Vieux are the consistory (council hall), decorated with some excellent 14th-century frescoes by Simone Martini; the Chapelle St-Jean, with original frescoes by Matteo Giovanetti; the Grand Tinel, or Salle des Festins, with a majestic vaulted roof and a series of 18th-century Gobelin tapestries; the Chapelle St-Martial, which has more Matteo frescoes; the Chambre du Cerf, with a richly decorated ceiling, murals featuring a stag hunt, and a delightful view of Avignon; the Chambre de Parement (papal antechamber); and the Chambre à Coucher (papal bedchamber).

The principal attractions of the Palais Nouveau are the Grande Audience, a magnificent two-naved hall on the ground floor, and, upstairs, the Chapelle Clémentine, where the college of cardinals gathered to elect the new pope. *Pl. du Palais des Papes. Admission: 32 frs. adults, 16 frs. students, children free. Guided tours only Mar.–Oct. Open Easter–June, daily 9–12:15 and 2–5:15; July–Sept., daily 9–6; Oct.–Easter, daily 9–11:30 and 2–5.*

2 The 12th-century **cathedral** nearby contains the Gothic tomb of
3 Pope John XII. Beyond is the **Rocher des Doms,** a large, attractive garden offering fine views of Avignon, the Rhône, and the
4 celebrated **Pont St-Bénezet**—built, according to legend, by a local shepherd named Bénezet in the 12th century. It was the first bridge to span the Rhône at Avignon and was originally 900 yards long. Though only half of the bridge remains, it's worth strolling along for the views and a visit to the tiny Chapelle St-Nicolas, which juts out over the river.

5 The medieval **Petit Palais,** situated between the bridge and the Rocher des Doms garden, was once home to cardinals and archbishops. Nowadays it contains an outstanding collection of Old Masters, led by the Italian schools of Venice, Siena, and Florence (note Sandro Botticelli's *Virgin and Child). 21 pl. du Palais. Admission: 18 frs. adults, 9 frs. children; free Sun. Open Wed.–Mon. 9:30–noon and 2–6.*

Double back past the Papal Palace and venture into the narrow, winding, shop-lined streets of old Avignon. Halfway down rue
6 de la République is the **Musée Lapidaire,** which displays a

Cathedral, **2**
Musée Calvet, **7**
Musée Lapidaire, **6**
Palais des Papes, **1**
Petit Palais, **5**
Pont St-Bénezet, **4**
Rocher des Doms, **3**

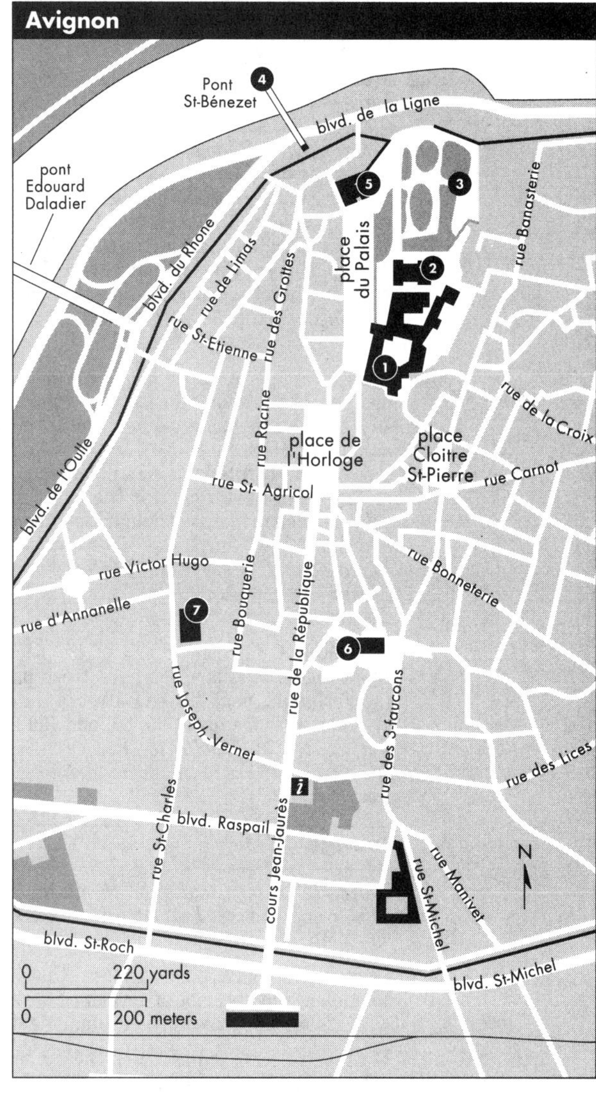

variety of archaeological finds—including the remains of Avignon's Arc de Triomphe—in a sturdy 17th-century Baroque chapel fronted by an imposing facade. *27 rue de la République. Admission: 9 frs. adults, children free. Open daily noon–7.*

7 Cross rue de la République and turn right onto rue Joseph-Vernet. A few minutes' walk will lead you to the **Musée Calvet,** an 18th-century town house featuring an extensive collection of mainly French paintings from the 16th century on; highlights include works by Théodore Géricault, Camille Corot, Edouard Manet, Raoul Dufy, Maurice de Vlaminck, and the Italian artist Amedeo Modigliani. Greek, Roman, and Etruscan statu-

ettes are also displayed. *65 rue Joseph-Vernet, tel. 90–86–33–84. Renovations were in progress at press time. Call for details.*

Lodging
Under 250 frs.

Médiéval. Since the building dates from the 17th century, the name of this hotel is almost appropriate, and its antique decor seems right at home among the narrow streets behind St-Pierre church. Rooms overlooking the street are predictably on the dark side; try for one overlooking the pretty patio-garden. *15 rue de la Petite-Saunerie, 84000, tel. 90–86–11–06. 20 rooms, some with shower. MC, V. Closed Jan.–Feb.*

Mignon. Located near the top of rue Joseph-Vernet, close to St-Agricol church, the small, cheerful Mignon provides excellent value in a hotel so central—rates start at just 165 francs. *12 rue Joseph-Vernet, 84000, tel. 90–82–17–30. 15 rooms, some with shower. Facilities: boutique. MC, V.*

Dining
Under 200 frs.
★

Hiély-Lucullus. According to most authorities, this establishment numbers among the top 50 restaurants in France. The upstairs dining room has a quiet, dignified charm and is run with aplomb by Madame Hiély. New chef André Chaussy's delights include crayfish tails in scrambled eggs hidden inside a puff-pastry case. Save room for the extensive cheese board. The prices, often moderate enough for a budgeting traveler, are an additional plus (have the 190-franc set menu). *5 rue de la République, tel. 90–86–17–07. Reservations required. AE, V. Closed most of Jan., last 2 weeks in June, Mon. lunch and Tues.*

Under 75 frs.

Férigoulo. A refreshing mix of traditional and nouvelle cuisine—snails, scallops, fish, and fresh pasta—draws diners to the Férigoulo, near Musée Calvet in the heart of the old town. There are set menus at 65, 85, and 150 francs. *30 rue Joseph-Vernet, tel. 90–82–10–28. Reservations recommended. AE, DC, MC, V. Closed Sun. evening, Mon., most of Nov., and two weeks in Mar.*

Orange

Trains to Orange make the 15-minute trip from Avignon at least every 2 hours. Tourist office: Cours Aristide-Briand, tel. 90–34–70–88.

Orange is a small, pleasant town that sinks into total siesta somnolence during hot afternoons but, at other times, buzzes with visitors who are keen on admiring its Roman remains.

The magnificent, semicircular **Théâtre Antique,** in the center of town, is the best-preserved remains of a theater from the ancient world. It was built just before the birth of Christ, to the same dimensions as that of Arles. Orange's theater, however, has a mighty screen-wall, over 100 yards long and 120 feet high, and steeply climbing terraces carved into the hillside. Seven thousand spectators can crowd in, and regularly do, for open-air concerts and operatic performances; the acoustics are superb. This is the only Roman theater that still possesses its original Imperial statue, of Caesar Augustus, which stands in the middle of the screen. At nearly 12 feet, it's one of the tallest Roman statues in existence. *Pl. des Frères-Mounet. Admission: 22 frs.; joint ticket with Musée Municipal. Open Apr.–Oct., daily 9–6:30; Nov.–Mar., daily 10–noon and 1:30–5.*

The **Parc de la Colline St-Eutrope,** the banked garden behind the theater, yields a fine view of the theater and of the 6,000-

foot Mont Ventoux to the east. Walk up cours Aristide-Briand, turn right at the top, then left immediately after to the venerable **Arc de Triomphe**—composed of a large central arch flanked by two smaller ones, the whole topped by a massive entablature. The 70-foot arch, the third-highest Roman arch still standing, towered over the old Via Agrippa between Arles and Lyon and was probably built around AD 25 in honor of the Gallic Wars. The carvings on the north side depict the legionnaires' battles with the Gauls and Caesar's naval showdown with the ships of Marseille. Today the arch presides over a busy traffic circle.

Dining
Under 125 frs.
★
Le Pigraillet. One of Orange's best lunch spots is Le Pigraillet, on the Chemin Colline St-Eutrope at the far end of the gardens. You may want to eat in the garden, but most diners seek shelter from the mistral in the glassed-in terrace. The modern cuisine includes crab ravioli, foie gras in port, and duck breast in the muscat wine of nearby Beaumes-de-Venise. Prices, which start in the moderate range, go high enough to raise your check if you don't watch it. *Colline St-Eutrope, tel. 90-34-44-25. Reservations advised. Jacket required. AE, DC. Closed Dec.–Feb., Sun. dinner, and Mon.*

Under 75 frs.
Le Bec Fin. While hardly elegant, Le Bec Fin is a perfect example of a small-town restaurant serving local specialties to tourists and locals alike. Try the rabbit with mustard for a real taste of Provençal cooking at its best. *14 rue Segond-Wéber, tel. 90-34-14-76. Reservations accepted. No credit cards. Closed Thurs., Fri., and Nov.*

Nîmes

Trains run to Nîmes from Avignon most hours and take around 25 minutes. Tourist office: 6 rue Auguste, tel. 66-67-29-11.

Numbers in the margins correspond to points of interest on the Nîmes map.

Few towns have preserved such visible links with their Roman past as **Nîmes.** Nemausus, as the town was then known, grew to prominence during the reign of Caesar Augustus (27 BC–AD 14) and still boasts a Roman amphitheater (Arènes), temple (Maison Carrée), and watchtower (Tour Magne). Luckily, these monuments emerged relatively unscathed from the cataclysmic flash flood that devastated Nîmes in 1988, leaving thousands homeless.

1 Start out at place des Arènes, site of the **Arènes,** over 140 yards long and 110 yards wide, with a seating capacity of 21,000. Despite its checkered history—it was transformed into a fortress by the Visigoths and used for housing in medieval times—the amphitheater has been restored to most of its original splendor. A roof has even been installed to facilitate its current use for theatrical performances, tennis matches, and bullfights. The arena is a smaller version of the Colosseum in Rome and is considered the world's best-preserved Roman amphitheater. *Blvd. Victor-Hugo. Admission: 20 frs. adults, 15 frs. children; joint ticket to all monuments and museums: 28 frs. adults, 17 frs. children. Open mid-June–mid-Sept., daily 8–8; mid-Sept.–Oct. and Apr.–mid-June, daily 9–noon and 2–6; Nov.–Mar., daily 9–noon and 2–5.*

Arènes, 1
Cathedral, 4
Jardin de la Fontaine, 7
Maison Carrée, 6
Musée Archéologique et d'Histoire Naturelle, 3
Musée des Beaux-Arts, 2
Musée du Vieux Nîmes, 5
Temple of Diana, 8
Tour Magne, 9

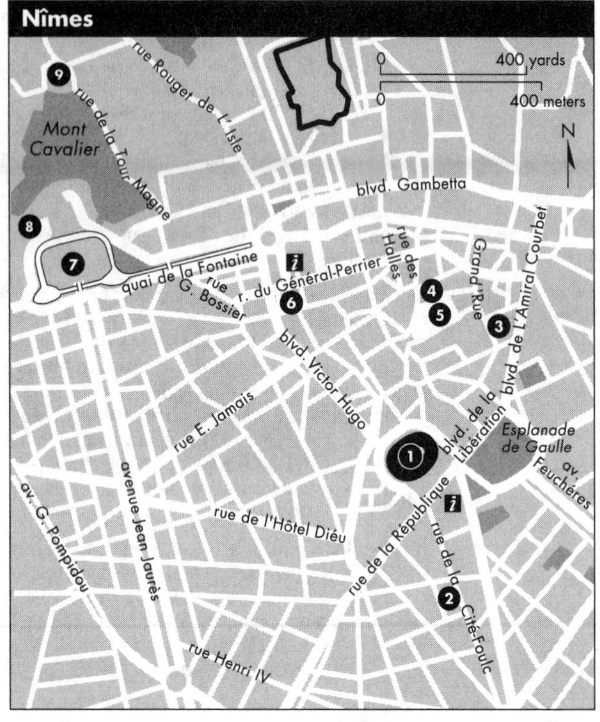

2 Take rue de la Cité-Foulc behind the Arènes to the **Musée des Beaux-Arts** (Fine Arts Museum), where you can admire a vast Roman mosaic discovered in Nîmes during the last century; the marriage ceremony depicted in the center of the mosaic provides intriguing insights into the Roman aristocratic lifestyle. Old Masters (Nicolas Poussin, Pieter Brueghel, Peter Paul Rubens) and sculpture (Auguste Rodin, and his pupil Emile Bourdelle) form the mainstay of the collection. *Rue de la Cité-Foulc. Admission: 15 frs. adults, 10 frs. children. Open daily 9:30–12:30 and 2–6.*

Return to the Arènes and head right, along boulevard de la Libération, which soon becomes boulevard de l'Amiral-Courbet.
3 A hundred and fifty yards down on the left is the **Musée Archéologique et d'Histoire Naturelle,** rich in local archaeological finds, mainly statues, busts, friezes, tools, glass, and pottery. It also houses an extensive collection of Greek, Roman, and medieval coins. *Blvd. de l'Amiral-Courbet. Admission free. Open Tues.–Sat. 9:30–12:30 and 2–6, Sun. and Mon. 1:30–6.*

Turn right into Grand' Rue behind the museum, then take the
4 second left up toward the **cathedral.** This uninspired 19th-century reconstruction is of less interest than either the sur-
5 rounding pedestrian streets or the **Musée du Vieux Nîmes** (Museum of Old Nîmes), housed opposite the cathedral in the 17th-century Bishop's Palace. Embroidered garments and woolen shawls fill the rooms in an exotic and vibrant display. Nîmes used to be a cloth-manufacturing center and lent its

name to what has become one of the world's most popular fabrics—denim (*de Nîmes*—from Nîmes). Two rooms contain colorful, sometimes grisly, exhibits on the regional sport of bullfighting. *Pl. aux Herbes. Admission free. Open daily 10–6.*

Head right from the cathedral along rue des Halles, then left
6 down rue du Général-Perrier, to reach the **Maison Carrée.** Despite its name (the "square house"), this Roman temple dating from the 1st century AD is oblong. Transformed down the ages into a stable, a private dwelling, a town hall, and a church, the building is now a museum that contains an imposing statue of Apollo and other antiquities. The exquisite carvings along the cornice and on the Corinthian capitals rank as some of the finest in Roman architecture. Thomas Jefferson admired the Maison Carrée's chaste lines of columns so much that he had them copied for the Virginia state capitol at Richmond. *Blvd. Victor-Hugo. Admission free. Open mid-June–mid-Sept., daily 9–7; mid-Sept.–Oct. and Apr.–mid-June, daily 9–noon and 2–6; Nov.–Mar., daily 9–noon and 2–5.*

Rue Molière and rue Boissier lead from the Maison Carrée to
7 the **Jardin de la Fontaine.** This elaborate formal garden was landscaped on the site of the Roman baths in the 18th century, when the Source de Nemausus, a once-sacred spring, was channeled into pools and a canal. Close by, you'll see a Roman ruin
8 known as the **Temple of Diana.** At the far end of the jardin is the
9 **Tour Magne**—a stumpy tower probably used as a lookout post, which, despite having lost 30 feet in the course of time, still provides fine views of Nîmes for anyone who is energetic enough to climb the 140 steps to the top. *Quai de la Fontaine. Admission to Tour Magne: 10 frs.; joint ticket as above. Open mid-June–mid-Sept., daily 9–7; mid-Sept.–Oct. and Apr.–mid-June, daily 9–noon and 2–6; Nov.–Mar., daily 9–noon and 2–5.*

Lodging and Dining
Under 350 frs.
★

Louvre. Occupying a 17th-century house on a leafy square near the Roman arena, the Louvre is the best sort of carefully run provincial hotel. The guest rooms are spacious and have high ceilings, and they manage to retain the feel of a private house; ask for one that faces the courtyard. The restaurant serves well-prepared traditional cuisine. The most tempting dishes are at the moderate level, though the inexpensive set menu is a remarkably good deal. Seafood addicts will enjoy the lobster or the mussels in a flaky pastry crust. *2 sq. de la Couronne, 30000, tel. 66–67–22–75. 33 rooms with bath. Facilities: restaurant. AE, DC, MC, V.*

Dining
Under 75 frs.
★

Nicolas. Locals have long known about this homey place, which is always packed; you'll hear the noise before you open the door. A friendly, frazzled staff serves up delicious *bourride* (a garlicky fish soup) and other local specialties—all at unbelievably low prices. *1 rue Poise, tel. 66–67–50–47. Reservations strongly advised. MC, V. Closed Mon., first 2 weeks July, and mid-Dec.–first week Jan.*

Pont du Gard

Eight buses make the ½-hour trip daily from Nîmes.

The **Pont du Gard** is a huge, three-tiered aqueduct erected 2,000 years ago as part of a 48-kilometer (30-mile) system for supplying water to Roman Nîmes. It is astonishingly well preserved. Its setting, spanning a rocky gorge 150 feet above the

River Gardon, is nothing less than spectacular. There is no entry fee or guide, and at certain times you can have it all to yourself: Early morning is best, when the honey-colored stone gleams in the sunlight. The best way to gauge the full majesty of the Pont du Gard is to walk right along the top.

Tarascon

Trains make the 15-minute run from Nîmes at least every 1½ hours.

Tarascon was once home of the mythical Tarasque, a monster that would emerge from the Rhône to gobble children and cattle. Luckily St. Martha, washed up with the three Maries at Stes-Maries-de-la-Mer, allegedly tamed the beast with a sprinkle of holy water, after which the inhabitants clobbered it senseless and slashed it to pieces. This dramatic event is celebrated on the last Sunday in June with a colorful parade.

Ever since the 12th century, Tarascon has possessed a formidable **castle** to protect it from any beast or man that might be tempted to emulate the Tarasque's fiendish deeds. The castle's massive stone walls, towering 150 feet above the rocky banks of the Rhône, are among the most daunting in France, so it's not surprising that the castle was used as a prison for centuries. Since 1926, however, the chapels, vaulted royal apartments, and stone carvings of the interior have been restored to less-intimidating glory. *Admission: 24 frs. adults, 13 frs. senior citizens, 5 frs. children. Open July and Aug., Wed.–Mon. 9–7; Sept.–June guided tours only 9–11 and 2–6 (last tour at 5 in Apr. and May; at 4, Oct.–Mar.).*

Arles

Trains run every 2 hours to Arles from Tarascon, 20 minutes away, and from Nîmes, 25 minutes away. Tourist office: 35 pl. de la République, tel. 90–93–49–11.

The first inhabitants of **Arles** were probably the Greeks, who arrived from Marseille in the 6th century BC. The Romans, however, left a stronger mark, constructing the theater and amphitheater that remain Arles's biggest tourist attractions. Arles used to be a thriving port before the Mediterranean receded over what is now the Camargue, a marshy realm of birds and beasts, pink flamingos and wild horses. It was also the site of the southernmost bridge over the Rhône, and became a commercial crossroads; merchants from as far afield as Arabia, Assyria, and Africa would linger here to do business on their way from Rome to Spain or northern Europe.

The Dutch painter Vincent van Gogh produced much of his best work—and chopped off his ear—in Arles during a frenzied 15-month spell (1888–90) just before his suicide at age 37. Unfortunately, the houses he lived in are no longer standing—they were destroyed during World War II—but one of his most famous subjects remains: the **Pont de Trinquetaille** across the Rhône. Van Gogh's rendering of the bridge, painted in 1888, was auctioned a century later for $20 million.

Local art museums such as the **Musée Réattu,** 300 yards from the bridge along quai Marx-Dormoy, can't compete with that type of bidding—which is one reason none of Van Gogh's works are displayed there. Another is that Arles failed to appreciate Van Gogh; he was jeered at and eventually packed off to the nearest lunatic asylum. To add insult to injury, Jacques Réattu, after whom the museum is named, was a local painter of dazzling mediocrity. His works fill three rooms, but of much greater interest is the collection of modern drawings and paintings by Pablo Picasso, Fernand Léger, and Maurice de Vlaminck, as well as the photography section containing images by some of the field's leading names. *Rue du Grand-Prieuré. Admission: 15 frs.; joint ticket to all monuments and museums: 44 frs. adults, 31 frs. students and senior citizens. Open June–Sept., daily 9:30–7; Nov.–Mar., daily 10–12:30 and 2–5; Apr.–May and Oct., daily 9:30–12:30 and 2–6.*

The museum facade, facing the Rhône, dates from the Middle Ages and formed part of a 15th-century priory. Beside it are the ruins of the **Palais Constantin,** site of Provence's largest Roman baths, the **Thèrmes de la Trouille.** *Entrance on rue Dominique-Maisto. Admission: 12 francs; joint ticket as above. Same opening times as above.*

Most of the significant sights and museums in Arles are set well away from the Rhône. The most notable is the 26,000-capacity **Arènes,** built in the 1st century AD to showcase circuses and to-the-death gladiator combats. The amphitheater is 150 yards long and as wide as a football field, with each of its two stories composed of 60 arches; the original top tier has long since crumbled, and the three square towers were added in the Middle Ages. Climb to the upper story for some satisfying views across the town and countryside. Despite its venerable age, the amphitheater still sees a lot of action, mainly Sunday-afternoon bullfights. *Rond-Point des Arènes. Admission: 17 frs.; joint ticket as above. Open June–Sept., daily 8:30–7; Nov.–Mar., daily 9–noon and 2–4:30; Apr.–May and Oct., daily 9–12:30 and 2–6:30.*

Just 100 yards from the Arènes are the scanty remains of Arles's **Théâtre Antique** (Roman theater); the bits of marble column scattered around the grassy enclosure hint poignantly at the theater's onetime grandeur. The capacity may have shrunk from 7,000 to a few hundred, but the orchestra pit and a few tiers of seats are still used for the city's Music and Drama festival each July. *Rue du Cloître, tel. 90–96–93–30 for ticket information. Admission: 12 frs.; joint ticket as above. Open June–Sept., daily 8:30–7; Nov.–Mar., daily 9–noon and 2–4:30; Apr.–May and Oct., daily 9–12:30 and 2–6:30.*

Follow rue de la Calade to place de la République. To the left is the church of **St-Trophime,** dating mainly from the 11th and 12th centuries; subsequent additions have not spoiled its architectural harmony. Take time to admire the accomplished 12th-century sculptures flanking the main portal, featuring the Last Judgment, the apostles, the Nativity, and various saints. There are other well-crafted sculptures in the cloisters. *Rue de l'Hôtel-de-Ville. Admission to cloisters: 21 frs.; joint ticket as above. Open June–Sept., daily 8:30–7; Nov.–Mar., daily 9–noon and 2–4:30; Apr.–May and Oct., daily 9–12:30 and 2–6:30.*

Opposite St-Trophime is the **Musée d'Art Païen** (Museum of Pagan Art), housed in a former church next to the 17th-century Hôtel de Ville (Town Hall). The "pagan art" displays encompass Roman statues, busts, mosaics, and a white marble sarcophagus. You'll also see a copy of the famous statue the *Venus of Arles;* Sun King Louis XIV waltzed off to the Louvre with the original. *Pl. de la République. Admission: 12 frs.; joint ticket as above. Open June–Sept., daily 8:30–7; Nov.–Mar., daily 9–noon and 2–4:30; Apr.–May and Oct., 9–12:30 and 2–6:30.*

Turn left alongside the Hôtel de Ville onto plan de la Cour. A hundred yards down, in a former 17th-century Jesuit chapel, is the **Musée d'Art Chrétien** (Museum of Christian Art). One of the highlights is a magnificent collection of sculpted marble sarcophagi, second only to the Vatican's, that date from the 4th century on. Downstairs, you can explore a vast double gallery built in the 1st century BC as a grain store and see part of the great Roman sewer built two centuries later. *Rue Balze. Admission: 12 frs.; joint ticket as above. Open June–Sept., daily 8:30–7; Nov.–Mar., daily 9–noon and 2–4:30; Apr.–May and Oct., daily 9–12:30 and 2–6:30.*

The **Museon Arlaten,** an old-fashioned folklore museum, is housed next door in a 16th-century mansion. The charming displays include costumes and headdresses, puppets, and waxworks, lovingly assembled by that great 19th-century Provençal poet, Frédéric Mistral. *29 rue de la République. Admission: 12 frs.; joint ticket as above. Open June–Sept., daily 8:30–7; Nov.–Mar., Tues.–Sun. 9–noon and 2–4:30; Apr.–May and Oct., Tues.–Sun. 9–12:30 and 2–6:30.*

Head down rue du Président-Wilson opposite the museum to the **boulevard des Luces,** a broad, leafy avenue flanked by trendy shops and sidewalk cafés. Locals favor it for leisurely strolls and aperitifs.

At the east end of the boulevard is the **Jardin d'Hiver,** a public garden whose fountains figure in several of Van Gogh's paintings. Cross the gardens to rue Fassin and head left to place de la Croisière and the start of the allée des Sarcophages, which leads to the **Alyscamps,** a Provençal term meaning "mythical burial ground." This was a prestigious burial site from Roman times through the Middle Ages. A host of important finds have been excavated here, many of which are exhibited in the town's museums. Empty tombs and sarcophagi line the allée des Sarcophages, creating a powerfully gloomy atmosphere in dull weather.

Lodging
Under 250 frs.

St-Trophime. This venerable town house, close to the Arènes and the eponymous church, has old-fashioned rooms and a nice courtyard. It can be a little noisy in the height of summer, but with prices as low as 170 francs for the smallest rooms, you can't complain. *16 rue Calade, 13200, tel. 90–96–88–38. 22 rooms, some with bath or shower. AE, DC, MC, V. Closed mid-Nov.–mid-Dec. and most of Jan.*

Dining
Under 200 frs.

Le Vaccarès. In an upstairs restaurant overlooking place du Forum, chef Bernard Dumas serves classical Provençal dishes with a touch of invention and some particularly good fish creations. Try his mussels dressed in herbs and garlic. The dining-room decor is as elegant as the cuisine, and many of the prices, though not all, will keep your tab to a moderate level. *11 rue Favorin, tel. 90–96–06–17. Reservations advised. MC, V. Closed end of Dec.–end of Jan., Sun. dinner, and Mon.*

Under 75 frs. **Côte d'Adam.** This country-style restaurant near place du Forum offers the best dining value in the historic town center: four different set menus for under 100 francs, showcasing such tasty, unpretentious fare as chicken salad and mussel soup. *12 rue de la Liberté, tel. 90–49–62–29. Reservations advised. AE, DC, MC, V. Closed Mon. and the second half of Nov.*

Les Baux-de-Provence

Four buses leave Arles daily on the ½-hour trip to Les Baux.

Perched on a mighty spur of rock high above the surrounding countryside of vines, olive trees, and quarries, **Les Baux-de-Provence** is an amazing place. The mineral bauxite was discovered here in 1821. Half of Les Baux is composed of tiny climbing streets and ancient stone houses inhabited, for the most part, by local craftsmen selling pottery, carvings, and assorted knickknacks. The other half, the **Ville Morte** (Dead Town), is a mass of medieval ruins, vestiges of Les Baux's glorious past, when the town boasted 6,000 inhabitants and the defensive impregnability of its rocky site far outweighed its isolation and poor access.

Close to the 12th-century church of St-Vincent (where local shepherds continue an age-old tradition by herding their lambs to midnight mass at Christmas) is the 16th-century **Hôtel des Porcelets,** featuring some 18th-century frescoes and a small but choice collection of contemporary art. *Pl. St-Vincent. Admission: 20 frs.; joint ticket with Musée Lapidaire and Ville Morte. Open Easter–Oct., daily 9–noon and 2–6.*

Rue Neuve leads around to the **Ville Morte.** Enter through the 14th-century Tour-de-Brau, which houses the **Musée Lapidaire,** displaying locally excavated sculptures and ceramics. You can wander at will amid the rocks and ruins of the Dead Town. A 13th-century castle stands at one end of the clifftop, and, at the other, the Tour Paravelle and the Monument Charloun Rieu. From here, you can enjoy a magnificent view of Arles and the Camargue as far as Stes-Maries-de-la-Mer. *Ville Morte admission: 20 frs.; joint ticket with museums. Open daily 9–noon and 2–6.*

St-Rémy-de-Provence

Two buses daily run between Les Baux and St-Rémy (15 minutes), and 3 between St-Rémy and Tarascon (30 minutes). Tourist office: Place Jean-Jaurès, tel. 90–92–05–22.

St-Rémy-de-Provence, founded in the 6th century BC and known as Glanum to the Romans, is renowned for its outstanding Roman remains: Temples, baths, forum, and houses have been excavated, and the **Roman Mausoleum** and **Arc Municipal** (Triumphal Arch) welcome visitors as they enter the town.

The Roman Mausoleum was erected around AD 100 to the memory of Caius and Lucius Caesar, grandsons of the emperor Augustus; the four bas-reliefs around its base, depicting ancient battle scenes, are stunningly preserved. The Mausoleum is composed of four archways topped by a circular colonnade. The nearby Arc Municipal is a few decades older and has suffered heavily; the upper half has crumbled away, although you can still make out some of the stone carvings.

Excavations since 1921 have uncovered about a tenth of the site of the adjacent Roman town. Many of the finds—statues, pottery, and jewelry—can be examined at the town museum, the **Musée Archéologique,** in the center of St-Rémy. *Hôtel de Sade, rue Parage. Admission: 12 frs. adults, 6 frs. children. Open June–Oct., daily 9–noon and 2–6; Apr.–May and Oct., weekends 10–noon, weekdays 3–6; closed Nov.–Mar.*

Opposite the Hôtel de Sade, in a grand 16th-century mansion, is the **Musée des Alpilles.** It boasts a fine collection of minerals found in the nearby hills (the Alpilles), plus items of regional folklore: costumes, furniture, and figurines. Exhibits also touch on the 16th-century astrologer Nostradamus, who was born in St-Rémy (his house can be seen on the other side of the church, on rue Hoche, but it's not open to the public). *Pl. Favier. Admission: 12 frs. Open Apr.–Oct., Wed.–Mon. 10–noon and 2–6; Mar. and Nov., weekends 10–noon and 2–4; closed Dec.–Feb.*

Tour 2: Marseille and Aix

The two towns in this tour, though just a short train ride apart, couldn't be more different. Marseille is big, brash, and busy, while Aix-en-Provence is elegant, proud, and almost haughty.

From Paris *By Train* TGV trains to Marseille leave Paris (Gare de Lyon) every 2 hours. The trip takes 4 hours 40 minutes.

By Car The 785-kilometer (490-mile) drive from Paris to Marseille via A6 and A7 takes around 7 hours.

Marseille

Tourist office: 4 La Canebière, close to the Vieux-Port, tel. 91–54–91–11.

Numbers in the margin correspond to points of interest on the Marseille map.

Marseille is not crowded with tourist goodies, nor is its reputation as a big, dirty city entirely unjustified, but it still has more going for it than many realize: a craggy mountain hinterland that provides a spectacular backdrop, superb coastal views of nearby islands, and the sights and smells of a Mediterranean melting pot where different peoples have mingled for centuries—ever since the Phocaean Greeks invaded around 600 BC. The most recent immigrants come from North Africa.

Marseille is the Mediterranean's largest port. The sizable, ugly industrial docks virtually rub shoulders with the intimate, pic-
1 turesque old harbor, the **Vieux-Port,** packed with fishing boats and pleasure craft. This is the heart of Marseille, with the Canebière avenue leading down to the water's edge.

Take the métro from Gare St-Charles to the Vieux-Port, or descend the majestic stone staircase outside the station and follow boulevard d'Athènes before turning right onto La Canebière. Pick up your leaflets and town plan at the tourist office and peruse them on a café terrace overlooking the Vieux-Port. Until the mid-19th century, this was the center of maritime activity in Marseille. These days, a forest of yacht and fishing-boat masts creates an impression of colorful bustle. A famous fish market is held here on Monday through Saturday

Basilique St-Victor, **3**
Cathedral, **2**
Château d'If, **8**
Fort St-Nicholas, **4**
Musée de la Marine, **6**
Musée des Beaux-Arts, **7**
Notre-Dame de la Garde, **5**
Vieux-Port, **1**

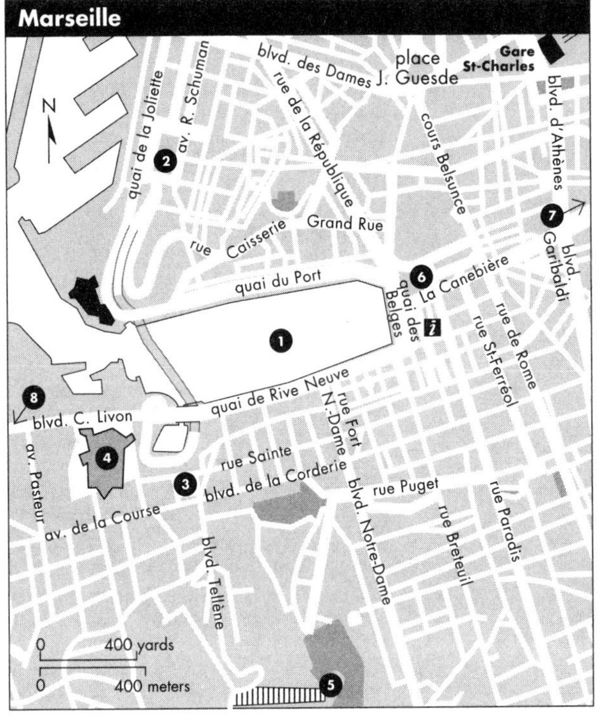

mornings. Restaurants line the quays, and fishwives spout incomprehensible Provençal insults as they serve gleaming fresh sardines each morning. The Marseillais can be an irascible lot: Louis XIV built the Fort St-Nicolas, at the entry of the Vieux-Port, with the guns facing inland to keep the citizens in order.

A short way down the right quay (as you look out to sea) is the elegant 17th-century Hôtel de Ville (Town Hall). Just behind, on rue de la Prison, is the Maison Diamantée, a 16th-century mansion with an elaborate interior staircase. The mansion now houses the **Musée du Vieux Marseille,** whose displays of costumes, pictures, and figurines depict old Marseille. *Rue de la Prison. Admission: 10 frs. adults, 5 frs. students and senior citizens. Open Tues.–Sun. 10–5.*

2 Marseille's pompous, striped neo-Byzantine **cathedral** stands
around the corner, but it is of considerably less interest than
3 the **Basilique St-Victor** (Rue Sainte) across the water, in the
4 shadow of the **Fort St-Nicolas** (which can't be visited). With its
powerful tower and thick-set walls, the basilica resembles a fortress and boasts one of southern France's oldest doorways (circa 1140), a 13th-century nave, and a 14th-century chancel and transept. Downstairs, you'll find the murky 5th-century underground crypt, with its collection of ancient sarcophagi.

Just up the street from the basilica at 136 rue Sainte is the **Four des Navettes**—a bakery that has been producing slender, orange-spiced, shuttle-shaped *navette* loaves for over 200 years. Since the navettes can last for up to a year, they make good take-home presents as well as on-the-spot snacks.

A brisk half-mile walk up boulevard Tellène, followed by a trudge up a steep flight of steps, will bring you to the foot of
5 **Notre-Dame de la Garde** (blvd. A. Aune). This church, a flashy 19th-century cousin of the Sacré-Coeur in Paris and Fourvière in Lyon, features a similar hilltop location. The expansive view, clearest in early morning (especially if the mistral is blowing), stretches from the hinterland mountains to the sea via the Cité Radieuse, a controversial '50s housing project by Swiss-born architect Le Corbusier. The church's interior is generously endowed with bombastic murals, mosaics, and marble, and at the top of the tower, the great gilded statue of the Virgin stands sentinel over the old port, 500 feet below.

Return to the Vieux-Port and venture along the legendary **La Canebière**—the "Can O' Beer" to prewar sailors—where stately mansions recall faded glory. La Canebière has been on the decline in recent years, but cafés and restaurants continue to provide an upbeat pulse. A hundred yards down on the left is the big white Palais de la Bourse (stock exchange) and, inside,
6 the **Musée de la Marine** (Nautical Museum), with a rundown on the history of the port and an interesting display of model ships. *Admission: 10 frs. Open Wed.–Mon. 9–noon and 2–6.*

Behind the bourse is the **Jardin des Vestiges,** a public garden that holds the remains of Roman foundations. Here you will find the little **Musée de l'Histoire de Marseille** (Town Museum), featuring exhibits related to the town's history. One of the highlights is the 60-foot Roman boat. *Cours Belsunce. Admission: 10 frs. adults, 5 frs. senior citizens and children. Open Tues.–Sat. 10–4:45.*

Continue past such busy shopping streets as rue Paradis, rue St-Ferréol, and rue de Rome, and turn right onto boulevard Garibaldi to reach **cours Julien,** a traffic-free street lined with sidewalk cafés, restaurants, bookshops, and boutiques. The atmosphere is that of a scaled-down St-Germain-des-Prés wafted from Paris to the Mediterranean.

Return to La Canebière and, when you reach the undistinguished church of St-Vincent de Paul, fork left along cours Jeanne-Thierry (which becomes boulevard Longchamp) to the imposing **Palais Longchamp,** built in 1860 by the same architect who built Notre-Dame de la Garde, Henri Espérandieu (1829–
7 74). The palais is home to the **Musée des Beaux-Arts** (Fine Arts Museum); its collection of paintings and sculptures includes works by 18th-century Italian artist Giovanni Battista Tiepolo, Rubens, and French caricaturist and painter Honoré Daumier. *Admission: 10 frs. adults, 5 frs. students and senior citizens. Open Tues.–Sun. 10–5.*

Marseille is no seaside resort, but a scenic coast road known as the **Corniche du Président J. F. Kennedy** links the Vieux-Port to the newly created Prado beaches in the swanky parts of southern Marseille 5 kilometers (3 miles) away. To get there, take any 19, 83, or 72 bus. There are breathtaking views across the sea toward the rocky Frioul Islands, which can be visited by boat. Boats leave the Vieux-Port hourly in summer and fre-
8 quently in winter for the 90-minute trip to the **Château d'If,** a castle in which various political prisoners were held captive down the ages. Alexandre Dumas condemned his fictional hero, the count of Monte Cristo, to be shut up in a cell here, before the wily count made his celebrated escape through a hole in the

wall. *Admission included in the boat fare (40 frs.). Open June–Sept., daily 8:30–noon and 1:30–6:30; Oct.–May, daily 8:30–noon and 1:30–4.*

Lodging
Under 250 frs.

Lutétia. There's nothing remarkable about this small hotel, but its rooms are quiet, airy, modernized, and a good value for the money, given the handy setting between La Canebière and St-Charles rail station. *38 allée Léon-Gambetta, 13001, tel. 91–50–81–78. 29 rooms with bath or shower. DC, MC, V.*

Splurge
★

Pullman Beauvau. Right on the Vieux-Port, a few steps from the end of La Canebière, the Beauvau is the ideal town hotel. The 200-year-old former coaching inn was totally modernized in 1986, and its charming, Old World opulence is enhanced by wood paneling, designer fabrics, fine paintings, genuine antique furniture—and exceptional service. The best rooms look out onto the Vieux-Port. There's no restaurant, but you can start your day in the cozy breakfast room. *4 rue Beauvau, 13001, tel. 91–54–91–00 (to make reservations toll-free from the U.S. call 800/223–9868; in the U.K., 071/621–1962). 71 rooms with bath. Facilities: bar, breakfast room. AE, DC, MC, V. 600–800 frs.*

Dining
Under 125 frs.

Chez Madie. Every morning the colorful *patronne*, Madie Minassian, bustles along the quayside to trade insults with the fishwives at the far end of the Vieux-Port—and to scour their catch for the freshest ingredients, which swiftly end up in her bouillabaisse, fish soup, *favouilles* sauce (made from tiny local crabs), and other dishes you'll savor from the menus at her restaurant, which are an excellent value. *138 quai du Port, tel. 91–90–40–87. Reservations advised. AE, DC, MC, V. Closed Mon., Sun. dinner, and most of Aug.*

Dar Djerba. This is perhaps the best of the North African restaurants that are scattered throughout Marseille. The cozy, white-walled Dar Djerba on bustling cours Julien specializes in couscous of all kinds (with lamb, chicken, or even quail) as well as in Arab coffees and pastries. The Moorish tile patterns and exotic aromas will waft you away on a Saharan breeze. *15 cours Julien, tel. 91–48–55–36. Reservations advised in summer. DC, MC, V. Closed Tues. and second half of Aug.*

Aix-en-Provence

Trains make the 30-minute run from Marseille to Aix every 1½ hours or so. Tourist office: 2 pl. du Gal-de-Gaulle, tel. 42–26–02–93.

Many villages, but few towns, are as well preserved as the traditional capital of Provence: elegant **Aix-en-Provence**. The Romans were drawn here by the presence of thermal springs; the name Aix originates from *Aquae Sextiae* (the waters of Sextius) in honor of the consul who reputedly founded the town in 122 BC. Twenty years later, a vast army of Germanic barbarians invaded the region but was defeated by General Marius at a neighboring mountain, known ever since as the Montagne Sainte-Victoire. Marius remains a popular local first name to this day.

Aix-en-Provence numbers two of France's creative geniuses among its sons: Paul Cézanne (1839–1906), many of whose paintings feature the nearby countryside, especially Montagne Sainte-Victoire (though Cézanne would not recognize it now, after the forest fire that ravaged its slopes in 1990), and novelist Emile Zola (1840–1902), who, in several of his works, described Aix (as "Plassans") and his boyhood friendship with Cézanne.

The celebrated **cours Mirabeau,** flanked by intertwining plane trees, is the town's nerve center, a gracious, lively avenue with the feel of a toned-down, intimate Champs-Elysées. It divides Old Aix into two, with narrow medieval streets to the north and sophisticated 18th-century mansions to the south. Begin your visit at the west end of cours Mirabeau (the tourist office is close by). Halfway down is the **Fontaine des Neuf Canons** (Fountain of the Nine Cannons), dating from 1691, and farther along is the **Fontaine d'Eau Thermale** (Fountain of Thermal Water), built in 1734.

Any route through the quaint pedestrian streets of the old town, north of cours Mirabeau, is rewarding. Wend your way up to the **Cathédrale St-Sauveur.** Its mishmash of styles lacks harmony, and the interior feels gloomy and dilapidated, but you may want to inspect the remarkable 15th-century triptych by Nicolas Froment, entitled *Tryptique du Buisson Ardent (Burning Bush),* depicting King René (duke of Anjou, Count of Provence, and titular king of Sicily) and Queen Joan kneeling beside the Virgin. Ask the sacristan to spotlight it for you (he'll expect a tip) and to remove the protective shutters from the ornate 16th-century carvings on the cathedral portals. Afterward, wander into the tranquil Romanesque cloisters next door to admire the carved pillars and slender colonnades.

The adjacent Archbishop's Palace is home to the **Musée des Tapisseries** (Tapestry Museum). Its highlight is a magnificent suite of 17 tapestries made in Beauvais that date, like the palace itself, from the 17th and 18th centuries. Nine woven panels illustrate the adventures of the bumbling Don Quixote. *28 pl. des Martyrs de la Résistance. Admission: 12 frs. Open Wed.–Mon. 10–noon and 2–6.*

Return past the cathedral and take rue de la Roque up to the broad, leafy boulevard that encircles Old Aix. Head up avenue Pasteur, opposite, then turn right onto avenue Paul-Cézanne, which leads to the **Musée-Atelier de Paul Cézanne** (Cézanne's studio). Cézanne's pioneering work, with its interest in angular forms, paved the way for the Cubist style of the early 20th century. No major pictures are on display here, but his studio remains as he left it at the time of his death in 1906, scattered with the great man's pipe, clothing, and other personal possessions, many of which he painted in his still lifes. *9 av. Paul-Cézanne. Admission: 13 frs. adults, 6 frs. senior citizens and children. Open Wed.–Mon. 10–noon and 2:30–6; closed Tues.*

Make your way back to cours Mirabeau and cross into the southern half of Aix. The streets here are straight and rationally planned, flanked by symmetrical mansions imbued with classical elegance. Rue du Quatre-Septembre, three-quarters of the way down cours Mirabeau, leads to the splendid **Fontaine des Quatre Dauphins,** where sculpted dolphins play in a fountain erected in 1667. Turn left along rue Cardinale to the **Musée Granet,** named after another of Aix's artistic sons: François Granet (1775–1849), whose works are good examples of the formal, at times sentimental, style of art popular during the first half of the 19th century. Granet's paintings show none of the fervor of Cézanne, who is represented here with several oils and watercolors. An impressive collection of European paintings from the 16th to the 19th century, plus archaeological finds from Egypt, Greece, and the Roman Empire, complete the museum's collections. *13 rue Cardinale. Admission: 14 frs. Open Wed.–Mon. 10–noon and 2–6.*

Lodging
Under 250 frs.

Caravelle. There is nothing remarkable about the Caravelle—except that it is just five minutes' walk from cours Mirabeau and one of the few affordable options in central Aix. Streetside rooms are small and sometimes noisy, but you'll have to pay about 350 francs for the quieter back rooms that look out over a cheerful flower garden. *29 blvd du Roi-René, 13100, tel. 42–21–53–05. 33 rooms, most with bath or shower. AE, DC, MC, V.*

Dining
Under 125 frs.

Brasserie Royale. This noisy, bustling eatery on cours Mirabeau serves up hearty Provençal dishes amid a background din of banging pots, vociferous waiters, and tumultuous cries for more wine. The best place to eat is in the glassed-in patio out front, so you can soak up the Champs-Elysées-style atmosphere of the leafy boulevard while enjoying your meal. *17 cours Mirabeau, tel. 42–26–01–63. Reservations advised. AE, V.*

Shopping

At **La Provence Gourmande** (66 rue Boulagon) you'll find a vast selection of soaps, as well as herbs, spices, and the marzipan delicacies known as *calissons d'Aix*, while **À La Reine Jeanne** (32 cours Mirabeau) makes marzipan its specialty. **Paul Fouque** (65 cours Gambetta) is a good source of *santons*, clay crêche figures. In addition, several **markets** are a delight to explore: the flower market on Tuesday, Thursday, and Saturday mornings at place de l'Hôtel-de-Ville; the fruit and vegetable market every morning at place Richelme; and the fruit, vegetable, and herb market on Tuesday, Thursday, and Saturday mornings at place des Prêcheurs. There is also an antiques market on Tuesday, Thursday, and Saturday mornings at place de Verdun.

12 The Riviera

Nice, Monaco

The Riviera is not the cheapest area of France. So before you make the journey, it's important to know what you'll really find when you get there. If you're expecting fabulous yachts and villas, movie stars and palaces, and budding starlets sunning themselves on ribbons of golden sand, think again. The truth is that most beaches, at least east of Cannes, are small and pebbly. And in summer, hordes of visitors are stuffed unglamorously into concrete high rises or roadside campsites—on weekends it can take two hours to drive the last 10 kilometers (6 miles) into St-Tropez. Yes, the film stars are here—but in their private villas. The merely wealthy wisely favor off-seasons—spring and fall.

That said, we can still recommend the Riviera, even in summer, as long as you're selective about the places you choose to visit. Cannes and Monaco are basically jet-set haunts; you visit quickly to soak up the atmosphere, then move on. But other resorts have something for every purse; Nice has downtown color and swing, and a wide choice of affordable hotels and restaurants. A few miles inland fortified medieval towns perch on mountaintops, high above the sea amid headily scented fields of roses and lavender. Craftspeople here still make and sell their wares, as their predecessors did in the Middle Ages. Only minutes from the beaches are some of the world's most famous museums of modern art, featuring the works of painters who were captivated by the colors here: Fernand Léger, Marc Chagall, Henri Matisse, Pablo Picasso, Auguste Renoir, Jean Cocteau. And the light is as magical as ever.

The only problem is accessibility—the spectacular rail line sticks stubbornly to the coast. Nonetheless, buses and trains serve most of the area's high points, so you don't need your own wheels to absorb the essence of this world-famous resort area.

Essential Information

Lodging The Riviera is unquestionably the most expensive region of France, so brace youself. Affordable hotels do exist—Nice is your best bet—but they fill up days in advance, if not weeks. Unless you're prepared to splurge, Cannes and Monaco are not places to spend a night.

Dining Though prices often scale Parisian heights, the Riviera shares its cuisine with Provence, enjoying the same vegetable and fish dishes prepared with the same vivid seasonings. The most famous is *bouillabaisse*, a fish stew from around Marseille. Genuine bouillabaisse combines *rascasse* (scorpion fish), eel, and half a dozen other types of seafood; crab and lobster are optional. Local fish is scarce, however, so dishes like *loup flambé* (sea bass with fennel and anise liqueur), braised tuna, and even fresh sardines are priced accordingly.

With Italy so close, it's no surprise that many menus feature such specialties as ravioli and potato gnocchi. Try vegetable *soupe au pistou*, an aromatic brew seasoned with basil, garlic, olive oil, and Parmesan cheese; or *pissaladière*, a pastry-based version of pizza, topped with tomato, olives, anchovy, and plenty of onion. Nice claims its own specialties: *pan bagna* (salad in a bun) and *poulpe à la niçoise* (octopus in a tomato sauce). Of the various vegetable dishes, the best is *ratatouille*, a stew of tomatoes, onions, eggplant, and zucchini.

Anise-flavored *pastis* is the Riviera's number-one drink.

Bicycling Bikes can be rented from train stations at Antibes, Cannes, Juan-les-Pins, and Nice. Two especially scenic trips on fairly level ground are from Nice to the area around Cap d'Antibes, and around Cap Ferrat from Cannes.

Hiking The hilly hinterland, spangled with old villages, makes good rambling country; write to the **Comité Départemental de la Randonnée Pédestre** (La Chenaie, Chemin Martourette, 06530 Le Tignet) for maps and recommended routes.

Beaches If you like your beaches sandy, stick to those between St-Tropez and Antibes; most of the others are pebbly, though Menton and Monaco have imported vast tons of sand to spread around their shores. Private beaches are everywhere. Though you'll have to pay between 55 and 120 francs a day to use them, you get value for money—a café or restaurant, cabanas and showers, mattresses and umbrellas, and the pleasure of watching the perpetual parade of stylish swimwear and languid egos.

La Napoule has no fewer than eight beaches, offering facilities for waterskiing, windsurfing, diving, and snorkeling, or you can just swim or stretch out on a lounge chair. In **Nice**, beaches extend along the Baie des Anges (Bay of Angels); **Ruhl Plage** is one of the most popular, with a good restaurant and facilities for waterskiing, windsurfing, and children's swimming lessons. Not to be outdone, **Neptune Plage** has all that plus a sauna.

The Arts The Riviera's cultural calendar is splashy and star-studded, and never more so than during the region's world-famous festivals. The biggest and most celebrated is the **Cannes Film Festival** in May, rivaled by Monte Carlo's arts festival, **Printemps des Arts** (late March through late April). Antibes and Nice both host **jazz festivals** during July, drawing international performers.

Nightlife Casinos are very much part of the scene in Cannes and Monaco, but a spell at the games table will be beyond the budget of all but the best-heeled travelers. And although Riviera resorts buzz after dark, discos require snappy dressing and ready funds.

Festivals The celebrated **Carnival** in Nice mixes parades and other revelry during the weeks preceding Lent. The two weekends preceding Mardi Gras are a swirl of parades, fireworks, and masked balls.

Highlights for First-time Visitors

A stroll down La Croisette, Cannes
Picasso Museum in the Château Grimaldi, Antibes
A walk along the Cap d'Antibes peninsula
St-Paul-de-Vence
Fondation Maeght, La Gardette
Old Town, Nice
The hill village of Peillon
Casino at Monte Carlo

Exploring the Riviera

Nice is a logical base for exploring the Riviera. By rail, you can then head west to Antibes, Cannes, and Fréjus; travel east to Monaco and Menton; and make excursions to ancient hinterland villages—St-Paul-de-Vence, accessible by bus, and Peillon, a train ride from Nice.

From Paris *By Train* Six TGV trains to Nice leave Paris (Gare de Lyon) each day. A change of trains at Marseille is often necessary, and the trip takes 7–7½ hours.

By Car Allow at least 8 hours for the 930-kilometer (580-mile) road journey from Paris via A6, A7, and A8.

Nice

Tourist office: Avenue Thiers, by the train station, tel. 93–87–07–07.

Numbers in the margin correspond to points of interest on the Nice map.

Nice is less glamorous, less sophisticated, and less expensive than Cannes. It's also older—weathered-old and faded-old—like a wealthy dowager who has seen better days but who still maintains a demeanor of dignity and poise. Nice is a big, sprawling city of 350,000 people—five times as many as Cannes—and has a life and vitality that survive when tourists pack their bags and go home.

Turn left out of the station, then right onto bustling avenue
1 Jean-Medécin, and on down to arcaded **place Masséna**, the

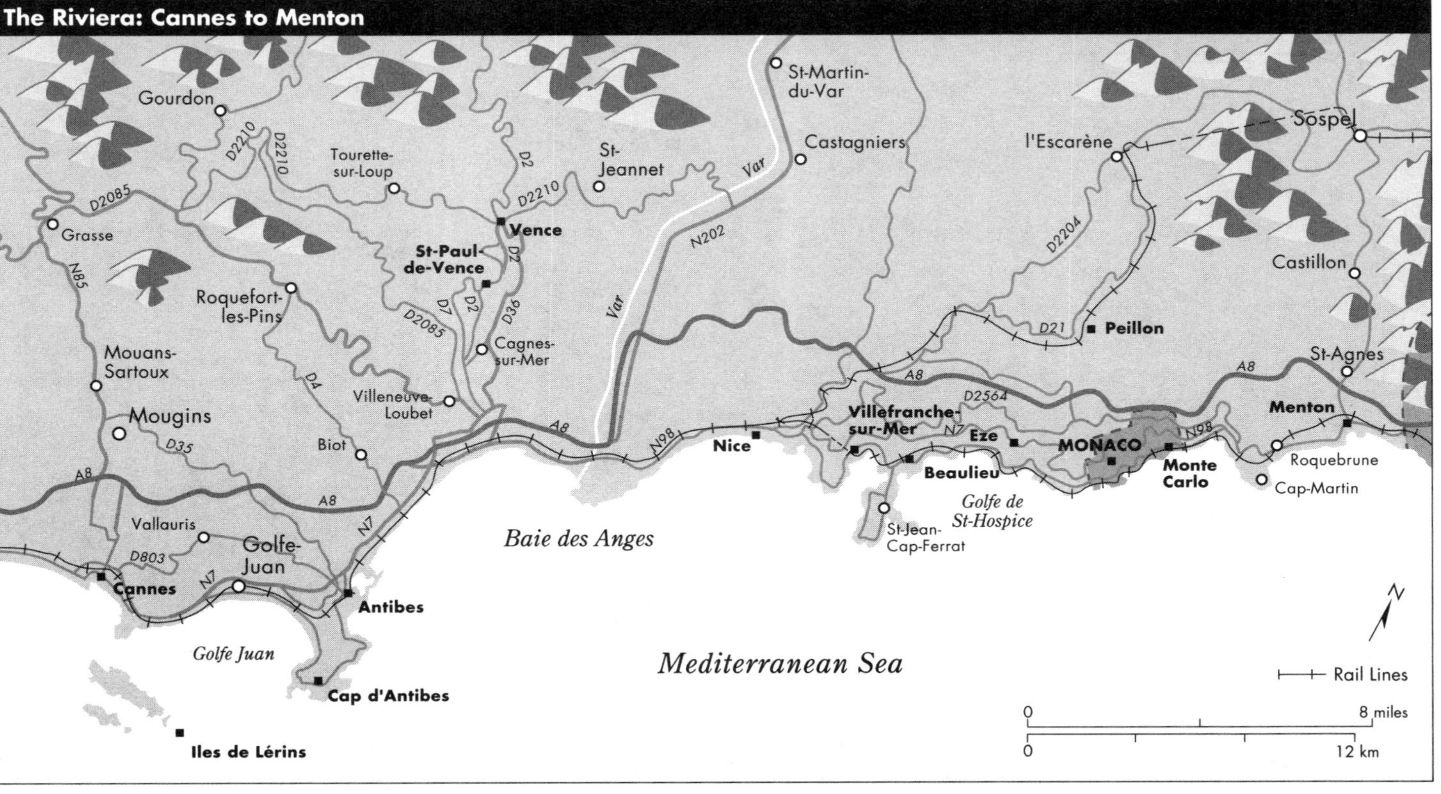
The Riviera: Cannes to Menton
Gourdon
D2210
Tourette-sur-Loup
D2
St-Jeannet
St-Martin-du-Var
Castagniers
Var
l'Escarène
Sospel
D2085
Grasse
D2210
Vence
St-Paul-de-Vence
N202
D2204
Castillon
N85
Roquefort-les-Pins
D7
D2
D36
D2085
Var
D21
Peillon
Mouans-Sartoux
D4
Cagnes-sur-Mer
A8
St-Agnes
Villeneuve-Loubet
D2564
Menton
Mougins
A8
Villefranche-sur-Mer
N7
Eze
MONACO
N98
D35
Biot
N98
Nice
Roquebrune
Beaulieu
Monte Carlo
Cap-Martin
A8
A8
Golfe de St-Hospice
Vallauris
N7
Golfe-Juan
Baie des Anges
St-Jean-Cap-Ferrat
D803
N7
Cannes
Antibes
N
Golfe Juan
Mediterranean Sea
Rail Lines
Cap d'Antibes
0
8 miles
0
12 km
Iles de Lérins

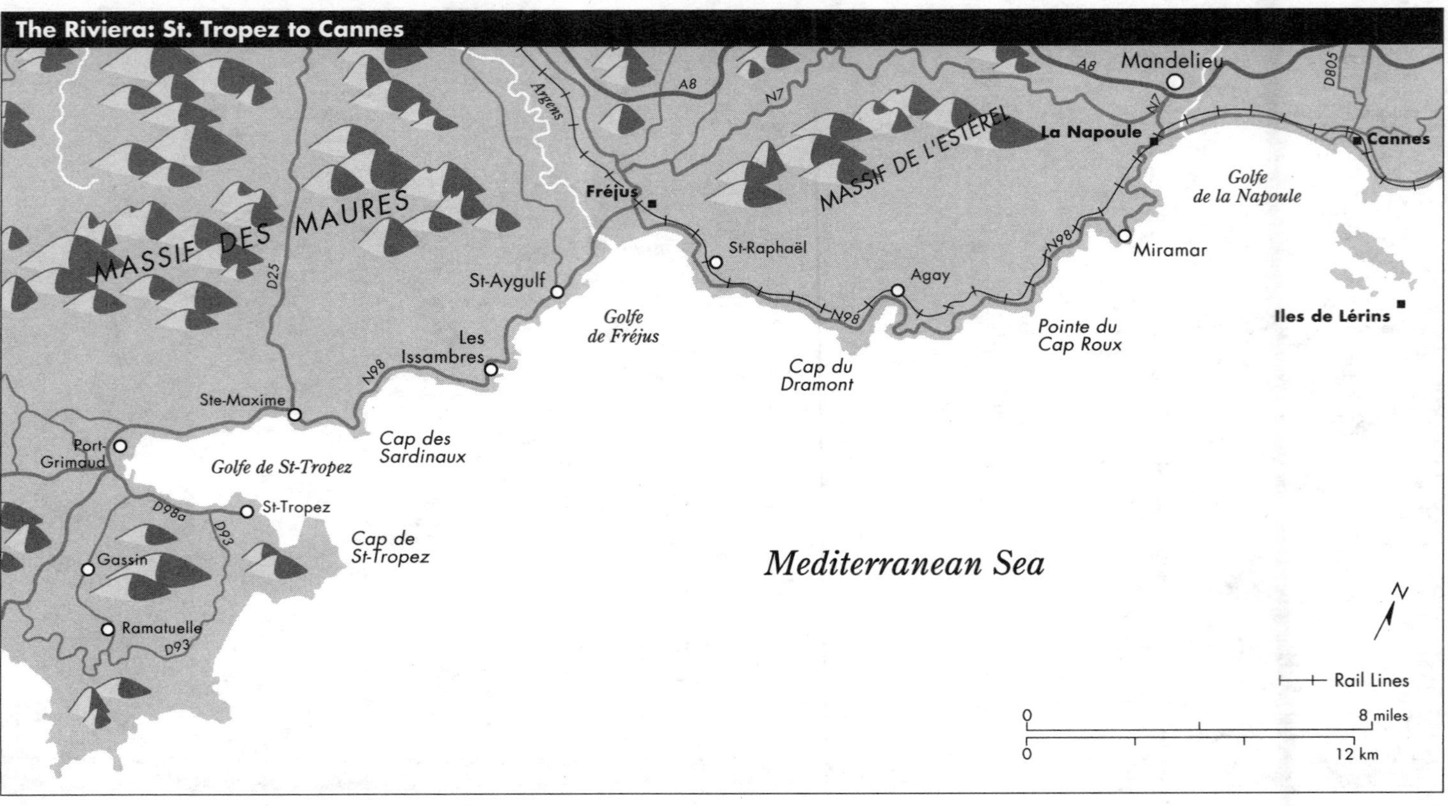

The Riviera: St. Tropez to Cannes
MASSIF DES MAURES
MASSIF DE L'ESTÉREL
Mandelieu
La Napoule
Cannes
Golfe de la Napoule
Iles de Lérins
Miramar
Pointe du Cap Roux
Agay
Cap du Dramont
St-Raphaël
Fréjus
Golfe de Fréjus
Argens
St-Aygulf
Les Issambres
Cap des Sardinaux
Ste-Maxime
Golfe de St-Tropez
Port-Grimaud
St-Tropez
Cap de St-Tropez
Gassin
Ramatuelle
Mediterranean Sea
A8
N7
D805
N98
D25
D98a
D93
N
Rail Lines
0
8 miles
0
12 km

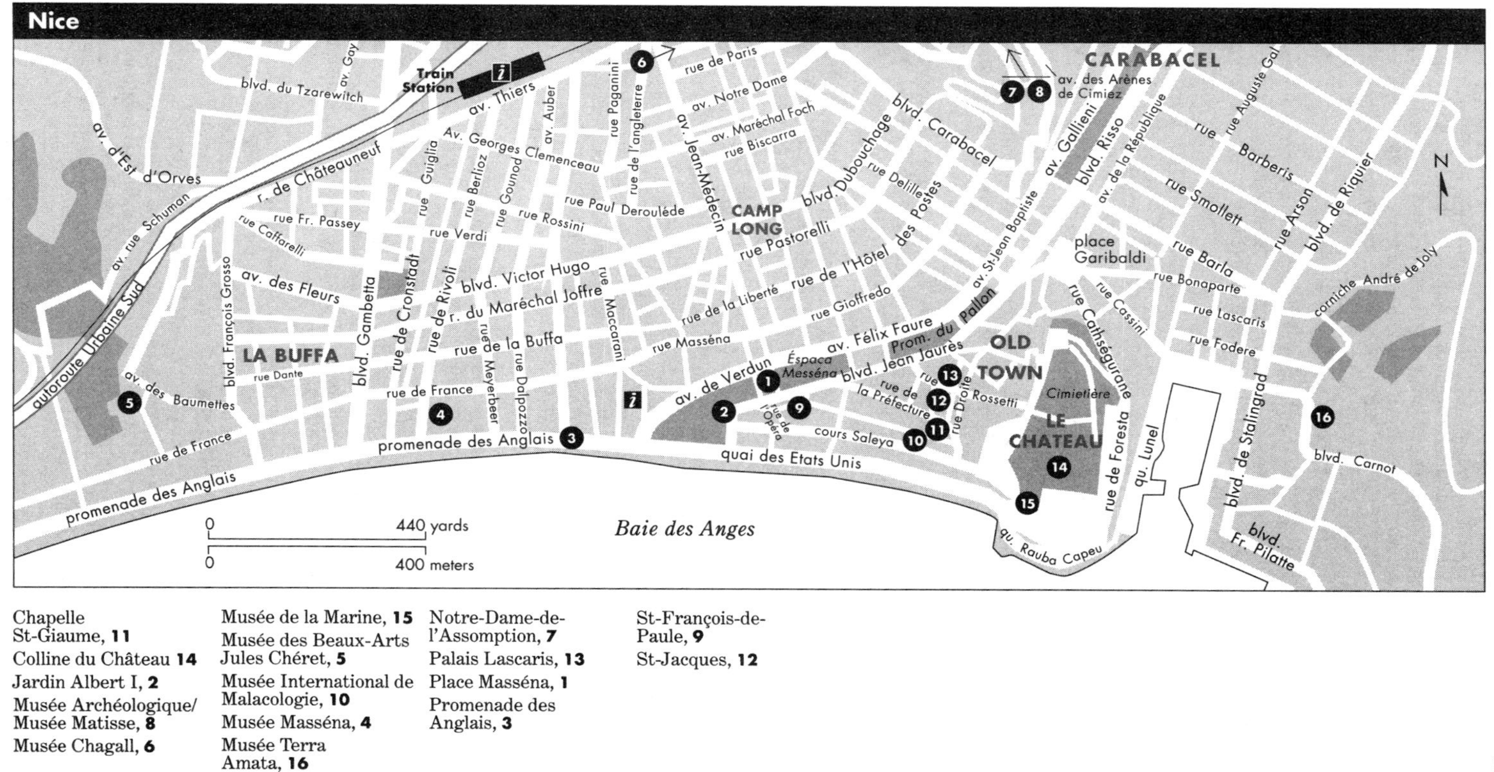

Chapelle St-Giaume, **11**
Colline du Château **14**
Jardin Albert I, **2**
Musée Archéologique/ Musée Matisse, **8**
Musée Chagall, **6**
Musée de la Marine, **15**
Musée des Beaux-Arts Jules Chéret, **5**
Musée International de Malacologie, **10**
Musée Masséna, **4**
Musée Terra Amata, **16**
Notre-Dame-de-l'Assomption, **7**
Palais Lascaris, **13**
Place Masséna, **1**
Promenade des Anglais, **3**
St-François-de-Paule, **9**
St-Jacques, **12**

city's main square and the logical starting point for the three Nice minitours we've mapped out. First, head west through the
2 3 fountains and gardens of the **Jardin Albert I** to the **Promenade des Anglais,** built, as the name indicates, by the English community in 1824. Traffic on this multilane highway can be heavy, but once you have crossed to the seafront, there are fine views, across private beaches, of the Baie des Anges.

Walk as far as the Neptune Plage (beach) and cross over to the **Hôtel Negresco** (37 Promenade des Anglais); spend a few dollars on a cup of coffee here and think of it as an admission charge to this palatial hotel.

4 Just up rue de Rivoli from the Hôtel Negresco is the **Musée Masséna,** concerned principally with the Napoleonic era and, in particular, with the life of local-born general André Masséna (1756–1817). Bonaparte rewarded the general for his heroic exploits during the Italian campaign with the sonorous sobriquet *l'enfant chéri de la victoire* (the cherished child of victory). Sections of the museum evoke the history of Nice and its cherished carnival; there are also some fine Renaissance paintings and objects. *67 rue de France. Admission free. Open Tues.–Sun. 10–noon and 2–5; closed Nov. and Mon.*

Head left along rue de France, then turn right up avenue des
5 Baumettes to the **Musée des Beaux-Arts Jules Chéret,** Nice's fine-arts museum, built in 1878 as a palatial mansion for a Russian princess. The rich collection of paintings includes works by Auguste Renoir, Edgar Degas, Claude Monet, Raoul Dufy, Oriental prints, sculptures by Auguste Rodin, and ceramics by Picasso. Jules Chéret (1836–1932) is best known for his Belle Epoque posters; several of his oils, pastels, and tapestries can be admired here. *33 av. des Baumettes. Admission free. Open May–Sept., Tues.–Sun. 10–noon and 3–6; Oct.–Apr., Tues.–Sun. 10–noon and 2–5; closed Mon.*

Nice's main shopping street, avenue Jean-Médecin, runs inland from place Masséna; all needs and most tastes are catered to in its big department stores (Nouvelles Galeries, Prisunic, and the split-level Etoile mall). Continue past the train station, on
6 avenue Thiers, then take the first right down to the **Musée Chagall**—built to show off the paintings of Marc Chagall (1887–1985) in natural light. The Old Testament is the primary subject of the works, which include 17 huge canvases covering a period of 13 years, together with 195 preliminary sketches, several sculptures, and nearly 40 gouaches. In summertime, you can buy snacks and drinks in the garden. *Av. du Dr-Ménard. Admission: 17 frs. adults, 9 frs. children and senior citizens (6-fr. supplement for special exhibitions). Open July–Sept., Wed.–Mon. 10–6:50; Oct.–July, Wed.–Mon. 10–12:20 and 2–5:20.*

Boulevard de Cimiez heads to the residential quarter of Nice—the hilltop site of **Cimiez,** occupied by the Romans 2,000 years ago. The foundations of the Roman town can be seen, along with vestiges of the arena, less spectacular than those at Arles or Nîmes but still in use (notably for a summer jazz festival).
7 Close by is the Franciscan monastery of **Notre-Dame-de-l'Assomption,** with some outstanding late-medieval religious pictures; guided tours include the small museum and an audio-visual show on the life and work of the Franciscans. *Admission free. Open weekdays 10–noon and 3–6.*

A 17th-century Italian villa amid the Roman remains contains
8 two museums: the **Musée Archéologique,** with a plethora of ancient objects, and the **Musée Matisse,** with paintings and
bronzes by Henri Matisse (1869–1954), illustrating the different stages of his career. The Matisse Museum is scheduled to
reopen in late 1992 or early 1993 after a four-year renovation
program. *164 av. des Arènes-de-Cimiez, tel. 93–53–17–70. Admission free. Open June–Aug., Tues.–Sat. 11–6; Apr., May,
and Sept., Tues.–Sat. 10–noon and 2–6; Oct. and Dec.–Mar.,
Tues.–Sat. 10–noon and 2–5; closed Sun., Mon., and Nov.*

The **old town** of Nice is one of the delights of the Riviera. Cars are forbidden on streets that are so narrow that their buildings crowd out the sky. The winding alleyways are lined with faded 17th- and 18th-century buildings, where families sell their wares. Flowers cascade from window boxes on soft pastel-colored walls. You wander down cobbled streets, proceeding with the logic of dreams, or sit in an outdoor café on a Venetian-looking square, basking in the purest, most transparent light.

To explore the old town, head south from place Masséna along
rue de l'Opéra, and turn left onto rue St-François-de-Paule.
9 You'll soon come to the 18th-century church of **St-François-de-
Paule,** renowned for its ornate Baroque interior and sculpted
decoration.

Rue St-François-de-Paule becomes the pedestrian-only cours
Saleya, with its colorful morning market selling seafood, flowers, and orange trees in tubs. Toward the far end of cours
10 Saleya is the **Musée International de Malacologie,** with a collection of seashells from all over the world (some for sale) and a
small aquarium of Mediterranean sea life. *3 cours Saleya. Admission free. Open Dec.–Oct., Tues.–Sat. 10:30–1 and 2–6
(until 6:30 June–Sept.); closed Sun., Mon., and Nov.*

Next, stroll left up rue la Poissonnerie and pop into the
11 **Chapelle St-Giaume** to admire its gleaming Baroque interior
and grand altarpieces. Continue to rue de Jésus; at one end is
12 the church of **St-Jacques,** featuring an explosion of painted an-
13 gels on the ceiling. Walk along rue Droite to the elegant **Palais
Lascaris,** built in the mid-17th century and decorated with
paintings and tapestries. The palace boasts a particularly
grand staircase and a reconstructed 18th-century pharmacy.
*15 rue Droite. Admission free. Open Dec.–Oct., Tues.–Sun.
9:30–noon and 2:30–6; closed Mon. and Nov.*

14 Old Nice is dominated by the **Colline du Château** (Castle Hill), a
romantic cliff fortified many centuries before Christ. The ruins
of a 6th-century castle can be explored and the views from the
surrounding garden admired. A small naval museum, the
15 **Musée de la Marine,** is situated in the 16th-century tower
known as the **Tour Bellanda,** with models, instruments, and
documents charting the history of the port of Nice. *Rue du
Château, tel. 93–80–47–61. Admission free. Open Oct.–May,
Wed.–Mon. 10–noon and 2–5; June–Sept., Wed.–Mon. 10–
noon and 2–7; closed Tues. Elevator between Tour Bellanda
and the quayside in operation daily 9–7 in summer, 2–7 in
winter.*

The back of Castle Hill overlooks the harbor. On the other side,
16 along boulevard Carnot, is the **Musée Terra Amata,** containing
relics of a local settlement that was active 400,000 years ago.
There are recorded commentaries in English and films explain-

ing the lifestyle of prehistoric dwellers. *25 blvd. Carnot, tel. 93–55–59–93. Admission free. Open Tues.–Sun. 9–noon and 2–6; closed first half of Sept.*

Lodging
Under 400 frs.

Little Palace. Monsieur and Madame Carlier run the closest thing to a country-house hotel in Nice. The old-fashioned decor, the jumble of bric-a-brac, and the heavy wooden furniture lend an Old World air; some may say it's like stepping onto a film set. *9 av. Baquis, 06000, tel. 93–88–70–49. 36 rooms, 35 with bath. AE, MC, V.*

Under 350 frs.

La Mer. This small hotel is handily situated on place Masséna, close to the old town and seafront. Rooms are Spartan (and carpets sometimes frayed), but all have a minibar and represent good value. Ask for a room away from the square to be sure of a quiet night. *4 pl. Masséna, 06000, tel. 93–92–09–10. 12 rooms with bath or shower. MC, V.*

Dining
Under 250 frs.

Barale. This is one of Nice's most fashionable restaurants, and eating here is almost like attending a theatrical performance. The tempestuous proprietress and chef, Hélène Barale, displays her varied menu on a blackboard hanging in the extraordinary dining room, a warehouse of artifacts and unusual odds and ends. The food blends elements of French cuisine with Italian; try the *salade Niçoise* or the stuffed poached veal. Madame Barale often makes appearances in the dining room and is known to sing to her guests. It sounds a bit hokey, but go in the right mood and you may love it. *39 rue Beaumont, tel. 93–89–17–94. Reservations essential. No credit cards. Closed Sun., Mon., and Aug.*

★ **La Mérenda.** This noisy bistro lies in the heart of the old town, and its down-to-earth Italo-Provençal food is a tremendously good value. The Giustis, who run the place, refuse to install a telephone, so go early to be sure of getting a table. House specials include pasta with *pistou* (a garlic-and-basil sauce) and succulent tripe. *4 rue de la Terrasse. No reservations or credit cards. Closed Sat., Sun., Mon., Feb., and Aug.*

Shopping

Crystallized fruit is a Nice specialty; there's a terrific selection at **Henri Auer** (7 rue St-François-de-Paule). Locals and visitors alike buy olive oil by the gallon from tiny **Alziari,** just down the street at no. 14; the cans sport colorful, old-fashioned labels, and you can also pick up lots of Provençal herbs and spices. In addition to plants, Nice's famous flower market at **cours Saleya** also features mounds of fish, shellfish, and other food items; on Monday, there's a flea market at the same spot.

Antibes

There are trains from Nice every 30 minutes. Expresses take 14 minutes, locals 40 minutes. Tourist office: 11 pl. Général-de-Gaulle, tel. 93–33–95–64.

Founded as a Greek trading port in the 4th century BC, **Antibes** is now a center for fishing and rose growing. Avenue de l'Amiral Grasse runs along the seafront from the harbor to the **market place,** a colorful sight most mornings, and to the church of the **Immaculate Conception,** with intricately carved portals (dating from 1710) and a 1515 altarpiece by Nice artist Louis Bréa (roughly 1455–1523).

The **Château Grimaldi,** built in the 12th century by the ruling family of Monaco and extensively rebuilt in the 16th century, is reached by nearby steps. Tear yourself away from the sun-baked terrace overlooking the sea to go inside to the Musée Picasso. There are stone Roman remains on show, but the works of Picasso—who occupied the château during his most cheerful and energetic period—hold center stage; they include an array of paintings, pottery, and lithographs inspired by the sea and Greek mythology. *Pl. du Château. Admission: 20 frs. adults, 10 frs. students and senior citizens. Open Dec.–Oct., Wed.–Mon. 10–noon and 2–6, 2–7 in summer; closed Tues. and Nov.*

Continue down avenue de l'Amiral Grasse to the St-André Bastion, constructed by Sébastien de Vauban in the late-17th century and home to the **Musée Archéologique.** Here 4,000 years of local history are illustrated by continually expanding displays. *Bastion St-André. Admission: 10 frs. adults, 5 frs. children and senior citizens. Open Dec.–Oct., Wed.–Mon. 10–noon and 2–6; closed Tues. and Nov.*

Antibes officially forms one town (dubbed "Juantibes") with the more recent resort of **Juan-les-Pins** to the south, where beach and nightlife attract a younger and less affluent crowd than in Cannes. In the summer, the mood is especially frenetic.

The **Cap d'Antibes** peninsula is rich and residential, with beaches, views, and large villas hidden in luxurious vegetation. Barely 3 kilometers (2 miles) long by 1 mile wide, it offers a perfect day's outing. An ideal walk is along the **Sentier des Douaniers,** the customs officers' path.

From Pointe Bacon, there is a striking view over the Baie des Anges toward Nice; climb up to the nearby Plateau de la Garoupe for a sweeping view inland over the Esterel massif and the Alps. The **Sanctuaire de la Garoupe** (sailors' chapel) has a 14th-century icon, a statue of Our Lady of Safe Homecoming, and numerous frescoes and votive offerings. The lighthouse alongside, which can be visited, has a powerful beam that carries over 40 miles out to sea. *Admission free. Open daily 10–noon and 2–6 in summer, 2:30–7 in winter.*

Nearby is the **Jardin Thuret,** established by botanist Gustave Thuret (1817–75) in 1856 as France's first garden for subtropical plants and trees. The garden, now run by the Ministry of Agriculture, remains a haven for rare, exotic plants. *41 blvd. du Cap. Admission free. Open weekdays 8:30–noon and 1:30–5 (5:30 in summer).*

At the southwest tip of the peninsula, opposite the luxurious and ultra-expensive Grand Hôtel du Cap d'Antibes, is the **Musée Naval & Napoléonien,** a former battery, where you can spend an interesting hour scanning Napoleonic proclamations and viewing scale models of oceangoing ships. *Batterie du Grillon, av. Kennedy. Admission: 15 frs. adults, 7 frs. children and senior citizens. Open Oct.–Apr., Wed.–Mon. 10–noon and 3–7; Dec.–Mar., Wed.–Mon. 10–noon and 2–5; closed Tues.*

Lodging and Dining
Under 400 frs.

Auberge de l'Esterel. The restaurant of this small auberge continues to offer one of the best quality–price ratios in town under the new management of Madame Bernier. The traditional French cuisine is all appealing, but you'll need to order carefully or your tab may rise higher than you expect. The secluded garden is a romantic setting for dinner under the stars. There are 15 bedrooms in the small attached hotel. *21 chemin des Iles,*

Juan-les-Pins, tel. 93-61-86-55. Reservations advised. AE, DC, MC, V. Closed mid-Nov.-mid-Dec., part of Feb., Sun. dinner, and Mon.

Cannes

Trains run every ½ hour from Antibes to Cannes and take 10 minutes. Trains from Nice take 23 minutes via express service or 50 minutes via local. Tourist office: Palais des Festivals, 1 La Croisette, tel. 93-39-24-53.

Unlike Nice, which is a city, **Cannes** is a resort town, existing only for the pleasure of its guests. Cosmopolitan, sophisticated, and smart, it's a tasteful and expensive breeding ground for the upscale (and those who are already "up"), and a sybaritic heaven for those who believe that life is short and that sin has something to do with the absence of a tan.

Alongside the long, narrow beach is a broad, elegant promenade called La Croisette, bordered by palm trees and flowers. At one end of the promenade is the modern Festival Hall, a summer casino, and an old harbor where pleasure boats are moored. At the other end is a winter casino and a modern harbor for some of the most luxurious yachts in the world. All along the promenade are cafés, boutiques, and luxury hotels like the Carlton and the Majestic. Speedboats and waterskiers glide by; little waves lick the beach, lined with prostrate bodies. Behind the promenade lies the town, filled with shops, restaurants, and hotels, and behind the town are the hills with the villas of the very rich.

The first thing to do is stroll along **La Croisette,** stopping at cafés and boutiques along the way. Near the eastern end (turning left as you face the water), before you reach the new port, is the **Parc de la Roserie,** where some 14,000 roses nod their heads in the wind. Walking west takes you past the **Palais des Festivals** (Festival Hall), where the famous film festival is held each May. Just past the hall is **Place du Général-de-Gaulle,** while on your left is the **old port.** If you continue straight beyond the port on **Allées de la Liberte,** you'll reach a tree-shaded area, where flowers are sold in the morning, *boules* is played in the afternoon, and a flea market is held on Saturday. If instead of continuing straight from the square you turn inland, you'll quickly come to rue Meynadier. Turn left. This is the old main street, which has many 18th-century houses—now boutiques and specialty food shops.

Lodging
Under 550 frs.

Mondial. A three-minute walk from the beach takes you to this six-story hotel, a haven for the traveler seeking solid, unpretentious lodging in a town that leans more to tinsel. Many guest rooms offer sea views. There's no restaurant. *77 rue d'Antibes, 06400, tel. 93-68-70-00. AE, DC, MC, V.*

Dining
Under 175 frs.

Au Bec Fin. A devoted band of regulars will attest to the quality of this family-run restaurant near the train station. Don't look for a carefully staged decor: It's the spirited local clientele and the homey food that distinguish this cheerful bistro. The fixed-price menus are a fantastic value at 76 or 96 francs; try the fish cooked with fennel or the *salade Niçoise. 14 rue du 24-Août, tel. 93-38-35-86. Reservations advised. AE, DC, MC, V. Closed Sat. dinner, Sun., Christmas-late Jan., and last week of June.*

Shopping Cannes is one of the Riviera's top spots for chic—and expensive—clothing. More fun is the local market, which sells everything from strings of garlic to secondhand gravy boats every Saturday on Allées de la Liberté.

Iles de Lérins

Ferries leave several times daily from Cannes harbor (near the Palais des Festivals); it's 15 minutes to Sainte-Marguerite and 30 minutes to St-Honorat. Call 93–39–11–89 for information.

Ste-Marguerite, the larger of the two **Iles de Lérins** (Lerin Islands), is all wooded hills, with a tiny main street lined with fishermen's houses. Visitors enjoy peaceful walks through a forest of enormous eucalyptus trees and parasol pines. Paths wind through a dense undergrowth of tree heathers, rosemary, and thyme. The main attraction is the dank cell in **Fort Royal,** where the Man in the Iron Mask was imprisoned (1687–98) before going to the Bastille, where he died in 1703. The mask, which he always wore, was in fact made of velvet. Was he the illegitimate brother of Louis XIV or Louis XIII's son-in-law? No one knows.

St-Honorat is less tamed but more tranquil than its sister island. It was named for a hermit-monk who came here to escape his followers; but when the hermit founded a monastery here in AD 410, his disciples followed and the monastery became one of the most powerful in all Christendom. It's worth taking the two-hour walk around the island to the **old fortified monastery,** where noble Gothic arcades are arranged around a central courtyard. Next door to the "new" 19th-century monastery (open on request) is a shop where the monks sell handicrafts, lavender scent, and a home-brewed liqueur called Lérina. There is also a small monastic museum. *Monastère de Lérins, tel. 93–48–68–68. Admission to museum and monastery free. Admission to fortress: 8 frs. Open daily 10:30–noon and 1:30–4:40 in winter; call for summer hours. Weekday mass in winter at 8:15 AM; Sun. mass at 9:50 AM year-round.*

La Napoule

Four trains run daily to La Napoule from Cannes, 8 minutes away, and from Nice, 50 minutes distant. Tourist office: 274 av. Henri-Clews, tel. 93–49–95–31.

La Napoule, forming a unit with the older, inland village of **Mandelieu,** boasts extensive modern sports facilities (swimming, boating, waterskiing, deep-sea diving, fishing, golf, tennis, horseback riding, and parachuting). It explodes with color during the Fête du Mimosa (Mimosa Festival) in February. Art lovers will want to stop in La Napoule at the **Château de La Napoule Art Foundation** to see the eccentric work of the American sculptor Henry Clews. A cynic and sadist, Clews had, as one critic remarked, a knowledge of anatomy worthy of Michelangelo and the bizarre imagination of Edgar Allan Poe. *Av. Henry-Clews. Admission: 25 frs. Guided tours only, Sept.–Oct. and Dec.–June, Wed.–Mon. at 3 and 4; July and Aug., Wed.–Mon. at 3, 4, and 5. Closed Tues. and Nov.*

Fréjus

Three trains run daily to Fréjus from Cannes, 30 minutes away, and from Nice, 70 minutes away. Tourist office: 325 rue Jean-Jaures, tel. 91–51–54–14.

Fréjus was founded by Julius Caesar as Forum Julii in 49 BC, and it is thought that the Roman city grew to 40,000 people—10,000 more than the population today. The Roman remains are unspectacular, if varied, and consist of part of the theater, an arena, an aqueduct, and city walls.

Fréjus Cathedral dates to the 10th century, although the richly worked choir stalls belong to the 15th century. The baptistry alongside it, square on the outside and octagonal inside, is thought to date from AD 400, making it one of France's oldest buildings. The adjacent cloisters feature an unusual contrast between round and pointed arches.

St-Raphaël, next door to Fréjus, is another family resort with holiday camps, best known to tourists as the railway stop to the teeming resort of St-Tropez, where Brigitte Bardot and her director Roger Vadim filmed *And God Created Woman* in 1956 (and changed the resort forever). It was in St-Raphaël that the Allied forces landed in their offensive against the Germans in August 1944.

Lodging and Dining
Under 400 frs.

Ligure. This large, modern hotel, a member of the Principal Hotel chain, lies a quick taxi ride from the center of Fréjus along the road to St-Raphaël. It has air-conditioning, a multilingual staff, and a great location just a half a mile from the Mediterranean sands. The restaurant serves light lunches and more substantial dinners; you may prefer to fill up at the start of the day with an English-style cooked breakfast, which costs just 60 francs and is too rare in France to go unheralded. There is a fixed-price lunch and dinner menu for 78 francs. *1074 av. du Mal-de-Lattre-de-Tassigny, 83600, tel. 94–53–73–72. 64 rooms with bath or shower. Facilities: restaurant. AE, DC, MC, V.*

St-Paul-de-Vence

Buses leave Nice's Gare Routière every ½ hour for St-Paul-de-Vence, 50 minutes away, continuing to Vence.

Not even hordes of tourists can destroy the ancient charm of **St-Paul-de-Vence**, a gem of a town whose medieval atmosphere has been perfectly preserved. You can walk the narrow, cobbled streets in perhaps 15 minutes, but you'll need another hour to explore the shops—mostly galleries selling second-rate landscape paintings, but also a few serious studios and gift shops offering everything from candles to dolls, dresses, and hand-dipped chocolate strawberries. Your best bet is to visit in the late afternoon, when the tour buses are gone, and enjoy a drink among the Klees and Picassos in the Colombe d'Or, a charming inn (*see below*). Be sure to visit the remarkable 12th-century Gothic church; you'll want to light a candle to relieve its wonderful gloom. The treasury is rich in 12th- to 15th-century pieces, including processional crosses, reliquaries, and an enamel Virgin and Child.

At La Gardette, within walking distance just northwest of the village, is the **Fondation Maeght,** one of the world's most famous small museums of modern art. Monumental sculptures are scattered around its pine-tree park, and a courtyard full of Alberto Giacometti's elongated creations separates the two museum buildings. The rooms inside showcase the works of Joan Miró, Georges Braque, Wassily Kandinsky, Bonnard, Matisse, and others. Few museums blend form and content so tastefully and imaginatively. There is also a library, cinema, and auditorium. *Admission: 40 frs. adults, 26 frs. children. Open July–Sept., daily 10–7; Oct.–June, daily 10–12:30 and 2:30–6.*

Lodging and Dining
Splurge
★

Colombe d'Or. Anyone who likes the ambience of a country inn will feel right at home here. You'll be paying for your meal with cash or credit cards; Picasso, Klee, Dufy, Utrillo—all friends of the former owner—paid with the paintings that now decorate the walls. The restaurant has a very good reputation. The Colombe d'Or is certainly on the tourist trail, but many of the tourists who stay here are rich and famous—if that's any consolation. *06570 St-Paul-de-Vence, tel. 93–32–80–02. 24 rooms with bath. Facilities: restaurant, pool. AE, DC, MC, V. Closed mid-Nov.–late Dec. 1010 frs. and up.*

Vence

Buses depart every ½ hour from St-Paul-de-Vence and take 5 minutes.

A few miles from St-Paul is **Vence**. The Romans were the first to settle on the 1,000-foot hill; the **cathedral** (built between the 11th and 18th century), rising above the medieval ramparts and traffic-free streets, was erected on the site of a temple to Mars. Of special note are a mosaic by Marc Chagall of Moses in the bullrushes and the ornate 15th-century wooden choir stalls.

At the foot of the hill, on the outskirts of Vence, is the **Chapelle du Rosaire,** a small chapel decorated with beguiling simplicity and clarity by Matisse between 1947 and 1951. The walls, floor, and ceiling are gleaming white and are pierced by small stained-glass windows in cool greens and blues. "Despite its imperfections I think it is my masterpiece . . . the result of a lifetime devoted to the search for truth," wrote Matisse, who designed and dedicated the chapel when he was in his eighties and nearly blind. *Av. Henri-Matisse. Admission free. Open Tues. and Thurs. 10–11:30 and 2:30–5.*

Lodging and Dining
Under 400 frs.

Le Roseraie. While there's no rose garden here, a giant magnolia spreads its venerable branches over the terrace. Chef Maurice Ganier hails from the southwest, as do the ducks that form the basis of his cooking. Polished service and sophisticated menus prove you don't have to be rich to enjoy life in this part of France. There are 12 guest rooms and a swimming pool. *Av. Henri-Giraud, 06140, tel. 93–58–02–20. 12 rooms with bath. Facilities: restaurant (closed Tues. lunch and Wed.), pool. AE, MC, V. Closed Jan.*

Peillon

Two trains run from Nice to Peillon daily. The trip, about 10 km (6 mi) inland, takes 25 minutes.

Situated on a craggy mountaintop more than 1,000 feet above the sea, the fortified medieval town of **Peillon** is the most spectacular and the least spoiled of all the Riviera's cliffside villages. Unchanged since the Middle Ages, it has only a few narrow streets and many steps and covered alleys. And since there's really nothing to do here but look, tour buses stay away, leaving Peillon uncommercialized for its 50 resident families—including professionals summering away from Paris and artists who want to escape the craziness of the world below. Stop at the charming **Auberge de la Madame** to pick up the key to the **Chapel of the White Penitents,** a short walk away; spend a half hour exploring the ancient streets; then head back down the mountain to Nice.

Villefranche-sur-Mer

Hourly trains to Villefranche take 6 minutes from Nice, 4 kilometers (2½ miles) to the west.

The harbor town of **Villefranche-sur-Mer** is a miniature version of old Marseille. The sort of place where *Fanny* could have been filmed, it's a stage set of brightly colored houses—orange buildings with lime-green shutters, yellow buildings with ice-blue shutters—with steep narrow streets winding down to the sea. (One, **rue Obscure,** is an actual tunnel.)

The 17th-century **St-Michel** church has a strikingly realistic Christ, carved of boxwood by an unknown convict. The chapel of St-Pierre-des-Pêcheurs, known as the **Cocteau Chapel,** is a small Romanesque chapel once used for storing fishing nets, which the French writer and painter Jean Cocteau decorated in 1957. Visitors walk through the flames of the Apocalypse (represented by staring eyes on either side of the door) and enter a room filled with frescoes of St. Peter, gypsies, and the women of Villefranche. *Admission: 10 frs. Open Oct.–Nov. 15 and Dec. 15–Apr., Tues.–Sun. 9:30–noon and 2–5; May–June, Tues.–Sun. 9:30–noon and 2–6; July–Sept., Tues.–Sun. 9:30–noon and 2–7. Closed Mon. and Nov. 15–Dec. 15.*

To see the chapel, arrive by 4 PM. If you skip the chapel, your best bet is to come at sundown (for dinner, perhaps) and enjoy an hour's walk around the harbor, when the sun turns the soft pastels to gold.

Beaulieu

There are hourly trains to Beaulieu from Villefranche, 3 minutes away, and from Nice, 9 minutes away.

Beaulieu, just next door to Villefranche, was a playground for high society at the turn of the century. Stop and walk along the promenade, sometimes called Petite Afrique (Little Africa) because of its magnificent palm trees, to get a flavor of how things used to be.

The one thing to do in Beaulieu is visit the **Villa Kérylos.** In the early part of the century, a rich amateur archaeologist named Theodore Reinach asked an Italian architect to build an authentic Greek house for him. The villa, now open to the public, is a faithful reproduction, made from cool Carrara marble, alabaster, and rare fruitwoods. The furniture, made of wood inlaid with ivory, bronze, and leather, is copied from drawings of Greek interiors found on ancient vases and mosaics. *Admission: 20 frs. Open July–Sept., Tues.–Sun. 2–7; Oct. and Dec.–June, Tues.–Sun. 2–6. Closed Mon. and Nov.*

519 M.P. H.

190 M.P. H.

S-HS 7469
75 M.P. H.

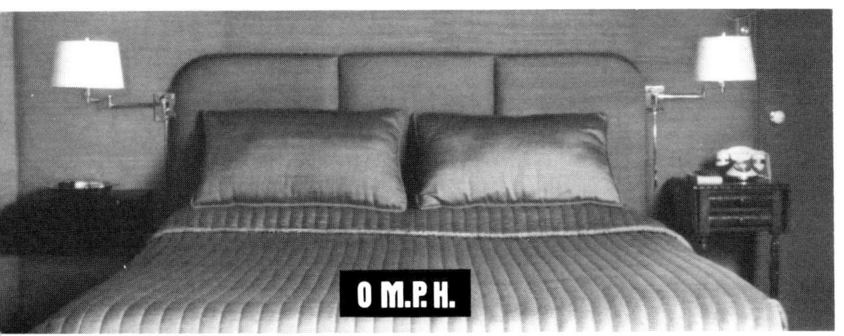
0 M.P. H.

Eze

There are hourly trains to Eze, which is 5 minutes from Beaulieu and 14 minutes from Nice.

Almost every tour from Nice to Monaco includes a visit to the medieval hill town of **Eze,** perched on a rocky spur some 1,300 feet above the sea. (Don't confuse Eze with the beach town of **Eze-sur-Mer,** which is down by the water.) Be warned that because of its accessibility the town is also crowded and commercial: Eze has its share of serious craftspeople, but most of its vendors make their living selling perfumed soaps and postcards to the package-tour trade.

Enter through a fortified 14th-century gate and wander down narrow, cobbled streets with vaulted passageways and stairs. The church is 18th century, but the small Chapel of the White Penitents dates to 1306 and contains a 13th-century gilded wooden Spanish Christ and some notable 16th-century paintings. Tourist and crafts shops line the streets leading to the ruins of a castle, which has a scenic belvedere. Some of the most tasteful crafts shops are in the hotel-restaurant **Chèvre d'Or.**

Near the top of the village is a garden with exotic flowers and cacti. (It's worth the admission price, but if you have time for only one exotic garden, visit the one in Monte Carlo.) Also stop in at **La Perfumerie Fragonard,** a branch of a Grasse perfumerie located in front of the public gardens.

Monaco

There are hourly trains to Monaco. The trip takes 8 minutes from Eze, 22 from Nice. Tourist office: 2-A blvd. des Moulins, tel. 93–30–87–01.

Numbers in the margin correspond with points of interest on the Monaco map.

Covering just 473 acres, the **Principality of Monaco** would fit comfortably inside New York's Central Park or a family farm in Iowa. Its 5,000 citizens would fill only a small fraction of the seats in Yankee Stadium. The country is so tiny that residents have to go to another country to play golf.

The present ruler, Prince Rainier III, traces his ancestry to Otto Canella, who was born in 1070. The Grimaldi dynasty began with Otto's great-great-great-grandson, Francesco Grimaldi, also known as Frank the Rogue. Expelled from Genoa, Frank and his cronies disguised themselves as monks and seized the fortified medieval town known today as the Rock in 1297. Except for a short break under Napoleon, the Grimaldis have been here ever since, which makes them the oldest reigning family in Europe. On the Grimaldi coat of arms are two monks holding swords (look up and you'll see them above the main door as you enter the palace).

Back in the 1850s, a Grimaldi named Charles III made a decision that turned the Rock into a figurative giant blue chip. Needing revenues but not wanting to impose additional taxes on his subjects, he contracted with a company to open a gambling facility. The first spin of the roulette wheel was on December 14, 1856. There was no easy way to reach Monaco then—no carriage roads or railroads—so no one came. Between March 15 and March 20, 1857, one person entered the casino—and won two francs. In 1868, however, the railroad reached Monaco, filled with wheezing Englishmen who came to escape the London fog. The effects were immediate. Profits were so great that Charles eventually abolished all direct taxes.

Almost overnight, a threadbare principality became an elegant watering hole for European society. Dukes and duchesses (and their mistresses and gigolos) danced and dined their way through a world of spinning roulette wheels and bubbling champagne—preening themselves for nights at the opera, where such artists as Vaslav Nijinsky, Sarah Bernhardt, and Enrico Caruso came to perform.

Monte Carlo—the modern gambling town with elegant shops, man-made beaches, high-rise hotels, and a few Belle Epoque hotels—is actually only one of four parts of Monaco. The second is the medieval town on the Rock (**Old Monaco**), 200 feet above the sea. It's here that Prince Rainier lives.

The third area is **La Condamine,** the commercial harbor area with apartments and businesses. The fourth is **Fontvieille,** the industrial district situated on 20 acres of reclaimed land.

Start at the Monte Carlo tourist office just north of the casino gardens, where you can pick up brochures on area attractions.
1 The **Casino** is a must-see, even if you don't bet a cent. You may find it fun to count the Jaguars and Rolls-Royces parked outside and breathe on the windows of shops selling Saint-Laurent dresses and fabulous jewels. Within the gold-leaf splendor of the casino, where fortunes have been won and shirts have been lost, the hopeful traipse in from tour buses to tempt fate at the slot machines beneath the gilt-edged Rococo ceiling.

The main gambling hall, once called the European Room, has been renamed the American Room and fitted with 150 one-armed bandits from Chicago. Adjoining it is the Pink Salon, now a bar where unclad nymphs float about on the ceiling smoking cigarillos. The Salles Privées (private rooms) are for high rollers. The stakes are higher here, so the mood is more sober, and well-wishers are herded farther back from the tables.

On July 17, 1924, black came up 17 times in a row on Table 5. This was the longest run ever. A dollar left on black would have grown to $131,072. On August 7, 1913, the number 36 came up three times in a row. In those days, if a gambler went broke, the casino bought him a ticket home.

The casino opens at 10 AM and continues until the last die is thrown. Ties and jackets are required in the back rooms, which open at 4 PM. Bring your passport.

Place du Casino is the center of Monte Carlo, and, in the true spirit of this place, it seems that the **Opera House,** with its 18-ton gilt bronze chandelier, is part of the casino complex. The designer, Charles Garnier, also built the Paris Opéra.

2 The serious gamblers, some say, play at **Loews Casino,** nearby. It opens weekdays at 4 PM and weekends at 1 PM. You may want to try parking here, as parking near the old casino is next to impossible in season.

From place des Moulins there is an escalator down to the Larvotto beach complex, artfully created with imported sand,

Casino, **1**
Cathedral, **5**
Jardin Exotique, **7**
Loews Casino, **2**
Musée Nationale, **3**
Musée Océanographique, **6**
Museum of Prehistoric Anthropology, **8**
Palace, **4**

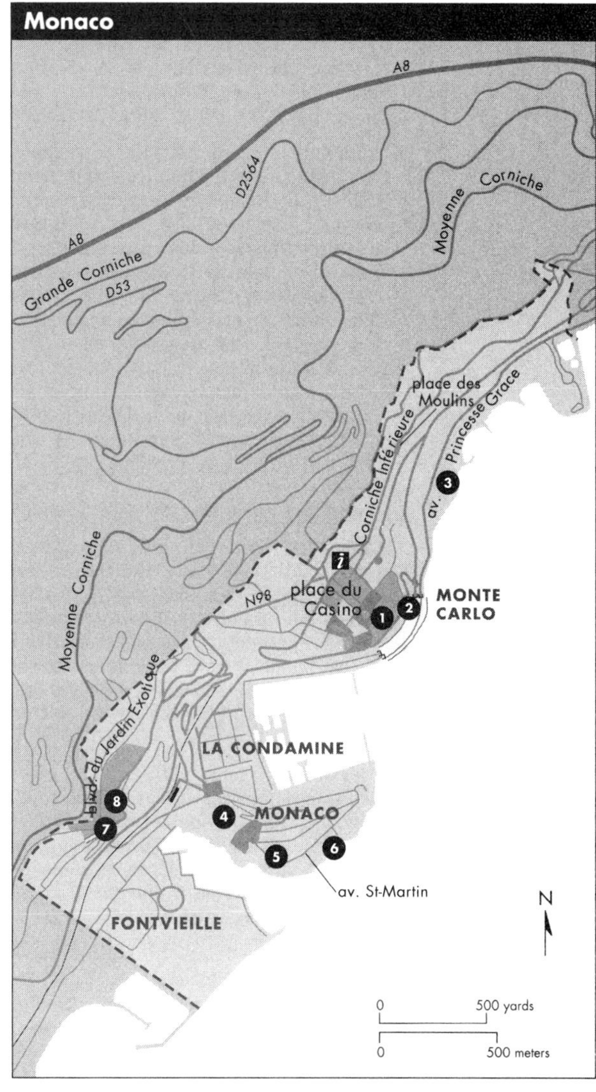

3 and the **Musée National,** housed in a Garnier villa within a rose garden. This museum has a beguiling collection of 18th- and 19th-century dolls and mechanical automatons, most in working order. *17 av. Princesse-Grace, tel. 93–30–91–26. Admission: 24 frs. adults, 14 frs. students. Open Apr.–Sept., daily 10–6:30; Oct.–Mar., daily 10–12:15 and 2:30–6:30. Closed holidays.*

4 Prince Rainier spends much of the year in his grand Italianate **Palace** on the Rock. The changing of the guard takes place here each morning at 11:55, and the State Apartments can be visited in summer. *Admission: 25 frs. Open June–Sept., daily 9:30–6:30; Oct., daily 10–5.*

One wing of the palace, open throughout the year, is taken up by a museum full of Napoleonic souvenirs and documents related to Monaco's history. *Admission: 15 frs. Open June–Sept., Tues.–Sun. 9:30–6:30; Oct., Tues.–Sun. 10–5; Dec.–May, Tues.–Sun. 10:30–12:30 and 2–5. Closed Mon. and Nov.*

From here, a stroll through the medieval alleyways takes you
5 past the **cathedral,** a neo-Romanesque monstrosity (1875–84),
with several important paintings of the Nice school. Continue
6 to one of Monaco's most outstanding showpieces, the **Musée Océanographique**—also an important research institute headed by celebrated underwater explorer and filmmaker Jacques Cousteau. Prince Rainier's great-grandfather Albert I (1848–1922), an accomplished marine biologist, founded the institute, which now boasts two exploration ships, laboratories, and a staff of 60 scientists. Nonscientific visitors may wish to make straight for the well-arranged and generously stocked aquarium in the basement. Other floors are devoted to Prince Albert's collection of seashells and whale skeletons, and to Cousteau's diving equipment. *Av. St-Martin, tel. 93–30–15–14. Admission: 50 frs. adults, 20 frs. students and children. Open daily, July–Aug. 9–9, Sept.–June 9:30–7.*

A brisk half-hour walk back past the palace brings you to the
7 **Jardin Exotique** (Tropical Garden), where 600 varieties of cacti
8 and succulents cling to a sheer rock face. The **Museum of Prehistoric Anthropology,** on the grounds, contains bones, tools, and other artifacts. Shapes of the stalactites and stalagmites in the cavernous grotto resemble the cacti outside. *Blvd. du Jardin-Exotique. Admission: 32 frs. adults, 28 frs. students, 16 frs. children. Open daily 9–6 (dusk in winter).*

Lodging
Splurge

Alexandra. Shades of the Belle Epoque linger in this comfortable hotel's spacious lobby and airy guest rooms. Tan and rose colors dominate the newer rooms, and the friendly proprietress, Madame Larouquie, makes foreign visitors feel right at home. If you're willing to do without a private bath, this place will cost you even less. Even so, remember that Monaco prices are sky high. *35 blvd. Princesse-Charlotte, 98000, tel. 93–50–63–13. 55 rooms, 46 with bath. AE, DC, MC, V. 550–750 frs.*

Dining
Under 250 frs.
★

Polpetta. This popular little trattoria is close enough to the Italian border to pass for the real McCoy and is an excellent value for the money. If it's on the menu, go for the vegetable *soupe au pistou. 2 rue Paradis, tel. 93–50–67–84. Reservations required in summer. V. Closed Sat. lunch and Tues. (except July–Sept.), last 2 weeks in Oct., and 3 weeks mid-Feb.–early Mar.*

Menton

Hourly trains operate from Monaco, 18 minutes away, and from Nice, 40 minutes away. Tourist office: Palais de l'Europe, av. Boyer, tel. 93–57–57–00.

Menton, a comparatively quiet all-year resort that likes to call itself the Pearl of the Riviera, boasts the area's warmest climate. Lemon trees flourish here, as do senior citizens, enticed by a long strand of beaches. It's beautiful, respectable, and not grossly expensive.

Walk eastward from the casino along promenade du Soleil to the harbor. There is a small 17th-century fort here, where writer, artist, and filmmaker Jean Cocteau (1889–1963) once worked. The fort now houses the **Cocteau Museum** of fantastical paintings, drawings, stage sets and a large mosaic. *Bastion du Port, 111 quai Napoléon III. Admission free. Open mid-June–mid-Sept., Wed.–Mon. 10–noon and 3–7; mid-Sept.–mid-June, Wed.–Mon. 10–noon and 2–6. Closed Tues.*

The quaint old town above the jetty has an Italian feel to it. Visit the church of **St-Michel** for its ornate Baroque interior and altarpiece of St. Michael slaying a dragon. Concerts of chamber music are held on the square on summer nights.

Higher still is the **Vieux Cimetière** (old cemetery), with a magnificent view of the old town and coast. Here lie Victorian foreigners—Russians, Germans, English—who hoped (in vain, as the dates on the tombstones reveal) that Menton's balmy climate would reverse the ravages of tuberculosis.

Return to the center and the pedestrian rue St-Michel. On avenue de la République, which runs parallel, is the **Hôtel de Ville** (Town Hall). The room where civil marriage ceremonies are conducted has vibrant allegorical frescoes by Cocteau; a tape in English helps to interpret them. *17 rue de la République. Admission 5 frs. adults; 2.50 frs. students and children. Open weekdays 8:30–12:30 and 1:30–5; closed weekends.*

Two other places of interest lie at opposite ends of Menton. To the west is the **Palais Carnolès,** an 18th-century villa once used as a summer retreat by the princes of Monaco. The gardens are beautiful, and the collection of European paintings spanning the 13th to 18th centuries is extensive. *3 av. Madone. Admission free. Open mid-June–mid-Sept., Wed.–Mon. 10–noon and 3–7; mid-Sept.–mid-June, Wed.–Mon. 10–noon and 2–6. Closed Tues.*

At the other end of Menton, above the Garavan harbor, lie the **Colombières Gardens,** where follies and statues lurk among 15 acres of hedges, yew trees, and Mediterranean flowers. *Chemin de Valleya. At press time gardens were closed for extensive renovation; check with tourist office for opening date, admission fee, and hours.*

Lodging and Dining
Under 250 frs.

Londres. This small hotel, close to the beach and casino, has its own restaurant. The cuisine is solid and traditional French fare, and there's a small garden for outdoor dining in summer. *15 av. Carnot, 06500, tel. 93–35–74–62. 26 rooms with shower or bath. Facilities: restaurant (closed Wed.), bar, ping-pong. AE, MC, V. Closed mid-Nov.–mid-Jan.*

13 Toulouse, the Midi-Pyrénées and Roussillon

Carcassonne, Lourdes, Pau

Toulouse is a long way from Paris, and the Pyrénées are poorly equipped with public transportation. But with 28,500 square miles stretching from the Massif Central in the north to the Spanish border in the south, the surrounding Midi-Pyrénées—the largest region in France—offers an abundance of historic towns and spectacular mountain scenery. In addition, skiing is less expensive in the Pyrénées than in the Alps, though ski stations are fewer and may have insufficient snow in mild winters.

The Pyrénées, western Europe's highest mountain range after the Alps, give birth to the Garonne, the great river of Toulouse and Bordeaux. The Garonne is joined by the Aveyron, Lot, and Tarn rivers, which cross the region from east to west, carving out steep gorges and wide green valleys. The Pyrenean foothills are riddled with streams, lakes, and spas established in Roman times. Armagnac brandy has its home among the gently undulating hills of the Gers while farther north, hearty red wine has been produced in the rugged country around Cahors for over 2,000 years.

Toulouse is a young, lively city, one of the few outside Paris whose nightlife doesn't grind to a halt at midnight. Smaller towns offer equal charms. Don't miss the fortified medieval bridge at Cahors or the extensive town walls at Carcassonne, where portions of Kevin Costner's *Robin Hood* were filmed. Pilgrims flock to Lourdes as they once flocked to the dramatic cliffside village of Rocamadour, the architectural embodiment of vertical takeoff. At Montauban is the Musée Ingres, devoted to one of France's most accomplished pre-Impressionist painters. Albi stands out for the Musée Toulouse-Lautrec, with its racy testimony to the leading observer of Belle Epoque cabaret, and the redbrick cathedral of Ste-Cécile, the most impressive monument in the Midi-Pyrénées, with slits for windows and walls like cliffs.

The attractive Mediterranean coast between Narbonne and the Spanish border can easily be reached from Toulouse and is covered on our tour of Roussillon. Perpignan, its capital, has a bustling, Spanish feel: Roussillon has strong linguistic and historic ties with Catalonia, across the Pyrénées, and was ceded by Spain to France as recently as 1659. The streets of even the smallest towns are awash with the proud Catalan colors of *sang et or* (blood and gold).

Essential Information

Lodging Hotels in this vast region range from Mediterranean-style modern to Middle Ages baronial; most are small and cozy rather than luxurious. Toulouse, the area's only major town, has the usual range of big-city hotels; make reservations well ahead if you plan to visit in spring or fall. As with most of France, many of the hotels we list offer excellent eating opportunities.

Dining The cuisine in Toulouse and the southwest is rich and strongly seasoned, making generous use of garlic and goose fat. This is the land of foie gras, especially delicious when sautéed with grapes. The most famous regional dish is *cassoulet,* a succulent white-bean stew with *confit* (preserved goose), spicy sausage, pork, and sometimes lamb; there are a number of local versions around Toulouse and Carcassonne. Goose and duck dishes are legion: Try a *magret de canard* (a steak of duck breast). Cheaper specialties include *garbure,* mixed vegetables served as a broth or puree; *farci du lauragais,* a kind of pork pancake; and *gigot de sept heures,* a leg of lamb braised with garlic for no fewer than seven hours. Béarn, around Pau, is great eating country, famous for richly marinated stews made with wood pigeon *(civet de palombes)* or wild goat *(civet d'isnard).* The local *poule au pot* of stuffed chicken poached with vegetables is memorable.

Shopping Don't leave the Midi-Pyrénées without buying some of the region's renowned foie gras and preserved duck *(confit de canard).* Two manufacturers in particular, **Aux Ducs de Gascogne** and **Comtesse de Barry,** offer beautifully packaged tins that make ideal gifts. You'll find their products in most good grocery stores and general food shops throughout the region.

Bicycling The attractive, varied terrain north of Toulouse and the desperately flat Garonne Valley makes for enjoyable cycling; you can rent bikes at the Cahors, Rocamadour, Albi, and Rodez rail stations. The banks and tow paths of the Canal du Midi offer less strenuous terrain (you can rent a bike from the Carcassonne station). Sturdier cyclists may opt to attack the Pyrenean foothills; contact **Cycles Fun** (3 pl. Comminges) in Bagnères-de-Luchon, or **Marc de Baudoine** (28 rue Polinaires) in Toulouse, which specializes in mountain bikes. You can also rent bikes at the Luchon, Foix, and Lourdes stations.

Hiking The Midi-Pyrénées offers more than 2,000 miles of marked paths for walkers and hikers, all designed to pass natural and historical sights. Local tourist offices have detailed maps, or, for advance information, contact **Comité de Randonnées Mi di-Pyrénées** (CORAMIP, 12 rue Salammbô, 31200 Toulouse, tel. 61–47–11–12).

The Arts Toulouse, the region's cultural high spot, is also recognized as one of France's most arty cities. Its classical, lyrical, and chamber music orchestras, dramatic-arts center, and ballet are all listed as national companies—no mean feat in this arts-oriented country. So many opera singers have come to sing here at the Théatre du Capitole or the Halle aux Grains that the city is known as the *capitale du bel canto*.

The medieval city of Carcassonne has a major arts festival in July, featuring dance, theater, classical music, and jazz; for details, contact the Théâtre Municipal (B.P. 236, rue Courtejaire, 11005 Carcassonne cedex, tel. 68–25–33–13).

Highlights for First-time Visitors

The town walls of Carcassonne, Tour 3
Lourdes, Tour 2
Musée Ingres, Montauban, Tour 1
Palais de la Berbie (Toulouse-Lautrec Museum), Albi, Tour 1
Rocamadour, Tour 1
Ste-Cécile, Albi, Tour 1
Château of Pau, Tour 2
St-Sernin, Toulouse, Tour 1

Tour 1: The Toulouse Region

Swinging Toulouse, rosy with its pink-brick buildings, is the base for a counterclockwise circle tour through Rodez, Cahors, and Montauban, with visits to other points of interest en route.

From Paris *By Train* Express trains to Toulouse leave Paris (Gare d'Austerlitz) 6 times daily. The trip takes 6–6½ hours.

By Car Allow 8–9 hours for the arduous 705-kilometer (440-mile) drive from Paris to Toulouse via A10 and A71, then N20 from Vierzon.

Toulouse

Tourist office: Donjon du Capitole, behind the Capitole itself, tel. 61–23–32–00.

Numbers in the margin correspond to points of interest on the Toulouse map.

Ebullient **Toulouse** lies just 96-odd kilometers (60 miles) from the Spanish border, and its flavor is more Spanish than French. The city's downtown sidewalks and restaurants are thronged way past midnight as foreign tourists mingle with immigrant workers, college students, and technicians from the giant Airbus aviation complex headquartered outside the city.

Head over the canal in front of Gare Matabiau and take rue de Bayard. Cross boulevard de Strasbourg and continue down rue de Remussat to the town center. **Place du Capitole**, a vast, open square lined with shops and cafés, is the best spot for getting

your bearings. One side of the square is occupied by the 18th-
1 century facade of the **Capitole** itself, home of the Hôtel de Ville
(Town Hall) and the city's highly regarded opera company. The
coats of arms of the Capitouls, the former rulers of Toulouse,
can be seen on the balconies in the Capitole's courtyard, and
the building's vast reception rooms are open to visitors when
not in use for official functions. Halfway up the Grand Escalier
(Grand Staircase) hangs a large painting of the *Jeux Floraux*,
the Floral Games organized by the Compagnie du Gai-
Savoir—a literary society created in 1324 to promote the local
language, Langue d'Oc. The festival continues to this day:
Poets give public readings here each May, the best receiving
silver- and gold-plated flowers as prizes. The pompous Salle
des Illustres, with its late-19th-century paintings, is used for
official receptions and uppercrust wedding ceremonies. Wed-
dings are also held in the Salle Gervaise, beneath a series of
paintings inspired by the theme of Love at ages 20, 40, and 60;
while the men age, the women stay young forever.

Four more giant paintings in the Salle Henri-Martin, named after the artist (1860–1943), show how important the River Garonne has always been to the region. Look out for Jean Jaurès, one of France's greatest Socialists (1859–1914), in *Les Rêveurs* (*The Dreamers*); he's wearing a boater and a beige-colored coat. *Pl. du Capitole. Tel. 61–22–29–22 (ext. 3412) to check opening times. Admission free. Closed Tues. and weekends.*

Head north from place du Capitole along rue du Taur, lined
with tiny shops. Half a block up, the 14th-century church of
2 **Notre-Dame du Taur** was built on the spot where St-Saturnin
(or Sernin), the martyred bishop of Toulouse, was dragged to
his death in AD 257 by a rampaging bull. The church is famous
for its *cloche-mur*, or wall tower; the wall looks more like an extension of the facade than a tower or steeple and has inspired
many similar versions throughout the Toulouse region.

3 The basilica of **St-Sernin,** Toulouse's most famous landmark, lies at the far end of rue du Taur. The basilica once belonged to a Benedictine abbey, built in the 11th century to house pilgrims on their way to Santiago de Compostela in Spain. When illuminated at night, St-Sernin's five-tiered octagonal tower glows red against the sky, dominating the city. Not all the tiers are the same: The first three, with their rounded windows, are Romanesque; the upper two, with their pointed Gothic windows, were added around 1300.

The size of the basilica—particularly the width of the transept, more than 68 feet—is striking. It's worth paying the token entry fee to the crypt and ambulatory to admire the tomb of St-Sernin and seven exquisitely preserved marble bas-reliefs of Christ and his apostles, dating from the end of the 11th century. *Rue du Taur. Admission to crypt: 8 frs. Open daily 10–11:30 and 2:30–5:30.*

4 Opposite the basilica is the **Musée St-Raymond,** the city's archaeological museum. The ground floor has an extensive collection of imperial Roman busts, and the second floor is devoted to the applied arts, featuring ancient and medieval coins, lamps, vases, and jewelry. *Pl. St-Sernin. Admission: 15 frs. adults, children free. Open Wed.–Mon. 8–noon and 2–6; closed Sun. morning and Tues.*

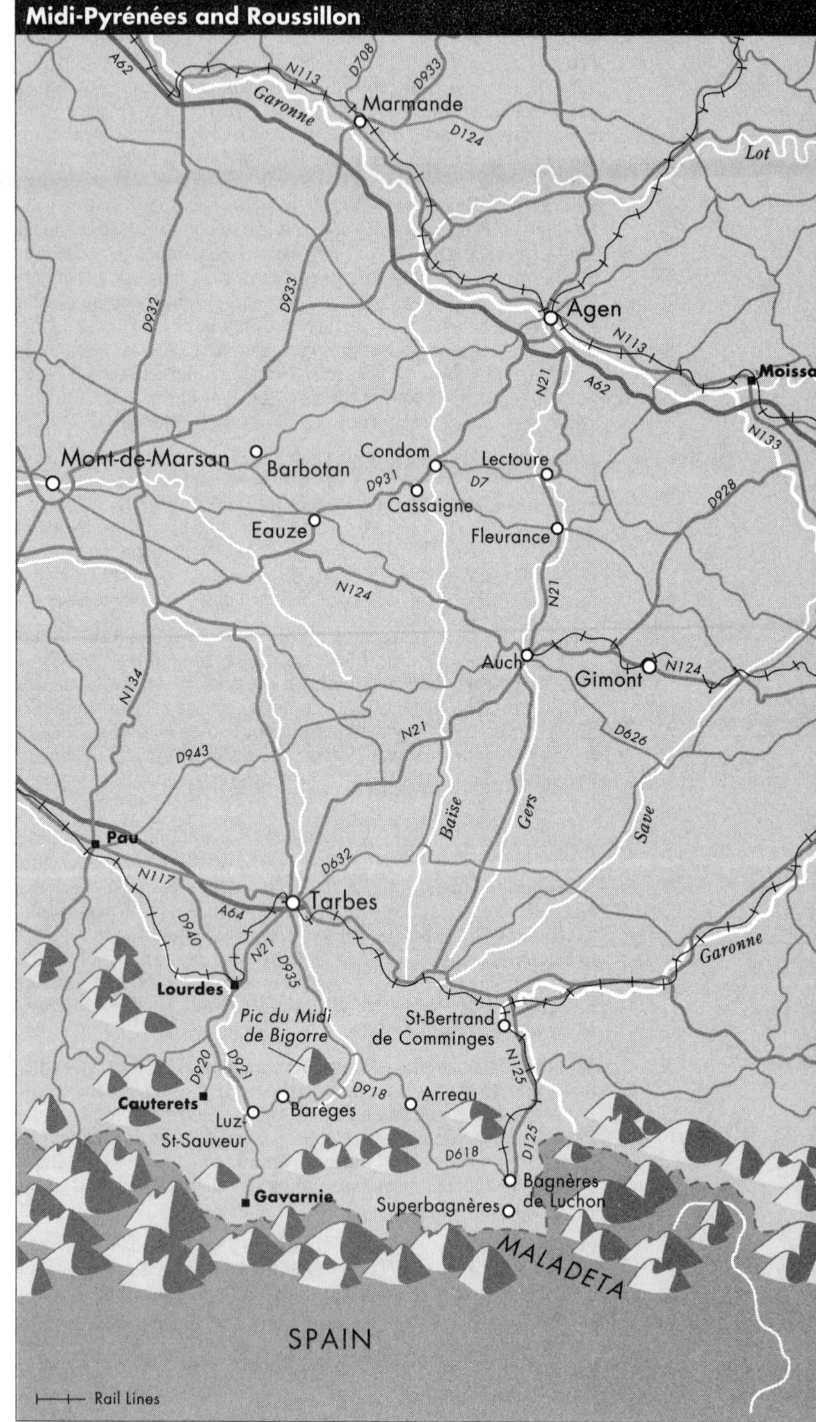

Midi-Pyrénées and Roussillon
A62
N113
D708
D933
Garonne
Marmande
D124
Lot
Agen
N113
Moissa
N21
A62
N133
D933
D932
Mont-de-Marsan
Barbotan
Condom
Lectoure
D931
D7
Cassaigne
D928
Eauze
Fleurance
N124
N21
Auch
Gimont
N124
N134
N21
D626
D943
Baïse
Gers
Save
Pau
D632
N117
Tarbes
A64
D940
N21
D935
Garonne
Lourdes
Pic du Midi
de Bigorre
St-Bertrand
de Comminges
D920
D921
N125
D918
Cauterets
Barèges
Arreau
Luz-
St-Sauveur
D618
D125
Bagnères
de Luchon
Gavarnie
Superbagnères
MALADETA
SPAIN
Rail Lines

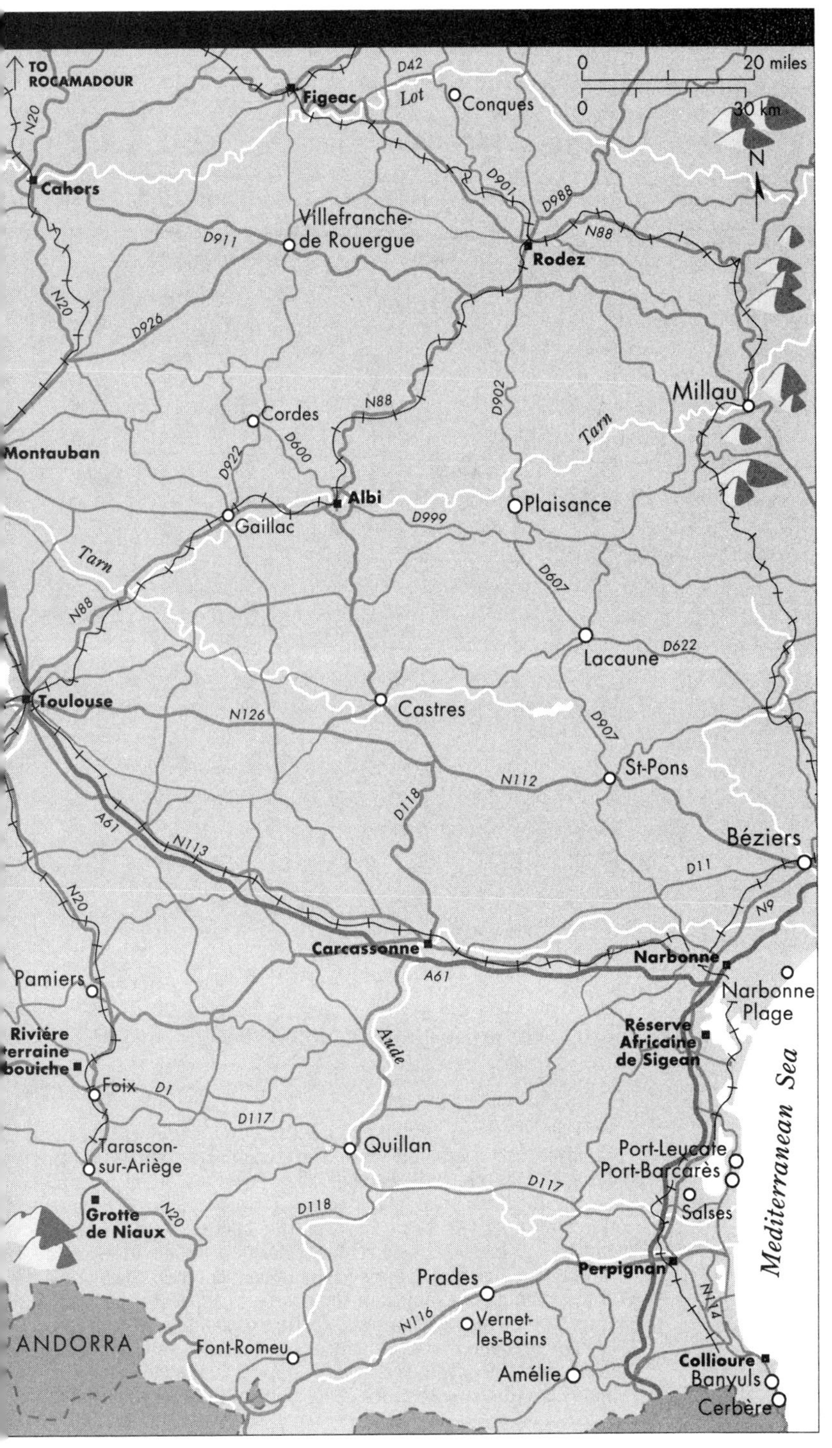
TO ROCAMADOUR
N20
Figeac
D42
Lot
Conques
0
20 miles
0
30 km
N
Cahors
D901
D988
Villefranche-de Rouergue
D911
Rodez
N88
N20
D926
N88
D902
Millau
Cordes
Tarn
Montauban
D600
D922
Albi
Plaisance
Gaillac
D999
Tarn
D607
N88
Lacaune
D622
Toulouse
Castres
N126
D907
St-Pons
N112
D118
A61
Béziers
N113
D11
N20
N9
Carcassonne
Narbonne
A61
Pamiers
Narbonne Plage
Rivière
Réserve Africaine de Sigean
Aude
Foix
D1
D117
Tarascon-sur-Ariège
Quillan
Mediterranean Sea
Port-Leucate
Port-Barcarès
D117
Salses
D118
Grotte de Niaux
N20
Perpignan
Prades
N114
N116
Vernet-les-Bains
ANDORRA
Font-Romeu
Collioure
Amélie
Banyuls
Cerbère

Capitole, **1**
Hôtel d'Assézat, **9**
Hôtel de Bernuy, **6**
Jacobins church, **5**
Musée des Augustins, **10**
Musée d'Histoire Naturelle, **12**
Musée St-Raymond, **4**
Notre-Dame de la Daurade, **7**
Notre-Dame du Taur, **2**
Pont Neuf, **8**
St-Etienne, **11**
St-Sernin, **3**

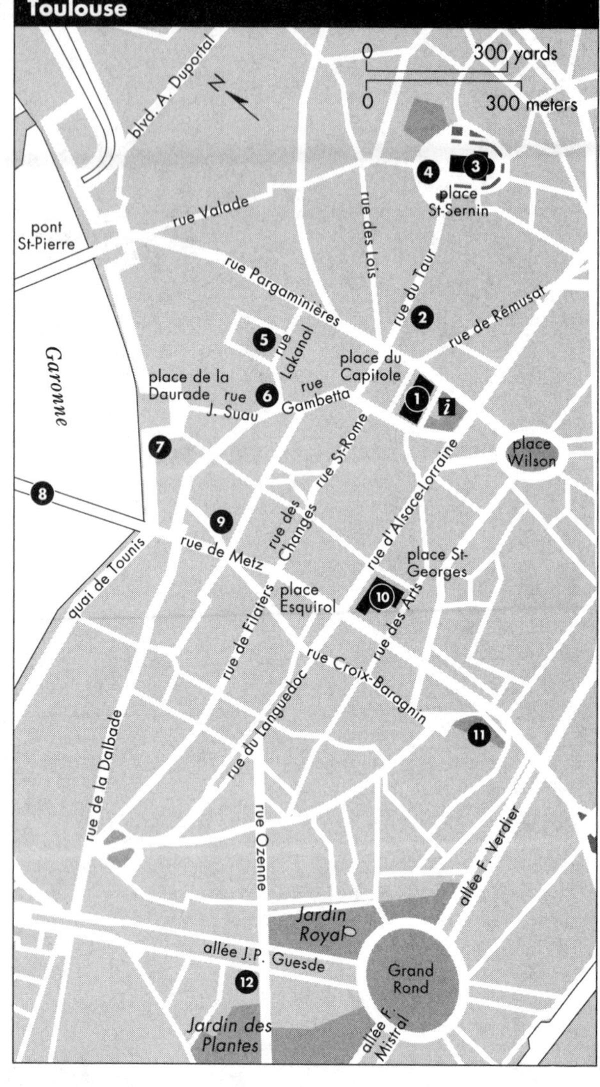

5 Retrace your steps down rue du Taur, turn right at place du Capitole and then left onto rue Lakanal to arrive at the **Jacobins church,** built in the 1230s for the Dominicans; the name "Jacobins" was given to the Dominicans in 1217 when they set up their Paris base at the Porte St-Jacques. The church was harmoniously restored in the 1970s, its interior retaining the original orange-ocher tones. The two rows of columns running the length of the nave—to separate the monks from their congregation—is a feature of Dominican churches, though this one is special, since the column standing the farthest from the entrance is said to support the world's finest example of palm-tree vaulting. The original refectory is used for

temporary art exhibitions, and the cloisters provide an atmospheric setting for the city's summer music festival.

6 Around the corner, on rue Gambetta, stands the **Hôtel de Bernuy,** built during the 16th century, when Toulouse was at its most prosperous. Merchant Jean de Bernuy made his fortune exporting pastel, a blue dye made from the leaves of a plant cultivated around Toulouse and Albi and used to color cloth, especially bed linen. Merchant wealth is reflected in the mansion's use of stone, a costly material in this region of brick, and by the octagonal stair tower, the highest in the city. Building such towers was a rarely bestowed privilege, and this one makes its opulent point by rising above the ceiling of the top floor. The Hôtel de Bernuy is now part of a school, but you may wander freely around its courtyard.

Walk down rue Jean-Suau to place de la Daurade and the 18th-
7 century church of **Notre-Dame de la Daurade,** overlooking the
River Garonne. The name "Daurade" comes from *doré* (gilt), referring to the golden reflection given off by the mosaics decorating the 5th-century temple to the Virgin that once stood on this site. The flowers presented to the winners of the Floral Games are blessed here.

Take time to saunter along quai de la Daurade, beside the
8 church, and admire the view from **Pont Neuf** across to the left
bank. Then head east along rue de Metz. A hundred yards
9 down, on the left, is the **Hôtel d'Assézat,** built in 1555 by
Toulouse's top Renaissance architect, Nicolas Bachelier. The facade is particularly striking: Superimposed classical orders frame alternating arcades and rectangular windows, with ornately carved doorways lurking below. Climb to the top of the tower for splendid views over the city rooftops. *Rue de Metz. Admission free. Open daily 10–noon and 2–6.*

Continue along rue de Metz. The second road on the left (rue des Changes, which becomes rue St-Rome) was once part of the Roman road that sliced through Toulouse from north to south; today it's a chic pedestrian shopping area. Running parallel is the swinging rue d'Alsace-Lorraine, a center of nightlife, luxury boutiques, and department stores. On the corner of rue d'Alsace-Lorraine and rue de Metz, just beyond busy place
10 Esquirol, is the largest museum in Toulouse: the **Musée des**
Augustins, housed in a medieval Augustinian convent whose sacristy, chapter house, and cloisters provide an attractive setting for an outstanding array of Romanesque sculpture and religious paintings by such renowned artists as Spain's Bartolomé Esteban Murillo (1618–82) and Flemish maestro Peter Paul Rubens (1577–1640). *21 rue de Metz. Admission: 7 frs., free Sun. Open Wed.–Mon. 10–noon and 2–6.*

From the Musée des Augustins, cross rue de Metz and head down rue des Arts, then turn left along rue Croix-Baragnin to place St-Etienne, site of both the city's oldest fountain, in mar-
11 ble (16th century), and of the cathedral of **St-Etienne,** erected
in stages between the 13th and the 17th centuries. The nave and choir languished unfinished for a lack of funds; they look awkward because they are not properly aligned. A fine collection of 16th- and 17th-century tapestries traces the life of St. Stephen (Etienne, in French).

The broad allée François-Verdier leads to the leafy, circular Grand Rond, flanked by the **Jardin Royal** (royal gardens) and

12 **Jardin des Plantes** (botanical gardens)—home of the **Musée d'Histoire Naturelle** (Natural History Museum) and its varied collection of stuffed birds and prehistoric exhibits. *35 allée Jules-Guesde. Gardens admission free; open daily dawn to dusk. Museum admission: 8 frs.; open daily 2–6.*

Lodging
Under 250 frs.
Taur. If you want to be in the hub of things without paying grand-hotel prices, the Taur, just a stone's throw from the Capitole, is a workmanlike option. Its labyrinthine corridors have a faded, creaky charm, and the welcome is courteous. But be prepared for soft mattresses, viewless rooms, and gaudily florid wallpaper. *2 rue du Taur, 31000, tel. 62–21–17–54. 41 rooms, most with shower. AE, MC, V.*

Dining
Under 200 frs.
La Belle Epoque. Owner Pierre Roudgé's approach to cooking is novel: Tell him what you don't like and he'll invent your menu on the spot. The ginger-spiced lobster in a flaky pastry is as good as it sounds, especially in the handsomely renovated 1920s setting. However, be prepared for prices that nudge toward the expensive range. *3 rue Pargaminières, tel. 61–23–22–12. Reservations advised. AE, DC, MC, V. Closed Sat. and Mon. lunch, Sun., and July.*

Under 125 frs.
Chez Emile. There are two dining rooms at this restaurant overlooking place St-Georges. The ground floor is modern and elegant, specializing in light, contemporary fish dishes that change daily; if it's on the menu, try the turbot in ginger. Upstairs is a cozy hideaway for those who appreciate a more traditional taste of Toulouse: *cassoulet, magrets de canard* (duck), and other filling fare. *13 pl. St-Georges, tel. 61–21–05–56. Reservations required. AE, DC, MC, V. Closed last week in Aug., Sun., and Mon.*

Shopping
The **Centre Commercial St-Georges**, a frenetic, modern shopping mall downtown (rue du Rempart St-Etienne), offers a vast array of clothing, jewelry, books, records—and just about anything else you'd possibly want to buy or admire. For upscale clothes, try the chic shops on **rue St-Rome** and **rue d'Alsace-Lorraine,** home to Toulouse's main department store, **Nouvelles Galeries,** which, like its sister store in Paris, Galeries Lafayette, provides a good range of services for foreign visitors (including overseas shipment and payment with any major credit card).

The Arts
The performing arts season here lasts from October until late May, though there are occasional summer presentations. Toulouse's **Ballet du Capitole** stages classical ballets, and the **Ballet-Théâtre Joseph Russilo** and **Compagnie Jean-Marc Matos** put on modern-dance performances. The **Centre National Chorégraphique de Toulouse** welcomes international companies each year in the St-Cyprien quarter. The main theaters all have performances in French. For performing arts schedules, get in touch with the city tourist office.

Nightlife
For a complete list of clubs and discos, buy a copy of *Toulouse Pratique* at any bookshop or newspaper stand. One of the best spots is **L'Art Club** (1 rue de l'Echarpe), a trendy, elegant vaulted brick cellar in the Esquirol quarter. If you like a more intimate setting, try **La Cendrée** (15 rue des Tourneurs), which has lots of cozy nooks and crannies. **L'Ubu** (16 rue St-Rome), the city's top night spot for 20 years, is where the local glitterati and concert and theater stars come to relax. Liber-

ated couples love **Victory-Clippers Club** (Canal de Brienne, 90 allée de Barcelone), though it may be a bit daring for some.

Le Café des Allées (64 allée Charles-de-Fitte) is a hot spot among local jazz musicians. **Café Le Griot** (34 rue des Blanchers) features jazz, blues, and a number of American duos and trios. **Le Père Bacchus** (20 pl. St.-Georges) is the trendiest jazz club on the city's trendiest square.

Albi

Trains make the 65-minute run from Toulouse every 2 hours. Tourist office: Place Ste-Cécile, tel. 63–54–22–30.

Albi, now a tastefully preserved town full of narrow streets and redbrick buildings, was once a major center for Cathars, members of an ascetic religious sect that rejected earthly life as evil and criticized the worldly ways of the Catholic Church; the town's huge cathedral of **Ste-Cécile** was meant to symbolize the Catholic Church's return to power after the crusade against the Cathars (or Albigensians, as they came to be known) at the start of the 13th century. With its intimidating clifflike walls, the cathedral appears as a cross between a castle, a power station, and an ocean liner.

Its interior is an ornate reply to the massive austerity of the ocher outer walls. Every possible surface has been painted; the leading contributors were a 16th-century team of painters from Bologna, Italy, who splattered the main vault with saints and Old Testament *venerati*, then lined the bays with religious scenes and brightly colored patterns. The most striking fresco, however, is a 15th-century depiction of the Last Judgment, which extends across the west wall beneath the 18th-century organ loft. Unfortunately, its central section was smashed through in 1693, to make the St-Clair chapel.

Climb the stairway to the right of the altar up to the bell tower. Here the view takes in the rooftops of the old town and, between the cathedral and the Pont Vieux (Old Bridge) spanning the River Tarn, the **Palais de la Berbie.** Built in 1265 as the Bishop's Palace, it was later transformed first into a fortress, then into a museum honoring Albi's most famous son: Belle Epoque painter Henri de Toulouse-Lautrec (1864–1901).

Toulouse-Lautrec left Albi for Paris in 1882 and soon made his name with racy evocations of the bohemian glamour of the cabarets, music halls, bars, and cafés in and around Montmartre. Despite his aristocratic origins (Lautrec is a town not far from Toulouse), Henri cut a far-from-noble figure. He stood under five feet tall (his growth was stunted by a childhood riding accident) and pursued a decadent life that led to an early grave. The Albi exhibit is the country's largest collection of works by Toulouse-Lautrec. These works are beautifully presented, notably in the lengthy Galérie Ambrie (holding his earliest efforts) and in the rooms leading from the Salon Rose (portraits and lithographs). *Just off pl. Ste-Cécile. Admission: 24 frs. adults, 12 frs. children. Open Easter–Oct., daily 10–noon and 2–6; Nov.–Easter, Wed.–Mon. 10–noon and 2–5; closed Tues.*

Before leaving Albi, stroll around the old town to admire its pedestrian streets and elegant shops. You can also visit Lautrec's birthplace, **Maison Natale de Toulouse-Lautrec** (along boulevard Sibille from the cathedral), to see more of his early works, as well as his personal possessions and memorabilia. *14 rue Henri de Toulouse-Lautrec. Admission: 16 frs. adults, 10 frs. children. Open July–Aug., daily 10–noon and 3–7.*

Lodging
Under 250 frs.

Orléans. Despite its ritzy modern facade, the Orléans is a large, traditional station hotel. Room rates that start at around 180 francs, the cheerful welcome, and the 90- and 130-franc set menus are the reasons to stay. *Pl. de Stalingrad, 81000, tel. 63–54–16–56. 48 rooms with bath or shower. Facilities: restaurant (closed Sun.), exercise room. AE, DC, MC, V. Closed Christmas through New Year's.*

Lodging and Dining
Under 350 frs.

Altéa. Ask for a room with a view in this converted 18th-century windmill, opposite the cathedral and overlooking the River Tarn. The ones on the second and fourth floor are best; those on the third and top floors have tiny windows. The hotel's restaurant is a stylish place to try Jean-Paul Devisi's regional specialties, such as *fritons*—peanut-size chunks of duck lard in flaky pastry with capers; they're a great deal more appetizing than they sound. Dine on the terrace in summer. *41 rue Porta, 81000, tel. 63–47–66–66. 56 rooms with bath. Facilities: restaurant, terrace. AE, DC, MC, V.*

Dining
Under 125 frs.

Le Jardin des Quatre Saisons. There are two reasons for this new restaurant's excellent reputation: value for the money and efficient service. Ask the wine waiter to help you choose a bottle from the extensive wine list to accompany one of the chef's fish dishes. House specialties include mussels baked with leeks, or *suprême de sandre* (a type of perch) in wine. Desserts are surprisingly light for this gastronomic region. Try for a table in the garden if the weather's fine. *19 blvd. de Strasbourg, tel. 63–60–77–76. Reservations advised. Jacket and tie required. AE, MC, V. Closed Mon., and Tues. lunch.*

Rodez

Five trains daily make the 85-minute run from Albi, 78 km (48 mi) away. Tourist office: Place du Mal-Foch, tel. 65–68–02–27.

Rodez, capital of the Aveyron département, sits on a windswept hill halfway between the arid, limestone Causses plateau and the verdant Ségala hills. Towering over the town is the pink sandstone cathedral of **Notre-Dame**, built over the 13th to 15th century. Its awesome bulk is lightened by the decorative upper stories, completed in the 17th century, and by the magnificently elaborate 285-foot bell tower. The interior contains ornamental altarpieces, an elaborate 15th-century choir screen, and a 17th-century organ within an intricate wooden casing.

The old but renovated **Cité quarter,** once ruled by medieval bishops, lies behind the cathedral; attractive pedestrian zones have been created around place du Bourg. One of the city's finest medieval mansions can be found on the tiny place de l'Olmet, just off place du Bourg: the 16th-century **House of Armagnac,** with its open courtyard and ornate facade covered in the medallion emblems of the counts of Rodez.

Farther on, at place de la Madeleine, is the 18th-century church of **St-Amans,** featuring finely preserved Romanesque capitals and, inside, some colorful 16th-century tapestries. The extensively modernized **Musée Denys Puech,** an art gallery noted for works by local painters and sculptors, lies just beyond the wide boulevard that encircles the old town. *Pl. Clemenceau. Admission: 18 frs. adults, 12 frs. children under 18. Open Wed.–Sat. and Mon. 10–noon and 3–7; Sun. 3–7; closed Tues.*

Lodging and Dining
Under 150 frs.

Midi. Pierre and Martine de Schepper are the enthusiastic hosts at this pleasant hotel near the cathedral in the old part of town. To savor the filling regional cuisine, you can't do better than to sample the 65- and 105-franc menus offered in the spacious dining room. *1 rue de Béteille, 12000, tel. 65–68–02–07. 34 rooms, most with shower. Facilities: restaurant (closed Sun. and Mon.). MC, V. Closed mid-Dec.–mid-Jan. and Sat. in winter.*

Figeac

Five trains daily make the 85-minute run from Rodez. The 3 daily trains from Toulouse take 2¼ hours. Tourist office: Place Vival, tel. 65–34–06–25.

Figeac, a charming old town with a lively Saturday-morning market, grew up around an abbey in the 9th century, becoming, in turn, a stopping point for pilgrims plodding from Conques to Compostela. Many houses in the older part of town date from the 13th, 14th, and 15th centuries and have been carefully restored. They retain their octagonal chimneys, rounded archways and arcades, and *soleilhos,* open attics used for drying flowers and stocking wood.

The 13th-century **Hôtel de la Monnaie,** a block in from the River Célé, is characteristic of such architecture. An elegant building probably used as a medieval money-changing office, it now houses the tourist office and a museum displaying fragments of sculpture and religious relics found in the town. *Pl. Vival. Admission free. Open July–Aug., daily 10–noon and 2:30–6:30; Sept.–June, Mon.–Sat. 3–5.*

Figeac was the birthplace of Jean-François Champollion (1790–1832), the first man to decipher Egyptian hieroglyphics. The **Musée Champollion,** in his house near place Champollion (walk right out of place Vival on rue 11-novembre, take the first left and follow it around as it bends right), contains a casting of the Rosetta Stone, discovered in the Nile Delta; the stone's three inscriptions—two in Egyptian and one in ancient Greek—enabled the mysteries of the pharaonic dialect to be penetrated for the first time. On the ground floor of the museum, a film traces Champollion's life. *4 impasse Champollion. Admission: 20 frs. adults, 10 frs. children. Open May–Sept., Tues.–Sat. 10–noon and 2:30–6:30.*

Rocamadour

There are 5 daily trains from Figeac; the trip takes 40 minutes. The station is 5 km (3 mi) from the village—walk or take a taxi. Tourist office: Hôtel de Ville, tel. 65–33–62–59.

The medieval village of **Rocamadour** seems to defy the laws of gravity as it surges out of a cliff 458 meters (1,500 feet) above the Alzou River gorge.

Rocamadour first made its name in 1166, when chronicles recorded the miraculous discovery of the body of St. Amadour "quite whole" under a sanctuary. This was a major event:

Amadour had died a thousand years earlier and, according to legend, was none other than Zaccheus, the tax collector of Jericho, who had come to live in Gaul as a hermit after Christ persuaded him to give up his money-grubbing ways. Amadour's body was moved into the church, displayed to pilgrims, and began to work miracles. Its fame soon spread to Portugal, Spain, and Sicily, and pilgrims flocked to the site and climbed the 216-step staircase leading up to the church—on their knees. Making the climb on foot is a sufficient reminder of the medieval penchant for agonizing penance, and today an elevator assists weary souls.

The staircase and elevator start from place de la Carreta; those making their way on foot can pause after the first 141 steps to admire the **Fort,** as the 14th-century Bishop's Palace is invitingly called. The remaining steps lead to tiny place St-Amadour and its seven sanctuaries: the basilica of **St-Sauveur** opposite the staircase; the **St-Amadour crypt** underneath the basilica; the chapel of **Notre-Dame** to the left; the chapels of **John the Baptist, St-Blaise,** and **Ste-Anne** to the right; and the Romanesque chapel of **St-Michel,** built into the overhanging cliff. St. Michel's two 12th-century frescoes—depicting the Annunciation and the Visitation—have survived in superb condition. *Centre d'Accueil Notre-Dame. English-speaking guide available. Guided tours Mon.–Sat. 9–5; tips at visitors' discretion.*

The village itself boasts beautifully restored medieval houses. One of the finest is the 15th-century **Hôtel de Ville** (Town Hall), near the Porte Salmon, which also houses the tourist office and a fine collection of tapestries. *Admission free. Open Mon.–Sat. 10–noon and 3–8.*

At the **Rocher des Aigles**, a hundred different species of birds of prey, including condors and vultures as well as eagles, swoop high and low at the command of their expert handlers. *Rte. du Château, tel. 65–33–65–45. Admission: 30 frs. adults, 15 frs. children. Open Apr.–mid-Nov. for demonstrations daily at 11, 3, 4, 5, and 6.*

Lodging and Dining
Under 250 frs.

Panoramic. Most restaurants and hotels in Rocamadour have terrific views. But this cheerful family hotel perched on the clifftop near the castle, a short stroll from the lift, has a better view than most—and a leafy dining terrace from which to enjoy it. There are 70- and 90-franc menus in the restaurant, and the management organizes excursions for guests along the Dordogne and Lot valleys. *L'Hospitalet, 46500, tel. 65–33–63–06. 21 rooms with bath or shower. Facilities: bar, restaurant, pool. AE, DC, MC, V. Closed Nov.–Feb.*

Dining
Under 125 frs.

Beau-Site et Notre-Dame. Within the ancient stone walls of this hotel (rue Roland-le-Preux), an exceptionally cozy restaurant serves richly flavored regional specialties as well as nouvelle dishes. The salmon *sashimi* (raw, with soy sauce) is a good bet—and leave room for some of Madame Menot's homemade desserts. *Rue Roland-le-Preux, la Cité, tel. 65–33–63–08. Reservations advised. Dress: casual. AE, DC, MC, V. Closed Oct.-Easter.*

Cahors

From Rocamadour, return to Figeac. Three trains daily make the 90-minute run to Cahors. The 8 direct trains per day from Toulouse to Cahors take about 70 minutes. Tourist office: Place Aristide-Briand, tel. 65–35–09–56.

Once an opulent Gallo-Roman settlement, **Cahors** sits snugly in a loop formed by the River Lot. The town is perhaps best known for its tannic red wine—often, in fact, a deep purple, and known to the Romans as "black wine"—which you can taste at many of the small estates in the surrounding region. The finest sight in Cahors is the **Pont Valentré** bridge, a spellbinding feat of medieval engineering whose tall, elegant towers have loomed over the river since 1360.

Rue du Président-Wilson cuts across town from the bridge to the old quarter of Cahors around the Cathedral of **St-Etienne,** easily recognized by its cupolas and fortresslike appearance. The tympanum over the north door was sculpted around 1135 with figures portraying the Ascension and the life of St-Etienne (St. Stephen). The cloisters, to the right of the choir, contain a corner pillar embellished with a charmingly sculpted Annunciation Virgin with long, flowing hair. The cloisters connect with the courtyard of the archdeaconry, awash with Renaissance decoration and thronged with visitors viewing its temporary art exhibits.

Lodging and Dining
Under 250 frs.

Terminus. This small hotel is deep in the heart of truffle country, yet just two minutes' walk from Cahors train station; the restaurant, La Balandre, is the city's best. The decor is mainly Roaring Twenties and the atmosphere is stylishly jazzy, but the windows have turn-of-the-century stained glass. Gilles Marre and his wife, Jacqueline, specialize in truffles but also serve an exceptional fresh cod *brandade* (mousse) and foie gras in flaky pastry. There's a good range of local wines, and the service is sophisticated yet friendly. The guest rooms are cozily traditional in feel. *5 av. Charles-de-Freycinet, 46000, tel. 65–35–24–50. 31 rooms. Facilities: restaurant (reservations advised; closed 2 weeks in Feb., 1 week in June, Sun. dinner and Mon. Jan.–Mar., and Sat. lunch July–Aug.) AE, MC, V.*

Dining
Under 75 frs.

Le Coq & La Pendule. This small, family-run café on a pedestrian street near the cathedral offers a classic example of homey French cooking served in a down-to-earth setting. Space is tight and it's all hustle-bustle, but service is friendly and portions generous. And a five-course meal with wine and coffee won't cost much above 50 francs. *10 rue St-James, tel. 65–35–28–84. No credit cards.*

Montauban

There are 7 daily trains from Cahors; the trip takes 45 minutes. Hourly trains make the 30-minute journey from Toulouse. Tourist office: 2 rue du Collège, tel. 63–63–60–60.

Montauban was the birthplace of the great painter Jean Auguste Dominique Ingres (1780–1867). Ingres was the last of the great French Classicists, who took their cue from Raphaël, favoring line over color and taking much of their subject matter from the antique world. Ingres's personal dislike of Eugène Delacroix (the earliest and most important French Romantic painter), his sour personality, and (for some) his arid painting style, with its worship of line and technical draftsmanship, led many contemporaries to ridicule his work. These days, Ingres is undergoing a considerable revival in popularity; looking at the works in Montauban's Ingres museum, with their quasi-photographic realism, it's easy to see why.

The **Musée Ingres** is housed in the sturdy, brick 17th-century Bishop's Palace overlooking the River Tarn. Ingres has the second floor to himself; note the contrast between his love of myth *(Ossian's Dream)* and his deadpan, uncompromising portraiture *(Madame Gonse)*, underscored by a closet eroticism (silky-skinned nudes) that belies the staid reputation of academic art. The exhibit also includes hundreds of Ingres's drawings, plus some of his personal possessions—including his beloved violin.

Most of the paintings in the museum are from Ingres's excellent private collection, ranging from his followers (Théodore Chassériau) and precursors (Jacques-Louis David) to Old Masters, who were active between the 14th and the 18th centuries (displayed on the third floor). *Pl. Bourdelle. Admission: 12 frs. adults, 8 frs. students. Open July–Aug., Mon.–Sat. 9:30–noon and 1:30–6, Sun. 1:30–6; Sept.–June, Tues.–Sat. 10–noon and 2–6.*

Take some time to explore the old streets of Montauban, especially the pedestrian zone around the restored place Nationale (home to a lively morning market). Check out the classical cathedral of **Notre-Dame** on place Roosevelt: Its white stone is an eye-catching contrast to the pink brick of other buildings, and inside lurks a major Ingres painting, the *Vow of Louis XIII*.

Lodging and Dining
Under 250 frs.

Midi. Thanks to a recent overhaul, this friendly, rambling old hotel near the cathedral now offers both spacious rooms with bath priced at all of 370 francs in addition to smaller, Spartan ones that go for as little as 180 francs a night. The restaurant's 75-franc menu is a good bet. *12 rue Notre-Dame, 82000, tel. 63–63–17–23. 64 rooms, some with bath or shower. Facilities: bar, restaurant (closed mid-Dec.–mid-Jan.). AE, DC, MC, V.*

Moissac

The 6 daily trains covering the 29 km (18 mi) from Montauban take 20 minutes. There are 5 trains daily from Toulouse, taking between 45 minutes and 1 hour.

Moissac holds one of the region's most remarkable abbey churches, **St-Pierre.** Little is left of the original 7th-century abbey, while religious wars laid waste its 11th-century replacement. Today's abbey, dating mostly from the 15th century, narrowly escaped demolition earlier in this century when the Bordeaux–Sète railroad was rerouted within feet of the cloisters, sparing the precious columns around the arcades, carved in different shades of marble. Each of the 76 capitals has its own unique pattern of animals, geometric motifs, and religious or historical scenes.

The museum, in the corner chapels, houses local religious sculpture and photographs of similar sculpture from throughout the Quercy region. The highlight of the abbey church is the 12th-century south portal, topped with carvings illustrating the Apocalypse. The sides and vaults of the porch are adorned with historical scenes sculpted in intricate detail. *6 bis rue de l'Abbaye. Admission to museum and cloisters: 20 frs. joint ticket. Open daily 9–noon and 2–5 (2–6 in June and Sept., 2–7 in July and Aug.); museum closed Tues. and Sun. morning.*

Tour 2: The Pyrénées

This tour, which follows the main Paris–Spain train route after it forks at Dax and turns left, hits the central Pyrénées and the towns of Pau and nearby Lourdes. Cauterets and Gavarnie can be reached by bus from Lourdes and are worthwhile visits.

From Paris
By Train
Eight TGVs daily make the 5½-hour run to Pau from Paris (Gare Montparnasse).

By Car
Pau is 785 kilometers (490 miles) from Paris: Take the A10 to Bordeaux, switch to the A63/N10 (in the direction of Spain), and then branch off along D947 via Dax to catch the A64 expressway at Orthez. Allow 8 hours for the trip.

Pau

Tourist office: Place Royale, tel. 59–27–27–08.

Elegant **Pau,** 160 kilometers (100 miles) southwest of Toulouse, is the historic capital of Béarn, a state annexed to France in 1620. Pau rose to prominence after being "discovered" in 1815 by British officers who were returning from the Peninsular War in Spain and was soon launched as a winter resort. Fifty years later, English-speaking inhabitants made up one-third of Pau's population. They launched the Pont-Long steeplechase, still one of the most challenging in Europe, in 1841; created France's first golf course here, in 1856; and introduced fox hunting to the region.

Paying tribute to Pau's regal past is the **château,** begun in the 14th century by Gaston Phoebus, the flamboyant Count of Béarn. The building was transformed into a Renaissance palace in the 16th century by the beautiful Marguerite d'Angoulême, sister of French king François I. Marguerite's grandson, the future King Henri IV, was born in the château in 1553. Temporary exhibits connected to Henri's life and times are mounted regularly here. His cradle—a giant turtle shell—is on show in his bedroom, one of the sumptuous, tapestry-lined royal apartments. Other highlights are the 16th-century kitchens and the imposing dining hall, which could seat up to 100 guests. *Rue du Château. Admission: 24 frs. (12 frs. Sun.). Open Apr.–Oct., daily 9:30–11:30 and 2–5:45; Nov.–Mar., daily 9:30–11:30 and 2–4:30.*

On the fourth floor of the château, the **Musée Béarnais** offers an overview of the region, encompassing everything from fauna to furniture to festival costumes. There is a reconstructed Béarn house and displays of such local crafts as cheese- and béret-making. *Admission: 6 frs. adults. Open Apr.–Oct., daily 9:30–12:30 and 2:30–6:30; Nov.–Mar., daily 9:30–12:30 and 2:30–5:30.*

Lodging
Under 250 frs.
Montpensier. This sturdy, old pink-brick mansion with well-kept rooms and a colorful garden has an air of calm despite its location in the bustling center of Pau, 600 yards from place Clemenceau via rue Serviez. *36 rue Montpensier, 64000, tel. 59–*

27–42–72. 22 rooms, some with bath or shower. AE, DC, MC, V.

Dining
Under 125 frs.

Fin Gourmet. This airy, elegant rotunda surrounded by its own garden strikes an incongruous note in its rather unbeautiful location near the station. Service is bashfully discreet, but the cuisine can be bold and inventive—take the veal with raspberry vinegar, for instance. There is a set menu at 160 francs (and another at 85 francs on weekdays); eating à la carte tends to be much more expensive. *24 av. Gaston-Lacoste, tel. 59–27–47–71. Reservations advised. AE, DC, MC, V. Closed Mon.*

Lourdes

Trains run from Pau to Lourdes, 25 minutes away, every 2 hours or so. Tourist office: Place du Champ-Commun, tel. 62–94–15–64.

More than 3 million pilgrims flock to **Lourdes** each year, many in quest of a miracle cure for their sickness or handicap. In February 1858, Bernadette Soubirous, a 14-year-old miller's daughter, claimed the Virgin Mary had appeared to her in the **Massabielle grotto** near the Gave de Pau river. The visions were repeated. During the night, Bernadette dug at the ground in the grotto, releasing a gush of water from a spot where no spring existed. From then on, pilgrims thronged the Massabielle rock in response to the water's supposed healing powers.

Church authorities reacted skeptically. It took four years of inquiry for the miracle to be authenticated by Rome and a sanctuary erected over the grotto. In 1864, the first organized procession was held. Today there are six official annual pilgrimages, the most important on August 15. In 1958, Lourdes celebrated the centenary of the apparitions by constructing the world's largest underground church, the basilica of **St-Pie X.** The basilica looks more like a parking lot than a church, but it can accommodate 20,000 people—more than the permanent population of the whole town. Above the basilica stand the neo-Byzantine basilica of **Rosaire** (1889) and the tall, white Basilique **Supérieure** (1871). Both are open throughout the day, but unfortunately, their spiritual function far outweighs their aesthetic appeal.

The area surrounding the churches and grotto (situated between the basilicas and the river) is woefully lacking in beauty. Out of season, the acres of parking space beneath the basilicas echo like mournful parade grounds to the steps of solitary visitors. Shops are shuttered and restaurants are closed. In season, a milling throng jostles for postcards, tacky souvenirs, and a glimpse of the famous grotto, lurking behind a forest of votive candles struggling to remain aflicker in the Pyrenean breeze.

The Pavillon Notre-Dame, across from the underground basilica, houses the **Musée Bernadette,** with mementoes of her life (she died at a convent in Nevers, Burgundy, in 1879) and illustrated history of the pilgrimages. In the basement is the **Musée d'Art Sacré du Gemmail,** *gemmail* being a modern approach to the stained-glass technique involving the assembly of broken glass, lit from behind, often by electric light. *72 rue de la Grotte. Admission free. Open July–Nov., daily 9:30–11:45 and 2:30–6:15; Dec.–June, Wed.–Mon. 9:30–11:45 and 2:30–5:45; closed Tues.*

Just across the river are the **Moulin des Boly,** where Bernadette was born on January 7, 1844, and, close to the parish church where she was baptized, the **Cachot,** a shabby little room where Bernadette and her family lived. *Moulin des Boly, rue Bernadette Soubirous. Open Easter–mid-Oct., daily 9:30–11:45 and 2:30–5:45. Cachot, 15 rue des Petits-Fossés. Admission free. Open Easter–mid-Oct., daily 9:30–11:45 and 2:30–5:30; mid-Oct.–Easter, daily 2:30–5:30.*

Though the story of Bernadette is compelling, Lourdes is lucky to have an authentic historic attraction to complement the commercialized aura of its pilgrim sites. **Lourdes Castle** stands on a hill above the town and can be reached on foot or by escalator. In the 17th and 18th centuries, the castle was used as a prison; now it contains the **Musée Pyrénéen,** one of France's best provincial museums, devoted to popular customs and arts throughout the Pyrénées region, from Bayonne on the Atlantic to Perpignan by the Mediterranean. *Admission: 18 frs. adults, 8 frs. students. Open Easter–mid-Oct., daily 9–noon and 2–7 (last admission at 6); mid-Oct.–Easter, Wed.–Mon. 9–noon and 2–7.*

Lodging
Under 150 frs.

Notre-Dame de Lorette. In Lourdes's mix of small, seedy hotels, and glitzy modern establishments, this featureless structure with small rooms is no great shakes. But the welcome is friendly, the housekeeping just fine, and the setting—across the river from the grotto—very pleasant. The restaurant serves honest French cuisine, and prices its three-course menu at 75 francs. *75 route de Pau, 65100, tel. 62–94–12–16. 20 rooms, some with shower. Facilities: restaurant. No credit cards. Closed mid-Oct.–Easter.*

Lodging and Dining
Under 250 frs.

Albret. Chef Claude Moreau's cabbage-and-bacon stew is excellent fuel for your own Lourdes pilgrimage—but lighter fish dishes are on the menu as well; prices start at 70 francs for a three-course meal. The modern hotel rooms are cheap and comfortable, if characterless, and from this town-center location you are only half a mile from the pilgrimage site. *21 pl. du Champ Commun, tel. 62–94–75–00. 27 rooms, some with shower. Facilities: restaurant (closed Sun.). AE, MC, V. Closed Nov.–Feb.*

Cauterets

Five coaches run daily from Lourdes 30 km (19 mi) south to Cauterets, 55 minutes away. Tourist office: 2 pl. Georges-Clemenceau, tel. 62–92–50–27.

The thermal springs at **Cauterets** have been revered since Roman times as a miracle cure for female sterility. Virile novelist Victor Hugo (1802–85) womanized here, and Lady Aurore Dudevant—better known as the writer George Sand (1804–76)—discovered the thrill of adultery. Poetic viscount François René Chateaubriand (1768–1848) stayed determinedly chaste, however, pining for his "inaccessible Occitan girl." It is still a spa-resort, but today's visitors often ski until May.

Gavarnie

Two coaches run daily from Cauterets to Gavarnie, via Pierrefitte.

Pretty **Gavarnie** makes a great base for hiking and stands at the foot of the **Cirque de Gavarnie,** one of the world's most remarkable examples of glacial erosion. When the upper snows melt, numerous streams whoosh down from the cliffs to form spectacular waterfalls; the greatest of them—the **Grande Cascade—** drops nearly 427 meters (1,400 feet). The Cirque presents a daunting challenge to mountaineers; if you've forgotten your climbing boots, a horse or donkey can take you partway into the mountains from the village.

Lodging and Dining
Under 250 frs.

Marboré. This family hotel is Gavarnie's most appealing. Its veranda offers splendid views of the magnificent Cirque, and the old-fashioned main restaurant serves filling meals from 80- and 160-franc set menus while an adjoining brasserie offers quicker, less expensive alternatives. The Marboré comes into its own in winter, when skiers warm up around the open hearth in the Swan Bar after their days on the nearby slopes. *Le Village, 65120, tel. 62–92–40–40. 24 rooms with shower. Facilities: restaurant, bar, exercise room. MC, V. Closed first half of Nov.*

Tour 3: Roussillon

We now head east from Toulouse to the historic region of Roussillon. This area was once part of Spain, and its culture and dialect retain close ties with neighboring Catalonia. We start at the hilltop town of Carcassonne and then visit Narbonne, Perpignan, and the pretty Mediterranean coastal town of Collioure.

From Paris
By Train

Two trains during the day (one requiring a change at Toulouse) and two more overnight make the 8-hour trip from Paris (Gare d'Austerlitz) to Carcassonne.

By Car

The Paris–Carcassonne drive is a very long one. You can travel either via Bordeaux/Toulouse (A10/A62), a journey of 870 kilometers (540 miles), or via Lyon/Montpellier (A6/A7/A9/A61), a 910-kilometer (570-mile) drive. Both routes take at least 8 hours.

Carcassonne

Tourist office: 15 blvd. Camille-Pelletan, tel. 68–25–07–04.

Carcassonne has Europe's longest **medieval town walls.** The mighty circle of towers and battlements stands high on a hilltop above the River Aude and is said to be the setting for Charles Perrault's *Puss in Boots*. The earliest sections of wall were built by the Romans in the 1st century AD, and the Visigoths later enlarged the settlement into a true fortress in the 5th century. In the 13th century, the French king St. Louis and his son, Philip the Bold, strengthened the fortifications and gave Carcassonne much of its present-day appearance. Much, but not all: In 1835, the Historic Monument Inspector (and poet) Prosper Mérimée was appalled by the dilapidated state of the walls, and by 1844 Viollet-le-Duc was at work restoring them.

You can spend several hours exploring the walls and peering over the battlements across sun-drenched plains toward the distant Pyrénées. The old streets inside the walls are lined with souvenir shops, crafts boutiques, and restaurants; be sure to visit the **Château Comtal,** with its drawbridge and Musée Lapidaire, home to stone sculptures found in the area. *Tel. 68–*

25–01–66. Admission: 25 frs. Open daily 9–noon and 2–5 (9–6 June–Sept.).

The *ville basse* (lower town), built between the River Aude and the Canal du Midi, is less captivating, but you may wish to visit the **Musée des Beaux-Arts,** housing a fine collection of porcelain, 17th- and 18th-century Flemish paintings, and works by local artists—including some stirring battle scenes by Jacques Gamelin (1738–1803). *Rue Verdun, tel. 68–72–47–22. Admission free. Open Mon.–Sat. 10–noon and 2–5.*

Lodging
Under 350 frs.

Montségur. This pretty little hotel lies just outside the old city walls. Rooms on the first two floors showcase elaborate 18th-century period furniture; those above are more romantic, with gilt-iron bedsteads set under sloping oak beams. *27 allée d'Iéna, 11000, tel. 68–25–31–41. 21 rooms with bath or shower. DC, MC, V. Closed mid-Dec.–mid-Jan.*

Dining
Under 200 frs.

Auberge du Pont-Levis. At the foot of the medieval city gateway, the Porte Narbonnaise, the Pont-Levis provides a welcome shelter from tourist crowds. Chef Henri Pautard serves traditional *cassoulet* (stew with beans and meat) and foie gras alongside a more inventive terrine marbled with artichokes and leeks, accompanied by a truffle vinaigrette. Otherwise, try the *méli-mélo du pêcheur,* a refreshing mix of mussels, cockles, and other seafood of the season. In summer you can eat on the terrace or in the garden. *Porte Narbonnaise, tel. 68–25–55–23. Reservations advised. Jacket required. AE, DC, MC, V. Closed Nov., Feb., Sun. dinner, and Mon.*

Narbonne

Trains make the 32-minute run from Carcassonne every 1½ hours. Tourist office: Place Roger-Salengro, tel. 68–65–15–60.

Back in Roman times Narbonne was the second-largest town in Gaul (after Lyon) and an important port. Until the sea receded in the Middle Ages, Narbonne prospered, and you will appreciate its one-time wealth when you enter the 14th-century cathedral; its vaults rise 41 meters (133 feet) from the floor, making it the tallest cathedral in southern France. Only Beauvais and Amiens, in Picardy, are taller, and as at Beauvais, the nave at Narbonne was never built. Richly sculpted cloisters link the cathedral to the former **Archbishop's Palace,** now home to the Museum of Archaeology and the Museum of Art and History. Note the enormous palace kitchen, with its ornate central pillar, and check out the late-13th-century *Donjon Gilles-Aycelin* (keep); climb the 180 steps to the top for a view of the region as well as the town. *Palais des Archevêques, tel. 68–90–30–30. Admission: 10 frs. adults, 5 frs. children (joint ticket for all town museums). Open May–Sept., daily 9–noon and 2–6; Oct.–Apr., Tues.–Sun. 10–noon and 2–5:30.*

Cross the nearby canal to visit the **Musée Lapidaire** (sculpture museum), housed in the handsome, 13th-century former church of Notre-Dame de la Mourguié. Classical busts, ancient sarcophagi, lintels, and Gallo-Roman inscriptions await you. *Place Lamourguier, tel. 68–65–53–58. Joint admission and same hours as for Palais des Archevêques, above.*

Lodging and Dining
Under 350 frs.

Languedoc. This old-fashioned, turn-of-the-century hotel in downtown Narbonne has a solid reputation. Most rooms have been renovated, but they vary in style and comfort; ask to check yours out before you book a room. La Coupole restaurant serves inexpensive regional dishes, and Sir John's Piano Bar stays open until 2 AM. *23 blvd. Gambetta, 11100, tel. 68–65–14–74. 45 rooms with bath or shower. Facilities: restaurant, piano bar, garage. AE, DC, MC, V.*

Perpignan

Trains make the 40-minute run from Narbonne every 1½ hours. Tourist office: Place Armand-Lanoux, tel. 68–66–30–30.

With a population of 120,000, Perpignan—Roussillon's historic capital—is the largest French town south of Toulouse. In medieval times, Perpignan was the Second City of Catalonia (after Barcelona) before falling to Louis XIII's French army in 1642.

Take avenue du Général-de-Gaulle from the station, turn right onto cours Escarguel, and follow this broad boulevard for 458 meters (500 yards). A left onto avenue Brutus will take you to Perpignan's leading monument, the fortified **Palais des Rois de Majorque** (Palace of the Majorcan Kings), begun in the 14th century by James II of Majorca. Highlights here are the majestic *Cour d'Honneur* (Hall of Honor), the two-tiered Flamboyant Gothic Chapel of Sainte-Croix, and the *Grande Salle* (Great Hall), containing monumental fireplaces. *Rue des Archers, tel. 68–34–48–29. Admission: 10 frs. Open daily 9–5.*

Head back across town toward the River Têt and the medieval monument of **Le Castillet,** with its tall, crenellated twin towers. The Casa Pairal, a museum devoted to Catalan art and traditions, is housed here. *Pl. de Verdun, tel. 68–35–42–05. Admission free. Open Wed.–Mon. 9–noon and 2–6.*

Across boulevard Wilson from Le Castillet, stroll along the **Promenade des Platanes,** a cheerful stretch of flowers, plane trees, and fountains. Perpignan may not be rich in outstanding tourist sites, but the streets near Le Castillet and the adjacent place de la Loge, the town's nerve center, contain interesting medieval buildings. Among them are the **Cathédrale St-Jean** (distinguished by a frilly, wrought-iron campanile and a dramatic medieval crucifix), the **Loge de Mer** (formerly a maritime exchange), and the **Palais de la Députation** (once home to the Spanish law courts). The **Petite Rue des Fabriques d'En Nabot,** opposite the Palais, is Perpignan's best-preserved medieval street.

Lodging and Dining
Under 350 frs.

Park. This family-run hotel with its own garden is unquestionably the smartest in Perpignan; although some rooms are small, most are positively luxurious, and all are soundproofed and air-conditioned. Locals pour into the excellent Chapon Fin restaurant to sample Claude Petry's subtle, understated cuisine; three set menus showcase authentic Mediterranean flavors and razor-fresh produce. Make the shellfish a priority: Try the crayfish with zucchini or oysters with asparagus. *18 blvd. Jean-Bourrat, 66000, tel. 68–35–14–14. 67 rooms with bath or shower. Facilities: restaurant (closed Sat. dinner, Sun., and mid-Aug.–early Sept.). MC, V.*

Dining
Under 125 frs.

La Serre. Regional dishes such as artichoke in pastry with garlic or duck with honey and grapefruit are showcased in this friendly restaurant in the old heart of town. We recommend the

80-franc menu. *2 bis rue Dagobert, tel. 68-34-33-02. Reservations advised. Dress: casual. MC, V. Closed Sat. lunch.*

Collioure

Nine trains daily make the 25-minute run from Perpignan. Tourist office: Place du 18-juin, tel. 68-82-15-47.

Collioure, with its sheltered natural harbor, was originally a fishing town; anchovies are still caught here at night using the *lamparo* technique (powerful lamps to which anchovies are irresistibly attracted). The town's picture-postcard setting makes it a mecca for tourists, the first of whom were such turn-of-the-century painters as Henri Matisse, André Derain, Henri Martin, Georges Braque, and Emile-Othon "Everyone" Friesz.

The view they admired remains largely unchanged today. To the north, the rocky Ilôt St-Vincent juts out into the sea, a modern lighthouse at its tip. The first building on the mainland is the 17th-century church of Notre-Dame-des-Anges—observe the exuberantly carved altar/pieces—whose pink-domed bell tower doubled as the original lighthouse. Behind the church lie the tumbling streets of the old Quartier du Mouré. A slender jetty divides the Boramar beach, beneath the church, from the small landing area at the foot of the **Château Royal.** This 15th-century castle, remodeled by Vauban 200 years later, can be visited and has fine views of the bay. *Tel. 68-82-06-43. Admission: 20 frs. Open Mar.-Oct., daily 10-noon and 2-5.*

The rail line hugs the Mediterranean on its way south from Collioure to **Cerbère** on the Spanish border, a tiny harbor town etched into the heart of the many travelers who have changed trains at its "international" station. There can be few less tedious places to wait for a connection, since the platform is a mere five-minute walk from the beach.

Lodging
Under 250 frs.

Les Caranques. There are no frills at this small seaside hotel, but service is efficient and friendly, and you'll enjoy the view from one of the rooms overlooking the picturesque bay. *Rte. de Port-Vendres, 66190, tel. 68-82-06-68. 16 rooms, 14 with bath or shower. Facilities: restaurant. MC, V. Closed Oct.-May.*

Dining
Under 200 frs.

La Balette. Patron Jean-Pierre de Gelder provides a warm welcome to this fine hotel-restaurant (rooms are pricey) in charming Collioure. Such local dishes as rabbit terrine and duck in a red berry sauce are served in the austere dining room and, in warm weather, on the terrace, which offers magnificent views of the old port and village. *Rte. de Port-Vendres, tel. 68-82-05-07. Reservations advised. Dress: casual. MC, V.*

14 The Atlantic Coast

Bordeaux and the Basque Country

It would be hard to visit the area of western France described in this chapter without finding something that captures your imagination. Poitou-Charentes, the rural, gently rolling region described in our first tour, contains France's finest Romanesque architecture, as the cathedrals of Poitiers, Saintes, and Angoulême testify. Those who love dramatic scenery and castles will find them on the second tour, heading east from Bordeaux along the Dordogne Valley—the best example is cliff-top Beynac. City lovers have just one choice, elegant Bordeaux: It's the only town with more than 80,000 inhabitants between Nantes and the Spanish border. It is also the wine capital of the world, and trips to the famous vineyards of St-Emilion and the Médoc are relatively easy by public transportation. Brandy drinkers can tour one of the world's most famous producers in Cognac. The third tour is for those interested in the Basque country.

Seafarers should make for La Rochelle, one of France's prettiest harbor towns. You'll sense the influence of the Atlantic on restaurant menus wherever you are: Shellfish predominate, especially oysters. If you enjoy rich, hearty food such as goose and duck, the Dordogne Valley will spoil you.

Note that the region is well served by trains and that Dax, Poitiers, and Bordeaux can be reached from Paris by the superfast TGV.

Essential Information

Lodging In summer, France's western coast provides extreme contrasts of crowds and calm. Vacationers flock to La Rochelle, Royan, and the islands of Ré and Oléron, and for miles around, hotels are booked solid months in advance. Farther inland the situation is easier, but note the dearth of hotel accommodations in Bordeaux. Advance booking is recommended here and in the Dordogne, whose few towns fill up quickly in summer.

Dining The cuisine of this ocean-facing region centers on fish and seafood. Oysters and mussels are major industries, while carp, eel, sardines, sole, and even sturgeon form the basis of menus in fish restaurants.

Heading inland into Périgord, along the Dordogne Valley, the cooking becomes richer. Truffles lead the way, followed by many types of game, fowl, and mushrooms. The goose market in the quaint old town of Sarlat is proof of the local addiction to foie gras. The River Dordogne is home to that rarest of western European fish, sturgeon, whose eggs—better known as caviar—surpass even foie gras as a sought-after delicacy.

The versatile wines of Bordeaux make fine accompaniments to most regional dishes, but don't overlook their less prestigious cousins (Bergerac, Pécharmant, Fiefs Vendéens, Monbazillac, Charentes). Cognac is de rigueur to finish a meal.

Shopping The Périgord region owes much of its fame to such gastronomic specialties as truffles, *fruits confits* (fruit preserved in brandy), and foie gras (ask for a sealed can rather than a glass jar, and it will last for months). Regional gifts include embroidery, wooden models, and, more exceptionally, the small green animals made from the stems of the wild angelica found around Poitiers and Niort.

Bicycling You can rent bikes from a number of train stations, notably La Rochelle, Bordeaux, Bergerac, Libourne, Le Verdon, and Sarlat. Homely Ile de Ré makes an excellent place for bike vacations (accessible from La Rochelle), as do the rolling vineyards around St-Emilion/Libourne or in the Médoc peninsula.

Hiking Enthusiastic walkers can choose a varied landscape of coast, vineyards, forest, and river valleys. For details of the best routes contact the **Grande Randonnée en Aquitaine** (Maison du Tourisme, Rond-Point du Figuier, 33115 Pila-sur-Mer, tel. 56–54–02–22).

Beaches The Atlantic coast presents an outstanding, uninterrupted vista of sandy beaches from Rochefort to Royan and from the Pointe de Grave to Biarritz, a stretch known as the **Côte d'Argent** (Silver Coast). Biarritz is an expensive resort—try St-Jean-de-Luz or Hendaye, as they're more affordable.

The Arts A wide range of music is available during **Bordeaux's International Musical May,** a leading event on France's cultural calendar (tel. 56–44–28–41). A smaller summer festival, the **Festival de la Musique Ancienne,** is held at **Saintes** in early July (tel. 46–92–51–35). Modern music gets a week-long airing at **La Rochelle's Franco-Folies** festival, also in July (tel. 46–50–56–39). Drama and music combine to make up the **Festival International de l'Entre-Deux-Mers** in August (tel. 56–71–51–35).

Festivals Other major festival activities in this ocean-bordered region are inspired by the sea. "Fêtes de la Mer"(Sea Festivals)—sometimes including carnival parades—are frequent, with one of the biggest at **La Rochelle** at Pentecost. A Bande Dessinée (comic book) festival takes place in **Angoulême** in January, and there's a Crime Film festival in **Cognac** each September.

Highlights for First-time Visitors

Beynac Castle, Tour 2
Bordeaux, Tour 2
Poitiers, Tour 1
La Rochelle, Tour 1
St-Emilion, Tour 2
St-Jean-de-Luz, Tour 3
Saintes, Tour 1
Sarlat, Tour 2

Tour 1: Poitou-Charentes

The region of Poitou-Charentes occupies the middle band of France's Atlantic coast. Excellent rail links mean easy access to the region's principal towns. Follow the main line from Poitiers to La Rochelle, veer south to stately Saintes, then return east along the Charente Valley branch line to the brandy towns of Cognac and Jarnac.

From Paris *By Train* TGV bullet trains to Poitiers leave Paris (Gare Montparnasse) every 2 hours. The trip takes 1 hour 40 minutes.

By Car The 335-kilometer (210-mile) drive to Poitiers from Paris via A10 takes 3¼ hours.

Poitiers

Tourist office: 15 rue Carnot, tel. 49–41–58–22.

Thanks to its majestic hilltop setting above the River Clain, and its position halfway along the Bordeaux–Paris trade route, **Poitiers** became an important commercial, religious, and university town in the Middle Ages. Since the 17th century, however, not much has happened in Poitiers, but visitors will find that this is not such a bad thing; stagnation equals preservation, and Poitiers's architectural heritage is correspondingly rich.

Boulevard Solférino climbs up from the station to the old town on the hilltop, continuing as rue Boncenne directly to the church of **Notre-Dame-la-Grande,** one of the most impressive examples of the Romanesque architecture so common in western France (rue des Cordeliers). Its 12th-century facade is framed by rounded arches of various sizes and decorated with a multitude of bas-reliefs and sculptures. The interior is dark. Its painted walls and pillars are not original; such decoration was a frequent ploy of mid-19th-century clerics keen to brighten up their otherwise austere churches.

Just off Grand'Rue, a few hundred yards beyond Notre-Dame-la-Grande, is the cathedral of **St-Pierre,** built during the 13th and 14th centuries (pl. de la Cathedrale). The largest church in Poitiers, it has a distinctive facade featuring two asymmetrical towers, as well as the usual rose window and carved portals.

The Atlantic Coast
La Roche-sur-Yon
Parthenay
Les Sables-d'Olonne
Fontenay-le-Comte
Poitiers
Le Blanc
Chauvigny
St-Savin
Lussac-les-Châteaux
Lusignan
Maillezais
Niort
St-Martin-de-Ré
Ile de Ré
La Rochelle
Melle
Civray
Surgères
Rochefort-sur-Mer
Aulnay
Bellac
Ile d'Oléron
Confolens
Brouage
Marennes
St-Jean-d'Angély
Mansle
St-Junien
Saintes
Cognac
Jarnac
Limoges
Royan
Angoulême
Châlus
Pointe de Grave
Talmont
Pons
Soulac-sur-Mer
Barbezieux-St-Hilaire
Gironde
Charente
Vienne
Thiviers
Brantôme
Dronne
Lesparre-Médoc
Hautefort
Ribérac
Chalais
Hourtin
The Médoc
Blaye
Montlieu-la-Garde
Périgueux
Auvézère
Margaux
Bourg
Montignac
Grotto of Lascaux
Lacanau
Isle
Libourne
Les Eyzies-de-Tayac
Sarlat
St-Emilion
Bergerac
Beynac
Bordeaux
Pessac
Dordogne
Garonne
Bay of Biscay
Léognan
Langoiran
Monbazillac
Lanquais
Arcachon
Haut-Bénauge
Domme
Labrède
Cadillac
Loupiac
Eymet
Monpazier
La Roque-Gageac
Cazaux
Barsac
Ste-Croix-du-Mont
Biron
Sauternes
Langon
Biscarosse
Monflanquin
Bazas
Lot
Parentis-en-Born
Casteljaloux
Damazan
Mimizan
Agen
Sabres
Nérac
Moissac
St-Julien-en-Born
Morcenx
Roquefort
Lévignacq
Castelsarrasin
Mont-de-Marsan
Cazaubon
Condom
Midour
Tartas
Villeneuve-de-Marsan
Eauze
Lectoure
Fleurance
Dax
Adour
St-Sever
Nogaro
Grenade
Auch
Biarritz
Gimont
Gesse
Bayonne
Orthez
Mirande
Leguevin
Maubourguet
Muret
St-Jean-de-Luz
Sauveterre-de-Béarn
Pau
Rieumes
St-Jean-Pied-de-Port
Gave de Pau
Boulogne-S.-Gesse
Tarbes
Oloron
SPAIN
N
Rail Lines
0
20 miles
0
30 km

The imposing interior is noted for its 12th-century stained glass, especially the Crucifixion in the chancel, and 13th-century wooden choir stalls, thought to be the oldest in France.

Head down Grand'Rue, taking the second left and first right onto rue Jean-Jaurès. The town museum, **Musée Ste-Croix,** is a modern building housing archaeological discoveries and European paintings from the 15th to the 19th centuries; these are of good, though not outstanding, quality. *61 rue St-Simplicien. Admission free. Open Wed.–Mon. 10–noon and 1–5 (2–6 weekends); closed Tues.*

Next to the museum is the 4th-century **Baptistère St-Jean,** the oldest Christian building in France. Its heavy stone bulk is sunk some 12 feet beneath ground level and consists of a rectangular chamber, used for baptisms, and an eastern end added during the 6th and 7th centuries. The porch, or narthex (restored in the 10th century), is linked to the main building by three archways. Go inside to see the octagonal basin, a larger version of a font for baptism by total immersion, and a collection of sarcophagi and works of sculpture. *Rue Jean-Jaurès. Admission: 8 frs. Open Mar.–Jan., daily 10–12:30 and 2–4; Feb., Thurs.–Tues. 10–12:30 and 2–4:30.*

Make your way back into the town center, pausing to admire the beautifully preserved houses lining the way, and turn left onto rue Carnot. Shortly after this street has become rue de la Tranchée, the oldest of Poitiers's churches, **St-Hilaire-le-Grand,** appears to the right (rue St. Hilaire). Parts of St-Hilaire date from the early 11th century. Unfortunately, the original church had to be reduced in width in the 12th century when its roof was destroyed by fire; local masons lacked the engineering know-how to cover large expanses with the fireproof stone vaults chosen as a replacement. The semicircular, mosaic-floor choir rises high above the level of the nave. Cupolas, mighty columns, frescoes, and finely carved capitals add to the church's interest.

Lodging
Under 250 frs.

Europe. An early 19th-century building in the middle of town holds this unpretentious hotel, though some rooms occupy a modern extension. Foreign visitors often stay here, attracted by the traditional decor and competitive prices. There is no restaurant. *39 rue Carnot, 86000, tel. 49–88–12–00. 78 rooms, some with bath. V.*

Dining
Under 125 frs.

Maxime. This crowd-pleaser lives up to its famous name, thanks to a wide choice of set menus, the personal recipes of chef Christian Rougier (foie gras and duck salad, for instance), and a pastel-toned decor featuring frescoes from the '20s and '30s. *4 rue St-Nicolas, tel. 49–41–09–55. Reservations required. AE, MC, V. Closed Sat., Sun., and much of July and Aug.*

Niort

Six trains daily make the 50-minute run from Poitiers, 72 km (45 mi) away. Niort tourist office: Rue Ernest-Perochon, tel. 49–24–18–79.

Niort, a complacent, middle-class town, is best known as the capital of the French insurance business. The massive keep, with its two square towers dominating the River Sèvre, is all that remains of the **castle** built at the end of the 12th century by

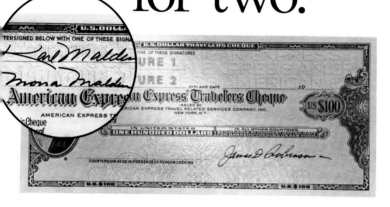

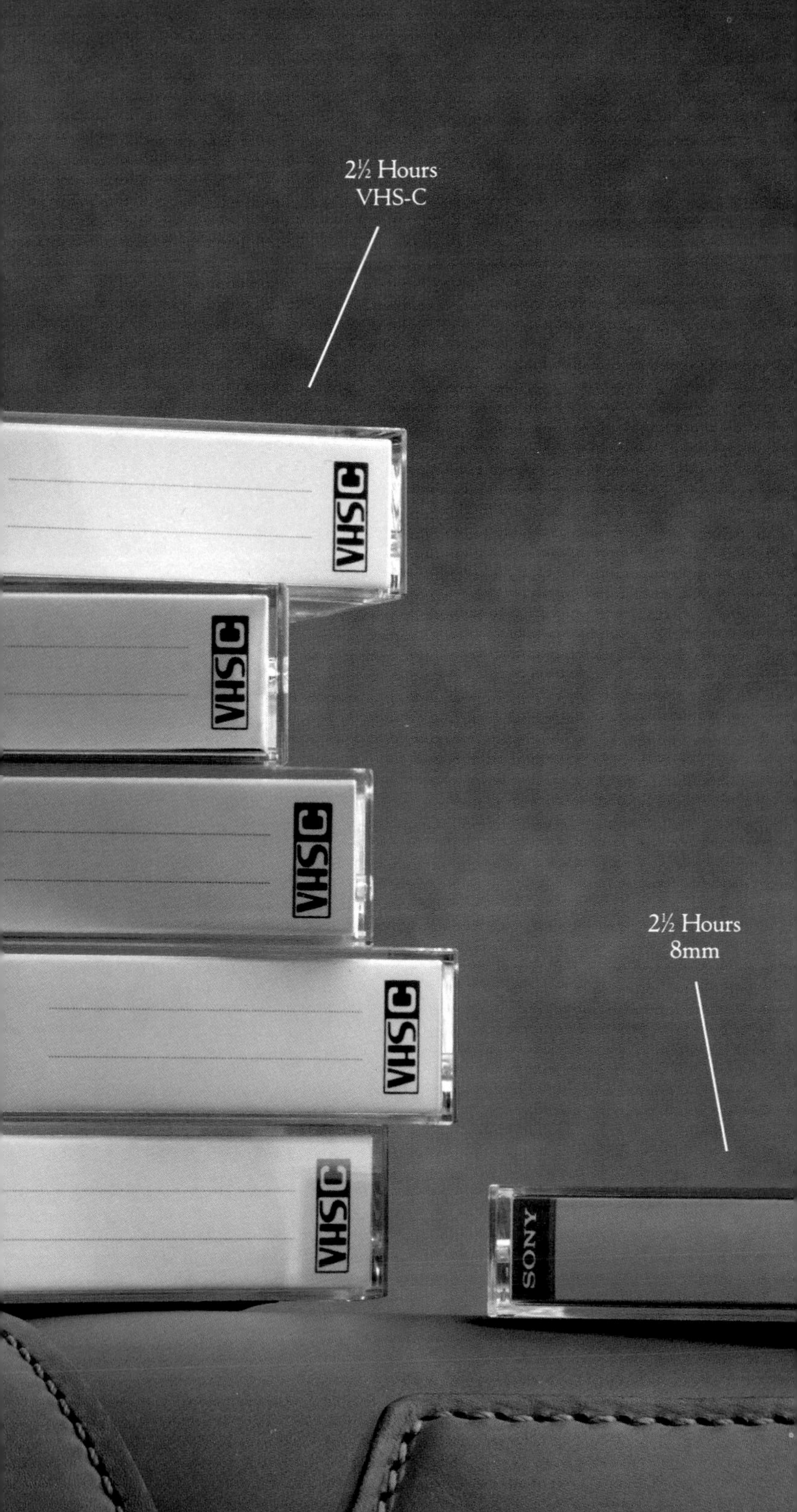
2½ Hours
VHS-C
VHS C
VHS C
VHS C
VHS C
VHS C
2½ Hours
8mm
SONY

SONY

PACK WISELY.

Given a choice, the seasoned traveler always carries less. Case in point: Sony Handycam® camcorders, America's most popular. They record up to 2½ hours on a single tape. VHS-C tapes record only 30 minutes.* And why carry five tapes when you can record everything on one? Which brings us to the first rule of traveling: pack a Sony Handycam camcorder.

*In standard play mode.

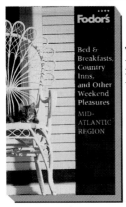

English kings Henry II and Richard the Lionheart. Inside there is a museum with an extensive collection of arms and local costumes. *Next to the Vieux-Ponts (Old Bridges). Admission: 13 frs. Open Apr.–Oct., Wed.–Mon 9–noon and 2–6; Nov.–Mar., Wed.–Mon. 9–noon and 2–5; closed Tues.*

Just off the nearby rue Victor-Hugo is the old town hall, a triangular building completed in 1535. It now houses the **Musée du Pilori,** with its collection of local archaeological finds and Renaissance artifacts. The highlight is an ebony chest encrusted with gold and silver. *Just off rue Victor-Hugo. Admission: 10 frs. Open Apr.–Oct., Wed.–Mon. 9–noon and 2–6; Nov.–Mar., Wed.–Mon. 9–noon and 2–5; closed Tues.*

Do an about-face and amble down rue St-Jean, the oldest street in Niort, to the **Musée des Beaux-Arts** (Fine Arts Museum), where tapestries, gold and enamelware, wooden statues and effigies, and 17th- to 18th-century paintings are on display. *Rue St-Jean. Admission: 14 frs. (free Wed.). Open Wed.–Mon. 9–noon and 2–6 (5 in winter).*

La Rochelle

Six trains daily link Niort to La Rochelle, 55 minutes away. Tourist office: Place de la Petite-Sirène, tel. 46–41–14–68.

La Rochelle is an appealing old town; its ancient streets are centered on its harbor, the remarkably picturesque Vieux-Port. Standing sentinel on either side of the harbor are the fortresslike 14th-century towers known as **Tour St-Nicholas** (to the left) and the **Tour de la Chaîne** (to the right). From the top of Tour St-Nicholas, visitors can admire the view over the surrounding bay toward the Ile d'Aix. *Admission: 18 frs. Open Wed.–Mon. 9:30–12:30 and 2:30–6 (until 5 in winter); closed Tues.*

Take cours des Dames, a spacious avenue lined with sturdy trees and 18th-century houses, back to the Porte de la Grosse-Horloge, a massive stone gate marking the entrance to the straight, narrow, bustling streets of the old town. Head down rue du Palais and onto rue Gargoulleau. Halfway down on the left is the 18th-century Bishop's Palace, now home to a museum of paintings. Opposite is the **Musée Lafaille,** housed in an elegant mansion and containing extensive collections of rocks, coral, and shellwork. Other items range from a tribal idol from Easter Island in the South Pacific to a giraffe (now stuffed) given as a gift to King Charles X (1824–30). *28 rue Albert-Ier. Admission: 12 frs. Open Apr.–Oct., Tues.–Sun. 10–noon and 2–6; Nov.–Mar., Tues.–Sat. 10–noon and 2–5, Sun. 2–5.*

Farther down rue du Palais (which becomes rue Albert-Ier) is another 18th-century building containing the **Musée du Nouveau-Monde** (New World Museum). Old maps, engravings, watercolors, and even wallpaper evoke the commercial links between La Rochelle and the New World. *10 rue Fleuriau. Admission: 12 frs. Open Wed.–Mon. 10:30–12:30 and 1:30–6, Sun. 3–6; closed Tues.*

Lodging
Under 250 frs.

Tour de Nesle. This modernized hotel may be a bit cramped, but it is clean, cheerful, and ideally placed for exploring the harbor and the old town. Ask for a room with a view across the canal toward St-Sauveur church. *2 quai Louis-Durand, 17000, tel. 46–41–30–72. 28 rooms with shower or bath. MC, V.*

Dining
Under 125 frs.

André. The salty decor is somewhat excessive—fishing nets flutter overhead, and posters of ocean liners billow from the walls—but the food and service have such gusto that you'll be caught up in the mood, especially if you order a monumental seafood platter to wash down with white Charentes wine. *5 rue St-Jean, tel. 46–41–28–24. Reservations advised. MC, V.*

Under 75 frs.

Pré Vert. Decorated throughout in shades of green, this restaurant is hidden down a discreet pedestrian street close to the harbor. It offers three inexpensive set menus and a good selection of regional specialties, such as foie gras, eel, and duck. *43 rue St-Nicolas, tel. 46–41–24–43. Reservations advised in summer. AE, DC, MC, V. Closed Sun., Nov.–Feb.*

Ile de Ré

Boats leave La Rochelle harbor daily in summer for the nearby islands of Ré (70 frs. adults, 49 frs. children, round-trip), Aix (120 and 84 frs.), and Oléron (135 and 95 frs.).

Cheerful **Ile de Ré** is just 26 kilometers (16 miles) long and never more than 6 kilometers (4 miles) wide. Vineyards sweep over the eastern part of the island while oyster beds straddle the shallow waters to the west. The largest village, **St-Martin de Ré** (population 3,000), has a lively harbor and a citadel built by ace military architect Sébastien de Vauban in 1681. Many of its streets also date from the 17th century, and the villagers' low, white houses, often embellished with window boxes full of flowers, are typical of the island as a whole.

Head down to the far end of the island to climb up the **Phare de la Baleine** (lighthouse) for sweeping views and check out the village of **Ars,** with its black-and-white church spire and cute harbor.

Dining
Under 75 frs.

Café du Phare. This spot at the foot of the lighthouse serves excellent meals and snacks in a surprising, art deco setting full of arty '30s lamps. Try the *poutargue*, a local specialty made from smoked cod roe and served with shallots and sour cream. *Route du Phare, St-Clément-des-Baleines, tel. 46–29–46–66. No reservations or credit cards. Closed Oct.–Easter.*

Saintes

Eight trains daily run down the coast from La Rochelle to Saintes, 50 minutes away. Tourist office: 62 cours National, tel. 46–74–23–82.

Saintes is a city of stately serenity. Its **cathedral** seems to stagger beneath the weight of its chunky tower, which climbs above the red roofs of the old town. Engineering caution foiled plans for the traditional pointed spire, so the tower was given a shallow dome—incongruous, perhaps, but distinctive. Angels, prophets, and saints decorate the Flamboyant Gothic main door of the cathedral, and the austere 16th-century interior is lined with circular pillars of formidable circumference.

The narrow pedestrian streets clustered around the cathedral contrast with the broad boulevard that slices through the town and over the River Charente, but both are full of life and color. Just across the bridge, to the right, is the impressive Roman **Arc de Germanicus,** built in AD 19. Ahead, reached by rue de l'Arc-de-Triomphe, is the sturdy octagonal tower of the **Abbaye**

aux Dames. Consecrated in 1047, this abbey church is fronted by an exquisite, arcaded facade, whose portals and capitals, carved with fantastic beasts, deserve more than a quick look. Although the Romanesque choir remains largely in its original form, the rest of the interior is less harmonious, having been periodically restored.

Saintes owes its development to the salt marshes that first attracted the Romans to the area some 2,000 years ago. The Romans left their mark with an arch, which we've already seen, and with an impressively restored amphitheater: There are several better-preserved examples in France, but few as old. To reach the amphitheater, take the boulevard back across the river and veer left onto cours Reverseaux. Access is via rue St-Eutrope.

Dining
Under 75 frs.

L'Abbatial. When the abbey complex was reopened in 1989 after a thorough overhaul, one consequence was the brasserie opposite the abbey portals. The design is state-of-the-art, and the set menus at lunchtime, priced at 55 and 90 francs, no less than astounding. Try the broccoli flan. *7 pl. de l'Abbaye, tel. 46-92-05-25. Reservations advised. V. Closed Sun.*

Cognac

Six trains daily make the 30-minute journey from Saintes. Cognac tourist office: 16 rue du XIV-Juillet, tel. 45-82-10-71.

Compared with Saintes, dull, black-walled **Cognac** seems an unlikely hometown for one of the world's most successful drink trades. You may be disappointed initially by its unpretentious appearance, but, like the drink, it tends to grow on you. Cognac owed its early development to the transport of salt and wine along the River Charente. When 16th-century Dutch merchants discovered that the local wine was both tastier and easier to transport if distilled, the town became the heart of the brandy industry and remains so to this day.

The leading monument in Cognac is its former **castle,** now part of the premises of Otard Cognac, a leading merchant. Volatile Renaissance monarch François I was born here in 1494. The castle has changed quite a bit since then. The remaining buildings are something of a hodgepodge, though the stocky towers that survey the Charente recall the site's fortified origins. The tour of Otard Cognac combines its own propaganda with historical comment on the drink itself. The slick audiovisuals are tastefully done, and you will visit some interesting rooms and receive a free taste of the firm's product, which is available for sale at vastly reduced prices. *Admission free. Guided tours daily on the hour 10–noon and 2–5 (except Sun. during Oct.–May).*

Most cognac houses organize visits of their premises and *chais* (warehouses). **Hennessy,** a little farther along the banks of the Charente (note the company's mercenary emblem: an ax-wielding arm carved in stone), and **Martell** both give polished guided tours, an ideal introduction to the mysteries of cognac. Martell's *chais* are perhaps more picturesque (pl. Martell, tel. 45-82-44-44), but the Hennessy tour includes a cheerful jaunt across the Charente in old-fashioned boats (rue Richonne, tel. 45-82-52-22). Wherever you decide to go, you will literally soak up the atmosphere of cognac; 3% of the precious cask-bound liquid evaporates every year! This has two consequences: Each *chais* smells delicious, and a small, black, funguslike mushroom, which feeds on cognac's alcoholic fumes, forms on walls throughout the town.

Rue Saulnier, alongside the Hennessy premises, is the most atmospheric of the somber, sloping, cobbled streets that compose the core of Cognac, dominated by the tower of **St-Léger,** a church with a notably large Flamboyant Gothic rose window. Busy boulevard Denfert-Rochereau twines around the old town, passing in front of the manicured lawns of the town hall and the gravelly drive of the neighboring **Musée du Cognac,** which contains good ceramics and art nouveau glass but is worth visiting mainly for its section on cognac itself. The history and production of cognac are clearly explained, and one room is devoted to amusing early advertising posters. *48 blvd. Denfert-Rochereau. Admission 11 frs. Open Wed.–Mon. 10–noon (summer only) and 2–5:30; closed Tues.*

Lodging and Dining

Under 350 frs.

Pigeons Blancs. "White Pigeons," a converted and modernized coaching inn standing in spacious grounds, has been owned by the same family since the 17th century. The welcome is warm, and the hotel is comfortable and intimate, worth the 1¼-mile trek from the train station. The highly rated restaurant offers a choice of three set menus of varying sophistication. The most expensive will not only titillate your taste buds but will keep you going for about a week! *110 rue Jules-Brisson, tel. 45–82–16–36. 10 rooms with bath. Facilities: restaurant (closed Sun. dinner). AE, DC, MC, V. Closed first half of Jan.*

Under 250 frs.

Auberge. The two-story Auberge occupies an old building on a quiet street in the heart of Cognac. The emphasis is on bourgeois comfort; the restaurant, decked out in earnest, 18th-century style, sets the tone. The food has a similarly serious ring to it: copious but unexceptional. *13 rue Plumejeau, 16100, tel. 45–32–08–70. 27 rooms, 20 with bath. Facilities: restaurant (closed Sat.). AE, MC, V. Closed Christmas–New Year's.*

Shopping

An old bottle of cognac makes a fine souvenir; try **La Cognathèque** (10 pl. Jean-Monnet). Though you'll find the same stuff, but infinitely cheaper, at any local producer, this is perhaps the most convenient source.

Jarnac

Trains continue from Cognac to Jarnac, 10 minutes and 16 km (10 mi) upriver.

Several cognac firms are found in the charming village of **Jarnac,** also famous as the birthplace of French president François Mitterrand. **Hine** (quai de l'Orangerie, tel. 45–81–11–38) and **Courvoisier** (pl. du Château, tel. 45–35–55–55) organize visits of their riverbank premises, though Hine's cozy buildings in local chalky stone have more appeal than does Courvoisier's bombastic redbrick factory by the bridge.

Angoulême

Six trains daily link Saintes to Angoulême via Cognac-Jarnac; the journey from Jarnac, 26 km (16 mi) away, lasts 20 minutes. Angoulême tourist office: Place de la Gare, tel. 45–92–27–57.

Angoulême is divided, as are many other French towns, between an old, picturesque sector perched around a hilltop cathedral and a modern, industrial part sprawling along the valley and railroad below.

Angoulême Cathedral, in place St-Pierre, bears little resemblance to the majority of its French counterparts because of a flattened dome that lends it an Oriental appearance. The cathedral dates from the 12th century, though it was partly destroyed by Calvinists in 1562, then restored in a heavy-handed manner in 1634 and 1866. Its principal attraction is the magnificent Romanesque facade, whose layers of rounded arches boast 70 stone statues and bas-reliefs illustrating the Last Judgment. The interior is austere and massive but of no great interest.

The cathedral dominates the *ville haute* (upper town), known as the "plateau." There are stunning views from the ramparts alongside, and a warren of quaint old streets to explore in the shadow of the Hôtel de Ville (Town Hall), with its colorful garden. Literary enthusiasts may like to note that 19th-century novelist Honoré de Balzac is one of the town's adopted sons; Balzac described Angoulême in his novel *Lost Illusions*.

Dining
Under 250 frs.

Terminus. Stay at this convenient, if run-of-the-mill, station hotel to avoid lugging your bags up Angoulême's steep hill to the old town. The ground-floor restaurant is actually under different management but makes an excellent venue for regional specialties like burbot with leeks or veal kidneys in a mustard sauce, showcased in a plethora of fixed-price menus. *1 pl. de la Gare, 16000, tel. 45-92-39-00. 33 rooms, some with bath or shower. Facilities: adjoining restaurant. AE, MC, V.*

Tour 2: Bordeaux and the Dordogne

Elegant Bordeaux is the base for this tour, which features rail excursions through the vineyards of the Médoc peninsula and along the picturesque castle-lined Dordogne Valley to St-Emilion, one of France's prettiest wine towns, and historic Sarlat, famed for its goose fair and foie gras.

From Paris
By Train

TGV bullet trains to Bordeaux leave Paris (Gare Montparnasse) just about every hour. The trip takes 3–3¼ hours.

By Car

The 575-kilometer (360-mile) drive from Paris to Bordeaux along A10 takes 5½ hours.

Bordeaux

Tourist office: 12 cours du XXX-Juillet, opposite the CIVB wine center, tel. 56-48-04-61.

Numbers in the margin correspond to points of interest on the Bordeaux map.

The capital of southwest France, **Bordeaux** is renowned worldwide for its wines. Vineyards extend on all sides: Graves and pretty Sauternes to the south; flat, dusty Médoc to the west; and Pomerol and St-Emilion to the east. Stylish châteaus loom above the most famous vines, but much of the wine-making area is unimpressive, with little sign of the extraordinary regional affluence it promotes.

There are signs enough in the city itself, however, where wine shippers have long based their headquarters along the banks of the Garonne. An aura of 18th-century elegance permeates the downtown area, whose fine shops and pedestrian precincts invite leisurely exploration.

But first, after turning right out of Gare St-Jean, head left
1 down rue de Tauzia into the heart of the **old dockland,** with its
narrow, sturdy, low-terraced streets. There is a forbidding feel
here, and indeed, Bordeaux as a whole is a less exuberant city
than most in France, with an almost British reserve. For a bet-
2 ter view of the picturesque quayside, stroll across the **Pont de
Pierre** bridge spanning the Garonne; built by Napoleon at the
start of the 19th century, the bridge makes spectacular viewing itself, thanks to a gracefully curving multitude of arches.

Two blocks from the riverbank, along cours Chapeau-Rouge, is
3 the city's leading 18th-century monument: the **Grand Théâtre,**
built between 1773 and 1780 to the plans of architect Victor
Louis. Its elegant exterior is ringed by graceful Corinthian columns and pilasters. The majestic foyer, with its two-winged
staircase and cupola, inspired Charles Garnier's design for the
Paris Opera. The theater hall itself has a frescoed ceiling and a
shimmering chandelier composed of 14,000 Bohemian crystals;
the acoustics are said to be perfect. *The theater was extensively
renovated in 1991–92; contact the tourist office for guided-tour
information.*

The allées de Tourny and cours du XXX-Juillet, haughty tree-
lined boulevards, reel off north from the Grand Théâtre. At the
4 start of the cours du XXX-Juillet is the **CIVB,** headquarters of
the Bordeaux wine trade, where information can be had and
samples tasted. The **Vinothèque,** opposite, sells Bordeaux by
the bottle to suit every purse. At the far end of the cours is the
Esplanade des Quinconces, a vast 400-yard-long square overlooking the Garonne.

Turn left from the esplanade and head 400 yards along the
5 quayside to the **Cité Mondiale du Vin** (entered at 25 quai des
Chartrons). This ambitious complex, opened in 1991, is part office block, part shopping mall, and part culture center; a museum, bars, and exhibition hall all have a common theme: the
world of wine.

6 Head back along the river, past the esplanade, as far as **place de
la Bourse,** the city's second most important 18th-century landmark after the Grand Théâtre. A provincial reply to Paris's celebrated place Vendôme, the square (built 1730–55) features
airy, large-windowed buildings designed by the country's most
esteemed architect of the era, Jacques-Ange Gabriel.

Head two blocks down rue F-Philippart to the 18th-century **place du Parlement,** and you'll have no problem finding a promising-looking lunch spot. No fewer than six bistros and restaurants, some with outdoor tables, line the square.

A maze of narrow streets wend their way from the river to the
7 **Cathédrale St-André,** located in place Pey-Berland. This hefty
edifice, 135 yards long, isn't one of France's better Gothic
cathedrals, and the outside has a dirty, neglected look. The interior, though, rewards your scrutiny as the soaring 14th-

Cathédrale St-André, **7**
Cité Mondiale du Vin, **5**
CIVB, **4**
Grand Théâtre, **3**
Hôtel de Ville, **8**
Musée des Beaux-Arts, **9**
Old dockland, **1**
Place de la Bourse, **6**
Pont de Pierre, **2**

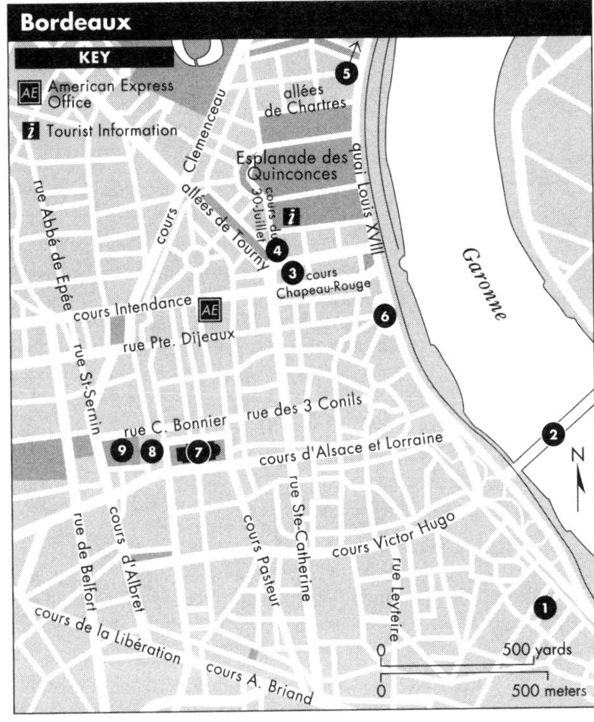

century chancel makes an interesting contrast with the earlier, more severe nave. Excellent—albeit grimy—stone carvings adorn the facade (notably that of the Porte Royale, to the right), as well as the 15th-century Pey-Berland Tower, which stands nearby.

8 Across the tidy gardens of the luxurious **Hôtel de Ville** (Town Hall) opposite the cathedral is the busy cours d'Albert and the
9 **Musée des Beaux-Arts.** This fine-arts museum has a notable collection of works spanning the 15th–20th centuries, with important paintings by Paolo Veronese *(Apostle's Head)*, Camille Corot *(Bath of Diana)*, and Odilon Redon *(Chariot of Apollo)*, and sculptures by Auguste Rodin. *20 cours d'Albret. Admission: 15 frs. Open Wed.–Mon. 10–6; closed Tues.*

Lodging
Under 250 frs.

Pyrénées. Located in a turn-of-the-century building close to theater and old town, Pyrénées provides typically earnest provincial comfort (deep, slightly worn armchairs and effusive decor). American and British guests are common. There is no restaurant. *12 rue St-Rémi, 33000, tel. 56–81–66–58. 18 rooms with bath. AE, V. Closed second half Aug. and Christmas–New Year's.*

Royal Médoc. This Bordeaux hotel is admirably situated near the majestic Esplanade de Quinconces in the city center, in a building that dates from 1720. English-speaking guests form the backbone of the foreign clientele attracted by the elegant, neoclassical architecture and cheerful, efficient service. There is no restaurant. *5 rue de Sèze, 33000, tel. 56–81–72–42. 45 rooms, many with bath. AE, MC, V.*

Under 200 frs. ★ **Vieux Bordeaux.** This much-acclaimed nouvelle cuisine haunt lies on the fringe of the old town. Chef Michel Bordage concentrates on fresh produce. His menu is therefore short but of high quality, complemented by three set-price menus. His fish dishes are particularly good; try the steamed turbot. The wine is well priced, the decor modern, and the ambience lively. *27 rue Buhan, tel. 56–52–94–36. Reservations advised. AE, MC, V. Closed Sat. lunch, Sun., Aug., and 1 week in Feb.*

Dining
Under 125 frs. ★ **Clavel.** The recently opened sister restaurant to a center-city establishment of the same name adds a note of gastronomic good value to the undistinguished St-Jean quarter near the train station. It is one of the few places in town where you can sample claret by the glass, though any number of fruity young Bordeaux are available by the bottle for under 100 francs. The squeaky-clean, modern-rustic decor, varied cuisine (including salmon, pig's feet, and lobster), and true bistro prices make this an excellent choice. *44 rue Charles-Domercq, tel. 56–92–91–52. Reservations advised. MC, V. Closed Sun., Mon., and second half of July.*

Under 75 frs. **Ombrière.** The friendly Ombrière looks out over one of the finest squares in old Bordeaux; during summer months, you can eat outside. The food is pleasant in an unexciting, brasserie sort of way (steak and fries), but for central Bordeaux, its set menu is fairly priced, and even a choice à la carte dinner won't seem extravagant. *14 pl. du Parlement, tel. 56–44–82–69. MC, V. Closed Sun., Mon., and Aug.*

Shopping Stylish shops abound in the commercial heart of Bordeaux, on the numerous pleasant pedestrian streets between the cathedral and Grand Théâtre. A top-ranking Bordeaux is not likely to represent top value, though at the **Vinothèque** in Bordeaux (8 cours du XXX-Juillet), you'll have a wide choice.

Médoc

Trains from Bordeaux plow up the Médoc peninsula 6 times daily to Margaux (45 minutes away) and Pauillac (70 minutes away). One midday train stops at St-Estèphe (80 minutes away), and 3 trains stop at Le Verdon, near Pointe de Grave (2 hours from Bordeaux).

Médoc is strange, dusty territory. Even the vines look dusty, and so does the ugly town of **Margaux,** the area's unofficial capital. Yet the soil hereabouts is sown with the seeds of grandeur. The small, arid communes and châteaus of Haut-Médoc feature such venerable names as Margaux, St-Julien, Pauillac, and St-Estèphe. Château Margaux, an elegant, coolly restrained classical building of 1802, and three wineries at Pauillac—Lafite-Rothschild, Latour, and Mouton-Rothschild—are recognized as producers of *Premiers Crus,* their wines qualifying with Graves's Haut-Brion as Bordeaux's top five reds.

Trains chug through the less prestigious wine fields of northern, or Bas, Médoc, toward **Pointe de Grave,** at the tip of the Médoc peninsula, the site of an American memorial commemorating the landing of U.S. troops in 1917. From the surrounding sand dunes, there are views over the Gironde estuary to Royan and back across the Atlantic. A car-ferry plows across to Royan four times daily (cost: 110 frs. per car, 30 frs. per passenger).

St-Emilion

Two trains each day make the ½-hour run from Bordeaux. There's 1 in the early morning, and 1 in early afternoon. St-Emilion tourist office: Place des Créneaux, tel. 57–24–72–03.

St-Emilion is a jewel of a town with its old buildings of golden stone, ruined town walls, well-kept ramparts offering charming views, and its church hewn into a cliff. Sloping vines invade from all sides, and lots and lots of tourists invade down the middle.

The medieval streets are filled with wine stores and crafts shops. Macaroons are a specialty. The local wines offer the twin advantages of reaching maturity earlier than other Bordeaux reds and representing better value for the money. Tours of the pretty **St-Emilion vineyard,** including wine tastings, are organized by the *Syndicat d'Initiative* (tourist office) on place des Créneaux, a bulky square with a terrace overlooking the lower part of St-Emilion. A stroll along the 13th-century ramparts helps you appreciate St-Emilion's ancient, unspoiled stone-walled houses, and soon brings you to the Royal Castle, or **Château du Roi,** built by occupying sovereign Henry III of England (1216–72).

Steps lead down from the ramparts to place du Marché, a wooded square where cafés remain open late into the balmy summer night. Lining one side are the east windows of the **Eglise Monolithe,** one of France's largest underground churches, hewn out of the rock face between the 9th and 12th century. *Visits organized by the Syndicat d'Initiative, tel. 57–24–72–03.*

Just south of the town walls is **Château Ausone,** an estate that is ranked with Cheval Blanc as producing the finest wine of St-Emilion.

Lodging and Dining
Under 250 frs.
★

Auberge de la Commanderie. For such a pretty town, St-Emilion is a bit short on accommodations. Luckily, this two-story, 19th-century hotel is admirable in every sense. It is close to the ramparts and has its own garden and views of the vineyards. The rooms are small but clean and individually decorated. The attractive restaurant is often frequented by nonresidents and boasts a good selection of local wines. *Rue des Cordeliers, 33300, tel. 57–24–70–19. 15 rooms, most with bath. Facilities: restaurant (closed Tues., Sept.–June), garden. MC, V. Closed Dec.–Jan.*

Dining
Under 125 frs.

Germaine. Family cooking and regional dishes are featured at this central St-Emilion eatery. The stylish upstairs dining room, candlelit and adorned with flowers, is a pleasant place to enjoy the reasonably priced set menus. Grilled meats and fish are house specialties; for dessert, try the almond macaroons. There's also a terrace for outdoor eating. *Pl. des Crénaux, tel. 57–24–70–88. Reservations advised. DC, V. Closed Sun., Mon., and mid-Dec.–mid-Jan.*

Bergerac

Seven trains operate daily from Bordeaux and take 75 minutes to reach Bergerac. There are 3 trains daily from St-Emilion, an hour away. Bergerac tourist office: 97 rue Neuve d'Argenson, tel. 53–57–03–11.

You expect vines to be cultivated around **Bergerac**—but not tobacco. Learn about this local industry at the **Musée du Tabac,** a museum housed in the haughty 17th-century Maison Peyrarède near the quayside. The manufacture, uses, and history of tobacco, from its American origins to its spread worldwide, are explained with the help of maps, pictures, documents, and other exhibits, including a collection of pipes and snuff bottles. *10 rue de l'Ancien Pont. Admission: 7 frs. Open Tues.–Fri. 10–noon and 2–6, Sat. 10–noon and 2–5, Sun. 2:30–6:30.*

Head left from the tobacco museum, past place de la Myrpe, to the **Couvent des Récollets.** This former convent's stone-and-brick buildings range in date from the 12th to the 17th century and include galleries, a large, vaulted cellar, and a cloister, where the Maison du Vin dishes out information on—and samples of—local wines. From the first floor of the convent, treat yourself to a view of the sloping vineyards of Monbazillac across the Dordogne. *Just off pl. de la Myrpe. Admission: 12 frs. Visits July–Aug., every hour from 10:30 to 11:30 and 1:30 to 5:30; mid-May–June and Sept.–mid-Oct., at 3:30 and 4:30. Closed Mon. and Sun., mid-May–June and Sept.–mid-Oct.*

The regional wines of Bergerac range from red and rosé to dry and sweet whites. While you're in town, you might like to purchase a bottle or two of the town's most famous vintage: Monbazillac, a sweet wine made from overripe grapes that enjoyed an international reputation long before its Bordeaux rival, Sauternes.

Lodging and Dining
Under 350 frs.

Bordeaux. You'll find a curious mixture here: Bordeaux is part typical French-provincial hotel, with stocky furniture and absurdly spacious rooms, and part city slicker, with the would-be modern design of the facade and reception area that might have worked a few decades ago but looks strangely unconvincing in a quiet square in a small country town. The recently refitted bathrooms, however, are just fine. The admirable restaurant serves regional dishes with nouvelle inventiveness, though guests are not obliged to eat here. English and American visitors are warmly and frequently welcomed. Rooms facing the garden courtyard are preferable to those with a view across undistinguished place Gambetta. *38 pl. Gambetta, 24100, tel. 53–57–12–83. 42 rooms with bath. Facilities: restaurant (closed Mon. and Sat., Nov.–Mar.), pool, garden. AE, DC, MC, V. Closed Jan.*

Sarlat

The 3 daily trains from Bergerac take 80 minutes. Sarlat tourist office: Place de la Liberté, tel. 53–59–27–67.

To do justice to the golden-stone splendor of **Sarlat**, you may want to take advantage of the guided tour offered by the tourist office on place de la Liberté. Rue de la Liberté leads to place du Payrou, occupied on one corner by the pointed-gable Renaissance house where writer-orator Etienne de la Boétie (1530–63) was born. Diagonally opposite is the entrance to **Sarlat Cathedral.** An elaborate turret-topped tower, begun in the 12th century, is the oldest part of the building and, along with the choir, all that remains of the original Romanesque church. A sloping garden behind the cathedral, the Cour de l'Evêché, affords good views of the choir and contains a strange, conical tower known as the **Lanterne des Morts** (Lantern of the Dead), which was occasionally used as a funeral chapel.

Rue d'Albusse, adjoining the garden, and rue de la Salamandre are narrow, twisty streets that head back to place de la Liberté and the 17th-century town hall. Opposite the town hall is the rickety former church of St-Marie, overlooking place des Oies and pointing the way to Sarlat's most interesting street, **rue des Consuls.** Among its medieval buildings are the Hôtel Plamon, with broad windows that resemble those of a Gothic church, and, opposite, the 15th-century Hôtel de Vassal.

Across the undistinguished rue de la République, which slices Sarlat in two, is the Quartier Ouest (Western Quarter), many of whose streets are too narrow to be used by cars. Rue Rousseau saunters past the Chapelle des Récollets and Abbaye St-Claire to the 16th-century Tour du Bourreau and a remnant of the former town walls.

Lodging and Dining
Under 250 frs.

St-Albert. At the edge of the old town, St-Albert provides functional accommodations and a friendly welcome from owner Michel Garrigou. The old-fashioned restaurant, with four moderately priced set menus, provides some of the best values on restaurant meals in Sarlat (though it's wise to keep your eye on your tab, since not all prices are equally modest). House specialties—duck foie gras with shallots, and *la mique,* dumplings with pork and vegetables—exemplify the kitchen's proclivity for hearty fare. *10 pl. Pasteur, 24200, tel. 56–59–01–09. 56 rooms, some with bath. Facilities: restaurant (closed Sun. dinner and Mon., Nov.–mid-Apr.).*

Dining
Under 125 frs.

Jardin des Consuls. If you feel like lunch or a snack, make your way to this establishment in the heart of old Sarlat. Part restaurant, part tearoom, it has a pleasant stone-walled dining room and a courtyard in back that's idyllic in sunny weather. Soups and *cassoulet* stews head the filling 100-franc menu, best accompanied by a young, *gouleyant* (fruity) Cahors. Or just enjoy the sorbets and crêpes. *4 rue des Consuls, tel. 53–59–18–77. Reservations not required. V. Closed Mon.*

Beynac

Three buses run daily from Sarlat to Le Buisson, stopping at La Roque-Gageac and Beynac.

The 13th-century castle of **Beynac** is daringly perched atop a sheer cliff face beside an abrupt bend in the Dordogne. Restoration of this privately owned castle is an ongoing process, but its muscular architecture and the staggering views from its battlements make a visit imperative. *Admission: 25 frs. Open daily Mar.–mid-Nov., 10–noon and 2:30–5 or 6 (7 in July and Aug.).*

A short distance upriver, huddled beneath a towering gray cliff, is **La Roque-Gageac,** one of the prettiest and best-restored villages in the Dordogne Valley. Full of low, narrow streets lined with craft shops, it is dominated by the outlines of the 19th-century, mock-medieval Château de Malartrie and the round-turreted Manoir de Tarde.

Lodging and Dining
Under 250 frs.

La Belle Etoile. This cozy old stone hotel fits snugly into La Roque-Gageac's spectacular cliffside setting on the banks of the Dordogne. Several rooms overlook the river—as does the restaurant, where you'll prefer the set menus (starting at 100 francs) to the pricey à la carte choices. *La Rogue-Gageac, 24250, tel. 53-29-51-44. 17 rooms, some with bath or shower. Facilities: restaurant. Closed mid-Oct.-Easter. MC, V.*

Tour 3: Basque Country

This tour, which follows the main Paris–Spain train route as it forks at Dax and heads right, leads you into Basque country and the attractive towns of Bayonne and St-Jean-de-Luz.

From Paris
By Train

Six TGV trains to Dax leave Paris (Gare Montparnasse) each day. The trip takes 4 hours 7 minutes.

By Car

The 735-kilometer (460-mile) drive from Paris takes about 7½ hours. Follow A10 and N10 from Bordeaux, then D947 from Castets.

Dax

Tourist office: Place Thiers, by the bridge, tel. 58-90-20-00.

Dax, known in Roman times as Aquae Tarbellicae, has been famous for 2,000 years on account of its thermal springs. The daughter of Caesar Augustus came here to soothe her aches and pains, and she was the first in a long line of seasonal guests whose numbers have swollen to 50,000 each year, making Dax the country's premier warm-water spa. Steaming water gushes out of the lion-headed Néhé fountain in the center of town. The local mud (containing radioactive algae) is also reputed to have healing qualities.

Dax, though short on outstanding sites, is an airy town ideal for peaceful walks through its parks and gardens or along the banks of the River Adour. Follow signs from the train station to the Centre Ville (town center), half-mile distant on the other side of the river. To the left as you cross the bridge is the Parc Denis with its bullring and traces of the old city walls. To the right along cours de Verdun is the ornate casino. Rue des Carmes, midway between the bridge and the casino, arrows through the old town toward the classical, 17th-century cathedral, which hosts a variety of fine sculpture, some inherited from the previous Gothic structure. (Architecture enthusiasts should make a trip to the church of St-Paul-lès-Dax across the river; 11th-century bas-reliefs adorn its east end.)

Lodging
Under 150 frs.

Nord. This clean but unremarkable hotel is not only very inexpensive but also the most convenient for rail travelers, since it's close to the station near the bridge across the Adour River to the town center. Rooms are smallish. *68 av. St-Vincent-de-Paul, 40100, tel. 58-74-19-87. 19 rooms, some with bath or shower. MC, V. Closed Christmas through New Year's.*

Lodging and Dining
Under 250 frs.

Richelieu. The smattering of elderly guests who come to Dax to take the waters across town seem right at home in the spacious, slightly old-fashioned rooms of this hotel, which is centrally located south of the cathedral. The solid, filling local specialties available in the restaurant—mainly variations on poultry and foie gras—have eternal appeal, and there are set menus at 100 and 150 francs. *13 av. Victor-Hugo, 40100, tel. 58–74–81–81. 17 rooms with bath or shower. Facilities: restaurant (closed Sat. out of season). AE, DC, MC, V.*

Régina. A heated corridor runs between the thermal baths and this large, calm, modern hotel. Rooms are individually decorated, and the best have balconies. In the restaurant, set menus start at 80 francs. *Blvd. des Sports, 40100, tel. 58–74–84–58. 88 rooms with bath or shower. Facilities: bar, restaurant. DC, MC, V. Closed Dec.–Feb.*

Bayonne

Eight trains daily make the ½-hour run from Dax, 48 km (30 mi) away. Most continue to Biarritz and St-Jean-de-Luz. Tourist office: Place de la Liberté, tel. 59–59–31–31.

Bayonne is the gateway to Basque country, a territory stretching across the Pyrénées to Bilbao in Spain. Bayonne stands at the confluence of the Rivers Adour and Nive; the port of Bayonne extends along the valley to the sea about 5 kilometers (3 miles) away. You could easily spend an enjoyable few hours here, admiring the town's 13th-century cathedral, cloisters, old houses, and 17th-century ramparts. The airy, modernized **Musée Bonnat** houses a notable collection of 19th-century paintings. *5 rue Jacques-Lafitte. Admission: 12 frs. Open Wed.–Mon. 10–noon and 3–7.*

Lodging and Dining
Under 350 frs.

Loustau. This comfortable, modernized hotel stands near the old town ramparts, just 100 yards from the station by Pont St-Esprit, the main bridge over the Adour River to the old town. Priced at 270 to 350 francs, its well-appointed rooms attract tourists and businessmen alike; the hotel's Clos St-Esprit restaurant offers a buffet at lunchtime, together with 75- and 95-franc menus. *1 pl. de la République, 64100, tel. 59–55–16–74. 44 rooms with bath or shower. Facilities: bar, restaurant (closed Jan. and weekends in winter). AE, DC, MC, V.*

St-Jean-Pied-de-Port

Three trains daily make the 55-minute run from Bayonne.

The journey itself is one good reason for making an excursion from Bayonne to **St-Jean-Pied-de-Port**, 8 kilometers (5 miles) from the Spanish border. The train hugs the banks of the sinuous River Nive as the valley grows ever steeper and the Pyrénées loom in the distance. Pilgrims once used St-Jean as a launching pad for their assault on the Pyrénées, preferring to tarry a while in the tumbling street of the old town. In fact, the winding main street is lined with century-old houses that are beautifully tended; its cobbled stones are worn smooth, and no cars are allowed to squeeze across the ancient bridge that once clattered with departures to Santiago de Compostela. Parts of the original town wall stand too, but this didn't prevent Vauban from erecting a muscular fort on a hill above the town, just in case. Scramble up for sweeping views across the valley and local vineyards, which produce Irouleguy wine.

Biarritz

Trains run from Bayonne to Biarritz every 1½ hours and take 10 minutes to travel the 8 km (5 mi) between towns. Tourist office: 1 square Ixelles, tel. 59–24–20–24.

The celebrated resort of **Biarritz**, set on a particularly sheltered part of the Atlantic coast, rose to prominence in the 19th century when upstart Emperor Napoleon III took to spending his holidays here. You'll soon understand why: The crowded Grande Plage and neighboring Miramar Beach provide fine sand and friendly breakers amid a setting of craggy natural beauty. Biarritz remains a high-brow resort, with no shortage of deluxe hotels or bow-tied gamblers ambling over to the casino. Yet the old down-to-earth charm of the former fishing village remains to counterbalance the uppercrust ambience. The narrow streets around the cozy 16th-century church of St-Martin are delightful to stroll and, together with the harbor of Port des Pêcheurs, offer a tantalizing glimpse of the Biarritz of old.

Lodging
Under 350 frs.

Windsor. Built in the 1920s, this hotel is handy for the casino and beach and boasts its own restaurant (fish predominates; the cheapest menu is around 100 francs). The guest rooms—some moderately priced and some more expensive—are modernized and cozy, and some offer sea views. Guests, including many foreigners, tend to come here because they can't afford the majestic Palais or the slick Miramar. *19 blvd. du Général-de-Gaulle, 64200, tel. 59–24–08–52. 37 rooms with bath. Facilities: restaurant. AE, MC, V. Closed mid-Nov.–mid Mar.*

St-Jean-de-Luz

Trains link Biarritz to St-Jean-de-Luz, 10 minutes away, every 2 hours. Six trains daily make the 80-minute journey between St-Jean-de-Luz and Dax. Tourist office: Place Foch, tel. 59–26–03–16.

St-Jean-de-Luz deserves a visit for its old streets, curious church, colorful harbor, and elegant beach. The tree-lined place Louis-XIV, alongside the Hôtel de Ville (Town Hall) with its narrow courtyard and dainty statue of Louis XIV on horseback, is the quaint hub of the town. Nearby are the Eglise St-Jean-Baptiste, where unusual wooden galleries line one wall to create a theaterlike effect, and the Maison de l'Infante, where Maria Teresa of Spain stayed prior to her wedding to the Sun King. The foursquare mansion contains worthy 17th-century furnishings. *Quai de l'Infante. Admission: 16 frs. Open June–Sept. 10:30–noon and 3–6:30; closed Sun. AM.*

Lodging and Dining
Under 350 frs.

Bel-Air. There's a family holiday mood at this large villa near the beach, next to the casino. Rooms are spacious, and the hotel has its own garden and a terrace overlooking the bay. In the restaurant, set menus are priced at 100 and 115 francs. *Promenade Jacques-Thibaut, 64500, tel. 59–26–04–86. 23 rooms with bath or shower. Facilities: restaurant (June–Sept. only). AE, DC, MC, V. Closed mid-Nov.–Apr.*

Conversion Tables

Clothing Sizes

Men
Suits

To change American suit sizes to French suit sizes, add 10 to the American suit size.
To change French suit sizes to American suit sizes, subtract 10 from the French suit size.

U.S.	36	38	40	42	44	46	48
French	46	48	50	52	54	56	58

Shirts

To change American shirt sizes to French shirt sizes, multiply the American shirt size by 2 and add 8.
To change French shirt sizes to American shirt sizes, subtract 8 from the French shirt size and divide by 2.

U.S.	14	14½	15	15½	16	16½	17	17½
French	36	37	38	39	40	41	42	43

Shoes

French shoe sizes vary in their relation to American shoe sizes.

U.S.	6½	7	8	9	10	10½	11
French	39	40	41	42	43	44	45

Women
Dresses and Coats

To change U.S. dress/coat sizes to French dress/coat sizes, add 28 to the U.S. dress/coat size.
To change French dress/coat sizes to U.S. dress/coat sizes, subtract 28 from the French dress/coat size.

U.S.	4	6	8	10	12	14	16
French	32	34	36	38	40	42	44

Blouses and Sweaters

To change U.S. blouse/sweater sizes to French blouse/sweater sizes, add 8 to the U.S. blouse/sweater size.
To change French blouse/sweater sizes to U.S. blouse/sweater sizes, subtract 8 from the French blouse/sweater size.

U.S.	30	32	34	36	38	40	42
French	38	40	42	44	46	48	50

Shoes

To change U.S. shoe sizes to French shoe sizes, add 32 to the U.S. shoe size.
To change French shoe sizes to U.S. shoe sizes, subtract 32 from the French shoe size.

U.S.	4	5	6	7	8	9	10
French	36	37	38	39	40	41	42

French Vocabulary

Words and Phrases

	English	*French*	*Pronunciation*
Basics	Yes/no	Oui/non	wee/no
	Please	S'il vous plaît	seel voo play
	Thank you	Merci	mare-**see**
	You're welcome	De rien	deh ree-**en**
	Excuse me, sorry	Pardon	pahr-**doan**
	Sorry!	Désolé(e)	day-zoh-**lay**
	Good morning/ afternoon	Bonjour	bone-**joor**
	Good evening	Bonsoir	bone-**swar**
	Goodbye	Au revoir	o ruh-**vwar**
	Mr. (Sir)	Monsieur	mih-see-**oor**
	Mrs. (Ma'am)	Madame	ma-dam
	Miss	Mademoiselle	mad-mwa-**zel**
	Pleased to meet you	Enchanté(e)	on-shahn-**tay**
	How are you?	Comment allez-vous?	ko-men-tahl-ay-**voo**
Numbers	one	un	un
	two	deux	dew
	three	trois	twa
	four	quatre	**cat**-ruh
	five	cinq	sank
	six	six	seess
	seven	sept	set
	eight	huit	wheat
	nine	neuf	nuf
	ten	dix	deess
	eleven	onze	owns
	twelve	douze	dooz
	thirteen	treize	trays
	fourteen	quatorze	ka-torz
	fifteen	quinze	cans
	sixteen	seize	sez
	seventeen	dix-sept	deess-**set**
	eighteen	dix-huit	deess-**wheat**
	nineteen	dix-neuf	deess-**nuf**
	twenty	vingt	vant
	twenty-one	vingt-et-un	vant-ay-**un**
	thirty	trente	trahnt
	forty	quarante	ka-**rahnt**
	fifty	cinquante	sang-**kahnt**
	sixty	soixante	swa-**sahnt**
	seventy	soixante-dix	swa-sahnt-**deess**
	eighty	quatre-vingts	cat-ruh-**vant**
	ninety	quatre-vingt-dix	cat-ruh-vant-**deess**
	one-hundred	cent	sahnt
	one-thousand	mille	meel

No matter what your travel style, the best trips start with Fodor's

Fodor's

TRAVEL GUIDES

The name that means smart travel

Available at bookstores everywhere.

See back pages for complete title listing.

	English	French	Pronunciation
Colors	black	noir	nwar
	blue	bleu	blu
	brown	brun/marron	brun
	green	vert	vair
	orange	orange	o-**ranj**
	red	rouge	rouge
	white	blanc	blahn
	yellow	jaune	jone
Days of the Week	Sunday	dimanche	dee-**mahnsh**
	Monday	lundi	lewn-**dee**
	Tuesday	mardi	mar-**dee**
	Wednesday	mercredi	mare-kruh-**dee**
	Thursday	jeudi	juh-**dee**
	Friday	vendredi	van-dra-**dee**
	Saturday	samedi	sam-**dee**
Months	January	janvier	jan-**vyay**
	February	février	feh-vree-**ay**
	March	mars	marce
	April	avril	a-**vreel**
	May	mai	meh
	June	juin	jwan
	July	juillet	jwee-**ay**
	August	août	oot
	September	septembre	sep-**tahm**-bruh
	October	octobre	oak-**toe**-bruh
	November	novembre	no-**vahm**-bruh
	December	décembre	day-**sahm**-bruh
Useful Phrases	Do you speak English?	Parlez-vous anglais?	par-lay vooz ahng-**glay**
	I don't speak French	Je ne parle pas français	jeh nuh parl pah fraun-**say**
	I don't understand	Je ne comprends pas	jeh nuh kohm-prahn **pah**
	I understand	Je comprends	jeh kohm-**prahn**
	I don't know	Je ne sais pas	jeh nuh say **pah**
	I'm American/ British	Je suis américain/ anglais	jeh sweez a-may-ree-**can**/ahng-**glay**
	What's your name?	Comment vous appelez-vous?	ko-mahn voo za-pel-ay-**voo**
	My name is . . .	Je m'appelle . . .	jeh muh-**pel** . . .
	What time is it?	Quelle heure est-il?	kel ur et-**il**
	How?	Comment?	ko-**mahn**
	When?	Quand?	kahnd
	Yesterday	Hier	yair
	Today	Aujourd'hui	o-zhoor-**dwee**
	Tomorrow	Demain	deh-**man**
	This morning/ afternoon	Ce matin/cet après-midi	seh ma-**tanh**/set ah-pray-mee-**dee**

Tonight	Ce soir	seh **swar**
What?	Quoi?	kwah
What is it?	Qu'est-ce que c'est?	kess-kuh-**say**
Why?	Pourquoi?	poor-**kwa**
Who?	Qui?	kee
Where is . . .	Où est . . .	oo ay
the train station? the subway station? the bus stop? the terminal (airport)? the post office? the bank? the . . . hotel? the . . . museum? the hospital? the elevator? the telephone?	la gare? la station de métro? l'arrêt de bus? l'aérogare? la poste? la banque? l'hôtel . . . ? le musée . . . ? l'hôpital? l'ascenseur? le téléphone?	la gar la sta-syon deh may-**tro** la-ray deh **booss** lay-ro-**gar** la post la bahnk low-**tel** leh mew-**zay** low-pee-**tahl** la-sahn-**seur** leh te-le-**phone**
Where are the restrooms?	Où sont les toilettes?	oo son lay twah-**let**
Here/there	Ici/lá	ee-**see**/la
Left/right	A gauche/à droite	a goash/a drwat
Is it near/far?	C'est près/loin?	say pray/lwan
I'd like . . .	Je voudrais . . .	jeh voo-**dray**
a room the key a newspaper a stamp	une chambre la clé un journal un timbre	ewn **shahm**-bra la clay un joor-**nahl** un **tam**-bruh
I'd like to buy . . .	Je voudrais acheter . . .	jeh voo-**dray** ahsh-**tay**
cigarettes matches city plan road map magazine envelopes writing paper airmail writing paper postcard	des cigarettes des allumettes un plan de ville une carte routière une revue des enveloppes du papier à lettres du papier avion une carte postale	day see-ga-**ret** days a-loo-**met** un plahn de la **veel** ewn cart roo-tee-**air** ewn reh-**view** dayz ahn-veh-**lope** deh-pa-pee-ay a **let**-ruh deh pa-pee-ay a-vee-**own** ewn cart post-**al**
How much is it?	C'est combien?	say comb-bee-**en**
It's expensive/cheap	C'est cher/pas cher	say sher/pa sher
A little/a lot	Un peu/beaucoup	un puh/bo-**koo**
More/less	Plus/moins	ploo/mwa

	Enough/too (much)	Assez/trop	a-**say**/tro
	I am ill/sick	Je suis malade	jeh swee ma-**lahd**
	Call a doctor	Appelez un docteur	a-pe-lay un dohk-**tore**
	Help!	Au secours!	o say-**koor**
	Stop!	Arrêtez!	a-ruh-**tay**
Dining Out	A bottle of . . .	une bouteille de . . .	ewn boo-**tay** deh
	A cup of . . .	une tasse de . . .	ewn tass deh
	A glass of . . .	un verre de . . .	un vair deh
	Ashtray	un cendrier	un sahn-dree-**ay**
	Bill/check	l'addition	la-dee-see-**own**
	Bread	du pain	due pan
	Breakfast	le petit déjeuner	leh pet-**ee** day-zhu-**nay**
	Butter	du beurre	due bur
	Cocktail/aperitif	un apéritif	un ah-pay-ree-**teef**
	Dinner	le dîner	leh dee-**nay**
	Fixed-price menu	le menu	leh may-**new**
	Fork	une fourchette	ewn four-**shet**
	I am on a diet	Je suis au régime	jeh sweez o ray-**jeem**
	I am vegetarian	Je suis végétarien(ne)	jeh swee vay-jay-ta-ree-**en**
	I cannot eat . . .	Je ne peux pas manger de . . .	jeh nuh puh pah mahn-**jay** deh
	I'd like to order	Je voudrais commander	jeh voo-**dray** ko-mahn-**day**
	I'd like . . .	Je voudrais . . .	jeh voo-**dray**
	I'm hungry/thirsty	J'ai faim/soif	jay fam/swahf
	Is service/the tip included?	Est-ce que le service est compris?	ess keh leh sair-veess ay comb-**pree**
	It's good/bad	C'est bon/mauvais	say bon/mo-**vay**
	It's hot/cold	C'est chaud/froid	say sho/frwah
	Knife	un couteau	un koo-**toe**
	Lunch	le déjeuner	leh day-juh-**nay**
	Menu	la carte	la cart
	Napkin	une serviette	ewn sair-vee-**et**
	Pepper	du poivre	due **pwah**-vruh
	Plate	une assiette	ewn a-see-**et**
	Please give me . . .	Donnez-moi . . .	doe-nay-**mwah**

Salt	du sel	dew sell
Spoon	une cuillère	ewn kwee-**air**
Sugar	du sucre	due **sook**-ruh
Wine list	la carte des vins	la cart day **van**

Menu Guide

English	*French*
Set menu	Menu à prix fixe
Dish of the day	Plat du jour
Drink included	Boisson comprise
Local specialties	Spécialités locales
Choice of vegetable accompaniment	Garniture au choix
Made to order	Sur commande
Extra charge	Supplément/En sus
When available	Selon arrivage

Breakfast

Jam	Confiture
Croissants	Croissants
Honey	Miel
Boiled egg	Oeuf à la coque
Bacon and eggs	Oeufs au bacon
Ham and eggs	Oeufs au jambon
Fried eggs	Oeufs sur le plat
Scrambled eggs	Oeufs brouillés
(Plain) omelet	Omelette (nature)
Rolls	Petits pains

Starters

Anchovies	Anchois
Chitterling sausage	Andouille(tte)
Assorted cold cuts	Assiette anglaise
Assorted pork products	Assiette de charcuterie
Small, highly seasoned sausage	Crépinette
Mixed raw vegetable salad	Crudités
Snails	Escargots
Ham (Bayonne)	Jambon (de Bayonne)
Bologna sausage	Mortadelle
Devilled eggs	Oeufs à la diable
Liver purée blended with other meat	Pâté
Tart with a rich, creamy filling of cheese, vegetables, meat or seafood	Quiche (lorraine)
Cold sausage	Saucisson
Pâté sliced and served from an earthenware pot	Terrine
Cured dried beef	Viande séchée

Salads

Diced vegetable salad	Salade russe
Endive salad	Salade d'endives
Green salad	Salade verte
Mixed salad	Salade panachée
Tuna salad	Salade de thon

Soups

Cold leek and potato cream soup	Vichyssoise
Cream of . . .	Crême de . . .
Cream of . . .	Velouté de . . .
Hearty soup	Soupe
day's soup	*du jour*
French onion soup	à l'oignon
Provençal vegetable soup	au pistou
Light soup	Potage
mashed red beans	*condé*
shredded vegetables	julienne
potato	parmentier
Fish and seafood stew	Bouillabaisse
Seafood stew (chowder)	Bisque
Stew of meat and vegetables	Pot-au-feu

Fish and Seafood

Bass	Bar
Carp	Carpe
Clams	Palourdes
Cod	Morue
Creamed salt cod	Brandade de morue
Crab	Crabe
Crayfish	Ecrevisses
Eel	Anguille
Fish stew from Marseilles	Bourride
Fish stew in wine	Matelote
Frog's legs	Cuisses de grenouilles
Herring	Harengs
Lobster	Homard
Mackerel	Maquereau
Mussels	Moules
Octopus	Poulpe
Oysters	Huîtres
Perch	Perche
Pike	Brochet
Dublin bay prawns (scampi)	Langoustines
Red mullet	Rouget
Salmon	Saumon
Scallops in creamy sauce	Coquilles St-Jacques
Sea bream	Daurade
Shrimps	Crevettes
Sole	Sole
Squid	Calmar
Trout	Truite
Tuna	Thon
Whiting	Merlan

Methods of Preparation

Baked	Au four
Fried	Frit
Grilled	Grillé
Marinated	Mariné
Poached	Poché
Sautéed	Sauté
Smoked	Fumé
Steamed	Cuit à la vapeur

Meat

Beef	Boeuf
Beef stew with vegetables, braised in red Burgundy wine	Boeuf bourguignon
Brains	Cervelle
Chops	Côtelettes
Cutlet	Escalope
Double fillet steak	Chateaubriand
Kabob	Brochette
Kidneys	Rognons
Lamb	Agneau
Leg	Gigot
Liver	Foie
Meatballs	Boulettes de viande
Pig's feet (trotters)	Pieds de cochon
Pork	Porc
Rib	Côte
Rib or rib-eye steak	Entrecôte
Sausages	Saucisses
Sausages and cured pork served with sauerkraut	Choucroute garnie
Steak (always beef)	Steak/steack
Stew	Ragoût
T-bone steak	Côte de boeuf
Tenderloin steak	Médaillon
Tenderloin of T-bone steak	Tournedos
Tongue	Langue
Veal	Veau
Veal sweetbreads	Ris de veau

Methods of Preparation

Very rare	Bleu
Rare	Saignant
Medium	A point
Well-done	Bien cuit
Baked	Au four
Boiled	Bouilli
Braised	Braisé
Fried	Frit
Grilled	Grillé
Roast	Rôti
Sautéed	Sauté
Stewed	A l'étouffée

Game and Poultry

Chicken	Poulet
Chicken breast	Suprême de volaille
Chicken stewed in red wine	Coq au vin
Chicken stewed with vegetables	Poule au pot
Spring chicken	Poussin
Duck/duckling	Canard/caneton
Duck braised with oranges and orange liqueur	Canard à l'orange
Fattened pullet	Poularde
Fowl	Volaille
Guinea fowl/young guinea fowl	Pintade/pintadeau
Goose	Oie

Partridge/young partridge	Perdrix/perdreau
Pheasant	Faisan
Pigeon/squab	Pigeon/pigeonneau
Quail	Caille
Rabbit	Lapin
Turkey/young turkey	Dinde/dindonneau
Venison (red/roe)	Cerf/chevreuil

Vegetables

Artichoke	Artichaut
Asparagus	Asperge
Brussels sprouts	Choux de Bruxelles
Cabbage (red)	Chou (rouge)
Carrots	Carottes
Cauliflower	Chou-fleur
Eggplant	Aubergines
Endive	Endives
Leeks	Poireaux
Lettuce	Laitue
Mushrooms	Champignons
Onions	Oignons
Peas	Petits pois
Peppers	Poivrons
Radishes	Radis
Spinach	Epinards
Tomatoes	Tomates
Watercress	Cresson
Zucchini	Courgette
White kidney/French beans	Haricots blancs/verts
Casserole of stewed eggplant, onions, green peppers, and zucchini	Ratatouille

Spices and Herbs

Bay leaf	Laurier
Chervil	Cerfeuil
Garlic	Ail
Marjoram	Marjolaine
Mustard	Moutarde
Parsley	Persil
Pepper	Poivre
Rosemary	Romarin
Tarragon	Estragon
Mixture of herbs	Fines herbes

Potatoes, Rice, and Noodles

Noodles	Nouilles
Pasta	Pâtes
Potatoes	Pommes (de terre)
matchsticks	*allumettes*
mashed and deep-fried	*dauphine*
mashed with butter and egg yolks	*duchesse*
in their jackets	*en robe des champs*
french fries	*frites*
mashed	*mousseline*
boiled/steamed	*nature/vapeur*

Rice	Riz
boiled in bouillon with onions	*pilaf*

Sauces and Preparations

Brown butter, parsley, lemon juice	Meunière
Curry	Indienne
Egg yolks, butter, vinegar	Hollandaise
Hot pepper	Diable
Mayonnaise flavored with mustard and herbs	Tartare
Mushrooms, red wine, shallots, beef marrow	Bordelaise
Onions, tomatoes, garlic	Provençale
Pepper sauce	Poivrade
Red wine, herbs	Bourguignon
Vinegar, egg yolks, white wine, shallots, tarragon	Béarnaise
Vinegar dressing	Vinaigrette
White sauce	Béchamel
White wine, mussel broth, egg yolks	Marinière
Wine, mushrooms, onions, shallots	Chasseur
With goose or duck liver purée and truffles	Périgueux
With Madeira wine	Madère

Cheeses

Mild:	Beaufort
	Beaumont
	Belle étoile
	Boursin
	Brie
	Cantal
	Comté
	Reblochon
	St-Paulin
	Tomme de Savoie
Sharp:	Bleu de Bresse
	Camembert
	Livarot
	Fromage au marc
	Munster
	Pont-l'Évêque
	Roquefort
Swiss:	Emmenthal
	Gruyère
	Vacherin
Goat's milk:	St-Marcellin
	Crottin de Chavignol Valençay
Cheese tart	Tarte au fromage
Small cheese tart	Ramequin
Toasted ham and cheese sandwich	Croque-monsieur

Fruits and Nuts

Almonds	Amandes
Apple	Pomme
Apricot	Abricot
Banana	Banane
Blackberries	Mûres
Blackcurrants	Cassis
Blueberries	Myrtilles
Cherries	Cerises
Chestnuts	Marrons
Coconut	Noix de coco
Dates	Dattes
Dried fruit	Fruits secs
Figs	Figues
Grapefruit	Pamplemousse
Grapes green/blue	Raisin blanc/noir
Hazelnuts	Noisettes
Lemon	Citron
Melon	Melon
Orange	Orange
Peach	Pêche
Peanuts	Cacahouètes
Pear	Poire
Pineapple	Ananas
Plums	Prunes
Prunes	Pruneaux
Raisins	Raisins secs
Raspberries	Framboises
Strawberries	Fraises
Tangerine	Mandarine
Walnuts	Noix
Watermelon	Pastèque

Desserts

Apple pie	Tarte aux pommes
Baked Alaska	Omelette norvégienne
Caramel pudding	Crème caramel
Chocolate cake	Gâteau au chocolat
Chocolate pudding	Mousse au chocolat
Custard tart	Flan
Custard	Creme anglaise
Ice cream	Glace
Layer cake	Tourte
Pear with vanilla ice cream and chocolate sauce	Poire Belle Hélène
Soufflé made with orange liqueur	Soufflé au Grand-Marnier
Sundae	Coupe (glacée)
Water ice	Sorbet
Whipped cream	Crème Chantilly
Creamy dessert of egg yolks, wine, sugar, and flavoring	Sabayon
Puff pastry filled with whipped cream or custard	Profiterole

Index

Personal Itinerary

Departure *Date*

Time

Transportation

Arrival *Date* *Time*

Departure *Date* *Time*

Transportation

Accommodations

Arrival *Date* *Time*

Departure *Date* *Time*

Transportation

Accommodations

Arrival *Date* *Time*

Departure *Date* *Time*

Transportation

Accommodations

Personal Itinerary

Arrival *Date* *Time*

Departure *Date* *Time*

Transportation

Accommodations

Arrival *Date* *Time*

Departure *Date* *Time*

Transportation

Accommodations

Arrival *Date* *Time*

Departure *Date* *Time*

Transportation

Accommodations

Arrival *Date* *Time*

Departure *Date* *Time*

Transportation

Accommodations

Personal Itinerary

Arrival *Date* *Time*

Departure *Date* *Time*

Transportation

Accommodations

Arrival *Date* *Time*

Departure *Date* *Time*

Transportation

Accommodations

Arrival *Date* *Time*

Departure *Date* *Time*

Transportation

Accommodations

Arrival *Date* *Time*

Departure *Date* *Time*

Transportation

Accommodations

Addresses

Name

Address

Telephone

Name

Address

Telephone

Name

Address

Telephone

Name

Address

Telephone

Name

Address

Telephone

Name

Address

Telephone

Name

Address

Telephone

Name

Address

Telephone

Name

Address

Telephone

Name

Address

Telephone

Name

Address

Telephone

Name

Address

Telephone

Name

Address

Telephone

Name

Address

Telephone

Name

Address

Telephone

Name

Address

Telephone

Addresses

Name	Name
Address	Address
Telephone	Telephone
Name	Name
Address	Address
Telephone	Telephone
Name	Name
Address	Address
Telephone	Telephone
Name	Name
Address	Address
Telephone	Telephone
Name	Name
Address	Address
Telephone	Telephone
Name	Name
Address	Address
Telephone	Telephone
Name	Name
Address	Address
Telephone	Telephone
Name	Name
Address	Address
Telephone	Telephone

Fodor's Travel Guides

U.S. Guides

Alaska

Arizona

Boston

California

Cape Cod, Martha's Vineyard, Nantucket

The Carolinas & the Georgia Coast

Chicago

Disney World & the Orlando Area

Florida

Hawaii

Las Vegas, Reno, Tahoe

Los Angeles

Maine, Vermont, New Hampshire

Maui

Miami & the Keys

New England

New Orleans

New York City

Pacific North Coast

Philadelphia & the Pennsylvania Dutch Country

San Diego

San Francisco

Santa Fe, Taos, Albuquerque

Seattle & Vancouver

The South

The U.S. & British Virgin Islands

The Upper Great Lakes Region

USA

Vacations in New York State

Vacations on the Jersey Shore

Virginia & Maryland

Waikiki

Washington, D.C.

Foreign Guides

Acapulco, Ixtapa, Zihuatanejo

Australia & New Zealand

Austria

The Bahamas

Baja & Mexico's Pacific Coast Resorts

Barbados

Berlin

Bermuda

Brazil

Budapest

Budget Europe

Canada

Cancun, Cozumel, Yucatan Penisula

Caribbean

Central America

China

Costa Rica, Belize, Guatemala

Czechoslovakia

Eastern Europe

Egypt

Euro Disney

Europe

Europe's Great Cities

France

Germany

Great Britain

Greece

The Himalayan Countries

Hong Kong

India

Ireland

Israel

Italy

Italy's Great Cities

Japan

Kenya & Tanzania

Korea

London

Madrid & Barcelona

Mexico

Montreal & Quebec City

Morocco

The Netherlands Belgium & Luxembourg

New Zealand

Norway

Nova Scotia, Prince Edward Island & New Brunswick

Paris

Portugal

Rome

Russia & the Baltic Countries

Scandinavia

Scotland

Singapore

South America

Southeast Asia

South Pacific

Spain

Sweden

Switzerland

Thailand

Tokyo

Toronto

Turkey

Vienna & the Danube Valley

Yugoslavia

Special Series

Fodor's Affordables

Affordable Europe

Affordable France

Affordable Germany

Affordable Great Britain

Affordable Italy

Fodor's Bed & Breakfast and Country Inns Guides

California

Mid-Atlantic Region

New England

The Pacific Northwest

The South

The West Coast

The Upper Great Lakes Region

Canada's Great Country Inns

Cottages, B&Bs and Country Inns of England and Wales

The Berkeley Guides

On the Loose in California

On the Loose in Eastern Europe

On the Loose in Mexico

On the Loose in the Pacific Northwest & Alaska

Fodor's Exploring Guides

Exploring California

Exploring Florida

Exploring France

Exploring Germany

Exploring Paris

Exploring Rome

Exploring Spain

Exploring Thailand

Fodor's Flashmaps

New York

Washington, D.C.

Fodor's Pocket Guides

Pocket Bahamas

Pocket Jamaica

Pocket London

Pocket New York City

Pocket Paris

Pocket Puerto Rico

Pocket San Francisco

Pocket Washington, D.C.

Fodor's Sports

Cycling

Hiking

Running

Sailing

The Insider's Guide to the Best Canadian Skiing

Fodor's Three-In-Ones (guidebook, language cassette, and phrase book)

France

Germany

Italy

Mexico

Spain

Fodor's Special-Interest Guides

Cruises and Ports of Call

Disney World & the Orlando Area

Euro Disney

Healthy Escapes

London Companion

Skiing in the USA & Canada

Sunday in New York

Fodor's Touring Guides

Touring Europe

Touring USA: Eastern Edition

Touring USA: Western Edition

Fodor's Vacation Planners

Great American Vacations

National Parks of the West

The Wall Street Journal Guides to Business Travel

Europe

International Cities

Pacific Rim

USA & Canada